CIMA
STUDY TEXT

Intermediate Paper 4

Finance

IN THIS JULY 2002 EDITION

- Targeted to the **syllabus** and **learning outcomes**
- **Quizzes** and **questions** to check your understanding
- Clear layout and style designed to save you time
- Plenty of **exam-style questions**
- **Chapter roundups** and summaries to help revision
- **Mind maps** to integrate the key points

NEW IN THIS JULY 2002 EDITION

- **Increased guidance** in the **exam question bank**

BPP's **MCQ cards** and **i-Learn** and **i-Pass** products also support this paper.

BPP Publishing
July 2002

First edition 2000
Third edition July 2002

ISBN 0 7517 3756 9 *(Previous edition 7517 3160 9)*

British Library Cataloguing-in-Publication Data
*A catalogue record for this book
is available from the British Library*

Published by

BPP Publishing Ltd
Aldine House, Aldine Place
London W12 8AW

www.bpp.com

Printed in Great Britain by Ashford Colour Press

All our rights reserved. No part of this publication may be reproduced, stored in a retrieval system or transmitted, in any form or by any means, electronic, mechanical, photocopying, recording or otherwise, without the prior written permission of BPP Publishing Limited.

We are grateful to the Chartered Institute of Management Accountants for permission to reproduce past examination questions and questions from the pilot paper. The suggested solutions to the illustrative questions have been prepared by BPP Publishing Limited.

©
*BPP Publishing Limited
2002*

Contents

	Page
THE BPP STUDY TEXT	(v)
HELP YOURSELF STUDY FOR YOUR CIMA EXAMS	(vii)
The right approach - developing your personal Study Plan- suggested study sequence	
SYLLABUS AND LEARNING OUTCOMES	(xii)
THE EXAM PAPER	(xix)
WHAT THE EXAMINER MEANS	(xxii)
TACKLING MULTIPLE CHOICE QUESTIONS	(xxiii)

PART A: THE FINANCE FUNCTION

1	Financial management and financial objectives	3
2	Securities market institutions	17
3	Determination of share prices	33
4	The treasury function	48

PART B: SOURCES OF LONG-TERM FINANCE

5	Share capital	63
6	Debt finance	85
7	Leasing	99
8	The cost of capital	112
9	Portfolios and diversification	131
10	The capital asset pricing model	144
11	Investor ratios	156

PART C: SOURCES OF SHORT-TERM FINANCE

12	Interest rates and the yield curve	173
13	Short-term investments	189
14	Short-term borrowing	210
15	Export finance	223

PART D: WORKING CAPITAL MANAGEMENT

16	Working capital characteristics	239
17	Cash flow forecasts	254
18	Cash management	282
19	Credit control policies	300
20	Assessing creditworthiness	320
21	Monitoring and collecting debtors	339
22	Remedies for bad debts	351
23	Managing creditors and stock	366

APPENDIX: MATHEMATICAL TABLES	387
EXAM QUESTION BANK	393
EXAM ANSWER BANK	406

Contents

	Page
MULTIPLE CHOICE QUESTIONS	445
ANSWERS TO MULTIPLE CHOICE QUESTIONS	453
INDEX	461
REVIEW FORM & FREE PRIZE DRAW	
ORDER FORM	

MULTIPLE CHOICE QUESTION CARDS

Multiple choice questions form a large part of the exam. To give you further practice in this style of question, we have produced a bank of **150 multiple choice question cards**, covering the syllabus. This bank contains exam style questions in a format to help you **revise on the move**.

COMPUTER-BASED LEARNING PRODUCTS FROM BPP

If you want to reinforce your studies by **interactive** learning, try BPP's **i-Learn** product, covering major syllabus areas in an interactive format. For **self-testing**, try **i-Pass,** which offers a large number of **objective test questions**, particularly useful where objective test questions form part of the exam.

See the order form at the back of this text for details of these innovative learning tools.

VIRTUAL CAMPUS

The Virtual Campus uses BPP's wealth of teaching experience to produce a fully **interactive** e-learning resource **delivered via the Internet**. The site offers comprehensive **tutor support** and features areas such as **study, practice, email service, revision** and **useful resources**.

Visit our website www.bpp.com/virtualcampus/cima to sample aspects of the campus free of charge.

LEARNING TO LEARN ACCOUNTANCY

BPP's ground-breaking **Learning to learn accountancy** book is designed to be used both at the outset of your CIMA studies and throughout the process of learning accountancy. It challenges you to consider how you study and gives you helpful hints about how to approach the various types of paper which you will encounter. It can help you **get your studies both subject and exam focused**, enabling you to **acquire knowledge, practice and revise efficiently and effectively**.

THE BPP STUDY TEXT

Aims of this Study Text

To provide you with the knowledge and understanding, skills and application techniques that you need if you are to be successful in your exams

This Study Text has been written around the **Finance** syllabus.

- It is **comprehensive**. It covers the syllabus content. No more, no less.
- It is written at the **right level**. Each chapter is written with CIMA's precise learning outcomes in mind.
- It is targeted to the **exam**. We have taken account of the pilot paper and the papers set to date, questions put to the examiner and the assessment methodology.

To allow you to study in the way that best suits your learning style and the time you have available, by following your personal Study Plan (see page (viii))

You may be studying at home on your own until the date of the exam, or you may be attending a full-time course. You may like to (and have time to) read every word, or you may prefer to (or only have time to) skim-read and devote the remainder of your time to question practice. Wherever you fall in the spectrum, you will find the BPP Study Text meets your needs in designing and following your personal Study Plan.

To tie in with the other components of the BPP Effective Study Package to ensure you have the best possible chance of passing the exam (see page (vi))

The BPP Study Text

Recommended period of use	Elements of the BPP Effective Study Package
From the outset and throughout	**Learning to learn accountancy** Read this invaluable book as you begin your studies and refer to it as you work through the various elements of the BPP Effective Study Package. It will help you to acquire knowledge, practice and revise, both efficiently and effectively.
Three to twelve months before the exam	**Study Text and i-Learn** Use the Study Text to acquire knowledge, understanding, skills and the ability to use application techniques. Use BPP's **i-Learn** product to reinforce your learning.
Throughout	**Virtual Campus** Study, practice, revise and take advantage of other useful resources with BPP's fully interactive e-learning site with comprehensive tutor support.
Throughout	**MCQ cards and i-Pass** Revise your knowledge and ability to use application techniques, as well as practising this key exam question format, with 150 multiple choice questions. **i Pass**, our computer based testing package, provides objective test questions in a variety of formats and is ideal for self-assessment.
One to six months before the exam	**Practice & Revision Kit** Try the numerous examination-format questions, for which there are realistic suggested solutions prepared by BPP's own authors. Then attempt the two mock exams.
From three months before the exam until the last minute	**Passcards** Work through these short, memorable notes which are focused on what is most likely to come up in the exam you will be sitting.
One to six months before the exam	**Success Tapes** These audio tapes cover the vital elements of your syllabus in less than 90 minutes per subject. Each tape also contains exam hints to help you fine tune your strategy.
Three to twelve months before the exam	**Breakthrough Videos** Use a Breakthrough Video to supplement your Study Text. They give you clear tuition on key exam subjects and allow you the luxury of being able to pause or repeat sections until you have fully grasped the topic.

HELP YOURSELF STUDY FOR YOUR CIMA EXAMS

Exams for professional bodies such as CIMA are very different from those you have taken at college or university. You will be under **greater time pressure before** the exam - as you may be combining your study with work. There are many different ways of learning and so the BPP Study Text offers you a number of different tools to help you through. Here are some hints and tips: they are not plucked out of the air, but **based on research and experience**. (You don't need to know that long-term memory is in the same part of the brain as emotions and feelings - but it's a fact anyway.)

The right approach

1 The right attitude

Believe in yourself	Yes, there is a lot to learn. Yes, it is a challenge. But thousands have succeeded before and you can too.
Remember why you're doing it	Studying might seem a grind at times, but you are doing it for a reason: to advance your career.

2 The right focus

Read through the Syllabus and learning outcomes	These tell you what you are expected to know and are supplemented by Exam Focus Points in the text.
Study the Exam Paper section	Past papers are a reasonable guide of what you should expect in the exam.

3 The right method

The big picture	You need to grasp the detail - but keeping in mind how everything fits into the big picture will help you understand better. • The **Introduction** of each chapter puts the material in context. • The **Syllabus content, learning outcomes** and **Exam focus points** show you what you need to **grasp**. • **Mind Maps** show the links and key issues in key topics.
In your own words	To absorb the information (and to practise your written communication skills), it helps to **put it into your own words**. • **Take notes.** • Answer the **questions** in each chapter. As well as helping you absorb the information, you will practise the assessment formats used in the exam and your written communication skills, which become increasingly important as you progress through your CIMA exams. • Draw **mind maps**. We have some examples. • Try 'teaching' a subject to a colleague or friend.

Help yourself study for your CIMA exams

Give yourself cues to jog your memory	The BPP Study Text uses **bold** to **highlight key points** and **icons** to identify key features, such as **Exam focus points** and **Key terms.** • Try **colour coding** with a highlighter pen. • Write **key points** on cards.

4 **The right review**

Review, review, review	It is a **fact** that regularly reviewing a topic in summary form can **fix it in your memory**. Because **review** is so important, the BPP Study Text helps you to do so in many ways. • **Chapter roundups** summarise the key points in each chapter. Use them to recap each study session. • The **Quick quiz** is another review technique to ensure that you have grasped the essentials. • Go through the **Examples** in each chapter a second or third time.

Developing your personal Study Plan

One thing that the BPP Learning to learn accountancy book emphasises (see page (iv)) is the need to prepare (and use) a study plan. Planning and sticking to the plan are key elements of learning success.

There are four steps you should work through.

Step 1. **How do you learn?**

First you need to be aware of your style of learning. The BPP Learning to learn accountancy book commits a chapter to this **self-discovery**. What types of intelligence do you display when learning? You might be advised to brush up on certain study skills before launching into this Study Text.

> BPP's **Learning to learn accountancy** book helps you to identify what intelligences you show more strongly and then details how you can tailor your study process through your preferences. It also includes handy hints on how to develop intelligences you exhibit less strongly, but which might be needed as you study accountancy.

Are you a **theorist** or are you more **practical**? If you would rather get to grips with a theory before trying to apply it in practice, you should follow the study sequence on page X. If the reverse is true (you like to know why you are learning theory before you do so), you might be advised to flick through Study Text chapters and look at questions, case studies and examples (Steps 7, 8 and 9 in the **suggested study sequence**) before reading through the detailed theory.

Step 2. **How much time do you have?**

Work out the time you have available per week, given the following.

- The standard you have set yourself
- The time you need to set aside later for work on the Practice & Revision Kit and Passcards
- The other exam(s) you are sitting

- Very importantly, practical matters such as work, travel, exercise, sleep and social life

Note your time available in box A.   A [ ] Hours

Step 3. Allocate your time

- Take the time you have available per week for this Study Text shown in box A, multiply it by the number of weeks available and insert the result in box B.   B [ ]

- Divide the figure in Box B by the number of chapters in this text and insert the result in box C.   C [ ]

Remember that this is only a rough guide. Some of the chapters in this book are longer and more complicated than others, and you will find some subjects easier to understand than others.

Step 4. Implement

Set about studying each chapter in the time shown in box C, following the key study steps in the order suggested by your particular learning style.

This is your personal **Study Plan**. You should try and combine it with the study sequence outlined below. You may want to modify the sequence a little (as has been suggested above) to adapt it to your **personal style**.

Suggested study sequence

It is likely that the best way to approach this Study Text is to tackle the chapters in the order in which you find them. Taking into account your individual learning style, you could follow this sequence.

Key study steps	Activity
Step 1 **Topic list**	Each numbered topic is a numbered section in the chapter.
Step 2 **Introduction**	This gives you the **big picture** in terms of the **context** of the chapter, the **content** you will cover, and the **learning outcomes** the chapter assesses - in other words, it sets your **objectives for study.**
Step 3 **Knowledge brought forward boxes**	In these we highlight information and techniques that it is assumed you have 'brought forward' with you from your earlier studies. If there are topics which have changed recently due to legislation for example, these topics are explained in more detail.
Step 4 **Explanations**	Proceed methodically through the chapter, reading each section thoroughly and making sure you understand.
Step 5 **Key terms and Exam focus points**	- **Key terms** can often earn you *easy marks* if you state them clearly and correctly in an appropriate exam answer (and they are highlighted in the index at the back of the text). - **Exam focus points** give you a good idea of how we think the examiner intends to examine certain topics.

Help yourself study for your CIMA exams

Key study steps	Activity
Step 6 **Note taking**	Take brief notes, if you wish. Avoid the temptation to copy out too much. Remember that being able to put something into your own words is a sign of being able to understand it. If you find you cannot explain something you have read, read it again before you make the notes.
Step 7 **Examples**	Follow each through to its solution very carefully.
Step 8 **Case examples**	Study each one, and try to add flesh to them from your own experience – they are designed to show how the topics you are studying come alive (and often come unstuck) in the real world.
Step 9 **Questions**	Make a very good attempt at each one.
Step 10 **Answers**	Check yours against ours, and make sure you understand any discrepancies.
Step 11 **Chapter roundup**	Work through it very carefully, to make sure you have grasped the major points it is highlighting.
Step 12 **Quick quiz**	When you are happy that you have covered the chapter, use the **Quick quiz** to check how much you have remembered of the topics covered and to practise questions in a variety of formats.
Step 13 **Question(s) in the Exam Question bank**	Either at this point, or later when you are thinking about revising, make a full attempt at the **Question(s)** suggested at the very end of the chapter. You can find these at the end of the Study Text, along with the **Answers** so you can see how you did. We highlight those that are introductory, and those which are of the standard you would expect to find in an exam. If you have purchased the **MCQ cards** or **i-Pass**, use these too.
Step 14 **Multiple choice questions**	Use the bank of MCQs at the back of this Study Text to practise this important assessment format and to determine how much of the Study Text you have absorbed. If you have bought the **MCQ cards** or **i-Pass**, use these too.

Short of time: Skim study technique?

You may find you simply do not have the time available to follow all the key study steps for each chapter, however you adapt them for your particular learning style. If this is the case, follow the **skim study** technique below (the icons in the Study Text will help you to do this).

- Study the chapters in the order you find them in the Study Text.
- For each chapter, follow the key study steps 1-3, and then skim-read through step 4. Jump to step 11, and then go back to step 5. Follow through steps 7 and 8, and prepare outline answers to questions (steps 9/10). Try the Quick quiz (step 12), following up any items you can't answer, then do a plan for the Question (step 13), comparing it against our answers. You should probably still follow step 6 (note-taking), although you may decide simply to rely on the BPP Passcards for this.

Moving on...

However you study, when you are ready to embark on the practice and revision phase of the BPP Effective Study Package, you should still refer back to this Study Text, both as a source of **reference** (you should find the index particularly helpful for this) and as a way to **review** (the Chapter roundups and Quick quizzes help you here).

And remember to keep careful hold of this Study Text – you will find it invaluable in your work.

Syllabus and learning outcomes

SYLLABUS MIND MAP

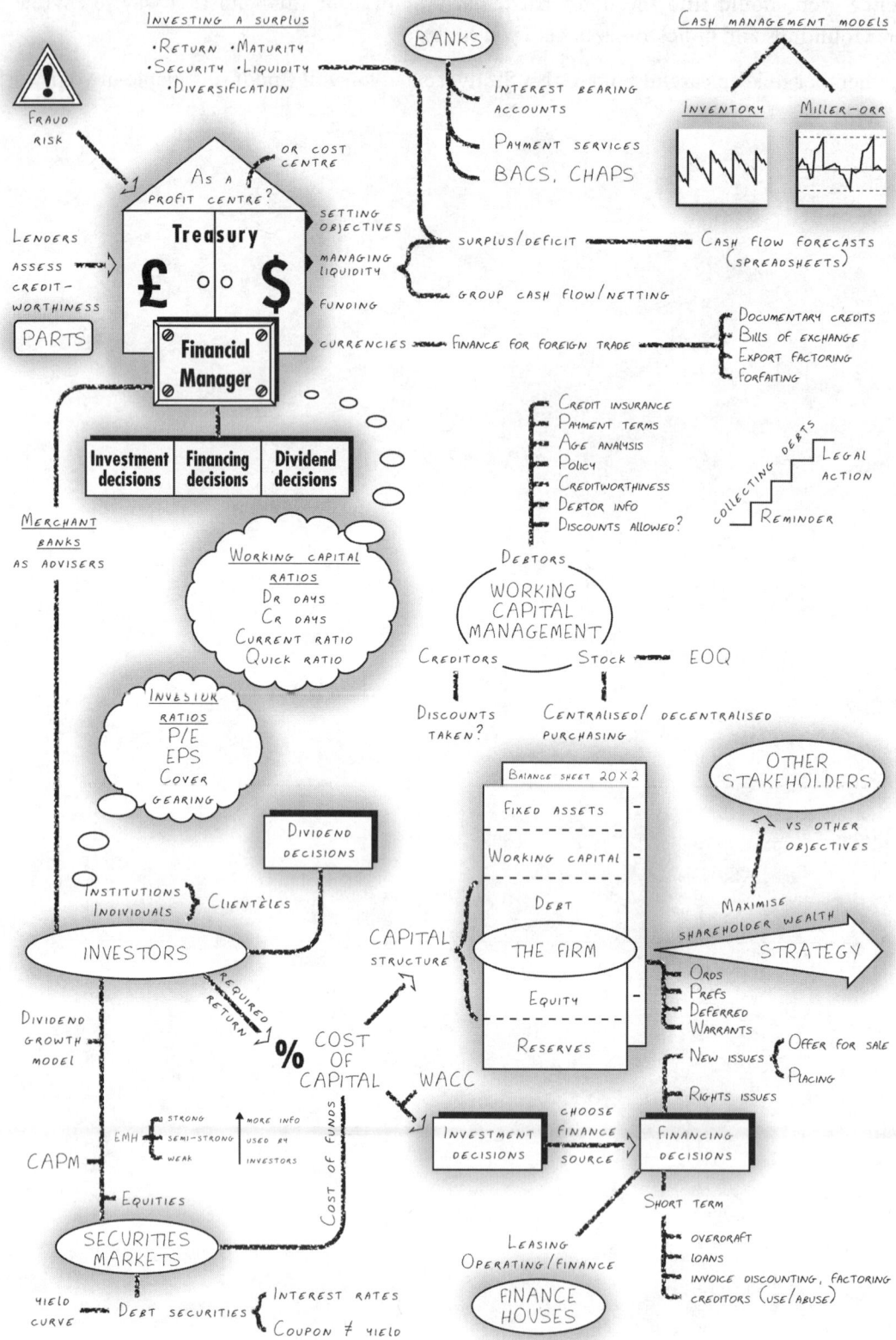

SYLLABUS AND LEARNING OUTCOMES

Syllabus overview

This is an introduction to financial management. It builds on the Foundation units of Economics for Business, Business Mathematics and Financial Accounting Fundamentals.

This syllabus deals with the evaluation of short and long term financing and requires an appreciation of the relevant theories underpinning this together with an understanding of working capital management.

The Finance paper underpins the Financial Strategy paper at the Final level.

Aims

This syllabus aims to test the student's ability to:

- Explain the role and purpose of financial management
- Identify and evaluate sources of finance
- Calculate cost of capital
- Analyse the overall management of working capital
- Evaluate debtor and creditor management policies

Assessment

There will be a written paper of 3 hours. The paper will comprise two sections.

Section A: 40% Objective testing. All questions will be compulsory.

Section B: 3 questions will be answered out of a choice of 5.

All learning outcomes may be tested in either section.

Formulae will be given as required.

Learning outcomes and syllabus content

4(i) The finance function - 10%

Learning outcomes

On completion of their studies students should be able to:

- Explain the interrelationships between decisions concerning investment, financing and dividends
- Describe and explain the operation of the securities markets
- Describe and explain the role and management of the treasury function
- Compare and contrast the services provided by financial institutions and recommend appropriate providers in different scenarios

Syllabus and learning outcomes

Syllabus content

	Covered in chapter
• The financial objectives of different organisations, eg value for money, maximising shareholder wealth, providing a surplus	1
• The three key decisions of financial management (ie investment, financing, dividend) and their links	1
• The operation of securities markets (stock exchanges) ie how share prices are determined and what causes share prices to rise or fall. (No detailed knowledge of any specific country's stock exchange will be tested.) Financial institutions, eg stock brokers, institutional investors, merchant banks, venture capitalists, money brokers	2, 3
• The efficient market hypothesis (EMH)	3
• The role of the treasury function in terms of setting corporate objectives, liquidity management, funding management, currency management	4
• The benefits and shortcomings of establishing treasury departments as profit centres or cost centres	4
• The control of treasury departments when established as cost centres or profit centres	4

4(ii) Sources of long term finance - 30%

Learning outcomes

On completion of their studies students should be able to:

- Recommend the sources of capital most appropriate for an organisation
- Evaluate the most appropriate method of funding an asset
- Calculate investor ratios and demonstrate the impact of changing capital structures on these ratios
- Calculate the cost of capital and demonstrate the impact of changing capital structures
- Explain the impact of interest rate changes on the cost of capital

Syllabus and learning outcomes

Syllabus content

	Covered in chapter
• Types of share capital, ie ordinary, preference, deferred, warrants	5
• Equity issues; new and rights issues	5
• Long-term debt finance (ie secured, unsecured, redeemable, irredeemable, convertibles and debt with warrants)	6
• Methods of issuing securities, eg rights, placing, offer for sale	5
• Fraud related to sources of finance (eg advance fee fraud and pyramid schemes)	4
• Operating and finance leases (One year lagged tax savings will be tested with leases and comparisons of the cost of a lease with the cost of buying.)	7
• The calculation of the cost of equity using the capital asset pricing model (CAPM) and the dividend growth model (knowledge of methods of calculating and estimating dividend growth will be expected)	8, 10
• An introduction to the relationship between risk, uncertainty and reward, eg use of CAPM (Beta, R_m and R_f will be given and a simple understanding of the CAPM is all that will be tested. Gearing and ungearing betas will not be tested.)	10
• The ideas of diversifiable risk (unsystematic risk) and systematic risk (Use of the two asset portfolio formula will not be tested.)	9, 10
• The cost of redeemable and irredeemable debt including the tax shield on debt (Numerical questions on the cost of convertible debt will not be tested.)	8
• The weighted average cost of capital (Modigliani and Miller will not be tested)	8
• Investor ratios, ie EPS, Price/Earnings(P/E) ratio, dividend cover, dividend yield, interest yield, earnings yield, redemption yield	11
• Gearing ratios (market and book values) and interest cover	11

4(iii) Sources of short term finance - 20%

Learning outcomes

On completion of their studies students should be able to:

- Identify alternatives for investment of short-term cash surpluses
- Identify sources of short-term funding
- Calculate and explain rates of interest
- Explain the yield curve and its practical use
- Analyse an organisation's creditworthiness from a lender's viewpoint
- Identify appropriate methods of finance for trading internationally

Syllabus and learning outcomes

Syllabus content

	Covered in chapter
• Interest rate arithmetic (compound, simple, annual, quarterly, monthly)	12
• The yield curve and theories concerning normal and inverse yield curves	12
• The principles of investing short term, ie maturity, return, security, liquidity and diversification	12
• Types of investments, eg interest bearing bank accounts, negotiable instruments (including certificates of deposit, short-term treasury bills), securities	13
• The difference between the coupon on debt and the yield of maturity	11
• Types of borrowing, eg overdrafts, short-term loans, invoice discounting	14
• The effect of short-term debt on the measurement of gearing	14
• Use and abuse of trade creditors as a source of finance	14
• The lender's assessment of creditworthiness	14
• Export finance, ie documentary credits, bills of exchange, export factoring, forfaiting	15

4(iv) Working capital management - 40%

Learning outcomes

On completion of their studies students should be able to:

- Calculate and interpret working capital ratios for business sectors
- Prepare and analyse cash flow forecasts over a 12 month period
- Identify measures to improve a cash forecast situation
- Compare and contrast the use and limitations of cash management models and identify when each model is most appropriate
- State and illustrate the main issues in group cash flow management
- Identify appropriate bank services to assist in cash management
- Identify debtor management policies and procedures for an organisation
- Interpret the creditworthiness of a customer
- Analyse trade debtor information
- Evaluate debtor and creditor policies
- Evaluate appropriate methods of stock management

Syllabus content

	Covered in chapter
• Working capital ratios, ie debtor days, stock days, creditor days, current ratio, quick ratio, and the working capital cycle	16
• The working capital characteristics of different businesses (eg supermarkets being heavily funded by creditors) and the importance of industry comparisons	16
• Cash flow forecasts, use of spreadsheets to assist in this in terms of changing variables (eg interest rates or inflation) and in consolidating forecasts	17
• Which variables are most easily changed, delayed or brought forward in a forecast	17
• The link between cash, profit and the balance sheet	17
• The Baumol and Miller Orr cash management models	18
• Group cash flow management eg netting	18
• Bank services available to organisations in order to help them manage cash eg investing overnight, Bankers' Automated Clearing Services (BACS), automated matching, minimising service charges	18
• Bank services and facilities and their impact on organisational activities and costs	18
• The credit cycle from receipt of customer order to cash receipt	19
• Payment terms	19
• Assessing a customer's creditworthiness eg sources of credit status information (eg bank references, trade references, internal credit rating information)	20
• Evaluating settlement discounts	19
• Methods of payment eg cash, BACS, cheque, banker's draft, standing order, direct debit, credit card, debit card	19
• Present and interpret an age analysis of debtors	21
• The stages in debt collection eg reminder, statement, telephone call, personal visit, legal action, debt collection agency, interest on overdue debts	21
• Establishing collection targets on an appropriate basis eg motivational issues in managing credit control	21
• Factoring and invoice discounting	21
• Remedies for bad debts eg credit insurance, debt collection agencies, specialist solicitors, guidance in taking legal action, negotiated settlements, an outline of the differences between bankruptcy and insolvency (no legal aspects to be examined)	22
• The payment cycle from agreeing the order to making payment	23
• Payment terms as part of the order	23

Syllabus and learning outcomes

	Covered in chapter
• Centralised versus decentralised purchasing	23
• Present and interpret an age analysis of creditors	23
• The link between purchasing and the budget for cost centres	23
• The relationship between purchasing and stock control	23
• The Economic Order Quantity (EOQ) model (ie reorder levels, reorder quantities, safety stocks and evaluating whether bulk order discounts should be accepted)	23

THE EXAM PAPER

Format of the paper - November 2002

		Number of marks
Section A:	20 Objective test questions 2 marks each	40
Section B:	Three questions from five 20 marks each	60
		100

Time allowed: 3 hours

STOP PRESS!

As this Text was going to print CIMA announced that the format of the Finance Paper was changing for the May 2003 exam.

Format of the paper - May 2003

		Number of marks
Section A:	10 Objective test questions 2 marks each	20
Section B:	One compulsory question	30
Section C:	Two questions from four 25 marks each	50
		100

Analysis of past papers

May 2002

Section A

1.1 Three Es
1.2 Quotation
1.3 Stock market efficiency
1.4 Terminal value with changing interest rates
1.5 Dividend cover
1.6 Theoretical ex rights price
1.7 Lease present value
1.8 Fraud
1.9 Dividend growth
1.10 Portfolio theory
1.11 Yield curve
1.12 Debt factoring
1.13 Interest rates
1.14 Working capital and current ratio
1.15 Economic order quantity
1.16 Baumol cash management model
1.17 Working capital
1.18 Bank overdraft
1.19 Cash receipts
1.20 Current and acid test ratios

The exam paper

Section B

2   Gearing; rights issues; convertible debt
3   Capital asset pricing model; marketable securities; investment of surplus funds
4   Creditor payment policy; just-in-time stock system
5   WACC; impact on cost of capital of change in gearing; bank loans and debentures
6   Operating cycle; cash movements; analysis of cash and working capital position

November 2001

Section A

1.1   Financial intermediary
1.2   Investment risk
1.3   Share prices
1.4   Rights issue
1.5   Debenture value
1.6   Financial gearing
1.7   CAPM
1.8   Yield curve
1.9   Present value
1.10 Commercial paper
1.11 Terminal value
1.12 Forfaiting
1.13 Current ratio
1.14 Working capital
1.15 Stock costs
1.16 Budget
1.17 Miller-Orr
1.18 Cash cycle
1.19 Economic order quantity
1.20 Working capital

Section B

2   Cost of debt; investment finance
3   Working capital management
4   Stock market ratios; investment and company valuation
5   Cash budget; bank finance
6   Rate of interest; finance of current assets

May 2001

Section A

1.1   Current ratio and cash operating cycle
1.2   Perpetuity
1.3   Cost of equity capital
1.4   Gearing theory
1.5   Price/earnings ratio
1.6   Equity warrants
1.7   Cash discounts
1.8   Working capital
1.9   Stock market efficiency
1.10 Investment risk
1.11 Interest rates
1.12 Payments to suppliers
1.13 Rights issues

The exam paper

1.14 Lease-buy decision
1.15 Venture capital
1.16 Cash received from debtors
1.17 Yield curve
1.18 Future dividends
1.19 Preference shares
1.20 Ex-dividend share prices

Section B

2 Cash budget; financing; working capital management
3 Weighted average cost of capital
4 Economic order quantity; stock/cost of sales ratio
5 Issue and ex-rights prices; value per ordinary share; working capital management
6 Capital asset pricing model; beta factors

Pilot paper

Section A

1.1 Yield curve
1.2 Dividend growth model
1.3 Price/earnings ratio
1.4 Stock market quotation
1.5 Finance lease
1.6 Cost of equity
1.7 Certificates of deposit
1.8 Ratios
1.9 Economic order quantity
1.10 BACS
1.11 Efficiency markets hypothesis
1.12 Price/earnings ratio
1.13 Miller-Orr cash management model
1.14 Share prices
1.15 Interest cover
1.16 Investment
1.17 Export sales funding
1.18 Warrants
1.19 Baumol cash management model
1.20 Venture capital

Section B

2 Treasury departments
3 Measures to improve cash flows; investing cash surpluses
4 Gearing ratios; WACC; debentures *versus* preference shares; merchant banks
5 Factoring services; cash discounts
6 Rights issue; issue of convertible loan stock

WHAT THE EXAMINER MEANS

The table below has been prepared by CIMA to help you interpret exam questions.

Learning objective	Verbs used	Definition
1 Knowledge What you are expected to know	• List • State • Define	• Make a list of • Express, fully or clearly, the details of/facts of • Give the exact meaning of
2 Comprehension What you are expected to understand	• Describe • Distinguish • Explain • Identify • Illustrate	• Communicate the key features of • Highlight the differences between • Make clear or intelligible/state the meaning of • Recognise, establish or select after consideration • Use an example to describe or explain something
3 Application Can you apply your knowledge?	• Apply • Calculate/compute • Demonstrate • Prepare • Reconcile • Solve • Tabulate	• To put to practical use • To ascertain or reckon mathematically • To prove with certainty or to exhibit by practical means • To make or get ready for use • To make or prove consistent/compatible • Find an answer to • Arrange in a table
4 Analysis Can you analyse the detail of what you have learned?	• Analyse • Categorise • Compare and contrast • Construct • Discuss • Interpret • Produce	• Examine in detail the structure of • Place into a defined class or division • Show the similarities and/or differences between • To build up or compile • To examine in detail by argument • To translate into intelligible or familiar terms • To create or bring into existence
5 Evaluation Can you use your learning to evaluate, make decisions or recommendations?	• Advise • Evaluate • Recommend	• To counsel, inform or notify • To appraise or assess the value of • To advise on a course of action

TACKLING MULTIPLE CHOICE QUESTIONS

Of the total marks available for this paper, multiple choice questions comprise:

A   10%
B   20%
C   30%
D   40%

The correct answer is D.

The multiple choice questions (MCQs) in your exam contain four possible answers. You have to **choose the option that best answers the question**. The three incorrect options are called distracters. There is a skill in answering MCQs quickly and correctly. By practising MCQs you can develop this skill, giving you a better chance of passing the exam.

You may wish to follow the approach outlined below, or you may prefer to adapt it.

Step 1.   **Skim read** all the MCQs and **identify** what appear to be the easier questions.

Step 2.   Attempt each question – **starting with the easier questions** identified in Step 1. Read the question thoroughly. You may prefer to work out the answer before looking at the options, or you may prefer to look at the options at the beginning. Adopt the method that works best for you.

Step 3.   Read the four options and see if one matches your own answer. **Be careful with numerical questions**, as the distracters are designed to match answers that incorporate common errors. Check that your calculation is correct. Have you followed the requirement exactly? Have you included every stage of the calculation?

Step 4.   You may **find that none of the options matches your answer**.

- Re-read the question to ensure that you understand it and are answering the requirement.
- Eliminate any obviously wrong answers.
- Consider which of the remaining answers is the most likely to be correct and select the option.

Step 5.   If you are still **unsure** make a note **and continue to the next question**.

Step 6.   **Revisit unanswered** questions. When you come back to a question after a break you often find you are able to answer it correctly straight away. If you are still unsure have a guess. You are not penalised for incorrect answers, so **never leave a question unanswered!**

Exam focus. After extensive practice and revision of MCQs, you may find that you recognise a question when you sit the exam. Be aware that the detail and/or requirement may be different. If the question seems familiar read the requirement and options carefully – do not assume that it is identical.

> BPP's **MCQ cards** and **i-Pass** for this paper provide you with plenty of opportunity for further practice of MCQs.

Part A
The finance function

Chapter 1

FINANCIAL MANAGEMENT AND FINANCIAL OBJECTIVES

Topic list	Syllabus reference	Ability required
1 The scope of financial management	(i)	Comprehension
2 Objectives of private sector companies	(i)	Comprehension
3 Non-financial objectives	(i)	Comprehension
4 Stakeholders in a company	(i)	Comprehension
5 Bodies which are not purely commercial	(i)	Comprehension
6 Value for money	(i)	Comprehension

Introduction

In this chapter, we examine the overall framework within which the financial manager operates. After introducing the **scope of financial management**, we consider the **objectives** of organisations.

In later chapters, we will be studying the **resources** available for an organisation to meet objectives and the methods available for doing so.

Learning outcomes covered in this chapter

- Explain the interrelationships between decisions concerning investment, financing and dividends

Syllabus content covered in this chapter

- The financial objectives of different organisations, eg value for money, maximising shareholder wealth, providing a surplus

- The three key decisions of financial management (ie investment, financing, dividend) and their links

1 THE SCOPE OF FINANCIAL MANAGEMENT

What is financial management?

> **KEY TERM**
>
> **Financial management** is the management of all the processes associated with the efficient acquisition and deployment of both short- and long-term financial resources.
> *(CIMA Official Terminology 2000 edition (OT 2000))*

3

Part A: The finance function

1.1 The usual assumption in financial management for the private sector is that the objective of the company is to **maximise shareholders' wealth**. There are two aspects of financial management:

- Financial planning
- Financial control

Financial planning

> **KEY TERMS**
>
> **Planning** is the establishment of objectives and the formulation, evaluation and selection of the policies, strategies, tactics and actions required to achieve them. Planning comprises long-term/strategic planning and short-term operation planning. The latter is usually for a period of up to one year.
>
> **Capital funding planning** is the process of selecting suitable funds to finance long-term assets and working capital.
>
> **Capital resource planning** is the process of evaluating and selecting long-term assets to meet strategies.
>
> **Financial planning** is planning the acquisition of funds to finance planned activities.
>
> *(OT 2000)*

1.2 The financial manager will need to **plan** to ensure that enough funding is available at the right time to meet the needs of the organisation.

(a) In the short term, funds may be needed to pay for purchases of stocks, or to smooth out changes in debtors, creditors and cash: the financial manager is here ensuring that **working capital requirements** are met.

(b) In the medium or long term, the organisation may have planned **purchases** of **fixed assets** such as plant and equipment, for which the financial manager must ensure that funding is available.

1.3 The financial manager contributes to decisions on the uses of funds raised by analysing financial data to determine uses which meet the organisation's financial objectives. For example: is project A to be preferred to Project B? Should a new asset be bought or leased?

Financial control

> **KEY TERM**
>
> **Financial control** is the control of divisional performance by setting a range of financial targets and the monitoring of actual performance towards these targets. *(OT 2000)*

1.4 The **control** function of the financial manager becomes relevant for funding which has been raised. For example: Are the various activities of the organisation meeting its objectives? Are assets being used efficiently? To answer these questions, the financial manager may compare data on **actual performance** with **forecast performance**.

Strategic financial management

1.5 Financial management concerns the strategy of the enterprise in meeting its objectives, and **strategic financial management** can be defined as follows.

> **KEY TERM**
>
> **Strategic financial management** is the identification of the possible strategies capable of maximising an organisation's net present value, the allocation of scarce capital resources among the competing opportunities and the implementation and monitoring of the chosen strategy so as to achieve stated objectives. *(OT 2000)*

Financial management decisions

1.6 A strategic plan will be required to implement strategic financial management decisions.

> **KEY TERM**
>
> A **strategic plan** is a statement of long-term goals along with a definition of the strategies and policies which will ensure achievement of those goals. *(OT 2000)*

1.7 The financial manager makes decisions relating to **investment, financing** and **dividends**.

EXAMPLES OF INVESTMENT DECISIONS	
• Internal decisions	• Undertaking new projects
	• Investment in new plant and machinery
	• Research and development
	• Marketing and advertising
• External parties	• Takeovers and mergers
	• Joint venture
• Divestment	• Sale of unprofitable segments
	• Sale of surplus plant and machinery
	• Sale of subsidiary companies

1.8 Investments in assets must be **financed** somehow. Financial management is also concerned with the management of short-term funds and with how funds can be raised over the long term, for example by the following methods.

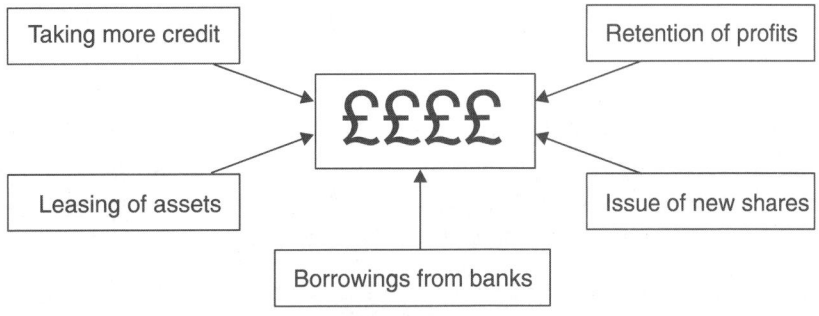

Part A: The finance function

1.9 Retention of profits was mentioned above as a financing decision. The other side of this decision is that if profits are retained, there is less to pay out to shareholders as **dividends**. An appropriate balance needs to be struck in addressing the **dividend decision**: how much of its profits should the company pay out as dividends and how much should it retain for investment to provide for future growth?

Question 1

Part of the job of the financial manager should be to identify surplus assets and dispose of them. Why do you think this should be done?

Answer

A surplus asset earns no return for the business. The business is likely to be paying the 'cost of capital' in respect of the money tied up in the asset, ie the money which it can realise by selling it.

If surplus assets are sold, the business may be able to **invest** the cash released in more productive ways, or alternatively it may use the cash to cut its liabilities. Either way, it will enhance the return on capital employed for the business as a whole.

Although selling surplus assets yields short-term benefits, the business should not jeopardise its activities in the medium or long term by **disposing** of **productive capacity** until the likelihood of it being required in the future has been fully assessed.

2 OBJECTIVES OF PRIVATE SECTOR COMPANIES

2.1 In much of economic theory, it is assumed that the firm behaves in such a way as to **maximise profits**, where profit is viewed in an economist's sense. To the economist, profit is the difference between the total revenue received by the firm and the total costs which it incurs. Unlike the accountant's concept of cost, total costs by this economist's definition includes an element of reward for the risk-taking of the entrepreneur, called 'normal profit'.

2.2 This is because entrepreneurship is viewed by the economist as one of the factors of production which the firm makes use of. Like the other factors of production - land, labour, and capital - entrepreneurship requires the prospect of a reward if it is to be prevented from being used elsewhere (in another firm) instead.

Profit maximisation and other objectives of firms

Profit maximisation

2.3 Where the entrepreneur is in full managerial control of the firm, as in the case of a small owner-managed company or partnership, the **economist's assumption of profit maximisation** would seem to be very reasonable. Even in companies owned by shareholders but run by non-shareholding managers, if the manager is serving the company's (ie the shareholders') interests, we might expect that the profit maximisation assumption should be close to the truth.

2.4 However, objectives other than profit maximisation might be pursued by firms. Managers are paid to make the decisions about prices and output, but it is the shareholders who expect to benefit from the profits. Managers, it is argued, will not necessarily make pricing decisions that will maximise profits, for these reasons.

(a) They have **no personal interests** at stake in the size of profits earned, except in so far as they are accountable to the shareholders for the profits they make.

1: Financial management and financial objectives

(b) There is **no competitive pressure** in the market to be efficient, minimise costs and maximise profits.

2.5 Given the **divorce of management from ownership**, it has been suggested that price and output decisions will be taken by managers with a **managerial aim** rather than the aim of profit maximisation, within the constraint that managers must take some account of shareholders' interests because they are formally responsible for them.

Sales maximisation

2.6 One 'managerial model' of the firm, *Baumol's* **sales maximisation model**, assumes that the firm acts to maximise sales revenue rather than profits (subject to the constraint that the profit level must be satisfactory). The management of a firm might opt for sales maximisation in order to maintain or increase its market share, to ensure survival and to discourage competition. Managers benefit personally because of the prestige of running a large and successful company, and also because salaries and other perks are likely to be higher in bigger companies than smaller ones.

Management discretion model

2.7 Another managerial model, *Williamson's* **management discretion model**, assumes that managers act to maximise their own utility, subject to a minimum profit requirement. The model states that utility, which a manager aims to maximise, is a function of the manager's own salary and also expenditure on his or her staff (prestige and influence depend on the numbers and pay levels of subordinate staff), the amount of perquisites (luxurious office, personal secretary, company car, expense account etc) and the authority to make 'discretionary investments' (ie new investments other than straightforward replacement decisions). The profit aimed for will not be maximum profit, because of management's wishes for expenditure on themselves, their staff and the perquisites of management.

Consensus theory

2.8 *Cyert* and *March's* **consensus theory** suggested that a firm is an organisational coalition of shareholders, managers, employees and customers, with each group having different goals, and so there is a need for political compromise in establishing the goals of the firm. Each group must settle for less than it would ideally want to have - shareholders must settle for less than maximum profit, and managers for less than maximum utility, and so on.

Maximisation of shareholder wealth

2.9 In the theory of company finance the assumption is that the financial manager's job is to maximise the market value of the company. Specifically, the **main financial objective of a company should be to maximise the wealth of its ordinary shareholders**. Within this context, the financial manager seeks to ensure that investments earn a **return**, for the benefit of shareholders.

2.10 All the surplus funds of a company belong to the legal owners of the company, its ordinary shareholders. Any retained profits are undistributed wealth of these equity shareholders.

Part A: The finance function

How are the wealth of shareholders and the value of a company measured?

2.11 If the financial objective of a company is to maximise the value of the company, and in particular the value of its ordinary shares, we need to be able to put values on a company and its shares. How do we do it?

2.12 Three possible methods for the valuation of a company might occur to us.

(a) **Balance sheet valuation, with assets valued on a going concern basis**

Balance sheet values are not a measure of 'market value', although retained profits might give some indication of what the company could pay as dividends to shareholders.

(b) **Break-up basis**

This method of valuing a business is only of interest when the business is threatened with liquidation, or when its management is thinking about selling off individual assets to raise cash.

(c) **Market values**

This is the method of valuation which is most relevant to the financial objectives of a company.

(i) When shares are traded on a recognised stock market, such as the Stock Exchange, the market value of a company can be measured by the **price** at which **shares** are currently being **traded**.

(ii) When shares are in a private company, and are not traded on any stock market, there is no easy way to measure their market value. Even so, the financial objective of these companies should be to maximise the wealth of their ordinary shareholders.

2.13 The wealth of the shareholders in a company comes from **dividends** received and the **market value of the shares**. A shareholder's return on investment is obtained in the form of dividends received and **capital gains** from increases in the market value of his or her shares.

> **KEY TERM**
>
> A **dividend** is an amount payable to shareholders from profits or other distributable reserves. Dividends are normally paid in cash but scrip dividends, paid by the issue of additional shares, are permissible. Listed companies normally pay two dividends per year: an interim dividend, based on interim profits reported during the accounting period, and a final dividend, based on the final audited accounts and approved at the Annual General Meeting.   *(OT 2000)*

How is the value of a business increased?

2.14 The price of a company's shares is likely to go up when the company makes attractive **earnings** (profits), which it pays out as dividends or re-invests in the business to achieve future profit growth and dividend growth. However, to increase the share price the company should achieve its attractive profits without taking business risks and financial risks which worry shareholders.

2.15 If there is an increase in earnings and dividends, management can hope for an increase in the share price too, so that shareholders benefit from both higher revenue (dividends) and

also capital gains (higher share prices). Management should set targets for factors which they can influence directly, such as **profits** and **dividend growth**.

Other financial targets

2.16 In addition to targets for earnings and dividends, a company might set **other financial targets**, such as the following.

(a) **Restriction on the company's level of debt**. For example, a company's management might decide that:

(i) The ratio of long-term debt capital to shares should never exceed, say, 1:1

(ii) The cost of interest payments should never be higher than, say, 25% of total profits before interest and tax

(b) **Target for profit retentions**. For example, management might set a target that dividend cover (the ratio of distributable profits to dividends actually distributed) should not be less than, say, 2.5 times.

(c) **Target for operating profitability**. For example, management might set a target for the profit/sales ratio.

2.17 Alternatively, a minimum return on capital employed may be set, of say 20%.

> **KEY TERM**
>
> Return on capital employed (ROCE) = $\dfrac{\text{Profit before interest and tax}}{\text{Average capital employed}} \times 100\%$

2.18 These financial targets are not primary long-term financial objectives, but they can act as subsidiary targets for individual years or constraints which should help a company to achieve its main financial objective without incurring excessive risks. Short-term measures of return can, however, encourage a company to pursue **short-term** objectives at the expense of **long-term** ones, for example by deferring new capital investments, or spending only small amounts on research and development and on training.

2.19 A major problem with setting a number of different financial targets, either primary targets or supporting secondary targets, is that they might not all be consistent with each other, and so might not all be achievable at the same time. When this happens, some compromises will have to be accepted.

3 NON-FINANCIAL OBJECTIVES

3.1 A company may have **non-financial objectives** as well as financial objectives. Examples of non-financial objectives are as follows.

(a) **The welfare of employees**. A company might try to provide good wages and salaries, comfortable and safe working conditions, good training and career development, and good pensions.

(b) **The welfare of management**. As we have seen, managers will often take decisions to improve their own circumstances, even though their decisions will incur expenditure and so reduce profits.

(c) **The welfare of society as a whole.** The management of some companies are aware of the role that their company has to play in providing for the well-being of society. Companies may be aware of their responsibility to minimise pollution and other harmful 'externalities' (to use the economist's term) which their activities generate. In delivering 'green' environmental policies, a company may improve its corporate image as well as reducing harmful externality effects.

(d) **The provision of a certain standard or level of service.** The major objectives of some companies will include fulfilment of a responsibility to provide a service to the public.

(e) **The fulfilment of responsibilities towards customers and suppliers.** Responsibilities towards **customers** include providing a product or service of a quality that customers expect, and dealing honestly and fairly with customers. Responsibilities towards **suppliers** are expressed mainly in terms of trading relationships. Suppliers might rely on getting prompt payment, in accordance with the agreed terms of trade.

Other non-financial objectives are **growth, diversification** and **leadership in research and development.**

Financial and non-financial objectives

3.2 Non-financial objectives do not negate financial objectives, but they do suggest that the simple theory of company finance, that the objective of a firm is to maximise the wealth of ordinary shareholders, is too simplistic. Financial objectives may have to be compromised in order to satisfy non-financial objectives.

4 STAKEHOLDERS IN A COMPANY

KEY TERM

Stakeholders are groups or individuals having a legitimate interest in the activities of an organisation, generally comprising customers, employees, the community, shareholders, suppliers and lenders. *(OT 2000)*

4.1 *Sharplin (Strategic Management)* has listed the following stakeholder groups in a firm.

Stakeholder groups	
• Common shareholders	• Competitors
• Preferred shareholders	• Neighbours
• Trade creditors	• The immediate community
• Holders of unsecured debt securities	• The national society
• Holders of secured debt securities	• The world society
• Intermediate (business) customers	• Corporate management
• Final (consumer) customers	• Organisational strategists
• Suppliers	• The chief executive
• Employees	• The board of directors
• Past employees	• Government
• Retirees	• Special interest groups

4.2 Stakeholder groups can exert influence on strategy. The greater the power of the stakeholder, the greater his influence will be.

4.3 Many managers acknowledge that the interests of some stakeholder groups - eg themselves and employees - should be recognised and provided for, even if this means that the interests of shareholders might be adversely affected. Not all stakeholder group interests can be given specific attention in the decisions of management, but those stakeholders for whom management recognises and accepts a responsibility are referred to as **constituents** of the firm.

Shareholders and management

4.4 Although ordinary shareholders (equity shareholders) are the owners of the company the **day-to-day** running of a company is the responsibility of the **management**.

4.5 **Shareholders** are often fairly ignorant about their company's current situation and future prospects. They have no right to inspect the books of account, and their forecasts of future prospects are gleaned from the annual report and accounts, stockbrokers, investment journals and daily newspapers. The relationship between management and shareholders is sometimes referred to as an **agency relationship**, in which managers act as agents for the shareholders.

> **KEY TERM**
>
> **Agency theory** is a hypothesis that attempts to explain elements of organisational behaviour through an understanding of the relationships between principals (such as shareholders) and agents (such as company managers and accountants). A conflict may exist between the actions undertaken by agents in furtherance of their own self-interest, and those required to promote the interests of the principals. Within the hierarchy of firms, the same goal incongruence may arise when divisional managers promote their own self-interest over those of other divisions and the company generally. *(OT 2000)*

4.6 However, if managers hold none or very few of the equity shares of the company they work for, what is to stop them from working inefficiently? **or** not bothering to look for profitable new investment opportunities? **or** giving themselves high salaries and perks?

4.7 One power that shareholders possess is the right to **remove the directors** from office. But shareholders have to take the initiative to do this, and in many companies, the shareholders lack the energy and organisation to take such a step. Even so, directors will want the company's report and accounts, and the proposed final dividend, to meet with shareholders' approval at the AGM.

4.8 Another reason why managers might do their best to improve the financial performance of their company is that managers' pay is often related to the size or profitability of the company. Managers in very big companies, or in very profitable companies, will normally expect to earn higher salaries than managers in smaller or less successful companies. There is also an argument for giving managers some **profit-related pay**, or providing incentives which are related to profits or share price.

4.9 **Advantages of having a wide range of shareholders**

   (a) There is likely to be **greater activity** in the market in the firm's shares.

Part A: The finance function

(b) There is **less likelihood** of one shareholder having a **controlling interest**.

(c) Since shareholdings are smaller on average, there is likely to be **less effect** on the **share price** if one shareholder sells his holding.

(d) There is a **greater likelihood** of a **takeover bid** being **frustrated**.

Disadvantages of a large number of shareholders

(a) **Administrative costs** will be high. These include the costs of sending out copies of the annual report and accounts, counting proxy votes, registering new shareholders and paying dividends.

(b) Shareholders will have **differing tax positions** and objectives in holding the firm's shares, which makes a dividend/retention policy more difficult for the management to decide upon.

Shareholders, managers and government

4.10 The government does not have a direct interest in companies (except for those in which it actually holds shares). However, the government does often have a strong indirect interest in companies' affairs.

(a) **Taxation.** The government raises taxes on sales and profits and on shareholders' dividends. It also expects companies to act as tax collectors for income tax and VAT. The tax structure might influence investors' preferences for either dividends or capital growth.

(b) **Encouraging new investments.** The government might provide funds towards the cost of some investment projects and offer tax incentives.

(c) **Encouraging a wider spread of share ownership.** In the UK, the government has made some attempts to encourage more private individuals to become company shareholders, by means of attractive privatisation issues and tax incentives, such as ISAs (Individual Savings Accounts).

(d) **Legislation.** The government also influences companies, and the relationships between shareholders, creditors, management, employees and the general public, through legislation.

(e) **Economic policy.** A government's economic policy will affect business activity. For example, exchange rate policy will have implications for the revenues of exporting firms and for the purchase costs of importing firms. Policies on economic growth, inflation, employment, interest rates and so on are all relevant to business activities.

5 BODIES WHICH ARE NOT PURELY COMMERCIAL

Nationalised industries

5.1 Following the privatisation programme of the 1980s and early 1990s, the UK's nationalised industries are much fewer in number than they were. One nationalised industry remaining in the UK is the Post Office. London Transport is another.

Strategic objectives for the nationalised industries

5.2 Nationalised industries are financed by **government loans**, and some **borrowing** from the capital markets. They do not have equity capital, and there is no stock exchange to give a day-by-day valuation of the business.

5.3 The financial objective cannot be to maximise the wealth of its owners, the government or the general public, because this is not a concept which can be applied in practice. Financial objectives will generally be subordinated to a number of political and social considerations.

   (a) A nationalised industry may be expected to provide a certain **standard of service** to all customers, regardless of the fact that some individuals will receive a service at a charge well below its cost. For example, the postal service must deliver letters to remote locations for the price of an ordinary first or second class stamp.

   (b) The need to provide a service may be of such overriding social and political importance that the government is prepared to **subsidise** the industry. There is a strong body of opinion, for example, which argues that public transport is a social necessity and a certain level of service must be provided, with losses made up by government subsidies.

Investment plans and investment appraisal in nationalised industries

5.4 Nationalised industries in the UK have generally been expected to aim at a **rate of return** (before interest and tax) on their new investment programmes of 5% in real terms. This is required so that the industries do not divert resources away from those areas where they could be used to best effect.

Corporate plans, targets and aims for nationalised industries

5.5 Each nationalised industry has **financial targets** and a series of **performance aims**. These targets and performance aims are set for a period of three to five years ahead, and may be included within a broader corporate plan.

External financing limits (EFLs) for nationalised industries

5.6 **External financing limits (EFLs)** control the flow of finance to and from nationalised industries. They set a limit on the amount of finance the industry can obtain from the government, and in the case of very profitable industries, they set requirements for the net repayment of finance to the government.

Not-for-profit organisations

5.7 Some organisations, such as **charities,** are set up with a prime objective which is not related to making profits. These organisations exist to pursue non-financial aims, such as providing a service to the community. However, there will be financial constraints which limit what any such organisation can do.

   (a) A not-for-profit organisation needs finance to pay for its operations, and the major financial constraint is the amount of funds that it can obtain.

   (b) Having obtained funds, a not-for-profit organisation should seek to use the funds so as to obtain **value for money**. Value for money is discussed further in the next section of this chapter.

Part A: The finance function

6 VALUE FOR MONEY

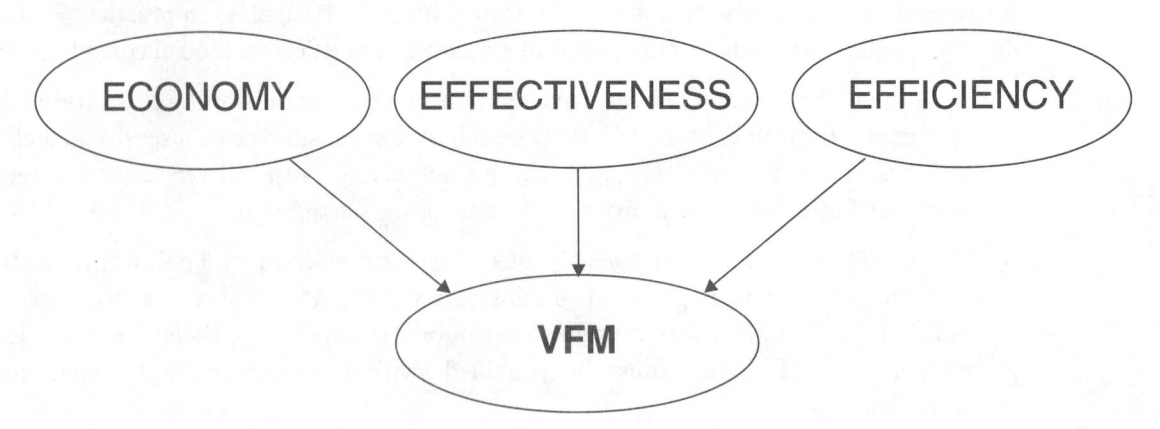

```
ECONOMY      EFFECTIVENESS      EFFICIENCY
       \           |           /
        \          |          /
         →        ↓        ←
              VFM
```

6.1 **Value for money (VFM)** means providing a service in a way which is economical, efficient and effective.

(a) **Economy** means doing things cheaply: not spending £2 when the same thing can be bought for £1.
(b) **Efficiency** means doing things well: getting the best use out of what money is spent on.
(c) **Effectiveness** means doing the right things: spending funds so as to achieve the organisation's objectives.

These are the **3 Es** of VFM.

6.2 In practice, evaluation of these elements of value for money is more often associated with not-for-profit organisations than commercial enterprises.

6.3 The term 'value for money' is used to cover all the three aspects. Public sector organisations are now under considerable pressure to prove that they operate economically, efficiently and effectively, and are encouraged from many sources to draw up action plans to achieve value for money as part of the continuing process of good management.

The three Es

6.4 In 1990, an Audit Brief on VFM audit defined the '**three Es**' as follows.

KEY TERMS

Economy means attaining the appropriate quantity and quality of physical, human and financial resources (**inputs**) at **lowest cost**. Economy does **not mean straightforward cost-cutting**, because resources must be acquired which are of a **suitable quality** to provide the service to the desired standard. Cost-cutting should not sacrifice quality to the extent that service standards fall to an unacceptable level. Economising by buying poor quality materials, labour or equipment is usually a false economy.

Efficiency is when an operation produces the **maximum output** for any **given set of resource** inputs; or it has **minimum inputs** for any **given quantity and quality** of output.

Effectiveness is concerned with how well an activity is **achieving its policy** objectives or other intended effects.

6.5 Value for money can often only be judged by **comparison**. In searching for value for money, present methods of operation and uses of resources must be compared with alternatives.

Studying and measuring the three Es

6.6 Economy, efficiency and effectiveness can be studied and measured with reference to the following.

(a) **Inputs, money**, or **resources** - the labour, materials, time and so on consumed, and their cost.

(b) **Outputs**, in other words the results of an activity, measurable as the services actually produced, and the quality of the services.

(c) **Impacts**, which are the **effect** that the outputs of an activity or programme have in terms of achieving policy objectives.

Question 2

Which of the following areas of decision-making would not normally be within the role of a financial manager?

A Dividends
B Financing
C Investment
D Marketing

Answer

D Marketing

Chapter roundup

- Financial management decisions cover **investment, financing** and **dividend** decisions.
- Financial targets may include targets for: **earnings; earnings per share; dividend per share; gearing level; profit retention; operating profitability**.
- Non-financial objectives may include: **employee welfare; management welfare; the welfare of society; service provision objectives; fulfilment of responsibilities to customers and suppliers**.
- **Stakeholders** are individuals or groups who are affected by the activities of the firm. They can be classified as **internal** (employees and managers), **connected** (shareholders, customers and suppliers) and **external** (local communities, pressure groups, government).
- The usual assumption in financial management for the private sector is that the primary financial objective of the company is to **maximise shareholders' wealth.**
- Particularly in not-for-profit organisations, providing **value for money** is a key objective. VFM involves doing things cheaply (**economy**), doing things well (**efficiency**) and doing the right thing (**effectiveness**).

Part A: The finance function

Quick quiz

1. In company finance, which of the following provides the best definition of the primary financial objective of a firm?

    A To maximise the wealth of its ordinary shareholders
    B To maximise the level of annual profits
    C To achieve long term growth in earnings
    D To maximise the level of annual dividends

2. Give a definition of financial management.

3. What are the 'Three Es' of value for money.

    E ………………..
    E ………………..
    E ………………..

4. What three broad types of decision does financial management involve?

5. ………………… planning is the process of evaluating and selecting long-term assets to meet strategies (OT 2000).

6. If earnings per share fall from one year to the next, so will the level of dividends.

    True ☐
    False ☐

7. Tick which are stakeholder groups for a company.

    Employees ☐
    Ordinary shareholders ☐
    The Board of Directors ☐
    Trade creditors ☐

8. In the context of managing performance in 'not for profit' organisations, which of the following definitions is incorrect?

    A Value for money means providing a service in a way which is economical, efficient and effective.
    B Economy means doing things cheaply: not spending £2 when the same thing can be bought for £1.
    C Efficiency means doing things quickly: minimising the amount of time that is spent on a given activity.
    D Effectiveness means doing the right things: spending funds so as to achieve the organisation's objectives.

Answers to quick quiz

1. A To maximise the wealth of its ordinary shareholders.
2. The management of the finances of an organisation in order to achieve the financial objectives of the organisation.
3. Efficiency. Economy. Effectiveness.
4. Investment decisions. Financing decisions. Dividend decisions.
5. Capital resource planning.
6. False. Dividends may still be maintained from payments out of profits retained in earlier periods.
7. You should have ticked all four boxes.
8. C Efficiency means doing things well: getting the best use out of what money is spent on.

Now try the question below from the Exam Question Bank

Number	Level	Marks	Time
1	Introductory	n/a	20 mins

Chapter 2

SECURITIES MARKET INSTITUTIONS

Topic list	Syllabus reference	Ability required
1 Financial intermediation and credit creation	(i)	Comprehension
2 Commercial banks and merchant banks	(i)	Comprehension
3 Money markets and capital markets	(i)	Comprehension
4 Venture capital	(i)	Comprehension
5 International money and capital markets	(i)	Comprehension

Introduction

Having discussed the scope of financial management and the objectives of firms and other organisations in the previous chapter, we now introduce the **markets** and **institutions** through which the financing of a business takes place.

Don't neglect this chapter. Your detailed knowledge of the institutions may be tested in an MCQ whilst a range of topics may be tested in the written parts of longer questions.

Learning outcomes covered in this chapter

- Describe and explain the operation of the securities markets
- Compare and contrast the services provided by financial institutions and recommend appropriate providers in different scenarios

Syllabus content covered in this chapter

- The operation of securities markets (stock exchanges), ie how share prices are determined and what causes share prices to rise or fall. (No detailed knowledge of any specific country's stock exchange will be tested.) Financial institutions, eg stock brokers, institutional investors, merchant banks, venture capitalists, money brokers

1 FINANCIAL INTERMEDIATION AND CREDIT CREATION

> **KEY TERM**
>
> **Financial intermediary** is a party bringing together providers and users of finance, either as broker or as principal.

1.1 A **financial intermediary** is an institution which links lenders with borrowers, by obtaining deposits from lenders and then re-lending them to borrowers.

Part A: The finance function

1.2 Not all intermediation takes place between savers and investors. Some institutions act mainly as intermediaries between other institutions. Almost all place part of their funds with other institutions, and a number (including finance houses, leasing companies and factoring companies) obtain most of their funds by borrowing from other institutions.

1.3 In the UK, financial intermediaries include the commercial banks, finance houses, building societies, the government's National Savings department and institutional investors such as pension funds and investment trusts.

The benefits of financial intermediation

1.4 Financial intermediaries perform the following functions.

(a) They provide obvious and **convenient** ways in which a **lender can save money**. Instead of having to find a suitable borrower for their money, lenders can deposit money with a bank, building society, pension fund, investment trust company, National Savings scheme etc. Financial intermediaries also provide a ready source of funds for borrowers. Even when money is in short supply, a borrower will usually find a financial intermediary prepared to lend some.

(b) They can aggregate or 'package' the amounts lent by savers and lend on to borrowers in different amounts. By aggregating the deposits of hundreds of small savers, a building society is able to package up the amounts and lend on to several borrowers in the form of larger mortgages. Through **aggregation**, institutions can use their size to exploit **economies of scale.**

(c) **Risk** for individual lenders is reduced by **pooling**. Since financial intermediaries lend to a large number of individuals and organisations, any losses suffered through default by borrowers or capital losses are effectively pooled and borne as costs by the intermediary. Such losses are shared among lenders in general.

(d) By pooling the funds of large numbers of people, some financial institutions are able to give investors access to **diversified portfolios** covering a varied range of different securities, such as unit trusts and investment trusts.

(e) Financial intermediaries, most importantly, provide **maturity transformation**; ie they bridge the gap between the wish of most lenders for liquidity and the desire of most borrowers for loans over longer periods.

Bank deposits and the creation of money ('credit creation')

1.5 An important aspect of financial intermediation affecting the workings of the economy as a whole is that of credit creation, which occurs as follows. Banks create money when they lend because when a bank lends money, most of the money will find its way back into the banking system as new customer deposits. This means that the amount lent by the bank adds to the money supply.

1.6 Suppose, for example, that in a country with a single bank, a customer C deposits £100,000. The bank, we will assume, re-lends all these deposits to another customer D. This customer D uses the money he has borrowed to buy goods and services from firm Y. If firm Y, after receiving payment, then puts the money into its own account with the bank, the bank's deposits will have doubled.

Liabilities of the bank		*Assets of the bank*	
	£		£
Deposit of customer C	100,000	Loan to customer D	100,000
Deposit of firm Y	100,000		
	200,000		

1.7 This will enable the bank to re-lend more money (another £100,000), to bring its assets up to £200,000 and this in turn will create even more bank deposits. This cycle could go on and on, with the bank making more and more loans, and the people who are paid for goods and services bought with the loans putting all their receipts back into the bank as extra deposits. In short, 'every loan creates a deposit'.

1.8 The situation is the same if we define money to include building society deposits.

1.9 Extra bank lending (and building society lending) therefore has a dual effect. It **increases the money supply**. It **provides credit** which borrowers use to increase their amount of spending. Lending adds to spending in the economy.

> **KEY TERM**
>
> **Credit creation** is the process whereby banks and other deposit-taking and lending institutions can, on the basis of an increase in reserve assets, expand the volume of lending and deposit liabilities by more than the initial increase in reserves.

2 COMMERCIAL BANKS AND MERCHANT BANKS

2.1 An important grouping of financial intermediaries is the **commercial banks**, which include both the retail banks, which include the well known 'High Street' banks, and the wholesale banks, which offer services mainly to larger customers, including large companies. The wholesale banks include merchant banks and overseas banks.

2.2 **Functions of the commercial banks**

(a) They provide a **payments mechanism**: a way in which individuals, firms and government can make payments to each other. The 'clearing system' of the clearing banks is the major payments mechanism in the UK, and it enables individuals and firms to make payments by cheque. The banks are also a source from which individuals and firms can obtain notes and coin.

(b) They provide a place for individuals, firms and government to store their wealth. Banks compete with other financial institutions to attract the funds of individuals and firms.

(c) They act as **providers of funds** by lending money in the form of loans or overdrafts.

Merchant banks

2.3 **Merchant** (or **investment**) banks engage in diverse activities, with individual banks having their specialised areas of expertise and interest. Merchant banking is perhaps best thought of in terms of its customers, who are generally corporate clients wanting particular financial services. The clearing banks carry out some merchant banking activities themselves.

The range of merchant banking activities

2.4 Merchant banking activities are various. The following list gives some examples.

- Involvement in the issue and underwriting of shares on the Stock Exchange
- Taking 'wholesale' deposits of funds, both in sterling and foreign currencies
- Large scale term lending to corporate borrowers

Part A: The finance function

- Dealing in foreign exchange
- Dealing in the gold and silver bullion markets
- Handling Stock Exchange business on behalf of clients
- Managing investments on behalf of clients
- Acting as trustees
- Advising business customers on takeovers and mergers
- Providing venture capital
- Share registration
- Dealing in stocks and shares as a market maker or stockbroker, through a subsidiary

Medium-term lending

2.5 Merchant banks compete for deposits of larger customers, and make large medium-term loans to borrowers. There is intense competition between banks in this area of activity with merchant banks, foreign banks and clearing banks vying with each other for 'wholesale' deposits and medium-term lending business.

Business advice on mergers and takeovers

2.6 Merchant banks have become increasingly involved in providing advice on business mergers and takeovers. If company A, for example, wants to take over company B by bidding for its shares, one merchant bank might advise the board of directors of company A in proceeding with the bid, and another bank might advise the board of company B, possibly on ways of contesting the takeover. Another function of a merchant bank might be to identify suitable candidates for a takeover by a customer.

Merchant banks and new capital issues by companies

2.7 The role of merchant banks in the issue of new share and loan capital is a major element of merchant banking. The banks provide not just advice but also the organisation for capital issues.

2.8 Capital issues business is not the exclusive preserve of merchant banks, however, and organisations other than merchant banks undertake capital issues. The regulatory body for capital issues is the Issuing Houses Association, and its members are known as **issuing houses**. The task of an issuing house is to supervise the issue of a company's stocks or shares.

3 MONEY MARKETS AND CAPITAL MARKETS

3.1 The **capital markets**, being markets for long-term capital, are distinguished from the **money markets**, which are markets for

- Trading short-term financial instruments
- Short-term lending and borrowing.

Differences between loan terms

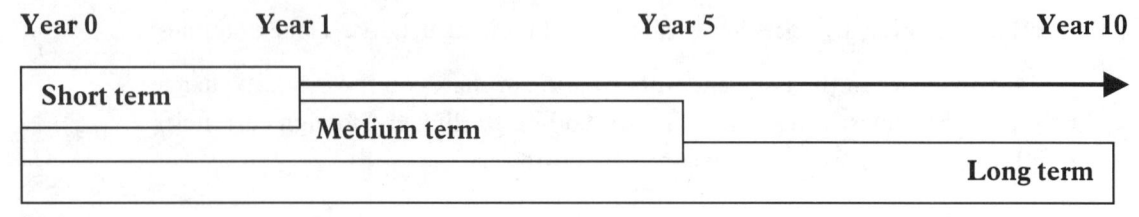

Year 0	Year 1	Year 5	Year 10
Short term			
	Medium term		
			Long term

The money markets

> **KEY TERM**
>
> **Money market** is a short-term wholesale market for securities maturing in one year, such as certificates of deposit, treasury bills and commercial paper. *(OT 2000)*

3.2 The money markets are operated by the banks and other financial institutions.

MONEY MARKETS	
Primary or official	Approved institutions buy bills of exchange/other short-term instruments in daily trading with Bank of England, which uses these open-market operations to control short-term interest rates
Interbank	Banks lend short-term funds to each other. **Money brokers** operate in the interbank market, acting as intermediaries between banks that wish to borrow and banks that wish to lend
Eurocurrency	Banks lend and borrow in foreign currencies
Certificate of deposit	Trading in certificates of deposits, negotiable instruments issued by banks acknowledging a deposit of money
Local authority	Local authorities borrow short-term from banks/other investors
Finance house	Finance houses raise short-term loans
Inter-company	Direct short-term lending between companies, without financial intermediary

The capital markets

3.3 Capital markets are markets for trading in **long-term finance**, in the form of long-term financial instruments. In the UK, the principal capital markets are the **Stock Exchange 'main market'** (for companies with a full Stock Exchange listing) and the more loosely regulated 'second tier' **Alternative Investment Market (AIM)** which is also regulated by the Stock Exchange. Apart from regulating these two markets, the Stock Exchange is also the market for dealings in **government securities** (gilts).

> **KEY TERMS**
>
> **Stock exchange** is a registered market in securities.
>
> **Alternative Investment Market** is a securities market designed primarily for small companies, regulated by the stock exchange but with less demanding rules than apply to the stock exchange official list of companies. *(OT 2000)*

3.4 Firms obtain long-term or medium-term capital in one of the following ways.

(a) They may raise **share capital**. Firms that issue ordinary share capital are inviting investors to take an equity stake in the business, or to increase their existing equity stake.

(b) They may raise **loan capital**. Long-term loan capital might be raised in the form of a mortgage or debenture. The lender will usually want some security for the loan, and

Part A: The finance function

the mortgage deed or debenture deed will specify the **security**. Most loans have a **fixed term** to maturity. Debenture stock, like shares, can be issued on the stock market and then bought and sold in 'secondhand' trading. Interest is paid on the stock and the loan is repaid when the stock reaches its maturity date.

3.5 The stock markets serve two main purposes.

(a) As **primary markets** they enable organisations to raise new finance, by issuing new shares or new debentures. Capital markets make it easier for companies to raise new long-term finance than if they had to raise funds privately by contacting investors individually. In the UK, a company must have public company status (be a plc) to be allowed to raise finance from the public on a capital market.

(b) As **secondary markets** they enable existing investors to sell their investments, should they wish to do so. The **marketability** of securities is a very important feature of the capital markets, because investors are more willing to buy stocks and shares if they know that they could sell them easily, should they wish to.

Stockbrokers are key figures in this process; as members of a Stock Exchange they buy and sell securities as agents for clients in return for a commission.

3.6 These are the main functions of a stock market, but we can add two more important ones.

(a) When a company comes to the stock market for the first time, and 'floats' its shares on the market, the **owners** of the company can **realise** some of the **value** of their shares in cash, because they will offer a proportion of their personally-held shares for sale to new investors.

(b) When one company wants to take over another, it is common to do so by issuing shares to finance the takeover. Takeovers by means of a share exchange are only feasible if the shares that are offered can be readily traded on a stock market, and so have an identifiable market value.

Question 1

Get hold of a copy of the Companies and Markets section of the weekday *Financial Times*, and look out for points relevant to your studies. Note the various London Money Rates in the Money Markets section, the parts covering the London Stock Exchange, and the share prices quotations on the London Share Service pages. This may help to put some of the topics covered here into context.

The Alternative Investment Market (AIM)

3.7 The London Stock Exchange launched the AIM in 1995 as a market for smaller, growing, companies that cannot qualify for or do not wish to join the Official List (or 'main market').

3.8 **Key characteristics of the AIM**

(a) There are no **eligibility criteria** for new entrants, whether in size, profitability or length of track record.

(b) **Any type of security** can be offered, provided there are no restrictions on transferability.

(c) There are no Stock Exchange requirements for the **percentage of shares** in public hands or the number of shareholders, although if too few shares are freely available, then there will be no realistic market price.

2: Securities market institutions

    (d) There are few obligations to issue **shareholder circulars**; public announcements will generally be sufficient.

    (e) Documents produced for admission to the AIM are the responsibility of the directors and are not reviewed by the Exchange.

    (f) Every company whose securities trade on the AIM must have (at all times) a **Nominated Adviser** chosen from an official list and a **Nominated Broker** which must be a member firm of the Exchange. The Adviser's role is to advise the directors of the issuer on their obligations under AIM rules. The Broker's role is to support trading if there is no market maker and to act as a point of contact for investors.

    (g) AIM shares are treated as **unquoted** for tax purposes, meaning that a number of reliefs are available to investors.

3.9 AIM companies might be new business 'start-ups' or well established family businesses, from high technology firms to traditional manufacturers. The AIM is designed to attract companies which wish to cut the cost of a stock market quotation. The Stock Exchange hopes that the failure rate among AIM companies will be minimised as a result of its careful vetting of Nominated Advisers.

3.10 The AIM offers the advantages of **wider access** to capital, enhanced credibility among financial institutions and a **higher public profile**, at a **much lower cost** than a full listing.

Over-the-counter markets

> **KEY TERM**
>
> The **over-the-counter (OTC) market** is a market in which trading takes place directly between licensed dealers rather than through an auction system as used in most organised exchanges. *(OT 2000)*

3.11 Shares and other financial instruments are bought and sold outside the supervised and regulated official exchanges in the **'over-the-counter' (OTC) markets**. Shares are traded 'off the market' to reduce costs as well as to maintain secrecy.

Institutional investors

> **KEY TERM**
>
> **Institutional investors** are institutions which have large amounts of funds which they want to invest, and they will invest in stocks and shares or any other assets (such as gold or works of art) which offer satisfactory returns and security.

3.12 The institutional investors are now the biggest investors on the stock market but they might also invest venture capital, or lend directly to companies. The major institutional investors in the UK are **pension funds, insurance companies, investment trusts, unit trusts** and venture capital organisations. Of these, pension funds and insurance companies have the largest amounts of funds to invest.

Part A: The finance function

Pension funds as institutional investors

3.13 **Pension funds** comprise funds set aside to provide for retirement pensions. They are financed from pension contributions paid by a company and its employees and by private individuals.

3.14 Pension funds are continually receiving large amounts of money from pension contributions and as dividends and interest. They are also continually paying out money for pensions, as lump sums and regular pension payments to beneficiaries. There will usually be an excess of contributions coming in over pensions going out, and this excess must be invested.

3.15 A **fund manager** is the person who makes the investment decisions, buying and selling securities. Fund managers must attempt to ensure that their investments will provide enough income to meet **future pension commitments**. Generally speaking, most holdings are considered to be long-term. Often a portion of the fund is invested in high yield securities, such as gilts which will, hopefully, give enough income to meet current commitments, and the balance is invested in growth assets such as equities or property.

Insurance companies

3.16 **Insurance companies** sell insurance policies (life assurance policies, car insurance, house insurance, pension policies and so on). They need cash to pay out for claims or other entitlements under the terms of their policies, but they will have substantial cash income to invest. The investment strategy of insurance companies is broadly similar to the investment strategy of pension fund managers.

Investment trusts

3.17 **Investment trusts** are companies whose business is to invest in the securities of a wide range of other companies. Their portfolios may change continually, as circumstances require.

(a) Having a capital structure, similarly to any other company they pay **dividends** to shareholders from profits which arise from their investment income, but not (if the investment company is listed) from sales arising from surpluses of investments.

(b) Most of the funds of investment trusts are invested directly through the Stock Exchange, and little money goes into unquoted shares.

Unit trusts

3.18 **Unit trusts** cater for small investors who wish to spread their investment risk over a wide range of securities, but have insufficient funds to create such a portfolio by themselves. A 'unit' is a portfolio of shares or other investments managed by a unit trust company in which individual investors are invited to take a stake (sub-unit).

3.19 Unit holders receive their income as a proportionate share of the investment income from the securities in the unit after deducting expenses of the management company. When unit holders want to realise their investment, they can sell their units.

Capital market participants

3.20 The various participants in the capital markets are summarised in the diagram below.

2: Securities market institutions

```
      Demand for funds           Capital markets              Suppliers
        comes from...             INTERMEDIARIES              of funds

      INDIVIDUALS         ←────    Banks           ←────     INDIVIDUALS
      (eg housing/consumer                                   (as savers and
       goods finance)     ←────    Building societies ←──── investors)

                                   Insurance companies
                          ←────    and pension funds   ←────
      FIRMS                                                   FIRMS
      (share capital;                                         (with long-term
       loans)             ←────    Unit trust/investment ←── funds to invest)
                                   trust companies

                          ←────    Stock exchanges       ←────
      GOVERNMENT                                              GOVERNMENT
      (budget deficit)    ←────    Venture capital       ←──── (budget surplus)
                                   organisations
```

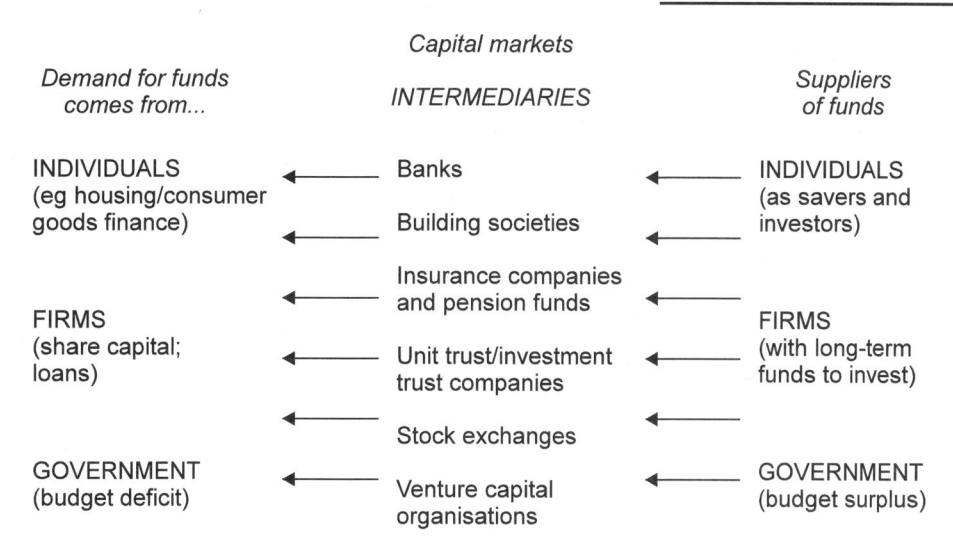

Question 2

What briefly is the Alternative Investment Market and how in general terms do its requirements for admission differ from those of the main market of the London Stock Exchange?

Answer

The Alternative Investment Market (AIM) was set up to **facilitate trading** in the securities of companies which do not qualify for a full listing on the main Stock Exchange. The requirements for admission to AIM are simpler and less stringent although still regulated and managed by a separate division of the London Stock Exchange.

AIM is open to a **wide range of companies** from old established family companies to management buy-outs and start-ups. It enables them to raise capital for further growth and to establish a market value for their shares as well as raising their visibility.

Companies coming to AIM **do not** have to have reached a **certain size** or demonstrate a **lengthy trading history**. There is no requirement for a specified percentage of the shares to be held by the public.

The two essential requirements for trading on AIM are that at all times the company must maintain a Nominated Broker and a Nominated Adviser who will assist and advise on admission, trading and ongoing obligations.

---

4 VENTURE CAPITAL

The role of venture capital

4.1 Compared to large companies, small companies have much more difficulty in obtaining funds. Smaller companies are perceived as being more risky, and investors either refuse to invest or expect a higher return on their investment, which the borrowing firm must then be able to pay.

4.2 Small and unquoted companies do not have ready access to new long-term funds, except for

- Cash from retained earnings
- Finance obtained by issuing more shares to private shareholders
- Bank borrowing

Part A: The finance function

4.3 The problems of finance for small businesses have received much publicity in recent years, and some efforts have been made to provide them with access to sources of funds. Most of these sources are referred to as '**venture capital**'.

> **KEY TERM**
>
> **Venture capital** is a specialised form of finance provided for new companies, buy-outs and small growth companies which are perceived as carrying above average risk.
>
> *(OT 2000)*

Venture capital organisations

4.4 **Venture capital organisations** have been operating for many years. There are now quite a large number of such organisations. The British Venture Capital Association is a regulatory body for all the institutions that have joined it as members. **Investors in Industry plc**, or the **3i group** as it is more commonly known, is the biggest and oldest of the venture capital organisations.

4.5 It was estimated that venture capital investment in the UK amounted to £18 billion by 1996. In 1999 and 2000, much venture capital investment has been in technology and 'e-commerce' internet ventures.

4.6 Like other venture capitalists, the 3i group wants to invest in companies that will be successful. The group's publicity material states that successful investments have three common characteristics.

- A **good basic idea**, a product or service which meets real customer needs
- **Finance**, in the right form, to turn the idea into a solid business
- **Commitment** and **drive** of an individual or group, and determination to succeed

4.7 The types of venture that the 3i group might invest in include the following.

(a) **Business start-ups**. When a business has been set up by someone who has already put time and money into getting it started, the group may be willing to provide finance to enable it to get off the ground. With start-ups, the 3i group often prefers to be one of several financial institutions putting in venture capital.

(b) **Business development**. The group may be willing to provide development capital for a company which wants to invest in new products or new markets or to make a business acquisition, and so which needs a major capital injection.

(c) **Management buyouts**. A management buyout is the purchase of all or parts of a business from its owners by its managers.

(d) **Investment realisation**. This will involve helping a company where one of its owners wants to **realise all or part of his investment**. The 3i group may be prepared to buy some of the company's equity.

Venture capital funds

4.8 Some other organisations are engaged in the creation of **venture capital funds,** whereby the organisation raises venture capital funds from investors and invests in management buyouts or expanding companies. The venture capital fund managers usually reward themselves by taking a percentage of the portfolio of the fund's investments.

2: Securities market institutions

4.9 **Venture capital trusts** are a special type of fund giving investors tax reliefs.

Finding venture capital

4.10 When a company's directors look for help from a venture capital institution, they must recognise the following.

(a) The institution will want an **equity stake** in the company.

(b) It will need convincing that the company can be **successful** (management buyouts of companies which already have a record of successful trading have been increasingly favoured by venture capitalists in recent years).

4.11 The directors of the company must then contact venture capital organisations, to try to find one or more which would be willing to offer finance. A venture capital organisation will only give funds to a company that it believes can succeed and before it will make any definite offer, it will want a number of details including a business plan stating how much finance is needed and how it would be used.

4.12 The venture capital organisation ('VC' below) will take account of various factors, as follows, in deciding whether to not to invest.

FACTORS DETERMINING VENTURE CAPITAL INVESTMENT	
Nature of the company's product	Viable production and sufficient sales potential
Expertise in production	Technical ability to produce efficiently
Expertise in management	Venture capitalists require commitment, skills and experience
The market and competition	Threat of rival producers and future new entrants
Future prospects	Do potential profits compensate for risks?
Board membership	Generally venture capitalist will require a place on the board of directors, to maintain interests & to have say in strategy
Risk borne by existing owners	Existing owners should bear substantial part of risk & their investment should be significant in terms of their own personal wealth.

4.13 The ways in which the venture capitalist can eventually realise its investment are called **exit routes**. Ideally the VC will try to ensure that there are a number of exit routes, such as the following.

(a) The sale of shares following a flotation of the company's shares on a recognised stock exchange, or on the Alternative Investment Market

(b) The sale of shares to another business in a takeover

(c) The sale of shares to the original owners, if they later have the necessary resources

Business angel financing

4.14 Business angel financing can be an important initial source of business finance. Business angels are wealthy individuals or groups of individuals who invest directly in small businesses.

Part A: The finance function

4.15 The main problem with business angel financing is that it is informal in terms of a market and can be difficult to set up. However informality can be a strength. There may be less need to provide business angels with detailed information about the company, since business angels generally have prior knowledge of the industry.

4.16 Surveys suggest that business angels are often more patient than providers of other sources of finance. However the money available from individual business angels may be limited, and large sums may only be available from a consortium of business angels.

5 INTERNATIONAL MONEY AND CAPITAL MARKETS

5.1 In this section, we consider (in outline) foreign currency and international borrowing.

5.2 Larger companies are able to borrow funds on the **eurocurrency markets** (which are international money markets) and on the markets for **eurobonds** (international capital markets).

> **Exam focus point**
>
> Don't suggest these international markets as possible sources of finance for a *smaller* business in an exam answer.

Eurocurrency markets

5.3 A UK company might borrow money from a bank or from the investing public, in sterling. But it might also borrow in a foreign currency, especially if it trades abroad, or if it already has assets or liabilities abroad denominated in a foreign currency. When a company borrows in a foreign currency, the loan is known as a **eurocurrency loan.**

> **KEY TERMS**
>
> **Eurocurrency** is currency which is held by individuals and institutions outside the country of issue of that currency.
>
> **Eurodollars** are US dollars deposited with, or borrowed from, a bank outside the USA.
>
> *(OT 2000)*

5.4 For example, if a UK company borrows US $50,000 from its bank, the loan will be a 'eurodollar' loan. London is a major centre for eurocurrency lending and companies with foreign trade interests might choose to borrow from their bank in another currency.

5.5 The **eurocurrency markets** involve the depositing of funds with a bank outside the country of the currency in which the funds are denominated and re-lending these funds for a fairly short term, typically three months. Most eurocurrency transactions in fact take place between banks of different countries and take the form of negotiable certificates of deposit. Money brokers operate in the various international markets.

International capital markets

5.6 Large companies may arrange borrowing facilities from their bank, in the form of bank loans or bank overdrafts. Instead, however, they might prefer to borrow from private investors. In other words, instead of obtaining a £10,000,000 bank loan, a company might issue 'bonds', or 'paper' in order to borrow directly from investors who will receive the interest.

5.7 In recent years, a strong international market has built up which allows very large companies to borrow in this way, long-term or short-term. As well as eurobonds, there is also a less highly developed market in international equity share issues ('**euro-equity**').

> **KEY TERM**
>
> A **eurobond** is a bearer bond, issued in a eurocurrency (see above), usually eurodollars.
> *(OT 2000)*

5.8 **Eurobonds** are long-term loans raised by international companies or other institutions and sold to investors in several countries at the same time. Such bonds can be sold by one holder to another. The term of a eurobond issue is typically ten to fifteen years.

5.9 Eurobonds may be the most suitable source of finance for a large organisation with an excellent credit rating, such as a large successful multinational company.

(a) It may require a long-term loan to finance a big **capital expansion programme** (with a loan for at least five years and up to twenty years).

(b) It may require borrowing which is not subject to the **national exchange controls** of any government (a company in country X could raise funds in the currency of country Y by means of a eurobond issue, and thereby avoid any exchange control restrictions which might exist in country X).

(c) Domestic capital issues may be **regulated** by the **government** or **central bank**, with an orderly queue for issues. In contrast, eurobond issues can be made whenever market conditions seem favourable.

5.10 The interest rate on a bond issue may be fixed or variable. Many variable rate issues have a minimum interest rate which the bond holders are guaranteed, even if market rates fall even lower. These bonds convert to a fixed rate of interest when market rates do fall to this level.

5.11 A borrower who is contemplating a eurobond issue must consider the **exchange risk** of a long-term foreign currency loan.

(a) If the money is to be used to purchase assets which will earn revenue in a currency **different to that of the bond issue,** the borrower will run the risk of exchange losses. These losses would be due to adverse movements in exchange rates, if the currency of the loan strengthens against the currency of the revenues out of which the bond (and interest) must be repaid.

(b) If the money is to be used to purchase assets which will earn revenue in the **same currency,** the borrower can match these revenues with payments on the bond, and so remove or reduce the exchange risk.

5.12 An **investor** subscribing to a bond issue will be concerned about the following factors.

(a) **Security**

The borrower must be of high quality. A standard condition of a bond issue is a 'negative pledge clause' in which the borrower undertakes not to give any prior charge

Part A: The finance function

over its assets, during the life of the bond issue, that would rank ahead of the rights of the investors in the event of a liquidation.

(b) **Marketability**

Investors will wish to have a ready market in which bonds can be bought and sold. If the borrower is of high quality the bonds or notes will be readily negotiable.

(c) **Anonymity**

Investors in eurobonds tend to be attracted to the anonymity of this type of issue, as the bonds are generally issued to bearer.

(d) **Return on the investment**

This is paid tax-free.

5.13 The period since World War II has seen the development of international financial centres as well as growth in international trade and multinational business activities. The most important such centres are London, New York and Tokyo. **International banks**, most of whom are themselves large multinational enterprises, are the most important financial intermediaries in these financial centres.

Question 3

What is 'a party bringing together providers and users of finance, either as broker or as principal' known as?

A   Financial intermediary
B   Financial institution
C   Bank
D   Venture capitalist

Answer

A   Financial institutions, banks and venture capitalists may all at times act as financial intermediaries.

Chapter roundup

- In this chapter, we have covered some important aspects of the **markets** and **institutions** which are relevant to the practice of financial management.

- A **financial intermediary** links those with surplus funds (eg **lenders**) to those with funds deficits (eg potential **borrowers**) thus providing **aggregation** and **economies of scale**, **risk pooling** and **maturity transformation**.

- **Commercial banks** provide payments mechanisms and means of storing wealth. They also act as providers of funds.

- **Merchant banks (investment banks)** provide various services, including business advice on mergers and takeovers.

- The **capital markets** and **money markets** are markets for long-term and short-term capital respectively.

- **Venture capital** is available to risky enterprises, usually in return for an equity stake. The venture capital company will often put a director on the board.

- A **stock market** (in the UK: the **main market** plus the **AIM**) acts as a **primary market** for raising finance, and as a **secondary market** for the trading of existing securities (ie stocks and shares).

- **International money and capital markets** are available for larger companies wishing to raise larger amounts of finance.

Quick quiz

1. Which of the following activities would **not** normally be undertaken by a merchant bank?

   A   Handling Stock Exchange business on behalf of clients
   B   Providing mortgage finance to individuals
   C   Acting as trustees
   D   Dealing in the gold and silver bullion markets

2. Match the four terms with their correct explanation. (b), (c) and (d) are all advantages of financial intermediation.

(a) Credit creation	(b) Maturity transformation	(c) Aggregation	(d) Pooling of risks
(i) Economy of scale in lending/ borrowing	(ii) Spreading of the costs of default	(iii) Growth in lending through lenders making use of 'multiplier' effect of increasing reserve assets	(iv) Linking of lenders and borrowers needing deposits/ funds over different periods

3. For short-term borrowing, a company will go to the **money markets/capital markets**? (Which?)

4. (a) From which does the **demand** for capital markets funds come: Individuals/Firms/Government? (Delete any that do not apply).

   (b) From which does the **supply** of capital market funds come: Individuals/Firms/Government? (Delete any that do not apply).

5. Identify five types of capital market intermediaries.

Part A: The finance function

6   Which of the following markets is **not** a money market?

    A   The interbank market
    B   The finance house market
    C   The Stock Exchange
    D   The inter-company market

7   Fill in the time periods.

    A   Short-term loans   0 - __ years
    B   Medium-term loans   0 - __ years
    C   Long-term loans   0 - __ years

8   List four factors that a venture capitalist will consider when deciding whether to invest in a company.

Answers to quick quiz

1   B   Merchant banks normally act for corporate clients, and not for individuals.

2   (a) (iii)
   (b) (iv)
   (c) (i)
   (d) (ii)

3   Money markets.

4   (a) and (b): You should have deleted none.

5   Any five of:

   (a) Banks   (e) Unit trust companies
   (b) Building societies   (f) Investment trusts
   (c) Insurance companies   (g) Stock Exchanges
   (d) Pension funds   (h) Venture capital organisations

6   C   The Stock Exchange is a capital market, not a money market.

7   A   Short-term loans   0 - 1 years
   B   Medium-term loans 0 - 5 years
   C   Long-term loans   0 - >5 years

8   Any four of:

   (a) Nature of the company's product
   (b) Production expertise
   (c) Management expertise
   (d) Future prospects
   (e) Board membership
   (f) Risk borne by existing owners

Now try the question below from the Exam Question Bank

Number	Level	Marks	Time
2	Introductory	n/a	20 mins

Chapter 3

DETERMINATION OF SHARE PRICES

Topic list	Syllabus reference	Ability required
1 Share prices and investment returns	(i)	Comprehension
2 The fundamental analysis theory of share values	(i)	Comprehension
3 Charting or technical analysis	(i)	Comprehension
4 Random walk theory	(i)	Comprehension
5 The efficient market hypothesis	(i)	Comprehension

Introduction

In this chapter, we look at methods of **valuing individual shares** and at the ways in which share prices are determined. This involves considering how participants in **stock markets** seem to respond to market information.

The most important part of this chapter is the **efficient market hypothesis**. You not only need to understand the various stages of the hypothesis, but also what will happen to share prices if an announcement or event occurs.

Learning outcomes covered in this chapter

- Describe and explain the operation of the securities markets

Syllabus content covered in this chapter

- The operation of securities markets (stock exchanges), ie how share prices are determined and what causes share prices to rise or fall

- The efficient market hypothesis (EMH)

1 SHARE PRICES AND INVESTMENT RETURNS

> **KEY TERM**
>
> A **share** is a fixed identifiable unit of capital which has a fixed nominal or face value, which may be quite different from the market value of the share. *(OT 2000)*

1.1 Investors will buy shares to obtain an income from dividends and/or to make a capital gain from an increase in share prices. The market price of a security will depend on the return that investors expect to get from it.

1.2 The return from an **ordinary share** consists of dividends plus any capital gain. The **capital gain (or loss)** is the difference between the price at which the investor bought the share, and the share's current market value.

1.3 We can compare this with returns on **fixed interest securities**, which consist of:

(a) Interest payments

(b) (i) **Either, changes in the market value** of the security, if the investor sells it before maturity

(ii) **Or,** the **redemption value** of the security when it eventually matures, less the price paid

1.4 Generally speaking, investors who buy ordinary shares are taking a bigger financial risk than investors in fixed interest securities. This is because holders of debt receive **interest** out of **pre-tax profits** and have a prior claim over shareholders in the event that the company goes into liquidation. Ordinary shareholders, in contrast, can only receive dividends if the company has enough distributable profits and might suffer capital losses if the share price goes down.

1.5 If the purpose of investing is to earn dividend income, an investor will try to buy shares which are expected to provide a satisfactory dividend in relation to their market value. The movement in share prices, which occurs from day to day on the stock market, means that an investor can improve his return by **buying at the right time**. For example, if the share price is £1.50 on day 1, rising to £1.55 on day 2, falling to £1.48 on day 3 and rising to £1.50 on day 4, the investor will obtain the best return if he buys shares on day 3.

1.6 Similarly, the prediction of share price movements may help an investor to **maximise** his or her **capital gain** from buying and selling shares. To make the most gain, shares should be bought when prices are at their lowest and sold when they are at their highest.

Theories of share price behaviour

1.7 There are the following differing views about share price movements.

- **The fundamental analysis theory**
- **Technical analysis (chartist theory)**
- **Random walk theory**

These different theories about how share prices are reached in the market, especially fundamental analysis, have important consequences for financial management.

2 THE FUNDAMENTAL ANALYSIS THEORY OF SHARE VALUES

2.1 The fundamental theory of share values is based on the theory that the 'realistic' market price of a share can be derived from a valuation of estimated future dividends. The value of a share will be the discounted present value of all future expected dividends on the share, discounted at the shareholders' cost of capital.

3: Determination of share prices

> **KEY TERM**
>
> **Fundamental analysis** is the analysis of external and internal influences upon the operations of a company with a view to assisting in investment decisions. Information accessed might include fiscal/monetary policy, financial statements, industry trends, competitor analysis, etc.
> *(OT 2000)*

2.2 (a) The formula below applies when the company is expected to pay constant dividends every year into the future, 'in perpetuity'.

> **EXAM FORMULA**
>
> Ordinary (equity) share paying a constant annual dividend d in perpetuity, where P_0 is the ex-div value.
>
> $$P_0 = \frac{d}{k_e}$$
>
> where k_e is the shareholders' cost of capital (the required rate of return).

Similar formulae can be used to find the price of preference share capital and debt.

> **EXAM FORMULAE**
>
> Irredeemable preference share, paying a constant annual dividend, d in perpetuity, where P_0 is the ex-div value:
>
> $$P_0 = \frac{d}{k_{pref}}$$
>
> where k_{pref} is the preference shareholders' cost of capital.
>
> Irredeemable (undated) debt, paying annual after tax interest, $i(1 - t)$ in perpetuity, where P_0 is the ex-interest value:
>
> $$P_0 = \frac{i(1 - t)}{k_d \text{ net}}$$
>
> Or, without tax:
>
> $$P_0 = \frac{i}{k_d}$$
>
> where k_d is the cost of debt.

(b) When the company is expected to pay a dividend which increases at a constant rate, g, every year into the future, the following **dividend growth model** may be used.

EXAM FORMULA

Ordinary (equity) share paying an annual dividend d, growing in perpetuity at a constant rate g, where P_0 is the ex-div value.

$$P_0 = \frac{d_0(1+g)}{k_e - g} = \frac{d_1}{k_e - g}$$

where d_0 is the dividend in the current year (year 0) and so $d_0(1+g)$ is the expected future dividend in year 1 (d_1).

2.3 EXAMPLE: CONSTANT DIVIDEND

Hocus plc expects to pay a constant dividend of £450,000 at the end of every year for ever (in perpetuity). Assuming that a dividend has just been paid, calculate what the market value of Hocus plc's shares ought to be if its shareholders' cost of capital is 15%.

2.4 SOLUTION

$$P_0 = \frac{£450,000}{(1.15)} + \frac{£450,000}{(1.15)^2} + \frac{£450,000}{(1.15)^3} + \ldots \text{ and so on, in perpetuity.}$$

EXAM FORMULAE

Present value of £1 per annum, payable or receivable in perpetuity, commencing in the year, discounted at r% per annum:

$$PV = \frac{1}{r}$$

Present value of £1 per annum, receivable or payable, commencing in one year, growing in perpetuity at a constant rate of g% per annum, discounted at r% per annum:

$$PV = \frac{1}{r - g}$$

Therefore, the present value of £450,000 a year at a rate of interest of 15%

is $£450,000 \times \frac{1}{0.15} = £3,000,000$.

The value of Hocus plc's shares will be £3,000,000.

Knowledge brought forward from Paper 3c Business Mathematics

The concept of present value was described in Paper 3c *Business Mathematics*. If you are unsure about this topic, read Chapter 12, Section 1 of this Text.

2.5 EXAMPLE: DIVIDEND GROWTH

Pocus plc paid a dividend this year of £3,000,000. The company expects the dividend to rise by 2% a year in perpetuity. This expectation is shared by the investors in the stock market. The current return expected by investors from shares in the same industry as Pocus plc is 11%.

(a) What would you expect the total market value of the shares of Pocus plc to be?

(b) If it is now rumoured in the stock market that interest rates are about to rise and so shareholders will want to earn an extra 1% on their shares. What change would you expect in the value of the shares of Pocus plc?

(c) What conclusion do you draw from this example?

2.6 SOLUTION

$$P_0 = \frac{d_0(1+g)}{k_e - g}$$

(a) Predicted share value (return of 11%) $= \frac{£3,000,000(1.02)}{(0.11-0.02)} = £34,000,000$

(b) Predicted share value (return of 12%) $= \frac{£3,000,000(1.02)}{(0.12-0.02)} = £30,600,000$

The value of the company's shares would fall by £3,400,000.

(c) When interest rates are expected to go up, there may well be a fall in share prices. Similarly, expectations of a fall in interest rates may well result in an increase in share prices. This is because the required return on shares is likely to move approximately in step with changes in rates of interest on other investments.

Question 1

The management of Crocus plc are trying to decide on the dividend policy of the company.

There are two options that are being considered.

(a) The company could pay a constant annual dividend of 8p per share.

(b) The company could pay a dividend of 6p per share next year, and use the retained earnings to achieve an annual growth of 3% in dividends for each year after that.

The shareholders' cost of capital is thought to be 18%. Which dividend policy would maximise the wealth of shareholders, by maximising the share price?

Answer

(a) With a constant annual dividend

$$\text{Share price} = \frac{8p}{0.18} = 44.4p$$

(b) With dividend growth

$$\text{Share price} = \frac{6p(1.03)}{(0.18-0.03)} = \frac{6.18}{0.15} = 41.2p$$

The constant annual dividend would be preferable.

Part A: The finance function

The importance of the fundamental theory of share values

2.7 In general terms, fundamental analysis seems to be valid. This means that if an investment analyst can foresee before anyone else that:

(a) A company's future profits and dividends are going to be different from what is currently expected, or

(b) Shareholders' cost of capital will rise or fall (for example in response to interest rate changes)

then the analyst will be able to predict a future share price movement, and so recommend clients to buy or sell the share before the price change occurs.

2.8 In practice however, share price movements are affected by day to day fluctuations, reflecting supply and demand in a particular period, investor confidence, market interest rate movements, and so on. Investment analysts want to be able to predict these fluctuations in prices, but **fundamental** analysis might be inadequate as a technique. Some analysts, known as **chartists**, therefore rely on **technical** analysis of share price movements.

3 CHARTING OR TECHNICAL ANALYSIS

3.1 **Chartists** or '**technical analysts**' attempt to predict share price movements by assuming that past price patterns will be repeated. There is no real theoretical justification for this approach, but it can at times be spectacularly successful. Studies have suggested that the degree of success is greater than could be expected merely from chance.

> **KEY TERM**
>
> **Technical analysis** is the analysis of past movements in the prices of financial instruments, currencies, commodities etc, with a view to, by applying analytical techniques, predict future price movements. *(OT 2000)*

3.2 Chartists do not attempt to predict every price change. They are primarily interested in trend reversals, for example when the price of a share has been rising for several months but suddenly starts to fall.

3.3 Moving averages help the chartist to examine overall trends. For example, he may calculate and plot moving averages of share prices for 20 days, 60 days and 240 days. The 20 day figures will give a reasonable representation of the actual movement in share prices after eliminating day to day fluctuations. The other two moving averages give a good idea of longer term trends.

4 RANDOM WALK THEORY

4.1 **Random walk theory** is consistent with the fundamental theory of share values. It accepts that a share should have an intrinsic price dependent on the fortunes of the company and the expectations of investors. One of its underlying assumptions is that **all relevant information about a company is available to all potential investors** who will act upon the information in a **rational** manner.

4.2 The key feature of random walk theory is that although share prices will have an **intrinsic or fundamental value,** this value will be altered as new information becomes available, and that the behaviour of investors is such that the actual share price will fluctuate from day to day around the intrinsic value.

4.3 Random walk theory emerged in the late 1950s as an attempt to disprove **chartist theory**. H V Roberts challenged the idea that share price movements were systematic, and showed how sequences of random numbers can exhibit the same pattern as actual recorded changes of share prices on the Stock Exchange.

Random walks and an efficient stock market

4.4 Research was carried out in the late 1960s to explain why share prices in the stock market display a random walk phenomenon. This research led to the development of the **efficient market hypothesis**. It can be shown that random movements in share prices will occur if the stock market operates 'efficiently' and makes information about companies, earnings, dividends and so on, freely (or cheaply) available to all customers in the market. In displaying efficiency, the stock market also lends support to the fundamental analysis theory of share prices.

5 THE EFFICIENT MARKET HYPOTHESIS 5/01

> **KEY TERM**
>
> **Efficient market hypothesis** is the hypothesis that the stock market responds immediately to all available information, with the effect that an individual investor cannot, in the long run, expect to obtain greater than average returns from a diversified portfolio of shares.
> *(OT 2000)*

5.1 It has been argued that the UK and US stock markets are efficient capital markets, that is, markets in which:

(a) The prices of securities bought and sold **reflect all the relevant information** which is available to the buyers and sellers, ie share prices change quickly to reflect all new information about future prospects

(b) No **individual dominates** the market

(c) **Transaction costs** of buying and selling are not so high as to discourage trading significantly

5.2 If the stock market is efficient at processing information, share prices should vary in a rational way.

(a) If a company makes an **investment** with a **positive net present value** (NPV), shareholders will get to know about it and the **market price** of its shares **will rise** in anticipation of future dividend increases.

(b) If a company makes a **bad investment** shareholders will find out and so the **price** of its shares will **fall**.

(c) If **interest rates rise**, shareholders will want a **higher return** from their investments, so **market prices** will **fall**.

Part A: The finance function

The definition of efficiency

5.3 Different types of efficiency can be distinguished in the context of the operation of financial markets.

TYPES OF EFFICIENCY	
Allocative	Direction of funds towards firms making best use of them
Operational	Minimisation of transaction costs such as commissions, interest rate margins and loan arrangement fees.
Information processing	Reflects ability of stock market to absorb information, achieved when market prices of all securities reflect all available information. It has three forms: • Weak • Semi-strong • Strong

Weak form tests and weak form efficiency

5.4 The weak form hypothesis suggests that share prices take into account all relevant information about past price movements and their implications. Share prices do **not** change **in anticipation** of new information being announced.

Semi-strong form tests and semi-strong form efficiency

5.5 Semi-strong form tests attempt to show that the stock market displays semi-strong efficiency, by which we mean that current share prices reflect both:

- All **relevant information** about past **price movements** and their implications, and
- All **knowledge** which is available **publicly**

5.6 Tests to prove semi-strong efficiency have concentrated on the ability of the market to **anticipate share price changes** before new information is formally announced.

5.7 For example, if two companies plan a merger, share prices of the two companies will inevitably change once the merger plans are formally announced. The market would show semi-strong efficiency, however, if it were able to **anticipate** such an announcement, so that share prices of the companies concerned would change in advance of the merger plans being confirmed.

5.8 Research in both the UK and the USA has suggested that market prices anticipate mergers several months before they are formally announced, and the conclusion drawn is that the stock markets in these countries **do** exhibit semi-strong efficiency.

Strong form tests and strong form efficiency

5.9 A strong form test of market efficiency attempts to prove that the stock market displays a strong form of efficiency, by which we mean that share prices reflect all information available:

- From past price changes
- From public knowledge or anticipation
- From specialists' or experts' insider knowledge (eg investment managers)

5.10 In order to maximise the wealth of shareholders, management should thus concentrate simply on **maximising** the **net present value** of its **investments**. They need not worry, for example, about the effect on share prices of financial results in the published accounts because investors will make allowances for low profits or dividends in the current year if higher profits or dividends are expected in the future. A company's real financial position will be reflected in its share price.

5.11 In theory an expert, such as an investment manager, should be able to use his privileged access to additional information about companies to earn a higher rate of return than an ordinary investor. Unit trusts should in theory therefore perform better than the average investor. Research has suggested, however, that this expert skill does not exist (or at least, that any higher returns earned by experts are offset by management charges).

How efficient are stock markets in reality?

5.12 Evidence so far collected suggests that stock markets show efficiency that is at least weak form, but tending more towards a semi-strong form. In other words, current share prices reflect all or most publicly available information about companies and their securities. However, it is very difficult to assess the market's efficiency in relation to shares which are not usually actively traded.

5.13 Fundamental analysis and technical analysis, which are carried out by analysts and investment managers, play an important role in creating an efficient stock market. This is because an efficient market depends on the widespread availability of cheap information about companies, their shares and market conditions, and this is what the firms of market makers and other financial institutions **do** provide for their clients and for the general investing public.

5.14 The **implication for an investor** is that if the market shows strong form or semi-strong form efficiency, he can rarely spot shares at a bargain price that will soon rise sharply in value. This is because the market will already have anticipated future developments, and will have reflected these in the share price. All the investor can do, instead of looking for share bargains, is to concentrate on building up a good spread of shares (a portfolio) in order to achieve a satisfactory balance between risk and return.

5.15 EXAMPLE: EFFICIENT MARKET HYPOTHESIS

Company X has 3,000,000 shares in issue and company Y 8,000,000.

(a) On day 1, the market value per share is £3 for X and £6 for Y.

(b) On day 2, the management of Y decide, at a private meeting, to make a takeover bid for X at a price of £5 per share. The takeover will produce large operating savings with a present value of £8,000,000.

(c) On day 5, Y publicly announces an unconditional offer to purchase all shares of X at a price of £5 per share with settlement on day 20. Details of the large savings are not announced and are not public knowledge.

(d) On day 10, Y announces details of the savings which will be derived from the takeover.

Ignoring tax and the time value of money between day 1 and 20, and assuming the details given are the only factors having an impact on the share price of X and Y, determine the day 2, day 5 and day 10 share price of X and Y if the market is:

Part A: The finance function

(a) Semi-strong form efficient
(b) Strong form efficient

in each of the following *separate* circumstances.

(a) The purchase consideration is cash as specified above.

(b) The purchase consideration, decided on day 2 and publicly announced on day 5, is five newly issued shares of Y for six shares of X.

5.16 SOLUTION

(a) **Semi-strong form efficient market (i) cash offer**

With a semi-strong form of market efficiency, shareholders know all the relevant historical data and publicly available current information.

(i) Day 1 Value of X shares: £3 each, £9,000,000 in total.
Value of Y shares: £6 each, £48,000,000 in total.

(ii) Day 2 The decision at the **private** meeting does not reach the market, and so share prices are unchanged.

(iii) Day 5 The takeover bid is announced, but no information is available yet about the savings.

(1) The value of X shares will rise to their takeover bid price of £5 each, £15,000,000 in total.

(2) The value of Y shares will be as follows.

	£
Previous value (8,000,000 × £6)	48,000,000
Add value of X shares to be acquired, at previous market worth (3,000,000 × £3)	9,000,000
	57,000,000
Less purchase consideration for X shares	15,000,000
New value of Y shares	42,000,000
Price per share	£5.25

The share price of Y shares will fall on the announcement of the takeover.

(iv) Day 10 The market learns of the potential savings of £8,000,000 (present value) and the price of Y shares will rise accordingly to:

$$\frac{£42,000,000 + £8,000,000}{8,000,000 \text{ shares}} = £6.25 \text{ per share.}$$

The share price of X shares will remain the same as before, £5 per share.

Semi-strong form efficient market (ii) share exchange offer

(i) The share price will not change until the takeover is announced on day 5, when the value of the combined company will be perceived by the market to be (48 + 9) £57,000,000.

The number of shares in the enlarged company Y would be as follows.

Current	8,000,000
Shares issued to former X shareholders (3,000,000 × 5/6)	2,500,000
	10,500,000

The value per share in Y would change to reflect what the market expects the value of the enlarged company to be.

$$\frac{£57,000,000}{10,500,000} = £5.43 \text{ per share}$$

The value per share in X would reflect this same price, adjusted for the share exchange terms.

$$\frac{5}{6} \text{ of } £5.43 = £4.52$$

(ii) Day 10 The value of the enlarged company would now be seen by the market to have risen by £8,000,000 to £65,000,000 and the value of Y shares would rise to:

$$\frac{£65,000,000}{10,500,000} = £6.19 \text{ per share}$$

The value per X share would be:

$$\frac{5}{6} \text{ of } £6.19 = £5.16$$

(b) **Strong form efficient market (i) cash offer**

In a strong form efficient market, the market would become aware of **all** the relevant information when the private meeting takes place. The value per share would change as early as **day 2** to:

(i) X: £5
(ii) Y: £6.25

The share prices would then remain unchanged until day 20.

Strong form efficient market (ii) share exchange offer

In the same way, for the same reason, the value per share would change **on day 2** to:

(i) X: £5.16
(ii) Y: £6.19

and remain unchanged thereafter until day 20.

5.17 The different characteristics of a semi-strong form and a strong form efficient market thus affect the timing of share price movements, in cases where the relevant information becomes available to the market eventually. The difference between the two forms of market efficiency concerns when the share prices change, not by how much prices eventually change.

5.18 You should notice, however, that in neither case would the share prices remain unchanged until day 20. In a **weak form** efficient market, the price of Y's shares would not reflect the expected savings until after the savings had been achieved and reported, so that the takeover bid would result in a fall in the value of Y's shares for a considerable time to come.

Explaining share price movements

5.19 Various types of anomaly appear to support the views that irrationality often drives the stock market, including the following.

(a) **Seasonal month-of-the-year effects**, day-of-the-week effects and also hour-of-the-day effects seem to occur, so that share prices might tend to rise or fall at a particular time of the year, week or day.

(b) There may be a **short-run overreaction** to recent events.

Part A: The finance function

(c) **Individual shares** or **shares in small companies** may be **neglected**.

5.20 According to **speculative bubble theory,** stock market behaviour is non-linear and based on inflating and bursting speculative bubbles, rather than economic forecasts. Security prices rise above their intrinsic prices reflecting expected cash returns because some investors believe that others will pay more for them in the future. This behaviour feeds upon itself and prices rise for a period, producing a bull market. However, at some point, investors will eventually react to all the information which they have previously ignored, losing confidence that prices can rise still further, and a market crash then occurs.

5.21 Zeeman (1974) divided all investors into two classes:

(a) '**Fundamentalists**', who are guided in their investment strategies by economic analyses to construct forecasts based on rational expectations

(b) '**Speculators**', whose decisions reflect adaptive behaviour in response to technical analysis of recent stock market patterns.

5.22 Instability in financial markets occurs if there is a substantial proportion of speculators, amplifying changes in market indices. If the index begins to rise/fall, there will be a rapid move into a bull/bear phase respectively.

Question 2

Briefly describe the main forms of market efficiency.

Answer

It is often argued that the UK and US stock markets are **efficient capital markets**, in which:

(a) The prices at which securities are traded **reflect all the relevant information** that is available to buyers and sellers, meaning that prices change quickly to reflect all new information about future prospects.

(b) **No individual dominates** the market.

(c) **Transaction costs are not so high** as to impact significantly on the level of trading activity.

If the market is efficient, then share prices should vary in a rational way.

The main forms of market efficiency are usually defined in relation to the varying degrees of efficiency with which the market processes information, and are as follows.

Weak form. This form of the hypothesis contends that share prices reflect all relevant information about past price movements. Share prices do not change in anticipation of new information being announced. Since new information arrives unexpectedly, it follows that share prices should be expected to change in a random manner and therefore that definable trends in share prices should not exist.

Semi-strong form. This form of the hypothesis contends that share prices reflect both **all relevant information** about past price movements and their implications, and all knowledge that is **publicly available**. This means that it will be expected that share prices can anticipate the formal announcement of new information. For example, if two companies plan a merger, their share prices will inevitably change once the merger plans are formally announced.

The market would show semi-strong efficiency if it were able to anticipate such an announcement, so that share prices of the two companies would change in advance of the merger plans being confirmed. Research in the UK and the US suggests that this does happen in practice, with the conclusion being drawn that the stock markets in these countries do demonstrate semi-strong form efficiency.

Strong form. If the market displays strong form efficiency, it would react in both the ways described above, but in addition, prices would also reflect **information** from **insider knowledge** available only to experts such as investment managers. If this is the case, then it would follow that managers should not need to worry overmuch about the presentation of information in one year's accounts provided that they are taking decisions aimed at maximising the net worth of the firm in the long term. This does not seem to be borne out by the short-term nature of much decision making in quoted companies. In addition, an expert such as an investment manager should be able to use his privileged access to additional information about companies to earn a higher rate of return than an ordinary investor. However, if unit trust results do out-perform the market, the excess returns would seem to be absorbed by management charges, since there is no evidence that such funds consistently beat the market.

Question 3

A stock market in which current share prices reflect all relevant information about past price movements, and all knowledge that is available publicly demonstrates which of the following types of market efficiency?

A   Operational efficiency
B   Weak form efficiency
C   Semi-strong form efficiency
D   Strong form efficiency

Answer

C   Semi-strong form efficiency

Chapter roundup

- **Fundamental analysis** is based on the theory that share prices can be derived from an analysis of **future dividends**.

- The theory behind the **movements in share prices** can be explained by the three forms of the **efficient market hypothesis, weak, semi-strong** and **strong**.

- Knowledge of **what** and **when** information will be incorporated into a quoted share price is likely to influence how and when information regarding financial management decisions is made public.

- In particular, since current share prices can be crucial to the success or otherwise of takeover **bids and new share issues**, it will be important to be aware of how the market is likely to react to varying levels of information released.

Quick quiz

1   Which theory of share price behaviour does the following statement describe?

   'The analysis of external and internal influences upon the operations of a company with a view to assisting in investment decisions.'

   A   Technical analysis
   B   Random walk theory
   C   Fundamental analysis theory
   D   Chartism

2   Who has a prior claim over assets when a company goes into liquidation: debt holders or shareholders?

3   In what two main ways do shareholders receive returns on their investment?

4   What is meant by 'efficiency', in the context of the efficient market hypothesis?

Part A: The finance function

5   The different 'forms' of the efficient market hypothesis state that share prices reflect *which* types of information? Tick all that apply.

	Form of EMH		
	Weak	Semi-strong	Strong
No information	☐	☐	☐
All information in past share price record	☐	☐	☐
All other publicly available information	☐	☐	☐
All information obtainable from fundamental analysis of the company and the economy	☐	☐	☐
Specialists' and experts' 'insider' knowledge	☐	☐	☐

6   Which theory makes which assertions?

(a) Chartism   (i) A share price can be expected to fluctuate around its 'intrinsic' value.

(b) Random walk theory   (ii) Past share price patterns tend to be repeated.

(c) Fundamental analysis theory   (iii) The value of a share is the discounted present value of all future expected dividends on the share, discounted at the shareholders' cost of capital.

7   Raybould plc expects to pay a constant dividend of 60 pence per share at the end of every year forever. Assuming that a dividend has just been paid, what should the market price of the shares be? The nominal value of the shares is £2, and the cost of capital is 12%.

    A   £10.00
    B   £5.00
    C   £2.50
    D   £2.40

8   What is the ex-dividend value of a share that is about to pay a dividend of £1.50 where the shareholder's cost of capital is 10% and the expected annual rate of dividend growth is 4%?

Answers to quick quiz

1   C   Fundamental analysis theory

2   Debt holders

3   Dividends, and capital gains

4   Efficiency in processing information in the pricing of stocks and shares

5

	Form of EMH		
	Weak	Semi-strong	Strong
No information	☐	☐	☐
All information in past share price record	✓	✓	✓
All other publicly available information	☐	✓	✓
All information obtainable from fundamental analysis of the company and the economy	☐	☐	✓
Specialists' and experts' 'insider' knowledge	☐	☐	✓

6   (a) (ii)
     (b) (i)
     (c) (iii)

7   B   Since the dividend is effectively a perpetuity, the expected market price is the present value of 60 pence, ie 60p/0.12 = £5.00. The nominal value of the shares is irrelevant.

8   $P_0 = \dfrac{d_0(1+g)}{k_e - g}$

   $= \dfrac{£1.50(1+0.04)}{0.1 - 0.04}$

   $= £26$

Now try the question below from the Exam Question Bank

Number	Level	Marks	Time
3	Introductory	n/a	20 mins

Chapter 4

THE TREASURY FUNCTION

Topic list	Syllabus reference	Ability required
1 Treasury departments	(i)	Comprehension
2 Centralised or decentralised cash management?	(i)	Comprehension
3 The treasury department as cost centre or profit centre	(i)	Comprehension
4 Fraud relating to sources of finance	(ii)	Comprehension

Introduction

In this chapter, we discuss the work of the **treasury function**, which in larger companies will form a separate department. More specific aspects of treasury work - for example **cash management techniques** - are covered later in this Study Text.

The key decisions relating to the treasury department – centralised or decentralised, cost centre or profit centre – are good territory for a discussion question in the exam.

Learning outcomes covered in this chapter

- Describe and explain the role and management of the treasury function

Syllabus content covered in this chapter

- The role of the treasury function in terms of setting corporate objectives, liquidity management, funding management, currency management
- The benefits and shortcomings of establishing treasury departments as profit centres or cost centres
- The control of treasury departments when established as cost centres or profit centres
- Fraud related to sources of finance (eg advance fee fraud and pyramid schemes)

1 TREASURY DEPARTMENTS   Pilot paper

1.1 Large companies rely heavily for both long-term and short-term funds on the financial and currency markets. To manage cash (funds) and currency efficiently, many large companies have set up a separate **treasury department**.

KEY TERM

The Association of Corporate Treasurers' definition of **treasury management** is 'the corporate handling of all financial matters, the generation of external and internal funds for business, the management of currencies and cash flows, and the complex strategies, policies and procedures of corporate finance'.

4: The treasury function

1.2 A treasury department, even in a large company, is likely to be quite small, with perhaps a staff of three to six qualified accountants, bankers or corporate treasurers working under a Treasurer, who is responsible to the Finance Director. In some cases, where the company or organisation handles very large amounts of cash or foreign currency dealings, and often has large cash surpluses, the treasury department might be larger.

The role of the treasurer

1.3 The diagrams below are based on the **Association of Corporate Treasurers'** list of experience it requires from its student members before they are eligible for full membership of the Association. Required experience gives a good indication of the roles of treasury departments.

(a) **Corporate financial objectives**

```
                    CORPORATE FINANCIAL OBJECTIVES
                    /              |              \
              Policies      Aims and         Systems
                            strategies
```

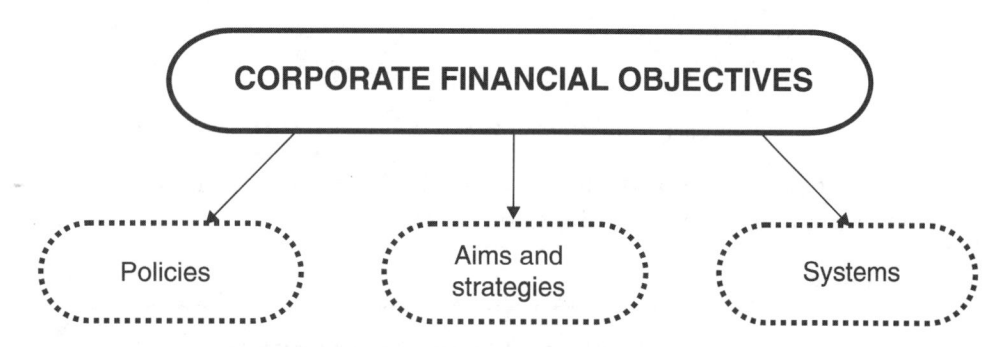

(b) **Liquidity management**: making sure the company has the liquid funds it needs, and invests any surplus funds, even for very short terms.

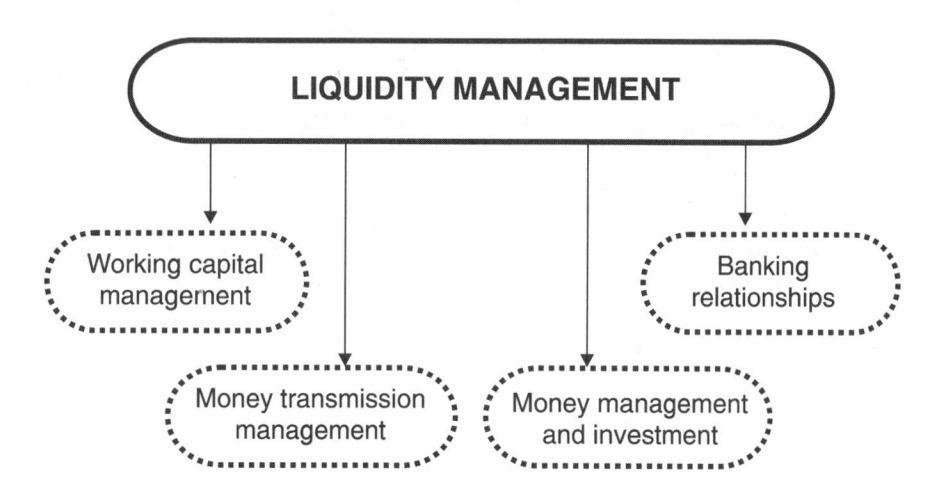

```
                         LIQUIDITY MANAGEMENT
              /           |            |           \
     Working capital                              Banking
      management                              relationships
              \                       /
         Money transmission    Money management
            management          and investment
```

Part A: The finance function

(c) **Funding management**

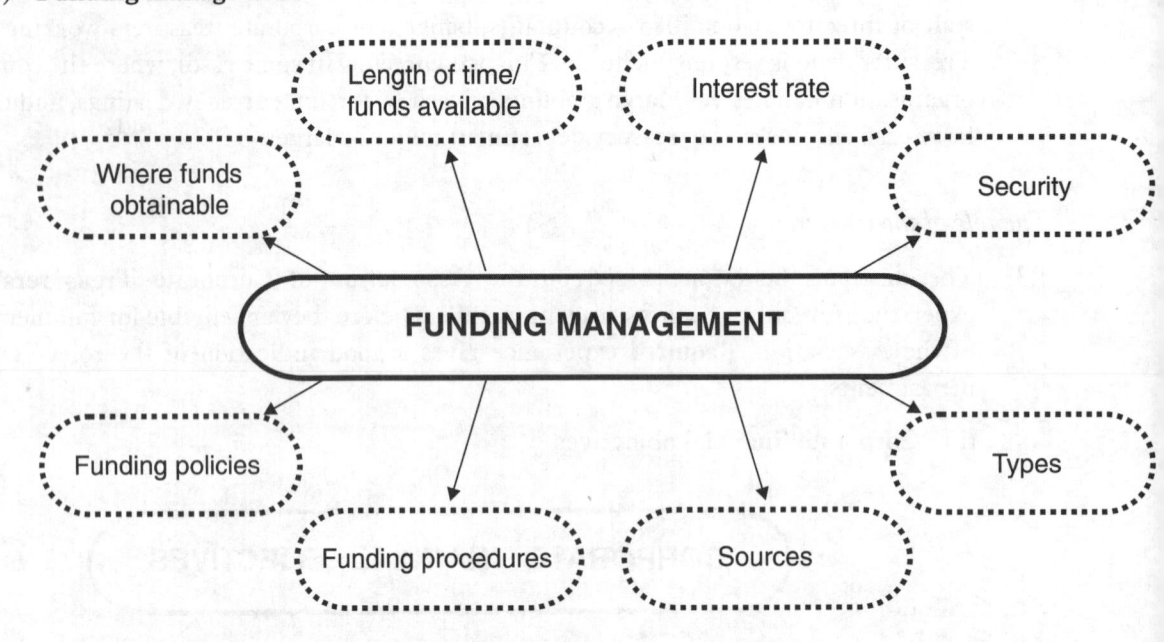

```
                    FUNDING MANAGEMENT
```
- Where funds obtainable
- Length of time/funds available
- Interest rate
- Security
- Funding policies
- Funding procedures
- Sources
- Types

Funding management is concerned with all forms of borrowing, and alternative sources of funds, such as leasing and factoring.

(d) **Currency management**

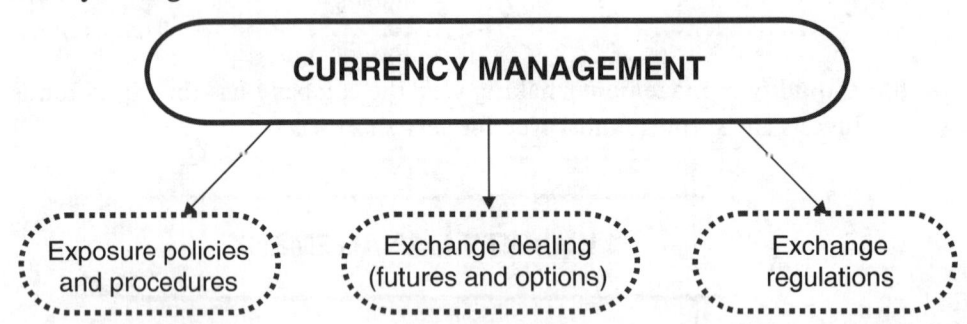

```
                    CURRENCY MANAGEMENT
```
- Exposure policies and procedures
- Exchange dealing (futures and options)
- Exchange regulations

Currency dealings can save or cost a company considerable amounts of money, and the success or shortcomings of the corporate treasurer can have a significant impact on the profit and loss account of a company which is heavily involved in foreign trade.

(e) **Corporate finance**

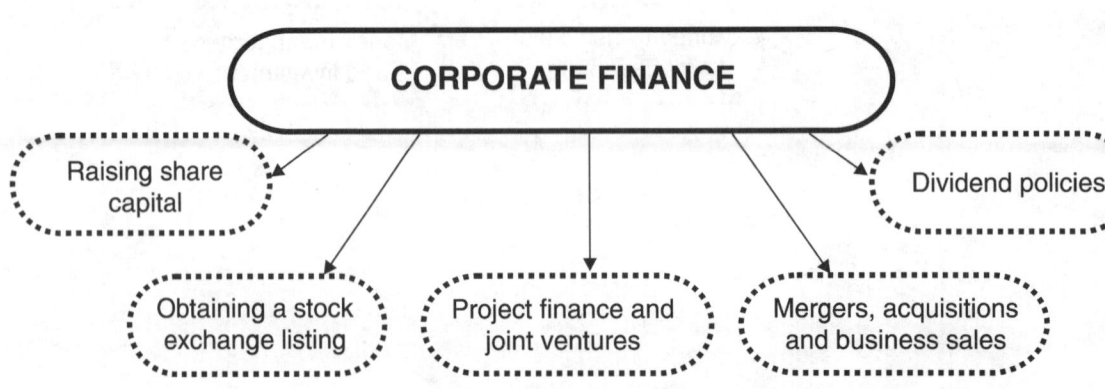

```
                    CORPORATE FINANCE
```
- Raising share capital
- Dividend policies
- Obtaining a stock exchange listing
- Project finance and joint ventures
- Mergers, acquisitions and business sales

The treasury department has a role in all levels of decision-making within the company. It is involved with **strategic** decisions such as dividend policy or the raising of capital, **tactical** decisions such as risk management, and **operational** decisions such as the investment of surplus funds.

Advantages of a separate treasury department

1.4 Advantages of having a treasury function which is **separate from the financial control function** are as follows.

(a) Centralised liquidity management avoids mixing cash surpluses and overdrafts in different localised bank accounts.

(b) Bulk cash flows allow **lower bank charges** to be negotiated.

(c) Larger volumes of cash can be invested, giving **better short-term investment opportunities**.

(d) Borrowing can be agreed in bulk, probably at **lower interest rates** than for smaller borrowings.

(e) Currency risk management should be improved, through **matching of cash flows in different subsidiaries**. There should be less need to use expensive hedging instruments such as option contracts.

(f) A specialist department can employ staff with a **greater level of expertise** than would be possible in a local, more broadly based, finance department.

(g) The company will be able to benefit from the use of **specialised cash management software**.

(h) Access to treasury expertise should **improve the quality of strategic planning and decision making**.

Outsourcing

1.5 Because of the specialist nature of treasury management, a number of businesses **outsource** the function to specialist institutions. The company receives the benefit of the **expertise** of the staff of the institution. The specialists can deal on a large scale and pass some of the benefit on in the form of fees that are lower than the cost of setting up an internal function would be. However whether the **same level of service** could be guaranteed from the external institution as from an internal department is perhaps questionable. The external institution may not have as much knowledge of the needs of the business that an internal department would have.

2 CENTRALISED OR DECENTRALISED CASH MANAGEMENT?

2.1 A large company may have a number of subsidiaries and divisions. In the case of a multinational, these will be located in different countries. It will be necessary to decide whether the treasury function should be centralised.

2.2 With **centralised cash management**, the central Treasury department effectively acts as the bank to the group. The central Treasury has the job of ensuring that individual operating units have all the funds they need at the right time.

2.3 **Advantages of a specialist centralised treasury department**

(a) **Centralised liquidity management:**

(i) Avoids having a mix of cash surpluses and overdrafts in different local bank accounts

(ii) Facilitates bulk cash flows, so that lower bank charges can be negotiated

Part A: The finance function

(b) Larger volumes of cash are available to invest, giving better **short-term investment opportunities** (for example, money market deposits, high interest accounts and Certificates of Deposit).

(c) Any borrowing can be arranged **in bulk**, at lower interest rates than for smaller borrowings, and perhaps on the eurocurrency or eurobond markets.

(d) **Foreign currency risk management** is likely to be improved in a group of companies. A central treasury department can match foreign currency income earned by one subsidiary with expenditure in the same currency by another subsidiary. In this way, the risk of losses on adverse exchange rate changes can be avoided without the expense of forward exchange contracts or other 'hedging' (risk-reducing) methods.

(e) A specialist treasury department will employ **experts** with knowledge of dealing in futures, eurocurrency markets, taxation, transfer prices and so on. Localised departments would not have such expertise.

(f) The centralised pool of **funds required for precautionary purposes** will be smaller than the sum of separate precautionary balances which would need to be held under decentralised treasury arrangements.

(g) Through having a separate **profit centre**, attention will be focused on the contribution to group profit performance that can be achieved by good cash, funding, investment and foreign currency management.

2.4 **Possible advantages of decentralised cash management**

(a) Sources of finance can be **diversified** and can be **matched with local assets**.

(b) Greater **autonomy** can be given to subsidiaries and divisions because of the closer relationships they will have with the decentralised cash management function.

(c) The decentralised Treasury function may be able to be **more responsive** to the needs of individual operating units.

However, since cash balances will not be aggregated at group level, there will be **more limited opportunities to invest** such balances on a short-term basis.

Centralised cash management in the multinational firm

2.5 If cash management within a **multinational firm** is centralised, each subsidiary holds only the minimum cash balance required for transaction purposes. All excess funds will be remitted to the central Treasury department.

2.6 Funds held in the central pool of funds can be returned quickly to the local subsidiary by telegraphic transfer or by means of worldwide bank credit facilities. The firm's bank can instruct its branch office in the country in which the subsidiary is located to advance funds to the subsidiary. Multinationals' central pools of funds are typically maintained in major financial centres such as London, New York, Tokyo and Zurich.

Question 1

Touten plc is a UK registered multinational company with subsidiaries in 14 countries in Europe, Asia and Africa. The subsidiaries have traditionally been allowed a large amount of autonomy, but Touten plc is now proposing to centralise most of the group treasury management operations.

4: The treasury function

Required

Acting as a consultant to Touten plc prepare a memo suitable for distribution from the group finance director to the senior management of each of the subsidiaries explaining:

(a) The potential benefits of treasury centralisation; and

(b) How the company proposes to minimise any potential problems for the subsidiaries that might arise as a result of treasury centralisation

Answer

MEMORANDUM

To: Directors of all foreign subsidiaries
From: Group Finance Director

Centralisation of treasury management operations

At its last meeting, the board of directors of Touten plc made the decision to centralise group treasury management operations. A further memo giving detailed plans will be circulated shortly, but my objective in this memo is to outline the potential benefits of treasury centralisation and how any potential problems arising at subsidiaries can be minimised. Most of you will be familiar with the basic arguments, which we have been discussing informally for some time.

What it means

Centralisation of treasury management means that most decisions on borrowing, investment of cash surpluses, currency management and financial risk management will be taken by an enhanced central treasury team, based at head office, instead of by subsidiaries directly. In addition we propose to set most transfer prices for inter-company goods and services centrally.

The potential benefits

The main benefits are:

(a) **Cost savings** resulting from reduction of unnecessary banking charges
(b) **Reduction of the group's total taxation charge**
(c) **Enhanced control over financial risk**

Reduction in banking charges will result from:

(a) **Netting off inter-company debts before settlement**. At the moment we are spending too much on foreign exchange commission by settling inter-company debts in a wide range of currencies through the banking system.

(b) **Knowledge of total group currency exposure from transactions**. Debtors in one subsidiary can hedge creditors in another, eliminating unnecessary hedging by subsidiaries.

(c) **Knowledge of the group's total cash resources and borrowing requirement**. This will reduce the incidence of one company lending cash while a fellow subsidiary borrows at a higher interest rate and will also eliminate unnecessary interest rate hedging. It will also facilitate higher deposit rates and lower borrowing rates.

Reduction in the group's tax charge will be made possible by a comprehensive centrally-set **transfer pricing policy**.

Enhanced control over financial risks will be possible because we will be able to develop a central team of specialists who will have a clear-cut strategy on hedging and risk management. Many of you have requested help in this area.

This team will be able to ensure that decisions are taken in line with **group strategy** and will also be able to provide you with enhanced financial information to assist you with your own decision making.

Potential problems for subsidiaries and their solution

Our group culture is one of **decentralisation** and **enablement of management at individual subsidiary level**. There is no intention to change this culture. Rather, it is hoped that releasing you from specialist treasury decisions will enable you to devote more time to developing your own business units.

The system can only work properly, however, if **information exchange** between head office and subsidiaries is swift and efficient. Enhanced computer systems are to be provided at all centres to assist you with daily reports. It is also important that you keep head office informed of all local

Part A: The finance function

conditions that could be beneficial to the treasury function, such as the availability of local subsidised loans, as well as potential local risks such as the threat of exchange control restrictions.

You will find that movements in your cash balances will be affected by **group policy**, as well as reported profitability. Any adjustments made by head office will be eliminated when preparing the performance reports for your own business units and we will ensure that joint venture partners are not penalised by group policy.

Please contact me with any further comments that you may have on our new treasury policy.

3 THE TREASURY DEPARTMENT AS COST CENTRE OR PROFIT CENTRE
Pilot paper

3.1 A treasury department might be managed either as a **cost centre** or as a **profit centre**. For a group of companies, this decision may need to be made for treasury departments in separate subsidiaries as well as for the central corporate treasury department.

3.2 In a cost centre, managers have an incentive only to **keep the costs** of the department within **budgeted spending targets**. The cost centre approach implies that the treasury is there to perform a service of a certain standard to other departments in the enterprise. The treasury is treated much like any other service department.

3.3 However, some companies (including BP, for example) are able to make significant profits from their treasury activities. Treating the treasury department as a profit centre recognises the fact that treasury activities such as speculation may earn **revenues** for the company, and may as a result make treasury staff more motivated.

3.4 The profit centre approach is probably going to be appropriate only if the company has a high level of foreign exchange transactions. Such companies may choose **not** to hedge against fluctuating exchange rates, depending on their perception of the current and future economic environment, in the hope of making higher-risk speculative gains.

Question 2

Suppose that your company is considering plans to establish its treasury function as a profit centre. Before reading the next paragraph, see if you can think of how the following issues are of potential importance to these plans.

(a) How can we ensure that high quality treasury staff can be recruited?

(b) How might costly errors and overexposure to risk be prevented?

(c) Why will the treasury team need extensive market information to be successful?

(d) Could there be a danger that attitudes to risk in the treasury team will differ from those of the Board? If so, how?

(e) What is the relevance of internal charges?

(f) What problems could there be in evaluating performance of the treasury team?

3.5 If a profit centre approach is being considered, the following issues should be addressed.

(a) **Competence of staff**

Local managers may not have sufficient expertise in the area of treasury management to carry out speculative treasury operations competently. Mistakes in this specialised field may be costly. It may only be appropriate to operate a larger **centralised** treasury as a profit centre, and additional specialist staff demanding high salaries may need to be recruited.

(b) **Controls**

Adequate controls must be in place to prevent costly errors and overexposure to risks such as foreign exchange risks. It is possible to enter into a very large foreign exchange deal over the telephone.

(c) **Information**

A treasury team which trades in futures and options or in currencies is competing with other traders employed by major financial institutions who may have better knowledge of the market because of the large number of customers they deal with. In order to compete effectively, the team needs to have detailed and up-to-date market information.

(d) **Attitudes to risk**

The more aggressive approach to risk-taking which is characteristic of treasury professionals may be difficult to reconcile with the more measured approach to risk which may prevail within the board of directors. The recognition of treasury operations as profit making activities may not fit well with the main business operations of the company.

(e) **Internal charges**

If the department is to be a true profit centre, then market prices should be charged for its services to other departments. It may be difficult to put realistic prices on some services, such as arrangement of finance or general financial advice.

(f) **Performance evaluation**

Even with a profit centre approach, it may be difficult to measure the success of a treasury team for the reason that successful treasury activities sometimes involve **avoiding** the incurring of costs, for example when a currency devalues. For example, a treasury team which hedges a future foreign currency receipt over a period when the domestic currency undergoes devaluation (as sterling did in 1992 when it left the European exchange rate mechanism) may avoid a substantial loss for the company.

4 FRAUD RELATING TO SOURCES OF FINANCE

Fraud

4.1 The incidence of **financial fraud**, including fraud in a computer environment, appears to be increasing fast. This trend, together with the increasing sophistication of fraudsters, creates difficult problems for management.

> **KEY TERM**
>
> In a famous court case, **fraud** was defined as:
>
> 'a false representation of fact made with the knowledge of its falsity, or without belief in its truth, or recklessly careless, whether it be true or false.'

Part A: The finance function

Types of fraud

4.2 Some methods of fraud relating especially to sources of finance are described briefly in the following paragraphs.

Teeming and lading

4.3 This is a 'rolling' fraud rather than a 'one-off' fraud. It occurs when a clerk has the chance to misappropriate payments from debtors or to creditors.

   (a) Cash received by the company is 'borrowed' by the cashier rather than being kept as petty cash or banked.

   (b) When the cashier knows that a reconciliation is to be performed, or audit visit planned, he pays the money back so that everything appears satisfactory at that point, but after the audit the teeming and lading starts again.

4.4 Surprise visits by auditors and independent checking of cash balances should discourage this fraud.

4.5 Another common fraud may arise when one employee has sole control of the sales ledger and recording debtors' cheques.

   (a) The employee pays cheques into a separate bank account, either by forged endorsement or by opening an account in a name similar to the employer's.

   (b) The clerk has to allocate cheques or cash received from other debtors against the account of the debtor whose payment was misappropriated. This prevents other staff from asking why the account is still overdue or from sending statements etc to the debtors. However, the misallocation has to continue as long as the money is missing.

   This fraud, therefore, never really stops. It can be detected by independent verification of debtors balances (eg by circulation) and by looking at unallocated payments, if the sales ledger is organised to show this. In addition, sending out itemised monthly statements to debtors should act as a deterrent.

Management fraud

4.6 While **employee fraud** is usually undertaken purely for the employee's financial gain, **management fraud** is often undertaken to **improve** the company's apparent **performance**, to reduce tax liabilities or to improve manager's promotion prospects. Managers are often in a position to override internal controls and to intimidate their subordinates into collusion or turning a blind eye. This makes it difficult to detect such frauds.

4.7 This clash of interest between loyalty to an employer and professional integrity can be difficult to resolve. Management fraud often comes to light after a takeover or on a change of internal audit staff or practices. Its consequences can be far reaching for the employing company in damaging its reputation or because it results in legal action. Because management usually have access to much larger sums of money than more lowly employees, the financial loss to the company can be immense.

Advance fee fraud

4.8 This type of fraud involves the fraudster taking a fee or deposit up-front, promising to deliver in the future goods and services which never materialise.

4.9 Many companies have been exposed to such frauds from international sources. In recent years, for example, the highest incidence of such fraud led to the Central Bank of Nigeria publishing warnings around the world. Hopefully, wide publicity about the details of such fraud schemes will mean that fewer such frauds will be perpetrated successfully.

Case example

Advance fee fraud in Nigeria

The advance fee fraud is normally perpetrated by the sending of a letter that promises to transfer million of US dollars to the addressee's bank account. In order to gain access to the funds, the addressee is requested to assist in paying various 'taxes' and 'fees' that will allow the funds to be processed. The fraudsters often make use of fake Government, Central Bank and Nigerian National Petroleum Corporation documents and go to considerable lengths to give the scam the appearance of a legitimate offer. They request confidentiality about the transaction.

The gathering of advance fees, made up of supposed legal fees, registration fees, VAT and so on, is the actual objective of the scam.

Two recent variants of the scam have been reported. The first, normally directed at religious and charitable organisations, is the request for fees to process bogus inheritances from a will. The second is an offer to use chemicals to transform paper into US dollar bills with the proceeds being shared by both parties.

Pyramid scheme frauds

4.10 **Pyramid scheme frauds** can take various forms. The schemes are based on the idea that the scope of the scheme continually widens to involve more people. People (or firms) newly recruited to the scheme may be induced to invest money which is not actually invested but goes towards paying returns to others already in the scheme. While the membership of the scheme multiplies, it appears that those in the scheme cannot lose.

4.11 However, such a scheme is destined to fail eventually as the flow of potential recruits dries up. Those setting up the scheme may have made themselves rich, at the expense of those recently recruited to the scheme.

Managing fraud risk

4.12 Fraud risk may be minimised by taking the following steps.

- Identify fraud risks in the industry
- Identify the fraud risks in the company
- Examine how particular circumstances within the organisation create fraud risk

Having analysed the risk in this way, management is in a position to **review how the company manages risk** and to **review how internal controls reduce the risk**.

4.13 To fight fraud effectively demands a coherent corporate strategy. **Fraud policy statements** communicate this through the organisation.

Prevention of fraud

4.14 Fraud will only be prevented successfully if potential fraudsters perceive the **risk of detection** as being high, and if **personnel** are adequately **screened** before employment and given no incentive to turn against the company once employed. The following safeguards should therefore be implemented:

- A good internal control system
- Continuous supervision of all employees
- Surprise audit visits
- Thorough personnel procedures

4.15 **Segregation of duties**, the dividing of key stages in the accounting process between different people, will be a key part of internal control.

4.16 The work of employees must be **monitored** as this will increase the perceived risk of being discovered. Actual results must regularly be compared against budgeted results, and employees should be asked to explain significant variances.

4.17 **Surprise audit visits** are a valuable contribution to preventing fraud. If the threat of a surprise visit is constantly present, the cashier will not be able to carry out a teeming and lading fraud without the risk of being discovered, and this risk is usually sufficient to prevent the fraud.

4.18 Finally, **personnel procedures** may be adequate to prevent the occurrence of frauds.

(a) Whenever a fraud is discovered, the **fraudster** should be **dismissed** and the police should be **informed**. Too often an employee is 'asked to resign' and then moves on to a similar job where the fraud is repeated.

(b) On recruitment, all new employees should be required to produce **adequate references** from their previous employers.

(c) If an employee's **lifestyle changes dramatically**, explanations should be sought.

(d) Every employee should take an **annual holiday entitlement**. Often in practice the employee who is 'so dedicated that he never takes a holiday' is in fact not taking his leave for fear of his fraud being discovered by his replacement while he is away.

(e) **Pay levels** should be **adequate** and **working conditions** of a **reasonable** standard. If employees feel that they are being paid an unfairly low amount or 'exploited', they may look for ways to supplement their pay dishonestly.

Question 3

Which of the following is an advantage of having a decentralised treasury function?

A   Foreign currency risk management is likely to be improved.
B   Better short-term investment opportunities will arise.
C   Lower bank charges can be negotiated.
D   It is possible to be more responsive to the needs of individual operating units.

Answer

D   All the other benefits are more likely to be associated with a centralised treasury function.

4: The treasury function

> **Chapter roundup**
>
> - Given the importance of **cash** to a business, we have looked at the skills needed to ensure its availability (**treasurership**).
>
> - **Treasury management** in a modern enterprise covers various areas, and in a large business it may be a **centralised** function. It may be a **cost** or **profit centre**.
>
> - The treasurer should be aware of the risk of **fraud** relating to sources of finance, including **advance fee fraud** and **pyramid schemes**.

Quick quiz

1. Which of the following functions is the **least likely** to be carried out by a treasury department?

   A Negotiating arrangements with bankers
   B Dealing in foreign exchange
   C Preparing the corporate budget and business plan
   D Involvement in business acquisitions and sales

2. **Fill in the blanks** in the statement below, using the words in the box. (Words may be used more than once.)

   - Treasury management may be defined as 'the corporate handling of all (1) .... matters, the generation of external and internal (2) .... for business, the management of (3) .... and cash flow, and the complex strategies, policies and procedures of (4) ....

   - A treasury department may be managed either as a (5) .... centre or a (6) .... centre.

   - A (7) .... treasury department has the role of ensuring that individual operating units have all the funds they need at the right time.

   - Futures and options might be employed in (8) .... risk management.

   - Acquisitions and sales of businesses fall within the area of (9) ....

   - Money transmission management is an aspect of (10) .... management.

• Corporate finance	• Centralised	• Profit	• Financial
• Liquidity	• Cost	• Currency/ies	• Funds

3. Why might a treasurer choose *not* to 'hedge' against the risk of a foreign exchange movement?

4. Which of the following principles would you say is the most important when designing systems to prevent fraud?

   A Ensuring that all receipts are banked daily
   B Segregation of duties between the various functions
   C Daily reconciliation of cash records
   D Obtaining of paid cheques from banks

5. What is an advance fee fraud?

6. What are the main things a treasurer needs to know to carry out funding management effectively?

7. Name three key elements in preventing fraud.

8. Teeming and lading frauds are based on the principle that the fraudulent scheme continually widens to involve more people.

   True ☐
   False ☐

59

Part A: The finance function

Answers to quick quiz

1   C   While the treasury department will be involved in the preparation of the cash budget, it is unlikely to have a major role in the wider budgeting and planning process.

2   (1) Financial (2) Funds (3) Currencies (4) Corporate finance (5) Cost (6) Profit (7) Centralised (8) Currency (9) Corporate finance (10) Liquidity

3   Because she thinks it likely that a profit will be made in refraining from hedging the risk.

4   B   Segregation of duties makes it much harder to commit a fraud without collusion between one or more employees.

5   A fraud where the fraudster takes the fee or deposit up front and promises to deliver, in the future, goods or services which never materialise.

6   (a)   Where funds are obtainable
    (b)   For how long
    (c)   At what interest rate
    (d)   Whether security will be required
    (e)   Whether interest rates would be fixed or variable

7   Any three of:
    (a)   A good internal control system
    (b)   Surprise audit visits
    (c)   Continuous supervision of all employees
    (d)   Thorough personnel procedures
    (e)   Segregation of duties

8   False. Pyramid schemes are based on the principle of continuous widening.

Now try the question below from the Exam Question Bank

Number	Level	Marks	Time
4	Examination	20	36 mins

Part B
Sources of long-term finance

Chapter 5

SHARE CAPITAL

Topic list	Syllabus reference	Ability required
1 Obtaining equity funds	(ii)	Evaluation
2 Rights issues	(ii)	Evaluation
3 Scrip dividends, scrip issues and stock splits	(ii)	Evaluation
4 Preference shares	(ii)	Evaluation
5 Dividend policy	(ii)	Evaluation
6 Warrants	(ii)	Evaluation

Introduction

The most important source of finance for companies is the cash that arises from **retaining profits** within the business. In the short term an **overdraft** is a flexible source of finance. In the case of long-term finance, the main choice is between **equity** (ordinary shares) and **debt** finance. In this chapter, we describe the different forms of **share capital**.

When sources of **long-term finance** are used, large sums are usually involved, and so the financial manager needs to consider all the options available with care, looking at the possible effects on the company in the long term.

You need a good knowledge of the different ways of obtaining equity; you may be asked to identify one in a MCQ or describe a number in a discussion question. Rights issues are also an important means of raising capital for many companies, and calculation of the theoretical rights price is a particularly important technique.

Learning outcomes covered in this chapter

- Recommend the sources of capital most appropriate for an organisation

Syllabus content covered in this chapter

- Types of share capital, ie ordinary, preference, deferred, warrants
- Equity issues; new and rights issues
- Methods of issuing securities, eg rights, placing, offer for sale

1 OBTAINING EQUITY FUNDS

1.1 A company might raise new funds from the following sources.

(a) Cash from retained earnings - the most important form of finance in practice

(b) The capital markets:
  (i)   New share issues
  (ii) Rights issues
  (iii) Issues of loan capital

Part B: Sources of long-term finance

    (c) Bank borrowings

    (d) Government sources

    (e) Business expansion scheme funds

    (f) Venture capital

    (g) The international money and capital markets (eurocommercial paper, eurobonds and eurocurrency borrowing)

Ordinary (equity) shares

> **KEY TERMS**
>
> **Equity** is the issued ordinary share capital plus reserves, statutory and otherwise, which represent the investment in a company by the ordinary shareholders.
>
> **Equity share capital** is a company's issued share capital less capital which carries preferential rights. Ordinary share capital normally comprises ordinary shares.
>
> *(OT 2000)*

1.2   **Ordinary (equity) shares** are those of the owners of a company.

> **KEY TERM**
>
> **Equity instrument** is an instrument that evidences an ownership interest in an entity, ie a residual interest in the assets of the entity after deducting all of its liabilities.
>
> Equity instrument has a wider meaning than equity shares because it includes some non-equity shares, as well as warrants (see later in this chapter) and options to subscribe for or purchase equity shares in the issuing company (FRS 13).   *(OT 2000)*

1.3   The ordinary shares of UK companies have a nominal or 'face' value, typically £1 or 50p. Outside the UK it is not uncommon for a company's shares to have no nominal value.

1.4   The market value of a quoted company's shares bears **no relationship** to their **nominal value**, except that when ordinary shares are issued for cash, the issue price must be equal to or (more usually) *more than* the nominal value of the shares.

> **KEY TERM**
>
> **Preferred ordinary shares** are entitled to a dividend at a fixed pre-agreed rate before the deferred ordinary shares. The dividend payable to deferred ordinary shares is not at a fixed rate.
>
> Alternatively, **deferred ordinary shares** may only be entitled to a dividend after a certain date or only if profits rise above a certain amount. Voting rights might also differ from those attached to other ordinary shares.

1.5   Ordinary shareholders put funds into their company by paying for a **new issue** of shares, or through **retained profits**. **Retained earnings** are a flexible source of finance, and will not involve a change in shareholding. However shareholders may be sensitive to the **loss of dividend** that will result from re-investing profits rather than paying them out.

1.6 A new issue of shares might be made in a variety of different circumstances.

(a) The company might want to **raise more cash**, for example for expansion of its operations. If, for example, a company with 200,000 ordinary shares in issue decides to issue 50,000 new shares to raise cash, should it offer the new shares to existing shareholders so that they can retain control, or should it sell them to new shareholders instead?

(i) If a company sells the new shares to existing shareholders in **proportion** to their existing shareholding in the company, we have a **rights issue**. The 50,000 shares would be issued as a one for four rights issue, by offering shareholders one new share for every four shares they currently hold. This is the method preferred by the London Stock Exchange as it avoids dilution of existing interests. We shall discuss rights issues further in Section 2.

(ii) If the number of new shares being issued is **small** compared to the number of shares already in issue, it might be decided instead to sell them to new shareholders, since ownership of the company would only be minimally affected.

(b) The company might want to issue new shares partly to raise cash but more importantly to obtain a **stock market listing**. When a UK company is floated, for example on the main stock market, it is a requirement of the Stock Exchange that at least a minimum proportion of its shares should be made available to the general investing public if the shares are not already widely held.

(c) The company might issue new shares to the shareholders of another company, in order to **take it over**.

Stock Exchange 'main market' listing

1.7 However, the owners of a private company which becomes a listed 'plc' (public limited company) must accept that the change is likely to involve a **significant loss of control** to a wider circle of investors and **greater public scrutiny** and **accountability**. The risk of the company being taken over will also increase following listing. The implications of this will need to be taken into account.

WHY SEEK A STOCK MARKET LISTING?
- Access to a wider pool of finance
- Improved marketability of shares
- Easier to seek growth by acquisition
- Enhanced public image
- Original owners selling holding to obtain funds for other projects
- Original owners realising holding

Obtaining a listing

1.8 An unquoted company can obtain a listing on the stock market by means of:

- Direct **offer by subscription** to the public
- **Offer for sale**
- **Placing**
- **Introduction**

1.9 Of these an **offer for sale** or a **placing** are the most common.

> **KEY TERMS**
>
> **Offer for sale** is an invitation to apply for shares in a company based on information contained in a prospectus.
>
> **Placing** is a method of raising share capital in which there is no public issue of shares, the shares being issued, rather, in a small number of large 'blocks', to persons or institutions who have previously agreed to purchase the shares at a predetermined price.
>
> *(OT 2000)*

Offers for sale

1.10 An **offer for sale** is a means of selling the shares of a company to the public at large. When companies 'go public' for the first time, a **large** issue will probably take the form of an offer for sale.

1.11 An offer for sale entails the acquisition by an issuing house of a large block of shares of a company, with a view to offering them for sale to the public.

1.12 An issuing house is usually a merchant bank (or sometimes a firm of stockbrokers). It may acquire the shares either as a direct allotment from the company or by purchase from existing members. In either case, the issuing house publishes an invitation to the public to apply for shares, either at a fixed price or on a tender basis.

1.13 The advantage of an offer for sale over a direct offer by the company to the public is that the issuing house accepts responsibility to the public, and gives to the issue the support of its own standing.

1.14 A smaller issue is more likely to be a placing, since the amount to be raised can be obtained more cheaply if the issuing house or other sponsoring firm approaches selected institutional investors privately.

1.15 A company whose shares are already listed might issue new shares to the general public. It is likely, however, that a new issue by a quoted company will be either a **placing** or a **rights issue**, which are described later.

Issuing houses and sponsoring member firms

1.16 When an unquoted company applies for a Stock Exchange listing:

(a) It must be sponsored by a firm that is a member of the Stock Exchange. This sponsoring member firm has the responsibility of ensuring that the company meets the **requirements for listing**, and carries out the necessary procedures.

(b) The company will also employ the services of an **issuing house**, which might well be the sponsoring member firm itself. An issuing house has the job of trying to ensure a successful issue for the company's shares, by advising on an issue price for the shares, and trying to interest institutional investors in buying some of the shares.

The issue price and offers for sale

1.17 The offer price must be **advertised a short time in advance**, so it is fixed without certain knowledge of the condition of the market at the time applications are invited. In order to ensure the success of an issue, share prices are often set **lower** than they might otherwise be. An issuing house normally tries to ensure that a share price rises to a **premium** above its issue price soon after trading begins. A target premium of 20% above the issue price would be fairly typical.

1.18 Companies will be keen to avoid over-pricing an issue, so that the issue is under-subscribed, leaving underwriters with the unwelcome task of having to buy up the unsold shares. On the other hand, if the issue price is too low then the issue will be oversubscribed and the company would have been able to raise the required capital by issuing fewer shares.

1.19 The share price of an issue is usually advertised as being based on a certain P/E ratio, the ratio of the price to the company's most recent earnings per share figure in its audited accounts. The issue's P/E ratio can then be compared by investors with the P/E ratios of similar quoted companies.

Offers for sale by tender

1.20 It is often very difficult to decide upon the price at which the shares should be offered to the general public. One way of trying to ensure that the issue price reflects the value of the shares as perceived by the market is to make an **offer for sale by tender**. A **minimum price** will be fixed and subscribers will be invited to tender for shares at prices equal to or above the minimum. The shares will be **allotted at the highest price** at which they will **all be taken up**. This is known as the **striking price**.

1.21 Offers by tender are less common than offers for sale. An offer for sale is more certain in the amount of finance that will be raised.

1.22 An increase in the use of offers for sale by tender might follow a general increase in share values. When share prices are generally rising, the striking price in an offer for sale by tender is likely to be higher than the issue price that would have been set if the issuing company were to select the issue price itself, since the issue price would have to be sufficiently low to be reasonably sure that the issue would be fully subscribed by investors.

1.23 EXAMPLE: OFFER FOR SALE BY TENDER

Byte Henderson plc is a new company that is making its first public issue of shares. It has decided to make the issue by means of an offer for sale by tender. The intention is to issue up to 4,000,000 shares (the full amount of authorised share capital) at a minimum price of 300 pence. The money raised, net of issue costs of £1,000,000, would be invested in projects which would earn benefits with a present value equal to 130% of the net amount invested.

Part B: Sources of long-term finance

The following tenders have been received. (Each applicant has made only one offer.)

Price tendered per share £	Number of shares applied for at this price
6.00	50,000
5.50	100,000
5.00	300,000
4.50	450,000
4.00	1,100,000
3.50	1,500,000
3.00	2,500,000

(a) How many shares would be issued, and how much in total would be raised, if Byte Henderson plc chooses:

    (i) To maximise the total amount raised?
    (ii) To issue exactly 4,000,000 shares?

(b) Harvey Goldfinger, a private investor, has applied for 12,000 shares at a price of £5.50 and has sent a cheque for £66,000 to the issuing house that is handling the issue. In both cases (a)(i) and (ii), how many shares would be issued to Mr Goldfinger, assuming that any partial acceptance of offers would mean allotting shares to each accepted applicant in proportion to the number of shares applied for? How much will Mr Goldfinger receive back out of the £66,000 he has paid?

(c) Estimate the likely market value of shares in the company after the issue, assuming that the market price fully reflects the investment information given above and that exactly 4,000,000 shares are issued.

1.24 SOLUTION

(a) We begin by looking at the cumulative tenders.

Price £	Cumulative number of shares applied for	Amount raised if price is selected, before deducting issue costs £
6.00	50,000	300,000
5.50	150,000	825,000
5.00	450,000	2,250,000
4.50	900,000	4,050,000
4.00	2,000,000	8,000,000
3.50	3,500,000	12,250,000
3.00	6,000,000	12,000,000

    (i) To maximise the total amount raised, the issue price should be £3.50. The total raised before deducting issue costs would be £12,250,000.

    (ii) To issue exactly 4,000,000 shares, the issue price must be £3.00. The total raised would be £12,000,000, before deducting issue costs.

(b) (i) Harvey Goldfinger would be allotted 12,000 shares at £3.50 per share. He would receive a refund of 12,000 × £2 = £24,000 out of the £66,000 he has paid.

    (ii) If 4,000,000 shares are issued, applicants would receive two thirds of the shares they tendered for. Harvey Goldfinger would be allotted 8,000 shares at £3 per share and would receive a refund of £42,000 out of the £66,000 he has paid.

(c) The net amount raised would be £12,000,000 minus issue costs of £1,000,000, £11,000,000.

The present value of the benefits from investment would be 130% of £11,000,000, £14,300,000. If the market price reflects this information, the price per share would rise to $\frac{£14,300,000}{4,000,000}$ = £3.575 per share.

A prospectus issue

1.25 In a **prospectus issue**, or public issue, a company offers its own shares to the general public. An issuing house or merchant bank may act as an agent, but not as an underwriter. This type of issue is therefore risky, and is very rare. Well known companies making a large new issue may use this method, and the company would almost certainly already have a quotation on the Stock Exchange.

A placing 5/01

1.26 A **placing** is an arrangement whereby the shares are not all offered to the public, but instead, the sponsoring market maker arranges for most of the issue to be bought by a **small number of investors**, usually institutional investors such as pension funds and insurance companies.

The choice between an offer for sale and a placing

1.27 When a company is planning a flotation on the AIM, or a full Stock Exchange listing, is it likely to prefer an offer for sale of its shares, or a placing?

(a) **Placings** are much **cheaper.**

(b) However, most of the shares will be placed with a **relatively small number** of **(institutional) shareholders**, which means that most of the shares are unlikely to be available for trading after the flotation.

A Stock Exchange introduction

1.28 By this method of obtaining a quotation, no shares are made available to the market, neither existing nor newly created shares; nevertheless, the Stock Exchange grants a quotation. This will only happen where shares in a large company are already widely held, so that a market can be seen to exist. A company might want an **introduction** to obtain greater marketability for the shares, a known share valuation for inheritance tax purposes and easier access in the future to additional capital.

Underwriting

1.29 A company about to issue new securities in order to raise finance might decide to have the issue underwritten. **Underwriters** are financial institutions which agree (in exchange for a fixed fee, perhaps 2.25% of the finance to be raised) to buy at the issue price any securities which are **not subscribed** for by the investing public.

1.30 Underwriters **remove** the **risk** of a share issue's being under-subscribed, but at a cost to the company issuing the shares. It is not compulsory to have an issue underwritten. Ordinary offers for sale are most likely to be underwritten although rights issues may be as well.

Part B: Sources of long-term finance

1.31 Because of the costs of underwriting, there has been a trend in recent years for companies whose securities are marketable to adopt the practice known as the '**bought deal**', whereby an investment bank buys the whole of a new issue at a small discount to the market.

Pricing shares for a stock market launch

1.32 Pricing shares for a stock market launch is a task for the company's sponsor. Factors that the sponsor will take into account are as follows.

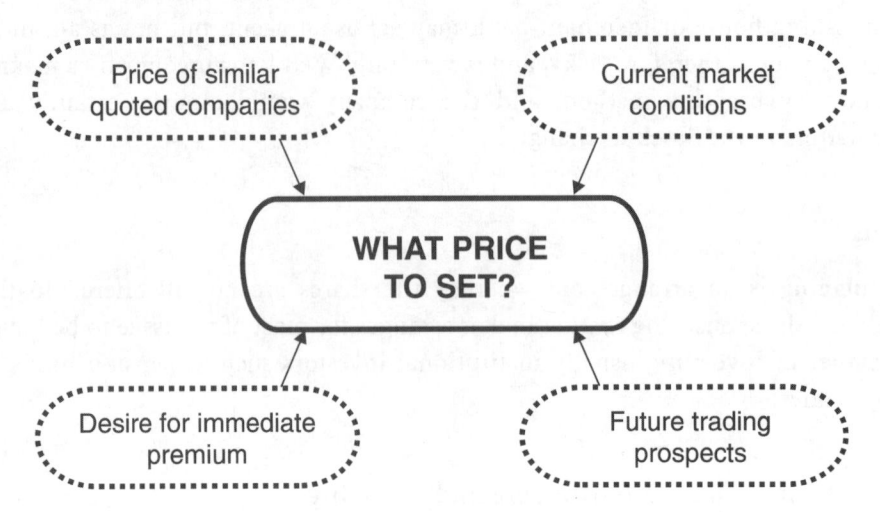

```
      Price of similar              Current market
      quoted companies              conditions
                  \                /
                   → WHAT PRICE ←
                     TO SET?
                  /                \
      Desire for immediate          Future trading
      premium                       prospects
```

2 RIGHTS ISSUES   Pilot paper, 5/01, 11/01

> **KEY TERM**
>
> **A rights issue** is the raising of new capital by giving existing shareholders the right to subscribe to new shares or debentures in proportion to their current holdings. These shares are usually issued at a discount to market price. A shareholder not wishing to take up a rights issue may sell the rights.   *(OT 2000)*

2.1 Existing shareholders have **pre-emption rights** when new shares are issued. So that existing shareholders' rights are not diluted by the issue of new shares, section 89 of Companies Act 1985 requires that before any equity shares are allotted for cash they must first be offered to existing shareholders.

> **KEY TERM**
>
> **A dilution** is the reduction in the earnings and voting power per share caused by an increase or potential increase in the number of shares in issue. For the purpose of calculating the diluted earnings per share, the net profit attributable to shareholders and the weighted average number of shares outstanding should be adjusted for the effects of all dilutive potential ordinary shares.   *(OT 2000)*

2.2 The major advantages of a rights issue are as follows.

(a) Rights issues are **cheaper** than offers for sale to the general public. This is partly because no **prospectus** is required (provided that the issue is for less than 10% of the class of shares concerned), partly because the **administration** is **simpler** and partly because the cost of underwriting will be less.

(b) Rights issues are **more beneficial** to **existing shareholders** than issues to the general public. New shares are issued at a **discount** to the current market price, to make them attractive to investors. A rights issue secures the discount on the market price for existing shareholders, who may either keep the shares or sell them if they wish.

(c) **Relative voting rights** are **unaffected** if shareholders all take up their rights.

(d) The finance raised may be used to **reduce gearing** in book value terms by increasing share capital and/or to pay off long-term debt which will reduce gearing in market value terms.

2.3 A company making a rights issue must set a price which is low enough to secure the acceptance of shareholders, who are being asked to provide extra funds, but not too low, so as to avoid excessive dilution of the earnings per share.

> **Exam focus point**
>
> A question might ask for discussion on the effect of a rights issue, as well as calculations, eg of the effect on EPS.

2.4 EXAMPLE: RIGHTS ISSUE (1)

Seagull plc can achieve a profit after tax of 20% on the capital employed. At present its capital structure is as follows.

	£
200,000 ordinary shares of £1 each	200,000
Retained earnings	100,000
	300,000

The directors propose to raise an additional £126,000 from a rights issue. The current market price is £1.80.

Required

(a) Calculate the number of shares that must be issued if the rights price is: £1.60; £1.50; £1.40; £1.20.

(b) Calculate the dilution in earnings per share in each case.

2.5 SOLUTION

The earnings at present are 20% of £300,000 = £60,000. This gives earnings per share of 30p. The earnings after the rights issue will be 20% of £426,000 = £85,200.

Rights price £	No of new share (£126,000 ÷ rights price)	EPS (£85,200 ÷ total no of shares) Pence	Dilution Pence
1.60	78,750	30.6	+ 0.6
1.50	84,000	30.0	–
1.40	90,000	29.4	– 0.6
1.20	105,000	27.9	– 2.1

2.6 Note that at a high rights price the earnings per share are increased, not diluted. The breakeven point (zero dilution) occurs when the rights price is equal to the capital employed per share: £300,000 ÷ 200,000 = £1.50.

Part B: Sources of long-term finance

The market price of shares after a rights issue: the theoretical ex-rights price

2.7 After the announcement of a rights issue, there is a tendency for share prices to fall. This temporary fall is due to uncertainty in the market about the consequences of the issue, with respect to future profits, earnings and dividends. After the issue has actually been made, the market price per share will normally fall, because there are more shares in issue and the new shares were issued at a discount price.

2.8 When a rights issue is announced, all existing shareholders have the right to subscribe for new shares, and so there are rights attached to the existing shares. The shares are therefore described as being traded as 'cum rights'. On the first day of dealings in the newly issued shares, the rights no longer exist and the old shares are now 'ex rights' (without rights attached).

2.9 In theory, the new market price will be the consequence of an adjustment to allow for the discount price of the new issue, and a theoretical ex rights price can be calculated.

> **EXAM FORMULA**
>
> Theoretical ex-rights price = $\dfrac{1}{N+1}\left((N \times \text{cum rights price}) + \text{issue price}\right)$
>
> where N = number of shares required to buy one new share.

2.10 EXAMPLE: RIGHTS ISSUE (2)

Fundraiser plc has 1,000,000 ordinary shares of £1 in issue, which have a market price on 1 September of £2.10 per share. The company decides to make a rights issue, and offers its shareholders the right to subscribe for one new share at £1.50 each for every four shares already held. After the announcement of the issue, the share price fell to £1.95, but by the time just prior to the issue being made, it had recovered to £2 per share. This market value just before the issue is known as the cum rights price. What is the theoretical ex-rights price?

2.11 SOLUTION

Theoretical ex-rights price = $\dfrac{1}{4+1}((4 \times £2) + £1.50) = \dfrac{£9.50}{5} = £1.90$

Yield adjusted ex-rights price

2.12 We have assumed so far that the additional funds raised by the rights issue will generate the same rate of return as existing funds. If the new funds are likely to earn a different return from what is currently being earned, the yield-adjusted theoretical ex-rights price should be calculated.

> **FORMULA TO LEARN**
>
> Yield-adjusted theoretical ex-rights price =
>
> $\left[\dfrac{\text{Cum rights price} \times N}{(N+1)}\right] + \left[\dfrac{\text{Issue price}}{(N+1)} \times \dfrac{\text{Yield on new funds}}{\text{Yield on existing funds}}\right]$

2.13 EXAMPLE: RIGHTS ISSUE (3)

Using the same data for Fundraiser as above, with the additional information that rate of return on new funds = 12%, and on existing funds = 8%, calculate the yield-adjusted theoretical ex-rights price.

2.14 SOLUTION

Yield-adjusted theoretical ex-rights price = $\left(\dfrac{2 \times 4}{5}\right) + \left[\dfrac{1.50}{5} \times \dfrac{0.12}{0.08}\right] = £2.05$

2.15 The yield-adjusted price demonstrates how the market will view the rights issue, and what will happen to the market value.

The value of rights

2.16 The value of rights is the **theoretical gain** a shareholder would make by exercising his rights.

- (a) (i) Using the above example, if the price offered in the rights issue is £1.50 per share, and the market price after the issue is expected to be £1.90, the value attaching to a right is £1.90 – £1.50 = £0.40. A shareholder would therefore be expected to gain 40 pence for each new share he buys.

  (ii) If he does not have enough money to buy the share himself, he could sell the right to subscribe for a new share to another investor, and receive 40 pence from the sale. This other investor would then buy the new share for £1.50, so that his total outlay to acquire the share would be £0.40 + £1.50 = £1.90, the theoretical ex rights price.

- (b) The value of rights attaching to existing shares is calculated in the same way. If the value of rights on a new share is 40 pence, and there is a one for four rights issue, the value of the rights attaching to each existing share is 40 ÷ 4 = 10 pence.

The theoretical gain or loss to shareholders

2.17 **Possible courses of action open to shareholders**

- (a) **'Take up' or 'exercise' the rights**, that is, to buy the new shares at the rights price. Shareholders who do this will maintain their percentage holdings in the company by subscribing for the new shares.

- (b) **'Renounce' the rights** and sell them on the market. Shareholders who do this will have lower percentage holdings of the company's equity after the issue than before the issue, and the total value of their shares will be less (on the assumption that the actual market price after the issue is close to the theoretical ex rights price).

- (c) **Renounce part of the rights and take up the remainder.** For example, a shareholder may sell enough of his rights to enable him to buy the remaining rights shares he is entitled to with the sale proceeds, and so keep the total market value of his shareholding in the company unchanged.

- (d) **Do nothing.** Shareholders may be protected from the consequences of their inaction because rights not taken up are sold on a shareholder's behalf by the company. The Stock Exchange rules state that if new securities are not taken up, they should be sold by the company to new subscribers for the benefit of the shareholders who were entitled to the rights.

Part B: Sources of long-term finance

Question 1

Gopher plc has issued 3,000,000 ordinary shares of £1 each, which are at present selling for £4 per share. The company plans to issue rights to purchase one new equity share at a price of £3.20 per share for every three shares held. A shareholder who owns 900 shares thinks that he will suffer a loss in his personal wealth because the new shares are being offered at a price lower than market value. On the assumption that the actual market value of shares will be equal to the theoretical ex rights price, what would be the effect on the shareholder's wealth if:

(a) He sells all the rights
(b) He exercises half of the rights and sells the other half
(c) He does nothing at all

Answer

The theoretical ex rights price = $\frac{1}{3+1}((3 \times £4) + £3.20)) = £3.80$ per share

	£
Theoretical ex rights price	3.80
Price per new share	3.20
Value of rights per new share	0.60

The value of the rights attached to each existing share is $\frac{£0.60}{3} = £0.20$.

We will assume that a shareholder is able to sell his rights for £0.20 per existing share held.

(a) If the shareholder **sells all his rights**:

	£
Sale value of rights (900 × £0.20)	180
Market value of his 900 shares, ex rights (× £3.80)	3,420
Total wealth	3,600
Total value of 900 shares cum rights (× £4)	£3,600

The shareholder would neither gain nor lose wealth. He would not be required to provide any additional funds to the company, but his shareholding as a proportion of the total equity of the company will be lower.

(b) If the shareholder **exercises half of the rights** (buys 450/3 = 150 shares at £3.20) and sells the other half:

	£
Sale value of rights (450 × £0.20)	90
Market value of his 1,050 shares, ex rights (× £3.80)	3,990
	4,080
Total value of 900 shares cum rights (× £4)	3,600
Additional investment (150 × £3.20)	480
	4,080

The shareholder would neither gain nor lose wealth, although he will have increased his investment in the company by £480.

(c) If the shareholder **does nothing**, but all other shareholders either exercise their rights or sell them, he would lose wealth as follows.

	£
Market value of 900 shares cum rights (× £4)	3,600
Market value of 900 shares ex rights (× £3.80)	3,420
Loss in wealth	180

It follows that the shareholder, to protect his existing investment, should either **exercise his rights** or **sell them** to another investor. If he does not exercise his rights, the new securities he was entitled to subscribe for might be sold for his benefit by the company, and this would protect him from losing wealth.

2.18 The decision by individual shareholders as to whether they take up the offer will therefore depend on:

(a) The expected rate of return on the investment (and the risk associated with it)
(b) The return obtainable from other investments (allowing for the associated risk)

Vendor placings

2.19 A **vendor placing** occurs when there is an issue of shares by one company to take over another, and these shares are then sold in a placing to raise cash for the shareholders in the target company, who are selling their shares in the takeover.

2.20 EXAMPLE: VENDOR PLACING

AB plc wants to take over Z Ltd. AB plc wants to finance the purchase by issuing more equity shares, and the shareholders of Z Ltd want to sell their shares for cash. AB plc can arrange a vendor placing whereby:

(a) AB plc issues new shares to finance the takeover.

(b) These shares are placed by AB plc's stockbrokers (market makers) with institutional investors, to raise cash.

(c) The cash that is raised is used to pay the shareholders in Z Ltd for their shares.

Other instances of issuing shares

2.21 There are some other methods of issuing shares on the Stock Exchange. These are as follows.

(a) An **open offer** is an offer to existing shareholders to subscribe for new shares in the company but, unlike a rights issue:

   (i) The offer is not necessarily *pro rata* to existing shareholdings

   (ii) The offer is not allotted on renounceable documents (With rights issues the offer to subscribe for new shares must be given on a renounceable letter, so that the shareholder can sell his rights if he so wishes.)

(b) A **capitalisation issue** is a 'scrip issue' of shares which does not raise any new funds (see later in this chapter).

(c) A **vendor consideration issue** is an issue of shares whereby one company acquires the shares of another in a takeover or merger. For example, if A plc wishes to take over B plc, A might make a 'paper' offer to B's shareholders, to try to buy the shares of B by offering B's shareholders newly issued shares of A. This is now a common form of share issue, because mergers and takeovers are fairly frequent events.

(d) **Employee share option schemes** are schemes for awarding shares to employees. For example, in an employee share option scheme, a company awards its employees share options, which are rights to subscribe for new shares at a later date at a predetermined price. When and if the options are eventually exercised, the employees will receive the newly issued shares at a price that ought by then to be below the market price.

The timing and costs of new equity issues

2.22 New equity issues in general will be more common when share prices are high than when share prices are low.

(a) When **share price are high, investors' confidence** will probably be **high**, and investors will be more willing to put money into companies with the potential for growth.

(b) By issuing shares at a high price, a company will **reduce** the **number of shares** it must issue to raise the amount of capital it wants. This will reduce the dilution of earnings for existing shareholders.

(c) Following on from (b), the company's **total dividend commitment** on the new shares, to meet shareholders' expectations, will be **lower**.

(d) If **share prices are low**, business **confidence** is likely to be **low** too. Companies may not want to raise capital for new investments until expectations begin to improve.

2.23 **Costs of a share issue**

- Underwriting costs
- Stock Exchange listing fee (the initial charge) for the new securities
- Fees of the issuing house, solicitors, auditors and public relations consultant
- Charges for printing and distributing the prospectus
- Advertising in national newspapers

3 SCRIP DIVIDENDS, SCRIP ISSUES AND STOCK SPLITS

3.1 Scrip dividends, scrip issues and stock splits are not methods of raising new equity funds, but they *are* methods of altering the share capital structure of a company, or in the case of scrip dividends and scrip issues, increasing the issued share capital of the company.

Scrip dividends

> **KEY TERM**
>
> **Scrip dividend** is a dividend paid by the issue of additional company shares, rather than by cash. *(OT 2000)*

3.2 A scrip dividend effectively converts profit and loss reserves into **issued share capital**. When the directors of a company would prefer to retain funds within the business but consider that they must pay at least a certain amount of dividend, they might offer equity shareholders the choice of a **cash dividend** or a **scrip dividend**. Each shareholder would decide separately which to take.

3.3 Recently **enhanced scrip dividends** have been offered by a number of companies. With enhanced scrip dividends, the value of the shares offered is much greater than the cash alternative, giving investors an incentive to choose the shares.

Bonus issues

> **KEY TERM**
>
> A **bonus/scrip issue** is the capitalisation of the reserves of a company by the issue of additional shares to existing shareholders, in proportion to their holdings. Such shares are normally fully paid-up with no cash called for from the shareholders. *(OT 2000)*

3.4 For example, if a company with issued share capital of 100,000 ordinary shares of £1 each made a one for five scrip issue, 20,000 new shares would be issued to existing shareholders, one new share for every five old shares held. Issued share capital would be increased by £20,000, and reserves (probably share premium account, if there is one) reduced by this amount.

3.5 By creating more shares in this way, a scrip issue does not raise new funds, but does have the advantage of making shares **cheaper** and therefore (perhaps) **more easily marketable** on the Stock Exchange. For example, if a company's shares are priced at £6 on the Stock Exchange, and the company makes a one for two scrip issue, we should expect the share price after the issue to fall to £4 each. Shares at £4 each might be more easily marketable than shares at £6 each.

Stock splits

3.6 The advantage of a scrip issue mentioned above is also the reason for a **stock split**. A stock split occurs where, for example, each ordinary share of £1 each is split into two shares of 50p each, thus creating cheaper shares with greater marketability. Investors also often expect a company which splits its shares in this way to be planning for substantial earnings growth and dividend growth in the future. As a consequence, the market price of shares may benefit.

4 PREFERENCE SHARES   Pilot paper

> **KEY TERM**
>
> **Preference shares** are shares carrying a fixed rate of dividends, the holders of which, subject to the conditions of issue, have a prior claim to any company profits available for distribution.
>
> Preference shareholders may also have a prior claim to the repayment of capital in the event of winding up.

4.1 As with ordinary shares, a preference dividend can only be paid if **sufficient distributable profits** are **available**, although with **cumulative preference shares** the right to an unpaid dividend is carried forward to later years. The arrears of dividend on cumulative preference shares must be paid before any dividend is paid to the ordinary shareholders. The stated dividend (such as 7%) on preference shares is the **cash dividend**, not grossed up.

4.2 Preference shares are an example of **prior charge capital**.

> **KEY TERM**
>
> **Prior charge capital** is capital which has a right to the receipt of interest or of preference dividends in precedence to any claim on distributable earnings on the part of the ordinary shareholders. On winding up, the claims of holders of prior charge capital also rank before those of ordinary shareholders.   *(OT 2000)*

4.3 Preference shares can be classified in various ways.

KEY TERMS

Cumulative preference shares are preference shares where any arrears of dividend are carried forward. When eventually the company decides to pay a dividend, the cumulative preference shareholders are entitled to all their arrears before ordinary shareholders are paid a dividend. However if a company goes into liquidation, the preference shareholders cease to be entitled to the arrears, unless a dividend has been declared prior to liquidation or there are provisions in the articles.

Preference shares are deemed to be cumulative unless the contrary is stated in the articles or terms of issue.

Participating preference shares are shares that have an additional entitlement to dividend over and above their specified rate. Normally preference shareholders have no such entitlement; once their dividend has been paid, the entire balance of available profit may be distributed to ordinary shareholders. Participating preference shareholders are however entitled to participate along with ordinary shareholders in available profits, normally once the ordinary shareholders have themselves received a specified level of dividend.

Why issue preference shares?

4.4 From the company's point of view, preference shares have some positive features.

(a) Dividends do **not have** to be **paid** in a year in which **profits are poor**, while this is not the case with interest payments on long-term debt (loans or debentures).

(b) Since they do not normally carry voting rights, preference shares **avoid diluting** the **control** of existing shareholders while an issue of equity shares would not.

(c) Unless they are redeemable, issuing preference shares will **lower** the company's **gearing**. Redeemable preference shares are normally treated as debt when gearing is calculated.

(d) The issue of preference shares does **not restrict** the company's **borrowing power**, at least in the sense that preference share capital is not secured against assets of the business.

(e) The non-payment of dividend does **not give** the preference shareholders the **right** to **appoint a receiver**, a right which is normally given to debenture holders.

4.5 However, **dividend payments on preference shares are not tax deductible** in the way that interest payments on debt are. Furthermore, for preference shares to be attractive to investors, the level of payment needs to be higher than for interest on debt to compensate for the additional risks.

4.6 From the point of view of the investor, preference shares are less attractive than loan stock because:

(a) They **cannot be secured** on the company's assets.

(b) The **dividend yield** traditionally offered on preference dividends has been much **too low** to provide an attractive investment compared with the interest yields on loan stock in view of the additional risk involved.

In recent years preference shares have formed a very small proportion only of new capital issues.

5 DIVIDEND POLICY

5/01, 5/02

5.1 For any company, the amount of earnings retained within the business has a direct impact on the amount of dividends. Profit re-invested as retained earnings is profit that could have been paid as a **dividend**. The major **reasons for using funds from retained earnings** to finance new investments, rather than to pay higher dividends and then raise new equity funds for the new investments, are as follows.

(a) The management of many companies believe that retained earnings are funds which do not cost anything, although this is not true. However, it is true that the use of retained earnings as a source of funds does **not lead** to a **payment of cash**.

(b) The dividend policy of a company is in practice determined by the directors. From their standpoint, retained earnings are an attractive source of finance because investment projects can be undertaken **without involving** either the **shareholders** or any **outsiders**.

(c) The use of retained earnings as opposed to new shares or debentures **avoids issue costs**.

(d) The use of retained earnings **avoids** the possibility of a **change in control** resulting from an issue of new shares.

5.2 Another factor that may be of importance is the **financial and taxation position** of the **company's shareholders**. If, for example, because of taxation considerations, they would rather make a capital profit (which will only be taxed when the shares are sold) than receive current income, then finance through retained earnings would be preferred to other methods.

5.3 A company must restrict its self-financing through retained profits because shareholders should be paid a **reasonable dividend**, in line with realistic expectations, even if the directors would rather keep the funds for re-investing. At the same time, a company that is looking for extra funds will not be expected by investors (such as banks) to pay generous dividends, nor over-generous salaries to owner-directors.

> **Exam focus point**
> On the other hand, dividends can be a mechanism for returning surplus funds to shareholders. Discussion of this course of action was part of Question 3 in May 2002.

Dividends as giving a 'signal'

5.4 Investors usually expect a **consistent** dividend policy from the company, with stable dividends each year or, even better, steady dividend growth. A large rise or fall in dividends in any year can have a marked effect on the company's share price. Stable dividends or steady dividend growth are usually needed for share price stability. A cut in dividends may be treated by investors as signalling that the future prospects of the company are weak.

Dividends and market values

5.5 What affects the market value of a company's shares? It seems reasonable to suppose that share values will depend upon:

- The amount in dividends that a company pays
- The rate of growth of dividends

Part B: Sources of long-term finance

- The rate of return which shareholders require

5.6 The purpose of a company's dividend policy should be to maximise shareholders' wealth, which depends on both current dividends and capital gains. Capital gains can be achieved by retaining some earnings for reinvestment and dividend growth in the future.

Question 2

Ochre plc is a company that is still managed by the two individuals who set it up 12 years ago. In the current year, the company acquired plc status and was launched on the Alternative Investment Market (AIM). Previously, all of the shares had been owned by its two founders and certain employees. Now, 40% of the shares are in the hands of the investing public. The company's profit growth and dividend policy are set out below. Will a continuation of the same dividend policy as in the past be suitable now that the company is quoted on the AIM?

	Profits £'000	Dividend £'000	Shares in issue
4 years ago	176	88	800,000
3 years ago	200	104	800,000
2 years ago	240	120	1,000,000
1 year ago	290	150	1,000,000
Current year	444	222 (proposed)	1,500,000

Answer

	Dividend per share p	Dividend as % of profit
4 years ago	11.0	50%
3 years ago	13.0	52%
2 years ago	12.0	50%
1 year ago	15.0	52%
Current year	14.8	50%

The company appears to have pursued a dividend policy of paying out half of after-tax profits in dividend.

This policy is only suitable when a company achieves a stable EPS or steady EPS growth. Investors do not like a fall in dividend from one year to the next, and the fall in dividend per share in the current year is likely to be unpopular, and to result in a fall in the share price.

The company would probably serve its shareholders better by paying a dividend of at least 15p per share, possibly more, in the current year, even though the dividend as a percentage of profit would then be higher.

6 WARRANTS

> **KEY TERMS**
>
> A **warrant** is an instrument that requires the issuer to issue shares (whether contingently or not) and contains no obligation for the issuer to transfer economic benefits. (FRS 4)
>
> The **exercise price** is the price at which an option to purchase or sell shares or other items (**call option** or **put option**) may be exercised. (OT 2000)

6.1 A **warrant** is a right given by a company to an investor, **allowing him** to **subscribe** for new shares at a future date at a fixed, pre-determined price (the **exercise price**).

6.2 **Warrants** are usually issued as part of a package with unsecured loan stock: an investor who buys stock will also acquire a certain number of warrants. The purpose of warrants is to make the loan stock more attractive.

6.3 Once issued, warrants are detachable from the stock and can be sold and bought separately before or during the 'exercise period' (the period during which the right to use the warrants to subscribe for shares is allowed). The market value of warrants will depend on expectations of actual share prices in the future.

6.4 During the exercise period, the price of a warrant should not fall below the higher of:

- **Nil**
- The '**theoretical value**', which equals:

(Current share price – Exercise price) × Number of shares obtainable from each warrant

6.5 If, for example, a warrant entitles the holder to purchase two ordinary shares at a price of £3 each, when the current market price of the shares is £3.40, the minimum market value ('theoretical value') of a warrant would be (£3.40 – £3) × 2 = 80p.

6.6 For a company with good growth prospects, the warrant will usually be quoted at a premium above the minimum prior to the exercise period. This premium is known as the **warrant conversion premium.** It is sometimes expressed as a percentage of the current share price.

6.7 **EXAMPLE: WARRANT CONVERSION PREMIUM**

An investor holds some warrants which can be used to subscribe for ordinary shares on a one for one basis at an exercise price of £2.50 during a specified future period. The current share price is £2.25 and the warrants are quoted at 50p. What is the warrant conversion premium?

6.8 **SOLUTION**

The easiest way of finding the premium is to deduct the current share price from the cost of acquiring a share using the warrant, treating the warrant as if it were currently exercisable:

	£
Cost of warrant	0.50
Exercise price	2.50
	3.00
Current share price	2.25
Premium	0.75

6.9 In the short run the warrant price and share price normally move fairly closely in line with each other. In the longer term the price of the warrant and hence the premium will depend on:

- The length of time before the warrants may be exercised
- The current price of the shares compared with the exercise price
- The future prospects of the company

As the exercise period approaches, the premium will reduce. Towards the end of the exercise period the premium will disappear because, if there were a premium, it would be cheaper to buy the shares directly rather than via the warrant.

6.10 You may be wondering why an investor would prefer to buy warrants at 50p when this means that it will cost him more to get the ordinary shares than if he bought them directly. The attractions of warrants to the investor are:

Part B: Sources of long-term finance

(a) **Low initial outlay**. He only has to spend 50p per share as opposed to £2.25. This means that he could buy 4½ times as many warrants as shares or, alternatively, he could invest the remaining £1.75 in other, less risky investments.

(b) **Lower downside potential**. His maximum loss per share is 50p instead of £2.25. Of course the risk of the loss of 50p is much greater than the risk of losing £2.25. The share price of £2.25 is below the exercise price. If it remained at this level until the beginning of the exercise period, the warrants would become worthless as it would not be worthwhile exercising them.

(c) **High potential returns**. Warrants offer the investor the possibility of making a high profit as a percentage of initial cost. This is because the price of the warrants will tend to move more or less in line with the price of the shares. Thus, if the share price rises by 50p the increase in the value of the warrant will be similar. Using the previous prices, a 50p increase in share price is about 22% but a 50p increase in the warrant price is 100%. This illustrates the gearing effect of warrants.

(d) **Capital gains**. As warrants provide no interest at all, all profits are in the **form of capital gains**, which will be attractive to higher-rate taxpayers who have not used up their annual tax-free allowance.

6.11 Let us now recalculate the premium, assuming a 50p rise in the share price and a 50p rise in the warrant price.

	£
Cost of warrant (50p + 50p)	1.00
Exercise price	2.50
	3.50
Current share price (£2.25 + 50p)	2.75
Premium	0.75

The premium has stayed the same.

6.12 Note also that the share price is now above the exercise price. The warrants now have an 'intrinsic' value of 25p (ie 275p – 250p).

Advantages of warrants

6.13 Advantages of warrants to the company

(a) Warrants themselves **do not involve** the **payment** of any **interest or dividends**. Furthermore, when they are initially attached to loan stock, the interest rate on the loan stock will be lower than for a comparable straight debt.

(b) Warrants make a loan stock issue more attractive and may make an issue of unsecured loan stock possible where adequate security is lacking. (**Loan stock**, as a form of debt finance, is covered in the next chapter.)

(c) Warrants provide a means of **generating additional equity** funds in the future without any immediate dilution in earnings per share.

Question 3

Garcha plc is making its first public issue of shares by means of an offer for sale by tender. It has an authorised share capital of 2m shares with a nominal value of £1. Garcha intends to issue up to the full amount of the authorised share capital at a minimum price of £4 per share.

The following tenders have been received:

Price tendered per share	Number of shares applied for at this price
£6.00	50,000
£5.50	150,000
£5.00	250,000
£4.50	800,000
£4.00	1,000,000

How much will be raised in total if Garcha decides to issue the whole of its authorised capital?

- A £2,000,000
- B £8,000,000
- C £8,975,000
- D £9,000,000

Answer

B The cumulative tenders are as follows:

Price	Cumulative number of shares applied for
£6.00	50,000
£5.50	200,000
£5.00	450,000
£4.50	1,250,000
£4.00	2,250,000

To issue exactly 2m shares, the issue price must be £4.00. The total raised will be 2m x £4.00 = £8m.

Chapter roundup

- A company can obtain a **stock market listing** for its shares through an offer for sale, a prospectus issue, a placing or an introduction.

- A **rights issue** is an offer to existing shareholders for them to buy more shares, usually at lower than the current share price.

- **Scrip dividend schemes** involve shareholders being issued with new shares in lieu of a cash dividend.

- **Bonus** or **scrip issues**, and **stock splits**, are ways of increasing the *number* of shares without raising any extra capital.

- **Preference shares** carry priority over shareholders with regard to dividend payments. They do not carry voting rights. They may be attractive to corporate investors, as (unlike interest receipts) dividends received are not subject to corporation tax. However, for the issuing company, dividend payments (unlike interest payments) are not tax-deductible.

- Practical considerations of **dividend policy** suggest that both **dividends** and **earnings** may be important in determining share price.

- Share **warrants** give their holder the right to apply for new shares at a specified exercise price in the future. They might be issued as an 'add-on' to a new issue of loan stock.

Part B: Sources of long-term finance

Quick quiz

1. Which of the following sources of finance to companies is the most widely used in practice?

   A Bank borrowings
   B Rights issues
   C New share issues
   D Retained earnings

2. Identify **four** reasons why a company may seek a stock market listing.

3. A company's shares have a nominal value of £1 and a market value of £3. In a rights issue, one new share would be issued for every three shares at a price of £2.60. What is the theoretical ex-rights price?

4. A company offers to pay a dividend in the form of new shares which are worth more than the cash alternative which is also offered. What is this dividend in the form of shares called?

5. Match A/B to (i)/(ii), to express the difference between a stock split and a scrip issue.

   A A scrip issue ....   (i)   .... converts equity reserves into share capital
   B A stock split ....   (ii) .... leaves reserves unaffected

6. Define a warrant.

7. Which of the following is least likely to be a reason for seeking a stock market flotation?

   A Improving the existing owners' control over the business
   B Access to a wider pool of finance
   C Enhancement of the company's image
   D Transfer of capital to other uses

8. Confirmation in writing is required to ensure preference shares are cumulative.

   True ☐
   False ☐

Answers to quick quiz

1. D Retained earnings

2. **Four** of the following **five**: access to a wider pool of finance; improved marketability of shares; transfer of capital to other uses (eg founder members liquidating holdings); enhancement of company image; making growth by acquisition possible

3. $((£3 \times 3) + £2.60) \div 4 = £2.90$

4. An enhanced scrip dividend

5. A(i); B(ii)

6. A right given by a company to an investor, allowing him to subscribe for new shares at a future date at a fixed, pre-determined price (the exercise price)

7. A Flotation is likely to involve a significant loss of control to a wider circle of investors.

8. False. Preference shares are deemed to be cumulative unless the terms of issue or articles say they are not.

Now try the question below from the Exam Question Bank

Number	Level	Marks	Time
5	Introductory	n/a	30 mins

Chapter 6

DEBT FINANCE

Topic list	Syllabus reference	Ability required
1 Loan capital	(ii)	Evaluation
2 Convertible securities	(ii)	Evaluation
3 Debt with warrants	(ii)	Evaluation
4 The capital structure decision	(ii)	Evaluation

Introduction

As well as being financed by its owners, the **shareholders,** a company is likely to be financed by lenders who provide it with **debt finance**. We look in this chapter at the most important forms of long-term debt finance. We finish off by examining the practical factors that determine the mix of finance that a company chooses.

MCQs may cover knowledge from any of the sections in this chapter, including the valuation of debentures. You also need to consider the advantages and disadvantages of the various forms of loan finance.

Learning outcomes covered in this chapter

- Recommend the sources of capital most appropriate for an organisation

Syllabus content covered in this chapter

- Long-term debt finance (ie secured, unsecured, redeemable, irredeemable, convertibles and debt with warrants)

1 **LOAN CAPITAL** Pilot paper, 5/02

> **KEY TERM**
>
> **Loan capital** (or loan stock) is debentures and other long-term loans to a business.
> *(OT 2000)*

1.1 Loan capital or stock has a **nominal value**, which is the debt owed by the company, and interest is paid at a stated '**coupon**' on this amount. For example, if a company issues 10% loan stock, the coupon will be 10% of the nominal value of the stock, so that £100 of stock will receive £10 interest each year. The rate quoted is the gross rate, before tax.

Part B: Sources of long-term finance

> **KEY TERM**
>
> **Stock** is an amount of fully paid up capital, any part of which can be transferred.
>
> *(OT 2000)*

1.2 Unlike shares, debt is often issued **at par**, ie with £100 payable per £100 nominal value. Where the coupon rate is fixed at the time of issue, it will be set according to prevailing market conditions given the credit rating of the company issuing the debt. Subsequent changes in market (and company) conditions will cause the market value of the bond to fluctuate, although the coupon will stay at the fixed percentage of the nominal value.

> **KEY TERM**
>
> A **debenture** is a written acknowledgement of a debt by a company, usually given under its seal and normally containing provisions as to payment of interest and the terms of repayment of principal. A debenture may be secured on some or all of the assets of the company or its subsidiaries.
>
> *(OT 2000)*

1.3 **Debentures** are a form of loan stock, legally defined as the written acknowledgement of a debt incurred by a company, normally containing provisions about the payment of interest and the eventual repayment of capital.

1.4 A **debenture trust deed** would empower a trustee (such as an insurance company or a bank) to **intervene** on behalf of debenture holders if the conditions of borrowing under which the debentures were issued are not being fulfilled. This might involve:

(a) **Failure** to **pay interest** on the due dates

(b) An **attempt** by the company to **sell off important assets** contrary to the terms of the loan

(c) A company taking out **additional loans** and thereby exceeding previously agreed borrowing limits established either by the Articles or by the terms of the debenture trust deed (A trust deed might place restrictions on the company's ability to borrow more from elsewhere until the debentures have been redeemed.)

> **Exam focus point**
>
> This topic was tested in the Pilot Paper.

1.5 **Advantages of debt over shares**

(a) Debentures are a **cheaper form of finance** than shares because, unlike preference shares, debenture interest is tax-deductible.

(b) Debentures should be **more attractive** to investors because they will be **secured** against the assets of the company.

(c) **Debenture holders** rank above **shareholders** in the event of a liquidation.

(d) **Issue costs** should be **lower** for debentures than for shares.

(e) There is **no immediate change** in the existing structure of control, although this will change over time as conversion rights are exercised.

(f) There is **no immediate dilution** in earnings and dividends per share.

1.6 **Disadvantages of debt**

(a) **Interest** has to be paid on debt no matter what the company's profits in a year are. In particular the company may find itself locked into long-term debt at unfavourable rates of interest. The company is not legally obliged to pay dividends.

(b) Money has to be made available for **redemption** or **repayment** of debt.

(c) Shareholders may demand a **higher rate of return** because an increased interest burden increases the risk that dividends will not be paid.

Debentures with a floating rate of interest

1.7 These are debentures for which the coupon rate of interest can be changed by the issuer, in accordance with changes in market rates of interest. They may be attractive to both lenders and borrowers when interest rates are volatile, and preferable to fixed interest loan stock or debentures.

(a) **Floating rate debentures** protect borrowers from having to pay high rates of interest on their debentures when market rates of interest have fallen. On the other hand, they allow lenders to benefit from higher rates of interest on their debentures when market rates of interest go up.

(b) The **market value** of debentures depends on the coupon rate of interest, relative to market interest rates. With floating rate debentures the market value should be fairly stable (and close to par) because interest rates are varied to follow market rate changes. Stable market prices **protect** the **value** of the lenders' investment.

1.8 For example, suppose that a company issues 6% fixed rate debentures at par when the market rate of interest is 6%, and the debentures have a term to maturity of 20 years. If interest rates suddenly rise to 12%, the market value of the debentures would fall by half to £50 per cent (that is, per £100 nominal value). However, if the debentures had carried a floating rate of interest, the interest rate would have been raised to 12% and the debentures would have retained their market value at par (£100 per cent).

Deep discount bonds

> **KEY TERM**
>
> **Deep discount bond** is a bond offered at a large discount on the face value of the debt so that a significant proportion of the return to the investor comes by way of a capital gain on redemption, rather than through interest payment. *(OT 2000)*

1.9 **Deep discount bonds** will be redeemable at par (or above par) when they eventually mature. For example a company might issue £1,000,000 of loan stock in 2002, at a price of £50 per £100 of stock, and redeemable at par in the year 2017. For a company with specific cash flow requirements, the low servicing costs during the currency of the bond may be an attraction, coupled with a high cost of redemption at maturity.

1.10 Investors might be attracted by the **large capital gain** offered by the bonds, which is the difference between the issue price and the redemption value. However, deep discount bonds will carry a much **lower rate of interest** than other types of loan stock. The only tax advantage is that the gain gets taxed (as **income**) in one lump on maturity or sale, not as

Part B: Sources of long-term finance

amounts of interest each year. The borrower can, however, deduct notional interest each year in computing profits.

Zero coupon bonds

> **KEY TERM**
>
> **Zero coupon bond** is a bond offering no interest payments, all investor return being gained through capital appreciation. *(OT 2000)*

1.11 **Zero coupon bonds** are bonds that are issued at a discount to their redemption value, but no interest is paid on them. The investor gains from the difference between the issue price and the redemption value, and there is an implied interest rate in the amount of discount at which the bonds are issued (or subsequently re-sold on the market).

(a) The advantage for borrowers is that zero coupon bonds can be used to **raise cash immediately**, and there is no cash repayment until redemption date. The cost of redemption is known at the time of issue, and so the borrower can plan to have funds available to redeem the bonds at maturity.

(b) The advantage for lenders is restricted, unless the rate of discount on the bonds **offers a high yield**. The only way of obtaining cash from the bonds before maturity is to sell them, and their market value will depend on the remaining term to maturity and current market interest rates.

The tax advantage of zero coupon bonds is the same as that for deep discount bonds (see Paragraph 1.10 above).

Security

1.12 Loan stock and debentures will often be secured. **Security** may take the form of either a **fixed charge** or a **floating charge**.

(a) **Fixed charge**

Security would be related to a specific asset or group of assets, typically land and buildings. The company would be unable to dispose of the asset without providing a substitute asset for security, or without the lender's consent.

(b) **Floating charge**

With a floating charge on certain assets of the company (for example stocks and debtors), the lender's security in the event of a default of payment is whatever assets of the appropriate class the company then owns (provided that another lender does not have a prior charge on the assets). The company would be able, however, to dispose of its assets as it chose until a default took place. In the event of default, the lender would probably appoint a receiver to run the company rather than lay claim to a particular asset.

1.13 Not all loan stock is secured. Investors are likely to expect a higher yield with **unsecured loan stock** to compensate them for the extra risk. The rate of interest on unsecured loan stock may be around 1% or more higher than for secured debentures.

The redemption of loan stock

1.14 Loan stock and debentures are usually **redeemable**. They are issued for a term of ten years or more, and perhaps 25 to 30 years. At the end of this period, they will 'mature' and become redeemable (at par or possibly at a value above par).

> **KEY TERM**
>
> **Redemption** is repayment, this term being most frequently used in connection with preference shares and debentures. *(OT 2000)*

1.15 Most redeemable stocks have an earliest and a latest redemption date. For example, 12% Debenture Stock 2007/09 is redeemable at any time between the earliest specified date (in 2007) and the latest date (in 2009). The issuing company can choose the date. The decision by a company when to redeem a debt will depend on **how much cash** is available to the company to repay the debt, and on the **nominal rate of interest** on the debt.

1.16 Some loan stock does not have a redemption date, and is '**irredeemable**' or '**undated**'. Undated loan stock might be redeemed by a company that wishes to pay off the debt, but there is no obligation on the company to do so.

Valuation of redeemable loan stock

1.17 The normal principles apply so that the valuation depends upon future expected receipts.

> **FORMULA TO LEARN**
>
> Value of debt = (Interest earnings × annuity factor) + (Redemption value × Discounted cash flow factor)

1.18 Similar principles apply to the valuation of convertible debt which we shall discuss later.

How will a company finance the redemption of long-term debt?

1.19 There is no guarantee that a company will be able to raise a new loan to pay off a maturing debt, and one item to look for in a company's balance sheet is the redemption date of current loans, to establish how much new finance is likely to be needed by the company, and when.

1.20 If the redemption is to take place using **current funds** (assuming there are enough available), the business needs to consider the **alternative uses** to which these funds could be put.

1.21 The company may decide to issue **new debt** to replace the old debt. The company will incur **issue costs** using new debt, and will also need to consider the **future pattern of interest rates**.

1.22 Alternatively the company could use an issue of **equity** to provide the funds for redemption. **Issue costs** will again be a factor, and the directors will need to consider whether to issue shares to **new shareholders**, or use a **rights issue** to existing shareholders.

Part B: Sources of long-term finance

1.23 If the redeemable debentures have been **issued** on the stock market, they can be bought and hence redeemed by the company at any time. The directors will choose to redeem these debentures if other possible sources of finance have a lower cost.

Companies that are unable to repay debt capital

1.24 A company might get into difficulties and be unable to pay its debts. The difficulty could be an inability to repay the debt capital when it is due for redemption or an inability, perhaps temporary, to pay interest on the debt, before the capital is due for redemption.

1.25 When this occurs, the debenture holders or loan stock holders could exercise their right to appoint a **receiver** and to make use of whatever **security** they have.

> **Exam focus point**
>
> Question 2 in the May 2002 exam asked candidates to calculate the effect on gearing (see Chapter 11) of the redemption of debt by means of a rights issue, and discuss the advantages and disadvantages of using this method.

Tax relief on loan interest

1.26 As far as companies are concerned, debt capital is a potentially attractive source of finance because interest charges reduce the profits chargeable to corporation tax.

   (a) A **new issue** of **loan stock** is likely to be **preferable** to a new issue of preference shares.

   (b) Companies might wish to avoid **dilution of shareholdings** and increase gearing (the ratio of fixed interest capital to equity capital) in order to improve their earnings per share by benefiting from tax relief on interest payments.

Mortgages

1.27 **Mortgages** are a specific type of secured loan. Companies place the title deeds of freehold or long leasehold property as security with a lender and receive cash on loan, usually repayable over a specified period, with interest payable at a fixed or floating rate. Most organisations owning property which is unencumbered by any charge should be able to obtain a mortgage up to two thirds of the value of the property.

2 CONVERTIBLE SECURITIES   Pilot paper

Convertible loan stock

> **KEY TERM**
>
> **Convertible loan stock** is a loan that gives the holder the right to convert to other securities, normally ordinary shares, at a pre-determined price/rate and time. *(OT 2000)*

2.1 Conversion terms often vary over time. For example, the conversion terms of convertible stock might be that on 1 April 2000, £2 of stock can be converted into one ordinary share, whereas on 1 April 2001, the conversion price will be £2.20 of stock for one ordinary share. Once converted, convertible securities cannot be converted back into the original fixed return security.

6: Debt finance

The conversion value and the conversion premium

2.2 The current market value of ordinary shares into which a unit of stock may be converted is known as the conversion value. The **conversion value** will be below the value of the stock at the date of issue, but will be expected to increase as the date for conversion approaches on the assumption that a company's shares ought to increase in market value over time. The difference between the issue value of the stock and the conversion value as at the date of issue is the implicit **conversion premium**.

> **Knowledge brought forward from paper 3c Business Mathematics**
>
> You need to use the Internal Rate of Return technique to answer Question 1 below. If you are unsure about this topic, which was covered in Paper 3c *Business Mathematics*, read Chapter 12, Section 1 of this Text.

Question 1

The 10% convertible loan stock of Starchwhite plc is quoted at £142 per £100 nominal. The earliest date for conversion is in four years time, at the rate of 30 ordinary shares per £100 nominal loan stock. The share price is currently £4.15. Annual interest on the stock has just been paid.

Required

(a) What is the average annual growth rate in the share price that is required for the stockholders to achieve an overall rate of return of 12% a year compound over the next four years, including the proceeds of conversion?

(b) What is the implicit conversion premium on the stock?

Answer

(a)

Year	Investment £	Interest £	Discount factor 12%	Terminal value £
0	(142)		1.000	(142.00)
1		10	0.893	8.93
2		10	0.797	7.97
3		10	0.712	7.12
4		10	0.636	6.36
				(111.62)

The value of 30 shares on conversion at the end of year 4 must have a present value of at least £111.62, to provide investors with a 12% return.

The money value at the end of year 4 needs to be £111.62 ÷ 0.636 = £175.50.

The current market value of 30 shares is (× £4.15) £124.50.

The growth factor in the share price over four years needs to be:

$$\frac{175.50}{124.50} = 1.4096$$

If the annual rate of growth in the share price, expressed as a proportion, is g, then:

$(1 + g)^4$ = 1.4096
$1 + g$ = 1.0896
g = 0.0896, say 0.09

Conclusion. The rate of growth in the share price needs to be 9% a year (compound).

(b) The conversion premium can be expressed as an amount per share or as a percentage of the current conversion value.

(i) As an amount per share $\dfrac{£142 - £(30 \times 4.15)}{30}$ = £0.583 per share

Part B: Sources of long-term finance

(ii) As a % of conversion value $\quad \dfrac{£0.583}{£4.15} \times 100\% = 14\%$

The issue price and the market price of convertible loan stock

2.3 A company will aim to issue loan stock with the **greatest possible conversion premium** as this will mean that, for the amount of capital raised, it will, on conversion, have to issue the lowest number of new ordinary shares. The premium that will be accepted by potential investors will depend on the company's growth potential and so on prospects for a sizeable increase in the share price.

2.4 Convertible loan stock issued at par normally has a **lower coupon rate of interest** than straight debentures. This lower yield is the price the investor has to pay for the conversion rights. It is, of course, also one of the reasons why the issue of convertible stock is attractive to a company.

2.5 When convertible loan stock is traded on a stock market, its *minimum* **market price** will be the price of straight debentures with the same coupon rate of interest. If the market value falls to this minimum, it follows that the market attaches no value to the conversion rights.

2.6 The actual market price of convertible stock will depend not only on the price of straight debt but also on the current conversion value, the length of time before conversion may take place, and the market's expectation as to future equity returns and the risk associated with these returns. If the conversion value rises above the straight debt value then the price of convertible stock will normally reflect this increase.

2.7 Most companies issuing convertible stocks expect them to be **converted**. They view the stock as delayed equity. They are often used either because the company's ordinary share price is considered to be particularly depressed at the time of issue or because the issue of equity shares would result in an immediate and significant drop in earnings per share.

2.8 There is no certainty, however, that the security holders will exercise their option to convert; therefore the stock may run its full term and need to be redeemed.

2.9 EXAMPLE: CONVERTIBLE DEBENTURES

CD plc has issued 50,000 units of convertible debentures, each with a nominal value of £100 and a coupon rate of interest of 10% payable yearly. Each £100 of convertible debentures may be converted into 40 ordinary shares of CD plc in three years time. Any stock not converted will be redeemed at 110 (that is, at £110 per £100 nominal value of stock).

Estimate the likely current market price for £100 of the debentures, if investors in the debentures now require a pre-tax return of only 8%, and the expected value of CD plc ordinary shares on the conversion day is:

(a) £2.50 per share
(b) £3.00 per share

2.10 SOLUTION

(a) *Shares are valued at £2.50 each*

If shares are only expected to be worth £2.50 each on conversion day, the value of 40 shares will be £100, and investors in the debentures will presumably therefore redeem their debentures at 110 instead of converting them into shares.

The market value of £100 of the convertible debentures will be the discounted present value of the expected future income stream.

Year		Cash flow £	Discount factor 8%	Present value £
1	Interest	10	0.926	9.26
2	Interest	10	0.857	8.57
3	Interest	10	0.794	7.94
3	Redemption value	110	0.794	87.34
				113.11

The estimated market value is £113.11 per £100 of debentures.

(b) *Shares are valued at £3 each*

If shares are expected to be worth £3 each, the debenture holders will convert their debentures into shares (value per £100 of stock = 40 shares × £3 = £120) rather than redeem their debentures at 110.

Year		Cash flow/value £	Discount factor 8%	Present value £
1	Interest	10	0.926	9.26
2	Interest	10	0.857	8.57
3	Interest	10	0.794	7.94
3	Value of 40 shares	120	0.794	95.28
				121.05

The estimated market value is £121.05 per £100 of debentures.

Question 2

Downon Howett plc is unable to pay the interest on its debt capital, which consists of £5,000,000 of 10% debenture stock. The debenture holders are entitled, under the terms of their trust deed, to appoint a receiver, but the current financial position of Downon Howett plc is so poor that the enforced liquidation of the company would not realise more than a small fraction of the amount owed to the debenture holders. The debenture holders are therefore willing to consider alternatives.

Downon Howett has suggested that either of two options might satisfy them. The debenture holders would surrender their debentures, in exchange for:

(a) 15,000,000 ordinary shares under option 1;

(b) £5,000,000 of non-interest-bearing convertible debentures under option 2. The debentures would be convertible into ordinary shares in two years time at the rate of 200 shares per £100 of stock. Alternatively, the debentures (which would not be secured) would be repayable at par after two years.

Estimates of the net realisable value of Downon Howett's assets in two years time are as follows.

Probability	Net realisable value £m
0.2	2
0.4	4
0.3	6
0.1	8

If Downon Howett does not go into liquidation, its value as a going concern after two years is estimated to be 150% of the net realisable value of its assets, and the share price will reflect this value. Downon

Part B: Sources of long-term finance

Howett would not be allowed to issue any additional shares, nor pay any dividend, for the next two years. There are currently 10,000,000 shares in issue.

Which option would the debenture holders prefer, on the assumption that they choose the one that maximises the expected value of their wealth?

Answer

(a) If option 1 is selected, the debenture holders would own:

$$\frac{15}{10 + 15} = 60\% \text{ of the shares.}$$

After two years, the EV of these shares would be as follows.

Break up value £m	Market value (going concern) 150% £m	Ex debenture holder's share 60% £m	Probability	EV £m
2	3	1.8	0.2	0.36
4	6	3.6	0.4	1.44
6	9	5.4	0.3	1.62
8	12	7.2	0.1	0.72
				4.14

(b) If option 2 is selected, the debenture holders could choose to demand repayment of the debentures, out of the proceeds of sale of the assets of the company, or to convert the debentures into shares.

They would own $\frac{10}{10 + 10} = 50\%$ of the total number of shares.

Break-up value £m	Going concern value £m	Value of convertibles as equity £m	Value of convertibles as debt £m	Convert? *yes or no	Value of debenture holders' securities £m	Probability	£m
2	3	1.5	2.0	No	2	0.2	0.4
4	6	3.0	4.0	No	4	0.4	1.6
6	9	4.5	5.0	No	5	0.3	1.5
8	12	6.0	5.0	Yes	6	0.1	0.6
							4.1

* The answer is 'no' if the break-up value or the total debt of £5,000,000, whichever is lower, exceeds the value of 50% of the equity of the going concern. The debenture holders will compare the value of their convertibles as debt and as shares, and opt to use them in the form that gives the greater value.

The debenture holders would prefer option 1 to option 2, but only marginally so (with a difference in expected value of only £40,000).

3 DEBT WITH WARRANTS

3.1 As noted in the previous chapter, **warrants** to buy shares at a future date may be issued as a 'sweetener' in conjunction with loan stock in order to make the loan stock more attractive to potential investors.

3.2 If the firm performs very well, the loan stock holder will be able to enjoy extra returns for the value of the warrants in addition to the loan stock interest. If the firm does not perform quite so well, the warrant may be worthless but the loan stock investor should still receive the interest due.

4 THE CAPITAL STRUCTURE DECISION

Principles of capital structure

> **KEY TERM**
>
> **Capital structure** refers to the way in which an organisation is financed, by a combination of long-term capital (ordinary shares and reserves, preference shares, debentures, bank loans, convertible loan stock) and short-term liabilities, such as a bank overdraft and trade creditors.

4.1 When a business is growing, the additional assets must be financed by additional capital. The question for businesses is finding the right **mix** of the various finance combinations available.

Matching assets with funds

4.2 As a general rule, **assets which yield profits over a long period of time should be financed** by **long-term funds**.

4.3 In this way, the returns made by the asset will be sufficient to pay either the interest cost of the loans raised to buy it, or dividends on its equity funding.

4.4 If, however a long-term asset is financed by short-term funds, the company cannot be certain that when the loan becomes repayable, it will have **enough cash** (from profits) to repay it.

4.5 A company may not finance all of its short-term assets with short-term liabilities, but instead finance short-term assets partly with short-term funding and partly with long-term funding.

Long-term capital requirements for replacement and growth

4.6 A distinction can be made between long-term capital that is needed to finance the replacement of worn-out assets, and capital that is needed to finance growth.

Aims	Main funding sources
Maintenance of current level of operations	Internal sources
Growth	External finance

Cost and flexibility

4.7 **Interest rates** on longer-term debt may be higher than interest rates on shorter-term debt. However **issue costs** or **arrangement fees** will be **higher** for shorter-term debt as it has to be renewed more frequently.

4.8 A business may also find itself locked into **longer-term debt**, with adverse interest rates and large penalties if it repays the debt early.

4.9 A high level of debt creates financial risk. **Financial risk** can be seen from different points of view.

Part B: Sources of long-term finance

(a) **The company** as a whole. If a company builds up debts that it cannot pay when they fall due, it will be forced into liquidation. Also the shorter the term of the debt, the greater the frequency of renewal, and the greater the risk that the finance will not be renewed, or only be available on disadvantageous terms.

(b) **Creditors**. If a company cannot pay its debts, the company will go into liquidation owing creditors money that they are unlikely to recover in full.

(c) **Ordinary shareholders**. A company will not make any distributable profits unless it is able to earn enough profit before interest and tax to pay all its interest charges, and then tax.

4.10 **Business confidence and expectations** of future profits are crucial factors in the determination of how much debt capital investors are prepared to lend. The level of gearing which the market will allow will therefore depend on the **nature** of the company wishing to borrow more funds, and the industry in which it is engaged.

(a) A company which is involved in a **cyclical business**, where profits are subject to periodic ups and downs, should have a relatively **low gearing**.

(b) A company in a business where **profits are stable** should be able to raise a **larger amount of debt**.

4.11 There may be **restrictions on further borrowing** contained in the debenture trust deed for a company's current debenture stock in issue or in the company's articles of association. Potential lenders may want **security** in the form of a legal charge over company assets that the borrowing company is unable to provide.

4.12 The options open to small and medium-sized enterprises (SMEs) may be particularly limited. They face **competition** for funds, as investors have opportunities to invest in all sizes of organisation, also overseas and in government debt. In this competition they are handicapped by the problem of uncertainty.

(a) Whatever the details provided to potential investors, SMEs have **neither** the **business history nor larger track record** that larger organisations possess.

(b) Larger enterprises are subject by law to **more public scrutiny**; their accounts have to contain more detail and be audited, they receive more press coverage and so on.

(c) Because of the uncertainties involved, banks often use **credit scoring** systems to **control exposure.**

4.13 A common problem is often that the banks will be **unwilling** to increase **loan funding** without an increase in **security given** (which the owners may be unwilling or unable to give), or an increase in **equity funding** (which may be difficult to obtain).

Question 3

Phoenix Construction is offering a new bond to investors. The nominal value of the bond is £10, the offer price is £6, interest is 2% pa, and the bond is redeemable at par in four years time. What type of stock is this?

A   Zero coupon bond
B   Deep discount bond
C   Debenture
D   Convertible loan stock

6: Debt finance

Answer

B   The bond is offered at a large discount to the face value of the debt so that a significant proportion of the return to the investor comes by way of a capital gain on redemption, rather than through interest payments. It differs from a zero coupon bond in that some of the return comes from interest, and some from capital gains, rather than all the return coming from capital gains.

Chapter roundup

- The term **bonds** describes various forms of long-term debt a company may issue, such as loan stock or debentures, which may be **redeemable** or **irredeemable**. Bonds or loans come in various forms, including **floating rate debentures, zero coupon bonds** and **convertible loan stock**.

- **Convertible securities** give investors the opportunity to turn their stock into shares at a later date if they wish and, because of this, they usually carry a lower rate of interest than a similar non-convertible security. For the companies issuing them, convertibles may be viewed as a delayed form of equity which does not immediately affect EPS.

Quick quiz

1   Which of the following comparisons between debentures and preference shares is not a true statement?

   A   Debentures are cheaper to service since interest is tax-deductible.
   B   Debentures are more attractive to investors because they are secured against assets.
   C   Debenture holders rank above preference shareholders in the event of a liquidation.
   D   Debentures are more similar to equity than preference shares.

2   Holders of loan stock are long-term debtors of the company.

   True ☐
   False ☐

3   A company has 12% debentures in issue, which have a market value of £135 per £100 nominal value. What is:

   (a)   The coupon rate?
   (b)   The amount of interest payable per annum per £100 (nominal) of stock?

4   An investor has the option of redeeming a company's 11% Debenture Stock 2006/2008 at any date between 1 January 2006 and 31 December 2008 inclusive.

   True ☐
   False ☐

5   Convertible securities are fixed return securities that may be converted into zero coupon bonds/ordinary shares/warrants. (Delete as appropriate.)

6   Which of the following statements about convertible securities is false?

   A   They are fixed return securities.
   B   They must be converted into shares before the redemption date.
   C   The price at which they will be converted into shares is predetermined.
   D   Issue costs are lower than for equity.

7   Do borrowers benefit from floating rate debentures when interest rates are rising or falling?

8   What is the value of £100 12% debt redeemable in 3 years time at a premium of 20p per £ if the loanholder's required return is 10%?

97

Part B: Sources of long-term finance

Answers to quick quiz

1. D This is not true – debentures are a form of loan stock.
2. False. They are long-term creditors of the company.
3. (a) 12%
   (b) £12
4. False. The company will be able to choose the date of redemption.
5. Ordinary shares
6. B The holder has the option to convert, but he will only convert if it is advantageous for him to do so. If the share price falls, the stock may run its full term and need to be redeemed in the same way as other forms of debt.
7. Falling
8.

Years		£	Discount factor 10%	Present value £
1-3	Interest	12	2.487	29.84
3	Redemption premium	120	0.751	90.12
				119.96

Value of debt = £119.96

Now try the question below from the Exam Question Bank

Number	Level	Marks	Time
6	Examination	20	36 mins

Chapter 7

LEASING

Topic list	Syllabus reference	Ability required
1 Leasing as a source of finance	(ii)	Evaluation
2 Lease or buy decisions	(ii)	Evaluation

Introduction

In this chapter, we consider the option of **leasing** an asset.

As well as looking at the **advantages** and **disadvantages** of different types of lease compared with **other forms of credit finance**, we shall be discussing the tax and cash flow implications of leasing. You need to know how to determine whether an organisation should **lease** or **buy** an asset.

Learning outcomes covered in this chapter

- Recommend the sources of capital most appropriate for an organisation
- Evaluate the most appropriate method of funding an asset

Syllabus content covered in this chapter

- Operating and finance leases (one year lagged tax savings will be tested with leases and comparisons of the cost of a lease with the cost of buying)

1 LEASING AS A SOURCE OF FINANCE

The nature of leasing

1.1 Rather than buying an asset outright, using either available cash resources or borrowed funds, a business may lease an asset. **Leasing** has become a popular source of finance in the UK.

> **KEY TERM**
>
> **Leasing** is a contract between lessor and lessee for hire of a specific asset selected from a manufacturer or vendor of such assets by the lessee.

(a) The **lessor** retains ownership of the asset.

(b) The **lessee** has possession and use of the asset on payment of specified rentals over a period.

(c) Many lessors are **financial intermediaries** such as banks and insurance companies.

(d) The **range of assets leased** is wide, including office equipment and computers, cars and commercial vehicles, aircraft, ships and buildings.

Types of leasing

> **KEY TERMS**
>
> **Finance lease** is a lease that transfers substantially all the risks and rewards of ownership of an asset to the lessee.
>
> **Operating lease** is a lease other than a finance lease. The lessor retains most of the risk and rewards of ownership. *(OT 2000)*

Operating leases

1.2 **Operating leases** are rental agreements between the user of the leased asset (the lessee) and a provider of finance (the lessor) whereby:

   (a) The **lessor supplies the equipment** to the lessee.

   (b) The **lessor is responsible** for **servicing and maintaining the leased equipment.**

   (c) The **period of the lease** is fairly **short, less** than the **expected economic life** of the asset, so that at the end of one lease agreement, the lessor can either lease the same equipment to someone else, and obtain a good rent for it, or sell the equipment second-hand.

1.3 Much of the growth in the UK leasing business in recent years has been in operating leases. With an operating lease, the lessor, often a finance house, purchases the equipment from the manufacturer and then leases it to the user (the lessee) for the agreed period.

Finance leases

1.4 **Finance leases** are lease agreements between a **lessor** and **lessee**, for most or all of the asset's expected useful life.

1.5 Suppose that a company decides to obtain a company car and to finance the acquisition by means of a finance lease. A **car dealer** will **supply the car**. A finance house will agree to act as lessor in a finance leasing arrangement, and so will purchase the car from the dealer and lease it to the company. The company will take possession of the car from the car dealer, and make regular payments (monthly, quarterly, six monthly or annually) to the finance house under the terms of the lease.

1.6 There are other important characteristics of a finance lease.

   (a) The **lessee** is **responsible** for the **upkeep**, servicing and maintenance of the asset. The lessor is not involved in this at all.

   (b) The **lease** has a **primary period**, which covers all or most of the useful economic life of the asset. At the end of this primary period, the lessor would not be able to lease the asset to someone else, because the asset would be worn out. The lessor must therefore ensure that the lease payments during the primary period pay for the full cost of the asset as well as providing the lessor with a suitable return on his investment.

   (c) It is usual at the end of the primary period to allow the lessee to continue to lease the asset for an **indefinite secondary period**, in return for a very low nominal rent, sometimes called a 'peppercorn rent'. Alternatively, the lessee might be allowed to sell the asset on a lessor's behalf (since the lessor is the owner) and to keep most of the sale proceeds, paying only a small percentage (perhaps 10%) to the lessor.

1.7 Returning to the example of the car lease, the primary period of the lease might be three years, with an agreement by the lessee to make three annual payments of £6,000 each. The lessee will be responsible for repairs and servicing, road tax, insurance and garaging. At the end of the primary period of the lease, the lessee might be given the option either to continue leasing the car at a nominal rent (perhaps £250 a year) or to sell the car and pay the lessor 10% of the proceeds.

1.8 **Sale and leaseback** is an arrangement which is similar to mortgaging. A business which already owns an asset, for example a building or an item of equipment, agrees to sell the asset to a financial institution and to lease it back on terms specified in the agreement. The business has the benefit of the funds from the sale while retaining use of the asset, in return for regular payments to the financial institution.

Attractions of leasing

1.9 The attractions of leases to the supplier of the equipment, the lessee and the lessor are as follows.

(a) The **supplier** of the **equipment** is **paid in full** at the **beginning**. The equipment is sold to the lessor, and apart from obligations under guarantees or warranties, the supplier has no further financial concern about the asset.

(b) The **lessor invests finance** by **purchasing assets** from suppliers and makes a return out of the lease payments from the lessee. Provided that a lessor can find lessees willing to pay the amounts he wants to make his return, the lessor can make good profits. He will also get capital allowances on his purchase of the equipment.

> **LINK WITH PAPER 5**
>
> You will learn in detail about capital allowances in Paper 5. For now you should note that the Inland Revenue does not regard depreciation as a tax-deductible expense, so the profits businesses make have to be adjusted by adding back depreciation for tax purposes.
>
> Instead of depreciation businesses can claim capital allowances on fixed assets, which can be deducted from profits. Capital allowances have however to be calculated in the ways prescribed by the taxation authorities.

(c) **Leasing** might be **attractive** to the **lessee**:

(i) If the lessee does not have enough cash to pay for the asset, and would have difficulty obtaining a bank loan to buy it, and so has to rent it in one way or another if he is to have the use of it at all, or

(ii) If finance leasing is cheaper than a bank loan (The cost of payments under a loan might exceed the cost of a lease).

The lessee may find the **tax relief** available advantageous.

1.10 Operating leases have these further advantages.

(a) The leased equipment does **not** have to be **shown** in the **lessee's published balance sheet**, and so the lessee's balance sheet shows no increase in its gearing ratio.

Part B: Sources of long-term finance

(b) The **equipment** is **leased** for a **shorter period** than its expected useful life. In the case of high-technology equipment, if the equipment becomes out of date before the end of its expected life, the lessee does not have to keep on using it, and it is the lessor who must bear the risk of having to sell obsolete equipment secondhand.

1.11 Not surprisingly perhaps, a major growth area in operating leasing in the UK has been in computers and office equipment (such as photocopiers and fax machines) where technology is continually improving.

Hire purchase

1.12 Hire purchase is similar to leasing, with the exception that ownership of the goods passes to the hire purchase customer on payment of the final credit instalment, whereas a lessee never becomes the owner of the goods.

> **KEY TERM**
>
> **Hire purchase contract** is a contract for the hire of an asset that contains a provision giving the hirer an option to acquire legal title to the asset upon the fulfilment of certain conditions stated in the contract (FRSSE). *(OT 2000)*

1.13 Hire purchase agreements nowadays usually involve a finance house.

- The supplier sells the goods to the finance house.
- The supplier delivers the goods to the customer who will eventually purchase them.
- The hire purchase arrangement exists between the finance house and the customer.

1.14 The finance house will nearly always insist that the hirer should pay a **deposit** towards the purchase price, perhaps as low as 10%, or as high as 33%. The size of the deposit will depend on the finance company's policy and its assessment of the hirer. This is in contrast to a finance lease, where the lessee might not be required to make any large initial payment.

1.15 An industrial or commercial business can use hire purchase as a source of finance. With **industrial hire purchase,** a business customer obtains hire purchase finance from a finance house in order to purchase a fixed asset. Goods bought by businesses on hire purchase include company vehicles, plant and machinery, office equipment and farming machinery. Hire purchase arrangements for fleets of motor cars are also quite common.

1.16 When faced with an investment opportunity, an organisation may have to decide whether to:
- Purchase the equipment
- Acquire it under a finance lease arrangement
- Acquire it under a hire purchase arrangement

1.17 When a company acquires a capital asset under a hire purchase agreement, it will eventually obtain **full legal title** to the asset. The HP payments consist partly of 'capital' payments towards the purchase of the asset, and partly of interest charges. For example, if a company buys a car costing £10,000 under an HP agreement, the car supplier might provide HP finance over a three year period at an interest cost of 10%, and the HP payments might be, say, as follows.

7: Leasing

	Capital element £	Interest element £	Total HP payment £
Year 0: down payment	2,540	0	2,540
Year 1	2,254	746	3,000
Year 2	2,479	521	3,000
Year 3	2,727	273	3,000
Total	10,000	1,540	11,540

1.18 The tax position on a hire purchase arrangement is as follows.

(a) The buyer obtains whatever **capital allowances** are available, based on the capital element of the cost. Capital allowances on the full capital element of the cost can be used from the time the asset is acquired.

(b) In addition, **interest payments** within the HP payments are an **allowable** expense against tax, spread over the term of the HP agreement.

(c) **Capital payments** within the HP payments, however, are **not allowable** against tax.

Question 1

Explain the cash flow characteristics of a finance lease, and compare it with the use of a bank loan. Your answer should include some comment on the significance of a company's anticipated tax position on lease versus buy decisions.

Answer

A finance lease is an agreement between the user of the leased asset and a provider of finance that covers the majority of the asset's useful life. Key features of a finance lease are as follows.

(a) The provider of finance is usually a **third party finance house** and not the original provider of the equipment.

(b) The **lessee is responsible for the upkeep**, servicing and maintenance of the asset.

(c) The lease has a **primary period**, which covers all or most of the useful economic life of the asset. At the end of the primary period the lessor would not be able to lease the equipment to someone else because it would be worn out.

(d) It is common at the end of the primary period to allow the lessee to continue to lease the asset for an indefinite **secondary period**, in return for a very low nominal rent, sometimes known as a 'peppercorn' rent.

The cash flow implications of this form of lease are therefore as follows.

(a) Regular payments to the lessor, which comprise interest and principal. This can be very useful to the lessee from a cash flow management point of view.

(b) Costs of maintenance and so on, which may be less predictable in terms of both timing and amount.

(c) Capital allowances cannot be claimed on the purchase cost of the equipment, but the lease payments are fully allowable for tax purposes. This may be of benefit to a company that is unable to make full use of its capital allowances.

If the equipment is acquired using a medium term bank loan, the cash flow patterns would be similar to those that would arise using a finance lease. However, if the loan were subject to a variable rate of interest, this would introduce a further source of variability into the cash flows. The main difference between the two approaches would be that the company could claim capital allowances on the purchase cost of the equipment. The interest element of the repayments would also be allowable against tax, but the repayments of principal would not.

2 LEASE OR BUY DECISIONS   11/01

2.1 For this topic, you will need to be familiar with the discounting and investment appraisal techniques that were covered in Paper 3c *Business Mathematics*. If you are unsure about these topics, go through Chapter 12, Section 1.

2.2 There are several ways of evaluating a decision whether to lease an asset, or to purchase it by another means of finance. The **traditional method** is to take the view that a decision to lease is a financing decision, which can only be made after a decision to acquire the asset has already been taken. It is therefore necessary to make a two-stage decision, as follows.

Step 1. An **acquisition decision** is made on whether the asset is worth having. The present values of operational costs and benefits from using the asset are found to derive a net present value (NPV).

Step 2. A **financing decision** is then made if the acquisition is justified by a positive NPV. This is the decision on whether to **lease or buy**.

2.3 The traditional method is complicated by the need to choose a discount rate for each stage of the decision. In the case of a non-taxpaying organisation, the method is applied as follows.

Step 1. The cost of capital that should be applied to the cash flows for the acquisition decision is the cost of capital that the organisation would normally apply to its **project evaluations**.

Step 2. The cost of capital that should be applied to the **(differential) cash flows** for the **financing** decision is the **cost of borrowing**.

(i) We assume that if the organisation decided to purchase the equipment, it would finance the purchase by borrowing funds (rather than out of retained funds).

(ii) We therefore compare the **cost of borrowing** with the **cost of leasing** (or hire purchase) by applying this cost of borrowing to the financing cash flows.

> **Exam focus point**
>
> The distinction between using the **cost of capital** to appraise the **investment** decision, and using the **cost of borrowing** to appraise the **finance** decision is important. Four marks were available in the November 2001 paper for explaining why the cost of debt should not be used to appraise an investment decision.

2.4 In the case of a tax-paying organisation, taxation should be allowed for in the cash flows, so that the traditional method would recommend:

(a) Discounting the **cash flows** of the **acquisition** decision at the firm's **after-tax cost of capital**

(b) Discounting the **cash flows** of the **financing** decision at the **after-tax cost of borrowing**

The tax treatment of finance leases in the UK under Finance Act 1991 rules is:

(a) To allow **depreciation** as **an expense**

(b) To allow the **interest** element of the **finance charge** as an expense over the period of the lease

7: Leasing

This treatment leads to some complex calculations, while the result may not be materially different from that obtained if we assume that the lease payments are allowable for tax in full.

> **Exam focus point**
>
> In the exam, it is acceptable to make this latter assumption provided that you state it in your answer and provided that the question does not direct otherwise. Detailed knowledge of the UK tax rules is not needed.

2.5 EXAMPLE: LEASE OR BUY DECISIONS (1)

Mallen and Mullins Ltd has decided to install a new milling machine. The machine costs £20,000 and it would have a useful life of five years with a trade-in value of £4,000 at the end of the fifth year. Additional cash profits from the machine would be £8,000 a year for five years. A decision has now to be taken on the method of financing the project. Three methods of finance are being considered.

(a) The company could purchase the machine for cash, using bank loan facilities on which the current rate of interest is 13% before tax.

(b) The company could lease the machine under an agreement which would entail payment of £4,800 at the end of each year for the next five years.

(c) The company could purchase the machine under a hire purchase agreement. This would require an initial deposit of £6,500 and payments of £4,400 per annum at the end of each of the next five years. The interest part of the payments, for tax purposes, would be £2,100 at the end of year 1 and £1,800, £1,400, £1,000 and £700 at the end of each of years 2, 3, 4 and 5 respectively.

The company's weighted average cost of capital, normally used for project evaluating, is 12% after tax. The rate of corporation tax is 30%. If the machine is purchased, the company will be able to claim an annual writing down allowance of 25% of the reducing balance.

Advise the management on whether to acquire the machine, on the most economical method of finance, and on any other matter which should be considered before finally deciding which method of finance should be adopted.

2.6 SOLUTION

The traditional method begins with the acquisition decision. The cash flows of the project should be discounted at 12%. The first writing down allowance is assumed to be claimed in the first year resulting in a saving of tax at year 2.

Capital allowances

Year		Allowance
		£
1	25% of £20,000	5,000
2	25% of £(20,000 – 5,000)	3,750
3	25% of £(15,000 – 3,750)	2,813
4	25% of £(11,250 – 2,813)	2,109
		13,672
5	£(20,000 – 13,672 – 4,000)	2,328
		16,000

Part B: Sources of long-term finance

Taxable profits and tax liability

Year	Cash profits £	Capital allowance £	Taxable profits £	Tax at 30% £
1	8,000	5,000	3,000	900
2	8,000	3,750	4,250	1,275
3	8,000	2,813	5,187	1,556
4	8,000	2,109	5,891	1,767
5	8,000	2,328	5,672	1,702

NPV calculation for the acquisition decision

Year	Equipment £	Cash profits £	Tax £	Net cash flow £	Discount factor 12%	Present value £
0	(20,000)			(20,000)	1.000	(20,000)
1		8,000		8,000	0.893	7,144
2		8,000	(900)	7,100	0.797	5,659
3		8,000	(1,275)	6,725	0.712	4,788
4		8,000	(1,556)	6,444	0.636	4,098
5	4,000	8,000	(1,767)	10,233	0.567	5,802
6			(1,702)	(1,702)	0.507	(863)
					NPV	6,628

2.7 The net present value (NPV) is positive, and so we conclude that the machine should be acquired, regardless of the method used to finance the acquisition.

2.8 The second stage is the financing decision, and cash flows are discounted at the after-tax cost of borrowing, which is at 13% × 70% = 9.1%, say 9%. The only cash flows that we need to consider are those which will be affected by the choice of the method of financing. The operating savings of £8,000 a year, and the tax on these savings, can be ignored.

(a) *The present value (PV) of purchase costs*

Year	Item	Cash flow £	Discount factor 9%	PV £
0	Equipment cost	(20,000)	1.000	(20,000)
5	Trade-in value	4,000	0.650	2,600
	Tax savings, from allowances			
2	30% × £5,000	1,500	0.842	1,263
3	30% × £3,750	1,125	0.772	869
4	30% × £2,813	844	0.708	598
5	30% × £2,109	633	0.650	411
6	30% × £2,328	698	0.596	416
			NPV of purchase	(13,843)

(b) *The PV of leasing costs*

It is assumed that the lease payments are fully tax-allowable.

Year	Lease payment £	Savings in tax (30%) £	Discount factor 9%	PV £
1-5	(4,800) pa		3.890	(18,672)
2-6		1,440 pa	3.569	5,139
			NPV of leasing	(13,533)

(c) *The PV of hire purchase*

Year	HP payments £	Capital allowances - tax saved £	Tax saved due to interest on HP payments at 30%	Net cash flow £	Discount factor at 9%	PV £
0	(6,500)			(6,500)	1.000	(6,500)
1	(4,400)			(4,400)	0.917	(4,035)
2	(4,400)	1,500	630	(2,270)	0.842	(1,911)
3	(4,400)	1,125	540	(2,735)	0.772	(2,111)
4	(4,400)	844	420	(3,136)	0.708	(2,220)
5	(400)*	633	300	533	0.650	346
6		698	210	908	0.596	541
				NPV of hire purchase		(15,890)

* £4,400 less £4,000 trade-in value

2.9 The cheapest option would be to lease the machine. However, there are other matters to be considered.

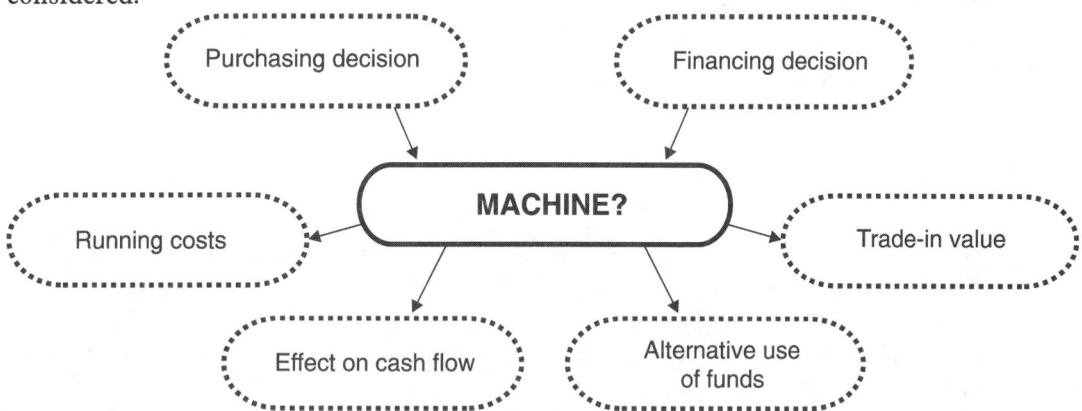

Factors around the MACHINE? decision: Purchasing decision, Financing decision, Running costs, Trade-in value, Effect on cash flow, Alternative use of funds.

2.10 A disadvantage of the traditional approach to making a lease or buy decision is that if there is a negative NPV when the operational cash flows of the project are discounted at the firm's cost of capital, the investment will be rejected out of hand, with no thought given to how the investment might be financed. It is conceivable, however, that the costs of leasing might be so low that the project would be worthwhile provided that the leasing option were selected. This suggests that an investment opportunity should not be **rejected** without first giving some thought to its financing costs.

2.11 **Other methods** of making lease or buy decisions are as follows.

(a) **Compare the cost of leasing** with the **cost of purchase**, and select the cheaper method of financing; then calculate the NPV of the project on the assumption that the cheaper method of financing is used. In other words, make the financing decision first and the acquisition decision afterwards.

(b) Calculate an NPV for the project if the machine is **purchased**, and secondly if the machine is **leased**. Select the method of financing which gives the higher NPV, provided that the project is viable (that is, has a positive NPV). In other words, combine the acquisition and financing decisions together into a single-stage decision. This method is illustrated in the following example.

2.12 EXAMPLE: LEASE OR BUY DECISIONS (2)

In the case of Mallen and Mullins Ltd, the NPV with purchase would be + £6,548. This was calculated above. The NPV with leasing would be as follows. A discount rate of 12% is used here.

Year	Profit less leasing cost £	Tax at 30% £	Net cash flow £	Discount factor 12%	PV £
1	3,200		3,200	0.893	2,858
2	3,200	(960)	2,240	0.797	1,785
3	3,200	(960)	2,240	0.712	1,595
4	3,200	(960)	2,240	0.636	1,425
5	3,200	(960)	2,240	0.567	1,270
6		(960)	(960)	0.507	(487)
				NPV	8,446

Using this method, leasing is preferable, because the NPV is £1,898 higher.

2.13 Since **operating leases** are a form of renting, the only cash flows to consider for this type of leasing are the lease payments and the tax saved. Operating lease payments are allowable expenses for tax purposes.

The position of the lessor

> **Exam focus point**
>
> So far, we have looked at examples of leasing decisions from the viewpoint of the lessee. You might be asked to evaluate a leasing arrangement from the position of the lessor. This is rather like a mirror image of the lessee's position.

2.14 Assuming that it is purchasing the asset, the lessor will receive capital allowances on the expenditure, and the lease payments will be taxable income.

2.15 EXAMPLE: LESSOR'S POSITION

Continuing the same case of Mallen and Mullins Ltd, suppose that the lessor's required rate of return is 12% after tax. The lessor's cash flows will be as follows.

	Cash flow £	Discount factor 12%	PV £
Purchase costs (see paragraph 2.7)			
Year 0	(20,000)	1.000	(20,000)
Year 5 trade-in	4,000	0.567	2,268
Tax savings			
Year 2	1,500	0.797	1,196
Year 3	1,125	0.712	801
Year 4	844	0.636	537
Year 5	633	0.567	359
Year 6	698	0.507	354
Lease payments: years 1-5	4,800	3.605	17,304
Tax on lease payments: years 2-6	(1,440)	3.218	(4,634)
NPV			(1,815)

2.16 *Conclusion.* The leasing payments proposed are not justifiable for the lessor if it seeks a required rate of return of 12%, since the resulting NPV is negative.

Question 2

The management of a company has decided to acquire Machine X which costs £63,000 and has an operational life of four years. The expected scrap value would be zero. Tax is payable at 30% on operating cash flows one year in arrears. Capital allowances are available at 25% a year on a reducing balance basis.

Suppose that the company has the opportunity either to purchase the machine or to lease it under a finance lease arrangement, at an annual rent of £20,000 for four years, payable at the end of each year. The company can borrow to finance the acquisition at 10%. Should the company lease or buy the machine?

Answer

Working

Capital allowances

Year		£
1	(25% of £63,000)	15,750
2	(75% of £15,750)	11,813
3	(75% of £11,813)	8,859
		36,422
4	(£63,000 – £36,422)	26,578

The financing decision will be appraised by discounting the relevant cash flows at the after-tax cost of borrowing, which is 10% × 70% = 7%.

(a) *Purchase option*

Year	Item	Cash flow £	Discount factor 7%	Present value £
0	Cost of machine	(63,000)	1.000	(63,000)
	Tax saved from capital allowances			
2	30% × £15,750	4,725	0.873	4,125
3	30% × £11,813	3,544	0.816	2,892
4	30% × £8,859	2,658	0.763	2,028
5	30% × £26,578	7,973	0.713	5,685
				(48,270)

(b) *Leasing option*

It is assumed that the lease payments are tax-allowable in full.

Year	Item	Cash flow £	Discount factor 7%	Present value £
1-4	Lease costs	(20,000)	3.387	(67,740)
2-5	Tax savings on lease costs (× 30%)	6,000	3.165	18,990
				(48,750)

The purchase option is cheaper, using a cost of capital based on the after-tax cost of borrowing. On the assumption that investors would regard borrowing and leasing as equally risky finance options, the purchase option is recommended.

Question 3

Robinson Ltd has just acquired a new production machine with an expected useful economic life of five years. The company has signed an agreement that requires it to be responsible for the servicing and maintenance of the machine. The agreement is for a period of five years, with the option at the end of that time for Robinson Ltd to continue to use the asset but with substantially reduced monthly payments. What type of agreement is this?

A Finance lease
B Operating lease
C Vendor credit
D Hire purchase

Part B: Sources of long-term finance

Answer

A Finance leases

Chapter roundup

- **Leasing** is a commonly used source of finance. We have distinguished three types of leasing: **operating leases** (**lessor** responsible for maintaining asset), **finance leases** (**lessee** responsible for maintenance), and **sale and leaseback** arrangements.
- The decision whether to **lease or buy** an asset involves two steps.
  - The **acquisition decision**: is the asset worth having? Test by discounting project cash flows at a suitable cost of capital.
  - The **financing decision**: if the asset should be acquired, compare the cash flows of purchasing and leasing or HP arrangements. The cash flows can be discounted at an after-tax cost of borrowing.

Quick quiz

1 Operating leases and finance leases are distinguished for accounting purposes. Which of the following statements is not true of an operating lease?

    A   The lessor supplies the equipment to the lessee.
    B   The period of the lease is less than the expected economic life of the asset.
    C   The lessee is normally responsible for servicing and maintaining the leased equipment.
    D   The lessor retains most of the risks and rewards of ownership.

2 Who is responsible for the servicing of a leased asset in the case of:

    (a)   An operating lease?
    (b)   A finance lease?

| The lessee | or | The lessor |

3 What two steps in a lease or buy decision evaluation may be distinguished?

4 Which discount rate should be used at each stage (delete as applicable)?

	(a)	Discount rate (b)
Step 1		Pre-tax/after-tax cost of capital/cost of borrowing
Step 2		Pre-tax/after-tax cost of capital/ cost of borrowing

5 Why should operating leases be popular for users of high technology equipment?

6 Cemstone Plc has decided to acquire a new grinding machine. It cannot afford to purchase the machine outright, and has therefore arranged to pay for it in regular instalments using a finance house. What type of arrangement is this?

    A   Finance lease
    B   Operating lease
    C   Lender credit
    D   Vendor credit

7 A hire purchase contract is a contract for the hire of an asset that contains a provision giving the hirer an option to acquire legal title to the asset upon the fulfilment of certain conditions stated in the contract.

    True ☐
    False ☐

8 .... credit occurs when the buyer borrows money and uses it to purchase goods outright.

Answers to quick quiz

1. C The lessor is normally responsible for maintaining the equipment.

2. (a) The lessor
   (b) The lessee

3/4. **Step 1.** The acquisition decision - discount at the firm's after-tax cost of capital
   Step 2. The financing decision - discount at the after-tax cost of borrowing

5. Because such equipment may soon become obsolete.

6. D This is also known as hire purchase.

7. True

8. Lender credit

Now try the question below from the Exam Question Bank

Number	Level	Marks	Time
7	Examination	20	36 mins

Chapter 8

THE COST OF CAPITAL

Topic list	Syllabus reference	Ability required
1 Investment decisions, financing and the cost of capital	(ii)	Comprehension
2 The costs of different sources of finance	(ii)	Application
3 Special problems	(ii)	Application
4 The weighted average cost of capital	(ii)	Application

Introduction

This chapter and the next chapter assume a basic understanding of **discounting of future cash flows**. We examine the concept of the **cost of capital**, which can serve as a **discount rate** in evaluating the investments of a firm. Calculation of the cost of capital is an important technique.

In this chapter, we base cost of capital calculations on what is called the **dividend valuation model**. In a later chapter, we look at a way of establishing the cost of capital which takes risk into account: the **capital asset pricing model.**

You need to have an appreciation of the effect on the cost of capital of a change in the financing mix of a company. This will be tested in more depth in Paper 13.

Learning outcomes covered in this chapter

- Calculate the cost of capital and demonstrate the impact of changing capital structures
- Explain the impact of interest rate changes on the cost of capital

Syllabus content covered in this chapter

- The calculation of the dividend growth model (knowledge of methods of calculating and estimating dividend growth will be expected)
- The cost of redeemable and irredeemable debt including the tax shield on debt (numerical questions on the cost of convertible debt will not be tested)
- The weighted average cost of capital (Modigliani and Miller will not be tested)

1 INVESTMENT DECISIONS, FINANCING AND THE COST OF CAPITAL

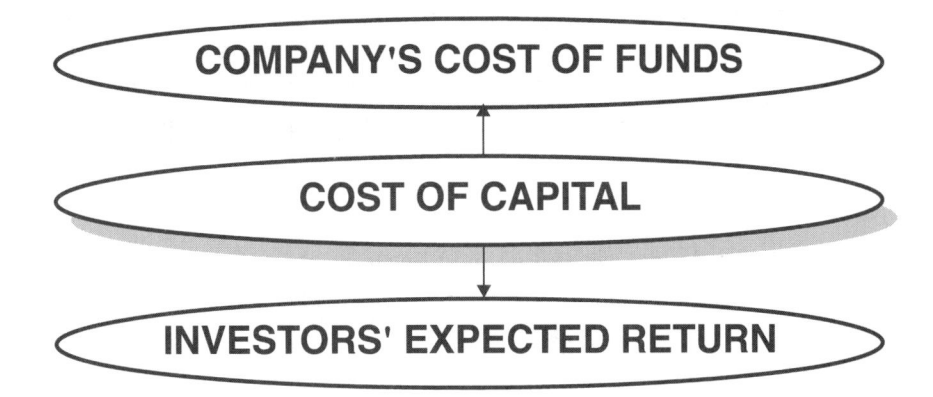

```
COMPANY'S COST OF FUNDS
           ↕
      COST OF CAPITAL
           ↕
  INVESTORS' EXPECTED RETURN
```

1.1 It is thus the **minimum return** that a company should make on its own investments, to earn the cash flows out of which investors can be paid their return.

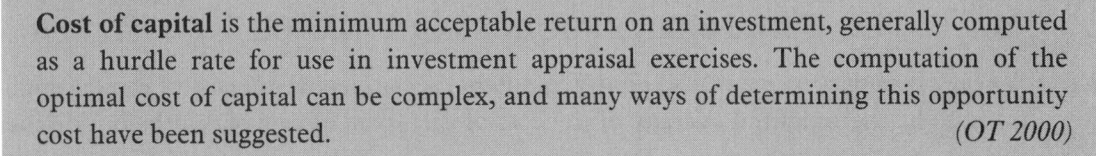

> **KEY TERM**
>
> **Cost of capital** is the minimum acceptable return on an investment, generally computed as a hurdle rate for use in investment appraisal exercises. The computation of the optimal cost of capital can be complex, and many ways of determining this opportunity cost have been suggested. *(OT 2000)*

The cost of capital as an opportunity cost of finance

1.2 The cost of capital, however it is measured, is an **opportunity cost of finance,** because it is the minimum return that investors require. If they do not get this return, they will transfer some or all of their investment somewhere else. Here are two examples.

(a) If a bank offers to lend money to a company, the interest rate it charges is the **yield** that the bank wants to receive from **investing** in the company, because it can get just as good a return from lending the money to someone else. In other words, the interest rate is the **opportunity cost** of lending for the bank.

(b) When shareholders invest in a company, the returns that they can expect must be sufficient to persuade them not to sell some or all of their shares and invest the money somewhere else. The yield on the shares is therefore the **opportunity cost** to the shareholders of not investing somewhere else.

The cost of capital and risk

1.3 The cost of capital has three elements.

Risk-free rate of return +

Premium for business risk +

<u>Premium for financial risk</u>

COST OF CAPITAL

(a) **Risk-free rate of return**

This is the return which would be required from an investment if it were completely free from risk. Typically, a risk-free yield would be the yield on government securities.

Part B: Sources of long-term finance

(b) **Premium for business risk**

This is an increase in the required rate of return due to the existence of uncertainty about the future and about a firm's business prospects. The actual returns from an investment may not be as high as they are expected to be. Business risk will be higher for some firms than for others, and some types of project undertaken by a firm may be more risky than other types of project that it undertakes.

(c) **Premium for financial risk**

This relates to the danger of high debt levels (high gearing). For ordinary shareholders, financial risk is evident in the variability of earnings after deducting payments to holders of debt capital. The higher the gearing of a company's capital structure, the greater will be the financial risk to ordinary shareholders, and this should be reflected in a higher risk premium and therefore a higher cost of capital.

1.4 Because different companies are in different types of business (varying **business risk**) and have different capital structures (varying **financial risk**) the cost of capital applied to one company may differ radically from the cost of capital of another.

2 THE COSTS OF DIFFERENT SOURCES OF FINANCE 5/01, 11/01, 5/02

2.1 Where a company uses a mix of **equity** and **debt** capital, its overall cost of capital might be taken to be the **weighted average** of the cost of each type of capital, but before discussing this we look first at the cost of each source of capital: ordinary shares (equity), preference shares, debt capital and so on.

The cost of ordinary share capital

2.2 New funds from equity shareholders are obtained either from **new issues of shares** or from **retained earnings**. Both of these sources of funds have a cost.

(a) Shareholders will **not** be prepared to **provide funds** for a **new issue** of **shares** unless the return on their investment is sufficiently attractive.

(b) Retained earnings also have a cost. This is an **opportunity cost**, the dividend forgone by shareholders.

The dividend valuation model

2.3 If we begin by ignoring share issue costs, the cost of equity, both for new issues and retained earnings, could be estimated by means of a **dividend valuation model**, on the assumption that the market value of shares is directly related to expected future dividends on the shares.

2.4 If the future dividend per share is expected to be **constant** in amount, then the **ex dividend** share price will be calculated by the formula:

$$p_o = \frac{d}{(1+k_e)} + \frac{d}{(1+k_e)^2} + \frac{d}{(1+k_e)^3} + \ldots = \frac{d}{k_e}, \text{ so } k_e = \frac{d}{p_o}$$

where k_e is the shareholders' cost of capital
        d is the annual dividend per share, starting at year 1 and then continuing annually in perpetuity.
        p_0 is the ex-dividend share price (the price of a share where the share's new owner is **not** entitled to the dividend that is soon to be paid).

8: The cost of capital

> **EXAM FORMULA**
>
> Cost of ordinary (equity) share capital, paying an annual dividend d in perpetuity, and having a current ex div price P_0:
>
> $$k_e = \frac{d}{P_0}$$

2.5 **Assumptions in the dividend valuation model**

(a) The dividends from projects for which the funds are required will be of **the same risk type or quality** as dividends from existing operations.

(b) There would be **no increase** in the **cost of capital**, for any other reason besides (a) above, from a new issue of shares.

(c) All shareholders have **perfect information** about the company's future, there is no delay in obtaining this information and all shareholders interpret it in the same way.

(d) **Taxation** can be **ignored**.

(e) All shareholders have the **same marginal cost of capital**.

(f) There would be **no issue expenses** for new shares.

Share issue costs and the cost of equity

2.6 The issue of shares, whether to the general public or as a rights issue, costs money and these costs should be considered in investment appraisal. Two approaches have been suggested.

(a) One approach is to **deduct issue costs** as a year 0 cash outflow of the project or projects for which the share capital is being raised. The issue costs would not affect the cost of equity capital.

(b) An alternative approach you might come across is to **calculate the cost of new equity** with the formula:

$$k_e = \frac{d}{P_0 - X}$$

where X represents the issue costs. Thus, if the issue price of a share is £2.50, issue costs are 20p per share, and new shareholders expect constant annual dividends of 46p, the cost of new equity would be:

$$\frac{46}{(250-20)} = 0.2 = 20\%$$

Approach (a) is recommended.

The dividend growth model

2.7 Shareholders will normally expect dividends to increase year by year and not to remain constant in perpetuity. The **fundamental theory of share values** states that the market price of a share is the present value of the discounted future cash flows of revenues from the share, so the market value given an expected constant annual growth in dividends would be:

$$P_0 = \frac{d_0(1+g)}{(1+k_e)} + \frac{d_0(1+g)^2}{(1+k_e)^2} + \ldots$$

Part B: Sources of long-term finance

where
P_0 is the current market price (ex div)
d_0 is the current net dividend
k_e is the shareholders' cost of capital
g is the expected annual growth in dividend payments
and both k_e and g are expressed as proportions.

2.8 This formula assumes a **constant growth rate** in dividends, but it could easily be adapted for uneven growth. Capital growth through increases in the share price will arise from changed expectations about future dividend growth, or changes in the required return.

2.9 It is often convenient to assume a constant expected dividend growth rate in perpetuity. The formula above then simplifies to:

$$P_0 = \frac{d_0(1+g)}{(k_e - g)}$$

2.10 Re-arranging this, we get a formula for the ordinary shareholders' cost of capital.

EXAM FORMULA

Cost of ordinary (equity) share capital, having a current ex div price, P_0, having just paid a dividend, d_0, with the dividend growing in perpetuity by a constant g% per annum:

$$k_e = \frac{d_0(1+g)}{P_0} + g, \text{ or } k_e = \frac{d_1}{P_0} + g$$

where d_1 is the dividend in year 1, so that:

$$d_1 = d_0(1+g)$$

Question 1

A share has a current market value of 96p, and the last dividend was 12p. If the expected annual growth rate of dividends is 4%, calculate the cost of equity capital.

Answer

$$\text{Cost of capital} = \frac{12(1 + 0.04)}{96} + 0.04$$
$$= 0.13 + 0.04$$
$$= 0.17$$
$$= 17\%$$

Exam focus point

If an examination question requires you to calculate a cost of equity using the growth model, it is likely that you will be expected to predict the future growth rate from an analysis of the growth in dividends over the past few years.

2.11 EXAMPLE: COST OF CAPITAL (1)

The dividends and earnings of Hall Shores plc over the last five years have been as follows.

Year	Dividends £	Earnings £
20X1	150,000	400,000
20X2	192,000	510,000
20X3	206,000	550,000
20X4	245,000	650,000
20X5	262,350	700,000

The company is financed entirely by equity and there are 1,000,000 shares in issue, each with a market value of £3.35 ex div. What is the cost of equity?

What implications does dividend growth appear to have for earnings retentions?

2.12 SOLUTION

The dividend growth model will be used.

(a) Dividends have risen from £150,000 in 20X1 to £262,350 in 20X5. The increase represents four years growth. (Check that you can see that there are four years growth, and not five years growth, in the table.) The average growth rate, g, may be calculated as follows.

$$\text{Dividend in 20X1} \times (1+g)^4 = \text{Dividend in 20X5}$$

$$(1+g)^4 = \frac{\text{Dividend in 20X5}}{\text{Dividend in 20X1}}$$

$$= \frac{£262,350}{£150,000}$$

$$= 1.749$$

$$1 + g = \sqrt[4]{1.749} = 1.15$$

$$g = 0.15, \text{ ie } 15\%$$

(b) The growth rate over the last four years is assumed to be expected by shareholders into the indefinite future, so the cost of equity, r, is:

$$\frac{d_0(1+g)}{P_0} + g$$

$$= \frac{0.26235(1.15)}{3.35} + 0.15 = 0.24, \text{ ie } 24\%$$

(c) Retained profits will earn a certain rate of return and so growth will come from the yield on the retained funds.

Assume $g = bR$

where b = proportion of profits retained for reinvestment

R = yield on new investments (this is often taken to be the accounting rate of return $\frac{\text{Profits}}{\text{Investment}}$ or $\frac{\text{Profits after taxation and preference dividends}}{\text{Equity}}$)

This is known as **Gordon's growth model**.

In our example, if we applied this assumption the future annual growth rate would be 15% if bR continued to be 15%. If the rate of return on new investments averages 24% (the cost of equity) and if the proportion of earnings retained is 62.5% (which it has been, approximately, in the period 20X1 – 20X5) then $g = bR = 62.5\% \times 24\% = 15\%$.

The cost of debt capital and the cost of preference shares

2.13 Estimating the cost of fixed interest or fixed dividend capital is much easier than estimating the cost of ordinary share capital because the interest received by the holder of the security is fixed by contract and will not fluctuate. The cost of debt capital already issued is the rate of interest (the internal rate of return) which equates the current market price with the discounted future cash receipts from the security.

2.14 Ignoring taxation for the moment, in the case of **irredeemable** debt (or preference shares) the future cash flows are the interest (or dividend) payments in perpetuity so that:

$$P_0 = \frac{i}{(1+k_d)} + \frac{i}{(1+k_d)^2} + \frac{i}{(1+k_d)^3} \ldots$$

where P_0 is the current market price of debt capital after payment of the current interest (dividend)
i is the interest (dividend) received
k_d is the cost of debt (preference share) capital net of tax

$$\frac{i}{(1+k_d)} + \frac{i}{(1+k_d)^2} + \frac{i}{(1+k_d)^3} \ldots$$

simplifies to $\frac{i}{k_d}$

2.15 Thus, the cost of irredeemable debt, assuming no tax, can be calculated as $k_d = \frac{i}{P_0}$.

EXAM FORMULA

Cost of irredeemable preference capital, paying an annual dividend d in perpetuity, and having a current ex-div price P_0:

$$k_{pref} = \frac{d}{P_0}$$

2.16 If interest is paid other than annually,

$$\text{Cost of loan capital} = \left(1 + \frac{\text{Interest}}{\text{Ex interest price}}\right)^n - 1$$

where n = number of times interest is paid per year

2.17 EXAMPLE: COST OF CAPITAL (2)

Henryted Ltd has 12% irredeemable debentures in issue with a nominal value of £100. The market price is £95 ex interest. Calculate the cost of capital if interest is paid half-yearly.

2.18 SOLUTION

If interest is 12% annually, therefore 6% is payable half-yearly.

$$\text{Cost of loan capital} = \left(1 + \frac{6}{95}\right)^2 - 1 = 13.0\%$$

8: The cost of capital

2.19 If the debt is **redeemable** then in the year of redemption the interest payment will be received by the holder as well as the amount payable on redemption, so:

$$P_0 = \frac{i}{(1+k_{d\,net})} + \frac{i}{(1+k_{d\,net})^2} + \ldots + \frac{i+p_n}{(1+k_{d\,net})^n}$$

where p_n = the amount payable on redemption in year n.

2.20 The above equation cannot be simplified, so 'r' will have to be calculated by trial and error, as an **internal rate of return (IRR)**.

2.21 The best trial and error figure to start with in calculating the cost of redeemable debt is to take the cost of debt capital as if it were irredeemable and then add the annualised capital profit that will be made from the present time to the time of redemption.

2.22 EXAMPLE: COST OF CAPITAL (2)

Owen Allot plc has in issue 10% debentures of a nominal value of £100. The market price is £90 ex interest. Calculate the cost of this capital if the debenture is:

(a) Irredeemable
(b) Redeemable at par after 10 years

Ignore taxation.

2.23 SOLUTION

(a) **The cost of irredeemable debt capital** is $\frac{i}{P_0} = \frac{£10}{£90} \times 100\% = 11.1\%$

(b) **The cost of redeemable debt capital**. The capital profit that will be made from now to the date of redemption is £10 (£100 – £90). This profit will be made over a period of ten years which gives an annualised profit of £1 which is about 1% of current market value. The best trial and error figure to try first is therefore 12%.

Year		Cash flow	Discount factor 12%	PV £	Discount factor 11%	PV £
0	Market value	(90)	1.000	(90.00)	1.000	(90.00)
1-10	Interest	10	5.650	56.50	5.889	58.89
10	Capital repayment	100	0.322	32.20	0.352	35.20
				(1.30)		+4.09

The approximate cost of redeemable debt capital is, therefore:

$$(11 + \frac{4.09}{(4.09 - -1.30)} \times 1) = 11.76\%$$

2.24 The cost of debt capital estimated above represents:

(a) The cost of **continuing to use the finance** rather than redeem the securities at their current market price.

(b) The cost of raising **additional fixed interest capital** if we assume that the cost of the additional capital would be equal to the cost of that already issued. If a company has not already issued any fixed interest capital, it may estimate the cost of doing so by

Part B: Sources of long-term finance

making a similar calculation for another company which is judged to be similar as regards risk.

Debt capital and taxation

2.25 The interest on debt capital is an allowable deduction for purposes of taxation and so the cost of debt capital and the cost of share capital are not properly comparable costs. This tax relief on interest ought to be recognised in computations. One way of doing this is to include tax savings due to interest payments in the cash flows of every project. A simpler method, and one that is normally used, is to allow for the tax relief in computing the cost of debt capital, to arrive at an 'after-tax' cost of debt. The after-tax cost of irredeemable debt capital is:

$$k_{d\ net} = \frac{i(1-t)}{P_0}$$

where $k_{d\ net}$ is the cost of debt capital
  i is the annual interest payment
  P_0 is the current market price of the debt capital ex interest (that is, after payment of the current interest)
  t is the rate of corporation tax

> **EXAM FORMULA**
>
> Cost of irredeemable debt capital, paying annual net interest $i(1 - t)$, and having a current ex-interest price P_0:
>
> $$k_{d\ net} = \frac{i(1-t)}{P_0}$$

2.26 Therefore if a company pays £10,000 a year interest on irredeemable debenture stock with a nominal value of £100,000 and a market price of £80,000, and the rate of corporation tax is 30%, the cost of the debentures would be:

$$\frac{10,000}{80,000}(1 - 0.30) = 0.0875 = 8.75\%$$

2.27 The higher the rate of corporation tax is, the greater the tax benefits in having debt finance will be compared with equity finance. In the example above, if the rate of tax had been 50%, the cost of debt would have been, after tax:

$$\frac{10,000}{80,000}(1 - 0.50) = 0.0625 = 6.25$$

2.28 In the case of **redeemable debentures**, the capital repayment is not allowable for tax. To calculate the cost of the debt capital to include in the weighted average cost of capital, it is necessary to calculate an internal rate of return which takes account of tax relief on the interest.

2.29 EXAMPLE: COST OF CAPITAL (3)

(a) A company has outstanding £660,000 of 8% debenture stock on which the interest is payable annually on 31 December. The stock is due for redemption at par on 1 January

20X6. The market price of the stock at 28 December 20X2 was 103 cum interest. Ignoring any question of personal taxation, what do you estimate to be the current market rate of interest?

(b) If a new expectation emerged that the market rate of interest would rise to 12% during 20X3 and 20X4 what effect might this have in theory on the market price at 28 December 20X2?

(c) If the effective rate of corporation tax was 30% what would be the percentage cost to the company of debenture stock in (a) above? Tax is paid each 31 December on profits earned in the year ended on the previous 31 December.

2.30 SOLUTION

(a) The current market rate of interest is found by calculating the pre-tax internal rate of return of the cash flows shown in the table below. We must subtract the current interest (of 8% per £100 of stock) from the current market price, and use this 'ex interest' market value. A discount rate of 10% is chosen for a trial-and-error start to the calculation.

Item and date		Year	Cash flow £	Discount factor 10%	Present value £
Market value (ex int)	28.12.X2	0	(95)	1.000	(95.0)
Interest	31.12.X3	1	8	0.909	7.3
Interest	31.12.X4	2	8	0.826	6.6
Interest	31.12.X5	3	8	0.751	6.0
Redemption	1.1.X6	3	100	0.751	75.1
NPV					0.0

By coincidence, the market rate of interest is 10% since the NPV of the cash flows above is zero.

(b) If the market rate of interest is expected to rise in 20X3 and 20X4 it is probable that the market price in December 20X2 will fall to reflect the new rates obtainable. The probable market price would be the discounted value of all future cash flows up to 20X6, at a discount rate of 12%.

Item and date		Year	Cash flow £	Discount factor 12%	Present value £
Interest	31.12.X2	0	8	1.000	8.0
Interest	31.12.X3	1	8	0.893	7.1
Interest	31.12.X4	2	8	0.797	6.4
Interest	31.12.X5	3	8	0.712	5.7
Redemption	1.1.X6	3	100	0.712	71.2
NPV					98.4

The estimated market price would be £98.4 per cent **cum** interest.

(c) Again we must deduct the current interest payable and use ex interest figures.

Part B: Sources of long-term finance

At a market value of 103

Item and date		Year	Cash flow ex int £	PV 5% £	PV 8% £
Market value		0	(95.0)	(95.0)	(95.0)
Interest	31.12.X3	1	8.0	7.6	7.4
Tax saved	31.12.X4	2	(2.4)	(2.2)	(2.1)
Interest	31.12.X4	2	8.0	7.3	6.9
Tax saved	31.12.X5	3	(2.4)	(2.1)	(2.0)
Interest	31.12.X5	3	8.0	6.9	6.4
Tax saved	31.12.X6	4	(2.4)	(2.0)	(1.8)
Redemption	1.1.X6	3	100.0	86.4	79.4
NPV				6.9	(0.8)

The estimated cost of capital is:

$$5\% + (\frac{6.9}{(6.9 - -0.8)} \times 3\%) = 7.7\%$$

The cost of floating rate debt

2.31 If a firm has variable or '**floating rate' debt**, then the cost of an equivalent fixed interest debt should be substituted. 'Equivalent' usually means fixed interest debt with a similar term to maturity in a firm of similar standing, although if the cost of capital is to be used for project appraisal purposes, there is an argument for using debt of the same duration as the project under consideration.

The cost of short-term funds

2.32 The cost of short term funds such as bank loans and overdrafts is the current interest being charged on such funds.

2.33 **Depreciation**, being a non-cash item of expense, is ignored in our cost of capital computations, but depreciation is a means of retaining funds within a business for new investments or replacements. For our purposes, it is sufficient to say that **the cost of funds retained by depreciation is ignored**, because it is argued that they should be taken as having a cost equal to the company's weighted average cost of capital, and so are irrelevant to the calculation of the cost of capital.

3 SPECIAL PROBLEMS

Private companies and the cost of equity

3.1 The cost of capital cannot be calculated from market values for **private companies** in the way that has been described so far, because the shares in a private company do not have a quoted market price. Since private companies do not have a cost of equity that can be readily estimated, it follows that a big problem for private companies which want to use DCF for evaluating investment projects is how to select a cost of capital for a discount rate.

3.2 **Suitable approaches**

(a) **Estimate** the **cost of capital** for similar public companies, but then add a **further premium** for additional business and financial risk

(b) Build up a cost of capital by adding **estimated premiums** for **business risk** and **financial risk** to the risk-free rate of return.

Government organisations and the cost of capital

3.3 The same problem faces government organisations. Government organisations do not have a market value, and most of them do not pay interest on much or all of the finance they receive. Government activities do not involve business risk, and there is no financial risk either for the investor, which is mainly the government itself. It is therefore impossible to calculate a cost of capital for government organisations. The problem is overcome in their case by using a target 'real' rate of return set by the Treasury.

The cost of equity capital: gross dividend or net dividend yield?

3.4 We have seen that the cost of equity is calculated on the basis of net dividends (perhaps with dividend growth). This selection of net dividends rather than gross dividends for the cost of equity requires some explanation. The net dividend is the appropriate choice because the **cost of capital** is used as the **discount rate** for the evaluation of capital projects by a company, and the company must have sufficient profits from its investments to pay shareholders the net dividends they require out of after-tax profits.

3.5 The taxation on profits is allowed for in the **cash flows** of each project. The discount rate is therefore applied to the cash flows of the project after tax. If a company were to make a payment of dividends out of profits, the amount available would be the net dividend, related to the after-tax profits earned. Since the company's cost of equity is connected with the net dividends payable by the company, the company need not be concerned with the net dividends received by the shareholders after personal taxation has been deducted from the shareholders' gross dividend income.

4 THE WEIGHTED AVERAGE COST OF CAPITAL   Pilot paper, 5/01, 5/02

Computing a discount rate

4.1 We have looked at the costs of individual sources of capital for a company. But how does this help us to work out the cost of capital as a whole, or the discount rate to apply in DCF investment appraisals?

4.2 In many cases it will be difficult to associate a particular project with a particular form of finance. A company's funds may be viewed as a pool of resources. Money is withdrawn from this pool of funds to invest in new projects and added to the pool as new finance is raised or profits are retained. Under these circumstances it might seem appropriate to use an average cost of capital as the discount rate.

4.3 The correct cost of capital to use in investment appraisal is the marginal cost of the funds raised (or earnings retained) to finance the investment. The weighted average cost of capital (WACC) might be considered the most reliable guide to the marginal cost of capital, but only on the assumption that the company continues to invest in the future, in projects of a standard level of business risk, by raising funds in the same proportions as its existing capital structure.

KEY TERM

Weighted average cost of capital is the average cost of the company's finance (equity, debentures, bank loans) weighted according to the proportion each element bears to the total pool of capital. Weighting is usually based on market valuations, current yields and costs after tax.

(OT 2000)

General formula for the WACC

4.4 A general formula for the weighted average cost of capital (WACC) k_0 is as follows.

EXAM FORMULA

$$k_0 = k_e \left(\frac{V_E}{V_E + V_D}\right) + k_d \left(\frac{V_D}{V_E + V_D}\right)$$

where k_e is the cost of equity
       k_d is the cost of debt
       V_E is the market value of equity in the firm
       V_D is the market value of debt in the firm

4.5 The above formula ignores taxation.

4.6 EXAMPLE: WEIGHTED AVERAGE COST OF CAPITAL

Prudence plc is financed partly by equity and partly by debentures. The equity proportion is always kept at two thirds of the total. The cost of equity is 18% and that of debt 12%. A new project is under consideration which will cost £100,000 and will yield a return before interest of £17,500 a year in perpetuity. Should the project be accepted? Ignore taxation.

4.7 SOLUTION

Since the company will maintain its gearing ratio unchanged, it is reasonable to assume that its marginal cost of funds equals its WACC. The weighted average cost of capital is as follows.

	Proportion	Cost	Cost × proportion
Equity	$\frac{2}{3}$	18%	12%
Debt	$\frac{1}{3}$	12%	4%
		WACC	16%

4.8 The present value of the future returns in perpetuity can be found using the WACC as the discount rate, as follows.

$$\text{Present value of future cash flows} = \frac{\text{Annual cash flow}}{\text{Discount rate}} = \frac{£17,500}{0.16} = £109,375$$

The NPV of the investment is £109,375 − £100,000 = £9,375.

4.9 Another way of looking at the investment shows how using the WACC as the discount rate ensures that equity shareholders' wealth is increased by undertaking projects with a positive NPV when discounted at the WACC.

The amount of finance deemed to be provided by the debenture holders will be $1/3 \times £100,000 = £33,333$. The interest on this will be $12\% \times £33,333 = £4,000$, leaving £13,500 available for the equity shareholders. The return they are receiving based on their 'investment' of £66,667 will be as follows.

Return to equity = $\dfrac{£13,500}{£66,667}$ = 0.2025 or 20.25%

As this return exceeds the cost of equity capital, the project is acceptable.

Weighting

4.10 In the last example, we simplified the problem of weighting the different costs of capital by giving the proportions of capital. Two methods of weighting could be used.

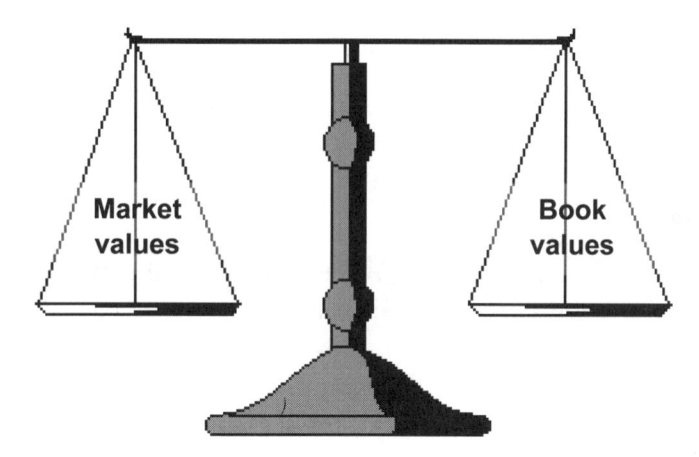

4.11 Although book values are often easier to obtain they are of doubtful economic significance. It is, therefore, more meaningful to use market values when data are available. For unquoted companies estimates of market values are likely to be extremely subjective and consequently book values may be used. When using market values it is not possible to split the equity value between share capital and reserves and only one cost of equity can be used. This removes the need to estimate a separate cost of retained earnings.

Using the WACC in investment appraisal

4.12 The weighted average cost of capital can be used in investment appraisal if we make the following assumptions.

(a) New investments must be **financed** by **new sources of funds**: retained earnings, new share issues, new loans and so on.

(b) The cost of capital to be applied to project evaluation must **reflect** the **marginal cost** of new capital.

(c) The weighted average cost of capital **reflects** the **company's long-term future capital structure**, and capital costs. If this were not so, the current weighted average cost would become irrelevant because eventually it would not relate to any actual cost of capital.

Arguments against using the WACC

4.13 The arguments against using the WACC as the cost of capital for investment appraisal (as follows) are based on criticisms of the assumptions that are used to justify use of the WACC.

(a) New investments undertaken by a company might have different **business risk** characteristics from the company's existing operations. As a consequence, the return required by investors might go up (or down) if the investments are undertaken, because their business risk is perceived to be higher (or lower).

(b) The finance that is raised to fund a new investment might substantially change the capital structure and the perceived **financial risk** of investing in the company. Depending on whether the project is financed by equity or by debt capital, the perceived financial risk of the entire company might change. This must be taken into account when appraising investments.

(c) Many companies raise **floating rate** debt capital as well as fixed interest debt capital. With floating rate debt capital, the interest rate is variable, and is altered every three or six months or so in line with changes in current market interest rates. The cost of debt capital will therefore fluctuate as market conditions vary.

Floating rate debt is difficult to incorporate into a WACC computation, and the best that can be done is to substitute an 'equivalent' fixed interest debt capital cost in place of the floating rate debt cost.

Effect of gearing

4.14 There are two main theories about the effect of changes in gearing on the weighted average cost of capital (WACC) and share values. These are the '**traditional**' view, and the **net operating income approach** (Modigliani and Miller – not covered in your syllabus).

4.15 The assumptions on which these theories are based are as follows:

(a) The company **pays out** all its **earnings** as **dividends.**

(b) The **gearing** of the company **can be changed immediately** by issuing debt to repurchase shares, or by issuing shares to repurchase debt. There are no transaction costs for issues.

(c) The earnings of the company are **expected to remain constant in perpetuity** and all investors share the same expectations about these future earnings.

(d) **Business risk** is also **constant**, regardless of how the company invests its funds.

(e) **Taxation**, for the time being, is **ignored**.

The traditional view of WACC   5/02

4.16 The **traditional view** is as follows:

(a) As the **level of gearing increases**, the **cost of debt remains unchanged** up to a certain level of gearing. Beyond this level, the cost of debt will increase.

(b) The **cost of equity** rises as the level of **gearing increases.**

(c) The **weighted average cost of capital** does **not remain constant**, but rather falls initially as the proportion of debt capital increases, and then begins to increase as the rising cost of equity (and possibly of debt) becomes more significant.

8: The cost of capital

(d) The **optimum level of gearing** is where the **company's weighted average cost of capital is minimised**.

4.17 The traditional view about the cost of capital is illustrated in the following figure. It shows that the weighted average cost of capital will be minimised at a particular level of gearing P.

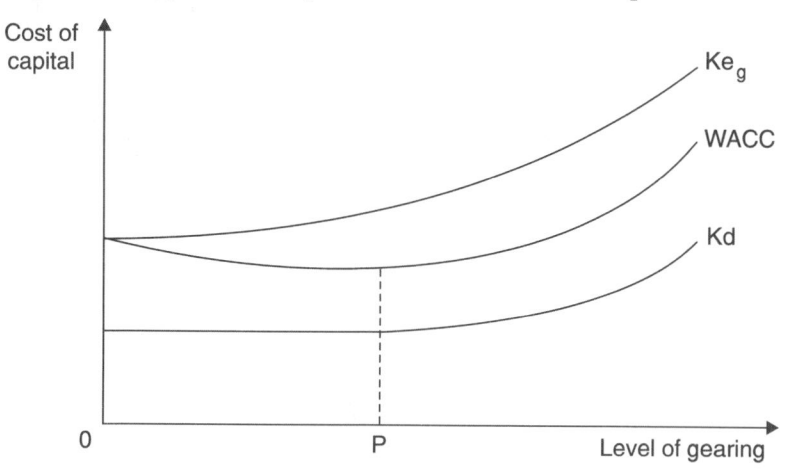

```
Cost of
capital
                                                Ke_g
                                                WACC
                                                Kd



0                      P              Level of gearing
```

Ke_g is the cost of equity in the geared company
Kd is the cost of debt
WACC is the weighted average cost of capital.

4.18 The traditional view is that the weighted average cost of capital, when plotted against the level of gearing, is saucer shaped. The optimum capital structure is where the weighted average cost of capital is lowest, at point P.

Marginal cost of capital approach

4.19 The **marginal cost of capital** approach involves calculating a marginal cut-off rate for acceptable investment projects by:

(a) **Establishing rates of return** for each component of capital structure, except retained earnings, based on its value if it were to be raised under current market conditions

(b) **Relating dividends or interest** to these values to obtain a marginal cost for each component

(c) **Applying the marginal cost** to each component depending on its proportionate weight within the capital structure and adding the resultant costs to give a weighted average

4.20 It can be argued that the current weighted average cost of capital should be used to evaluate projects, where a company's capital structure changes only very slowly over time; then the marginal cost of new capital should be roughly equal to the weighted average cost of current capital.

4.21 Where gearing levels fluctuate significantly, or the finance for new project carries a significantly different level of risks to that of the existing company, there is good reason to seek an alternative marginal cost of capital.

Question 2

(a) What is meant by the 'weighted average cost of capital' of a company. Why do many companies use it as a discount rate in investment appraisal?

Part B: Sources of long-term finance

(b) Explain how this cost of capital is calculated and discuss the components required. (Detailed mathematical calculations are not required.)

Answer

(a) The **weighted average cost of capital** (WACC) is the **average cost** of the different elements within the capital structure of a company, using weightings based on the market values of each of the different elements.

In many cases it will be difficult to associate a particular project with a particular form of finance. A company's funds may be viewed as a pool of resources. Money is withdrawn from this pool of funds to invest in new projects and added to the pool as new finance is raised or profits are retained. Under these circumstances it might seem appropriate to use an average cost of capital as a discount rate.

The correct cost of capital to use in investment appraisal is the **marginal cost** of the funds raised (or earnings retained) to finance the investment. The WACC might be considered the most reliable guide to the marginal cost of capital, but only on the assumption that the company continues to invest in the future, in projects of a standard level of business risk, by raising funds in the same proportions as its existing capital structure.

(b) The WACC can be expressed using the formula:

$$\text{WACC} = k_e \left(\frac{V_E}{V_E + V_D} \right) + k_d \left(\frac{V_D}{V_E + V_D} \right)$$

where k_e = cost of equity
k_d = cost of debt
V_E = market value of equity in the firm
V_D = market value of debt in the firm

The cost of capital is the **cost of funds** that a company raises and uses, and the return that investors expect to be paid for putting funds into the company. It is therefore the minimum return that a company should make on its own investments to earn the cash flows out of which investors can be paid their return.

New equity funds are obtained from new issues of shares and from retained earnings. The costs of these funds are effectively the rate of return required by shareholders. In the case of retained earnings, the cost is the opportunity cost of the dividend foregone by the shareholders.

The cost of equity, both for new issues and retained earnings, is often estimated using the **dividend valuation model**, on the assumption that the market value of shares is directly related to expected future dividends on the shares.

Estimating the cost of **fixed interest** or fixed dividend capital is much easier than estimating the cost of ordinary share capital because the interest received by the holder of the security is fixed by contract and will not fluctuate.

The cost of debt capital already issued is the **rate of interest** (the internal rate of return) which equates the current market price with the discounted future cash receipts from the security.

Since the interest on debt capital is an allowable deduction for tax purposes, this should be taken into account in computing the cost of debt capital so as to make it properly comparable with the cost of equity.

If a firm has floating rate debt, the cost of an equivalent fixed interest debt should be substituted. This means debt with a similar term to maturity in a firm of similar standing. The cost of short-term funds such as bank loans and overdrafts is the current rate of interest being charged on such funds.

Weightings should be based on market values where possible because they have greater economic significance than book values.

8: The cost of capital

Question 3

The following figures have been extracted from the accounts of Mezzo Ltd:

Year	Dividends £	Earnings £
20X1	100,000	350,000
20X2	125,000	400,000
20X3	125,000	370,000
20X4	160,000	450,000
20X5	200,000	550,000

You have been asked to calculate the cost of equity for the company. What growth rate would you use in the calculations?

A 12%
B 14%
C 19%
D 25%

Answer

C   Let 'g' = rate of growth in dividends.

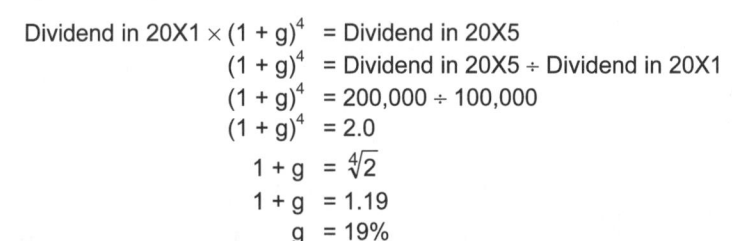

$$\text{Dividend in 20X1} \times (1+g)^4 = \text{Dividend in 20X5}$$
$$(1+g)^4 = \text{Dividend in 20X5} \div \text{Dividend in 20X1}$$
$$(1+g)^4 = 200,000 \div 100,000$$
$$(1+g)^4 = 2.0$$
$$1+g = \sqrt[4]{2}$$
$$1+g = 1.19$$
$$g = 19\%$$

Chapter roundup

- The **cost of capital** is the rate of return that the enterprise must pay to satisfy the providers of funds, and it reflects the riskiness of the funding transaction.

- The **dividend valuation model** can be used to estimate a cost of equity, on the assumption that the market value of share is directly related to the expected future dividends on the shares.

- Expected **growth in dividends** can be allowed for, using Gordon's growth model.

- The **cost of debt** is the return an enterprise must pay to its lenders.
  - For **irredeemable debt**, this is the (post-tax) interest as a percentage of the ex int market value of the loan stock (or preference shares).
  - For **redeemable debt**, the cost is given by the internal rate of return of the cash flows involved.

- The **weighted average cost of capital** can be used to evaluate a company's investment projects if:
  - The project is small relative to the company.
  - The existing capital structure will be maintained (same financial risk).
  - The project has the same business risk as the company.

Quick quiz

1 The cost of capital has three elements. Which of the following is not one of these elements?

A The market rate of return
B The premium for business risk

Part B: Sources of long-term finance

  C The premium for financial risk
  D The risk-free rate of return

2 'The minimum acceptable return on an investment, generally computed as a hurdle rate for use in investment appraisal exercises' *(CIMA Official Terminology)*. What does this define?

3 What does Gordon's yields and growth model illustrate?

4 Explain how gearing affects the risk borne by ordinary shareholders.

5 Identify the variables r, d_1, P_0 and g in the following dividend valuation model formula.

$$r = \frac{d_1}{P_0} + g$$

6 Identify the variables k_e, k_d, V_E and V_D in the following weighted average cost of capital formula.

$$k_0 = k_e \left(\frac{V_E}{V_E + V_D}\right) + k_d \left(\frac{V_D}{V_E + V_D}\right)$$

7 When calculating the weighted average cost of capital, which of the following is the preferred method of weighting?

  A Book values of debt and equity
  B Average levels of the market values of debt and equity (ignoring reserves) over five years
  C Current market values of debt and equity (ignoring reserves)
  D Current market values of debt and equity (plus reserves)

8 What is the cost of £1 irredeemable debt capital paying an annual rate of interest of 7%, and having a current market price of £1.50?

Answers to quick quiz

1 A The market rate of return

2 The cost of capital

3 The relationship of the cost of equity share capital to its price and the expected growth rate in its dividends.

4 If gearing is higher, the variability of earnings after deducting payments to holders of debt capital is higher. If the rate of return exceeds the rate of interest paid on debt, this works to ordinary shareholders' advantage. If it does not, ordinary shareholders' returns are reduced by gearing.

5 r is the shareholders' cost of capital (as a proportion)
  d_1 is the dividend in year 1
  P_0 is the current market price (ex div)
  g is the expected annual growth in dividend payments (as a proportion)

6 k_e is the cost of equity
  k_d is the cost of debt
  V_E is the market value of equity in the firm
  V_D is the market value of debt in the firm

7 C Current market values of debt and equity (ignoring reserves)

8 Cost of debt = $\frac{0.07}{1.50}$ = 4.67%

Now try the question below from the Exam Question Bank

Number	Level	Marks	Time
8	Introductory	n/a	35 mins

Chapter 9

PORTFOLIOS AND DIVERSIFICATION

Topic list	Syllabus reference	Ability required
1 Portfolios and portfolio theory	(ii)	Evaluation
2 Investors' preferences	(ii)	Evaluation
3 Portfolio theory and financial management	(ii), (iii)	Evaluation

Introduction

The **diversification of portfolios** of investments is an important concept in financial management. In this chapter, we examine the benefits of portfolio diversification. **Modern portfolio theory**, which has gained much popularity since 1970, concludes that a well diversified portfolio of investments is optimal. We explain here some key aspects of portfolio theory, its relevance and its limitations.

Learning outcomes covered in this chapter

- Calculate the cost of capital and demonstrate the impact of changing capital structures.

Syllabus content covered in this chapter

- The ideas of diversifiable risk (unsystematic risk) and systematic risk (use of the two asset portfolio formula will not be tested)

1 PORTFOLIOS AND PORTFOLIO THEORY

1.1 A **portfolio** is the collection of different investments that make up an investor's total holding. A portfolio might be:

- The investments in stocks and shares of an investor
- The investments in capital projects of a company

1.2 **Portfolio theory**, which originates from the work of Markowitz, is concerned with establishing guidelines for building up a portfolio of stocks and shares, or a portfolio of projects. The same theory applies to both stock market investors and to companies with capital projects to invest in.

Factors in the choice of investments

1.3 There are five major factors to be considered when any investor chooses investments.

Part B: Sources of long-term finance

CHOOSING INVESTMENTS	
Security	Investments at least maintaining their capital value
Liquidity	If investments are with short-term funds, should be convertible back into cash at short notice
Return	Make highest return compatible with safety
Spreading risks	Spreading investments over several types of security, so losses on some offset by gains on others
Growth prospects	Most profitable investments are in businesses with good growth prospects

Portfolios: expected return and risk

1.4 When an investor has a portfolio of securities, he will expect the portfolio to provide a certain return on his investment.

1.5 The **expected return of a portfolio** will be a weighted average of the expected returns of the investments in the portfolio, weighted by the proportion of total funds invested in each.

1.6 The **risk** in an investment, or in a portfolio of investments, is the risk that the actual return will not be the same as the expected return. The actual return may be higher, but it may be lower. A prudent investor will want to avoid too much risk, and will hope that the actual returns from his portfolio are much the same as what he expected them to be.

1.7 The risk of a security, and the risk of a portfolio, can be measured as the standard deviation of expected returns, given estimated probabilities of actual returns.

1.8 EXAMPLE: PORTFOLIOS (1)

Suppose that the return from an investment has the following probability distribution.

Return x %	Probability p	Expected value px
8	0.2	1.6
10	0.2	2.0
12	0.5	6.0
14	0.1	1.4
		11.0

The expected return is 11%, and the standard deviation of the expected return is as follows. The symbol $\bar{x}$ refers to the expected value of the return, 11%.

Return

x %	$x - \bar{x}$ %	p	$p(x - \bar{x})^2$
8	−3	0.2	1.8
10	−1	0.2	0.2
12	1	0.5	0.5
14	3	0.1	0.9
	Variance		3.4

Standard deviation = $\sqrt{3.4}$ = 1.84%

Thus, the expected return is 11% with a standard deviation of 1.84%.

9: Portfolios and diversification

1.9 The risk of an investment might be high or low, depending on the nature of the investment.

(a) Low risk investments usually give low returns.

(b) High risk investments might give high returns, but with more risk of disappointing results.

So how does holding a **portfolio of investments** affect expected returns and investment risk?

Diversification as a means of reducing risk

1.10 Portfolio theory states that individual investments cannot be viewed simply in terms of their risk and return. The relationship between the return from one investment and the return from other investments is just as important.

1.11 The relationship between investments can be one of three types.

(a) **Positive correlation**

When there is positive correlation between investments, if one investment does well (or badly) it is likely that the other will perform likewise. Thus if you buy shares in one company making umbrellas and in another which sells raincoats you would expect both companies to do badly in dry weather.

(b) **Negative correlation**

If one investment does well the other will do badly, and vice versa. Thus if you hold shares in one company making umbrellas and in another which sells ice cream, the weather will affect the companies differently.

(c) **No correlation**

The performance of one investment will be independent of how the other performs. If you hold shares in a mining company and in a leisure company, it is likely that there would be no relationship between the profits and returns from each.

1.12 This relationship between the returns from different investments is measured by the correlation coefficient. A figure close to +1 indicates high positive correlation, and a figure close to −1 indicates high negative correlation. A figure of 0 indicates no correlation.

1.13 If investments show high negative correlation, then by combining them in a portfolio overall risk would be reduced. Risk will also be reduced by combining in a portfolio investments which have no significant correlation.

2 INVESTORS' PREFERENCES

2.1 Investors must choose a portfolio which gives them a satisfactory balance between:

- The **expected returns** from the **portfolio,** and
- The **risk** that **actual returns** from the **portfolio** will be **higher or lower** than expected

Some portfolios will be more risky than others.

2.2 Traditional investment theory suggests that rational investors wish to maximise return and minimise risk. Thus if two portfolios have the same element of risk, the investor will choose the one yielding the higher return. Similarly, if two portfolios offer the same return the investor will select the portfolio with the lesser risk. This is illustrated by Figure 1.

Part B: Sources of long-term finance

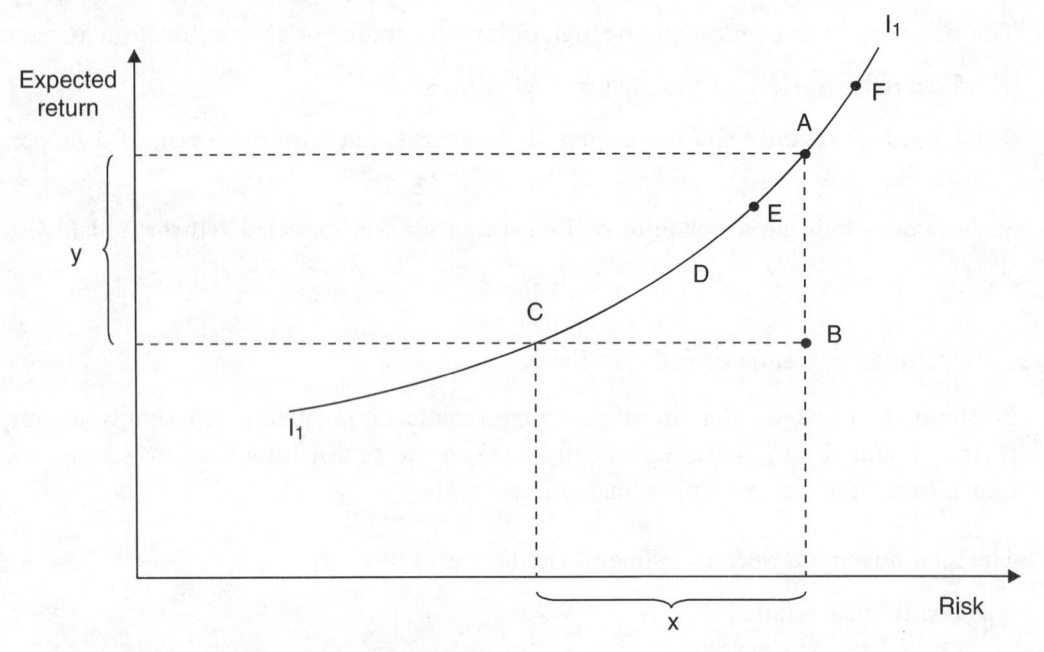

Figure 1 An investor's indifference curve

2.3 Portfolio A will be **preferred** to portfolio B because it offers a higher expected return for the same level of risk. Similarly, portfolio C will be preferred to portfolio B because it offers the same expected return for lower risk. (A and C are said to **dominate** portfolio B). But whether an investor chooses portfolio A or portfolio C will depend on the individual's attitude to risk: whether he wishes to accept a greater risk for a greater expected return.

2.4 The curve I_1 is an **investor's indifference curve**. The investor will have no preference between any portfolios which give a mix of risk and expected return which lies on the curve, since he derives **equal utility** from each of them.

2.5 Thus, to the investor the portfolios A, C, D, E and F are all just as good as each other, and all of them are better than portfolio B. Remembering that the risk of a portfolio can be measured as the standard deviation of expected returns, this may be expressed by saying that portfolio B is dispreferred on grounds of **mean-variance inefficiency**.

2.6 An investor would prefer combinations of return and risk on indifference curve A to those on curve B (Figure 2) because curve A offers higher returns for the same degree of risk (and less risk for the same expected returns). For example, for the same amount of risk x, the expected return on curve A is y_1, whereas on curve B it is only y_2.

9: Portfolios and diversification

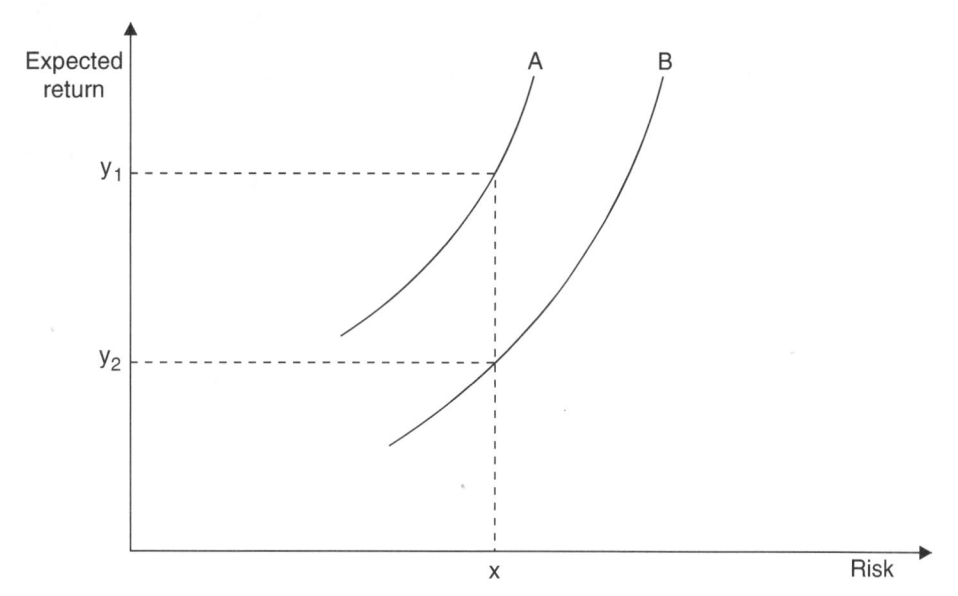

Figure 2 Indifference curves compared

Efficient portfolios

2.7 If we drew a graph (Figure 3) to show the expected return and the risk of the many possible portfolios of investments, we could (according to portfolio theory) plot an egg-shaped cluster of dots on a scattergraph as follows.

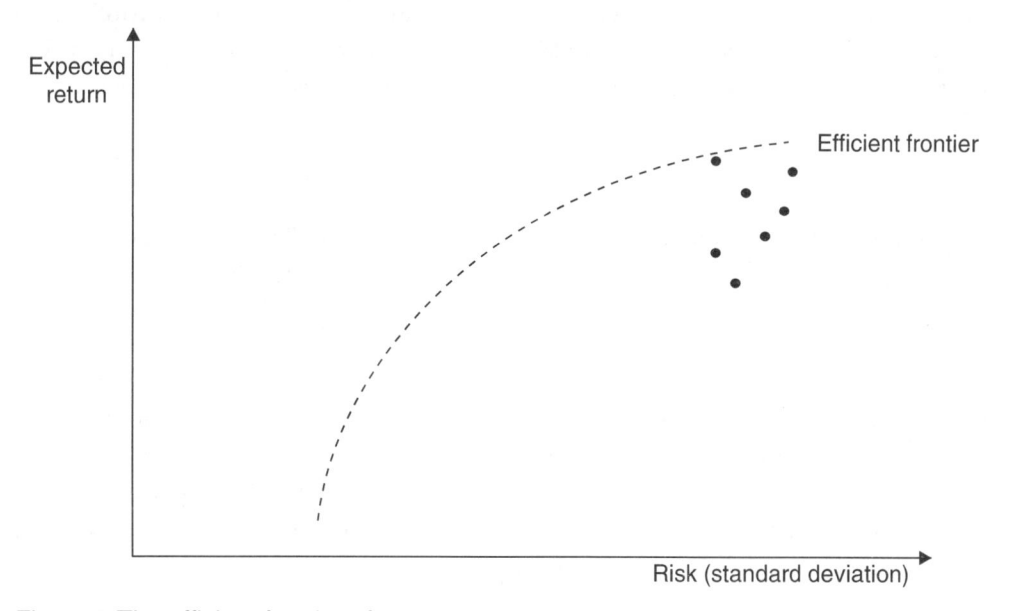

Figure 3 The efficient frontier of available investment portfolios

2.8 In this graph, there are some portfolios which would not be as good as others. However, there are other portfolios which are neither better nor worse than each other, because they have either a higher expected return but a higher risk, or a lower expected return but a lower risk. These portfolios lie along the so-called 'efficient frontier' of portfolios which is shown as a dotted line in Figure 3. Portfolios on this efficient frontier are called 'efficient' portfolios.

2.9 We can now place an investor's indifference curves on the same graph as the possible portfolios of investments (the **egg-shaped scatter graph**), as in Figure 4.

Part B: Sources of long-term finance

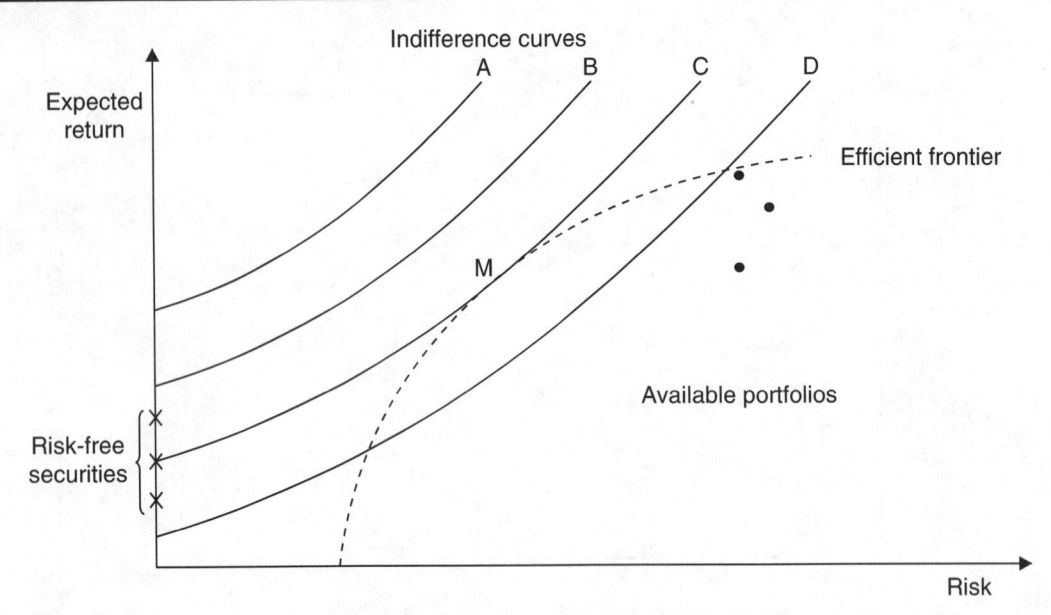

Figure 4 The optimum portfolio (ignoring risk-free securities)

2.10 An investor would prefer a portfolio of investments on indifference curve A to a portfolio on curve B, which in turn is preferable to a portfolio on curve C which in turn is preferable to curve D. No portfolio exists, however, which is on curve A or curve B.

2.11 The optimum portfolio (or portfolios) to select is one where an indifference curve touches the efficient frontier of portfolios at a tangent. In Figure 4, this is the portfolio marked M, where indifference curve C touches the efficient frontier at a tangent. Any portfolio on an indifference curve to the right of curve C, such as one on curve D, would be worse than M.

Risk-free investments

2.12 The efficient frontier is a curved line, not a straight line. This is because the additional return for accepting a greater level of risk will not be constant. The curve eventually levels off because a point will be reached where no more return can be offered to an investor for accepting more risk.

2.13 All the portfolios under consideration carry some degree of risk. But some investments are risk-free. It is extremely unlikely that the British Government would default on any payment of interest and capital on its stocks. Thus government stocks can be taken to be risk-free investments. If we introduce a risk-free investment into the analysis we can see that the old efficient frontier is superseded (Figure 5).

2.14 The straight line XZME is drawn at a tangent to the efficient frontier and cuts the y axis at the point of the risk-free investment's return. The line (known as the 'capital market line' (CML)) becomes the new efficient frontier.

2.15 Portfolio M is the same as in Figure 4. It is the efficient portfolio which will appeal to the investor most, ignoring risk-free investments. Portfolio Z is a mixture of the investments in portfolio M and risk-free investments. Investors will prefer portfolio Z (a mixture of risky portfolio M and the risk-free investment) to portfolio P because a higher return is obtained for the same level of risk. The only portfolio consisting entirely of **risky investments** a rational investor should want to hold is portfolio M. All other risky portfolios are inefficient (because they are below the CML).

9: Portfolios and diversification

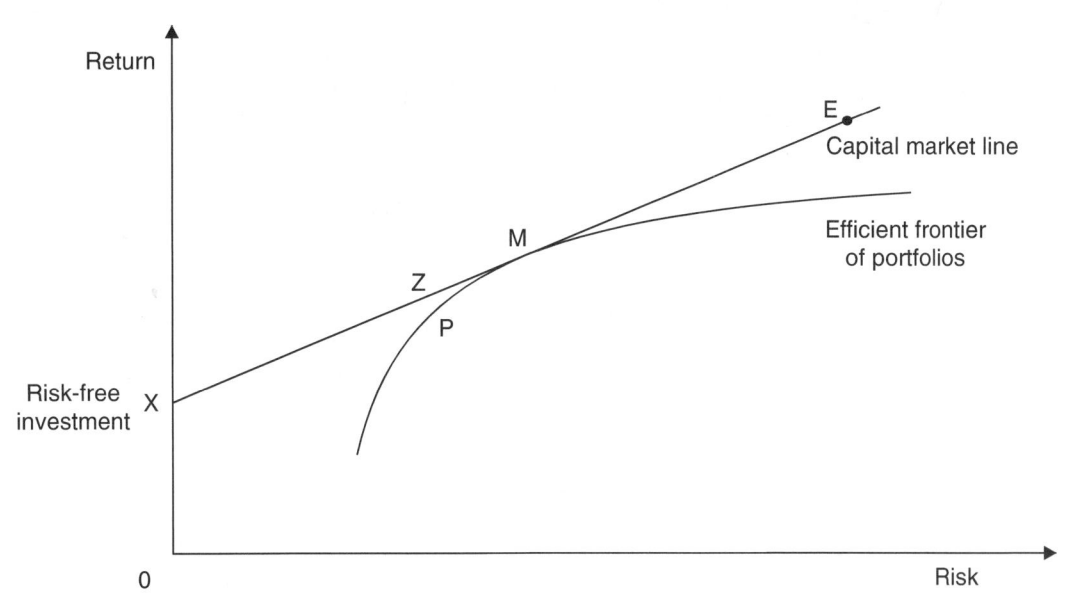

Figure 5 The capital market line

2.16 As with the curvilinear frontier, one portfolio on the capital market line is as attractive as another to a rational investor. One investor may wish to hold portfolio Z, which lies 2/3 of the way along the CML between risk-free investment X and portfolio M (that is, a holding comprising 2/3 portfolio M and 1/3 risk-free securities). Another investor may wish to hold portfolio E, which entails putting all his funds in portfolio M and borrowing money at the risk-free rate to acquire more of portfolio M.

2.17 We have said that investors will only want to hold one portfolio of risky investments: portfolio M. This may be held in conjunction with a holding of the risk-free investment (as with portfolio Z). Alternatively, an investor may borrow funds to augment his holding of M (as with portfolio E). Therefore:

- Since all investors wish to hold portfolio M, and
- All shares quoted on the Stock Exchange must be held by investors, it follows that
- All shares quoted on the Stock Exchange must be in portfolio M

2.18 Thus **portfolio M is the market portfolio** and each investor's portfolio will contain a proportion of it. However, in practice, investors **might** be able to build up a small portfolio that 'beats the market' or might have a portfolio which performs worse than the market average. The following question illustrates this.

Question 1

The following data relate to four different portfolios of securities.

Portfolio	Expected rate of return %	Standard deviation of return on the portfolio %
K	11	6.7
L	14	7.5
M	10	3.3
N	15	10.8

The expected rate of return on the market portfolio is 8.5% with a standard deviation of 3%. The risk-free rate is 5%.

Identify which of these portfolios could be regarded as 'efficient'.

Part B: Sources of long-term finance

Answer

To answer this question, we can start by drawing the CML (see below).

(a) When risk = 0, return = 5.
(b) When risk = 3, return = 8.5.

These points can be plotted on a graph and joined up, and the line can be extended to produce the CML. The individual portfolios K, L, M and N can be plotted on the same graph.

(a) Any portfolio which is above the CML is efficient.
(b) Any portfolio which is below the CML is inefficient.

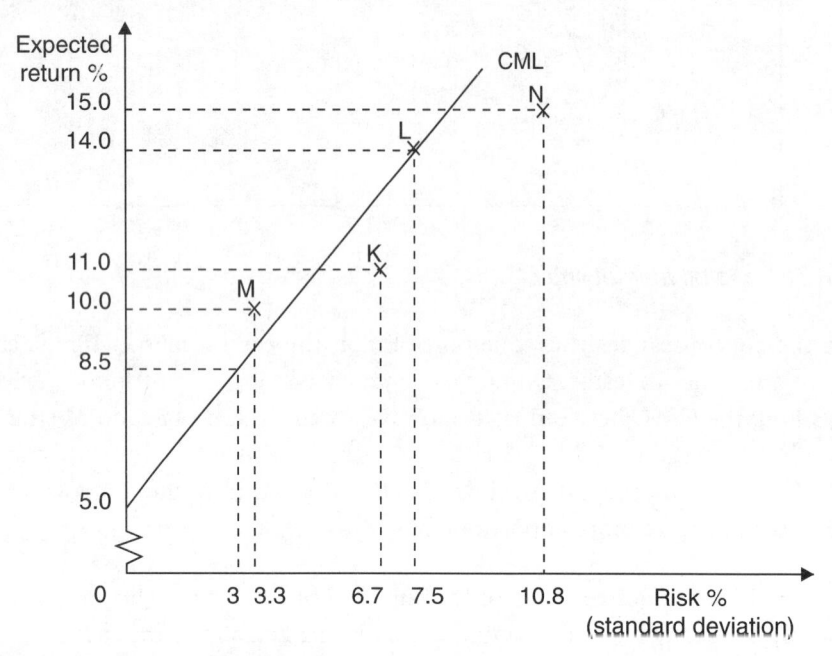

(a) Portfolio M is very efficient.
(b) Portfolio L is also efficient.
(c) Portfolios K and N are inefficient.

If you prefer numbers to graphs, we can tackle the problem in a slightly different way, by calculating the equation of the CML.

Let the standard deviation of a portfolio be x.

Let the return from a portfolio be y.

The CML equation is $y = r_f + bx$.

where r_f is the risk-free rate of return. Here, this is 5.

To calculate b, we can use the high-low method.

When   x = 3, y = 8.5
When   x = 0, y = 5

Therefore $b = \dfrac{(8.5 - 5)}{(3 - 0)} = \dfrac{3.5}{3} = 1.16667$

The CML is y = 5 + 1.16667x

Portfolio	Standard deviation x	CML return	%	Actual return %	Efficient or inefficient portfolio
K	6.7	(5 + 1.16667 × 6.7)	12.8	11	Inefficient
L	7.5	(5 + 1.16667 × 7.5)	13.8	14	Efficient
M	3.3	(5 + 1.16667 × 3.3)	8.9	10	Very efficient
N	10.8	(5 + 1.16667 × 10.8)	17.6	15	Inefficient

If the actual return exceeds the CML return for the given amount of risk, the portfolio is efficient.

Here, L is efficient and M is even more efficient, but K and N are inefficient.

The return on the market portfolio M

2.19 The expected returns from portfolio M will be higher than the return from risk-free investments because the investors expect a greater return for accepting a degree of investment risk. The size of the risk premium will increase as the risk of the market portfolio increases. We can show this with an analysis of the capital market line (CML) as in Figure 6.

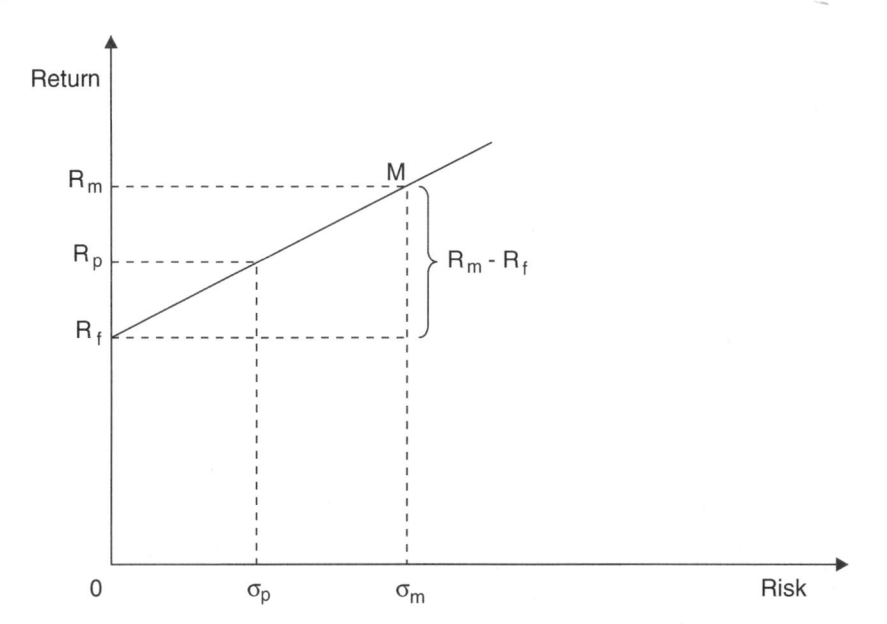

R_m = return from portfolio M
R_f = risk-free return
σ_m = risk of the portfolio M

Figure 6 The risk premium in required returns from a portfolio

2.20 Let
R_f = the risk-free rate of return
R_m = the return on market portfolio M
R_p = the return on portfolio P, which is a mixture of investments in portfolio M and risk-free investments
σ_m = the risk (standard deviation) of returns in portfolio M
σ_p = the risk (standard deviation) of returns in portfolio P

The gradient of the CML can be expressed as $\dfrac{R_m - R_f}{\sigma_m}$

This represents the extent to which the required returns from a portfolio should exceed the risk-free rate of return, to compensate investors for risk.

The beta factor

2.21 The equation of the CML can be expressed as: $R_p = R_f + \left(\dfrac{R_m - R_f}{\sigma_m}\right)\sigma_p$

where $\left(\dfrac{R_m - R_f}{\sigma_m}\right)\sigma_p$ is the risk premium that the investor should require as compensation for accepting portfolio risk σ_p.

Part B: Sources of long-term finance

2.22 The risk premium can be arranged into:

$$\frac{\sigma_p}{\sigma_m}(R_m - R_f)$$

The expression $\frac{\sigma_p}{\sigma_m}$ is referred to as a **beta factor**, so that an investor's required return from a portfolio can be stated as:

FORMULA TO LEARN

$R_p = R_f + (R_m - R_f)\beta$

2.23 The beta factor (β) can therefore be used to measure the extent to which a portfolio's return (or indeed an individual investment's return) should **exceed** the **risk-free rate of return**. This risk premium will include both a business risk and a financial risk element in it. This equation forms the basis of the **capital asset pricing model (CAPM)**, which we shall look at in the next chapter.

3 PORTFOLIO THEORY AND FINANCIAL MANAGEMENT 5/02

3.1 Our discussion of portfolio theory has concentrated mainly on portfolios of stocks and shares. Investors can reduce their investment risk by diversifying, but what about individual companies choosing a range of businesses or projects to invest in?

Should companies try to diversify?

3.2 You can probably think of examples of large companies today which concentrate mainly on a single industry or product range (for example, British Telecom) and **conglomerates** which are **widely diversified** (for example, the so-called 'guns-to-buns' Tomkins group).

KEY TERM

Conglomerate is an entity comprising a number of dissimilar businesses. *(OT 2000)*

3.3 There are a number of reasons why a company should not try to diversify too far.

(a) A company may employ people with particular skills, and it will get the best out of its employees by allowing them to stick to doing **what they are good at**. A manager with expert knowledge of the electronics business, for example, might not be any good at managing a retailing business.

(b) When companies try to grow, they will often find the **best opportunities** to make extra profits in **industries or markets** with which they are **familiar.**

(c) Conglomerates are vulnerable to takeover bids where the buyer plans to '**unbundle**' the **companies** in the group and **sell them off individually** at a profit. Conglomerate's returns will often be mediocre rather than high, and so the stock market will value the shares on a fairly low P/E ratio, making them vulnerable to acquirers. Separate companies within the group would be valued according to their individual performance and prospects, often at P/E ratios that are much higher than for the conglomerate as a whole.

(d) A company can reduce its business risk by diversifying and **lower business risk** would **protect the company's shareholders**; however, a shareholder does not need the company to reduce investment risk on his behalf. The shareholder can reduce risk himself by diversifying into shares in a range of different companies.

(e) Investors can probably **reduce investment risk more efficiently** than companies. They have a wider range of investment opportunities. Investments with uncorrelated or negatively correlated returns will be easier to identify. Estimates of beta factors will be more reliable for quoted companies' shares than for companies' capital expenditure projects.

Limitations of portfolio analysis for the financial manager

3.4 **Portfolio analysis** offers a way in which the financial manager can deal with risk by diversifying through the investment decisions which are made by the firm. However, portfolio theory applied to the selection of investment proposals has a number of limitations.

(a) In practice, it may require guesswork to **estimate probabilities** of different outcomes, for example when a new product is to be developed. In other cases, such as machine replacement, sufficient information may however be available to make relatively good probability estimates.

(b) It will be difficult in practical cases to know what are **shareholders' preferences** between risk and return and therefore to reflect these preferences in decision-making.

(c) The '**agency problem**' in management's relationship to the company is relevant. Portfolio theory is based on the notion of managers assessing the relevant probabilities and deciding the combination of activities that a business will be involved in. Managers have the security of their jobs to consider, while the shareholder can easily buy and sell securities. It is arguable that managers are as a result more risk-averse than shareholders, and this may distort managers' investment decisions.

(d) Projects may be of such a size that they are not **easy to divide** in accordance with recommended diversification principles.

(e) The theory assumes that there are **constant returns** to scale, in other words that the percentage returns provided by a project are the same however much is invested in it. In practice, there may be economies of scale to be gained from making a larger investment in a single project.

(f) **Other aspects** of risk **not covered** by the theory may need to be considered, eg bankruptcy costs.

Question 2

Which of the following measures the risk premium on a portfolio of investments?

A The correlation coefficient of expected returns
B The beta factor
C A weighted average of expected returns on portfolio investments
D The standard deviation of expected returns

Answer

B The beta factor

Part B: Sources of long-term finance

Chapter roundup

- Both individuals and firms diversify their investments. Individuals have **portfolios of shares** and firms have **portfolios of business operations**.

- **Portfolio theory** takes account of the fact that many investors have a range of investments which are unlikely all to changes values in step. The investor should be concerned with his or her overall position, not with the performance of individual investments.

- **Diversification** is equally an important consideration for the financial manager in making investment decisions. Portfolio theory has limitations in its use by the financial manager, although it provides the basis of the more sophisticated **CAPM** approach to making investment decisions under risk, which we turn to in the next chapter.

Quick quiz

1 Which of the following factors is the least important when choosing investments to include in a portfolio?

   A Security of returns
   B Liquidity of investments
   C Expected returns
   D Geographical location

2 Match each of A, B, C and D to its equivalent: one of 1, 2, 3 or 4.

A	the expected return of a portfolio	1	the correlation coefficient of expected returns
B	the risk of a portfolio	2	the beta factor
C	relationship between returns from different investments	3	a weighted average of expected returns on portfolio investments
D	extent to which return exceeds the risk-free rate of return	4	the standard deviation of expected returns

3 Give an example of a risk-free security.

4 What do the initials 'CAPM' stand for?

5 Which of the following is an argument in favour of diversification by a company?

   A Employees of the company are likely to possess specialised skills.
   B Investors can probably reduce investment risk more efficiently than companies.
   C Conglomerates are vulnerable to takeover bids with the purpose of 'unbundling'.
   D The risk of variable profits may be reduced.

6 Negative correlation is where the performance of the investment is independent of how the other performs.

   True ☐
   False

7 What is the significance of the equation $\dfrac{R_m - R_f}{\sigma_m}$

8 ……………………………… is an entity comprising a number of dissimilar businesses.

Answers to quick quiz

1. D This will only be relevant if it impacts on one of the other primary factors, such as security or the expected level of returns.

2. A3; B4; C1; D2

3. Government stocks are generally considered to be virtually risk-free.

4. Capital asset pricing model

5. D The risk of variable profits may be reduced.

6. False; no correlation is the situation where performance is independent.

7. The equation is the gradient of the capital market line, the extent to which the required returns from a portfolio should exceed the risk-free rate of return.

8. Conglomerate

Now try the question below from the Exam Question Bank

Number	Level	Marks	Time
9	Introductory	n/a	15 mins

Chapter 10

THE CAPITAL ASSET PRICING MODEL

Topic list	Syllabus reference	Ability required
1 Risk and the CAPM	(ii)	Application
2 CAPM and portfolio management	(ii)	Application
3 Practical implications of the CAPM	(ii)	Application

Introduction

The **Capital Asset Pricing Model** (CAPM) brings together aspects of topics already raised in earlier chapters: **portfolio theory**, **share valuations**, the **cost of capital** and **gearing**. You need to be comfortable with using the CAPM equation $k_e = R_f + (R_m - R_f)\beta$, and also to be able to explain how CAPM can be used by investors, and what its limitations are.

Learning outcomes covered in this chapter

- Recommend the sources of capital most appropriate for an organisation
- Calculate the cost of capital and demonstrate the impact of changing capital structures

Syllabus content covered in this chapter

- The calculation of the cost of equity using the capital asset pricing model (CAPM)
- An introduction to the relationship between risk, uncertainty and reward, eg use of CAPM (Beta, R_m and R_f will be given and a simple understanding of the CAPM is all that will be tested. Gearing and ungearing betas will not be tested)
- The ideas of diversifiable risk (unsystematic risk) and systematic risk (use of the two asset portfolio formula will not be tested)

1 RISK AND THE CAPM 11/01

1.1 The uses of the **capital asset pricing model (CAPM)** include:

(a) Trying to **establish** the **'correct' equilibrium market value** of a company's shares

(b) Trying to **establish** the **cost of a company's equity** (and the company's average cost of capital), taking account of the risk characteristics of a company's investments, both business and financial risk

The CAPM thus provides an approach to establishing a cost of equity capital which is an alternative to the dividend valuation model which we looked at earlier.

Systematic risk and unsystematic risk

1.2 Whenever an investor invests in some shares, or a company invests in a new project, there will be some risk involved. The actual return on the investment might be better or worse than that hoped for. To some extent, risk is unavoidable (unless the investor settles for risk-free securities such as gilts). Provided that the investor diversifies his investments in a suitably wide portfolio, the investments which perform well and those which perform badly should tend to cancel each other out, and much risk can be diversified away. In the same way, a company which invests in a number of projects will find that some do well and some do badly, but taking the whole portfolio of investments, average returns should turn out much as expected.

1.3 Risks that can be diversified away are referred to as **unsystematic risk**. But there is another sort of risk too. Some investments are by their very nature more risky than others. This has nothing to do with chance variations up or down in actual returns compared with what an investor should expect. This **inherent risk** - the **systematic risk** or **market risk** - cannot be diversified away (see Figure 1).

> **KEY TERMS**
>
> **Market** or **systematic risk** is risk that cannot be diversified away. **Non-systematic** or **unsystematic risk** applies to a single investment or class of investments, and can be reduced by diversification.
>
> Studies suggest that up to 95% of non-systematic risk can be diversified away by increasing, randomly, the number of shares in the portfolio to between about 25 and 30. Non-systematic risk can be eliminated by holding a portfolio that reflects exactly the composition of the market. *(OT 2000)*

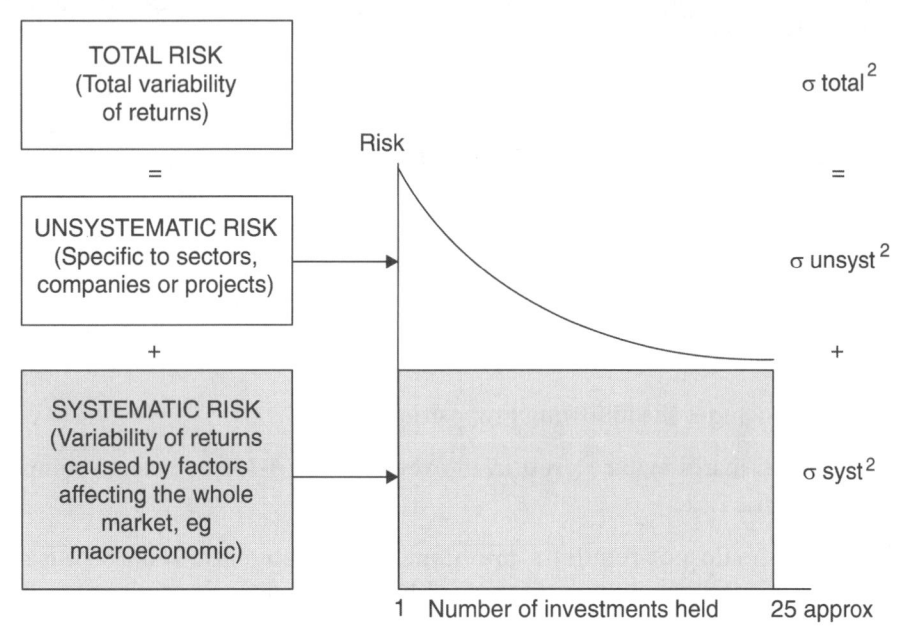

Figure 1

1.4 In return for accepting systematic risk, a **risk-averse investor** will expect to earn a return which is higher than the return on a risk-free investment.

1.5 The amount of systematic risk in an investment varies between different types of investment.

Part B: Sources of long-term finance

Systematic risk and unsystematic risk: implications for investments

1.6 The implications of systematic risk and unsystematic risk are as follows.

(a) If an investor wants to **avoid risk** altogether, he must **invest entirely** in **risk-free securities**.

(b) If an investor **holds shares in just a few companies**, there will be **some unsystematic risk** as well as systematic risk in his portfolio, because he will not have spread his risk enough to diversify away the unsystematic risk. To eliminate unsystematic risk, he must build up a well diversified portfolio of investments.

(c) If an investor holds a **balanced portfolio** of all the stocks and shares on the stock market, he will incur systematic risk which is exactly equal to the average systematic risk in the stock market as a whole.

(d) **Shares in individual companies** will have **different systematic risk characteristics** to this market average. Some shares will be less risky and some will be more risky than the stock market average. Similarly, some investments will be more risky and some will be less risky than a company's 'average' investments.

Systematic risk and the CAPM 5/01

1.7 The capital asset pricing model is mainly concerned with how systematic risk is measured, and how systematic risk affects required returns and share prices. **Systematic risk** is measured using **beta factors**.

> **KEY TERM**
>
> **Beta factor** is the measure of the volatility of the return on a share relative to the market. If a share price were to rise or fall at double the market rate, it would have a beta factor of 2.0. Conversely, if the share price moved at half the market rate, the beta factor would be 0.5.
>
> The beta factor is defined mathematically as a share's covariance with the market portfolio divided by the variance of the market portfolio. *(OT 2000)*

1.8 CAPM theory includes the following propositions.

(a) Investors in shares require a **return** in **excess of the risk-free rate**, to compensate them for systematic risk.

(b) Investors should **not require** a **premium** for **unsystematic risk**, because this can be diversified away by holding a wide portfolio of investments.

(c) Because systematic risk varies between companies, investors will require a **higher return** from shares in those companies where the systematic risk is bigger.

1.9 The same propositions can be applied to capital investments by companies.

(a) Companies will want a **return on a project** to **exceed** the **risk-free rate**, to compensate them for systematic risk.

(b) **Unsystematic risk** can be **diversified away**, and so a premium for unsystematic risk should not be required.

10: The capital asset pricing model

(c) Companies should want a **bigger return** on projects where **systematic risk is greater**.

> **Exam focus point**
>
> Question 4 in November 2001 required candidates to explain the difference between systematic risk (the risk that is correlated with market returns and cannot be diversified away) and unsystematic risk (the risk of a project that can be diversified).

Market risk and returns

1.10 Market risk (systematic risk) is the average risk of the market as a whole. Taking all the shares on a stock market together, the total expected returns from the market will vary because of systematic risk. The market as a whole might do well or it might do badly.

Risk and returns from an individual security

1.11 In the same way, an individual security may offer prospects of a return of x%, but with some risk (business risk and financial risk) attached. The return (the x%) that investors will require from the individual security will be higher or lower than the market return, depending on whether the security's systematic risk is greater or less than the market average. A major **assumption in CAPM** is that there is a linear relationship between the return obtained from an individual security and the average return from all securities in the market.

1.12 EXAMPLE: CAPM (1)

The following information is available about the performance of an individual company's shares and the stock market as a whole.

	Individual company	Stock market as a whole
Price at start of period	105.0	480.0
Price at end of period	110.0	490.0
Dividend during period	7.6	39.2

1.13 The expected return on the company's shares R_j and the expected return on the 'market portfolio' of shares R_m may be calculated as:

$$\frac{\text{Capital gain (or loss)} + \text{dividend}}{\text{Price at start of period}}$$

$$R_j = \frac{(110-105)+7.6}{105} = 0.12 \qquad R_m = \frac{(490-480)+39.2}{480} = 0.1025$$

1.14 A statistical analysis of 'historic' returns from a security and from the 'average' market may suggest that a linear relationship can be assumed to exist between them. A series of comparative figures could be prepared (month by month) of the return from a company's shares and the average return of the market as a whole. The results could be drawn on a scattergraph and a 'line of best fit' drawn (using linear regression techniques) as shown in Figure 1.

Part B: Sources of long-term finance

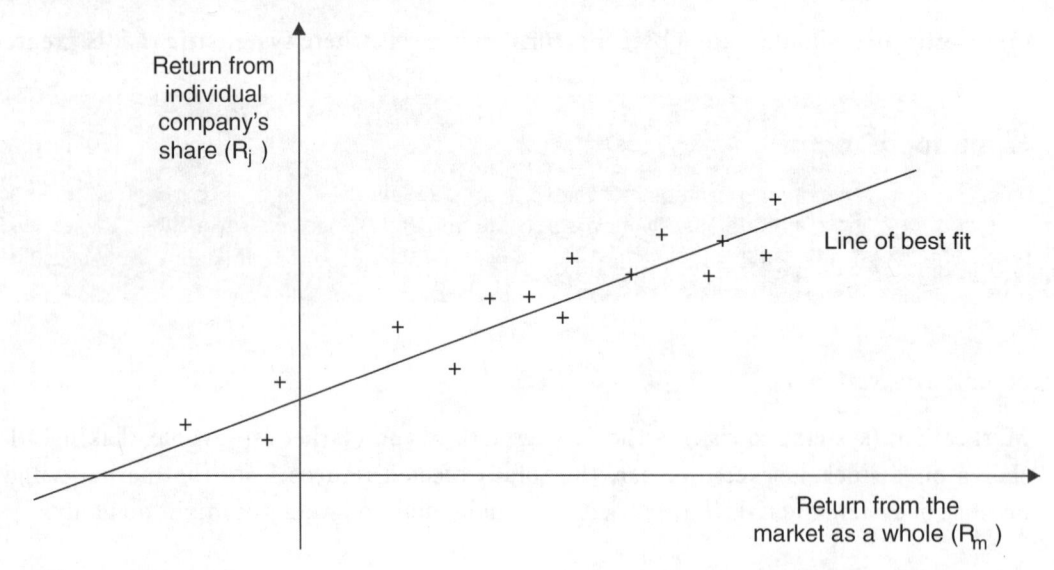

Figure 1

1.15 This analysis would show three things.

(a) The **return from** the **security** and the **return from** the **market as** a whole **will tend to rise or fall together**.

(b) The **return from the security** may be **higher or lower** than the **market return**. This is because the systematic risk of the individual security differs from that of the market as a whole.

(c) The scattergraph may **not give** a **good line of best fit**, unless a large number of data items are plotted, because actual returns are affected by unsystematic risk as well as by systematic risk.

Note that returns can be negative. A share price fall represents a capital loss, which is a negative return.

1.16 The conclusion from this analysis is that individual securities will be either more or less risky than the market average in a fairly predictable way. The measure of this relationship between market returns and an individual security's returns, reflecting differences in systematic risk characteristics, can be developed into a beta factor for the individual security.

The beta factor and the market risk premium

> **KEY TERM**
>
> **Market risk premium** is the extra return required from a share to compensate for its risk compared with the average risk of the market. *(OT 2000)*

1.17 Suppose that returns on shares in XYZ plc tend to vary twice as much as returns from the market as a whole, so that if market returns went up 3%, say, returns on XYZ plc shares would be expected to go up by 6% and if market returns fell by 3%, returns on XYZ plc shares would be expected to fall by 6%. The beta factor of XYZ plc shares would be 2.0.

1.18 Thus if the average market return rises by, say, 2%, the return from a share with a beta factor of 0.8 should rise by 1.6% in response to the **same conditions** which have caused the

10: The capital asset pricing model

market return to change. The **actual return** from the share might rise by, say, 2.5%, or even fall by, say, 1%, but the difference between the actual change and a change of 1.6% due to general market factors would be attributed to unsystematic risk factors unique to the company or its industry.

1.19 It is an essential principle of CAPM theory that **unsystematic** risk can be **cancelled** out by diversification.

Excess returns over returns on risk-free investments

1.20 The CAPM also makes use of the principle that **returns on shares** in the **market** as a whole are expected to be higher than the returns on risk-free investments. The difference between market returns and risk-free returns is called an **excess return**. For example, if the return on British Government stocks is 9% and market returns are 13%, the **excess** return on the market's shares as a whole is 4%.

1.21 The difference between the risk-free return and the expected return on an individual security can be measured as the **excess return for the market as a whole multiplied** by **the security's beta factor.**

The CAPM formula 5/01

1.22 The capital asset pricing model is a statement of the principles explained above. It can be stated as follows.

> **EXAM FORMULA**
>
> $k_e = R_f + (R_m - R_f)\beta$
>
> where k_e is the cost of equity capital – expected equity return
> R_f is the risk-free rate of return
> R_m is the return from the market as a whole
> β is the beta factor of the individual security

> **KEY TERMS**
>
> **Capital asset pricing model (CAPM)** is a theory which predicts that the expected risk premium for an individual stock will be proportional to its beta, such that:
>
> Expected risk premium on a stock = beta × expected risk premium in the market.
>
> **Risk premium** is defined as the expected incremental return for making a risky investment rather than a safe one. *(OT 2000)*

> **Exam focus point**
>
> In the *Finance* exam, the beta factor, the risk-free rate of return and the market rate of return will be given in any question. Only a basic understanding of the CAPM will be required.

Part B: Sources of long-term finance

Question 1

The risk-free rate of return is 7%. The average market return is 11%.

(a) What will be the return expected from a share whose β factor is 0.9?

(b) What would be the share's expected value if it is expected to earn an annual dividend of 5.3p, with no capital growth?

Answer

(a) $7\% + (11\% - 7\%) \times 0.9 = 10.6\%$

(b) $\dfrac{5.3p}{10.6\%} = 50$ pence

2 CAPM AND PORTFOLIO MANAGEMENT 5/02

2.1 Just as an individual security has a beta factor, so too does a portfolio of securities.

(a) A **portfolio** consisting of **all the securities** on the stock market (in the same proportions as the market as a whole), **excluding risk-free securities,** will have an expected return equal to the expected return for the market as a whole, and so will have a **beta factor of 1**.

(b) A portfolio consisting entirely of **risk-free securities** will have a **beta factor of 0**.

(c) The **beta factor** of an **investor's portfolio** is the **weighted average** of the **beta factors** of the **securities in the portfolio**.

2.2 EXAMPLE: CAPM

A portfolio consisting of five securities could have its beta factor computed as follows.

Security	Percentage of portfolio	Beta factor of security	Weighted beta factor
A plc	20%	0.90	0.180
B plc	10%	1.25	0.125
C plc	15%	1.10	0.165
D plc	20%	1.15	0.230
E plc	35%	0.70	0.245
	100%	Portfolio beta =	0.945

2.3 If the risk-free rate of return is 12% and the average market return is 20%, the expected return from the portfolio would be $12\% + (20 - 12) \times 0.945\% = 19.56\%$

2.4 The calculation could have been made as follows.

Security	Beta factor	Expected return $E(r_j)$	Weighting %	Weighted return
A plc	0.90	19.2	20	3.84
B plc	1.25	22.0	10	2.20
C plc	1.10	20.8	15	3.12
D plc	1.15	21.2	20	4.24
E plc	0.70	17.6	35	6.16
			100	19.56

Question 2

(a) What does beta measure, and what do betas of 0.5, 1 and 1.5 mean?
(b) What factors determine the level of beta which a company may have?

Answer

(a) **Beta measures** the systematic risk of a risky investment such as a share in a company. The total risk of the share can be sub-divided into two parts, known as systematic (or market) risk and unsystematic (or unique) risk. The systematic risk depends on the sensitivity of the return of the share to general economic and market factors such as periods of boom and recession. The capital asset pricing model shows how the return which investors expect from shares should depend only on systematic risk, not on unsystematic risk, which can be eliminated by holding a well-diversified portfolio.

Beta is calibrated such that the average risk of stock market investments has a beta of 1. Thus shares with betas of 0.5 or 1.5 would have half or 1½ times the average sensitivity to market variations respectively.

This is reflected by higher volatility of share prices for shares with a beta of 1.5 than for those with a beta of 0.5. For example, a 10% increase in general stock market prices would be expected to be reflected as a 5% increase for a share with a beta of 0.5 and a 15% increase for a share with a beta of 1.5, with a similar effect for price reductions.

(b) The beta of a company will be the **weighted average** of the beta of its shares and the beta of its debt. The beta of debt is very low, but not zero, because corporate debt bears default risk, which in turn is dependent on the volatility of the company's cash flows.

Factors determining the beta of a company's equity shares include:

(i) **Sensitivity** of the company's **cash flows** to economic factors, as stated above. For example sales of new cars are more sensitive than sales of basic foods and necessities.

(ii) The company's **operating gearing**. A high level of fixed costs in the company's cost structure will cause high variations in operating profit compared with variations in sales.

(iii) The company's **financial gearing**. High borrowing and interest costs will cause high variations in equity earnings compared with variations in operating profit. This effect will, of course, be cancelled out by the low beta of debt when computing the weighted average beta of the whole company.

3 PRACTICAL IMPLICATIONS OF THE CAPM   5/01, 5/02

3.1 Practical implications of CAPM theory for an investor are as follows.

(a) He should decide what **beta factor** he would like to have for his portfolio. He might prefer a portfolio beta factor of greater than 1, in order to expect above-average returns when market returns exceed the risk-free rate, but he would then expect to lose heavily if market returns fall. On the other hand, he might prefer a portfolio beta factor of 1 or even less.

(b) He should seek to invest in shares with **low beta factors** in a bear market, when **average market returns** are **falling**. He should then also sell shares with high beta factors.

(c) He should seek to **invest in shares** with **high beta factors** in a **bull market**, when average market returns are rising.

An investor can measure the beta factor of his portfolio by obtaining information about the beta factors of individual securities. These are obtainable from a variety of investment analysts, or from the London Business School's Risk Management Service.

Part B: Sources of long-term finance

> **Exam focus point**
>
> Question 3 of the May 2002 paper combined calculations using CAPM with discussions about investment policy and marketable securities.

Limitations of the CAPM for the selection of a portfolio of securities

3.2 Under the CAPM, the return required from a security is related to its systematic risk rather than its total risk. If we relax some of the assumptions upon which the model is based, as follows, then the **total risk** may be important.

(a) The model assumes that the costs of insolvency are zero, or in other words, that all assets can be sold at going concern prices. In practice, the costs of insolvency cannot be ignored. Furthermore, the risk of insolvency is related to a firm's total risk rather than just its systematic risk.

(b) The model assumes that the investment market is efficient. If it is not, this will limit the extent to which investors are able to eliminate unsystematic risk.

(c) The model also assumes that portfolios are well diversified and so need only be concerned with systematic risk. However, this is not necessarily the case, and undiversified or partly diversified shareholders should also be concerned with unsystematic risk.

3.3 **Sources of difficulty in applying the CAPM in practice**

(a) The need to **determine** the **excess return** ($R_m - R_f$). Expected, rather than historical, returns should be used, although historical returns are used in practice.

(b) The need to **determine** the **risk-free rate**. A risk-free investment might be a government security. However, interest rates vary with the term of the lending.

(c) **Errors** in the **statistical analysis used** to calculate β values. Betas may also change over time.

(d) The CAPM is also unable to forecast accurately returns for companies with low price/earnings ratios and to take account of seasonal 'month-of-the-year' effects and 'day-of-the-week' effects that appear to influence returns on shares.

Question 3

In the graph below, what does area 'a' represent?

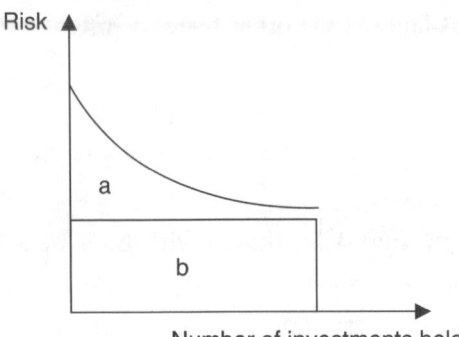

```
Risk ▲
     │
     │╲
     │ ╲
     │  ╲ a
     │   ╲_____
     │   │           │
     │   │     b     │
     │   │           │
     └───┴───────────┴──►
           Number of investments held
```

A   Total risk
B   Unsystematic risk
C   Systematic risk
D   Inherent risk

Answer

B Unsystematic risk

> **Chapter roundup**
>
> - The **capital asset pricing model** has many applications. However, you should not think of it as the only approach to the cost of equity, or to project appraisal. You should learn the formulae, not only to be able to use them but also to be able to criticise the CAPM.
>
> - The **risk** involved in holding securities (shares) divides into risk **specific** to the company and risk due to **variations in market activity**.
>
> - **Unsystematic or business risk** can be diversified away, while **systematic or market risk** cannot. Investors may mix a diversified market portfolio with risk-free assets to achieve a preferred mix of risk and return.

Quick quiz

1   Which of the following risks can be eliminated by diversification?

   A Inherent risk
   B Systematic risk
   C Market risk
   D Unsystematic risk

2   Systematic risk is the risk arising from variability in returns caused by factors affecting the whole market.

   True ☐
   False ☐

3   An investor can virtually eliminate unsystematic risk by building up a well diversified portfolio of investments.

   True ☐
   False ☐

4   Unsystematic risk is measured by beta factors.

   True ☐
   False ☐

5   A portfolio consisting entirely of risk-free securities will have a beta factor of (tick one box):

   −1 ☐
   0 ☐
   1 ☐

6   If k_e = cost of equity capital
       R_f = risk-free rate of return
       R_m = return from the market as a whole
       β = beta factor of the individual security

   What is the correct formula for the capital asset pricing model?

   A $k_e = R_f + (R_m - R_f)\beta$
   B $k_e = R_f - (R_m - R_f)\beta$
   C $k_e = R_m + (R_m - R_f)\beta$
   D $k_e = R_m - (R_m - R_f)\beta$

7   The risk free rate of return is 8%. Average market return is 14%. A share's beta factor is 0.5. What will be its expected return?

Part B: Sources of long-term finance

8   An investor should seek to invest in shares with a high beta factor in a bull market.

   True ☐
   False ☐

Answers to quick quiz

1   D   This is risk that is specific to sectors, companies or projects. Systematic risk (also known as inherent risk or market risk) affects the whole market and therefore cannot be reduced by diversification.

2   True

3   True

4   False. Beta factors measure systematic risk.

5   Zero

6   A $k_e = R_f + [R_m - R_f]\beta$

7   Expected return = $8 + (14 - 8)0.5 = 11\%$

8   True

Now try the question below from the Exam Question Bank

Number	Level	Marks	Time
10	Examination	20	36 mins

Mind map: Risk and the CAPM

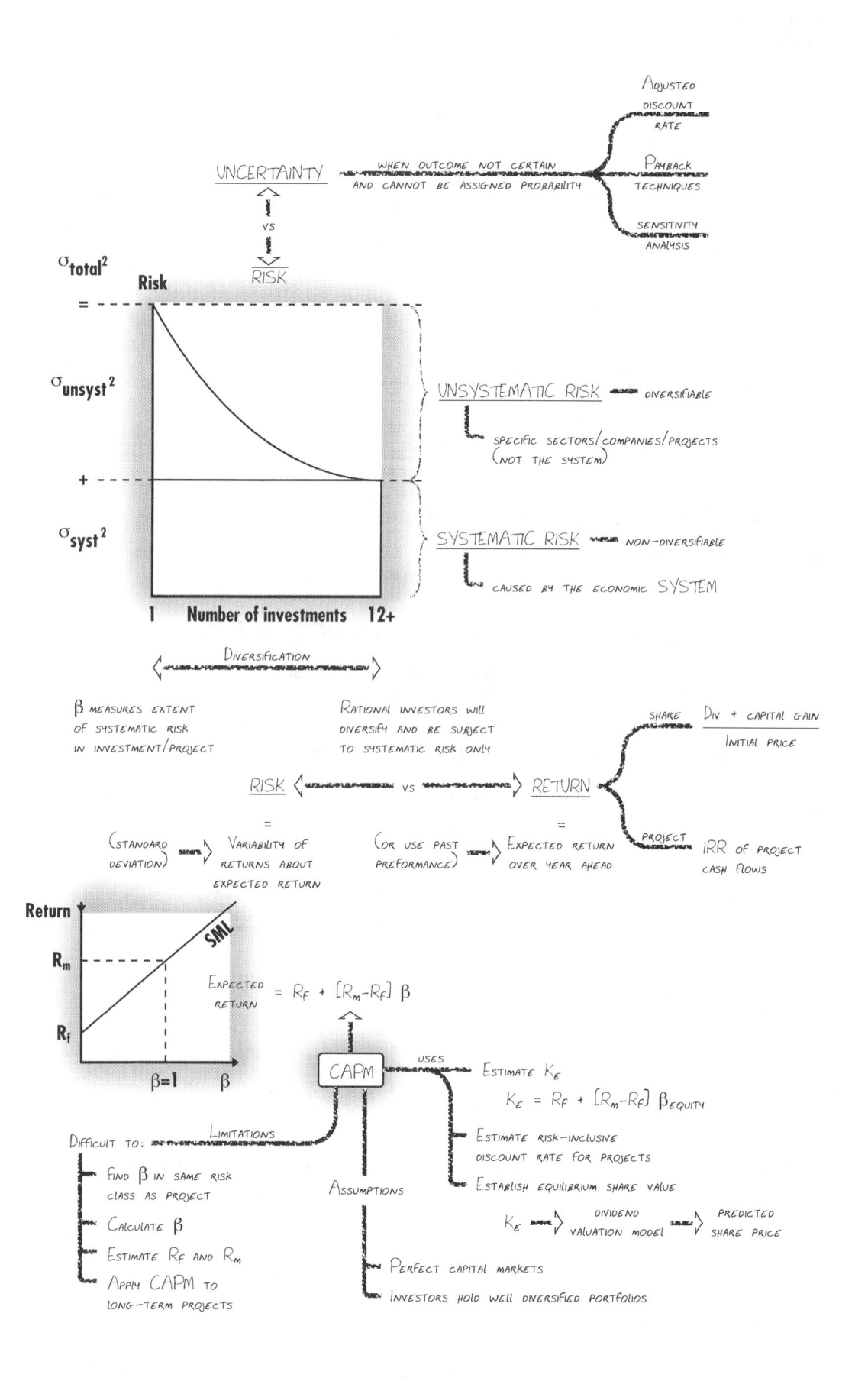

UNCERTAINTY — WHEN OUTCOME NOT CERTAIN AND CANNOT BE ASSIGNED PROBABILITY
- Adjusted discount rate
- Payback techniques
- Sensitivity analysis

vs

RISK

σ_{total}^2 = σ_{unsyst}^2 + σ_{syst}^2

Risk (graph: Number of investments 1 to 12+)

Diversification

UNSYSTEMATIC RISK — diversifiable
 — specific sectors/companies/projects (not the system)

SYSTEMATIC RISK — non-diversifiable
 — caused by the economic SYSTEM

β measures extent of systematic risk in investment/project

Rational investors will diversify and be subject to systematic risk only

RISK vs RETURN

RISK = (standard deviation) → Variability of returns about expected return

RETURN = (or use past performance) → Expected return over year ahead
- SHARE: $\dfrac{\text{Div + capital gain}}{\text{Initial price}}$
- PROJECT: IRR of project cash flows

SML graph: Return vs β, showing R_f, R_m at $\beta = 1$

Expected return = $R_f + [R_m - R_f]\beta$

CAPM

Uses:
- Estimate K_E: $K_E = R_f + [R_m - R_f]\beta_{EQUITY}$
- Estimate risk-inclusive discount rate for projects
- Establish equilibrium share value: K_E → dividend valuation model → predicted share price

Limitations — Difficult to:
- Find β in same risk class as project
- Calculate β
- Estimate R_f and R_m
- Apply CAPM to long-term projects

Assumptions:
- Perfect capital markets
- Investors hold well diversified portfolios

Chapter 11

INVESTOR RATIOS

Topic list	Syllabus reference	Ability required
1 Stock market ratios	(ii), (iii)	Application
2 Gearing ratios	(ii)	Application

Introduction

In this chapter, we are concerned with measures by which investors may assess their investment, and at how the mix of debt and equity in a business – its **gearing** – may be measured.

You will need to carry out ratio calculations in MCQs, but you also have to understand what each ratio **shows** and what might cause the different ratios to **change**.

Learning outcomes covered in this chapter

- Calculate investor ratios and demonstrate the impact of changing capital structures on these ratios

Syllabus content covered in this chapter

- Investor ratios, ie EPS, price/earnings (P/E) ratio, dividend cover, dividend yield, interest yield, earnings yield, redemption yield
- Gearing ratios (market and book values) and interest cover
- The difference between the coupon on debt and the yield to maturity

1 STOCK MARKET RATIOS   11/01

1.1 A company will only be able to raise finance if investors think that the returns they can expect are satisfactory in view of the risks they are taking. We must therefore consider how investors appraise companies. We will concentrate on quoted companies.

1.2 Information that is relevant to market prices and returns is available from published stock market information, and in particular from certain **stock market ratios**. Key stock market ratios are the **dividend yield, interest yield, earnings per share**, the **price/earnings ratio** and the **dividend cover**. The **redemption yield**, also mentioned in the syllabus, is covered in Chapter 13.

1.3 The first term to consider is **dividend per share**.

KEY TERM

Dividend per share is the total amount declared as dividends per share. The dividend per share actually paid in respect of a financial year *(OT 2000)*

The dividend yield

KEY TERM

$$\text{Dividend yield} = \frac{\text{Gross dividend per share}}{\text{Market price per share}} \times 100\%$$

1.4 The gross dividend is the dividend paid plus the appropriate tax credit. The (net) dividend yield (using the dividend per share net of taxes deducted at source) can also be used. The reason for preferring the (gross) dividend yield to the (net) dividend yield is so that investors can make a direct comparison with (gross) **interest yields** from loan stock and gilts.

1.5 EXAMPLE: DIVIDEND YIELD

A company pays a dividend of 15p (net) per share. The market price is 240p. What is the dividend yield if the rate of tax credit is 10%?

$$\text{Gross dividend per share} = 15p \times \frac{100}{(100-10)} = 16.67p$$

$$\text{Dividend yield} = \frac{16.67p}{240p} \times 100\% = 6.95\%$$

Interest yield

KEY TERM

$$\text{Interest yield} = \frac{\text{Gross interest}}{\text{Market value of loan stock}} \times 100\%$$

1.6 EXAMPLE: INTEREST YIELD

An investment buys £1,000 (nominal value) of a bond with a **coupon** of 8% for the current market value of £750.

$$\text{Interest yield} = \frac{1{,}000 \times 8\%}{750} \times 100\% = 10.67\%$$

Exam focus point

Note carefully that the interest yield, which is the investor's rate of return, is different from the coupon rate of 8%. Many students confuse these in their exam answers.

Part B: Sources of long-term finance

1.7 In practice, we usually find with quoted companies that the dividend yield on shares is less than the interest yield on debentures and loan stock (and also less than the yield paid on gilt-edged securities). The share price often rises each year, giving shareholders capital gains. In the long run, shareholders will want the return on their shares, in terms of dividends received plus capital gains, to exceed the return that investors get from fixed interest securities.

Earnings yield

1.8 The earnings yield is an alternative measure to the interest yield.

> **KEY TERM**
>
> $$\text{Earnings yield} = \frac{\text{EPS}}{\text{Market price of share}} \times 100\%$$
>
> *(OT 2000)*

1.9 This indicates as a percentage the total earnings in respect of each equity share, in relation to its market price.

1.10 Alternatively the earnings yield computation can be based on the aggregate earnings and the market value of the equity capital.

Earnings per share (EPS)

> **KEY TERM**
>
> **Basic earnings per share** should be calculated by dividing the net profit or loss for the period attributable to ordinary shareholders by the weighted average number of ordinary shares outstanding during the period.

1.11 **Earnings per share (EPS)** is widely used as a measure of a company's performance and is of particular importance in comparing results over a period of several years. A company must be able to sustain its earnings in order to pay dividends and re-invest in the business so as to achieve future growth. Investors also look for **growth** in the EPS from one year to the next.

Question 1

Walter Wall Carpets plc made profits before tax in 20X8 of £9,320,000. Tax amounted to £2,800,000.

The company's share capital is as follows.

	£
Ordinary shares (10,000,000 shares of £1)	10,000,000
8% preference shares	2,000,000
	12,000,000

Calculate the EPS for 20X8.

Answer

	£
Profits before tax	9,320,000
Less tax	2,800,000
Profits after tax	6,520,000
Less preference dividend (8% of £2,000,000)	160,000
Earnings	6,360,000
Number of ordinary shares	10,000,000
EPS	63.6p

1.12 EPS on its own does not tell us anything. It must be seen in the context of several other matters.

(a) EPS is used for **comparing results** of a company over time. Is its EPS growing? What is the rate of growth? Is the rate of growth increasing or decreasing?

(b) Is there likely to be a **significant dilution of EPS** in the **future**, perhaps due to the exercise of share options or warrants, or the conversion of convertible loan stock into equity?

(c) EPS should not be **used blindly** to compare the earnings of one company with another. For example, if A plc has an EPS of 12p for its 10,000,000 10p shares and B plc has an EPS of 24p for its 50,000,000 25p shares, we must take account of the numbers of shares. When earnings are used to compare one company's shares with another, this is done using the P/E ratio or perhaps the earnings yield.

(d) If EPS is to be a reliable basis for comparing results, it must be **calculated consistently**. The EPS of one company must be directly comparable with the EPS of others, and the EPS of a company in one year must be directly comparable with its published EPS figures for previous years. Changes in the share capital of a company during the course of a year cause problems of comparability.

1.13 Note the following points.

(a) EPS is a figure **based** on **past data**.

(b) It is easily **manipulated** by **changes** in **accounting policies** and by mergers or acquisitions.

The price earnings ratio

1.14 The **price earnings (P/E) ratio** is the most important yardstick for assessing the relative worth of a share.

> **KEY TERM**
>
> Price earnings (P/E) ratio = $\dfrac{\text{Market price per share}}{\text{Earnings per share}}$

This is the same as:

$$\frac{\text{Total market value of equity}}{\text{Total earnings}}$$

1.15 This is of course the reciprocal of the earnings yield.

1.16 The **value of the P/E ratio** reflects the market's appraisal of the share's future prospects. It is an important ratio because it relates two key considerations for investors, the **market price** of a **share** and its **earnings capacity**.

1.17 EXAMPLE: PRICE EARNINGS RATIO

A company has recently declared a dividend of 12p per share. The share price is £3.72 cum div and earnings for the most recent year were 30p per share. Calculate the P/E ratio.

1.18 SOLUTION

$$\text{P/E ratio} = \frac{\text{MV ex div}}{\text{EPS}} = \frac{£3.60}{30p} = 12$$

Changes in EPS: the P/E ratio and the share price

1.19 The P/E ratio approach is based on the following ideas.

(a) The **relationship** between the **EPS** and **the share price is measured** by the **P/E ratio**.

(b) The P/E ratio does **not vary much** over time **normally**.

(c) So if the EPS goes up or down, the share price should be expected to move up or down too, and the new share price will be the new EPS multiplied by the constant P/E ratio.

1.20 For example, if a company had an EPS last year of 30p and a share price of £3.60, its P/E ratio would have been 12. If the current year's EPS is 33p, we might expect that the P/E ratio would remain the same, 12, and so the share price ought to go up to 12 × 33p = £3.96.

1.21 EXAMPLE: EFFECTS OF A RIGHTS ISSUE

Annette Cord Sports Goods plc has 6,000,000 ordinary shares in issue, and the company has been making regular annual profits after tax of £3,000,000 for some years. The share price is £5. A proposal has been made to issue 2,000,000 new shares in a rights issue, at an issue price of £4.50 per share. The funds would be used to redeem £9,000,000 of 12% debenture stock. The rate of corporation tax is 30%.

What would be the predicted effect of the rights issue on the share price, and would you recommend that the issue should take place?

1.22 SOLUTION

If the stock market shows semi-strong form efficiency, the share price will change on announcement of the rights issue, in anticipation of the change in EPS. The current EPS is 50p per share, and so the current P/E ratio is 10.

	£	£
Current annual earnings		3,000,000
Increase in earnings after rights issue		
Interest saved (12% × £9,000,000)	1,080,000	
Less tax on extra profits (30%)	324,000	
		756,000
Anticipated annual earnings		3,756,000
Number of shares (6,000,000 + 2,000,000)		8,000,000
EPS		46.95 pence
Current P/E ratio		10

The anticipated P/E ratio is assumed to be the same.

Anticipated share price 469.5 pence

The proposed share issue is a one for three rights issue, and we can estimate the theoretical ex rights price.

	£
Current value of three shares (× £5)	15.00
Rights issue price of one share	4.50
Theoretical value of four shares	19.50

Theoretical ex rights price $\dfrac{£19.50}{4} = £4.875$

1.23 The anticipated share price after redeeming the debentures would be 469.5 pence per share, which is less than the theoretical ex rights price. If the rights issue goes ahead and the P/E ratio remains at 10, shareholders should expect a fall in share price below the theoretical ex rights price, which indicates that there would be a capital loss on their investment. The rights issue is for this reason not recommended.

Changes in the P/E ratio over time

1.24 Changes in the P/E ratios of companies over time will depend on several factors.

(a) If **interest rates rise**, investors will be attracted **away from shares** and into debt capital. Share prices will fall, and so P/E ratios will fall. The contrary applies if interest rates fall.

(b) If **prospects** for company **profits improve**, share prices will go up, and P/E ratios will rise.

(c) **Investors' confidence might alter**.

Dividend cover

1.25 The **dividend cover** is the number of times the actual dividend could be paid out of current profits.

> **KEY TERM**
>
> Dividend cover = $\dfrac{\text{Earnings per share}}{\text{Dividend per share}}$

1.26 The dividend cover indicates the proportion of **distributable profits** for the year that is being retained by the company, and the level of risk that the company will not be able to maintain the same dividend payments in future years, should earnings fall. A high dividend cover means that a high proportion of profits are being retained, which might indicate that the company is investing to achieve earnings growth in the future.

Dividend payout ratio

1.27 The **dividend payout ratio** is closely related to the dividend cover, as it calculates the percentage of post-tax earnings that are distributed as dividends.

Part B: Sources of long-term finance

> **KEY TERM**
>
> $$\text{Dividend payout ratio} = \frac{\text{Ordinary dividends for the year}}{\text{Earnings attributable to ordinary shareholders}}$$

1.28 EXAMPLE: DIVIDEND COVER AND DIVIDEND PAYOUT RATIO

The EPS of York plc is 20p. The dividend was 20% on the 25p ordinary shares. Calculate the dividend cover and the dividend payout ratio.

1.29 SOLUTION

$$\text{Dividend cover} = \frac{20p}{20\% \text{ of } 25p} = 4$$

A dividend cover of 4 means that the company is retaining 75% of its earnings for reinvestment.

$$\text{Dividend payout ratio} = \frac{20\% \text{ of } 25p}{20p} = 0.25$$

2 GEARING RATIOS

Pilot paper, 5/01

Principles of capital structure

2.1 The assets of a business must be financed somehow, and when a business is growing, the additional assets must be financed by additional capital. As we have seen **capital structure** refers to the way in which an organisation is **financed**, by a combination of long-term capital (ordinary shares and reserves, preference shares, debentures, bank loans, convertible loan stock and so on) and short-term liabilities, such as a bank overdraft and trade creditors.

The appraisal of capital structures

2.2 We discussed in chapter 6 that a high level of debt creates financial risk. The financial risk of a company's capital structure can be measured by a **gearing ratio**, a **debt ratio** or **debt/equity ratio** and by the **interest cover**. A gearing ratio should not be given without stating how it has been defined.

> **Exam focus point**
>
> You need to be able to explain *and calculate* the level of financial gearing using alternative measures.

Debt ratios

2.3 Debt ratios are concerned with how much the company owes in relation to its size and whether it is getting into heavier debt or improving its situation.

(a) When a company is heavily in debt, and seems to be getting even more heavily into debt, banks and other would-be lenders are very soon likely to **refuse further borrowing** and the company might well find itself in trouble.

(b) When a company is earning only a modest profit before interest and tax, and has a **heavy debt burden**, there will be **very little profit** left over for **shareholders** after the interest charges have been paid. And so if interest rates were to go up or the company were to borrow even more, it might soon be incurring interest charges in excess of PBIT. This might eventually lead to the liquidation of the company.

Financial gearing

2.4 **Financial gearing** measures the relationship between shareholders' capital plus reserves, and either prior charge capital or borrowings or both.

> **KEY TERM**
>
> **Financial leverage/gearing** is the use of debt finance to increase the return on equity by deploying borrowed funds in such a way that the return generated is greater than the cost of servicing the debt. If the reverse is true, and the return on deployed funds is less than the cost of servicing the debt, the effect of gearing is to reduce the return on equity.
> *(OT 2000)*

2.5 Gearing measures the relationships between shareholders' capital plus reserves, and either prior charge capital or borrowings or both.

> **KEY TERM**
>
> **Prior charge capital** is capital which has a right to the receipt of interest or of preference dividends in precedence to any claim on distributable earnings on the part of the ordinary shareholders. On winding up, the claims of holders of prior charge capital also rank before those of ordinary shareholders. *(OT 2000)*

2.6 Prior charge capital consists of:

   (a) Any preference share capital

   (b) Interest-bearing long-term capital

   (c) Interest-bearing short-term debt capital with less than 12 months to maturity, including any bank overdraft

   However, (c) might be excluded.

2.7 Commonly used measures of financial gearing are based on the **balance sheet values** (**book values**) of the fixed interest and equity capital. They include:

$$\frac{\text{Prior charge capital}}{\text{Equity capital (including reserves)}}$$

$$\frac{\text{Prior charge capital}}{\text{Equity plus prior charge capital}}$$

and $\quad\dfrac{\text{Prior charge capital}}{\text{Total capital employed}^*}$

* Either including or excluding minority interests, deferred tax and deferred income.

Part B: Sources of long-term finance

2.8 With the first definition above, a company is low geared if the gearing ratio is less than 100%, highly geared if the ratio is over 100% and neutrally geared if it is exactly 100%. With the second definition, a company is neutrally geared if the ratio is 50%, low geared below that, and highly geared above that.

Question 2

From the following balance sheet, compute the company's financial gearing ratio.

	£'000	£'000	£'000
Fixed assets			12,400
Current assets		1,000	
Creditors: amounts falling due within one year			
Loans	120		
Bank overdraft	260		
Trade creditors	430		
Bills of exchange	70		
		880	
Net current assets			120
Total assets less current liabilities			12,520
Creditors: amounts falling due after more than one year			
Debentures		4,700	
Bank loans		500	
			(5,200)
Provisions for liabilities and charges: deferred taxation			(300)
Deferred income			(250)
			6,770

	£'000
Capital and reserves	
Called up share capital	
Ordinary shares	1,500
Preference shares	500
	2,000
Share premium account	760
Revaluation reserve	1,200
Profit and loss account	2,810
	6,770

Answer

	£'000
Prior charge capital	
Preference shares	500
Debentures	4,700
Long-term bank loans	500
Prior charge capital, ignoring short-term debt	5,700
Short-term loans	120
Overdraft	260
Prior charge capital, including short-term interest bearing debt	6,080

Either figure, £6,080,000 or £5,700,000, could be used. If gearing is calculated with capital employed in the denominator, and capital employed is net fixed assets plus **net** current assets, it would seem more reasonable to exclude short-term interest bearing debt from prior charge capital. This is because short-term debt is set off against current assets in arriving at the figure for net current assets.

Equity = 1,500 + 760 + 1,200 + 2,810 = £6,270,000

The gearing ratio can be calculated in any of the following ways.

(a) $\dfrac{\text{Prior charge capital including short-term debt}}{\text{Equity}} \times 100\% = \dfrac{6,080}{6,270} \times 100\% = 97\%$

(b) $\dfrac{\text{Prior charge capital including short-term debt}}{\text{Equity plus prior charge capital}} \times 100\% = \dfrac{6,080}{(6,080 + 6,270)} \times 100\% = 49.2\%$

(c) $\dfrac{\text{Prior charge capital excluding short-term debt}}{\text{Total capital employed (total assets less current liabilities)}} \times 100\% = \dfrac{5{,}700}{12{,}520} \times 100\% = 45.5\%$

Gearing ratios based on market values

2.9 An alternative method of calculating a gearing ratio is one based on **market values**.

$$\dfrac{\text{Market value of debt (including preference shares)}}{\text{Market value of equity} + \text{Market value of debt}}$$

2.10 The advantage of this method is that potential investors in a company are able to judge the further debt capacity of the company more clearly by reference to **market values** than they could by looking at balance sheet values.

2.11 The disadvantage of a gearing ratio based on market values of debt and equity is that it disregards the value of the company's assets, which might be used to secure further loans. A gearing ratio based on balance sheet values arguably gives a better indication of the security for lenders of fixed interest capital.

2.12 Capital gearing is concerned with a company's **long-term capital structure**. As with the debt ratio, there is no absolute limit to what a **gearing ratio** ought to be. Many companies are highly geared, but if a highly geared company is increasing its gearing, it is likely to have difficulty in the future when it wants to borrow even more, unless it can also boost its shareholders' capital, either with retained profits or with a new share issue.

The effect of gearing on earnings

2.13 The level of gearing has a considerable effect on the earnings attributable to the ordinary shareholders. A highly geared company must earn enough profits **to cover its interest charges** before anything is available for equity. On the other hand, if borrowed funds are invested in projects which provide returns in excess of the cost of debt capital, then shareholders will enjoy increased returns on their equity.

2.14 Gearing, however, also increases the probability of **financial failure** occurring through a company's inability to meet interest payments in poor trading circumstances.

2.15 EXAMPLE: GEARING

Suppose that two companies are identical in every respect except for their gearing. Both have assets of £20,000 and both make the same operating profits (profit before interest and tax: PBIT). The only difference between the two companies is that Nonlever Ltd is all-equity financed and Lever Ltd is partly financed by debt capital, as follows.

	Nonlever Ltd £	Lever Ltd £
Assets	20,000	20,000
10% Loan stock	0	(10,000)
	20,000	10,000
Ordinary shares of £1	20,000	10,000

Because Lever Ltd has £10,000 of 10% loan stock it must make a profit before interest of at least £1,000 in order to pay the interest charges. Nonlever Ltd, on the other hand, does not have any minimum PBIT requirement because it has no debt capital. A company, which is lower geared, is considered less risky than a higher geared company because of the greater

Part B: Sources of long-term finance

likelihood that its PBIT will be high enough to cover interest charges and make a profit for equity shareholders.

Operating gearing

2.16 Financial risk, as we have seen, can be measured by financial gearing. **Business risk** refers to the risk of making only low profits, or even losses, due to the nature of the business that the company is involved in. One way of measuring business risk is by calculating a company's **operating gearing** or 'operational gearing'.

> **KEY TERM**
>
> Operating gearing or leverage = $\dfrac{\text{Contribution}}{\text{Profit before interest and tax (PBIT)}}$
>
> Contribution is sales minus variable cost of sales.

2.17 The significance of operating gearing is as follows. **If contribution is high but PBIT is low**, fixed costs will be high, and only just covered by contribution. Business risk, as measured by operating gearing, will be high. **If contribution is not much bigger than PBIT**, fixed costs will be low, and fairly easily covered. Business risk, as measured by operating gearing, will be low.

Interest cover

2.18 **Interest cover** is a measure of financial risk, which is designed to show the risks in terms of profit rather than in terms of capital values. It indicates the number of times by which interest payable is 'covered' by profits earned by the company.

> **KEY TERM**
>
> Interest cover = $\dfrac{\text{Profit before gross interest and tax}}{\text{Gross interest}}$ *(OT 2000)*

2.19 The reciprocal of this, the interest to profit ratio, is also sometimes used, as is the financial leverage ratio: $\dfrac{\text{Profit before interest payable and tax}}{\text{Profit before tax}}$

As a general guide, an interest cover of **less than three times** is considered low, indicating that profitability is too low given the gearing of the company.

The debt ratio (debt/equity ratio)

> **KEY TERM**
>
> The **debt ratio** is the ratio of a company's total debts to its total assets.
>
> (a) Assets consist of fixed assets at their balance sheet value, plus current assets.

> (b) Debts consist of all creditors, whether amounts falling due within one year or after more than one year.

2.20 You can ignore long-term provisions and liabilities, such as deferred taxation.

2.21 Another way of expressing the **debt ratio** is as the ratio of debt to equity (the **debt/equity ratio**). (Long-term provisions and liabilities, such as deferred taxation, can be ignored.)

2.22 There is no firm rule on the maximum safe debt ratio but, as a general guide, you might regard 50% as a safe limit to debt. In practice, many companies operate successfully with a higher debt ratio than this, but 50% is a helpful benchmark. If the debt ratio is over 50% and getting worse, the company's debt position will be worth looking at more closely.

2.23 An alternative way of looking at the security provided to borrowers is to consider **asset cover**.

> **KEY TERM**
>
> $$\text{Asset cover} = \frac{\text{Net tangible assets before deducting overdrafts and other borrowings}}{\text{Total borrowings including overdrafts}}$$
>
> This indicates the safety of lenders' money. *(OT 2000)*

2.24 When investing, equity shareholders might also consider the asset value per share.

> **KEY TERM**
>
> $$\text{Asset value per share} = \frac{\text{Total assets less liabilities}}{\text{Number of issued equity shares}}$$
>
> This shows the value of assets per share, to assist with investment and divestment decisions, usually for the benefit of equity shareholders. *(OT 2000)*

Question 3

The following figures have been extracted from the accounts of Frobisher plc. What is the dividend cover?

	£
Profit on ordinary activities	2,000,000
Interest	150,000
	1,850,000
Taxation	650,000
	1,200,000
Dividend	200,000
Retained profit	1,000,000
Ordinary shares (£1 nominal)	2,000,000
Share premium account	250,000
Profit and loss account	2,500,000
8% debentures	500,000
Mortgage on property	200,000

Part B: Sources of long-term finance

Current market price of ordinary shares   £6.00

A   10.00
B   9.25
C   6.00
D   5.00

Answer

C   The dividend cover can be found by dividing the maximum possible equity dividend that could be paid out of current profits by the actual dividend paid to ordinary shareholders.

In this case:

Maximum possible dividend	£1,200,000
Actual dividend	£200,000
Dividend cover	6

Chapter roundup

- Indicators such as **dividend yield**, **EPS**, **PE ratio** and **dividend cover** can be used to assess investor returns.
- **Debt and gearing ratios** measure how much debt there is in an enterprise.
- **Financial gearing** measures the extent of a business's debt financing.
- **Operating gearing** measures the relationship of contribution to profit before interest and tax.

Quick quiz

1   Beattie plc has just returned annual profits before tax of £700,000. Tax amounted to £130,000.

The company's share capital is as follows:

	£
Ordinary shares (2.5m shares of £2)	5,000,000
7% preference shares (1m shares of £1)	1,000,000
	6,000,000

What is the EPS for the year?

A   28 pence
B   23 pence
C   20 pence
D   10 pence

2   Complete the following definitions using the terms (1) to (11) in the boxes.

Earnings per share = _____   P/E = _____

Dividend cover = _____   Dividend yield = _____

Earnings yield = _____   Financial gearing = _____

Interest cover = _____

11: Investor ratios

(1) Prior charge capital	(2) Interest	(3) Capital employed
(4) Distributable profits	(5) Profit after tax	(6) Dividends paid
(7) Number of shares	(8) Market value of one share	(9) Profit before interest and tax
(10) Earnings per share	(11) Gross dividend per share	

3   On a day when there are no relevant company announcements, a company's quoted share price increases by 5%. The P/E ratio will be higher/lower/the same as before the price rise.

4   A company retains 80% of its earnings for reinvestment. What is the dividend cover?

5   Which of the following formulae could **not** be used to calculate the gearing ratio?

   A   Prior charge capital : equity
   B   Prior charge capital : equity plus prior charge capital
   C   Equity plus prior charge capital : equity
   D   Prior charge capital : total capital employed

6   .... is the use of debt finance to increase the return on equity by deploying borrowed finds in such a way that the return generated is greater than the cost of servicing the debt.

7   Operating gearing = $\dfrac{\text{Contribution}}{\text{Profit before interest and tax}}$

   True   ☐
   False ☐

8   Are preference shares equity or prior charge capital?

Answers to quick quiz

1   C

	£
Profits before tax	700,000
Less tax	130,000
Profits after tax	570,000
Less preference dividend (7% of £1m)	70,000
Earnings	500,000
Number of ordinary shares	2,500,000 shares
EPS = 500,000 ÷ 2,500,000 =	20 pence

2   EPS = (5)/(7)

   P/E = (8)/(10)

   Dividend cover = (4)/(6)

   Dividend yield = ((11)/(8)) × 100%

   Earnings yield = (10)/(8)

   Financial gearing = (1)/(3)

   Interest cover = (9)/(2)

3   The P/E ratio will be higher: earnings are not increased, but the share price has increased.

4   5

5   C   Equity plus prior charge capital : equity

6   Financial leverage

7   True

8   Prior charge capital

Part B: Sources of long-term finance

Now try the question below from the Exam Question Bank

Number	Level	Marks	Time
11	Examination	20	36 mins

Part C
Sources of short-term finance

Chapter 12

INTEREST RATES AND THE YIELD CURVE

Topic list	Syllabus reference	Ability required
1 Interest rate and present value arithmetic	(iii)	Application
2 Rates of interest and rates of return	(iii)	Application

Introduction

In this chapter, we revise **interest rate arithmetic**. You are expected to be familiar with compound, simple, annual, quarterly and monthly interest; these calculations are often tested in MCQs.

We also explain the different shapes that might be taken by the **yield curve**, which shows the interest rates applying to assets maturing over different periods of time. Again, MCQs are often used to test your understanding of the yield curve.

Learning outcomes covered in this chapter

- Calculate and explain rates of interest
- Explain the yield curve and its practical use

Syllabus content covered in this chapter

- Interest rate arithmetic (compound, simple, annual, quarterly, monthly)
- The yield curve and theories concerning normal and inverse yield curves
- The principles of investing short term, ie maturity, return, security, liquidity and diversification

1 INTEREST RATE AND PRESENT VALUE ARITHMETIC

> **KEY TERM**
>
> **Interest** is the amount of money which an investment earns over time.

1.1 We covered interest rate and present value arithmetic in detail in Paper 3c *Business Mathematics*. We summarise below the main points of the chapter dealing with interest rates, and follow the summary by a number of questions. If you have difficulty with these questions, you should work through the chapter in the *Business Mathematics* text.

Part C: Sources of short-term finance

Knowledge brought forward from Paper 3c Business Mathematics

Simple interest

- Interest which is earned in equal amounts each period and which is a given proportion of the original investment (principal)
- $S = X + nrX$

    where
    - X = original sum invested
    - r = interest rate expressed as a proportion
    - n = number of periods
    - S = sum invested after n periods (X + interest)

Compound interest

- Interest which, as it is earned, is added to the original investment and earns interest itself

EXAM FORMULA

$$S = X(1 + r)^n$$

- Formula above can be used to predict future prices after allowing for inflation
- If r changes during the period of an investment the formula becomes $S = X(1 + r_1)^y (1 + r_2)^{n-y}$

    where y = the period of time for which the initial interest rate r_1 applies and n–y = the (balancing) period of time for which the next rate of interest r_2 applies

- The basic compound interest formula can be used to calculate the net book value of an asset depreciated using the **reducing balance method of depreciation** by applying a 'negative' rate of interest

    Example: An item cost £500 and is to be depreciated at a fixed rate of 25% pa. At the end of five years its value =
    £500 $(1 - 0.25)^5$ = £119

Regular investments

- An investment into which equal annual instalments are paid in order to earn interest, so that by the end of a given number of years, the investment is large enough to pay off a known commitment (eg replace an asset) at that time

    The required value of a sinking fund at the end of n years is a sum of a geometric progression:

    $$S = A\left[\frac{R^n - 1}{R - 1}\right]$$

    where
    - A = annual payment into the fund
    - R = the common ratio, 1 + r

- Example: Sinking fund to replace an asset (bought for £30,000 and depreciated on a straight line basis to an expected scrap value of £9,000) in three years' time. Value of fund must be £50,000. Fund will earn interest at 10%

    $$A = \frac{50,000 \times 0.1}{1.1^3 - 1} = £15,106$$

12: Interest rates and the yield curve

> *Mortgages*
>
> - The annual repayment (A) under a repayment mortgage can be calculated (using the formula for the sum of a geometric progression with 'A' = A and 'R' = (1 + r)) as:
>
> $Sr(1 + r)^n/((1 + r)^n - 1)$,
>
> where S is the initial amount borrowed
>
> **Annual Percentage Rate (APR)**
>
> - When interest is compounded at intervals shorter than a year (daily, weekly, monthly), an **effective** (that is, equivalent) **annual rate** can be calculated as:
>
> $[(1 + r)^n - 1]$
>
> where n is the number of time periods in the year
>
> An annual rate can be expressed as a **nominal rate** rather than an effective rate.
>
> Example: If a bank offers depositors 10% per annum interest payable half-yearly, 10% is the nominal rate of interest, the bank would pay 5% every six months and the effective rate of interest would be $[(1.05)^2 - 1] = 0.1025 = 10.25\%$ pa. The APR is the effective rate shortened to one decimal place.

Question 1

What would be the total value of £5,000 invested now:

(a) After three years, if the interest rate is 20% per annum?
(b) After four years, if the interest rate is 15% per annum?
(c) After three years, if the interest rate is 6% per annum?

Answer

(a) £5,000 × 1.20^3 = £8,640
(b) £5,000 × 1.15^4 = £8,745.03
(c) £5,000 × 1.06^3 = £5,955.08

Question 2

At what annual rate of compound interest will £2,000 grow to £2,721 after four years?

A 7%　　　　　　　B 8%　　　　　　　C 9%　　　　　　　D 10%

Answer

Using the formula for compound interest, $V = X(1 + r)^n$, we know that X = £2,000, V = £2,721 and n = 4. We need to find r. It is essential that you are able to rearrange equations confidently when faced with this type of multiple choice question - there is not a lot of room for guessing!

$$2,721 = 2,000 \times (1 + r)^4$$
$$(1 + r)^4 = 2,721/2,000 = 1.3605$$
$$1 + r = \sqrt[4]{1.3605} = 1.08$$
$$r = 0.08 = 8\%$$

The correct answer is B.

Question 3

(a) If £8,000 is invested now, to earn 10% interest for three years and 8% thereafter, what would be the size of the total investment at the end of five years?

Part C: Sources of short-term finance

(b) An investor puts £10,000 into an investment for ten years. The annual rate of interest earned is 15% for the first four years, 12% for the next four years and 9% for the final two years. How much will the investment be worth at the end of ten years?

(c) An item of equipment costs £6,000 now. The annual rates of inflation over the next four years are expected to be 16%, 20%, 15% and 10%. How much would the equipment cost after four years?

Answer

(a) £8,000 × 1.10^3 × 1.08^2 = £12,419.83
(b) £10,000 × 1.15^4 × 1.12^4 × 1.09^2 = £32,697.64
(c) £6,000 × 1.16 × 1.20 × 1.15 × 1.10 = £10,565.28

Nominal rates of interest and the annual percentage rate

1.2 **Most interest rates are expressed as per annum figures** even when the interest is compounded over periods of less than one year. In such cases, the given interest rate is called a **nominal rate**. We can, however, work out the **effective rate**. It is this effective rate (shortened to one decimal place) which is quoted in advertisements as the **annual percentage rate (APR),** sometimes called the **compound annual rate (CAR).**

Exam focus point

Students often become seriously confused about the various rates of interest.

- The **NOMINAL RATE** is the interest rate expressed as a per annum figure, eg 12% pa nominal even though interest may be compounded over periods of less than one year.

- Adjusted nominal rate = **EQUIVALENT ANNUAL RATE**

- Equivalent annual rate (the rate per day or per month adjusted to give an annual rate) = **EFFECTIVE ANNUAL RATE**

- Effective annual rate = **ANNUAL PERCENTAGE RATE (APR) = COMPOUND ANNUAL RATE (CAR)**

1.3 EXAMPLE: NOMINAL AND EFFECTIVE RATES OF INTEREST

A building society may offer investors 6% per annum interest payable half-yearly. If the 6% is a nominal rate of interest, the building society would in fact pay 3% every six months, compounded so that the effective annual rate of interest would be

$[(1.03)^2 - 1] = 0.0609 = 6.09\%$ per annum.

1.4 Similarly, if a bank offers depositors a nominal 12% per annum, with interest payable quarterly, the effective rate of interest would be 3% compound every three months, which is

$[(1.03)^4 - 1] = 0.1255 = 12.55\%$ per annum.

Question 4

Calculate the effective annual rate of interest of:

(a) 15% nominal per annum compounded quarterly;
(b) 24% nominal per annum compounded monthly.

Answer

(a) 15% per annum (nominal rate) is 3.75% per quarter. The effective annual rate of interest is

$[1.0375^4 - 1] = 0.1587 = 15.87\%$

(b) 24% per annum (nominal rate) is 2% per month. The effective annual rate of interest is

$[1.02^{12} - 1] = 0.2682 = 26.82\%$

Question 5

A bank adds interest monthly to investors' accounts even though interest rates are expressed in annual terms. The current rate of interest is 12%. Fred deposits £2,000 on 1 July. How much interest will have been earned by 31 December (to the nearest £)?

A £123.00   B £60.00   C £240.00   D £120.00

Answer

The nominal rate is 12% pa payable monthly.

∴ The effective rate = $\dfrac{12\%}{12 \text{ months}}$ = 1% compound monthly.

∴ In the six months from July to December, the interest earned = (£2,000 × $(1.01)^6$) − £2,000 = £123.04.

The correct answer is A.

Money and real rates of interest

1.5 The difference between money and real rates of interest is significant in times of inflation where the minimum return required by investors will rise along with prices. The two rates of return are linked by the equation:

FORMULA TO LEARN

(1 + money rate) = (1 + real rate) × (1 + inflation rate)

where all the rates are expressed as proportions.

1.6 EXAMPLE: MONEY AND REAL RATES OF INTEREST

What return in real terms would a company require if it required a money return of 20% and inflation was running at 10%?

1.7 SOLUTION

$(1 + \text{real rate}) = \dfrac{1 + \text{money rate}}{1 + \text{inflation rate}} = \dfrac{1 + 0.2}{1 + 0.1} = 1.091$

Real rate required = 9.1%

1.8 You may be wondering when the real rate is used and when the money rate is used.

(a) If the cash flows are expressed in terms of the **actual number of pounds** that will be received or paid on the various **future dates,** the **money rate** should be used for discounting.

Part C: Sources of short-term finance

(b) When cash flows are expressed in terms of the **value of the pound at time 0**, the **real rate** should be used for discounting.

Discounting

> **Knowledge brought forward from Paper 3c Business Mathematics**
>
> - Discounting involves determining the equivalent worth today (present value) of a future cash flow.

EXAM FORMULA

Present value of £1 payable or receivable in n years, discounted at r% per annum = $\dfrac{1}{[1+r]^n}$

- Example: present value of £100,000 received in five years' time, if r = 6% = $\dfrac{100,000}{[1+0.06]^5}$

  = £74,726

EXAM FORMULA

Present value of an annuity of £1 per annum, receivable or payable for n years, commencing in one year, discounted at r% per annum = $\dfrac{1}{r}\left[1 - \dfrac{1}{[1+r]^n}\right]$

- Example: present value of an annuity of £5,000 receivable for ten years, if r = 8%

  = $\dfrac{5,000}{0.08}\left[1 - \dfrac{1}{[1+0.08]^{10}}\right]$

  = £33,550

- **Discount factors** are shown in present value tables provided in the exam and in the appendix to this Text.

- The rows in the present value table represent years, the columns interest rates. Thus if you are looking for the present value of £10,000 received in 6 years time, with a cost of capital of 17%, the figure from the tables is 0.390:

  Present value = £10,000 × 0.390
  = £3,900

- In the cumulative present value tables, the rows represent the number of periods for which the same sum (the annuity) is received, **starting at year 1**. Thus if a sum of £500 is to be received for 7 years, starting at year 1, with a cost of capital of 12%:

  Present value = 500 × 4.564
  = £2,282

- If this annuity was first received at **year 0**, and then for years 1-7, then:

  Present value = 500 × (4.564 + 1)
  = £2,782

Question 6

What is the present value at 10% interest of £20,000 in year 7?

Answer

Present value $= \dfrac{20{,}000}{(1+1.10)^7}$

$= £10{,}263$

Question 7

What is the present value of an annuity of £5,000, with payment starting in year 1 and receivable for five years, at 12% interest?

Answer

Present value $= \dfrac{5{,}000}{0.12}\left[1 - \dfrac{1}{[1+0.12]^5}\right]$

$= £18{,}024$

Investment appraisal

Knowledge brought forward from Paper 3c Business Mathematics

- Discounted cash flow (DCF) techniques can be applied to the cash flows associated with an investment to ascertain whether the investment is worth undertaking.

Net present value (NPV) method

- **Work out present values** of all cash flows (income and expenditure) related to an investment
- **Work out a net total (NPV)**
    - Positive NPV – investment acceptable
    - Negative NPV – investment unacceptable
    - Choice of one or more options – choose one with highest NPV
- Cash flows spread over a year are assumed to occur at the year end

Internal rate of return (IRR) method

- IRR = investment's rate of return = rate of interest at which NPV is 0
- To determine the IRR of a one- or two-year investment, equate the PV of costs with the PV of benefits
- If the investment is longer, use interpolation

    Step 1. Calculate a rough estimate of the IRR using $^2/_3 \times$ (profit ÷ initial investment)

    Step 2. Calculate the NPV using r = rough estimate of the IRR
    - If the NPV negative, recalculate the NPV using a lower rate
    - If the NPV positive, recalculate the NPV using a higher rate

    Step 3. Calculate the IRR using $a\% + \left[\dfrac{A}{A-B} \times (b-a)\right]\%$ where

    a, b = two interest rates
    A = NPV at rate a
    B = NPV at rate b

Part C: Sources of short-term finance

1.9 EXAMPLE: NPV

Slogger Ltd is considering a capital investment, where the estimated cash flows are as follows.

Year	Cash flow £
0 (ie now)	(100,000)
1	60,000
2	80,000
3	40,000
4	30,000

The company's cost of capital is 15%. You are required to calculate the NPV of the project and to assess whether it should be undertaken.

1.10 SOLUTION

Year	Cash flow £	Discount factor 15%	Present value £
0	(100,000)	1.000	(100,000)
1	60,000	$\frac{1}{(1.15)} = 0.870$	52,200
2	80,000	$\frac{1}{(1.15)^2} = 0.756$	60,480
3	40,000	$\frac{1}{(1.15)^3} = 0.658$	26,320
4	30,000	$\frac{1}{(1.15)^4} = 0.572$	17,160
		NPV =	56,160

Question 8

LCH Limited manufactures product X which it sells for £5 per unit. Variable costs of production are currently £3 per unit, and fixed costs 50p per unit. A new machine is available which would cost £90,000 but which could be used to make product X for a variable cost of only £2.50 per unit. Fixed costs, however, would increase by £7,500 per annum as a direct result of purchasing the machine. The machine would have an expected life of 4 years and a resale value after that time of £10,000. Sales of product X are estimated to be 75,000 units per annum. LCH Limited expects to earn at least 12% per annum from its investments. Ignore taxation.

You are required to decide whether LCH Limited should purchase the machine.

Answer

Savings are 75,000 × (£3 − £2.50) = £37,500 per annum.

Additional costs are £7,500 per annum.

Net cash savings are therefore £30,000 per annum. (Remember, depreciation is not a cash flow and must be ignored as a 'cost'.)

The first step in calculating an NPV is to establish the relevant costs year by year. All future cash flows arising as a direct consequence of the decision should be taken into account. It is assumed that the machine will be sold for £10,000 at the end of year 4.

Year	Cash flow £	PV factor 12%	PV of cash flow £
0	(90,000)	1.000	(90,000)
1	30,000	0.893	26,790
2	30,000	0.797	23,910
3	30,000	0.712	21,360
4	40,000	0.636	25,440
			7,500

The NPV is positive and so the project is expected to earn more than 12% per annum and is therefore acceptable.

1.11 EXAMPLE: NPV INCLUDING USE OF ANNUITY TABLES

Elsie Limited is considering the manufacture of a new product which would involve the use of both a new machine (costing £160,000) and an existing machine, which cost £80,000 two years ago and has a current net book value of £60,000. There is sufficient capacity on this machine, which has so far been under-utilised. Each unit would make a contribution of £11, and annual sales of the product would be 5,000 units.

The project would have a five-year life, after which the new machine would have a net residual value of £25,000.

The company's cost of capital is 20%. Ignore taxation.

You are required to assess whether the project is worthwhile.

1.12 SOLUTION

The relevant cash flows are as follows.

(a) Year 0   Purchase of new machine   £150,000

(b) Years 1-5 Contribution from new product
               (5,000 units × £11)   £55,000

(c) The NPV is calculated as follows.

Year	Equipment £	Contribution £	Net cash flow £	Discount factor 20%	PV of net cash flow £
0	(160,000)		(160,000)	1.000	(160,000)
1-5		55,000	55,000	2.991	164,505
5	25,000		25,000	0.402	10,050
				NPV =	14,555

The NPV is positive and the project is worthwhile, although there is not much margin for error. Some risk analysis of the project is recommended.

1.13 EXAMPLE: THE IRR METHOD

A company is trying to decide whether to buy a machine for £80,000 which will save costs of £20,000 per annum for 5 years and which will have a resale value of £10,000 at the end of year 5. If it is the company's policy to undertake projects only if they are expected to yield a DCF return of 10% or more, ascertain whether this project be undertaken.

Part C: Sources of short-term finance

1.14 SOLUTION

Annual depreciation would be £(80,000 – 10,000)/5 = £14,000.

Step 1. Calculate the first NPV, using a rate that is two thirds of the return on investment.

The return on investment would be:

$$\frac{20{,}000 - \text{depreciation of } 14{,}000}{\frac{1}{2} \text{ of } (80{,}000 + 10{,}000)} = \frac{6{,}000}{45{,}000} = 13.3\%$$

Two thirds of this is 8.9% and so we can start by trying 9%.

The IRR is the rate for the cost of capital at which the NPV = 0.

Year	Cash flow £	PV factor 9%	PV of cash flow £
0	(80,000)	1.000	(80,000)
1-5	20,000	3.890	77,800
5	10,000	0.650	6,500
		NPV	4,300

This is fairly close to zero. It is also **positive**, which means that the actual **rate of return** is **more than 9%**. We can use 9% as one of our two NPVs close to zero.

Step 2. Calculate the second NPV, using a rate that is **greater** than the first rate, as the first rate gave a positive answer.

Suppose we try 12%.

Year	Cash flow £	PV factor 12%	PV of cash flow £
0	(80,000)	1.000	(80,000)
1-5	20,000	3.605	72,100
5	10,000	0.567	5,670
		NPV	(2,230)

This is fairly close to zero and **negative**. The real rate of return is therefore greater than 9% (positive NPV of £4,300) but less than 12% (negative NPV of £2,230).

Step 3. Use the two NPV values to estimate the IRR.

The interpolation method assumes that the NPV rises in linear fashion between the two NPVs close to 0. The real rate of return is therefore assumed to be on a straight line between NPV = £4,300 at 9% and NPV = –£2,230 at 12%.

Using the formula

$$\text{IRR} \approx a + \left[\left(\frac{A}{A-B}\right)(b-a)\right]\%$$

$$\text{IRR} \approx 9 + \left[\frac{4{,}300}{4{,}300 + 2{,}230} \times (12-9)\right]\% = 10.98\%, \text{ say } 11\%$$

If it is company policy to undertake investments which are expected to yield 10% or more, this project would be undertaken.

Question 9

Find the IRR of the project given below and state whether the project should be accepted if the company requires a minimum return of 17%.

Time		£
0	Investment	(4,000)
1	Receipts	1,200
2	"	1,410
3	"	1,875
4	"	1,150

Answer

The total receipts are £5,635 giving a total profit of £1,635 and average profits of £409. The average investment is £2,000. The ARR is £409 ÷ £2,000 = 20%. Two thirds of the ARR is approximately 14%. The initial estimate of the IRR that we shall try is therefore 14%.

Time	Cash flow	Try 14% Discount factor	PV	Try 16% Discount factor	PV
	£		£		£
0	(4,000)	1.000	(4,000)	1.000	(4,000)
1	1,200	0.877	1,052	0.862	1,034
2	1,410	0.769	1,084	0.743	1,048
3	1,875	0.675	1,266	0.641	1,202
4	1,150	0.592	681	0.552	635
		NPV	83	NPV	(81)

The IRR must be less than 16%, but higher than 14%. The NPVs at these two costs of capital will be used to estimate the IRR.

Using the interpolation formula:

$$IRR = 14\% + \left[\frac{83}{83 + 81} \times (16\% - 14\%)\right] = 15.01\%$$

The IRR is, in fact, almost exactly 15%. The project should be rejected as the IRR is less than the minimum return demanded.

1.15 You will meet more complicated NPV and IRR calculations in CIMA Paper 9 *Management Accounting: Decision-Making*. For this paper you may need to use the techniques in questions involving leasing or debt capital.

2 RATES OF INTEREST AND RATES OF RETURN

The money markets and rates of interest

2.1 The **money markets** are markets for **short-term** lending and borrowing, in contrast with the **capital markets**, which provide **long-term** capital. **Interest rates** are effectively the 'prices' governing lending and borrowing. The borrower pays interest to the lender at a certain percentage of the capital sum, as the price for the use of the funds borrowed. As with other prices, supply and demand effects apply.

The pattern of interest rates

2.2 The pattern of interest rates refers to the variety of interest rates on different financial assets, and the margin between interest rates on lending and deposits that are set by banks. Note that the **pattern of interest rates** is a different thing from the **general level of interest rates**.

Part C: Sources of short-term finance

FACTORS DETERMINING THE TERM STRUCTURE OF INTEREST RATES	
Risk	Higher risk borrowers will pay higher yields, to compensate for greater risk. Banks assess creditworthiness and set rate at LIBOR plus markup
Need to make profit on lending	Relending is at higher rate than borrowing; before making profit, banks must pay costs including bad debts & admin charges
Duration of lending	Generally longer-dated assets earn higher yield than similar shorter-dated assets, known as **term structure** of interest rates
Size of loan or deposit	More generous rates may be offered by banks on larger sums borrowed or deposited, because of savings in administration costs
Different types of financial asset	Different types of asset attract different borrowers eg bank deposits individuals and companies, government securities institutional investors

2.3 The rates of interest paid on government borrowing (the Treasury bill rate for short-term borrowing and the gilt-edged rate for long-dated government stocks) provide benchmarks for other interest rates. For example:

(a) Clearing banks might set the three months **inter-bank rate (LIBOR)** at about 1% above the Treasury bill rate

(b) Banks in turn lend (wholesale) at a **rate higher** than **LIBOR**.

The term structure of interest rates: the yield curve

2.4 Suppose that an investor decides to buy some government securities (gilts). The rate of interest offered on a new issue of securities will depend on **conditions in the market** at the time. This will explain why the nominal interest rate on new gilt-edged securities might be 12% on one occasion, 10% on another and 8% on another.

2.5 There is another important reason why interest rates on the same type of financial asset might vary. This is that interest rates depend on the **term to maturity** of the asset. For example, government stock – also called 'gilts' (eg Treasury Stock) – might be short-dated, medium-dated, or long-dated.

2.6 The **term structure of interest rates** refers to the way in which the yield on a security varies according to the term of the borrowing, that is the length of time until the debt will be repaid as shown by the **yield curve**. Normally, the longer the term of an asset to maturity, the higher the rate of interest paid on the asset.

2.7 The reasons why, in theory, the yield curve will normally be upward sloping, so that long-term financial assets offer a higher yield than short-term assets, are as follows.

(a) The investors must be compensated for **tying up their** money in the asset for a longer period of time. If the government were to make two issues of 9% Treasury Stock on the same date, one with a term of five years and one with a term of 20 years, then the **liquidity preference** of investors would make them prefer the five year stock. The only way to overcome the liquidity preference of investors is to compensate them for the loss of liquidity; to offer a higher rate of interest on longer dated stock.

(b) There is a greater risk in lending long-term than in lending short-term. To compensate investors for this risk, they might require a higher yield on longer dated investments.

12: Interest rates and the yield curve

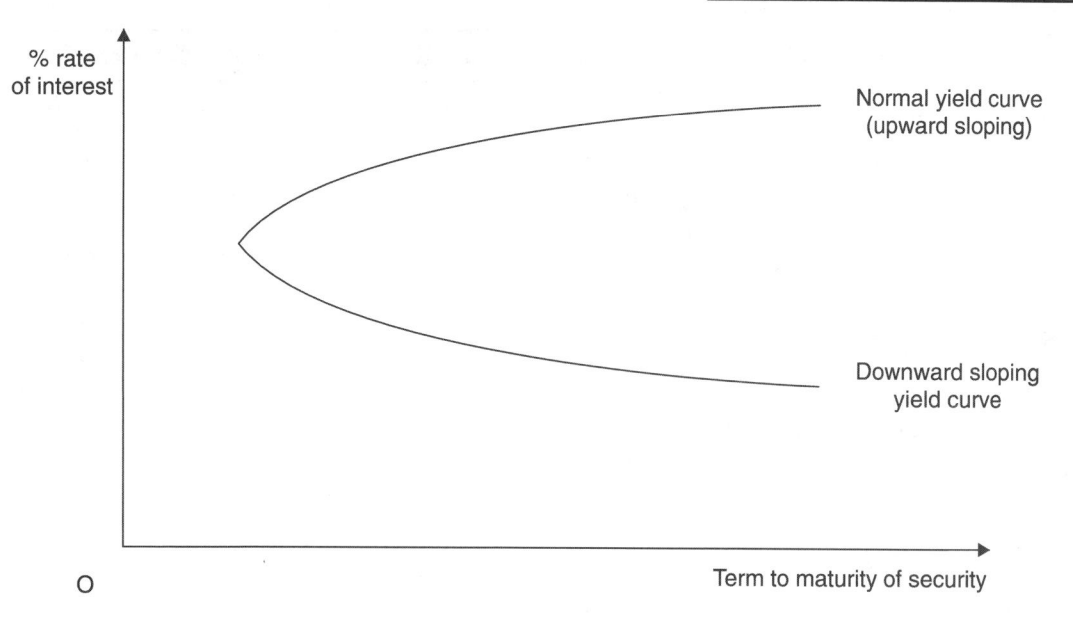

[Figure: Yield curves showing Normal yield curve (upward sloping) and Downward sloping yield curve, with % rate of interest on y-axis and Term to maturity of security on x-axis]

2.8 So why might a yield curve slope downwards, with short-term rates higher than longer-term rates?

(a) **Expectations** about the way that interest rates will move in the future affect the term structure of interest rates. When interest rates are expected to fall, short-term rates might be higher than long-term rates, and the yield curve would be downward sloping. Thus, the shape of the yield curve gives an indication to the financial manager about how interest rates are expected to move in the future.

(b) **Government policy** on interest rates might be significant too. In the UK, government influence over interest rates is directed mainly towards short-term interest rates. A policy of keeping interest rates relatively high might therefore have the effect of forcing short-term interest rates higher than long-term rates.

(c) The **market segmentation theory** of interest rates suggests that the slope of the yield curve will reflect conditions in different segments of the market. This theory holds that the major investors are confined to a particular segment of the market and will not switch segment even if the forecast of likely future interest rate changes.

2.9 Interest rates on any one type of financial asset will vary over time.

FACTORS AFFECTING THE GENERAL LEVEL OF INTEREST RATES	
Need for a real return	Level depends on various factors eg investment risk
Inflation	Nominal rates should exceed inflation & provide real rate of return
Uncertainty about future inflation	If significant uncertainty exists, higher interest yields required to compensate for risk
Investors' liquidity preference	Higher interest rates required to persuade investors to invest surplus cash
Demand for borrowing	Increased demand by private sector or government will mean higher interest rates
Balance of payments	Combination of current account deficit & unwillingness to devalue exchange rate mean interest rates must rise to attract capital into country so that deficit can be financed by borrowing from abroad

FACTORS AFFECTING THE GENERAL LEVEL OF INTEREST RATES	
Monetary policy	Interest rate levels may change to influence volume of credit
Interest rates abroad	When overseas interest rates are high, domestic interest rates must be high to avoid capital transfers abroad/currency depreciation

The risk-return trade-off

2.10 We have explained how rates of interest, and therefore rates of return to lenders, will be affected by the risk involved in lending. The idea of a risk-return trade-off can, however, be extended beyond a consideration of interest rates.

2.11 An investor has the choice between different forms of investment. The investor may earn interest by depositing funds with a financial intermediary who will lend on to, say, a company, or it may invest in loan stock of a company. Alternatively, the investor may invest directly in a company by purchasing shares in it.

2.12 The current market price of a security is found by discounting the future expected earnings stream at a rate suitably adjusted for risk. This rate of return or yield has two components:

- **Annual income** (dividend or interest)
- **Expected capital gain**

2.13 In general, the higher the risk of the security, the more important is the capital gain component of the expected yield. We discuss this issue further in the next chapter.

The reverse yield gap

2.14 Because debt involves lower risk than equity investment, we might expect yields on debt to be lower than yields on shares. More usually, however, the opposite applies and the yields on shares are lower than on low-risk debt: this situation is known as a **reverse yield gap**. A reverse yield gap can occur because shareholders may be willing to accept lower returns on their investment in the short term, in anticipation that they will make capital gains in the future.

Interest rates and shareholders' required rates of return

2.15 Given that equity shares and interest-earning investments stand as alternatives from the investor's point of view, changes in the general level of interest rates can be expected to have an effect on the rates of return which shareholders will expect.

2.16 If the return expected by an investor from an equity investment is 11% and the dividend paid on the shares is 15 pence, the market value of one share will be 15 pence ÷ 11% = £1.36.

2.17 Suppose that interest rates then fall. Because the option of putting the funds on deposit has become less attractive, the shareholders' required return will fall, to say, 9%. Then the market value of one share will increase to 15 pence ÷ 9% = £1.67.

2.18 You can see from this that an **increase** in the **shareholders' required rate** of return will lead to **a fall in** the **market value** of the share.

12: Interest rates and the yield curve

Question 10

Mr Lafite has invested £10,000 at 0.5% simple interest per month. How much will his investment be worth at the end of one year?

A £600
B £10,050
C £10,500
D £10,600

Answer

D   Using the formula:

S = X + nrX

where   S = sum invested after 'n' periods
        X = original sum invested
        r = interest rate
        n = number of periods

In this case S = £10,000 + (12 × 0.5% × £10,000)

S = £10,600

Chapter roundup

- **Simple interest** is interest which is earned in equal amounts every year (or month) and which is a given proportion of the principal. The simple interest formula is **S = X + nrX**.

- **Compounding** means that, as interest is earned, it is added to the original investment and starts to earn interest itself. The basic formula for compound interest is $S = X(1 + r)^n$.

- If the **rate of interest changes during the period** of an investment, the compounding formula must be amended slightly to $S = X(1+r_1)^n(1 + r_2)^{n-y}$

- The **final value** (or **terminal value**), S, of an investment to which equal annual amounts will be added is found using the formula $S = A\left[\dfrac{R^n - 1}{R - 1}\right]$ (the formula for a geometric progression).

- An **effective annual rate of interest** is the corresponding annual rate when interest is compounded at intervals shorter than a year.

- A **nominal rate** of interest is an interest rate expressed as a per annum figure although the interest is compounded over a period of less than one year. The corresponding effective rate of interest shortened to one decimal place is the **annual percentage rate (APR).**

- The pattern of **interest rates** on financial assets is influenced by the risk of the assets, the duration of the lending, and the size of the loan.

- The **yield curve** shows the **term structure** of interest rates on assets of different periods to maturity.

- There is a **trade-off between risk and return.** Investors in riskier assets expect to be compensated for the risk. In the case of ordinary shares, investors hope to achieve their return in the form of an increase in the share price (a capital gain) as well as from dividends.

Part C: Sources of short-term finance

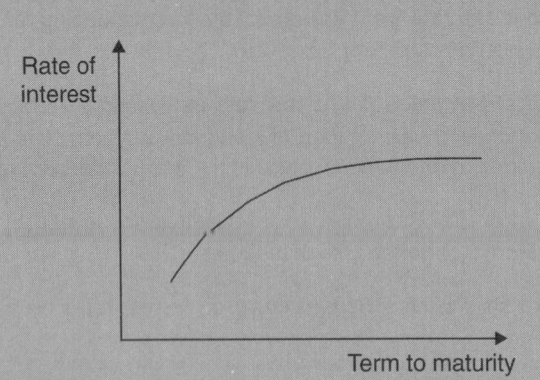

Quick quiz

1. The Typhoon Bank has offered you a loan at 3% over base with interest payable quarterly. Base rate is currently 5%. What is the effective annual rate of interest?

    A 8.00%
    B 8.24%
    C 32.0%
    D 36.0%

2. If a sum X is invested earning a simple annual interest rate of r, how much (S) will the investor have after n years?

3. If a sum X is invested earning a compound annual interest rate of r, how much (S) will the investor have after n years?

4. How should changes in the rate of interest (from r_1 to r_2) be dealt with in compound interest calculations?

5. The Annual Percentage Rate of Interest (APR) is the same thing as the Compound Annual rate (CAR).

    True ☐
    False ☐

6. Sketch a yield curve where it is expected that interest rates will rise in the future.

7. Which of the following types of investment carries the highest level of risk?

    A Company loan stock
    B Preference shares
    C Government stock
    D Ordinary shares

8. Which of the following is not an explanation for a downward slope in the yield curve?

    A Liquidity preference
    B Expectations
    C Government policy
    D Market segmentation

Answers to quick quiz

1. B $(1.02)^4 - 1 = 0.0824 = 8.24\%$
2. $S = X + nrX$
3. $S = X(1 + r)^n$
4. $S = X(1 + r_1)^y (1 + r_2)^{n-y}$
5. True
6.

7. D Ordinary shares
8. A Liquidity preference (and thus compensating investors for a longer period of time) is an explanation of why the liquidity curve slopes upwards.

Now try the question below from the Exam Question Bank

Number	Level	Marks	Time
12	Examination	20	36 mins

Chapter 13

SHORT-TERM INVESTMENTS

Topic list	Syllabus reference	Ability required
1 Cash surpluses	(iii)	Comprehension
2 Cash investments: bank and building society accounts	(iii)	Comprehension
3 Marketable securities: prices and interest rates	(iii)	Comprehension
4 Government securities	(iii)	Comprehension
5 Local authority stocks	(iii)	Comprehension
6 Certificates of deposit	(iii)	Comprehension
7 Bills of exchange	(iii)	Comprehension
8 Other commercial stocks	(iii)	Comprehension
9 Risk and exposure	(iii)	Comprehension

Introduction

In this chapter, we look at the ways in which cash can be invested in the short-term, and identify the purpose and main features of various types of short-term investment. The characteristics of different types of instrument may be tested in an MCQ. Alternatively in a longer question you might be asked to explain which types of investment an investor might choose.

Learning outcomes covered in this chapter

- Identify alternatives for investment of short-term cash surpluses

Syllabus content covered in this chapter

- Types of investments, eg interest bearing bank accounts, negotiable instruments (including certificates of deposit, short-term treasury bills), securities

1 CASH SURPLUSES   Pilot paper, 5/02

1.1 Many companies have temporary cash surpluses which they need to manage so as to earn a return. **Banks** provide one avenue for investment, but larger firms can invest in other forms of financial instrument in the money markets. Generally speaking, the greater the return offered, the riskier the investment.

1.2 A business's management of cash should be conducted with:
- Liquidity
- Safety
- Profitability

in mind.

Part C: Sources of short-term finance

1.3 Clearly a company which runs persistent cash surpluses has little problem with liquidity: it should be able to pay its debts as they fall due. Moreover the firm's expenses are lower as it does not have to pay overdraft charges. However, the other factors identified still apply. Cash is an asset of a business; if it is to be invested, and it must be invested profitably, the investment must be secure.

What should be done with a cash surplus?

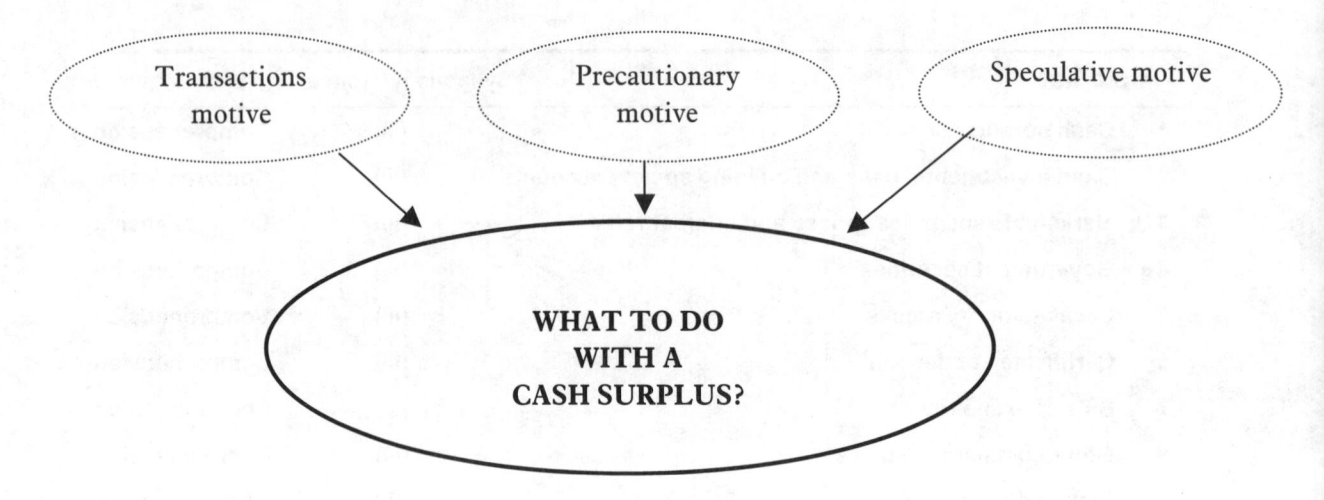

```
  Transactions          Precautionary         Speculative motive
    motive                motive
       \                    |                    /
        \                   |                   /
         v                  v                  v
              ┌─────────────────────────┐
              │      WHAT TO DO         │
              │       WITH A            │
              │    CASH SURPLUS?        │
              └─────────────────────────┘
```

1.4 Firstly, a business needs cash to meet its **regular commitments** of paying its creditors, its employees' wages, its taxes, its annual dividends to shareholders and so on. This reason for holding cash is what the economist J M Keynes called the **transactions motive**.

1.5 Keynes identified the **precautionary motive** as a second motive for holding cash. This means that there is a need to maintain a 'buffer' of cash for **unforeseen contingencies**. In the context of a business, this buffer may be provided by an **overdraft facility**, which has the advantage that it will cost nothing until it is actually used.

1.6 Keynes identified a third motive for holding cash - the **speculative motive**. However, most businesses do not hold surplus cash as a speculative asset (eg in the hope that interest rates will rise).

1.7 The cash management policy of a business will reflect its **strategic position**.

 (a) Thus, if a company is planning future major **fixed asset purchases,** or if it is planning to **acquire another business**, it will consider whether any cash surplus should be retained and invested in marketable securities until it is needed. Using surplus cash to make such future investments will reduce the extent to which it may need to borrow.

 (b) If a company has no plans to grow or to invest, then surplus cash not required for transactions or precautionary purposes should be returned to shareholders.

1.8 Surplus cash may be returned to shareholders by the following methods.

```
                    ┌─────────────┐
                    │   COMPANY   │
                    └─────────────┘
```

(Diagram: Company connected to Shareholders via three options — "Increasing annual dividends", "Making one-off dividend payment", "Buying back own shares")

```
                    ┌──────────────┐
                    │ SHAREHOLDERS │
                    └──────────────┘
```

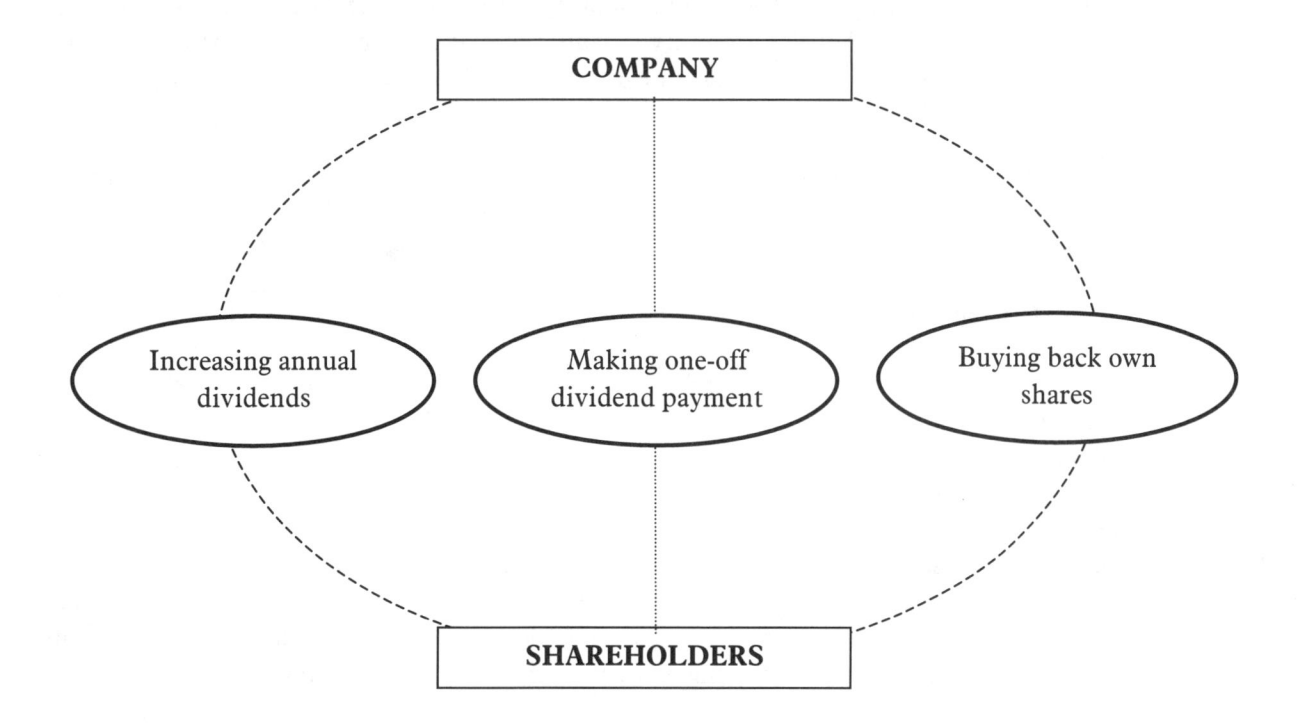

How much cash will a business require for transactions and precautionary purposes?

1.9 We noted earlier that a number of mathematical **cash management models** have been developed to try to establish a theoretical basis to the idea of an **optimal cash balance.**

1.10 Although many larger companies use such models in practice, for the medium-sized or smaller business, deciding how to manage cash balances is more often a matter left to the judgement and skill of the financial manager, in the light of the cashflow forecast. Once an 'optimal' cash balance is established, the remainder of a surplus should be invested in marketable securities.

Liquidity

1.11 We need to consider what we mean by surplus. Take the following example.

1.12 EXAMPLE: LIQUIDITY

(a) Drif Ltd receives money every month from cash sales and from debtors for credit sales of £1,000. It makes payments, in the normal course of events of £800 a month. In January, the company uses an overdraft facility to buy a car for £4,000.

	Jan £	Feb £	March £
Brought forward	-	(3,800)	(3,600)
Receipts	1,000	1,000	1,000
Payments	(800)	(800)	(800)
Car	(4,000)	0	0
Overdrawn balance	(3,800)	(3,600)	(3,400)

The company has been left with a persistent overdraft, even though, in operating terms it makes a monthly surplus of £200.

Part C: Sources of short-term finance

(b) Guide Ltd on the other hand has monthly cash receipts of £1,200 and monthly cash payments of £1,050. The company sets up a special loan account: it borrows £5,000 to buy a car. This it pays off at the rate of £80 a month.

	Jan £	Feb £	March £
Brought forward	-	70	140
Receipts	1,200	1,200	1,200
Payments	(1,050)	(1,050)	(1,050)
Loan repayment	(80)	(80)	(80)
Operating surplus	70	140	210

1.13 Which do you consider has the healthier finances? Clearly Drif Ltd produces an operating surplus (before the motor purchase) of £200 (£1,000 – £800) a month, which is more than Guide (£150, ie £1,200 – £1,050). Furthermore Guide Ltd has a much higher net debt, the loan for the car being £5,000 as opposed to £4,000.

1.14 Yet, in effect the financing arrangements each has chosen has turned the tables. Drif Ltd is relying on normal overdraft finance which will be **repayable on demand**. Its normal **operating surplus** of receipts from sales and debtors over payments to purchasers and creditors has been completely swamped by the long-term financing of a car.

1.15 On the other hand, Guide Ltd, by arranging a separate term loan, which is more secure from Guide Ltd's point of view, is able to run an **operating surplus** of £70 a month. It has effectively separated an operating surplus arising out of month to month business expenses from its cash requirements for capital investment (in the car), a **financial inflow**.

1.16 This shows the following.

(a) A 'surplus' can sometimes be created by the way in which **financial information** is **presented**.

(b) It is often necessary to distinguish **different kinds** of cash transaction (eg capital payments).

(c) Different types of debt have **different risks** for the company attached to them.

1.17 Cash surpluses may arise from **seasonal factors,** so that surpluses generated in good months are used to cover shortfalls later. In this case, the management of the business needs to ensure that the surpluses are big enough to cover the later deficits. The mere existence of a surplus in one or two months in a row is no guarantee of liquidity in the long term.

Safety

1.18 Considerations of **safety** are also important. Cash surpluses are rarely hoarded on the company's premises, where they can be stolen: but what should be done with them, in the short term?

(a) They are assets of the company, and do need to be **looked after** as well as any other asset.

(b) In time of inflation, money effectively **falls in value**.

(c) Any surplus must be kept **secure**: as depositors in the collapsed Bank of Credit and Commerce International must be painfully aware, some banks are not as secure as others. Some investments are riskier than others.

Profitability

1.19 We can approach this aspect by means of a question (Question 1).

Question 1

Compare the following two situations. Steve and Andy are both in the car repair business. Both own equipment worth £4,000 and both owe £200 to creditors. Steve, however, has accumulated £1,000 in cash which is deposited in a non interest bearing current account at his bank. Andy has £100 in petty cash.

	Steve £	Andy £
Fixed assets	4,000	4,000
Cash at bank	1,000	100
Creditors	(200)	(200)
Net assets	4,800	3,900
Profit for the year	1,200	1,200

Which would you say is the more profitable?

Answer

(a) Both obviously have made the same amount of profit in the year in question. In absolute terms they are equal.

(b) However, if we examine more closely, we find that the relative performance of Steve and Andy differs.

	Steve	Andy
Profit	£1,200	£1,200
Net assets	£4,800	£3,900
%	25%	30.7%

In other words, Andy is making the same amount out of more limited resources. Steve could have easily increased his profit if he had invested his spare cash and earned interest on it.

1.20 There is the other question about cash surpluses: what do you do with them, to make a profit? They are business assets like any other.

(a) In the long term, a company with an ever increasing cash balance can:

   (i) **Invest it in new business opportunities** for profit
   (ii) **Return it to owners/shareholders** by way of increased drawings/dividends

(b) In the short term, surplus funds need to be invested so that they can earn a return when they are not being used for any other purpose.

   (i) A return can be earned perhaps by an earlier payment of business debts. The return is the **'interest' saved**.

   (ii) Otherwise, there is a variety of deposit accounts and financial instruments which can be used to earn a return on the cash surpluses until they are needed. These are discussed in the next section of this chapter.

Guidelines for investing

1.21 Any business will normally have a number of guidelines as to how the funds are invested. A firm will try and maximise the return for an **acceptable** level of risk. What is acceptable depends on the preferences of the firm in question.

Part C: Sources of short-term finance

1.22 To maintain liquidity, it is often company policy that the surplus funds should be **invested** in financial instruments which are **easily converted** into cash; in effect, enough of the surplus funds should be invested to maintain liquidity.

1.23 There have been a number of reported incidents where a firm's corporate treasury department took too many risks with the firm's funds, investing them in risky financial instruments to gain a profit. These went sour, and firms have been left with high losses, arising solely out of treasury operations, with little relevance to the firm's main business.

1.24 Guidelines can cover issues such as the following.

(a) Surplus funds can only be invested in **specified types of investment** (eg no equity shares).

(b) All investments must be **convertible into cash** within a set number of days.

(c) Investments should be **ranked**: surplus funds to be invested in higher risk instruments only when a sufficiency has been invested in lower risk items (so that there is always a cushion of safety).

(d) If a firm invests in certain financial instruments, a **credit rating** should be obtained. Credit rating agencies, discussed in a later chapter, issue gradings according to risk.

Legal restrictions on investments

1.25 The type of investments an organisation can make is restricted by law in certain special cases:

(a) Where public (ie taxpayers') money is invested by a **public sector** (central or local government) institution

(b) Where the money is invested by a company on behalf of personal investors in cases such as **pension schemes**

(c) In the case of **trusts** (as determined by the Trustee Investment Act)

2 CASH INVESTMENTS: BANK AND BUILDING SOCIETY ACCOUNTS

High street bank deposits

2.1 All of the retail 'High Street' banks offer a wide range of different types of interest earning account, the variety having increased in recent years in competition with the building societies. The main clearers and many building societies also pay interest on some types of current account. Some of these may be of limited relevance to large corporations, but for sole traders and small businesses, high street bank products are important.

2.2 For someone who wishes to invest a small sum for a short period, **deposit account** facilities are available from the banks. However, the interest rate is relatively low, and many of these accounts are now being discontinued.

High interest deposit accounts and high interest cheque accounts

2.3 If you have a larger amount of money to invest (typically a minimum of £500), you can place the money in a high interest account. Access is usually still immediate, but the rate of interest offered will be higher.

Option deposits

2.4 These arrangements are for predetermined periods of time ranging from 2 to 7 years with minimum deposits of (say) £2,500. The interest rates, which may be linked to base rates, reflect the longer term nature of the arrangement and the corresponding lack of withdrawal facilities before the expiry of the agreed term. For businesses, these might be of limited relevance.

Other facilities

2.5 All banks can offer special facilities for larger amounts.

(a) For example, with amounts of, say, over £50,000 it is usually possible to get fixed rate quotes for **money market deposits** for varying intervals from seven days up to eighteen months or longer.

(b) For still larger amounts it is possible to arrange for the money to be deposited with the bank's finance company at better rates than that available for normal deposits.

2.6 In general, seven days remains the minimum unless the funds deposited are over £100,000 in which case overnight rates can be obtained. Normally rates increase with the term of the deposit.

Finance company deposits

2.7 All of the larger finance companies will accept cash deposits for varying periods from 7 days upwards. Most of them insist on a minimum deposit of (say) £10,000 but they do pay a higher rate of interest than for basic bank deposits. Finance companies are involved in lending of above average risk.

Question 2
It was stated above that lending by finance companies is of above average risk. What sort of return would you expect by depositing money with a finance company?

Answer
A slightly higher return than offered by a bank: risk and reward are related.

The Banking Act 1987

2.8 The Banking Act 1987 created a single set of criteria for authorisation and a supervisory regime applicable to all banks and other deposit-taking bodies, collectively known as **authorised institutions**. These institutions must pass tests concerned with their **solvency** and the **competence** of their management.

Building societies deposits

2.9 The Building Societies Act 1986 allowed building societies to compete with banks over a much wider range of activities than they used to, and increasingly the societies are offering cheque or credit card facilities. Like the banks, the building societies have developed a wide range of different investment facilities, which are mainly for non-corporate investors.

Part C: Sources of short-term finance

3 MARKETABLE SECURITIES: PRICES AND INTEREST RATES

3.1 In the cash investments discussed in the previous section, the investor's initial capital is secure. He cannot get back less than he put in. Another common feature is that such investments are not marketable.

3.2 However, there are also **marketable securities**, such as gilts, bills and certificates of deposit. Such securities are bought and sold, and they earn interest. What determines their price?

Prices of fixed interest stocks

3.3 The price of marketable securities is affected by the following.

(a) The **interest rate** on a stock is normally fixed at the outset, but it may become more or less attractive when compared with the interest rates in the money markets as a whole. Let us take an example. Suppose that investors in the market expect a return of 6.47%.

(i) $2^1/_2$% Consolidated Stock was issued in 1883, paying £2.50 interest for every £100 of the stock's nominal value. However, the increased return means that:

$$\frac{£2.50}{\text{Price of £100 nominal}} = 6.47\% \therefore \text{ the expected price is } £2.50/0.0647 = £38.64$$

Where general interest rates rise, the price of stocks will fall.

(ii) Where general interest rates fall, the price of stocks will rise. For example, if the market required a return of 6.47%, the price of £100 nominal of a non-redeemable 8% stock would be:

$$\frac{£8}{\text{Price}} = 6.47\% \therefore \text{the expected price is } £123.65.$$

Both these examples ignore two other features affecting prices of stocks.

(b) The **risk** associated with the payment of interest and the **eventual repayment of capital**. British Government securities are considered virtually risk-free but other fixed interest stocks may not be.

(c) The **length of time to redemption** or **maturity**. Suppose the following market values were quoted on 25 March 20X2.

9% Treasury Stock 20X5	£113.8029
9% Treasury Stock 20X9	£142.6311

The first stock is due to be redeemed in 20X5, whereas the second will not be redeemed until the year 20X9. In both cases, as with all government securities except those that are index-linked, the stocks will be redeemed at their nominal value of £100. The closer a stock gets to its redemption date the closer will the price approach £100. This is known as the **pull to maturity**.

Yields on fixed interest stocks

3.4 The paragraphs below concentrate on gilts but the principles involved apply equally to any other fixed interest stocks including, for example company debentures.

Interest yield

3.5 The yield for a particular gilt is an expression for the return on the stock if it was bought at the price ruling and held for one year. We looked at the calculation of interest yield in an earlier chapter.

13: Short-term investments

> **KEY TERM**
>
> The **interest yield** (also known as the flat yield or running yield) is the interest or coupon rate expressed as a percentage of the market price.

Question 3

On 19 March 2000 the market price of 9% Treasury Stock 2010 is £134.1742. What is the interest yield?

Answer

$$\text{Interest yield} = \frac{\text{Gross interest}}{\text{Market price}} \times 100\%$$

$$= \frac{9}{134.1742} \times 100\% = 6.71\%$$

3.6 The interest yield in practice is influenced by two other factors.

(a) **Accrued interest**

The interest on 10% Treasury Stock 2003, is paid in two equal instalments on 8 March and 8 September each year. Thus, if an investor were to sell his stock on 1 June 2000, in the absence of any other rules he would be forgoing a considerable amount of interest which will be received on 8 September 2000 by the purchaser. **The price paid by the purchaser must reflect this amount of accrued interest**, and this type of calculation is tested in Question 4 below.

(b) **Cum div (int) and Ex div (int)**

For administrative reasons, issuers of securities (eg the government) must close their books some time before the due date for the payment of interest or dividends so that they can prepare and send out the necessary interest or dividend warrants in time for them to reach the registered owner of the security before the due dates.

(i) Any person who buys stocks or shares **ex div** or **ex int** will not receive the next interest or dividend payment. This will be sent to the former owner. Government stocks normally go ex div about five weeks before the interest payment date. During that period the stock is quoted 'ex div'.

(ii) The purchaser of a stock **cum div** will receive the next interest or dividend payment.

Redemption yields

> **KEY TERM**
>
> **Redemption yield** is the rate of interest at which the total of the discounted values of any future payments of interest and capital is equal to the current price of a security.
>
> *(OT 2000)*

3.7 The interest yield takes no account of the fact that most Government stocks are redeemable (ie that their face value will be repaid) nor of the proximity of the redemption date although we have seen how the pull to maturity can affect the price. A more realistic measure of the overall return available from a stock is the **gross redemption yield**. This takes account of both the **interest payable until redemption** and the **redemption value**.

3.8 Yields are determined by **market prices** which in turn reflect the **demand for particular stocks**. Thus, if a yield is relatively low it can be concluded that the price is relatively high and that the demand for the stock is also relatively high. Conversely, a high yield means that a stock is relatively unpopular.

3.9 The major factors affecting choice are these.

(a) Whether the investor is looking for **income or capital appreciation**

(b) The investor's **tax position**

(c) The investor's **attitude to the risk** inherent in gilts resulting from changes in interest rates. (It is important to remember that although the eventual repayment of a gilt is not in doubt, the market price may fluctuate widely between the date of purchase and the eventual redemption)

(d) **Other aspects** of the **investor's business** (The banks and building societies tend traditionally to concentrate on holding short-dated stocks (redeemable soon) while the insurance companies and pension funds which have long-term liabilities often match these with long-dated gilts (redeemable further in the future).)

4 GOVERNMENT SECURITIES

KEY TERM

The term **gilts** is short for 'gilt-edged securities' and refers to marketable British Government securities. These stocks, although small in number (around 100), dominate the fixed interest market.

4.1 The *Financial Times* classifies gilts as follows.

(a) Shorts - lives up to five years (Stock Exchange up to seven years)

(b) Mediums - lives from five to fifteen years (Stock Exchange seven to fifteen years)

(c) Longs - lives of more than fifteen years

(d) Undated stocks (Issued many years ago these are sometimes known as irredeemable or one-way option stocks. These include *War Loan $3^1/_2$%, Conversion Loan $3^1/_2$%, Consolidated Stock $2^1/_2$%*. Each has certain other peculiarities)

(e) Index-linked stocks

By 'life' is meant the **number of years** before the issuer repays the principal amount.

Fixed interest gilts

4.2 Most gilts are fixed interest, and their prices and yields follow the principles outlined in Section 3 above. There are some other types of gilt, outlined below.

13: Short-term investments

Treasury bills

> **KEY TERM**
>
> A **treasury bill** is government short-term debt, maturing in less than one year, and generally issued at a discount. *(OT 2000)*

4.3 **Treasury bills** are issued weekly by the government to finance short-term cash deficiencies in the government's expenditure programme. They are IOUs issued by the government, giving a promise to pay a certain amount to their holder on maturity. Treasury bills have a term of 91 **days to maturity**, after which the holder is paid the full value of the bill. A company can arrange through its bank to invest in Treasury bills. Since they are negotiable, they can be re-sold, if required, before their maturity date.

4.4 Treasury bills do not pay interest, but the purchase price of a Treasury bill is less than its face value, the amount that the government will eventually pay on maturity. There is thus an **implied rate of interest** in the price at which the bills are traded.

Index-linked stocks

4.5 There are various **index-linked Treasury stocks** in issue. The first such stock, 2% Treasury Stock 1996, was issued in March 1981.

4.6 Both the interest and the eventual redemption value are linked to inflation. The half yearly interest payment is calculated on the basis of the value of the Retail Prices Index eight months before the interest payment date. Thus if a 2% index-linked stock was issued 8 months after the index had stood at 100 and the index stood at 150 eight months before a particular interest payment date, then the interest payable would be:

$$\text{Interest payable} = \tfrac{1}{2} \times \frac{150}{100} \times 2\% = 1.5\%$$

The ½ is needed as the **interest is payable half-yearly**. The redemption value is similarly indexed.

4.7 From the above, it should be apparent that these gilts offer a **guaranteed real return** equal to the **coupon rate**. Many investment fund managers would have considered such a return highly satisfactory over the last fifteen years.

Convertible gilts

4.8 There are a small number of **convertible gilts**. These stocks are redeemable on the date shown or, at the holder's option, convertible into a new longer dated stock. Convertible stocks have gross redemption yields lower than those of similar unconvertible stocks with the same redemption date. The difference arises because of the terms of conversion which, so as to be attractive to investors, offer an enhanced yield from the new stock.

Gilt prices in the Financial Times

4.9 **Gilt prices** are to be found in the *Financial Times*. For all categories other than index-linked gilts, the information is presented as follows.

Part C: Sources of short-term finance

Monday edition

Notes	Price (£)	Wk% +/-	Amount £m	Interest due	Last xd
Treas 10pc 2003	121.0801	0.4	2,506	Mr 8 Se 8	22.2

Tuesday to Saturday editions

	Yield				52 week	
Notes	Int	Red	Price (£)	+ or −	High	Low
Treas 10pc 2003	8.27	4.72	120.9273	+0.0600	123.52	115.44

4.10 The first (Monday) example (from Monday 22 March 1999) above shows that:

   (a) 10% Treasury Stock 2003 was quoted at £121.0801 at the close of business on the previous Friday, a change of +0.4% in the week.

   (b) £2,506 million of the stock was in issue.

   (c) Interest is due on 8 March and 8 September.

   (d) The stock last went **ex-dividend** on 22 February. In other words, if you bought the stock after 22 February 1999, you will not receive the interest due on 8 March 1999. This interest will be paid to whoever held the stock up to 22 February.

4.11 The second (Tuesday to Saturday) example shows that:

   (a) The current price of the same stock was £120.9273 at the close of business on the previous day, which is £0.06 higher than the price on the day before.

   (b) The highest quoted price in the 52 weeks to date is £123.52; the lowest is £115.44.

   (c) The gross interest yield and the gross redemption yield are given in the first two columns.

Index-linked gilts

4.12 For **index-linked gilts**, it is not possible to calculate exact yields because, of course, the rate of inflation in the future is not known. As a rough guide to the yield of index-linked gilts, the *Financial Times* shows the prospective real redemption yield based on projected inflation at rates of 10% and 5%. The RPI base used for indexing (ie eight months prior to issue) is also shown, in brackets next to the title of the gilt.

Purchase, sale and issue of gilts

Question 4

Suppose that a client wishes to purchase 13¾% Treasury Stock 2002-05 with a nominal value of £5,000. The transaction is executed by a stockbroker, who charges commission of 0.8%, in March 2001 at a price of £111.5064. Accrued interest is 56 days. What will be the total cost?

Answer

	£
Purchase consideration	
£5,000 @ 111.5064 per £100	5,575.32
Accrued interest: 56 days at 13¾% (£5,000 × 0.1375 × 56/365)	105.48
Broker's commission on consideration	
0.8% on £5,575.32	44.60
Total purchase cost	5,725.40

4.13 Gilts can be dealt in any amount down to 1p. It is therefore quite possible to buy, say, £13,456.83 worth of a particular stock. This facility is often useful to investors who wish to round up an existing holding to some convenient figure. Similarly, it is quite possible to spend an exact amount on a particular stock. For example, an investor might ring up his stockbroker and ask him to buy £5,000 worth of the 13¾% Treasury Stock on the day referred to in the Question above. The broker would then buy stock with a nominal value of:

$$£5,000 \times \frac{£100}{£111.5064} = £4,484.05$$

5 LOCAL AUTHORITY STOCKS

5.1 We have already mentioned that it is possible for investors to deposit their money with local authorities. In addition to these investments there are a very large number of marketable local authority securities. Stocks may be issued by any size of authority from County Councils to Borough Councils.

5.2 Some of the **local authority stocks** are issued with long lives (eg 13½% Leeds 2006) and there are several one way option stocks and even a handful of genuinely irredeemable stocks. These stocks may, in most respects, be considered as being very similar to British Government Stocks. The main differences are as follows.

(a) The security of a local authority is not considered quite as **good** as that of the central government.

(b) The market in most of the stocks is **much thinner**: (ie there are not many transactions) than for gilts, since the amounts involved are smaller and the stocks tend to be held by just a few institutions.

As a result of the points listed above, the yield on local authority stocks tends to be rather higher than on gilts.

6 CERTIFICATES OF DEPOSIT

> **KEY TERM**
>
> A **certificate of deposit** is a negotiable instrument that provides evidence of a fixed term deposit with a bank. Maturity is normally within 90 days, but can be longer. *(OT 2000)*

6.1 **Certificates of deposit (CDs)** are issued by an institution (bank or building society), certifying that a specified sum has been deposited with the issuing institution, to be repaid on a specific date. The term may be as short as seven days, or as long as five years. Most are for a term of six months. The minimum nominal amount is usually £50,000, or its foreign currency equivalent.

6.2 Since CDs are negotiable, if the holder of a CD cannot wait until the end of the term of the deposit and wants cash immediately, the CD can be sold. The certificates of deposit market is one of the London money markets, and there is no difficulty for a CD holder to sell if the wish to do so arises. The appeal of a CD is that it offers an attractive rate of interest, *and* can be easily sold. CDs are sold on the market at a discount which reflects prevailing interest rates.

6.3 The document recognises the obligation of the amount to the **bearer** (with or without interest) at a future date. The holder of a certificate is therefore entitled to the money on deposit, usually with **interest,** on the stated date. Payment is obtained by presenting the CD on the appropriate date to a recognised bank (which will in turn present the CD for payment to the bank or building society that issued it).

6.4 CDs have one major advantage over a money-market time deposit with the same bank or building society, namely **liquidity**. Unlike a money market deposit which cannot be terminated until it matures, CDs can be liquidated **at any time** at the prevailing market rate. In return for this liquidity, the investor must, however, accept a lower yield than a money market deposit would command.

7 BILLS OF EXCHANGE

7.1 A **bill of exchange** is similar to a cheque although, strictly speaking, a cheque is a type of bill of exchange.

> **KEY TERM**
>
> A **bill of exchange** is a negotiable instrument, drawn by one party on another, for example, by a supplier of goods on a customer, who by accepting (signing) the bill, acknowledges the debt, which may be payable immediately (a sight draft) or at some future date (a time draft). The holder of the bill can, thereafter, use an accepted time draft to pay a debt to a third party, or can discount it to raise cash. *(OT 2000)*

7.2 Term bills of exchange have the following features.

(a) Their **duration or maturity** may be from **two weeks** to **six months**.
(b) They can be **denominated** in any **currency**.
(c) They can be for a value of up to **£500,000** per bill.

Bills may be drawn in any currency.

Definitions

7.3 (a) The **bill** is **drawn** on the company or person who is being ordered to pay.

(b) The **drawer** orders payment of the money.

(c) The **drawee** is the party who is to pay, and to whom the bill is addressed.

(d) The **payee** receives the funds.

7.4 Let us take the example of a cheque. A (**the drawer**), writes out a cheque to B (the payee). The cheque instructs A's bank (**the drawee**), to pay B a sum of money. The drawee of a bill of exchange does not have to be a bank, and the payment date does not have to be immediate.

7.5 The **date of the bill** is normally the date when it is signed by the drawer. The place of drawing (which might be shown just as a town or city name) is also included. The amount payable must be shown in words and figures as in a cheque).

7.6 There are three ways of specifying the **due date for payment** of a term bill.

(a) On a stated date

(b) A stated period after sight (sighting date is when the drawee signs his acceptance of the bill)

(c) A stated period after the date of the bill

7.7 A bill is an unconditional order to pay, and it will always include the word 'pay' and be phrased so as to make it clear that the order is unconditional. The bill must also specify the name of the payee, which might be the drawer ('Pay... to our order') or a third party ('Pay.... to XYZ Limited or order....').

7.8 For a term bill with a future payment date, the **drawee** signs his acceptance of the order to pay (**accepts the bill** in other words, agrees to pay) and returns the bill to the drawer or the drawer's bank. When a bill is accepted, it becomes an IOU or promise to pay. Acceptance of a term bill is by signature across the front of the bill. To an accepted bill there will also be added details of where the payment will be made.

7.9 For example, an accepted bill might have wording such as 'Accepted payable at Epsilon Bank, Moorgate, London, for and on behalf of Omega Tango Limited' followed by the signature of an authorised person.

7.10 An example of an accepted bill is shown below. The name of the drawee is shown in the example on the bottom left-hand side.

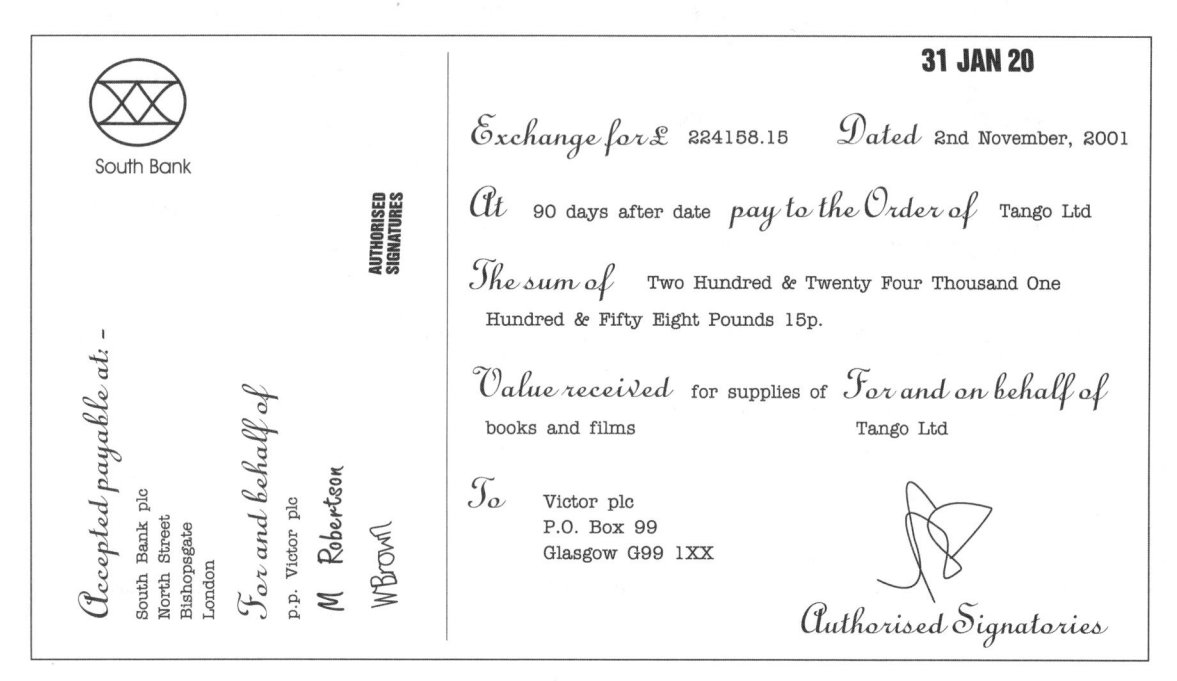

Discounting bills

7.11 As an IOU, an accepted bill of exchange is a form of debt. It is a **negotiable instrument**.

(a) The holder of the bill can hold on to the bill until maturity, then present it to the specified bank for payment.

(b) Alternatively, the bill holder can **sell the bill** before **maturity**, for an amount below its payment value (ie at a discount). A bill of exchange can be transferred by a simple endorsement. (An authorised signatory of the drawer or bill holder signs the back of the bill, and gives the bill to the buyer. The buyer, as the new bill holder, will claim payment at maturity, unless the bill is sold on again.)

Part C: Sources of short-term finance

7.12 The ability of a bill holder to sell the bill for a reasonable price depends on:

(a) The **credit quality** of the drawee
(b) The existence of a liquid secondary market in bills

7.13 The **buyer** of a bill expects to make a profit by purchasing the bill at a discount to its face value and then either receiving full payment at maturity on presenting the bill for payment, or reselling the bill before maturity. The profit from buying a bill therefore represents an **interest yield** on a short-term investment (to maturity of the bill).

7.14 The seller obtains immediate cash from the buyer of the bill, but in effect is borrowing short-term funds, with the interest rate for borrowing built into the discount price.

7.15 Bills of exchange are also used to finance domestic and international trade, because they are tradeable instruments for short-term credit. There are two main types of sterling-denominated bills of exchange.

(a) **Trade bills** are bills drawn by one non-bank company on another company, typically demanding payment for a trade debt. The ability of the drawer (bill holder) to discount a trade bill before maturity (ie resell the bill at a discount) depends on the financial status of the two companies concerned. Institutions will only buy the 'finest' trade bills, where both companies have a high credit standing.

(b) **Bank bills** are bills of exchange drawn and payable by a bank. The most common form of bank bill is a **banker's acceptance**, whereby a bank accepts a bill on behalf of a customer, and promises to pay the bill at maturity.

7.16 Money market instruments are traded on either an interest rate basis or a discount basis.

(a) When an **interest rate** basis applies, a **principal sum** is lent and the borrower repays the **principal plus interest** at maturity. The interest rate is specified and applied to the principal amount for the term of the loan to calculate the amount of interest payable. Bank loans are made on this basis.

(b) When a **discount basis** applies, a **specified sum** is **payable at maturity** to the holder of a money market instrument. If the instrument is purchased before maturity, the price will be less than the amount payable at maturity. For example, a bill of exchange for £50,000 payable in six months' time might be discounted (sold) for £47,500.

Size of discount

7.17 The **size of the discount** will reflect the interest rate that the buyer of the instrument wishes to receive, and the term to the instrument's maturity.

8 OTHER COMMERCIAL STOCKS

> **KEY TERMS**
>
> A **bond** is a debt instrument normally offering a fixed rate of interest (coupon) over a fixed period of time, with a fixed redemption value.
>
> **Coupon** is the annual interest payable on a bond, expressed as a percentage of the nominal value. *(OT 2000)*

8.1 **Bond** is a term given to any fixed interest (mostly) security, whether it be issued by the government, a company, a bank or other institution. (Gilts are therefore **UK government bonds**.) Businesses also issue bonds. They are usually for the long term. They may or may not be secured.

> **KEY TERM**
>
> **Commercial paper** is unsecured short-term loan note issued by companies, and generally maturing within three months.

8.2 Like a gilt, CP is traded often at a discount reflecting the yield required. It is a type of promissory note, and companies find them useful for short term borrowing (usually 3 months), and is unsecured. It is therefore risky. Although formal **credit ratings** are not required in some countries, they do help investors make rational choices: a firm's CP is therefore given credit rating by third party agencies to assess its risk.

8.3 **Debenture stocks** are issued in return for loans **secured on a particular asset of the business**. The factory, for example, may be offered as **security**. The loan is for the long term. Debenture holders take priority over other creditors when a business is wound-up. They can force a liquidation.

> **KEY TERM**
>
> **Permanent interest bearing shares (PIBS)** are a type of security specially created to enable **building societies** to raise funds while improving their capital ratios.

8.4 PIBS are quoted on the London Stock Exchange and the market totals about £1 billion.

9 RISK AND EXPOSURE 5/02

9.1 Risk may be considered in terms of its effect on income, capital or both.

(a) **Income only**

For *most* cash investments there is virtually no risk that the *capital* invested will not be repaid. Also while there may be little doubt that the interest will be paid, those cash investments which carry a variable rate of interest also carry the risk that the rate will fall in line with conditions prevailing in the market.

(b) **Capital only**

With an investment in gilts or other 'undoubted' marketable fixed interest stocks, there is always a risk of a capital loss if prices fall, even though the payment of interest may be considered completely secure.

(c) **Capital and income**

For many investments both income and capital are at risk. Often a loss of income will precede a loss of capital. A company may reduce its ordinary share dividend, precipitating a fall in the share price.

9.2 Risk may be caused by general factors, or by factors specific to an individual security or sector.

(a) **General factors**

All investments are affected, to some extent, by changes in the political and economic climate. In October 1987 all major stockmarkets fell dramatically, apparently taking their cue from one another.

(b) **Inflation**

Investments are also at risk from inflation. A fall in the value of money may affect both income and capital. Cash and other non-equity investments are particularly susceptible, although the high yield may provide some compensation.

(c) **Special factors**

The results of an individual company will be affected not only by general economic conditions but also by:

(i) Its type of products or services
(ii) Its competitive position within the industry
(iii) Management factors

The relationship between risk and return

9.3 The return expected by an investor will, as you will now be aware, depend on the level of risk. The higher the risk, the higher the required return. This can be illustrated as in the diagram below.

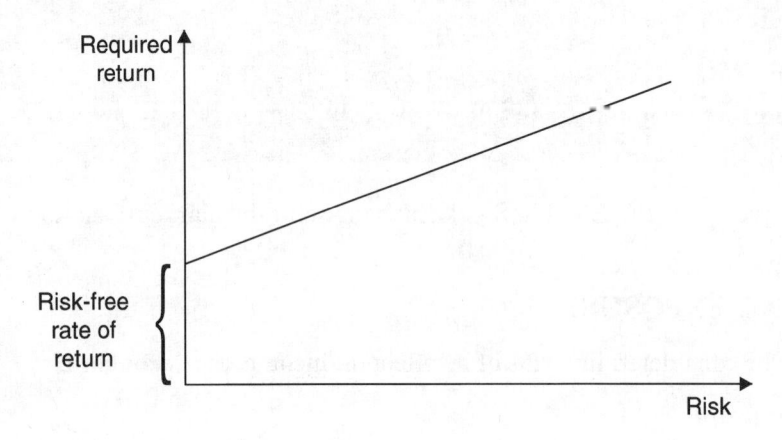

9.4 Marketable UK securities can be ranked in order of increasing risk and increasing expected return.

- Government securities — *Low risk*
- Local authority stocks
- Other 'public' corporation stocks
- Company mortgage debentures
- Other secured loans
- Unsecured loans
- Convertible loan stocks
- Preference shares
- Equities — *High risk*

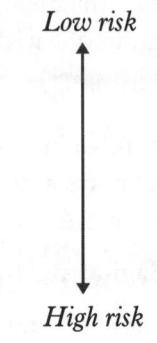

(a) **Government stock**

The risk of default is negligible and hence this tends to form the base level for returns in the market. The only uncertainty concerns the movement of interest rates over time, and hence longer dated stocks will tend to carry a higher rate of interest.

(b) **Company loan stock**

Although there is some risk of default on company loan stock (also called corporate bonds), the stock is usually secured against corporate assets.

(c) **Preference shares**

These are generally riskier than loan stock since they rank behind debt in the event of a liquidation, although they rank ahead of equity. The return takes the form of a fixed percentage dividend based on the par value of the share. Sometimes it is possible for investors to receive a higher rate of return if distributable profits exceed a given level. However, the dividend may be missed if results are particularly poor.

(d) **Ordinary shares**

Ordinary shares carry a high level of risk. Dividends are paid out of distributable profits after all other liabilities have been paid and can be subject to large fluctuations from year to year. However, there is the potential for significant capital appreciation in times of growth. In general, the level of risk will vary with the operational and financial gearing of the company and the nature of the markets in which it operates.

(e) **CDs and Bills of Exchange**

The riskiness of CDs and bills of exchange varies with the creditworthiness of the issuers. They are riskier than government (and probably local government) securities, but less risky than shares.

9.5 **What combination of risk and return is appropriate?** Given that an investor is faced with a range of investments with differing risk/return combinations, what sort of investment should he choose? This is very difficult question to answer. Whilst it is safe to assume that most investors are risk-averse (they prefer less risk to more risk, given the same return), the intensity of that aversion varies between individuals.

Diversification and holding a portfolio

9.6 As we saw earlier, holding more than one investment always carries less risk than holding only one. If only one investment is held, the investor could lose a lot if this one investment fails. The extent to which risk can be reduced will depend on the relationship which exists between the different returns. Recall that the process of reducing risk by increasing the number of separate investments in a portfolio is known as **diversification**.

Question 5

One of the reasons for which a business holds cash is to meet its regular commitments of paying its creditors, wages, taxes and so on. How did Keynes describe this reason?

A   Transactions motive
B   Precautionary motive
C   Speculative motive
D   Liquidity preference

Answer

A   Transactions motive

Part C: Sources of short-term finance

Chapter roundup

- A company has a variety of opportunities for using its **cash surpluses**, but the choice of obtaining a return is determined by considerations of **profitability**, **liquidity** and **safety**.

- Surplus funds can be deposited in **interest bearing accounts** offered by banks, finance houses or building societies. Generally speaking:

  ○ These are for a fixed period of time
  ○ Withdrawal may not be permitted, or may result in a penalty
  ○ The principal does not decline in monetary value

- The **yield** (profitability) of a money market instrument depends on:

  ○ Its face value
  ○ The interest rate offered
  ○ The period of time before it is redeemed (ie converted into cash) by the issuer

- **Gilts** are securities issued by the UK government. Other fixed interest marketable securities included **local authority bonds**, and **corporate debt**.

- **Commercial paper** and **debenture stock** are debt instruments issued by companies: commercial paper is unsecured.

- A **certificate of deposit** is a certificate indicating that a sum of money has been deposited with a bank and will be repaid at a later date. As CDs can be bought and sold, they are a liquid type of investment.

- A **bill of exchange** is like a cheque, only it is not drawn on a bank. It orders the drawee to pay money.

- The relative attractiveness of investing in any of these securities derives from their **return** and the **risk**. **Diversification** across a range of separate investments can reduce risk for the investor.

Quick quiz

1. Apart from liquidity, what are the other two key considerations which a business should bear in mind in managing cash?

2. .... is unsecured short-term loan note issued by companies, and generally maturing within three months.

3. Interest yield = $\dfrac{\boxed{}}{\boxed{}} \times 100\%$. Fill in the boxes.

4. On a particular day, 9% Treasury Stock 2012 is quoted at price of £141. What is the coupon rate?

5. Government stocks generally go 'ex div' about five weeks after the interest payment date.

   True ☐
   False ☐

6. The market prices of gilts will generally fall if interest rates rise.

   True ☐
   False ☐

13: Short-term investments

7   Rank the following in order of risk (1 for the lowest risk).

	Preference shares
	Government securities
	Company debentures
	Ordinary shares
	Local authority stocks

8   Ms Archer is intending to purchase 8% Treasury Stock 2003-06 with a nominal value of £10,000. The transaction is executed by a broker, who charges commission of 0.8%, at a price of £105.50. Accrued interest is 30 days. What will be the total cost?

   A   £10,700
   B   £10,634
   C   £10,616
   D   £10,550

Answers to quick quiz

1   Safety; profitability

2   Commercial paper

3   Interest yield = $\frac{\text{Coupon rate}}{\text{Market price}} \times 100\%$

4   9%

5   False. Gilts generally go ex div about five weeks before the date for the interest payment.

6   True

7   Preference shares, 4; Government securities, 1; Company debentures, 3; Ordinary shares, 5; Local authority stocks, 2.

8   A

Purchase consideration:	
£10,000 @ £105.50 per £100	10,550
Accrued interest:	
30 days at 8% (£10,000 × 0.08 × 30/365)	66
Broker's commission:	
£10,550 × 0.8%	84
	10,700

Now try the question below from the Exam Question Bank

Number	Level	Marks	Time
13	Introductory	n/a	35 mins

Chapter 14

SHORT-TERM BORROWING

Topic list	Syllabus reference	Ability required
1 Budgeting for borrowings	(iii)	Comprehension
2 Banks' criteria for lending	(iii)	Analysis
3 Overdrafts	(iii)	Comprehension
4 Short- and long-term borrowing	(iii)	Comprehension
5 Trade creditors as a source of finance	(iii)	Comprehension
6 Short-term borrowing and capital structure	(iii)	Comprehension

Introduction

In this chapter, we discuss short/medium/long-term finance. This involves us in looking at the use of bank loans and overdrafts. You should concentrate on understanding when different forms of borrowing might be most appropriate for businesses, and what banks consider when deciding whether or not to lend money.

Learning outcomes covered in this chapter

- Identify sources of short-term funding
- Analyse an organisation's creditworthiness from a lender's viewpoint

Syllabus content covered in this chapter

- Types of borrowing, eg overdrafts, short-term loans, invoice discounting
- The effect of short-term debt on the measurement of gearing
- Use and abuse of trade creditors as a source of finance
- The lender's assessment of creditworthiness

1 BUDGETING FOR BORROWINGS

1.1 As far as borrowing is concerned, there are three aspects to the **maintenance of liquidity**.

(a) The firm needs enough money to function operationally, pay salaries, creditors and so on. Of course, eventually it will receive funds from debtors, but the length of the cash cycle can mean reliance on **overdraft finance** at times.

(b) The firm also needs to minimise the **risk** that some of its sources of finance will be removed from it.

(c) The firm also needs to provide against the **contingency** of any sudden movements in cash. Contingency measures can take the form of special arrangements with the bank, insurance policies and so on.

1.2 Some of these needs are more pressing than others.

(a) **Working capital**

Working capital is often financed by an overdraft - this is a result of lagged payments and receipts as discussed earlier and the willingness of businesses to offer credit.

(b) **Long-term finance**

This is used for major investments. Capital expenditure is easier to put off than, say, wages in a crisis, but a long-term failure to invest can damage the business and reduce its capacity.

(c) **Overseas finance**

The borrowing might be required to finance **assets overseas**, in which case the **currency** of the borrowing might be important.

> **KEY TERMS**
>
> Bank borrowing can be obtained in the following ways.
>
> (a) **Overdraft facility**. A company, through its current account, can borrow money on a short-term basis up to a certain amount. Overdrafts are repayable on demand.
>
> (b) **Term loan**. The customer borrows a fixed amount and pays it back with interest over a period or at the end of it.
>
> (c) **Committed facility**. The bank undertakes to make a stipulated amount available to a borrower, on demand.
>
> (d) A **revolving facility** is a facility that is renewed after a set period. Once the customer has repaid the amount, the customer can borrow again.
>
> (e) **Uncommitted facility**. The bank, if it feels like it, can lend the borrower a specified sum. The only purpose of this is that all the paperwork has been done up front. The bank has no obligation to lend.
>
> (f) **Banker's acceptance facilities**. This relates to bills of exchange, which were discussed in Chapter 13.

2 BANKS' CRITERIA FOR LENDING   11/01

2.1 If the bank makes a loan which is not repaid, a bank's profits suffer in a number of ways.

- The expected interest from the loan is not earned.
- The amount advanced and not recoverable is written off as a bad debt.
- The costs of administering the account are much increased.
- There are legal costs in chasing the debt.

Lending criteria

2.2 A bank's decision whether or not to lend will be based on the following factors. The mnemonic is **CAMPARI**.

Character of the customer
Ability to borrow and repay
Margin of profit
Purpose of the borrowing
Amount of the borrowing
Repayment terms
Insurance against the possibility of non-payment

Part C: Sources of short-term finance

Character of the borrower

2.3 The **character of the borrower** can be established and judged.

(a) The borrower's **past record** with the bank is examined.

(b) **Personal interviews** are mainly used for business lending.

(c) Personal lending is more often **credit scored** (by computer).

(d) In the case of a company, the bank may look at **key ratios** which indicate the company's performance. We looked at **ratio analysis** in an earlier Chapter.

Ability to borrow and repay

2.4 The bank will look at a business customer's **financial performance** as an indication of **future trends**. Hopefully the loan will be invested in such a way as to generate profit.

2.5 **Re-investment** of **retained profits** is a sign of the owner's faith in the business. (In other words, the owner does not take out all profits as dividends or drawings.) Revaluations (eg of buildings) would be viewed cautiously.

2.6 Bankers scour financial statements for signs of:

- Low/declining profitability
- Increased dependence on borrowing
- Overtrading
- Inadequate control over working capital
- Sudden provisions
- Delays

2.7 Although a bank will use published accounts and management accounts, it will not lend *solely* on that basis: in other words the viability of the loan itself will be assessed.

2.8 The bank should check whether the company has the **legal capacity** to borrow. A company might be prohibited by its Articles of Association (the legal instrument setting it up) from certain types of borrowing.

Margin of profit

2.9 Remember, banks want to lend money to make money! It is therefore important to consider the rate of interest at which they are prepared to lend.

(a) **Fixed rates**. The lending policies of most banks stipulate different rates for different purposes to customers.

(b) **Discretionary rates**. The bank will decide on the return which it requires from the lending. A loan for a risky venture (such as a new business) will be offered at a higher rate of interest, so as to compensate the bank for the risk it takes that the lending will not be repaid, than a loan perceived to be of low risk.

Purpose of the borrowing

2.10 The customer must specify the **purpose of the borrowing**. (Bankers do not lend money unless they know what it is going to be used for, other than with overdrafts.) Loans for certain purposes will normally not be granted at all. Some will be granted only on certain conditions.

(a) **Illegal loans**. A loan which is for an illegal purpose such as drug smuggling obviously must be refused.

(b) **Lending to finance working capital**. Lending money (usually on overdraft) to finance some of the working capital of a business is quite normal. However, when the intended purpose of an advance is to finance a big increase in stock-holding or debtors, the bank will consider the liquidity of the business, and whether the customer will need more and more financial assistance from the bank as time goes on.

(c) **Loans for new business ventures**. A loan to set up a new business venture should be viewed in the context that all new ventures are risky; while many do succeed a considerable number of them fail to make profits and survive.

Amount of the borrowing

2.11 The lending proposition must state exactly **how much** the customer wants to borrow. This might seem self-evident, but there are two important points to consider.

(a) The banker will check that the customer is not asking for **too much**, or **more than** is **needed** for the particular purpose. This is especially important with requests for an overdraft facility. Clearly this consideration is linked in with the customer's wealth and ability to repay.

(b) The banker checks that the customer has not asked for *less* than he or she really needs. Otherwise the bank may later have to lend more, purely to safeguard the original advance.

2.12 The bank's lending policy will indicate limits on the amount of certain loans and the amount which must be paid 'up front' by the customer.

Repayment terms

2.13 The likelihood that the advance will be repaid is the most important requirement for a loan. A bank should not lend money to a person or business who has not got the resources to repay it with interest, even if it also has **security** for the loan. Security for the loan gives the lender the right to take certain assets if the borrower defaults. Security is only a **safety net**.

2.14 The timescale for repayment is very important. Overdrafts are technically repayable **on demand** (though it is rare for a bank to insist on this without first having discussed a different timescale). Other loans might be payable in instalments, especially loans to acquire assets.

Insurance against the possibility of non-payment

2.15 If a bank **needs** to take **insurance** against the possibility that the loan will not be repaid (in the form of security, such as title deeds or a life policy) then the loan should not be made - as stated above, **security** is only a safety net. That said, many customers might take out payment protection insurance, for peace of mind.

Security for lending

2.16 The **security for a loan** should have the following characteristics.

(a) **Easy to take**. The bank will want to have, or to obtain easily, title to the secured property so that it may be sold and the loan repaid.

(b) **Easy to value**. The security should have an identifiable value which:

Part C: Sources of short-term finance

    (i)   Is stable or increasing, and
    (ii) Fully covers the lending plus a margin

(c) **Easy to realise**. The ideal security is one which can readily be sold and converted to cash. Banks prefer readily realisable security for the following reasons.

    (i)   The administrative costs are thereby kept to a minimum.
    (ii) There is less danger of deterioration (say, of premises) between the time of default and that of realisation.
    (iii) A quick pay-off reduces the length of time over which interest accrues on the unpaid advance.

Personal guarantees

2.17 Often, in its search for security, the bank will ensure that a business loan is supported by a **personal guarantee**. Such requirements are mainly a concern of smaller or medium sized businesses, largely run by their owners.

2.18 For example, Mr Badger is Managing Director of Setts Ltd. Setts Ltd has an overdraft arrangement with the bank, but Mr Badger has to give a personal guarantee of the overdraft. This means that if Setts Ltd fails to pay its debt **to the bank**, the bank can call in the guarantee, and Mr Badger will have to pay the debt out of his own resources.

Question 1

Grog Ltd is a wholesaler, selling alcoholic beverages to shopkeepers for resale to the general public. Grog Ltd has a large warehouse at Ponders End, North London. Its cash cycle is such that most of the time it makes a cash surplus but recently a number of thefts and unexplained account movements have reduced the size of the surplus. The managing director, Lil Drop, has recently decided that she wants to move house. Rather than take out a mortgage, she suggests to the bank that the company borrows money, on overdraft, to buy her a house. She will personally guarantee the loan, although at the moment her only asset she can pledge as security is a port wine making firm in Portugal, which she inherited from a great aunt: other members of the family are suing her for a share. What chance do you think Grog Ltd has of obtaining the loan?

Answer

The banker will pour himself a glass of CAMPARI, as it were, and say no. Lil Drop can pledge no security, and the purpose of the loan is not for business reasons. Furthermore, Grog Ltd's ability to repay looks increasingly in doubt.

3 OVERDRAFTS

OVERDRAFTS	
Amount	Should not exceed limit, usually based on known income
Margin	Interest charged at base rate plus margin on daily amount overdrawn and charged quarterly. Fee may be charged for large facility
Purpose	Generally to cover short-term deficits
Repayment	Technically repayable on demand
Security	Depends on size of facility
Benefits	Customer has flexible means of short-term borrowing; bank has to accept fluctuation

14: Short-term borrowing

3.1 Where payments from a current account exceed income to the account for a temporary period, the bank finances the deficit by means of an **overdraft**. It is very much a form of **short-term lending**, available to both personal and business customers.

3.2 By providing an overdraft facility to a customer, the bank is committing itself to provide an overdraft to the customer whenever the customer wants it, up to the agreed limit. The bank will earn interest on the lending, but only to the extent that the customer uses the facility and goes into overdraft. If the customer does not go into overdraft, the bank cannot charge interest.

3.3 The bank will generally charge a **commitment fee** when a customer is granted an overdraft facility or an increase in his overdraft facility. This is a fee for granting an overdraft facility and agreeing to provide the customer with funds if and whenever he needs them.

Overdrafts and the operating cycle

3.4 Many businesses require their bank to provide financial assistance for normal trading over the **operating cycle**.

3.5 For example, suppose that a business has the following operating cycle.

	£	£
Stocks and debtors		10,000
Bank overdraft	1,000	
Creditors	3,000	
		4,000
Working capital		6,000

The business now buys stocks costing £2,500 for cash, using its overdraft. Working capital remains the same, £6,000, although the bank's financial stake has risen from £1,000 to £3,500.

	£	£
Stocks and debtors		12,500
Bank overdraft	3,500	
Creditors	3,000	
		6,500
Working capital		6,000

A bank overdraft provides support for normal trading finance. In this example, finance for normal trading rises from £(10,000 − 3,000) = £7,000 to £(12,500 − 3,000) = £9,500 and the bank's contribution rises from £1,000 out of £7,000 to £3,500 out of £9,500.

3.6 A feature of bank lending to support normal trading finance is that the amount of the overdraft required at any time will depend on the **cash flows of the business**: the timing of receipts and payments, seasonal variations in trade patterns and so on. An overdraft will increase in size if the customer writes more cheques, but will reduce in size when money is paid into the account.

3.7 There should be times when there will be no overdraft at all, and the account is in credit for a while. In other words, the customer's account may well **swing** from overdraft into credit, back again into overdraft and again into credit, and so on. The account would then be a **swinging account**. The purpose of the overdraft is to bridge the gap between cash payments and cash receipts.

3.8 When a business customer has an overdraft facility, and the account is always in overdraft, then it has a **solid core** (or **hard core**) instead of swing. For example, suppose that the account of Blunderbuss Ltd has the following record for the previous year:

Part C: Sources of short-term finance

Quarter to	Average balance £	Range £		£	Debit turnover £
31 March 20X5	40,000 debit	70,000 debit	-	20,000 debit	600,000
30 June 20X5	50,000 debit	80,000 debit	-	25,000 debit	500,000
30 September 20X5	75,000 debit	105,000 debit	-	50,000 debit	700,000
31 December 20X5	80,000 debit	110,000 debit	-	60,000 debit	550,000

These figures show that the account has been permanently in overdraft, and the hard core of the overdraft has been rising steeply over the course of the year (from a minimum overdraft of £20,000 in the first quarter to one of £60,000 in the fourth quarter).

3.9 If the hard core element of the overdraft appears to be becoming a long-term feature of the business, the bank might wish, after discussions with the customer, to convert the hard core of the overdraft into a medium-term loan, thus giving formal recognition to its more permanent nature. Otherwise annual reductions in the hard core of an overdraft would typically be a requirement of the bank.

The purpose of an advance for day-to-day trading

3.10 The purpose of a bank overdraft for normal day-to-day trading is to help with the financing of current assets. However, there are a number of different reasons why a business might need an overdraft facility. Only **some** of these reasons will be sound and acceptable to a bank.

3.11 Borrowing by a business will either:

- Increase the assets of the business, or
- Decrease its liabilities

Increasing business assets

3.12 If borrowing is to increase the business assets, a bank will first check whether the purpose is to acquire more **fixed assets** or more **current assets**. A customer might ask for an overdraft facility to help with day to day trading finance, when the *real* cause of his shortage of liquidity is really a decision to purchase a new fixed asset. There is nothing wrong with asking a bank for financial assistance with the purchase of fixed assets. But borrowing to purchase a fixed asset reduces the liquidity of the business, and might even make it illiquid.

Question 2

The directors of Wrong Wreason Ltd have asked their bank for a £50,000 overdraft which they say will be used for normal trading operations. They present two balance sheets, one indicating the firm's position before the loan and one after. What do you think the bank's response will be?

WRONG WREASON LIMITED - BALANCE SHEET (BEFORE)

	£	£
Fixed assets		200,000
Current assets	120,000	
Current liabilities: trade creditors	60,000	
Working capital		60,000
		260,000
Share capital and reserves		260,000

WRONG WREASON LIMITED - BALANCE SHEET (AFTER)

	£	£	£
Fixed assets (200,000 + 50,000)			250,000
Current assets		120,000	
Current liabilities: bank overdraft	50,000		
trade creditors	60,000		
		110,000	
Working capital			10,000
			260,000
Share capital and reserves			260,000

Answer

Although the directors might believe that they are asking the bank to help with financing their current assets, they are really asking for assistance with the purchase of a fixed asset, because the bank lending would leave the total current assets of the company unchanged, but will increase the current liabilities. Consequently, bank borrowing on overdraft to buy a fixed asset would reduce the working capital of Wrong Wreason Limited from £60,000 to £10,000. In contrast, borrowing £50,000 to finance extra current assets would have increased current assets from £120,000 to £170,000, and with current liabilities going from £60,000 to £110,000, total working capital would have remained unchanged at £60,000 and liquidity would arguably still be adequate.

3.13 An overdraft facility for **day-to-day trading** should therefore be either to **increase total current assets**, or to **reduce other current liabilities.**

Increasing total current assets

3.14 A request for an overdraft facility to increase total current assets can be pinpointed more exactly, to a wish by the company:

- To increase its stock levels
- To increase its overall debtors
- To increase its overall sales turnover

3.15 The underlying guide to a bank's attitude to lending (in addition to avoiding risk) is whether the finance will be temporary (and 'swinging') or longer term. There might be a number of reasons for a business **increasing its stock levels** without increasing its total sales.

REASONS FOR INCREASING STOCK LEVELS	
Large order	Overdraft suitable, temporary finance to enable business to fulfil order
Stock build up anticipating seasonal peak	Overdraft suitable, temporary finance to support cost of stock
Speculative purchase, eg buying raw materials	Overdraft suitable, provided finance temporary and not unacceptably risky
Permanent increase without increase in sales	Overdraft probably not suitable; need for review of finance facilities; stock may be unsaleable

3.16 Reasons for a business wanting to **increase its total debtors** without increasing its sales turnover might be:

(a) A loss of efficiency in the credit control, invoicing and debt collection procedures of the business, or

(b) The inability of existing customers to pay without being allowed more credit

Part C: Sources of short-term finance

3.17 In both cases, the bank will be cautious about agreeing to an increased overdraft facility. Delays in invoicing should be eliminated by the business; however, if more credit must be allowed to maintain sales, a bank might agree to an overdraft facility for this purpose.

3.18 When a business **increases its sales turnover**, it will almost certainly have to increase its investment in stocks and debtors. It will probably be able to obtain more credit from trade creditors, but the balance of the extra finance required will have to be provided out of extra proprietors' capital or other lending. A danger with business expansion is **overtrading**, and a bank will be wary of requests to support ambitious expansion schemes.

Using an overdraft to reduce other current liabilities

3.19 A bank might be asked to provide an overdraft facility to enable a business to pay its tax bills, or to reduce its volume of trade creditors. The payment of tax might be VAT (generally every quarter) or year end corporation tax. An overdraft facility to help a business to pay tax when it falls due is a 'legitimate' and acceptable purpose for an overdraft, although the bank might wish to know why the business had not set funds aside to pay the tax. A bank should be able to expect that the overdraft would soon be paid off out of profits from future trading.

3.20 An **extension** to an overdraft in order to pay trade creditors must be for the purpose of **reducing the overall average volume of trade creditors**, which in turn implies a significant change in the trade credit position of the business, all other things being equal. Why might such a reduction in total trade creditors be required?

 (a) **To take advantage of attractive purchase discounts offered by suppliers for early settlement of debts.** This should be an acceptable purpose for an extra overdraft to a bank, because taking the discount would reduce the costs and so increase the profits of the business.

 (b) **To pay creditors who are pressing for payment**. A bank will deal cautiously with such a request. It might be because the creditor is desperate for money. If the business *customer* is getting into difficulties, and is falling behind with paying his debts, a banker would take the view that agreeing to an increased overdraft would simply mean taking over debts that might one day never be paid, and so may not agree to such a proposition.

4 SHORT- AND LONG-TERM BORROWING 5/01, 11/01, 5/02

4.1 A customer might ask the bank for an overdraft facility when the bank would wish to suggest a loan instead; alternatively, a customer might ask for a loan when an overdraft would be more appropriate.

 (a) In most cases, when a customer wants finance to help with 'day to day' trading and cash flow needs, an **overdraft** would be the **appropriate method** of financing. The customer should not be short of cash all the time, and should expect to be in credit in some days, but in need of an overdraft on others.

 (b) When a customer wants to borrow from a bank for only a **short period of time**, even for the purchase of a major fixed asset such as an item of plant or machinery, an overdraft facility might be more suitable than a loan, because the customer will stop paying interest as soon as his account goes into credit.

 (c) When a customer wants to borrow from a bank, but cannot see his way to repaying the bank except over the course of a few years, the **medium- or long-term nature** of the financing is best catered for by the provision of a loan rather than an overdraft facility.

4.2 Advantages of an overdraft over a loan

(a) The customer **only pays interest when he is overdrawn**.

(b) The bank has the flexibility to **review** the customer's overdraft facility periodically, and perhaps agree to additional facilities, or insist on a reduction in the facility.

(c) An overdraft can do the same job as a loan: a facility can simply be **renewed every** time it comes up **for review**.

(d) Being short-term debt, an overdraft will not **affect** the calculation of a company's **gearing**.

Bear in mind, however, that overdrafts are normally **repayable on demand**.

4.3 Advantages of a loan

(a) Both the customer and the bank **know exactly** what the repayments of the loan will be and how much interest is payable, and when. This makes planning (budgeting) simpler.

(b) The customer does not have to worry about the bank deciding to reduce or **withdraw** an overdraft facility before he is in a position to repay what is owed. There is an element of 'security' or 'peace of mind' in being able to arrange a loan for an agreed term.

(c) Loans normally carry a **facility letter** setting out the precise terms of the agreement.

4.4

For purchases of a fixed asset it is important, however, that the **term of the loan should not exceed** the **economic or useful life** of the asset purchased with the money from the loan. A businessman will often expect to use the revenues earned by the asset to repay the loan, and obviously, an asset can only do this as long as it is in operational use.

5 TRADE CREDITORS AS A SOURCE OF FINANCE

> **Exam focus point**
>
> It may seem an obvious point, but take care not to confuse debtors and creditors, as many students do under exam pressure.

Trade creditors as a source of short-term finance

5.1 Taking trade credit from suppliers is one way in which a company can obtain some *short-term* finance, in addition to its longer term sources. Remember that short-term finance can also be obtained:

(a) With a **bank overdraft**

(b) By **raising finance** from a bank or other organisation against the security of trade debtors, for example through factoring or invoice discounting (both described later in this Study Text)

(c) For larger companies, by issuing **short-term debt instruments**, such as 'commercial paper'

6 SHORT-TERM BORROWING AND CAPITAL STRUCTURE

6.1 Current and fixed assets can be funded in different ways by employing different capital structures with different proportions of long and short-term sources of funding.

6.2 The diagram below illustrates three alternative types of policy A, B and C. The dotted lines A, B and C are the cut-off levels between short-term and long-term financing for each of the policies A, B and C respectively. Assets above the relevant dotted line are financed by short-term funding while assets below the dotted line are financed by long-term funding.

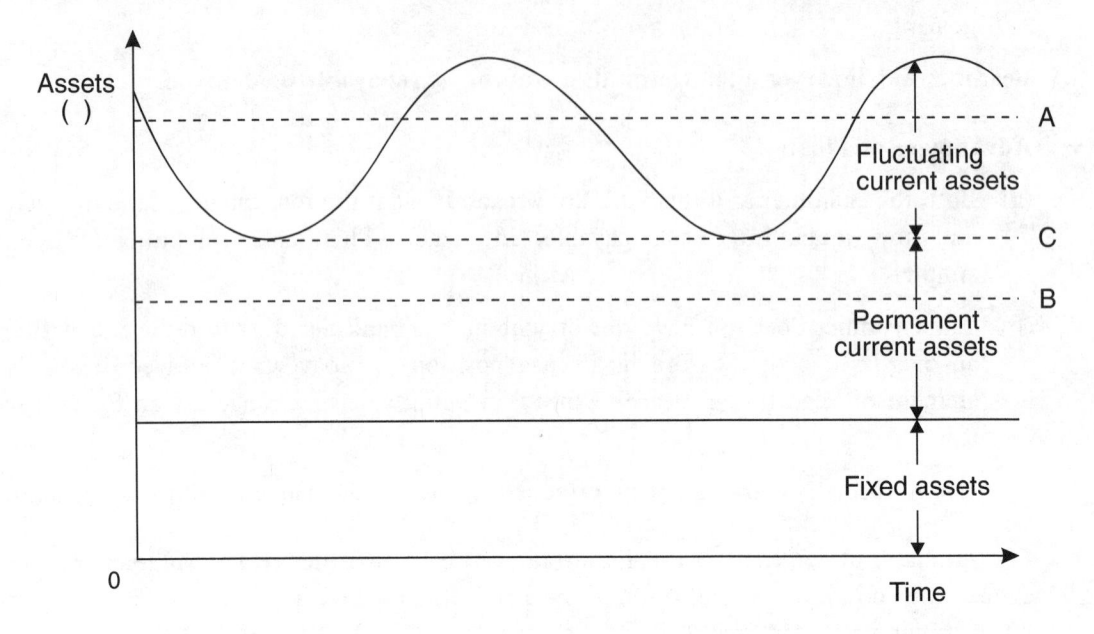

6.3 Fluctuating current assets together with permanent current assets form part of the working capital of the business. This may be financed by either long-term funding (including equity capital) or by current liabilities (short-term funding). This can be seen in terms of policies A, B and C.

(a) Policy A can be characterised as **conservative**. All fixed assets and permanent current assets, as well as part of fluctuating current assets, are financed by long-term funding. The company will only call upon short-term financing at times when fluctuations in current assets push total assets above the level of dotted line A. At times when fluctuating current assets are low and total assets fall below line A, there will be surplus cash which the company will be able to invest in marketable securities.

(b) Policy B is more **aggressive** in its approach to financing working capital. Not only are fluctuating current assets all financed out of short-term sources, but also a part of the permanent current assets. This policy presents an increased risk of liquidity and cash flow problems, although potential returns will be increased if short-term financing can be obtained more cheaply than long-term finance.

(c) A **balance** between risk and return might be best achieved by policy C, in which long-term funds finance permanent assets while short-term funds finance non-permanent assets.

Question 3

For which of the following purposes would a bank be **least likely** to grant an overdraft facility to a company?

- A To increase its stock levels
- B To increase its overall debtors
- C To increase its fixed assets
- D To increase its sales turnover

Answer

C Long-term assets should normally be financed using long-term capital.

Chapter roundup

- Maintenance of **liquidity** is an important corporate objective. Organisations may have problems due to **timing differences**, **risk** and **contingencies**.
- Banks make lending decisions according to various criteria including **ability to repay, purpose and amount of borrowing,** and **security available.**
- **Overdrafts** are a form of short-term lending, technically repayable on demand. Businesses may not need to use the overdraft facilities that they have been granted.
- **Trade credit** from suppliers is another possible short-term source.

Quick quiz

1. Which of the following is **not** a type of bank borrowing?

    - A Term loan
    - B Certificate of deposit
    - C Revolving facility
    - D Uncommitted facility

2. Match the name of the bank borrowing facilities detailed below with the relevant description.

    Facility

    - A Overdraft
    - B Revolving facility
    - C Term loan

    Description

    1. Renewable after a set period.
    2. Borrowing of a fixed amount.
    3. Borrowing through the customer's current account up to a certain limit. Repayable on demand.

3. Identify the list of factors a bank may consider in a lending decision.

    C ....
    A ....
    M ....
    P ....
    A ....
    R ....
    I ....

4. What reasons may make a business ask for an overdraft to reduce trade creditors?

5. Which of the following is normally an advantage of an overdraft over a term loan?

    - A No risk of the bank withdrawing the facility
    - B Interest only paid to the extent that funds are required
    - C Better for borrowing to finance purchase of fixed assets
    - D Planning and budgeting are simpler

6. What three characteristics should security for a loan have?

Part C: Sources of short-term finance

7   Banks are generally likely to grant an overdraft facility when a business is building up its stock.

    True ☐
    False ☐

8   Why might a bank seek a personal guarantee from a director for a company's debts?

> **Answers to quick quiz**
>
> 1   B   This is a type of investment, not a debt.
>
> 2   A3; B1; C2
>
> 3   Character of the customer
>   Ability to borrow and repay
>   Margin of profit
>   Purpose of the borrowing
>   Amount of the borrowing
>   Repayment terms
>   Insurance against possible non-payment
>
> 4   (a) To take advantage of early settlement discounts
>   (b) To pay suppliers who are pressing for payment
>
> 5   B   Interest only being paid to the extent funds are required
>
> 6   (a) Easy to take
>   (b) Easy to value
>   (c) Easy to realise
>
> 7   False. Some reasons for building up stocks (coping with seasonal demand, taking advantage of favourable purchase terms) will probably be acceptable to the bank, but generally such build-ups will be temporary. Banks are less likely to grant an increase to support a permanent increase in stock level.
>
> 8   Because the company and director are separate legal entities, the director can normally only be liable for the company's debts if he or she gives a personal guarantee.

Now try the question below from the Exam Question Bank

Number	Level	Marks	Time
14	Introductory	n/a	30 mins

Chapter 15

EXPORT FINANCE

Topic list	Syllabus reference	Ability required
1 Methods of international finance	(iii)	Comprehension
2 Export credit insurance	(iii)	Comprehension
3 Countertrade	(iii)	Comprehension
4 Foreign exchange risk	(iii)	Comprehension

Introduction

In this chapter, we look at different methods of **financing foreign trade** and at methods of **insuring** against the risk of non-payment by enterprises overseas. You may be asked to identify a certain method of finance in an MCQ, or describe the various methods of finance in more detail in a longer question.

Learning outcomes covered in this chapter

- Identify appropriate methods of finance for trading internationally

Syllabus content covered in this chapter

- Export finance, ie documentary credits, bills of exchange, export factoring, forfaiting

1 METHODS OF INTERNATIONAL FINANCE

Finance for foreign trade

1.1 **Foreign trade** raises special **financing problems**, including the following.

(a) When goods are sold abroad, the customer might ask for credit. The period of credit might be 30 days or 60 days, say, after receipt of the goods; or perhaps 90 days after shipment. Exports take time to arrange, and there might be **complex paperwork**. Transporting the goods can be slow, if they are sent by sea. These delays in foreign trade mean that exporters often build up large investments in stocks and debtors.

(b) The risk of bad debts can be greater with foreign trade than with domestic trade. If a foreign debtor refuses to pay a debt, the exporter must pursue the debt in the debtor's own country, where procedures will be subject to the laws of that country.

There are various measures available to exporters to overcome these problems. (Apart from credit risks, there are other risks, including the risk of currency (exchange rate) fluctuations and political risks.)

Part C: Sources of short-term finance

Reducing the investment in foreign debtors

1.2 A company can reduce its **investment in foreign debtors** by insisting on earlier payment for goods. Another approach is for an exporter to **arrange for a bank to give cash for a foreign debt**, sooner than the exporter would receive payment in the normal course of events. There are several ways in which this might be done.

METHODS OF OBTAINING CASH FOR FOREIGN DEBTS	
Advances against collections	Exporter asks bank to handle, and bank makes 80-90% advance against value of collection. Banks expect repayment from proceeds. Used when bill/cheque payable in exporter's own country
Documentary credits	Described later in the chapter
Negotiation of bills or cheques	Similar to advance against collection, used when the bill/cheque is payable outside exporter's country (eg in foreign buyer's country)

1.3 **Advantages of using bills of exchange in international trade**

(a) They provide a **convenient method** of **collecting payments** from foreign buyers.

(b) The exporter can seek **immediate finance**, using term bills of exchange, instead of having to wait until the period of credit expires (ie until the maturity of the bill). At the same time, the foreign buyer is allowed the full period of credit before payment is made.

(c) On payment, the foreign buyer keeps the bill as **evidence of payment,** so that a bill of exchange also serves as a receipt.

(d) If a bill of exchange is dishonoured, it may be used by the drawer to **pursue payment** by means of legal action in the drawee's country.

(e) The buyer's bank might add its name to a term bill, to indicate that it **guarantees payment** at maturity. On the continent of Europe, this procedure is known as 'avalising' bills of exchange.

Reducing the bad debt risk

1.4 Methods of minimising bad debt risks are broadly similar to those for domestic trade. An exporting company should vet the creditworthiness of each customer, and grant credit terms accordingly. Methods of reducing the risks of bad debts in foreign trade are described below.

Export factoring

1.5 **Export factoring** relates to export trade and is similar to the factoring of domestic trade debts, which we examine in more detail in a later chapter.

> **KEY TERM**
>
> **Factoring** is the sale of debts to a third party (the factor) at a discount, in return for prompt cash. A factoring service may be with recourse, in which case the supplier takes the risk of the debt not being paid, or without recourse when the factor takes the risk.
>
> *(OT 2000)*

15: Export finance

1.6 **Main aspects of factoring**

(a) **Administration** of the **client's invoicing**, **sales accounting** and debt collection services are generally involved.

(b) The arrangement is likely to provide **credit protection** for the client's debts, whereby the factor takes over the risk of loss from bad debts and so 'insures' the client against such losses.

(c) The factor will **make payments** to the client **in advance** of collecting the debts. This is sometimes referred to as 'factor finance' because the factor is providing cash to the client against outstanding debts.

1.7 A factoring service typically offers prepayment of up to 80% against approved invoices. Service charges vary between around 0.75% and 3% of total invoice value, plus finance charges at levels comparable to bank overdraft rates for those taking advantage of prepayment arrangements.

1.8 Factoring, as compared with forfaiting (which we discuss below), is widely regarded as an appropriate mechanism for trade finance and collection of receivables for small to medium-sized exporters, especially where there is a flow of small-scale contracts.

Forfaiting

> **KEY TERM**
>
> **Forfaiting** is a method of export finance whereby a bank purchases from a company a number of sales invoices or promissory notes, usually obtaining a guarantee of payment of the invoices or notes.

1.9 **Forfaiting** is the most common method of providing medium-term (say, three to five years) export finance. It has normally been used for export sales involving capital goods (machinery etc), where payments will be made over a number of years.

1.10 Forfaiting works as follows.

(a) An exporter of capital goods finds an overseas buyer who wants medium-term credit to finance the purchase. The buyer must be willing:

- To pay **some of the cost** (perhaps 15%) at once
- To pay the balance in **regular instalments** normally for the next five years

(b) The buyer will either:

- Issue a **series** of **promissory notes,** or
- Accept a **series of drafts**

with a final maturity date, say, **five years ahead** but providing for regular payments over this time: in other words, a series of promissory notes maturing every six months, usually each for the same amount.

(c) In most cases, however, the buyer will be required to find a bank which is willing to guarantee (**avalise**) the notes or drafts.

(d) At the same time, the exporter must find a bank that is willing to be a '**forfaiter**'.

Part C: Sources of short-term finance

(e) The exporter will deliver the goods and receive the avalised promissory notes or accepted bills. He will then sell them to the forfaiter, who will purchase them **without recourse to the exporter**. The forfaiter must now bear the risk, ie:

- Risks of non-payment
- Political risks in the buyer's country
- Transfer risk, the buyer's country not meeting its foreign exchange obligations
- Foreign exchange risk
- The collection of payment from the avalising bank

1.11 The diagram below should help to clarify the procedures.

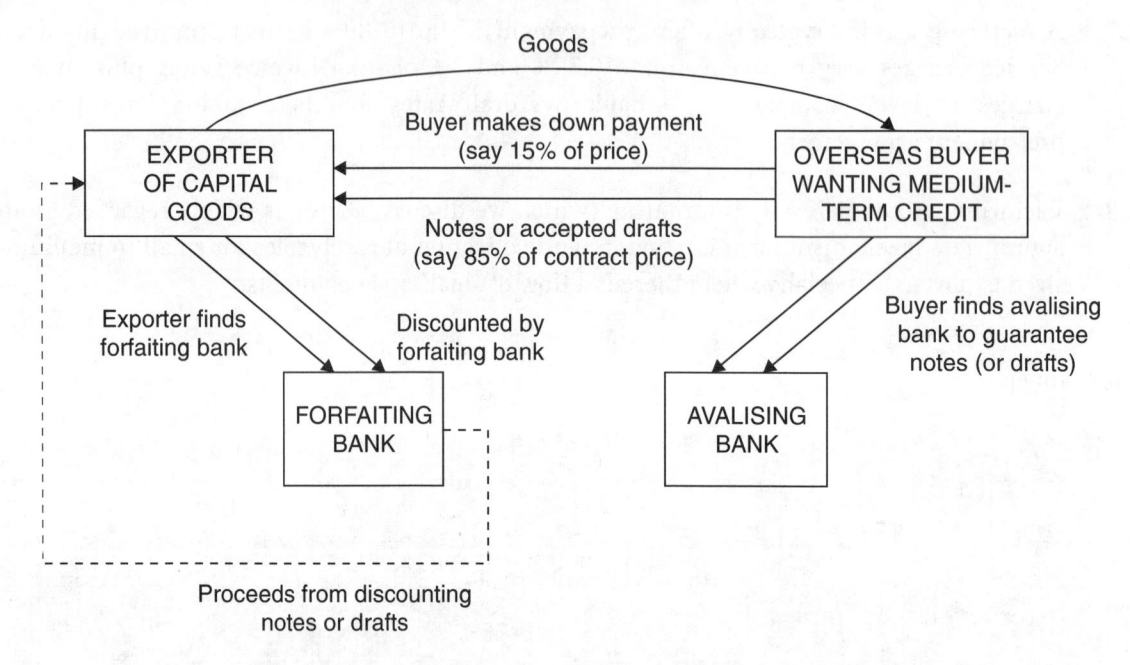

```
                            Goods
                ┌─────────────────────────────────┐
                │                                 ↓
                │    Buyer makes down payment
   ┌──────────────┐    (say 15% of price)    ┌──────────────┐
   │  EXPORTER    │◄─────────────────────────│ OVERSEAS BUYER│
 ┌▶│  OF CAPITAL  │                          │ WANTING MEDIUM│
 │ │   GOODS      │◄─────────────────────────│ -TERM CREDIT  │
 │ └──────────────┘   Notes or accepted     └──────────────┘
 │        │            drafts (say 85%            │
 │        │            of contract price)         │
 │  Exporter finds    Discounted by         Buyer finds avalising
 │  forfaiting bank   forfaiting bank       bank to guarantee
 │        │                                 notes (or drafts)
 │        ▼                                       ▼
 │   ┌───────────┐                          ┌───────────┐
 │   │FORFAITING │                          │ AVALISING │
 │   │   BANK    │                          │   BANK    │
 │   └───────────┘                          └───────────┘
 │        │
 └────────┘
   Proceeds from discounting
      notes or drafts
```

1.12 Forfaiting can be an expensive choice, and arranging it takes time. However, it can be a useful way of enabling trade to occur in cases where other methods of ensuring payment and smooth cash flow are not certain, and in cases where trade may not be possible by other means.

Documentary credits

1.13 **Documentary credits** ('letters of credit') provide a method of payment in international trade which gives the exporter a risk-free method of obtaining payment. At the same time, documentary credits are a method of obtaining short-term finance from a bank, for working capital. This is because a bank might agree to discount or negotiate a bill of exchange.

(a) The exporter receives **immediate payment** of the amount due to him, less the discount, instead of having to wait for payment until the end of the credit period allowed to the buyer.

(b) The buyer is able to get a **period of credit** before having to pay for the imports.

1.14 The process works as follows:

(a) The buyer (a foreign buyer, or a UK importer) and the seller (a UK exporter or a foreign supplier) first of all agree a contract for the sale of the goods, which provides for payment through a documentary credit.

(b) The **buyer** then requests a bank in his country to issue a **letter of credit** in favour of the exporter. This bank which issues the letter of credit is known as the **issuing bank**.

The buyer is known as the **applicant** for the credit and the exporter is known as the **beneficiary** (because he receives the benefits).

(c) The issuing bank, by issuing its letter of credit, guarantees payment to the beneficiary. Banks are involved in the credits, not in the underlying contracts.

(d) The issuing bank asks a bank in the exporter's country to advise the credit to the exporter. This bank is known as the **advising bank**. The advising bank agrees to handle the credit (on terms arranged with the issuing bank) but does not normally make any commitment itself to guarantee payment to the exporter.

(e) The advising bank (in the exporter's country) might be required by the issuing bank to add its own 'confirmation' or guarantee of payment, in addition to the guarantee already provided by the issuing bank. If it does confirm the credit, it is then known as the **confirming bank**.

1.15 A documentary credit arrangement must be made between the exporter, the buyer and participating banks **before the export sale takes place**. Documentary credits are slow to arrange, and administratively cumbersome; however, they might be considered essential where the risk of non-payment is high, or when dealing for the first time with an unknown buyer.

International credit unions

1.16 **International credit unions** are organisations or associations of finance houses or banks in different countries (in Europe). The finance houses or banks have reciprocal arrangements for providing instalment credit finance. When a buyer in one country wants to pay for imported goods by instalments the exporter can approach a member of the credit union in his own country which will then arrange for the finance to be provided through a credit union member in the importer's country. The exporter receives immediate payment without recourse to himself. The buyer obtains instalment credit finance.

1.17 This type of scheme has advantages for small exporters who cannot afford to allow lengthy credit periods to their overseas customers. Examples of international credit unions are the European Credit Union and Eurocredit.

2 EXPORT CREDIT INSURANCE

The purpose of export credit insurance

> **KEY TERM**
>
> **Export credit insurance** is insurance against the risk of non-payment by foreign customers for export debts.

2.1 Not all exporters take out export credit insurance because premiums are very high and the benefits are sometimes not fully appreciated; but, if they do, they will obtain an insurance policy from a private insurance company that deals in **export credit insurance**. The largest provider of export credit insurance in the UK is **NCM UK,** which insures more than 6,000 British companies in trade with 200 countries. The government's **Export Credit Guarantee Department (ECGD),** provides long-term guarantees to banks on behalf of exporters.

2.2 Export credit insurance is not essential, if exporters are reasonably confident that all their customers are trustworthy, but it helps cover for some of the special risks involved in exporting. If an export customer defaults on payment, the task of pursuing the case through the courts will be lengthy, and it might be a long time before payment is eventually obtained.

The short-term guarantee

2.3 NCM UK provides credit insurance for short-term export credit business. A credit insurance policy for export trade on short-term credit (up to 180 days) or on cash terms is known as a short-term guarantee.

2.4 Exporters can choose to obtain credit insurance **for all their export business on a regular basis,** for **selected parts of their export business** or for **occasional, high-value export sales.**

2.5 The **risks covered by the short-term guarantee** are non-payment by an overseas customer in the circumstances described below.

2.6 These risks fall into two broad categories:

- The creditworthiness of the foreign buyer (**buyer risks**)
- Economic and political risks in the overseas country (**country risks**)

EXPORTING RISKS

Risks covered by short-term guarantee	Risks not covered by short-term guarantee
Insolvency of buyer	Non-payment due to exporter's failure to comply with insurance policy provisions
Buyer's failing to pay within six months of due date when accepted goods	Non-payment due to causes within exporter's control
Buyer's failure to accept goods (except when caused/excused by exporter)	Losses due to exporter breaching sales contract
Moratorium on debts to overseas suppliers by buyers' government	Losses covered by normal commercial insurance policy (damage/theft)
Other government action preventing contract performance	Losses due to exporter's illegal activities
Political, economic, legal events outside UK preventing/delaying payment	Insolvency/default over payment by collecting bank/exporter's agent
Exchange losses on local currency payment which should've been in sterling	Exchange risks covered by forward exchange contracts
War and similar disturbances preventing performance	Losses due to breach of exchange control regulations in buyer's country
Cancellation/non-renewal of export licence, or legal prohibition of exports	Failure of buyer to obtain authority to import goods/ make payment for them
Failure or refusal by foreign government buyers to perform contract	Losses incurred on contract itself due to exporter's own costs in UK

2.7 Unless the exporter has additional pre-credit risk cover, this policy does not protect him from cancellation of the contract by the buyer before the goods are dispatched from the UK.

15: Export finance

The percentage of cover

2.8 The **percentage of the loss incurred** by the exporter that this policy covers varies according to the cause of the loss. For example, the short-term guarantee covers 90% of the loss arising from the insolvency of the buyer, or the buyer's failure to pay within six months of the due date, that is losses due to poor creditworthiness of the buyer.

Premiums

2.9 As a general guide, the **premiums** payable by the exporter for a comprehensive short-term guarantee comprise a **fixed basic premium** at the start of the year, plus **additional monthly premiums** that vary with the amount of exports declared by the exporter during the month.

Question 1

Cameracase Ltd has expanded rapidly in recent years and has started to venture into the export market. However, the Finance Director, Mr Zoom, explains to you that the company is having some difficulty in collecting its overseas debts.

Mr Zoom mentions that Cameracase Ltd's total annual exports amount to £500,000,000 of which 20% are paid in advance of despatch and the remainder, the credit sales, are paid on open account terms of sixty days credit. However, on average these latter payments have been running eighteen days late. Moreover, 0.6% by value of the credit sales have been unrecoverable bad debts. Mr Zoom also mentions that the company can borrow unsecured from its bank at base rate plus 2.25% by using the existing overdraft facility.

The company has so far had no specific arrangements to deal with export sales and is currently considering the following alternatives.

(a) Insure the exports against non-payment through a recognised overseas trade credit insurer. The insurer offers a comprehensive insurance policy which costs 45p per £100 insured and provides cover for 85% of the risk of non-payment. The insurer will allow Cameracase to assign its rights to a bank in return for which the bank will advance 75% of the sales value of the insured debts at a cost of base rate plus 1.75% (base rate is currently 6%).

(b) Use the services of a non-recourse export factor. If required the factor can offer immediate finance of 80% of the export credit sales at a rate of 2% over base rate. A debt collection service fee is chargeable amounting to 2% of credit sales. Mr Zoom estimates the use of a factor would produce administrative savings of £60,000 per annum.

Required

Evaluate the options available to Mr Zoom to deal with the export sales and recommend the most cost-effective combination of export administration and financing in the circumstances. Clearly state any assumptions made. You may assume a 360 day year.

Answer

Cameracase Ltd

Total annual export sales:		5,000,000
Cash received in advance	20%	1,000,000
Balance on 60 days credit	80%	4,000,000
Irrecoverable bad debts	0.6% × £4m	(24,000)

Assuming a 360-day year, average export debtors = £4m × 78/360 = £866,667.

Alternative 1: credit insurer

	£
Annual insurance cost: £0.45/£100 × £4,000,000	(18,000)
Bad debts saved: 85% × £24,000	20,400
Interest saving of (2.25% − 1.75%) = 0.5% on 75% of debtors:	
0.5% × 75% × £866,667	3,250
Net improvement in annual cash position	5,650

229

Part C: Sources of short-term finance

Alternative 2: non-recourse export factor

With a non-recourse factoring agreement all the bad debts will be saved. The company can choose between:

(a) Using just the debt collection service ('service factoring') or
(b) Using the service in conjunction with the cash advance ('service and finance factoring').

In this case, the company should take advantage of the factor's cash advance because it is below the overdraft rate by 2.25% –2% = 0.25%.

Service factoring	£
Annual service fee: 2% × £4,000,000	(80,000)
Administrative costs saved	60,000
Bad debts saved (all)	24,000
Net improvement on current position	4,000
Cash advance	
Interest saving of 0.25% on 80% of debtors:	
£866,667 × 80% × 0.25%	1,733
Total improvement on current position	5,733

Conclusion. Both alternatives are estimated to improve the company's cash position and save annual costs. If the factor's financing option is taken up, then factoring is estimated to produce marginally better results. However the uncertainty of the cash flows must be considered. Whereas the agreement with the credit insurer appears to involve no additional uncertainties, the viability of the factoring agreement is heavily dependent on saving administrative costs, which can be rather difficult to reduce in practice.

3 COUNTERTRADE

What is countertrade?

> **KEY TERM**
>
> **Countertrade** is a form of trading activity based on other than an arm's-length goods for cash exchange. *(OT 2000)*

3.1 **Countertrade** is a general term used to describe a variety of commercial arrangements for reciprocal international trade or barter between companies or other organisations (eg state controlled organisations) in two or more countries.

3.2 Countertrade involving exchange of petroleum and manufacturing goods became popular in the early 1980s as such deals provided a way of avoiding OPEC export quotas for oil-producing countries. It is also common in deals with East European countries which are short of foreign exchange.

3.3 Countertrade is costly for the exporter; it creates lengthy and cumbersome administrative problems, just to set up a countertrade arrangement. It is fraught with uncertainty, and deals can easily collapse or go wrong. However, in some situations, countertrade might be the only way of securing export orders.

Question 2

Countertrade can involve problems for the exporter, in addition to 'normal' export risks. See if you can think what specific problems might arise, before looking at the next paragraph.

Problems with countertrade

3.4 Problems which may arise in countertrade include the following.

(a) The **costs** of countertrade (see below) might exceed the exporter's expectations. The exporter might increase the export price to cover the extra costs, or he might try to absorb the extra costs himself.

(b) The exporter might be pushed into agreeing to accept large quantities of **unmarketable goods** without any means of disposing of them.

(c) The importer's country might place an **unrealistically high value** on the goods they wish to countertrade.

(d) **Several parties** are likely to be involved in a countertrade arrangement, and this increases the risks of cancellation of the export order, due to one party failing to fulfil its contractual obligations.

What are the extra costs of countertrade?

3.5 The costs of countertrade include:

(a) Fees of **specialist consultants** who advise on countertrade negotiations

(b) The **discount** or 'disagio' necessary to dispose of the goods in countertrade (The size of the discount could vary from 2-3% for high grade materials and commodities to 25-30% and sometimes as much as 40-50%) for low-quality manufactured goods.)

(c) **Counterpurchase** undertakings can be dealt with by assigning the counterpurchase obligations for a fee, to a third party trading house or broker

(d) **Insurance costs**

(e) **Bank fees**, where a bank provides advice and help on countertrade matters (for example on negotiations or disposal of countertraded goods)

Question 3

What type of arrangement does the following statement define?

'A method of export finance whereby a bank purchases from a company a number of sales invoices or promissory notes, usually obtaining a guarantee of payment of the invoices or notes.'

A   Factoring
B   Invoice discounting
C   Export credit insurance
D   Forfaiting

Answer

D   Forfaiting

4 FOREIGN EXCHANGE RISK

4.1 A company may become exposed to risk from movements in exchange rates in a number of ways, including the following:

- As an exporter of goods or services
- As an importer of goods or services
- Through having an overseas subsidiary
- Through being the subsidiary of an overseas company

Part C: Sources of short-term finance

- Through transactions in overseas capital markets

4.2 Perhaps the most important aspect of **managing overseas debtors** is the problem that **exchange rates** may **change** before payment is received. Hedging involves measures to reduce exposure to such **foreign exchange risk**.

Transaction exposure

4.3 Much international trade involves credit. An importer will take credit often for **several months** and **sometimes longer**, and an exporter will **grant credit**. One consequence of taking and granting credit is that international traders will know in advance about the receipts and payments arising from their trade. They will know:

- What foreign currency they will receive or pay
- When the receipt or payment will occur
- How much of the currency will be received or paid

4.4 **Importers and exporters** alike will be concerned about the profit they can expect to make from trade. An exporter who invoices a foreign buyer in the buyer's currency will expect to be able to exchange his foreign currency proceeds from the buyer for his domestic currency and earn **enough domestic currency** to **cover his costs** and **make a profit**. Similarly, an importer might buy goods from abroad for which he is invoiced in foreign currency. If he plans to sell the imports, he will produce a price list for his customers, or agree prices to earn **enough domestic currency** from selling the goods to **pay** the **foreign supplier** in foreign currency, and make a profit.

4.5 The great danger to profit margins is the movement in exchange rates. The risk faces

- Exporters who invoice in a foreign currency, and
- Importers who pay in a foreign currency

Matching receipts and payments

4.6 A company can reduce or eliminate its foreign exchange transaction exposure by matching receipts and payments. Wherever possible, a company that expects to make payments and have receipts in the same foreign currency should plan to **offset** its **payments** against its **receipts** in the currency.

4.7 Since the company will be setting off foreign currency receipts against foreign currency payments, it does not matter whether the currency strengthens or weakens against the company's 'domestic' currency because there will be no purchase or sale of the currency.

4.8 The process of matching is made simpler by having **foreign currency accounts** with a bank. UK residents are allowed to have bank accounts in any foreign currency. Receipts of foreign currency can be credited to the account pending subsequent payments in the currency.

4.9 Since a company is unlikely to have exactly the same amount of receipts in a currency as it makes payments, it will still be exposed to the extent of the surplus of income, and so the company may wish to avoid exposure on this surplus by arranging forward exchange cover.

4.10 **Offsetting** (matching payments against receipts) will be cheaper than arranging a forward contract to buy currency and another forward contract to sell the currency, provided that:

- **Receipts occur before payments**, and
- The **time difference** between receipts and payments in the currency is **not too long**

Leads and lags

4.11 Companies might try to use:

- **Lead payments**: payments in advance, or
- **Lagged payments**: delaying payments beyond their due date

in order to take advantage of foreign exchange rate movements.

4.12 With a lead payment, paying in advance of the due date, there is a finance cost to consider. This is the interest cost on the money used to make the payment.

Currency of invoice

4.13 One way of avoiding exchange rate risk is for an exporter to **invoice** his foreign customer in his **domestic currency**, or for an importer to **arrange** with his **foreign supplier** to be **invoiced** in his **domestic currency**. However, although either the exporter or the importer can avoid any exchange risk in this way, only one of them can deal in his domestic currency. The other must accept the exchange risk, since there will be a period of time elapsing between agreeing a contract and paying for the goods (unless payment is made with the order).

Forward exchange contracts

4.14 Forward exchange contracts allow a trader who knows that he will have to buy or sell foreign currency at a date in the future, to make the purchase or sale at a predetermined rate of exchange. The trader will therefore know in advance either how much **local currency** he will **receive** (if he is selling foreign currency to the bank) or how much local currency he must **pay** (if he is buying foreign currency from the bank).

Money market hedges

4.15 An exporter who invoices foreign customers in a foreign currency can hedge against the exchange risk by:

- **Borrowing** an amount in the foreign currency **immediately**
- **Converting** the **foreign currency** into **domestic currency** at the **spot rate**
- **Repaying the loan** with **interest** out of the eventual foreign currency receipts

4.16 Similarly, if a company has to make a foreign currency payment in the future, it can **buy the currency now** at the spot rate and **put it on deposit**, using the principal and the interest earned to make the foreign currency payment when it falls due.

Part C: Sources of short-term finance

> **Chapter roundup**
>
> - The various methods of providing export and import finance should be understood. **Export factoring** provides all the advantages of factoring generally and is especially useful in assessing credit risk. **International credit unions** and **forfaiting** provide medium term finance for importers of capital goods.
>
> - It is worth remembering that the exporter can obtain finance from the foreign buyer (by insisting on **cash with order**) and the importer can obtain finance from the foreign supplier (by means of normal trade credit, perhaps evidenced by a term bill of exchange).
>
> - Various forms of **credit insurance** are available to exporters.
>
> - **Countertrade** is a potentially complex means of trading with poor and less developed countries. It can take several forms.
>
> - Companies can manage their exposure to **foreign exchange risk** by **matching, leading and lagging, forward exchange contracts** and **money market hedges**.

Quick quiz

1   Which of the following methods could not be used to reduce the risks of bad debts in foreign trade?

   A   Export factoring
   B   Forfaiting
   C   Advances against collections
   D   Documentary credits

2   Fill in the blanks below, using the following terms: documentary credit, forfaiting, invoice discounting, factoring

   (A) .... is an arrangement to have debts collected by a company providing the service, which advances a proportion of the money it is due to collect. With (B) ...., the company providing the service does not administer the sales ledger but only advances cash. (C) .... is a method of export finance whereby a bank purchases from a company a number of sales invoices or promissory notes, usually obtaining a guarantee of payment of the invoices or notes. (D) .... gives an exporter a risk-free method of obtaining payment from another country.

3   Identify the benefits of factoring for a business customer.

4   Define export credit insurance.

5   What can be defined as 'a form of trading activity based on other than arm's-length goods for cash exchange?

6   A credit insurance policy for export trade on short-term credit or on cash terms is known as a short-term guarantee. Which of the following risks would normally be covered by such a policy?

   A   Failure or refusal of a 'public buyer' in an overseas country to perform the contract through no fault of the exporter.

   B   Losses due to adverse movements in exchange rates

   C   Insolvency or default over payment by the collecting bank

   D   Insolvency or default over payment by the exporters' agent

7   What is the main purpose of International Credit Unions?

8   Give three examples of costs of countertrade.

Answers to quick quiz

1. C   This can reduce the investment in foreign debtors, but it does not reduce the risk of bad debts.

2. (A) Factoring; (B) Invoice discounting; (C) Forfaiting; (D) Documentary credit

3. (a) Enables prompt payment for own supplies, taking advantage of discounts.
   (b) There is cash to finance stocks.
   (c) Injections of fresh capital to assist growth may be avoided.
   (d) Finance is linked to volume of sales.
   (e) Management time is saved.
   (f) Administration costs are reduced.

4. Insurance against the risk of non-payment by foreign customers for export debts

5. Countertrade

6. A   Failure or refusal of a public buyer to perform the contract

7. To provide reciprocal arrangements for providing instalment credit finance

8. Any three of:
   (a) Fees of specialist consultants
   (b) Discount to dispose of goods
   (c) Counterpurchase undertakings
   (d) Bank fees
   (e) Insurance costs

Now try the question below from the Exam Question Bank

Number	Level	Marks	Time
15	Introductory	n/a	20 mins

Part D
Working capital management

Chapter 16

WORKING CAPITAL CHARACTERISTICS

Topic list	Syllabus reference	Ability required
1 Working capital	(iv)	Application
2 Working capital (liquidity) ratios	(iv)	Analysis
3 Working capital requirements	(iv)	Analysis

Introduction

In this chapter, we consider functions of the financial manager relating to the **management of working capital** in general terms.

In later chapters, we shall be looking at specific aspects of the management of **cash**, **debtors** and **stocks** (inventories).

MCQs often test the effect on working capital of certain transactions or events.

Learning outcomes covered in this chapter

- Calculate and interpret working capital ratios for business sectors

Syllabus content covered in this chapter

- Working capital ratios, ie debtor days, stock days, creditor days, current ratio, quick ratio, and the working capital cycle
- The working capital characteristics of different businesses (eg supermarkets being heavily funded by creditors) and the importance of industry comparisons

1 WORKING CAPITAL

Pilot paper

What is working capital?

> **KEY TERM**
>
> **Working capital** is the capital available for conducting the day-to-day operations of an organisation; normally the excess of current assets over current liabilities. *(OT 2000)*

1.1 Every business needs adequate **liquid resources** to maintain day-to-day cash flow. It needs enough to pay wages and salaries as they fall due and enough to pay creditors if it is to keep its workforce and ensure its supplies. Maintaining adequate working capital is not just important in the short term. Sufficient liquidity must be maintained in order to ensure the survival of the business in the long term as well. Even a profitable company may fail if it does not have adequate cash flow to meet its liabilities as they fall due.

Part D: Working capital management

Working capital characteristics of different businesses

1.2 Different businesses will have different working capital characteristics. There are three main aspects to these differences.

(a) Holding stocks (from their purchase from external suppliers, through the production and warehousing of finished goods, up to the time of sale)

(b) Taking time to pay suppliers and other creditors

(c) Allowing customers (debtors) time to pay

1.3 Here are some examples.

(a) Supermarkets and other retailers receive much of their sales in cash or by credit card or debit card. However, they typically buy from suppliers on credit. They may therefore have the advantage of significant cash holdings, which they may choose to invest.

(b) A company which supplies to other companies, such as a wholesaler, is likely to be selling and buying mainly on **credit**. Co-ordinating the flow of cash may be quite a problem. Such a company may make use of short-term borrowings (such as an overdraft) to manage its cash.

(c) Smaller companies with a limited trading record may face particularly severe problems. Lacking a long track record, such companies may find it difficult to obtain credit from suppliers. At the same time, customers will expect to receive the length of credit period that is normal for the particular business concerned. The firm may find itself squeezed in its management of cash.

What is working capital management?   5/01

1.4 Ensuring that sufficient liquid resources are maintained is a matter of working capital management. This involves achieving a balance between the requirement to minimise the risk of insolvency and the requirement to maximise the return on assets. An excessively conservative approach to working capital management resulting in high levels of cash holdings will harm profits because the opportunity to make a return on the assets tied up as cash will have been missed.

> **Exam focus point**
>
> Working capital management - covered in Chapters 16 to 23 of this Study Text - is the largest section of the *Finance* syllabus, accounting for 40% of the paper.

The working capital cycle   5/02

> **KEY TERM**
>
> **Working capital cycle** is the period of time which elapses between the point at which cash begins to be expended on the production of a product and the collection of cash from a purchaser. *(OT 2000)*

1.5 The connection between investment in working capital and cash flow may be illustrated by means of the **working capital cycle** (also called the **cash cycle, operating cycle** or **trading cycle**).

1.6 The working capital cycle in a manufacturing business equals:

The average time that raw materials remain in stock
Less the period of credit taken from suppliers
Plus the time taken to produce the goods
Plus the time taken by customers to pay for the goods

1.7 If the turnover periods for stocks and debtors lengthen, or the payment period to creditors shortens, then the operating cycle will lengthen and the investment in working capital will increase.

Cash flow planning

1.8 Since a company must have adequate cash inflows to survive, management should plan and control cash flows as well as profitability. **Cash budgeting** is an important element in short-term cash flow planning.

1.9 The purpose of cash budgets is to make sure that the organisation will have **enough cash inflows** to meet its cash outflows. If a budget reveals that a short-term cash shortage can be expected, steps will be taken to meet the problem and avoid the cash crisis (perhaps by arranging a bigger bank overdraft facility).

1.10 Cash budgets and cash flow forecasts on their own do not give full protection against a cash shortage and enforced liquidation of the business by creditors. There may be unexpected changes in cash flow patterns. When unforeseen events have an adverse effect on cash inflows, a company will only survive if it can maintain adequate cash inflows despite the setbacks.

Question 1

Give examples of unforeseen changes which may affect cash flow patterns.

Answer

Your list probably included some of the following.

(a) A **change** in the **general economic environment**. An economic recession will cause a slump in trade.

(b) A **new product**, launched by a competitor, which takes business away from a company's traditional and established product lines.

(c) **New cost-saving product technology**, which forces the company to invest in the new technology to remain competitive.

(d) **Moves by competitors** which have to be countered (for example a price reduction or a sales promotion).

(e) **Changes in consumer preferences**, resulting in a fall in demand.

(f) **Government action** against certain trade practices or against trade with a country that a company has dealings with.

(g) **Strikes** or other industrial action.

(h) **Natural disasters**, such as floods or fire damage, which curtail an organisation's activities.

2 WORKING CAPITAL (LIQUIDITY) RATIOS 11/01

The current ratio and the quick ratio

2.1 The standard test of liquidity is the **current ratio**. It can be obtained from the balance sheet.

> **KEY TERM**
>
> $$\text{Current ratio} = \frac{\text{Current assets}}{\text{Current liabilities}}$$

2.2 A company should have enough current assets that give a promise of 'cash to come' to meet its commitments to pay its current liabilities. Obviously, a ratio in excess of 1 should be expected; an ideal is probably about 2. Otherwise, there would be the prospect that the company might be unable to pay its debts on time. In practice, a ratio comfortably in excess of 1 should be expected, but what is 'comfortable' varies between different types of businesses.

2.3 Some manufacturing companies might hold large quantities of raw material stocks, which must be used in production to create finished goods. Finished goods might be warehoused for a long time, or sold on lengthy credit. In such businesses, where stock turnover is slow, most stocks are not very liquid assets, because the cash cycle is so long. For these reasons, we calculate an additional liquidity ratio, known as the quick ratio or acid test ratio.

> **KEY TERM**
>
> $$\text{Quick ratio, or acid test ratio} = \frac{\text{Current assets less stocks}}{\text{Current liabilities}}$$

2.4 This ratio should ideally be at least 1 for companies with a slow stock turnover. For companies with a fast stock turnover, a quick ratio can be less than 1 without suggesting that the company is in cash flow difficulties.

The debtors' payment period

2.5 A rough measure of the average length of time it takes for a company's debtors to pay what they owe is the '**debtor days**' ratio.

> **KEY TERM**
>
> $$\text{Debtors' days ratio} = \frac{\text{Average trade debtors}}{\text{Average daily turnover on credit terms}} \qquad (OT\ 2000)$$

2.6 An alternative measure is the debtors' payment period.

KEY TERM

Debtors' payment period, or **debtors' turnover period**

$$= \frac{\text{Average trade debtors}}{\text{Credit sales turnover for year}} \times 365 \text{ days}$$

2.7 The trade debtors are not the **total** figure for debtors in the balance sheet, which includes prepayments and non-trade debtors. The trade debtors figure will be itemised in an analysis of the total debtors, in a note to the accounts.

2.8 The estimate of debtors' days is only approximate.

(a) The balance sheet value might be used instead of the average. However, don't forget that the balance sheet value of debtors might be abnormally high or low compared with the 'normal' level the company usually has.

(b) Turnover in the profit and loss account excludes value added tax (VAT), but the debtors' figure in the balance sheet includes VAT. We are not strictly comparing like with like. If the figures are too distorted by VAT adjustment will be needed.

(c) Average debtors may not be representative of year-end sales if sales are growing rapidly.

The creditors' payment period

2.9 Similar measures can be used for creditors.

KEY TERM

Creditors' days ratio $= \dfrac{\text{Average trade creditors}}{\text{Average daily purchases on credit terms}}$ *(OT 2000)*

2.10 This indicates the average time taken, in calendar days, to pay for supplies received on credit. Again, the distortion effect of VAT needs to be taken into account.

KEY TERM

Creditors' payment period, or **creditors' turnover period**

$$= \frac{\text{Average trade creditors}}{\text{Purchases on credit terms for year}} \times 365 \text{ days}$$

2.11 If the credit purchases information is not readily available, cost of sales can be used instead. Don't forget however that some elements of cost of sales (for example, labour costs) are not relevant to trade creditors.

The stock turnover period

2.12 Another ratio worth calculating is the stock turnover period, or stockholding period days. This is another estimated figure, obtainable from published accounts, which indicates the average number of days that items of stock are held for. As with the average debt collection period, it is only an approximate figure; there may be distortions caused by seasonal variations in stock levels. However it should be reliable enough for finding changes over time.

> **KEY TERM**
>
> $$\text{Stock turnover} = \frac{\text{Stock value}}{\text{Average daily cost of sales in period}}$$
>
> The stock turnover period can also be calculated:
>
> $$\text{Stock turnover period} = \frac{\text{Stock value}}{\text{Cost of sales}} \times 365 \text{ days}$$

2.13 The ratio $\frac{\text{Average stock}}{\text{Cost of sales}}$ is called the stock turnover, and is another measure of how vigorously a business is trading. A lengthening stock turnover period indicates:

(a) A slowdown in trading, or

(b) A build-up in stock levels, perhaps suggesting that the investment in stocks is becoming excessive

2.14 If we add together the stock days and the debtor days, this should give us an indication of how soon stock is convertible into cash, thereby giving a further indication of the company's liquidity.

2.15 All the ratios calculated above will **vary industry by industry**; hence **comparisons** of ratios calculated with other similar companies in the same industry are important.

3 WORKING CAPITAL REQUIREMENTS   Pilot paper

The need for funds for investment in current assets

3.1 As we have seen, current assets may be financed either by long-term funds or by current liabilities.

3.2 Liquidity ratios are a guide to the risk of cash flow problems and insolvency. If a company suddenly finds that it is unable to renew its short-term liabilities (for example, if the bank suspends its overdraft facilities, or creditors start to demand earlier payment), there will be a danger of insolvency unless the company is able to turn enough of its current assets into cash quickly.

3.3 Current liabilities are often a cheap method of finance (trade creditors do not usually carry an interest cost) and companies may therefore consider that, in the interest of higher profits, it is worth accepting some risk of insolvency by increasing current liabilities, taking the maximum credit possible from suppliers.

The volume of current assets required

3.4 The volume of current assets required will depend on the nature of the company's business. For example, a manufacturing company may require more stocks than a company in a

service industry. As the volume of output by a company increases, the volume of current assets required will also increase.

3.5 Even assuming efficient stock holding, debt collection procedures and cash management, there is still a certain degree of choice in the total volume of current assets required to meet output requirements. Policies of low stock-holding levels, tight credit and minimum cash holdings may be contrasted with policies of high stocks (to allow for safety or buffer stocks) easier credit and sizeable cash holdings (for precautionary reasons).

Over-capitalisation and working capital

3.6 If there are excessive stocks, debtors and cash, and very few creditors, there will be an over-investment by the company in current assets. Working capital will be excessive and the company will be in this respect over-capitalised. The return on investment will be lower than it should be, and long-term funds will be unnecessarily tied up when they could be invested elsewhere to earn profits.

3.7 **Over-capitalisation** with respect to working capital should not exist if there is good management, but the warning signs of excessive working capital would be unfavourable accounting ratios, including the following.

(a) **Sales/working capital**

The volume of sales as a multiple of the working capital investment should indicate whether, in comparison with previous years or with similar companies, the total volume of working capital is too high.

(b) **Liquidity ratios**

A current ratio greatly in excess of 2:1 or a quick ratio much in excess of 1:1 may indicate over-investment in working capital.

(c) **Turnover periods**

Excessive turnover periods for stocks and debtors, or a short period of credit taken from suppliers, might indicate that the volume of stocks or debtors is unnecessarily high, or the volume of creditors too low.

3.8 **EXAMPLE: WORKING CAPITAL RATIOS**

Calculate liquidity and working capital ratios from the following accounts of a manufacturer of products for the construction industry, and comment on the ratios.

	20X8 £m	20X7 £m
Turnover	2,065.0	1,788.7
Cost of sales	1,478.6	1,304.0
Gross profit	586.4	484.7
Current assets		
Stocks	119.0	109.0
Debtors (note 1)	400.9	347.4
Short-term investments	4.2	18.8
Cash at bank and in hand	48.2	48.0
	572.3	523.2
Creditors: amounts falling due within one year		
Loans and overdrafts	49.1	35.3
Corporation taxes	62.0	46.7
Dividend	19.2	14.3
Creditors (note 2)	370.7	324.0

Part D: Working capital management

	20X8	20X7
	501.0	420.3
Net current assets	71.3	102.9

Notes

		20X8 £m	20X7 £m
1	Trade debtors	329.8	285.4
2	Trade creditors	236.2	210.8

3.9 SOLUTION

	20X8		20X7	
Current ratio	$\frac{572.3}{501.0}$	= 1.14	$\frac{523.2}{420.3}$	= 1.24
Quick ratio	$\frac{453.3}{501.0}$	= 0.90	$\frac{414.2}{420.3}$	= 0.99
Debtors' payment period	$\frac{329.8}{2,065.0} \times 365$	= 58 days	$\frac{285.4}{1,788.7} \times 365$	= 58 days
Stock turnover period	$\frac{119.0}{1,478.6} \times 365$	= 29 days	$\frac{109.0}{1,304.0} \times 365$	= 31 days
Creditors' turnover period	$\frac{236.2}{1,478.6} \times 365$	= 58 days	$\frac{210.8}{1,304.0} \times 365$	= 59 days

The company is a manufacturing group serving the construction industry, and so would be expected to have a comparatively lengthy debtors' turnover period, because of the relatively poor cash flow in the construction industry. It is clear that the company compensates for this by ensuring that they do not pay for raw materials and other costs before they have sold their stocks of finished goods (hence the similarity of debtors' and creditors' turnover periods).

The company's current ratio is a little lower than average but its quick ratio is better than average and very little less than the current ratio. This suggests that stock levels are strictly controlled, which is reinforced by the low stock turnover period. It would seem that working capital is tightly managed, to avoid the poor liquidity which could be caused by a high debtors' turnover period and comparatively high creditors.

Overtrading 11/01

> **KEY TERM**
>
> **Overtrading** is the condition of a business which enters into commitments in excess of its available short-term resources. This can arise even if the company is trading profitably, and is typically caused by financing strains imposed by a lengthy operating cycle or production cycle.
> *(OT 2000)*

3.10 In contrast with over-capitalisation, overtrading happens when a business tries to do too much too quickly with too little long-term capital, so that it is trying to support too large a volume of trade with the capital resources at its disposal.

3.11 Even if an overtrading business operates at a profit, it could easily run into serious trouble because it is short of money. Such liquidity troubles stem from the fact that it does not have enough capital to provide the cash to pay its debts as they fall due.

16: Working capital characteristics

> **Exam focus point**
> Question 6 in May 2002 is an example of a question where candidates were expected to diagnose overtrading from information given to them about a company.

3.12 EXAMPLE: OVERTRADING   5/02

Great Ambition Ltd appoints a new managing director who has great plans to expand the company. He wants to increase turnover by 100% within two years, and to do this he employs extra sales staff. He recognises that customers do not want to have to wait for deliveries, and so he decides that the company must build up its stock levels. There is a substantial increase in the company's stocks. These are held in additional warehouse space which is now rented. The company also buys new cars for its extra sales representatives.

The managing director's policies are immediately successful in boosting sales, which double in just over one year. Stock levels are now much higher, but the company takes longer credit from its suppliers, even though some suppliers have expressed their annoyance at the length of time they must wait for payment. Credit terms for debtors are unchanged, and so the volume of debtors, like the volume of sales, rises by 100%.

In spite of taking longer credit, the company still needs to increase its overdraft facilities with the bank, which are raised from a limit of £40,000 to one of £80,000. The company is profitable, and retains some profits in the business, but profit margins have fallen. **Gross profit margins** are lower because some prices have been reduced to obtain extra sales. **Net profit margins** are lower because overhead costs are higher. These include sales representatives' wages, car expenses and depreciation on cars, warehouse rent and additional losses from having to write off out-of-date and slow-moving stock items.

3.13 The balance sheet of the company might change over time from (A) to (B).

	\multicolumn{3}{c}{Balance sheet (A)}	\multicolumn{3}{c}{Balance sheet (B)}
	£	£	£	£	£	£
Fixed assets			160,000			210,000
Current assets						
Stock		60,000			150,000	
Debtors		64,000			135,000	
Cash		1,000			-	
		125,000			285,000	
Current liabilities						
Bank	25,000			80,000		
Creditors	50,000			200,000		
	75,000			280,000		
			50,000			5,000
			210,000			215,000
Share capital			10,000			10,000
Profit and loss account			200,000			205,000
			210,000			215,000
Sales			£1,000,000			£2,000,000
Gross profit			£200,000			£300,000
Net profit			£50,000			£20,000

In situation (B), the company has reached its overdraft limit and has four times as many creditors as in situation (A) but with only twice the sales turnover. Stock levels are much higher, and stock turnover is lower.

Part D: Working capital management

The company is overtrading. If it had to pay its next trade creditor, or salaries and wages, before it received any income, it could not do so without the bank allowing it to exceed its overdraft limit. The company is profitable, although profit margins have fallen, and it ought to expect a prosperous future. But if it does not sort out its cash flow and liquidity, it will not survive to enjoy future profits.

3.14 Suitable solutions to the problem would be measures to reduce the degree of overtrading. **New capital** from the shareholders could be injected. Short-term finance could be converted to longer-term finance. **Better control** could be applied to stocks and debtors. The company could **abandon ambitious plans** for increased sales and more fixed asset purchases until the business has had time to consolidate its position, and build up its capital base with retained profits. It partly requires the business to take a long-term view of future prospects, and **avoid short-termism**.

> **KEY TERM**
>
> **Short-termism** is a bias towards paying particular attention to short-term performance, with a corresponding relative disregard to the long term. *(OT 2000)*

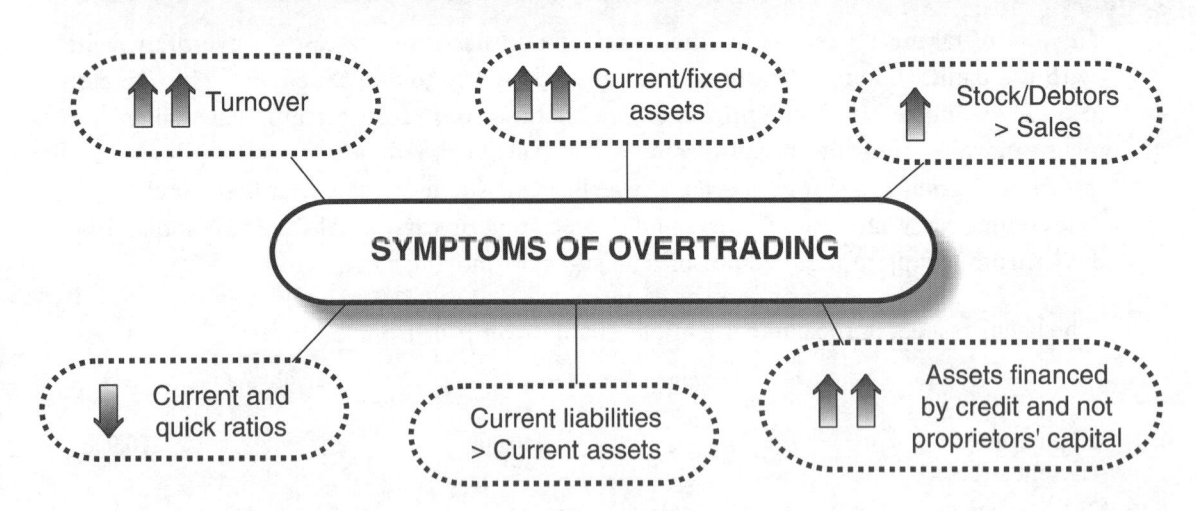

SYMPTOMS OF OVERTRADING
- ↑↑ Turnover
- ↑↑ Current/fixed assets
- ↑ Stock/Debtors > Sales
- ↓ Current and quick ratios
- Current liabilities > Current assets
- ↑↑ Assets financed by credit and not proprietors' capital

3.15 Apart from the danger of overtrading when a business seeks to increase its turnover too rapidly without an adequate capital base, **other causes** are as follows.

(a) When a business repays a loan, it often replaces the old loan with a new one. However a business might **repay a loan** without **replacing it**, with the consequence that it has **less long-term capital** to finance its current level of operations.

(b) A business might be profitable, but in a period of inflation, its **retained profits** might be **insufficient** to pay for replacement fixed assets and stocks, which now cost more because of inflation. The business would then rely increasingly on credit, and find itself eventually unable to support its current volume of trading with a capital base that has fallen in real terms.

> **Exam focus point**
>
> Question 3 in November 2001 described an over-trading situation, allowing the examiner to test various ways of improving working capital control to correct the problem.

The working capital requirement

3.16 **Computing the working capital requirement** is a matter of calculating the value of current assets less current liabilities, perhaps by taking averages over a one year period.

3.17 EXAMPLE: WORKING CAPITAL REQUIREMENTS

The following data relate to Corn Ltd, a manufacturing company.

Turnover for the year	£1,500,000
Costs as percentages of sales	%
Direct materials	30
Direct labour	25
Variable overheads	10
Fixed overheads	15
Selling and distribution	5

On average:

(a) Debtors take 2.5 months before payment.

(b) Raw materials are in stock for three months.

(c) Work-in-progress represents two months worth of half produced goods.

(d) Finished goods represents one month's production.

(e) Credit is taken as follows.

(i)	Direct materials	2 months
(ii)	Direct labour	1 week
(iii)	Variable overheads	1 month
(iv)	Fixed overheads	1 month
(v)	Selling and distribution	0.5 months

Work-in-progress and finished goods are valued at material, labour and variable expense cost.

Compute the working capital requirement of Corn Ltd assuming the labour force is paid for 50 working weeks a year.

3.18 SOLUTION

(a) The annual costs incurred will be as follows.

		£
Direct materials	30% of £1,500,000	450,000
Direct labour	25% of £1,500,000	375,000
Variable overheads	10% of £1,500,000	150,000
Fixed overheads	15% of £1,500,000	225,000
Selling and distribution	5% of £1,500,000	75,000

Part D: Working capital management

(b) The average value of current assets will be as follows.

		£	£
Raw materials	3/12 × £450,000		112,500
Work-in-progress			
Materials (50% complete)	1/12 × £450,000	37,500	
Labour (50% complete)	1/12 × £375,000	31,250	
Variable overheads (50% complete)	1/12 × £150,000	12,500	
			81,250
Finished goods			
Materials	1/12 × £450,000	37,500	
Labour	1/12 × £375,000	31,250	
Variable overheads	1/12 × £150,000	12,500	
			81,250
Debtors	2.5/12 × £1,500,000		312,500
			587,500

(c) Average value of current liabilities will be as follows.

		£
Materials	2/12 × £450,000	75,000
Labour	1/50 × £375,000	7,500
Variable overheads	1/12 × £150,000	12,500
Fixed overheads	1/12 × £225,000	18,750
Selling and distribution	0.5/12 × £75,000	3,125
		116,875

(d) Working capital required is (£(587,500 − 116,875)) = 470,625

It has been assumed that all the direct materials are allocated to work-in-progress when production starts.

Predicting business failure

3.19 Investors will wish to know whether additional funds could be lent to the company with reasonable safety, and whether the company would fail without additional funds.

3.20 One method of predicting business failure is the use of **liquidity ratios** (the current ratio and the quick ratio). A company with a current ratio well below 2:1 or a quick ratio well below 1:1 might be considered illiquid and in danger of failure. Research seems to indicate, however, that the current ratio and the quick ratio and trends in the variations of these ratios for a company, are poor indicators of eventual business failure.

Z scores

3.21 E I Altman researched into the simultaneous analysis of several financial ratios as a combined predictor of business failure. Altman analysed 22 accounting and non-accounting variables for a selection of failed and non-failed firms in the USA and from these, five key indicators emerged. These five indicators were then used to derive a **Z score**. Firms with a Z score above a certain level would be predicted to be financially sound, and firms with a Z score below a certain level would be categorised as probable failures. Altman also identified a range of Z scores in between the non-failure and failure categories in which eventual failure or non-failure was uncertain.

3.22 Altman's Z score model (derived in 1968) emerged as:

$$Z = 1.2X_1 + 1.4X_2 + 3.3X_3 + 0.6X_4 + 1.0X_5$$

where

X_1 = working capital/total assets
X_2 = retained earnings/total assets

X_3 = earnings before interest and tax/total assets
X_4 = market value of equity/book value of total debt (a form of gearing ratio)
X_5 = sales/total assets

Question 2

Define what is meant by the term 'overtrading' and describe some of the typical symptoms.

Answer

'**Overtrading**' refers to the situation where a company is **over-reliant** on **short-term finance** to support its operations. This is risky because short-term finance may be withdrawn relatively quickly if creditors lose confidence in the business, or if there is a general tightening of credit in the economy, and this may result in a liquidity crisis and even bankruptcy, even though the firm is profitable. The fundamental solution to overtrading is to replace short term finance with longer term finance such as term loans or equity funds.

The term overtrading is used because the condition commonly arises when a company is **expanding rapidly**. In this situation, because of increasing volumes, more cash is frequently needed to pay input costs such as wages or purchases than is currently being collected from debtors. The result is that the company runs up its overdraft to the limit and sometimes there is insufficient time to arrange an increase in facilities to pay other creditors on the due dates.

These problems are often compounded by a general lack of attention to cost control and working capital management, such as debt collection, because most management time is spent organising selling or production. The result is an unnecessary drop in profit margins.

When the overdraft limit is reached the company frequently raises funds from other expensive short term sources, such as debt factoring or debtor's prompt payment discounts, and delays payment to creditors, instead of underpinning its financial position with equity funds or a longer term loan. The consequent under-capitalisation delays investment in fixed assets and staff and can further harm the quality of the firm's operations.

Question 3

The figures below have been extracted from the accounts of Premier Ltd.

	£
Turnover	750,000
Cost of sales	500,000
Gross profit	250,000
Current assets	
Stocks	75,000
Trade debtors	100,000
Other debtors	10,000
Cash at bank and in hand	5,000
	190,000
Current liabilities	
Overdraft	30,000
Dividend	40,000
Trade creditors	80,000
Other creditors	10,000
	160,000
Net current assets	30,000

A 0.69
B 0.72
C 0.82
D 1.19

What is the quick ratio?

Part D: Working capital management

Answer

B   The quick ratio is the ratio of current assets excluding stocks to current liabilities.

In this case: $\dfrac{190{,}000 - 75{,}000}{160{,}000} = 0.72$

Chapter roundup

- The amount tied up in **working capital** is equal to the value of raw materials, work-in-progress, finished stocks and debtors less creditors. The size of this net figure has a direct effect on the **liquidity** of an organisation.

- **Liquidity ratios** may help to indicate whether a company is **over-capitalised**, with excessive working capital, or if a business is likely to fail. A business which is trying to do too much too quickly with too little long-term capital is **overtrading**.

- **Liquidity ratios** might be used, as in Altman's model, to predict whether a business is likely to fail.

Quick quiz

1   Which of the following is the most likely to be a symptom of overtrading?

    A   Static levels of stock turnover
    B   Rapid increase in profits
    C   Increase in the level of the current ratio
    D   Rapid increase in sales

2   The operating cycle is:

	A The time	
Less	B The time	
Plus	C The time	
Plus	D The time	

    Fill in the blanks.

3   Fill in the blanks with the following:

    Current liabilities; current assets; stocks; 2; 1.

    Quick ratio = $\dfrac{\text{............ less ....}}{\text{................................}}$ (This should be at least ....)

4   Which of the following describes *overcapitalisation* and which describes *overtrading*?

    A   A company with excessive investment in working capital
    B   A company trying to support too large a volume of trade with the capital resources at its disposal

5   Which of the following statements best defines the current ratio?

    A   The ratio of current assets to current liabilities.
        For the majority of businesses it should be at least 2.

    B   The ratio of current assets to current liabilities.
        For the majority of businesses it should be at least 1.

    C   The ratio of current assets excluding stock to current liabilities.
        For the majority of businesses it should be at least 1.

    D   The ratio of current assets excluding stock to current liabilities.
        For the majority of businesses it should be at least 2.

16: Working capital characteristics

6   The debtors' payment period is a calculation of the time taken to pay by all debtors.

   True ☐
   False ☐

7   A company has a current ratio of 2:1. It decides to use surplus cash balances to settle 40% of its total current liabilities. The current ratio will:

   A   Increase by more than 40%
   B   Decrease by more than 40%
   C   Increase by less than 40%
   D   Decrease by less than 40%

8   What is the working capital requirement of a company with the following average figures over a year?

	£
Stock	3,750
Trade debtors	1,500
Cash and bank balances	500
Trade creditors	1,800

Answers to quick quiz

1   D   Rapid increase in sales

2   A   The time raw materials remain in stock
    B   The time period of credit taken from suppliers
    C   The time taken to produce goods
    D   The time taken by customers to pay for goods

3   Quick ratio = $\dfrac{\text{Current assets less stocks}}{\text{Current liabilities}}$ (This should be at least 1)

4   A   Overcapitalisation
    B   Overtrading

5   A   The ratio of current assets to current liabilities: 2

6   False; the calculation normally only includes trade debtors.

7   C   Current ratio = 2
        Settlement = 0.4
        New current ratio = 1.6/0.6 = 2.67

        Increase = (2.67/2) – 1 = 33.3%

8   Working capital requirement = current assets less current liabilities

    = 3,750 + 1,500 + 500 – 1,800
    = £3,950

Now try the question below from the Exam Question Bank

Number	Level	Marks	Time
16	Examination	20	36 mins

Chapter 17

CASH FLOW FORECASTS

Topic list	Syllabus reference	Ability required
1 Cash flows and profit	(iv)	Application
2 The purpose of cash forecasts	(iv)	Application
3 Cash budgets in receipts and payments format	(iv)	Application
4 Cleared funds cash forecasts	(iv)	Application
5 Cash forecasts based on financial statements	(iv)	Application
6 Inflation and cash budgeting	(iv)	Application
7 Computer models and sensitivity analysis	(iv)	Application

Introduction

Survival in business depends on the ability to generate cash. **Cash flow information** directs attention towards this critical issue. Cash flow is a more comprehensive concept than 'profit' which is dependent on accounting conventions and concepts.

The **cash budget** is an extremely important mechanism for monitoring cash flows, and cash budgets will appear frequently in this paper. Various complications about timing of cash flows or lack of particular figures will be included in cash budget questions, or will be tested individually in MCQs.

Learning outcomes covered in this chapter

- Prepare and analyse cash flow forecasts over a 12 month period

Syllabus content covered in this chapter

- Cash flow forecasts, use of spreadsheets to assist in this in terms of changing variables (eg interest rates or inflation) and in consolidating forecasts
- Which variables are most easily changed, delayed or brought forward in a forecast
- The link between cash, profit and the balance sheet

1 CASH FLOWS AND PROFIT

Types of cash transaction

1.1 There are many types of cash transaction. They can be distinguished by their purpose (ie what they are for), their form (how they are implemented), and their frequency. Sometimes the following distinctions are made.

(a) **Capital** and **revenue** items

    (i) Capital items relate to the long-term functioning of the business, such as raising money from shareholders, or acquiring fixed assets.

    (ii) Revenue items relate to day-to-day operations, as in the operating cycle, including other matters such as overdraft interest.

(b) **Exceptional** and **unexceptional** items

    (i) Exceptional items are unusual. An example would be the costs of closing down part of a business.

    (ii) Unexceptional items include everything else. You have to be careful using this distinction, as the phrase 'exceptional item' has a precise meaning in the preparation of a company's financial statements.

(c) **Regular** and **irregular** items

    (i) Regular items occur at predictable intervals. Such intervals might be frequent such as the payment of wages every week or month, or relatively infrequent, such as the disbursement of interim and final dividends twice a year. A capital item might be the regular repayment of principal and interest on leased property. Annual disbursements are sums of money paid at yearly intervals.

    (ii) Irregular items do not occur at regular intervals.

Cash flows and profit

1.2 **Trading profits** and **cash flows** are different. A company can make losses but still have a net cash income from trading. A **company** can also make profits but have a net cash deficit on its trading operations.

(a) Cash may be obtained from a transaction which has **nothing** to do with **profit or loss**. For example, an issue of shares or loan stock for cash has no immediate effect on profit but is obviously a source of cash. Similarly, an increase in bank overdraft provides a source of cash for payments, but it is not reported in the profit and loss account.

(b) Cash may be paid for the **purchase of fixed assets**, but the charge in the profit and loss account is depreciation, which is only a part of an asset's cost.

(c) When a fixed asset is sold there is a profit or loss on sale **equal to the difference** between the **sale proceeds** and the '**net book value**' of the asset in the balance sheet at the time it is sold.

(d) One reason is changes in the amount of the company's stocks, debtors and creditors.

    (i) **Profit** is sales minus the cost of sales.

    (ii) **Operational cash flow** is the difference between cash received and cash paid from trading.

    (iii) Cash received differs from sales because of changes in the amount of debtors.

	£
Debtors owing money at the start of the year	X
Sales during the year	X
Total money due from customers	X
Less debtors owing money at the end of the year	(X)
Cash receipts from debtors during the year	X

    (iv) Cash paid differs from the cost of sales because of changes in the amount of stocks and creditors.

Part D: Working capital management

	£
Closing stocks at the end of the year	X
Add cost of sales during the year	X
	X
Less opening stocks at the start of the year	(X)
Equals purchases	Y

	£
Payments owing to creditors at the start of the year	X
Add purchases	Y
	X
Less payments still owing to creditors at the end of the year	(X)
Equals **cash payments** to creditors during the year	X

(v) Operational cash flow therefore differs from profit because of changes in the amount of debtors, stocks and creditors between the start and end of a period.

Question 1

Assume that Beta achieved sales turnover in a particular year of £200,000 and the cost of sales was £170,000. Stocks were £12,000, creditors £11,000 and debtors £15,000 at the start of the year. At the end of the year, stocks were £21,000, creditors were £14,000 and debtors £24,000.

Required

Find out the profits and the operational cash flow resulting from the year's trading.

Answer

	Profit £	Operational cash flow £
Sales	200,000	200,000
Opening debtors (∴ received in year)		15,000
Closing debtors (outstanding at year end)		(24,000)
Cash in		191,000
Cost of sales	170,000	170,000
Closing stock (bought, but not used, in year)		21,000
Opening stock (used, but not bought, in year)		(12,000)
Purchases in year		179,000
Opening creditors (∴ paid in year)		11,000
Closing creditors (outstanding at year end)		(14,000)
Cash out		176,000
Profit/operational cash flow	30,000	15,000

1.3 The difference between profit and cash flow has important implications.

(a) If a company is profitable but short of cash, one reason could be an increase in the other elements of working capital. If a company were to seek credit from a bank to finance the growth in working capital, the bank might ask the management whether **operational cash flows could be improved** by squeezing working capital, and:

- Reducing debtors
- Reducing stocks, or
- Taking more trade credit from suppliers

Better control over working capital could remove the need to borrow.

(b) If a company is making losses, it could try to maintain a positive operational cash flow by **taking more credit** (ie by increasing its creditors and so reducing working capital).

The credit managers of supplier companies should then consider whether to give the extra credit required, or whether to refuse because the risk would be too great.

Question 2

Write brief notes on why the reported profit figure of a business for a period does not normally represent the amount of cash generated in that period.

Answer

The principal reasons why profit will not equal cash flow are as follows.

(a) The '**matching concept**' means that costs and revenues do not equal payments and receipts. Revenue is recognised in the profit statement when goods are sold, and any revenue not received is recorded as a debtor. Similarly, costs are incurred when a resource is acquired or subsequently used, not when it happens to be paid for.

(b) **Some items appearing** in the profit statement do not **affect cash flow**. For example, depreciation is a 'non-cash' deduction in arriving at profit.

(c) Similarly, items may **affect cash flow** but not profit. Capital expenditure decisions (apart from depreciation) and stock level adjustments are prime examples.

2 THE PURPOSE OF CASH FORECASTS

2.1 **Cash forecasting** ensures that sufficient funds will be available when they are needed to sustain the activities of an enterprise.

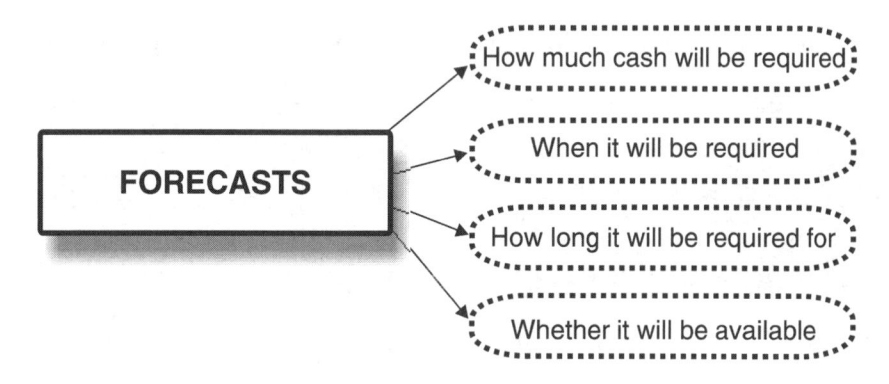

FORECASTS
- How much cash will be required
- When it will be required
- How long it will be required for
- Whether it will be available

2.2 **Banks** have increasingly insisted that customers provide cash forecasts (or a business plan that includes a cash forecast) as a precondition of lending. A newly established company wishing to open a bank account will also normally be asked to supply a **business plan**. The cash and sales forecasts will also allow the bank to **monitor** the **progress** of the new company, and control its lending more effectively.

Deficiencies

2.3 Any forecast **deficiency** of cash will have to be funded.

(a) **Borrowing**. If borrowing arrangements are not already secured, a source of funds will have to be found. If a company cannot fund its cash deficits it could be wound up.

(b) The firm can make arrangements to **sell any short-term financial investments** to raise cash.

(c) The firm can delay payments to creditors, or pull in payments from customers. This is sometimes known as **leading and lagging**.

2.4 Because cash forecasts cannot be entirely accurate, companies should have **contingency funding**, available from a surplus cash balance and liquid investments, or from a bank facility

2.5 Forecasting gives management time to arrange its funding. If planned in advance, instead of a panic measure to avert a cash crisis, a company can more easily choose **when to borrow**, and will probably obtain a **lower interest rate**.

Forecasting a cash surplus

2.6 Many cash-generative businesses are less reliant on high quality cash forecasts. If a cash surplus is forecast, having an idea of both its size and how long it will exist could help decide how best to invest it.

2.7 In some cases, the amount of interest earned from surplus cash could be significant for the company's earnings. The company might then need a forecast of its interest earnings in order to indicate its prospective earnings per share to stock market analysts and institutional investors.

Types of forecast   5/01

2.8 There are two broad types of cash forecast.

- Cash flow based forecasts (or cash budgets) in **receipts and payments format**
- **Balance sheet and financial statement based** forecasts

We discuss these later on in this chapter, but some introductory points are in order here.

> **KEY TERM**
>
> A **cash budget** is a detailed budget of estimated cash inflows and outflows, incorporating both revenue and capital items. *(OT 2000)*

2.9 In companies that use cash flow reporting for control purposes, there will probably be:

- A cash budget divided into monthly or quarterly periods
- A statement comparing actual cash flows against the monthly or quarterly budget
- A revised cash forecast
- A statement comparing actual cash flows against a revised forecast

2.10 Revised forecasts should be prepared to keep forecasts relevant and up-to-date. Examples would be a revised three-month forecast every month for the next three-month period, or a revised forecast each month or each quarter up to the end of the annual budget period.

2.11 A **rolling forecast** is a forecast that is **continually updated**. When actual results are reported for a given time period (say for one month's results within an annual forecast period) a further forecast period is added and forecasts for intermediate time periods are updated. A rolling forecast can therefore be a 12-month forecast which is updated at the end of every month, with a further month added to the end of the forecast period and with figures for the intervening 11 months revised if necessary.

17: Cash flow forecasts

> **Exam focus point**
>
> In the *Finance* exam, you may be asked to prepare and analyse a cash flow forecast over a period of up to twelve months.

Cash flow control with budgets and revised forecasts

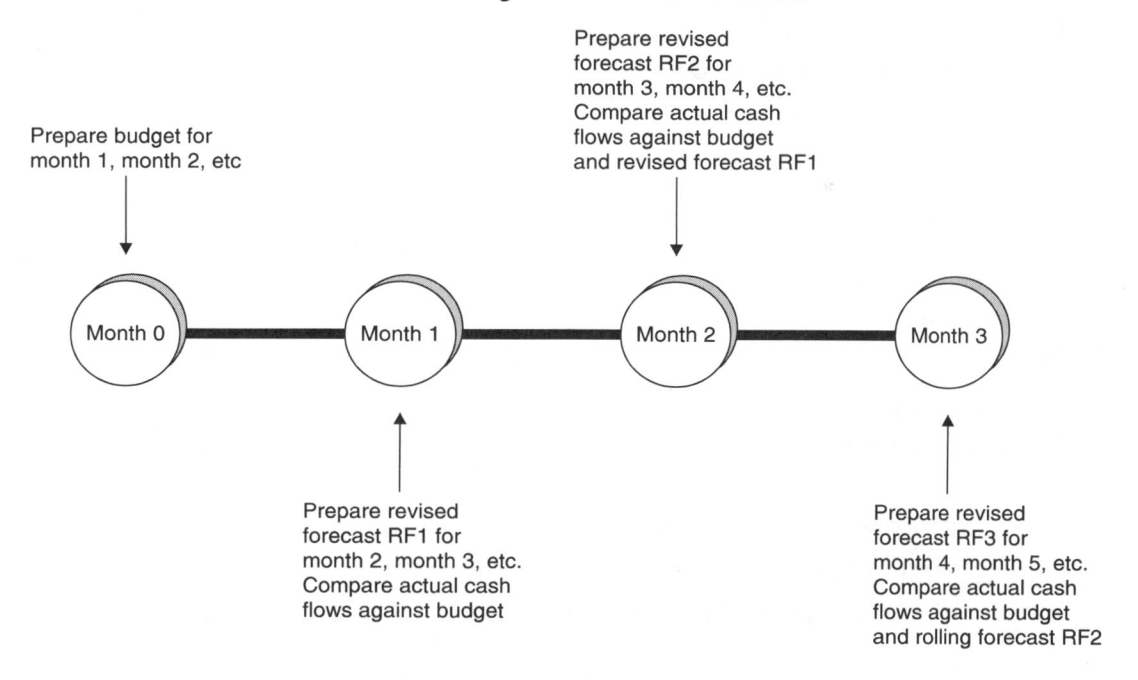

Prepare budget for month 1, month 2, etc → Month 0

Prepare revised forecast RF1 for month 2, month 3, etc. Compare actual cash flows against budget → Month 1

Prepare revised forecast RF2 for month 3, month 4, etc. Compare actual cash flows against budget and revised forecast RF1 → Month 2

Prepare revised forecast RF3 for month 4, month 5, etc. Compare actual cash flows against budget and rolling forecast RF2 → Month 3

Strategic forecasts

2.12 In **strategic forecasts**, a 'cash surplus' or 'funds deficit' is the **balancing item** after a forecast has been made for *all* the *other* items in the balance sheet.

2.13 For example, if a firm increases its credit period offered, leading to an increase in debtors, and intends to purchase fixed assets, what will be its requirements for cash. Such plans express the company's or group's likely future balance sheet as a consequence of adopting certain strategies.

2.14 Strategic forecasts should consider:

- The amount of funds required to pursue the chosen strategies
- The sources of those funds, including internally generated cash flows
- The strategy's potential consequences for liquidity and financial gearing

Assumptions of a forecast

2.15 Even fairly predictable items of income and spending (eg salary payments, and NI/tax deductions) cannot usually be forecast with total accuracy. Any forecast should therefore include a clear statement of the **assumptions** on which the figures are based. With clearly stated assumptions, a forecast can be tested for **reasonableness**.

2.16 For example, cash receipts from sales and debtors might be forecast on the assumption that sales will be a certain level, and debtors will take a certain time to pay.

Part D: Working capital management

3 CASH BUDGETS IN RECEIPTS AND PAYMENTS FORMAT   5/01, 11/01

> **Knowledge Brought Forward from Paper 2 Management Accounting Fundamentals**
>
> Chapter 13 of the Paper 2 *Management Accounting Fundamentals* text covered the preparation of cash budgets. The steps are as follows:
>
> Preparation
>
> - Set up a proforma cash budget
>
> | | Month 1 £ | Month 2 £ | Month 3 £ |
> |---|---|---|---|
> | Cash receipts | | | |
> | Receipts from debtors | X | X | X |
> | Loan etc | X | X | X |
> | | X | X | X |
> | Cash payments | | | |
> | Payments to creditors | X | X | X |
> | Wages etc | X | X | X |
> | | X | X | X |
> | Opening balance | X | X | X |
> | Net cash flow (receipts - payments) | X | X | X |
> | Closing balance | X | X | X |
>
> - Sort out cash receipts from debtors
> - Establish budgeted sales month by month
> - Establish the length of credit period taken by debtors
>
> $$\text{Debtors collection period (no. of days credit)} = \frac{\text{average (or year-end) debtors during period}}{\text{total credit sales in period}} \times \text{no of days in period}$$
>
> - Hence determine when budgeted sales revenue will be received as cash (by considering cash receipts from total debtors, ignoring any provision for doubtful debts)
> - Establish when opening debtors will pay
> - Establish when any other cash income will be received
> - Sort out cash payments to creditors
> - Establish production quantities and materials usage quantities each month
> - Establish materials stock changes and hence the quantity and cost of materials purchases each month
> - Establish the length of credit period taken from suppliers and hence calculate when cash payments to suppliers will be made and when the amount due to opening creditors will be paid
>
> $$\text{Creditors payment period (no of days credit)} = \frac{\text{average (or year-end) creditors during period}}{\text{total purchases on credit in period}} \times \text{no of days in period}$$
>
> - Establish when any other cash payments (excluding non-cash items such as depreciation) will be made
> - The bottom of the budget must show clearly opening position, net cash flow and closing position
> - If an overdraft is shown, suggest delaying payments to suppliers, reducing production volumes or arranging further overdraft facilities

3.1 You are likely to have to prepare more complex cash budgets for Paper 4, and the assumptions you make will be important.

Assumptions

3.2 For each item of cash inflows or outflows, assumptions must be made about the **quantity** and timing of the flows. The total amount of receipts and payments will be derived from other budgets, such as the company's operating budgets and capital expenditure budget. Assumptions will already have been made for these to prepare the profit or loss budget. Assumptions about the **time to pay** must be introduced for cash forecasting.

3.3 The forecasting method can be either one or a combination of the following.

- Identifying a particular cash flow, and scheduling when it will be received or paid
- Projecting future trends and seasonal cycles in business activity and cash flows
- Analysing historical payment patterns of regular repeat payments

> **Exam focus point**
>
> A list of the assumptions, once made, should be included with any cash forecast you prepare in an assessment.

Cash payments

3.4 **Assumptions about payments** are easier to make than assumptions about income. Assumptions about payments to suppliers can take account of:

(a) The **credit terms** given by suppliers (or groups of suppliers), company policy on purchase orders and the administration of cheque payments, etc

(b) Any **specific supply arrangements**, (such as a delivery once every two months, with payment for each delivery at the end of the following month)

(c) **Past practice** (eg the proportion of invoices (by value) paid in the month of supply and invoice, the proportion paid in the month following, and so on)

(d) **Predictable dates** for certain payments, such as payments for rent, business rates, telephones, electricity and corporation tax

As a guideline, assumptions about payments should lean towards caution, ie if in doubt, budget for earlier payments.

Fixed cost expenditures

3.5 Some items of expenditure will be regarded as **fixed costs** in the operating budget. Salaries, office expenses and marketing expenditure are three such items. With some fixed costs, it could be assumed that there will be an **equal monthly expenditure** on each item, with cash payment in the month of expenditure perhaps, or in the month following. Other costs may not be monthly. If annual building rental is payable quarterly in advance, the budget should plan for payments on the specific dates.

Receipts

3.6 **Assumptions about receipts** might be more difficult to formulate than assumptions about payments.

(a) For a company that depends almost entirely on consumer sales by cash, credit card and debit card, the major uncertainty in the cash flow forecast will be the **volume of sales**.

The timing of receipts from a large proportion of those sales will be predictable (payment with sale).

(b) Companies that have a **mixture of cash and credit sales** must attempt to **estimate** the **proportion** of **each** in the total sales figure, and then formulate assumptions for the timing pattern of receipts from credit sales.

(c) There are several ways of estimating when receipts will occur.

  (i) If the company has **specific credit terms,** such as a requirement to pay within 15 days of the invoice date, it could assume that:

   (1) Invoices will be sent out at the time of sale

   (2) A proportion, say 25%, will be paid within 15 days (1/2 month)

   (3) A proportion, say 65%, will be paid between 16 days and 30 days (one month after invoice)

   (4) A proportion (say 9%) will pay in the month following

   (5) There will be some bad debts (say 1%, a proportion that should be consistent with the company's budgeted expectations)

  (ii) If there is a policy of cash discounts for early payment, the **discounts allowed** should be provided for in the forecasts of receipts.

  (iii) The time **customers take to pay** can be estimated from past experience. Care should be taken to allow for seasonal variations and the possibility that payments can be slower at some times of the year than at others (for example, delays during holiday periods).

  (iv) **Payment patterns** can also vary from one country to another. Companies in France and Italy for example will often take several months after the invoice date to pay amounts due.

Calendar variations

3.7 Assumptions could be required to take account of calendar variations.

(a) **Days-in-the-month effect.** It could be assumed that receipts will be the same on every day of the 20th/21st/22nd/23rd etc working day each month. Alternatively, it could be assumed that receipts will be twice as high in the first five days of each month. Assumptions should generally be based on past experience.

(b) **Days-in-the-week effect.** Where appropriate, assumptions should be made about the cash inflows on each particular day of the week, with some days regularly producing higher cash inflows than other days. Such forecasts should be based on historical analysis.

3.8 Receipts for some companies, particularly retailers, follow a regular weekly pattern (with some variations for holidays and seasons of the year). Companies should be able to estimate total weekly takings in cash (notes and coins), cheques and credit card vouchers, the number of cheques and credit card vouchers handled and the deposit spread (for each day, the percentage of the total takings for the week, eg 10% on Monday, 15% on Tuesday).

Time periods and overdraft size

3.9 Dividing the forecast period into time periods should coincide as closely as possible with significant cash flow events, to provide management with information about the **high or**

low points for cash balances. In other words, as well as predicting the **month end surplus or overdraft,** the **maximum overdraft** *during* **the month** should be predicted.

3.10 EXAMPLE: TIMING OF CASH FLOWS

Oak Tree Villa Ltd operates a retail business. Purchases are sold at cost plus $33^1/_3\%$. Or put another way, purchases are 75% of sales.

(a)

	Budgeted sales £	Labour cost £	Expenses incurred £
January	40,000	3,000	4,000
February	60,000	3,000	6,000
March	160,000	5,000	7,000
April	120,000	4,000	7,000

(b) It is management policy to have sufficient stock in hand at the end of each month to meet sales demand in the next half month.

(c) Creditors for materials and expenses are paid in the month after the purchases are made or the expenses incurred. Labour is paid in full by the end of each month.

(d) Expenses include a monthly depreciation charge of £2,000.

(e) (i) 75% of sales are for cash.
    (ii) 25% of sales are on one month's interest-free credit.

(f) The company will buy equipment for cash costing £18,000 in February and will pay a dividend of £20,000 in March. The opening cash balance at 1 February is £1,000.

Required

(a) A profit and loss account for February and March
(b) A cash budget for February and March

3.11 SOLUTION

(a) PROFIT AND LOSS ACCOUNT

	February £	£	March £	£	Total £	£
Sales		60,000		160,000		220,000
Cost of purchases (75%)		45,000		120,000		165,000
Gross profit		15,000		40,000		55,000
Less: labour	3,000		5,000		8,000	
expenses	6,000		7,000		13,000	
		9,000		12,000		21,000
		6,000		28,000		34,000

(b) *Workings*

(i) *Receipts:*

			£
in February	75% of Feb sales (75% × £60,000)		45,000
	+ 25% of Jan sales (25% × £40,000)		10,000
			55,000

			£
in March	75% of Mar sales (75% × £160,000)		120,000
	+25% of Feb sales (25% × £60,000)		15,000
			135,000

Part D: Working capital management

(ii)

	Purchases in January		Purchases in February
	£		£
Purchases:			
For Jan sales (50% of £30,000)	15,000		
For Feb sales (50% of £45,000)	22,500	(50% of £45,000)	22,500
For Mar sales	-	(50% of £120,000)	60,000
	37,500		82,500

These purchases are paid for in February and March.

(iii) *Expenses.* Cash expenses in January (£4,000 – £2,000) and February (£6,000 – £2,000) are paid for in February and March respectively. Depreciation is not a cash item.

CASH BUDGET

	February	March	Total
	£	£	£
Receipts from sales	55,000	135,000	190,000
Payments			
Trade creditors	37,500	82,500	120,000
Expenses creditors	2,000	4,000	6,000
Labour	3,000	5,000	8,000
Equipment purchase	18,000	-	18,000
Dividend	-	20,000	20,000
Total payments	60,500	111,500	172,000
Receipts less payments	(5,500)	23,500	18,000
Opening cash balance b/f	1,000	(4,500)★	1,000
Closing cash balance c/f	(4,500)★	19,000	19,000

Notes

★ The cash balance at the end of February is carried forward as the opening cash balance for March.

1 The profit in February and March does means that there is sufficient cash to operate the business as planned.

2 Steps should be taken either to ensure that an overdraft facility is available for the cash shortage at the end of February, or to defer certain payments so that the overdraft is avoided.

Cash budgets and opening debtors and creditors

3.12 One situation which can be problematic is if you are required to analyse an **opening balance sheet** to decide how many outstanding debtors will pay what they owe in the first few months of the cash budget period, and how many outstanding creditors must be paid.

3.13 EXAMPLE: DEBTORS AND CREDITORS

For example, suppose that a balance sheet as at 31 December 20X4 shows that a company has the following debtors and creditors.

Debtors	£150,000
Trade creditors	£ 60,000

You are informed of the following.

(a) Debtors are allowed two months to pay.

(b) 1½ months' credit is taken from trade creditors.

(c) Sales and materials purchases were both made at an even monthly rate throughout 20X4.

Required

Determine in which months of 20X5 the debtors will eventually pay and the creditors will be paid.

3.14 SOLUTION

(a) Since debtors take two months to pay, the £150,000 of debtors in the balance sheet represent credit sales in November and December 20X4, who will pay in January and February 20X5 respectively. Since sales in 20X4 were at an equal monthly rate, the cash budget should plan for receipts of £75,000 each month in January and February from the debtors in the opening balance sheet.

(b) Similarly, since creditors are paid after 1½ months, the balance sheet creditors will be paid in January and the first half of February 20X5, which means that budgeted payments will be as follows.

	£
In January (purchases in second half of November and first half of December 20X4)	40,000
In February (purchases in second half of December 20X4)	20,000
Total creditors in the balance sheet	60,000

(The balance sheet creditors of £60,000 represent 1½ months' purchases, so that purchases in 20X4 must be £40,000 per month, which is £20,000 per half month.)

3.15 EXAMPLE: A MONTH-BY-MONTH CASH BUDGET IN DETAIL

Now you have some idea as to the underlying principles, let us put these to work. From the following information which relates to George and Zola Ltd, you are required to prepare a month by month cash budget for the second half of 20X5 and to append such brief comments as you consider might be helpful to management.

(a) The company's only product, a calfskin vest, sells at £40 and has a variable cost of £26 made up as follows.

    Material £20   Labour £4   Variable overhead £2

(b) Fixed costs of £6,000 per month are paid on the 28th of each month.

(c) *Quantities sold/to be sold on credit*

May	June	July	Aug	Sept	Oct	Nov	Dec
1,000	1,200	1,400	1,600	1,800	2,000	2,200	2,600

(d) *Production quantities*

May	June	July	Aug	Sept	Oct	Nov	Dec
1,200	1,400	1,600	2,000	2,400	2,600	2,400	2,200

(e) Cash sales at a discount of 5% are expected to average 100 units a month.

(f) Customers are expected to settle their accounts by the end of the second month following sale.

(g) Suppliers of material are paid two months after the material is used in production.

(h) Wages are paid in the same month as they are incurred.

Part D: Working capital management

(i) 70% of the variable overhead is paid in the month of production, the remainder in the following month.

(j) Corporation tax of £18,000 is to be paid in October.

(k) A new delivery vehicle was bought in June, the cost of which, £8,000 is to be paid in August. The old vehicle was sold for £600, the buyer undertaking to pay in July.

(l) The company is expected to be £3,000 overdrawn at the bank at 30 June 20X5.

(m) The opening and closing stocks of raw materials, work in progress and finished goods are budgeted to be the same.

3.16 SOLUTION

CASH BUDGET FOR 1 JULY TO 31 DECEMBER 20X5

	July £	Aug £	Sept £	Oct £	Nov £	Dec £	Total £
Receipts							
Credit sales	40,000	48,000	56,000	64,000	72,000	80,000	360,000
Cash sales	3,800	3,800	3,800	3,800	3,800	3,800	22,800
Sale of vehicles	600						600
	44,400	51,800	59,800	67,800	75,800	83,800	383,400
Payments							
Materials	24,000	28,000	32,000	40,000	48,000	52,000	224,000
Labour	6,400	8,000	9,600	10,400	9,600	8,800	52,800
Variable overhead (W1)	3,080	3,760	4,560	5,080	4,920	4,520	25,920
Fixed costs	6,000	6,000	6,000	6,000	6,000	6,000	36,000
Corporation tax				18,000			18,000
Purchase of vehicle		8,000					8,000
	39,480	53,760	52,160	79,480	68,520	71,320	364,720
Excess of receipts over payments	4,920	(1,960)	7,640	(11,680)	7,280	12,480	18,680
Balance b/f	(3,000)	1,920	(40)	7,600	(4,080)	3,200	(3,000)
Balance c/f	1,920	(40)	7,600	(4,080)	3,200	15,680	15,680

Working

Variable overhead

	June £	July £	Aug £	Sept £	Oct £	Nov £	Dec £
Variable overhead production cost	2,800	3,200	4,000	4,800	5,200	4,800	4,400
70% paid in month		2,240	2,800	3,360	3,640	3,360	3,080
30% in following month		840	960	1,200	1,440	1,560	1,440
		3,080	3,760	4,560	5,080	4,920	4,520

Comments

(a) There will be a small overdraft at the end of August but a much larger one at the end of October. It may be possible to delay payments to suppliers for longer than two months or to reduce purchases of materials or reduce the volume of production by running down existing stock levels.

(b) If neither of these courses is possible, the company may need to negotiate overdraft facilities with its bank.

(c) The cash deficit is only temporary and by the end of December there will be a comfortable surplus. The use to which this cash will be put should ideally be planned in advance.

Question 3

Tom Ward has worked for some years as a sales representative, but has recently been made redundant. He intends to start up in business on his own account, using £15,000 which he currently has invested with a building society. Tom maintains a bank account showing a small credit balance, and he plans to approach his bank for the necessary additional finance. Tom asks you for advice and provides the following additional information.

(a) Arrangements have been made to purchase fixed assets costing £8,000. These will be paid for at the end of September and are expected to have a five-year life, at the end of which they will possess a nil residual value.

(b) Stocks costing £5,000 will be acquired on 28 September and subsequent monthly purchases will be at a level sufficient to replace forecast sales for the month.

(c) Forecast monthly sales are £3,000 for October, £6,000 for November and December, and £10,500 from January 20X7 onwards.

(d) Selling price is fixed at the cost of stock plus 50%.

(e) Two months' credit will be allowed to customers but only 1 month's credit will be received from suppliers of stock.

(f) Running expenses, including rent, are estimated at £1,600 per month.

(g) Tom intends to make monthly cash drawings of £1,000.

Required

Prepare a cash budget for the 6 months October 20X6 to March 20X7.

Answer

The opening cash balance at 1 October will consist of Tom's initial £15,000 less the £8,000 expended on fixed assets purchased in September, ie the opening balance is £7,000. Cash receipts from credit customers arise two months after the relevant sales.

Payments to suppliers are a little more tricky. We are told that cost of sales is 100/150 × sales. Thus for October cost of sales is 100/150 × £3,000 = £2,000. These goods will be purchased in October but not paid for until November. Similar calculations can be made for later months. The initial stock of £5,000 is purchased in September and consequently paid for in October.

The cash budget can now be constructed.

CASH BUDGET FOR THE SIX MONTHS ENDING 31 MARCH 20X7

	October £	*November* £	*December* £	*January* £	*February* £	*March* £
Payments						
Suppliers	5,000	2,000	4,000	4,000	7,000	7,000
Running expenses	1,600	1,600	1,600	1,600	1,600	1,600
Drawings	1,000	1,000	1,000	1,000	1,000	1,000
	7,600	4,600	6,600	6,600	9,600	9,600
Receipts						
Debtors	-	-	3,000	6,000	6,000	10,500
Surplus/(shortfall)	(7,600)	(4,600)	(3,600)	(600)	(3,600)	900
Opening balance	7,000	(600)	(5,200)	(8,800)	(9,400)	(13,000)
Closing balance	(600)	(5,200)	(8,800)	(9,400)	(13,000)	(12,100)

Question 4

You are presented with the following budgeted data for your organisation for the period November 20X1 to June 20X2. It has been extracted from functional budgets that have already been prepared.

Part D: Working capital management

	Nov X1 £	Dec X1 £	Jan X2 £	Feb X2 £	Mar X2 £	Apr X2 £	May X2 £	June X2 £
Sales	80,000	100,000	110,000	130,000	140,000	150,000	160,000	180,000
Purchases	40,000	60,000	80,000	90,000	110,000	130,000	140,000	150,000
Wages	10,000	12,000	16,000	20,000	24,000	28,000	32,000	36,000
Overheads	10,000	10,000	15,000	15,000	15,000	20,000	20,000	20,000
Dividends		20,000						40,000
Capital expenditure			30,000			40,000		

You are also told the following.

(a) Sales are 40% cash, 60% credit. Credit sales are paid two months after the month of sales.
(b) Purchases are paid the month following purchase.
(c) 75% of wages are paid in the current month and 25% the following month.
(d) Overheads are paid the month after they are incurred.
(e) Dividends are paid three months after they are declared.
(f) Capital expenditure is paid two months after it is incurred.
(g) The opening cash balance is £15,000.

The managing director is pleased with the above figures as they show sales will have increased by more than 100% in the period under review. In order to achieve this he has arranged a bank overdraft with a ceiling of £50,000 to accommodate the increased stock levels and wage bill for overtime worked.

Required

(a) Prepare a cash budget for the six month period January to June 20X2.

(b) Comment upon your results in the light of your managing director's comments and offer advice.

(c) If you have access to a computer spreadsheet package and you know how to use it, try setting up the cash budget on it. Then make a copy of the budget and try making changes to the estimates to see their effect on cash flow.

Answer

(a)

	January £'000	February £'000	March £'000	April £'000	May £'000	June £'000
Sales revenue						
Cash (40%)	44	52	56	60	64	72
Credit (60%, 2 months)	48	60	66	78	84	90
	92	112	122	138	148	162
Purchases	60	80	90	110	130	140
Wages						
75%	12	15	18	21	24	27
25%	3	4	5	6	7	8
Overheads	10	15	15	15	20	20
Dividends				20		
Capital expenditure			30			40
	85	114	178	152	181	235
b/f	15	22	20	(36)	(50)	(83)
Net cash flow	7	(2)	(56)	(14)	(33)	(73)
c/f	22	20	(36)	(50)	(83)	(156)

(b) The overdraft arrangements are quite inadequate to service the cash needs of the business over the six-month period. If the figures are realistic then action should be taken now to avoid difficulties in the near future. The following are possible courses of action.

    (i) **Activities** could be **curtailed**.

    (ii) Other **sources of cash** could be **explored**, for example a long-term loan to finance the capital expenditure and a factoring arrangement to provide cash due from debtors more quickly.

    (iii) Efforts to **increase the speed of debt collection** could be made.

    (iv) **Payments to creditors** could be **delayed**.

(v) The **dividend payments** could be **postponed** (the figures indicate that this is a small company, possibly owner-managed).

(vi) Staff might be **persuaded to work at a lower rate** in return for, say, an annual bonus or a profit-sharing agreement.

(vii) **Extra staff** might be taken on to reduce the amount of overtime paid.

(viii) The **stockholding policy** should be **reviewed**; it may be possible to meet demand from current production and minimise cash tied up in stocks.

4 CLEARED FUNDS CASH FORECASTS

Cleared funds

4.1 **Float** refers to the amount of money tied up between the time a payment is initiated and **cleared funds** become available in the recipient's bank account for immediate spending.

4.2 Knowing what **cleared funds** are likely to be has a direct and immediate relevance to cash management in the **short-term**. If a company expects to have insufficient cleared funds in the next few days to meet a payment obligation, it must either borrow funds to meet the obligation or (if possible) defer the payment until there are cash receipts to cover it.

4.3 A **cleared funds cash forecast** is a short-term cash forecast of the cleared funds available to a company in its bank accounts, or of the funding deficit that must be met by **immediate borrowing**. Cleared funds forecasts should be reviewed and updated regularly, *daily* for companies with large and uncertain cash flows. Uncertainty might be caused by the internal organisation of the recipient.

(a) The recipient might delay the banking of cheques.
(b) Cheques do sometimes get held up by bureaucracy.

Preparing a cleared funds forecast

4.4 There should be relatively few items in a cleared funds forecast, and each forecast should generally relate to a **particular bank account** unless balances can be netted against each other.

4.5 A cleared funds forecast can be prepared by a combination of three methods.

(a) **Obtaining information** from the **company's banks**.

(b) **Forecasting for other receipts and payments** that have occurred but have not yet been lodged with a bank. You should be already familiar with bank reconciliations.

(c) **Adapting the cash budget**.
- Analyse the cash budget into suitable time periods.
- Identify cash book payments and receipts.
- Adjust these for float times

Question 5

Kim O'Hara runs an import/export retail business, largely on a cash basis. He likes to negotiate the best possible deals from his suppliers and this generally means a strict adherence to any payment terms so as to benefit from any settlement discounts: he also orders his supplies at the last possible moment, as he is a firm believer in 'just-in-time' philosophy. On the other hand Creighton plc is a large

Part D: Working capital management

software house, dealing with major clients. Which type of forecast would be most appropriate to each business?

Answer

Kim O'Hara would be best served by a **cleared funds forecast**, Creighton plc by a **cash book based forecast**.

5 CASH FORECASTS BASED ON FINANCIAL STATEMENTS

Balance sheet

5.1 The balance sheet is produced for **management accounting purposes** and so not for external publication or statutory financial reporting. **It is not an estimate of cash inflows and outflows**. A number of sequential forecasts can be produced, for example a forecast of the balance sheet at the end of each year for the next five years.

5.2 A balance sheet based forecast is an estimate of the company's balance sheet at a future date. It is used to identify either the cash surplus or the funding shortfall in the company's balance sheet at the **forecast date**.

Estimating a future balance sheet

5.3 A balance sheet estimate calls for some prediction of the amount/value of each item in the company's balance sheet, **excluding cash and short-term investments,** as these are what we are trying to predict. A forecast is prepared by taking each item in the balance sheet, and estimating what its value might be at the future date. The assumptions used are critical, and the following guidelines are suggested.

(a) Intangible **fixed assets** (gross book value) and long term investments, if there are any, should be taken at their current value unless there is good reason for another treatment.

(b) Some estimate of **fixed asset purchases** (and disposals) will be required. Revaluations can be ignored as they are not cash flows.

(c) **Current assets**. Balance sheet estimates of stocks and debtors can be based on fairly simple assumptions. The estimated value for stocks and debtors can be made in any of the following ways.

(i) **Same as current amounts**. This is unlikely if business has boomed.

(ii) **Increase by a certain percentage,** to allow for growth in business volume. For example, the volume of debtors might be expected to increase by a similar amount.

(iii) **Decrease by a certain percentage**, to allow for tighter management control over working capital.

(iv) **Assume to be a certain percentage** of the company's estimated **annual turnover** for the year.

(v) The firm can assume that the operating cycle will more or less **remain the same**. In other words, if a firm's debtors take two months to pay, this relationship can be expected to continue.

(d) **Current liabilities.** Some itemising of current liabilities will be necessary, because no single set of assumptions can accurately estimate them collectively.

(i) **Trade creditors and accruals** can be estimated in a similar way to current assets, as indicated above.

(ii) Current liabilities include **bank loans** due for repayment within 12 months. These can be identified individually.

(iii) **Bank overdraft facilities** might be in place. It could be appropriate to assume that there will be no overdraft in the forecast balance sheet. Any available overdraft facility can be considered later when the company's overall cash requirements are identified.

(iv) **Taxation.** Any corporation tax payable should be estimated from anticipated profits and based on an estimated percentage of those profits.

(v) **Dividends payable.** Any ordinary dividend payable should be estimated from anticipated profits, and any preference dividend payable can be predicted from the coupon rate of dividend for the company's preference shares.

(vi) **Other creditors** can be included if required and are of significant value.

(e) **Long-term creditors.** Long-term creditors are likely to consist of long-term loans, and any other long-term finance debt. Unless the company has already arranged further long-term borrowing, this item should include just existing long-term debts, minus debts that will be repaid before the balance sheet date.

(f) **Share capital and reserves.** With the exception of the profit and loss account reserves (retained profits), the estimated balance sheet figures for share capital and other reserves should be the same as their current amount unless it is expected or known that a new issue of shares will take place before the balance sheet date.

(g) An estimate is required of the change in the company's **retained profits** in the period up to the balance sheet date. This reserve should be calculated as:

(i) The existing value of the profit and loss reserve

(ii) Plus further retained profits anticipated in the period to the balance sheet date (ie post tax profits minus estimated dividends)

5.4 The various estimates should now be brought together into a balance sheet. The figures on each side of the balance sheet will not be equal, and there will be one of the following.

(a) A surplus of share capital and reserves over net assets (total assets minus total creditors). If this occurs, the company will be forecasting a **cash surplus**.

(b) A surplus of net assets over share capital and reserves. If this occurs, the company will be forecasting a **funding deficit**.

5.5 Alpha Limited has an existing balance sheet and an estimated balance sheet in one year's time before the necessary extra funding is taken into account, as follows.

	Existing		Forecast after one year	
	£	£	£	£
Fixed assets		100,000		180,000
Current assets	90,000		100,000	
Short-term creditors	(60,000)		(90,000)	
Net current assets		30,000		10,000
		130,000		190,000
Long-term creditors		(20,000)		(20,000)
Deferred taxation		(10,000)		(10,000)
Total net assets		100,000		160,000

Part D: Working capital management

	Existing £	£	Forecast after one year £	£
Share capital and reserves				
Ordinary shares capital		50,000		50,000
Other reserves		20,000		20,000
Profit and loss account		30,000		50,000
		100,000		120,000

5.6 The company is expecting to increase its net assets in the next year by £60,000 (£160,000 – £100,000) but expects retained profits for the year to be only £20,000 (£50,000 – £30,000). There is an excess of net assets over share capital and reserves amounting to £40,000 (£160,000 – £120,000), which is a funding deficit. The company must consider ways of obtaining extra cash (eg by borrowing) to cover the deficit. If it cannot, it will need to keep its assets below the forecast amount, or to have higher short-term creditors.

5.7 A revised projected balance sheet can then be prepared by introducing these new sources of funds. This should be checked for realism (eg by ratio analysis) to ensure that the proportion of the balance sheet made up by fixed assets and working capital, etc is sensible.

5.8 **Main uses of balance sheet-based forecasts**

(a) As longer-term (strategic) estimates, to assess the scale of funding requirements or cash surpluses the company expects over time

(b) To act as a check on the realism of cash flow-based forecasts (The estimated balance sheet should be **roughly** consistent with the net cash change in the cash budget, after allowing for approximations in the balance sheet forecast assumptions)

Deriving cash flow from profit and loss account and balance sheet information

5.9 The previous paragraphs concentrated on preparing a forecast balance sheet, with estimated figures for debtors, creditors and stock. Cash requirements might therefore be presented as the '**balancing figure**'. However, it is possible to derive a forecast figure for cash flows using both the balance sheet and profit and loss account.

5.10 This is examined in the example below, which is based on Question 1 in this chapter. For the time being, assume that there is no depreciation to worry about. The task is to get from profit to operational cash flow, by taking into account movements in working capital.

	Profit £	Operational cash flow £
Sales	200,000	200,000
Opening debtors (∴ received in year)		15,000
Closing debtors (outstanding at year end)		(24,000)
Cash in		191,000
Cost of sales	170,000	170,000
Closing stock (purchased, but not used, in year)		21,000
Opening stock (used, but not purchased, in year)		(12,000)
Purchases in year		179,000
Opening creditors (∴ paid in year)		11,000
Closing creditors (outstanding at year end)		(14,000)
Cash out		176,000
Profit/operational cash flow	30,000	15,000

17: Cash flow forecasts

		Profit £	Operational cash flow £
Profit			30,000
(Increase)/Decrease in stocks	Opening	12,000	
	Closing	(21,000)	
			(9,000)
(Increase)/Decrease in debtors	Opening	15,000	
	Closing	(24,000)	
			(9,000)
Increase/(Decrease) in creditors	Closing	14,000	
	Opening	(11,000)	
			3,000
Operational cash flow			15,000

5.11 In practice, a business will make many other adjustments. The profit figure includes items which do not involve the movement of cash, such as the annual depreciation charge, which will have to be added back to arrive at a figure for cash.

5.12 Both 'receipts and payments' forecasts and forecasts based on financial statements could be used alongside each other. The cash management section and the financial controller's section should reconcile differences between forecasts on a continuing basis, so that the forecast can be made more accurate as time goes on.

6 INFLATION AND CASH BUDGETING

Index numbers

6.1 When results of a business are being compared over a period of time for internal management purposes, it is up to managers of the business to agree and use an appropriate method of allowing for changing price levels. The usual method is to use a series of index numbers.

> **KEY TERM**
>
> An **index** is a measure, over a period of time, of the average **changes** in the values (prices or quantities) of a group of items.

The use of index numbers in cash forecasting and budgeting

6.2 What is the use of index numbers in **cash budgeting and forecasting**? The person preparing the cash budget is not particularly interested in prices in 'real terms': instead, it is the exact monetary amount that he or she is interested in. After all, bank overdrafts, for example, are expressed in fixed monetary amounts which do not allow for inflation.

6.3 Index numbers are still useful, however.

(a) Index numbers might be used to **predict future cash inflows**. For example, if it is assumed that 500,000 units will be sold in three or four months time, an estimate of future monetary prices gives some idea of the amount **in cash terms** that can be expected if a forecast index of prices is applied to estimated sales volumes.

(b) Similarly, with cash outflows, an **estimated future price index** can suggest the **likely size of cash payments**.

Part D: Working capital management

(c) Their use in forecasting can also suggest a need for **increased borrowing limits**, which might be fixed in monetary terms.

6.4 Different items, such as capital items, costs of various kinds, and revenues, are likely to be subject to differing rates of inflation, and different indices may therefore be appropriate for different items. As well as the RPI, the UK Office for National Statistics publishes various **producer price indices** to reflect the levels of different types of cost faced by businesses.

Question 6

You are assisting with the work on a maintenance department's budget for the next quarter of 20X4. The maintenance department's budget for the current quarter (just ending) is £200,000.

	Quantity used in current quarter	Average price payable per unit	
		Current quarter	Next quarter
	Units	£	£
Material A	9	10	10.20
Material B	13	12	12.50
Material C	8	9	9.00
Material D	20	25	26.00

A base weighted index for the next quarter stands at 103.5, compared to 100 for this quarter, for the price of input quantities.

Required

(a) Estimate the budget for the next quarter, assuming that the quantities of each material to be used:

    (i) remain the same;
    (ii) increase by 10%.

(b) Give reasons why your budget estimate could be in error.

Answer

(a) (i) The index suggests prices will increase by 3.5% and so produces a budget of £200,000 × 1.035 = £207,000.

    (ii) The budget in (i) assumes that quantities consumed remain the same. If quantities increase by 10% the budget will be £207,000 × 110% = £227,700.

(b) The budget estimates could be in error for a number of reasons.

    (i) The **estimates** of quantities and prices for next quarter could be inaccurate.

    (ii) The **current budget** (of £200,000) may not be a **suitable basis** on which to base the next quarter's budget. It may have been incorrectly set or next period's workload may not reflect that of the current period.

    (iii) The maintenance department may have a **budget limit** imposed on it and may not be allowed to increase its budget.

    (iv) The **weightings** on which the index is made may **go out of date**.

7 COMPUTER MODELS AND SENSITIVITY ANALYSIS

KEY TERM

Sensitivity analysis is a modelling and risk assessment procedure in which changes are made to significant variables in order to determine the effect of these changes on the planned outcome. Particular attention is thereafter paid to variables identified as being of special importance.

(OT 2000)

7.1 **Sensitivity analysis** is a method commonly used in planning, especially by companies using a **spreadsheet model** or other **financial modelling package**. The method may also be used manually - without a computer. Changes are made to estimates of key variables to establish how they could critically affect the outcome of the plan.

7.2 Sensitivity analysis tests the 'responsiveness' of profitability or cash flow to changes in one of the budget variables. For example, it would be possible to test the profit and loss account budget and cash budget for:

- An unforeseen 10% rise in material costs
- An unforeseen 5% drop in productivity
- A shortfall in sales volumes of, say, 10%
- A labour strike of, say, one month
- A delay of six months in opening a new plant or operation

7.3 **Computer cash forecast models** allow the user to test different assumptions and ask questions about the consequences of different future events or outcomes. Alternative methods of uncertainty analysis include:

(a) **Preparing** a **series** of **different forecasts**, each assuming a different scenario

(b) **Preparing cash forecasts** as a **range of possible outcomes**, from most pessimistic through most likely, to most optimistic

(c) **Carrying out sensitivity analysis** on key items of cash flow (in terms of quantity and timing) to identify the consequences for borrowing/investing

(d) **Using probability analysis** by assigning probabilities to a range of values for key uncertain cash flow items

7.4 EXAMPLE: SENSITIVITY ANALYSIS

A company setting up a subsidiary prepared a cash budget. As with many start-ups, initial expenditures were expected to be high in comparison with first year revenues. The company's budget year ended on 31 March and the operation was planned to commence on 1 June of the previous year. Selling to customers would not begin until 1 September. Revenue was forecast at £2 million for the period to 31 March.

The initial cash budget, illustrated below along with the revised budget, indicated a maximum deficit of about £750,000–£800,000 in September and October. The main areas of uncertainty were sales revenue, one major item of production cost and marketing costs.

7.5 Lower than anticipated revenues, and excessive production costs, would possibly create a bigger cash deficit than the company could afford. Management believed, however, that controls over marketing expenditure would ensure that such costs should not exceed budget.

7.6 The cash flow model was used for sensitivity analysis. Assumptions were changed. Estimated sales revenue was reduced by 25% and production costs increased by 50%. The output from the revised model indicated a resulting cash deficit of about £1.5 million, **just** within the funding limit the company would allow for the new operation. Management concluded that the budget was acceptable, but that revenue, production costs and marketing costs should be continually reviewed.

Part D: Working capital management

Original cash budget	Jun £'000	Jul £'000	Aug £'000	Sept £'000	Oct £'000	Nov £'000	Dec £'000	Total £'000
Sales	0	0	160	210	280	360	490	1,500
Total inflows	0	0	160	210	280	360	490	1,500
Set-up costs	120	20	0	0	0	0	0	140
Production	100	100	100	100	100	100	100	700
Distribution	0	0	20	20	20	20	20	100
Marketing and advertising	0	150	150	75	75	75	75	600
Staff costs	10	20	24	24	24	24	24	150
General overheads	6	14	16	16	16	16	16	100
Accommodation	0	25	0	0	25	0	0	50
Capital equipment	30	0	0	10	0	0	0	40
Total outflows	266	329	310	245	260	235	235	1,880
Net inflow/(outflow)	(266)	(329)	(150)	(35)	20	125	255	(380)
Cumulative cash flow	(266)	(595)	(745)	(780)	(760)	(635)	(380)	(380)

Revised cash budget	Jun £'000	Jul £'000	Aug £'000	Sept £'000	Oct £'000	Nov £'000	Dec £'000	Total £'000
Sales	0	0	120	158	210	270	367	1,125
Total inflows	0	0	120	158	210	270	367	1,125
Set-up costs	120	20	0	0	0	0	0	140
Production	150	150	150	150	150	150	150	1,050
Distribution	0	0	20	20	20	20	20	100
Marktg & advertising	0	150	150	75	75	75	75	600
Staff costs	10	20	24	24	24	24	24	150
General overheads	6	14	16	16	16	16	16	100
Accommodation	0	25	0	0	25	0	0	50
Capital equipment	30	0	0	10	0	0	0	40
Total outflows	316	379	360	295	310	285	285	2,230
Net inflow/(outflow)	(316)	(379)	(240)	(137)	(100)	(15)	82	(1,105)
Cumulative cash flow	(316)	(695)	(935)	(1,072)	(1,172)	(1,187)	(1,105)	(1,105)

Spreadsheets

> **Exam focus point**
>
> You should be familiar with spreadsheets already. We provide below an example of how a spreadsheet can be used in cash budgeting and forecasting.

7.7 EXAMPLE: PREPARING A CASH FLOW PROJECTION

A loan officer of a bank advising a small company wishes to assess the company's cash flow using a spreadsheet model. The cash flow projection is to provide a monthly cash flow analysis over a 5 year period. The following data is relevant.

(a) On 1 January 20X4 the company expects to have £15,000 in the bank. Sales in January are expected to be £25,000, and a growth rate of 1.25% per month in sales is predicted throughout the forecast period.

(b) The company buys stock one month in advance and pays in cash. All sales are on credit. There are no bad debts.

(c) On average, payment is received from customers as follows.

   (i) 60% one month in arrears
   (ii) 40% two months in arrears

(d) The cost of sales is 65% of sales value. Overhead costs (cash expenses) are expected to be £6,500 per month, rising by 5% at the start of each new calendar year.

(e) Purchases of capital equipment and payments of tax, interest charges and dividends must also be provided for within the model. The loans officer has advised the company that the interest rate on bank overdrafts is expected to be 1.695% per month.

The loans officer might decide to label the spreadsheet rows and columns as follows.

	A	B	C	D	E	F
1:		20X4				
2:		Jan	Feb	March	April	May
3:		£	£	£	£	£
4:	Sales					
5:	Cash receipts:					
6:	One months in arrears					
7:	Two months in arrears					
8:	Three months in arrears					
9:	Total receipts					
10:						
11:	Cash payments:					
12:	Stock					
13:	Overheads					
14:	Interest					
15:	Tax					
16:	Dividends					
17:	Capital purchases					
18:	Total payments					
19:						
20:	Cash receipts less payments					
21:	Balance b/f					
22:	Balance c/f					

Your task is to construct the formulae necessary.

7.8 SOLUTION

The formulae required can be constructed in a variety of ways. One way would be to insert some 'constant' values into cells of the spreadsheet and then cross-refer each formula to these constants, or absolutes.

	Column A	B
Row		
23:	Sales growth factor per month	1.0125
24:	Interest rate per month	0.01695
25:	Debts paid within 1 month	0.6
26:	Debts paid within 2 months	0.4
27:	Debts paid within 3 months	0
28:	Bad debts	0
29:	Cost of sales as proportion of sales	0.65

Part D: Working capital management

Alternatively, these values could be specified in the formulae in the spreadsheet. The advantage of setting up key data like this separately is that in the event of a change in say, interest rates, only one figure needs to be changed and there is no need for a search through the spreadsheet for relevant formulae.

Examples of constructing formulae for the spreadsheet are as follows.

(a) The formulae for sales in February 20X4, in this example, would be (+B4 * B23), in March 20X1 (+C4 * B23), in April 20X4 (+D4 * B23) etc. Replication of the formula could be used to save input time.

(b) The formula for cash receipts in April 20X4 would be:

E6 = D4 * B25
E7 = C4 * B26
E8 = B4 * B27
E9 = + E6 + E7 + E8

(c) Cash payments for stock would be expressed as the cost of sales in the previous month; for February 20X4, the formula in cell C12 would be:

+ B4 * B29

(d) Total cash payments in May 20X4 would be the sum of cells F12 to F17, ie the formula in cell F18 would be:

@ SUM (F12..F17)

and so on.

Input data would include the opening cash balance on 1 January 20X4, dividend and tax payments, capital purchases, sales in January 20X4, the constant values (in our example in column B, rows 23 to 29) and the other data needed to establish cash receipts and payments in the first month or so of the forecast period (eg receipts in January 20X4 will depend on sales in November and December 20X3, which the simplified model shown here has not provided for).

With this input data, and the spreadsheet formulae, a full cash flow projection for the five year period can be produced and, if required, printed out.

Question 7

Whenever a forecast or budget is made, management should consider asking 'what if' questions, and so carry out a form of sensitivity analysis. Using the example above, how would you take account of the following changed assumptions? Describe what amendments would need to be made to the contents of individual cells.

(a) What if the payment pattern from debtors is:

1 month in arrears	40%
2 months in arrears	50%
3 months in arrears	10%?

(b) What if sales growth is only ½% per month?

Answer

Using the spreadsheet model, the answers to these questions can be obtained simply and quickly, using the editing facility in the program.

(a) To test the consequences of slower payments by debtors, it would merely be necessary to alter the contents of cells B25, B26 and B27 in our example from 0.6, 0.4 and 0 to 0.4, 0.5 and 0.1 respectively, and then to run the model again.

17: Cash flow forecasts

(b) Similarly, the consequences for cash flow of slower sales growth of only ½% per month can be tested by altering the value of Cell B23 in our example from 1.0125 to 1.005.

Quality control of forecasts

7.9 When actual results differ from budget, it can be tempting to conclude that plans never work out in practice. However, as planning is a vital management activity, and if actual results differ from the plan, it is important to find out whether the *planning* processes can be improved.

7.10 Accuracy of cash flow forecasts can be enhanced by:

(a) **Reviewing actual cash flows** against the **forecasts**, learning from past mistakes, and
(b) **Updating rolling forecasts** or **revised forecasts**, where useful, to replace earlier, less reliable forecasts

7.11 A constant monthly amount for receipts and payments will often indicate either sloppy cash forecasting practice, or a high degree of uncertainty in the forecast, since it is rare for specific receivables and payables to remain unchanged except where there is a formal arrangement.

7.12 As a financial year progresses, the actual cash flows for the past months could show large variances from budget, but a rolling forecast indicates that the original budget for the end-of-year cash balance will still be achieved. This could occur if the rolling forecast has been prepared by adjusting the forecast for the unexpired months of the year, in order to keep the annual budget (on paper at least) for the end-of-year cash position. Where this occurs, suspicion must arise that the rolling forecast has been prepared with little thought.

7.13 Unchanged figures over a number of months of revised forecast submissions are also an indication of a **weak forecasting system**. It could be that business expectations have not changed; however there are few businesses that do not fluctuate with market conditions. A more likely explanation is that the rolling cash forecast has been prepared by copying the figures from the previous forecast or that a new revised forecast has not been prepared at all.

Question 8

Frosty Ice Cream Ltd had sales in the last year of £150,000, and purchases of £115,000. At the start of the year stocks were £15,000, debtors were £5,000 and creditors were £10,000. At the end of the year stocks were £10,000, debtors were £8,000 and creditors were £12,000.

What was the operating cash flow for the period?

A £30,000
B £32,000
C £34,000
D £40,000

Part D: Working capital management

Answer

C

	£
Sales	150,000
Add opening debtors	5,000
Less closing debtors	(8,000)
	147,000
Less purchases	(115,000)
Less opening creditors	(10,000)
Add closing creditors	12,000
Operating cash flow	34,000

Chapter roundup

- **Trading profits** need to be distinguished from cash flows.

- **Cash flow forecasts** provide an early warning of liquidity problems and funding needs. **Banks** often expect business customers to provide a cash forecast as a condition of lending.

- There are **two main ways** of preparing a cash forecast.

    ○ A forecast can be prepared of cash receipts and payments, and net cash flows (cash flow based forecasts).

    ○ Alternatively, a cash surplus or funding requirement can be prepared by constructing a forecast balance sheet (balance sheet-based forecast), or adjusting other financial statements.

- **Cash flow based forecasts** include **cash budgets**; **cleared funds forecasts for the short term**.

- Cash budgets and forecasts can be used for **control reporting**. Balance sheet based forecasts are used for long-term strategic analysis.

- A **cash budget** is a detailed forecast of cash receipts, payments and balances over a planning period. It is formally adopted as part of the business plan or master budget for the period.

- Cash budgets are prepared by taking **operational budgets** and converting them into forecasts as to when receipts and payments occur. The forecast should indicate the highest and lowest cash balance in a period as well as the balance at the end.

- **Cleared funds** are used for short-term planning. They take clearance delays into account.

- A number of **statistical and modelling techniques** can be used to reduce uncertainty in cash flow forecasting.

- **Sensitivity analysis** tests the results of a forecast to see how sensitive the results are to changes in inputs (eg lower or higher interest rates). **Spreadsheet modelling** is used for this purpose.

Quick quiz

1. Operational cash flows of a business could be improved directly by:

    - *Reducing/Increasing* debtors
    - *Reducing/Increasing* stocks
    - *Reducing/Increasing* the credit period for the company's trade creditors

    Delete the word in italics that does not apply.

2. What is a rolling forecast?

3. The 'float' is the time between (A) .... and (B) .... (Fill in the blanks)

17: Cash flow forecasts

4   List the components of current liabilities which should normally be taken into account when preparing a balance sheet based forecast for a limited company which is trading. (Fill in the blanks)

   • Trade creditors and ....
   • ....
   • ....
   • ....
   • ....
   • ....

5   'Changes are made to estimates of key variables to establish how they could critically affect the outcome of the plan.' What technique does this describe?

6   What is an index?

7   Heavy Metal Ltd is preparing its cash flow forecast for the next quarter. Which of the following items should be excluded from the calculations?

   A   The receipt of a bank loan that has been raised for the purpose of investment in a new rolling mill
   B   Depreciation of the new rolling mill
   C   A tax payment that is due to be made, but which relates to profits earned in a previous accounting period
   D   Disposal proceeds from the sale of the old rolling mill

8   The cash flow forecast prepared by Heavy Metal Ltd suggests that the overdraft limit will be exceeded during the second month of the forecast period due to the timing of the asset purchase. However, by the end of the quarter the overdraft should be back to a level similar to that at the start of the period. Which of the following courses of action would you recommend to overcome this problem?

   A   Acquire the asset using a finance lease rather than by outright purchase
   B   Seek help from a venture capital company
   C   Make a rights issue to raise the additional funds
   D   Negotiate with the bank for a short-term loan to cover the deficit

Answers to quick quiz

1   The following words are those which you should *not* have deleted.

   • *Reducing* debtors
   • *Reducing* stocks
   • *Increasing* credit period for the company's trade creditors

2   A forecast that is continually updated

3   (A)   Initiation of a payment
    (B)   When cleared funds become available in the recipient's bank account

4   Trade creditors and accruals; Bank overdraft; Bank loans; Taxation; Dividends payable; Other creditors

5   Sensitivity analysis

6   A measure over a period of time of the average changes in the values (prices or quantities) of a group of items

7   B   This is a non-cash item and should therefore be excluded.

8   D   Since the cash flow problems appear to be temporary in nature, it is appropriate to use a short-term solution. Additional long-term capital should not be required.

Now try the question below from the Exam Question Bank

Number	Level	Marks	Time
17	Introductory	n/a	30 mins

Chapter 18

CASH MANAGEMENT

Topic list	Syllabus reference	Ability required
1 The need for cash management	(iv)	Comprehension
2 Cash management services	(iv)	Comprehension
3 Inventory approach to cash management	(iv)	Analysis
4 Applying probabilities in cash management	(iv)	Analysis
5 Pooling and netting	(iv)	Comprehension
6 Other bank services	(iv)	Comprehension

Introduction

How much cash should a company keep on hand or 'on short call' at a bank? The more cash which is on hand, the easier it will be for the company to meet its bills as they fall due and to take advantage of discounts. However, holding cash or near equivalents to cash has a cost in terms of the loss of earning which would otherwise have been obtained by using the funds in another way. The financial manager must try to balance **liquidity** with **profitability**. Crucially the manager must also be aware of means to ease cash shortages.

Use of the Baumol or Miller-Orr models of cash management can assist the financial manager. You need to understand how these work therefore, as both will be regularly tested in the *Finance* paper.

Learning outcomes covered in this chapter

- Identify measures to improve a cash forecast situation
- Compare and contrast the use and limitations of cash management models and identify when each model is most appropriate
- State and illustrate the main issues in group cash flow management
- Identify appropriate bank services to assist in cash management

Syllabus content covered in this chapter

- The Baumol and Miller-Orr cash management models
- Group cash flow management, eg netting
- Bank services available to organisations in order to help them manage cash, eg investing overnight, Bankers' Automated Clearing Services (BACS), automated matching, minimising service charges
- Bank services and facilities and their impact on organisational activities and costs

1 THE NEED FOR CASH MANAGEMENT

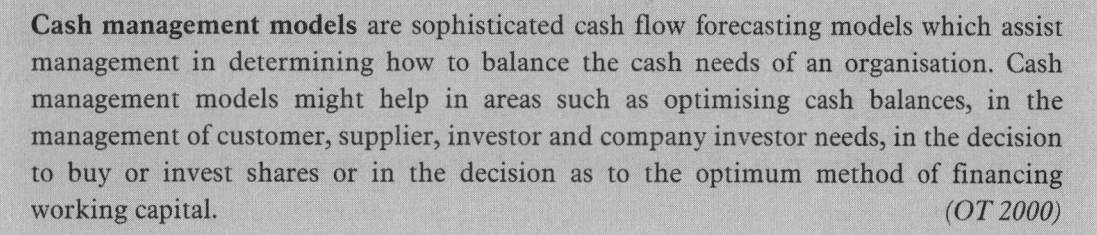

> **KEY TERMS**
>
> **Cash management models** are sophisticated cash flow forecasting models which assist management in determining how to balance the cash needs of an organisation. Cash management models might help in areas such as optimising cash balances, in the management of customer, supplier, investor and company investor needs, in the decision to buy or invest shares or in the decision as to the optimum method of financing working capital.
>
> *(OT 2000)*

1.1 We have already used the concept of the **operating cycle**, which connects investment in working capital with cash flows. Cash flow problems can arise in several ways.

CASH FLOW PROBLEMS	
Making losses	Continual losses will eventually mean problems, timing depends on size of losses and whether depreciation is significant; if it is problems arise on replacement of assets
Inflation	Ever-increasing cash flows required just to replace used-up and worn out assets
Growth	Growth means business needs to support more debtors and stock
Seasonal business	Cash flow difficulties may occur at certain times when cash inflows are low and outflows high, as stocks are being built up
One-off items of expenditure	Large item such as loan repayment or purchase of expensive fixed asset such as freehold land

Methods of easing cash shortages

Improving the business

1.2 Cash deficits can arise out of **basic trading factors** underlying the business such as falling sales or increasing costs. Clearly, the way to deal with these items is to take normal business measures, rectifying the fall in sales by marketing activities or, if this cannot be achieved, by cutting costs.

Controlling the operating cycle: short-term deficiencies

1.3 Cash deficits can also arise out of the business's management of the operating cycle and from timing differences. The following are possibilities.

(a) **Borrowing** from the bank. This is only a short-term measure. It is possible that a bank will convert an overdraft into a long-term loan, or perhaps new overdraft limits can be set up.

(b) **Raising capital.** This is likely to be expensive and should be generally used for long-term investment, not short term cash management.

(c) **Different sources of finance** (such as leasing) might be used.

1.4 When a company cannot obtain resources from any other source such as a loan or an increased overdraft, it can take the following steps.

Part D: Working capital management

(a) **Postponing capital expenditure**

   (i) It might be imprudent to postpone expenditure on fixed assets which are needed for the **development** and **growth** of the business.

   (ii) On the other hand, some **capital expenditures** might be **postponable** without serious consequences. The routine replacement of motor vehicles is an example. If a company's policy is to replace company cars every two years, it may decide, if cash is short, to replace cars every three years.

(b) **Accelerating cash inflows which would otherwise be expected in a later period**

   The most obvious way of bringing forward cash inflows would be to press debtors for earlier payment (leading and lagging debtors).

(c) **Reversing past investment decisions by selling assets previously acquired**

   Some assets are less crucial to a business than others and so if cash flow problems are severe, the option of selling short-term investments or even property might have to be considered.

(d) **Negotiating a reduction in cash outflows, so as to postpone or even reduce payments**

   There are several ways in which this could be done.

   (i) **Longer credit** might be taken from suppliers (leading and lagging creditors).

   (ii) **Loan repayments** could be rescheduled by agreement with a bank.

   (iii) A **deferral of the payment of tax** could be agreed with the taxation authorities.

   (iv) **Dividend payments** could be **reduced**. Dividend payments are discretionary cash outflows, although a company's directors might be constrained by shareholders' expectations.

   (v) **Stock levels** could decrease to reduce the amount of money tied up in their production cost.

1.5 EXAMPLE: LEADING AND LAGGING

Assume that Gilbert Gosayne Ltd sells Nullas. Each Nulla costs £50 to make and is sold for £100. The bank has refused an overdraft to Gilbert Gosayne. Creditors are normally paid at the end of Month 1; the Nullas are sold on the 15th of Month 2. Payment is received on the first day of Month 3.

(a) Under this system we have the following forecast.

	Inflows £	Outflows £	Balance £
Month 1 (end)	-	50	(50)
Month 2	-	-	(50)
Month 3 (beginning)	100	-	50

In other words the cash cycle means that the firm is in deficit for all of Month 2. As the bank has refused an overdraft, the creditors will not be paid.

(b) If, however, Gilbert Gosayne Ltd persuades its creditors to wait for two weeks until the 15th of Month 2 and offers a settlement discount of £5 to debtors to induce them to pay on the 15th of Month 2, the situation is transformed.

	Inflows	Outflows	Balance
	£	£	£
Month 1	-	-	-
Month 2	95	50	45
Month 3	-	-	45

1.6 In practice, it is not that simple.

(a) Creditors can object to their customers taking extra credit and it can also harm their businesses, thus jeopardising their ability to make future supplies. The customer also loses the possibility of taking advantage of trade discounts.

(b) Debtors might refuse to pay early, despite the inducement of a discount.

In fact, a firm's debtors and creditors might be 'leading and lagging' themselves.

1.7 A firm might be in a position to choose which of its creditors should be paid now rather than later. Certain creditors have to be paid early, if they are powerful. The bank is a powerful creditor: it is worth keeping the bank happy even if the firm loses out on a few trade discounts in the process.

1.8 Shortening the operating cycle is helpful in dealing with **short-term deficiencies** and saving interest costs, but it is not necessarily a long term solution to the business's funding problems. This is because a shorter operating cycle time will **reduce the amount of cash** that a company needs to invest in its operating activities.

2 CASH MANAGEMENT SERVICES

Computerised cash management

2.1 A relatively recent development in banking services is that of cash management services for corporate customers. A company with many different bank accounts can obtain information about the cash balance in each account through a computer terminal in the company's treasury department linked to the bank's computer. The company can then arrange to move cash from one account to another and so manage its cash position more efficiently.

2.2 The cash management services provided by the banks comprise three basic services.

(a) **Account reporting**

(i) Information is given about the balances on sterling or currency accounts whether held in the UK or overseas, including details of the cleared balance for the previous day and any uncleared items.

(ii) Forecast balance reports, which take into account uncleared items and automated entries (BACS credits and debits, standing orders and direct debits) can be obtained.

(iii) Reports giving details of individual transactions can be obtained.

(b) **Funds transfer**

The customer can initiate sterling and currency payments through his terminal. Banks will also give customers with substantial cash floats the opportunity to get in touch with money market dealers directly and deposit funds in the money markets.

(c) **Decision support services**

A rates information service, giving information on foreign exchange rates and money market (sterling deposit) interest rates, can be used.

Part D: Working capital management

Float

2.3 As already mentioned, the term 'float' is sometimes used to describe the amount of time between:

(a) The time when a **payment** is **initiated** (for example when a debtor sends a cheque in payment, probably by post), and

(b) The time when the **funds** become **available** for use in the recipient's bank account.

	REASONS FOR LENGTHY FLOAT
Transmission delay	Postal delays of a day, maybe longer
Lodgement delay	Delay in banking payments received, payee delaying presentation to bank of cash/cheques received
Clearance delay	Time for bank to clear cheque, payment not available for use by recipient until clearance (2-3 days in UK, longer abroad)

2.4 There are several measures that could be taken to reduce the float.

(a) The payee should ensure that the **lodgement delay** is kept to a minimum. **Cheques** received should be presented to the bank on the day of receipt.

(b) The payee might, in some cases, arrange to **collect cheques** from the payer's premises. This would only be practicable, however, if the payer is local. The payment would have to be large to make the extra effort worthwhile.

(c) The payer might be asked to pay through his own branch of a bank. The payer can give his bank detailed payment instructions, and use the credit clearing system of the bank giro. The **bank giro** is a means of making credit transfers for customers of other banks and other branches. The payee may include a bank giro credit slip on the bottom of his invoice, to help with this method of payment.

(d) **BACS** (Bankers' Automated Clearing Services Ltd), a system which provides for the computerised transfer of funds between banks, could be used. BACS is available to corporate customers of banks for making payments. The customer must supply a magnetic tape or disk to BACS, which contains details of payments, and payment will be made in two days.

(e) For regular payments **standing orders** or **direct debits** might be used.

(f) **CHAPS** (Clearing House Automated Payments System) is a computerised system for banks to make same-day clearances (that is, immediate payment) between each other. Each member bank of CHAPS can allow its own corporate customers to make immediate transfers of funds through CHAPS. However, there is a large minimum size for payments using CHAPS.

2.5 EXAMPLE: CASH MANAGEMENT

Ryan Coates owns a chain of seven clothes shops in the London area. Takings at each shop are remitted once a week on Thursday evening to the head office, and are then banked at the start of business on Friday morning. As business is expanding, Ryan Coates has hired an accountant to help him. The accountant gave him the following advice.

'Turnover at the seven shops totalled £1,950,000 last year, at a constant daily rate, but you were paying bank overdraft charges at a rate of 11%. You could have reduced your overdraft costs by banking the shop takings each day, except for Saturday's takings. Saturday takings could have been banked on Mondays.'

18: Cash management

Comment on the significance of this statement, stating your assumptions. The shops are closed on Sundays.

2.6 SOLUTION

(a) A bank overdraft rate of 11% a year is approximately 11/365 = 0.03% a day.

(b) Annual takings of £1,950,000 would be an average of £1,950,000/312 = £6,250 a day for the seven shops in total, on the assumption that they opened for a 52 week year of six days a week (312 days).

(c) Using the approximate overdraft cost of 0.03% a day, the cost of holding £6,250 for one day instead of banking it is 0.03% × £6,250 = £1.875.

(d) Banking all takings up to Thursday evening of each week on Friday morning involves an unnecessary delay in paying cash into the bank. The cost of this delay would be either:

  (i) The opportunity cost of investment capital for the business, or
  (ii) The cost of avoidable bank overdraft charges

It is assumed here that the overdraft cost is higher and is therefore more appropriate to use. It is also assumed that, for interest purposes, funds are credited when banked.

Takings on	Could be banked on	Number of days delay incurred by Friday banking
Monday	Tuesday	3
Tuesday	Wednesday	2
Wednesday	Thursday	1
Thursday	Friday	0
Friday	Saturday	6
Saturday	Monday	4
		16

In one week, the total number of days delay incurred by Friday banking is 16. At a cost of £1.875 a day, the weekly cost of Friday banking was £1.875 × 16 = £30.00, and the annual cost of Friday banking was £30.00 × 52 = £1,560.

(e) *Conclusion*. The company could have saved about £1,560 a year in bank overdraft charges last year. If the overdraft rate remains at 11% and turnover continues to increase, the saving from daily banking would be even higher next year.

3 INVENTORY APPROACH TO CASH MANAGEMENT

Baumol's model

3.1 There are a number of different formal cash management models designed to indicate the optimum amount of cash that a company should hold. One such model, **Baumol's model**, is based on the idea that deciding on optimum cash balances is a similar question to deciding on optimum stock levels (which we look at in Chapter 23).

3.2 We can distinguish two types of cost which are involved in obtaining cash:

(a) The **fixed cost** represented, for example, by the issue cost of equity finance or the cost of negotiating an overdraft

(b) The **variable cost** (opportunity cost) of keeping the money in the form of cash

3.3 The average total cost incurred for a period in holding a certain average level of cash (C) is:

Part D: Working capital management

$$\frac{Qi}{2} + \frac{FS}{Q}$$

Where S = the amount of cash to be used in each time period
F = the fixed cost of obtaining new funds (cost per sale/purchase of securities)
i = the interest cost of holding cash or near cash equivalents
Q = the total amount to be raised to provide for S

3.4 We can then establish that the optimum amount of cash to obtain each time that new funds are needed is given by the following formula, whose derivation you do not need to know. Whenever cash holdings fall to a low 'safety' level, the 'optimum sale' quantity of securities such as shares or gilts would be sold in order to replenish holdings of cash.

EXAM FORMULA

$$\text{Optimal sale} = \sqrt{\frac{2 \times \text{annual cash disbursements} \times \text{cost per sale of securities}}{\text{interest rate}}}$$

ie $Q = \sqrt{\frac{2FS}{i}}$

3.5 EXAMPLE: INVENTORY APPROACH TO CASH MANAGEMENT

Finder Limited faces a fixed cost of £4,000 to obtain new funds. There is a requirement for £24,000 of cash over each period of one year for the foreseeable future. The interest cost of new funds is 12% per annum; the interest rate earned on short-term securities is 9% per annum. How much finance should Finder Limited raise at a time?

3.6 SOLUTION

The cost of holding cash is 12% − 9% = 3%
The optimum level of Q (the 're-order quantity') is:

$$\sqrt{\frac{2 \times 4,000 \times 24,000}{0.03}} = £80,000$$

The optimum amount of new funds to raise is £80,000.

This amount is raised every 80,000 ÷ 24,000 = $3^{1}/_{3}$ years.

Drawbacks of the inventory approach

3.7 The inventory approach has the following drawbacks.

(a) In reality, **amounts required** over **future periods** will be **difficult to predict** with much certainty.

(b) There may be **costs** associated with running out of cash.

(c) There may be **other normal costs of holding cash** which increase with the average amount held.

(d) The model works satisfactorily for a firm which uses up its cash inventory at a **steady rate**, but not if there are larger inflows and outflows of cash from time to time.

The Miller-Orr model

3.8 In an attempt to produce a more realistic approach to cash management, various models more complicated than the inventory approach have been developed. One of these, the **Miller-Orr model**, manages to achieve a reasonable degree of realism while not being too elaborate.

3.9 We can begin looking at the Miller-Orr model by asking what will happen if there is no attempt to manage cash balances. Clearly, the cash balance is likely to 'meander' upwards or downwards. The Miller-Orr model imposes limits to this meandering. If the cash balance reaches an upper limit (point A in Figure 1) the firm buys sufficient securities to return the cash balance to a normal level (called the 'return point'). When the cash balance reaches a lower limit (point B in Figure 1), the firm sells securities to bring the balance back to the return point.

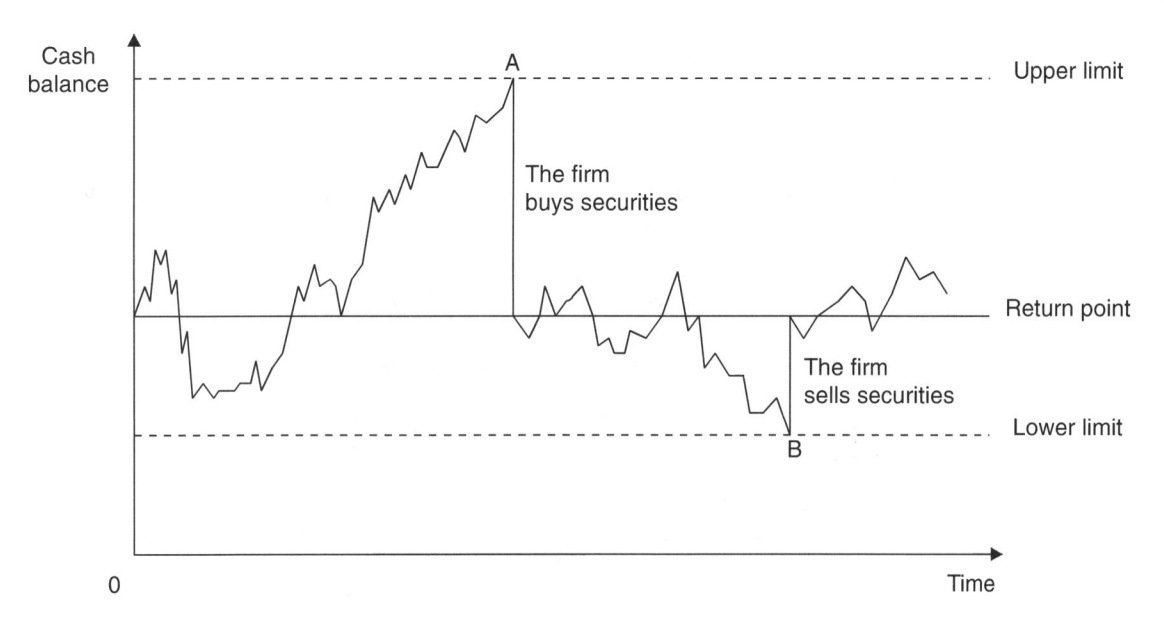

Figure 1 Applying the Miller-Orr model

3.10 How are the upper and lower limits and the return point set? Miller and Orr showed that the answer to this question depends on three factors:

- The variance of cash flows
- Transaction costs
- Interest rates

If the day-to-day variability of cash flows is high or the transaction cost in buying or selling securities is high, then wider limits should be set. If interest rates are high, the limits should be closer together.

3.11 To keep the interest costs of holding cash down, the return point is set at one-third of the distance (or 'spread') between the lower and the upper limit.

$$\text{Return point} = \text{Lower limit} + \frac{1}{3} \times \text{spread}$$

Part D: Working capital management

> **EXAM FORMULA**
>
> Spread between upper and lower cash balance limits, Miller-Orr model:
>
> $$\text{Spread} = 3\left(\frac{3}{4} \times \frac{\text{transaction cost} \times \text{variance of cash flows}}{\text{interest rate}}\right)^{\frac{1}{3}}$$

3.12 To use the Miller-Orr model, it is necessary to follow the steps below.

(a) **Set** the **lower limit** for the **cash balance**. This may be zero, or it may be set at some minimum safety margin above zero.

(b) **Estimate** the **variance of cash flows**, for example from sample observations over a 100-day period.

(c) **Note the interest rate** and the **transaction cost** for each sale or purchase of securities (the latter is assumed to be fixed).

(d) **Compute** the **upper limit** and the return point from the model and instruct an employee to implement the limits strategy.

3.13 Now try applying the Miller-Orr equations yourself in the following exercise.

Question 1

The following data applies to a company.

(a) The minimum cash balance is £8,000.
(b) The variance of daily cash flows is 4,000,000, equivalent to a standard deviation of £2,000 per day.
(c) The transaction cost for buying or selling securities is £50.
(d) The interest rate is 0.025 per cent per day.

Required

Formulate a decision rule using the Miller-Orr model.

Answer

The spread between the upper and the lower cash balance limits is calculated as follows.

$$\text{Spread} = 3\left(\frac{3}{4} \times \frac{\text{transaction cost} \times \text{variance of cash flows}}{\text{interest rate}}\right)^{\frac{1}{3}}$$

$$= 3\left(\frac{3}{4} \times \frac{50 \times 4,000,000}{0.00025}\right)^{\frac{1}{3}} = £25,303, \text{ say } £25,300$$

The upper limit and return point are now calculated.

Upper limit = Lower limit + £25,300 = £8,000 + £25,300 = £33,300

Return point = lower limit + $^1/_3$ × spread

= £8,000 + $^1/_3$ × £25,300 = £16,433, say £16,400

The decision rule is as follows. If the cash balance reaches £33,300, buy £16,900 (= 33,300 − 16,400) in marketable securities. If the cash balance falls to £8,000, sell £8,400 of marketable securities for cash.

18: Cash management

Advantages and disadvantages of the Miller-Orr model

3.14 The usefulness of the Miller-Orr model is limited by the **assumptions** on which it is based. In practice, cash inflows and outflows are **unlikely** to be **entirely unpredictable** as the model assumes: for example, for a retailer, seasonal factors are likely to affect cash inflows; for any company, dividend and tax payments will be known well in advance. However, the Miller-Orr model may save management time which might otherwise be spent in responding to those cash inflows and outflows which cannot be predicted.

Use of cash management models in practice

3.15 Some banks, especially in the USA, make cash management models available to their customers. These models vary from relatively simple spreadsheet-based models to more sophisticated systems such as those provided for multinational companies by the Chemical Bank.

3.16 Sophisticated models, such as that used by the Chemical Bank, can take account of user's risk preferences by allowing limits to be set on the amount of funds allocated to any single investment. Users can manipulate variables to trace the effect on the short-term plan, which can help them to increase their awareness of the factors affecting day-to-day management decisions and the liquidity/profitability trade-off.

> **Exam focus point**
>
> You could be asked to discuss advantages and disadvantages of cash management models, but any formulae required to apply them would be provided in the exam.

4 APPLYING PROBABILITIES IN CASH MANAGEMENT

4.1 We can see how probabilities can be applied to cash management problems by looking at an example.

4.2 EXAMPLE: PROBABILITIES IN CASH MANAGEMENT

Sinkos Wim Ltd has an overdraft facility of £100,000, and currently has an overdraft balance at the bank of £34,000. The company maintains a cash float of £10,000 for transactions and precautionary purposes. It is unclear whether a long awaited economic recovery will take place, and the company has prepared cash budgets as set out below for the next three months using two different assumptions about economic events. The cash flows in months 2 and 3 depend on the cash flows in the previous month.

Estimated net cash flows

Month 1		Month 2		Month 3	
Probability	Cash flow £'000	Probability	Cash flow £'000	Probability	Cash flow £'000
		0.8	25	0.5	30
0.7	(40)			0.5	20
		0.2	10	0.5	10
				0.5	0

Part D: Working capital management

	Month 1		Month 2		Month 3	
	Probability	Cash flow £'000	Probability	Cash flow £'000	Probability	Cash flow £'000
			0.8	0	0.5	(10)
	0.3	(60)			0.5	(20)
			0.2	(10)	0.5	(40)
					0.5	(50)

Required

If the company intends to maintain a cash float of £10,000 at the end of each month, what is the probability that this will be possible at the end of each of months 1, 2 and 3 given the current overdraft limit?

4.3 SOLUTION

The opening balance at the beginning of month 1 is £10,000.

	Month 1				Month 2				Month 3		
Prob.	Cash flow £'000	Clos. bal. £'000	Over-draft £'000	Prob.	Cash flow £'000	Clos. bal. £'000	Over-draft £'000	Prob.	Cash flow £'000	Clos. bal. £'000	Over-draft £'000
								0.28	30	10	19
				0.56	25	10	49	0.28	20	10	29
0.7	(40)	10	74								
								0.07	10	10	54
				0.14	10	10	64	0.07	0	10	64
								0.12	(10)	6	100
				0.24	0	10	94	0.12	(20)	(4)	100
0.3	(60)	10	94								
								0.03	(40)	(34)	100
				0.06	(10)	6	100	0.03	(50)	(44)	100

The probabilities that the cash float of £10,000 can be maintained at the end of each month are as follows.

Month 1: 0.7 + 0.3 = 1.0
Month 2: 0.56 + 0.14 + 0.24 = 0.94
Month 3: 0.28 + 0.28 + 0.07 + 0.07 = 0.7

Question 2

Using the figures in the above example, state the probabilities that the company completely runs out of cash at the end of each month.

Answer

Under none of the projected outcomes for months 1 and 2 does the company run out of cash.

For month 3, the probability of the company running out of cash is:

0.12 + 0.03 + 0.03 = 0.18

5 POOLING AND NETTING

5.1 If an organisation has a large number of different bank accounts with the same bank, it can make arrangements with the bank to **minimise** the **service charges** and **maximise interest**. These include the bank pooling balances when calculating interest and taking into account total balances held when it decides whether overdraft limits have been breached.

Multilateral netting

5.2 Where there is a large number of separate transactions in different currencies between different subsidiaries, in a multinational company the obligations of different subsidiaries may be netted off against each other on a **multilateral** basis. This may bring the advantage of reduced transaction costs because there will be a reduced level of transfers between different currencies.

5.3 **EXAMPLE: MULTILATERAL NETTING**

A group of companies controlled from the USA has subsidiaries in the UK, South Africa and Denmark. Below, these subsidiaries are referred to as UK, SA and DE respectively. At 30 June 20X5, inter-company indebtedness is as follows.

Debtor	Creditor	Amount
UK	SA	1,200,000 South African rand (R)
UK	DE	480,000 Danish kroners (KR)
DE	SA	800,000 South African rand
SA	UK	£74,000 sterling
SA	DE	375,000 Danish kroners

It is the company's policy to net off inter-company balances to the greatest extent possible. The central treasury department is to use the following exchange rates for this purpose.

US$1 equals R 6.1260 / £0.6800 / KR 5.880.

You are required to calculate the net payments to be made between the subsidiaries after netting off of inter-company balances.

5.4 **SOLUTION**

The first step is to convert the balances into US dollars as a common currency.

Debtor	Creditor	Amount in US dollars
UK	SA	1,200,000 ÷ 6.126 = $195,886
UK	DE	480,000 ÷ 5.880 = $81,633
DE	SA	800,000 ÷ 6.126 = $130,591
SA	UK	£74,000 ÷ 0.6800 = $108,824
SA	DE	375,000 ÷ 5.880 = $63,776

	Paying subsidiaries			
Receiving subsidiaries	UK	SA	DE	Total
	$	$	$	$
UK	-	108,824	-	108,824
SA	195,886	-	130,591	326,477
DE	81,633	63,776	-	145,409
Total payments	(277,519)	(172,600)	(130,591)	580,710
Total receipts	108,824	326,477	145,409	
Net receipt/(payment)	(168,695)	153,877	14,818	

Part D: Working capital management

The UK subsidiary should make payments of $153,877 to the South African subsidiary and $14,818 to the Danish subsidiary.

6 OTHER BANK SERVICES

6.1 The ease with which payments can be transferred between enterprises and between enterprises and its customers who are private individuals has been enhanced by the development of various electronic funds transfer operations.

> **KEY TERM**
>
> **Electronic funds transfer (EFT)** is the system used by banking organisations for the movement of funds between accounts and for the provision of services to customers.
>
> *(OT 2000)*

6.2 These include **BACS** and **CHAPS**, which we looked at earlier in this chapter. Other payment methods are described in the following paragraphs.

SWIFT

6.3 **SWIFT** (Society for Worldwide Interbank Financial Telecommunications) provides an electronic funds transfer (EFT) and payment system for its shareholder banks worldwide. Most major North American and Western European banks are members. Other users include securities houses, recognised exchanges, central clearing institutions, moneybrokers and fund managers.

6.4 SWIFT is a secure telecommunications network which facilitates rapid international transfers between the member banks. SWIFT now handles about one and three-quarter million messages a day. To do so, it imposes standard formats on certain types of message to facilitate **Electronic Data Interchange (EDI)**. These include purchase and sales orders, clearing instructions, foreign exchange confirmations, balance reporting, securities statements and trade confirmations.

Visa International

6.5 Visa's system allows individuals and small companies to make payments across European borders, and focuses on **low value cross-border payments**. Visa uses its existing data network, currently used by member banks to debit each other for credit card payments. Under the new system, banks are able to transmit credits as well. Visa expect the service to be used primarily by individuals, although small companies, such as retailers making VAT refunds to overseas customers, may also be a source of business.

Factors to consider in making international payments

Payment by cheque

6.6 Payment by cheque is a **slow** method of settlement, because the payee must wait for the cheque to be returned to the drawer's bank for clearance before his own account is credited. The exporter will arrange for his bank to collect the payment. (In international trade, cheques must always be sent for collection.) The collection procedures for a cheque are as follows.

(a) **If a foreign buyer draws a cheque in favour of a UK exporter**

    (i) The buyer will **post** the **cheque** to the **UK exporter**

    (ii) The **exporter** will **present the cheque** to his bank in the UK

    (iii) The bank in the UK will **send** the **cheque** to the **buyer's bank** in the **buyer's own country**, which will then pay the amount of the cheque and debit its customer's account, ie the buyer's account

    (iv) On **receiving payment** from the **buyer's bank**, the bank in the UK will **pay** the **exporter** (or credit his account) after deducting collection charges

(b) If the foreign buyer writes a cheque for an amount in sterling, he will have to arrange with his bank to have his account debited with an **appropriate amount** of his **local** currency.

If the cheque is written in the buyer's own currency (or a third currency)

    (i) The UK exporter may have a foreign currency bank account in that currency with a bank in the UK. He would then arrange to have this account **credited** with the **cheque payment**.

    (ii) Otherwise the exporter will have to arrange with his UK bank to have his **sterling account credited** with an **appropriate amount of sterling**. The bank would buy the foreign currency in exchange for sterling.

6.7 If a UK importer wished to pay an overseas supplier by cheque, much the same procedures operate in reverse.

6.8 Payment by cheque of a debt in international trade might be unsatisfactory for the following reasons.

(a) The long time it takes to collect payment by cheque is a serious inconvenience.

(b) The exporter (payee) will have to ask his bank to arrange to collect the payment for him, and the bank will make a **collection charge**.

(c) The cheque might **contravene** the **exchange control regulations** of the buyer's country, so that settlement would be delayed until the necessary authorisation to make payment has been obtained.

(d) Many companies are unaware that they are **receiving** an **advance** if their account is credited immediately in domestic currency when they present a cheque drawn on an overseas bank to their bank. The bank will charge interest on their advance.

(e) The cheque might **not be paid** when **presented**. If the cheque is unpaid, the bank will reclaim the advance, converting the domestic currency into the currency of the cheque at the prevailing exchange rate, possibly resulting in an exchange loss.

Payment by bill of exchange

6.9 **Bills of exchange** are a fairly commonly used method of settlement in international trade.

6.10 **Advantages of payment by bill of exchange**

(a) They provide a **convenient method of collecting payments** from foreign buyers.

(b) The exporter can seek **immediate finance**, using term bills of exchange, instead of having to wait until the period of credit expires (ie until the maturity of the bill). At the same time, the foreign buyer is allowed the full period of credit before payment is made.

Part D: Working capital management

   (c) On payment, the foreign buyer **keeps the bill** as **evidence of payment**, so that a bill of exchange also serves as a receipt.

   (d) If a **bill of exchange** is **dishonoured**, it may be used by the drawer to **pursue payment** by means of legal action in the drawee's country.

   (e) The buyer's bank might **add its name** to a **term bill,** to indicate that it *guarantees* payment at maturity. On the continent of Europe, this procedure is known as 'avalising' bills of exchange.

Payment by banker's draft

6.11 A **banker's draft** is a cheque drawn by a bank on one of its **own bank accounts**. For example, a banker's draft might be issued by a UK bank instructing payment out of its own bank account with a 'correspondent' bank in an overseas country. The draft may be denominated in a foreign currency but alternatively a banker's draft could be issued authorising payment in sterling, in which case the overseas supplier would present the draft to his bank in France and ask the bank to collect the payment.

6.12 Banker's drafts are fairly commonly used, but they are a **slow** method of payment and would not be used when **quick payment is required**. An advantage of a banker's draft is that the exporter receives direct notification that the payment is now available to him. If the draft is for an advance payment, and the exporter is waiting to receive it before shipping the goods abroad, this direct notification to the exporter might help to speed up the shipment.

Mail transfer (mail payment orders)

6.13 A mail transfer (MT) is:

   (a) A **payment order in writing**

   (b) **Sent by one bank** to **another bank** (overseas)

   (c) Which can be **authenticated** as having been authorised by a proper official in the sending bank

   (d) And which **instructs** the other **bank to pay a certain sum** of money

   (e) To a **specified beneficiary** (or on application by a specified beneficiary)

   The payment order is sent from the instructing bank to the overseas bank by airmail.

6.14 As is the case with banker's drafts, the overseas bank will have an account in the name of the instructing bank, and it is this account which will be debited with the amount paid to the beneficiary. Unlike a banker's draft, a mail transfer is sent by the bank itself to another bank, not by the bank's customer to the overseas supplier.

6.15 Because mail transfer (MT) involves airmail communication between one bank and another, it is a quicker method of payment than a banker's draft at no extra cost. However, there is always a possibility that instructions sent by airmail will be delayed or lost in the post, and there are quicker methods of arranging payment.

Telegraphic transfer (TT): cable or telex payment orders

6.16 Telegraphic transfers (TT) or 'cable payment orders' are the same as mail transfers, except that instructions are sent by cable or telex instead of by airmail. TT is therefore slightly more costly to the paying bank's customer than mail transfer, but it speeds up payment.

18: Cash management

Large payments should be made by TT or by SWIFT (see below) because the marginal extra cost of TT over MT might be outweighed by the extra interest earnings or savings in interest costs which would be achievable if TT were used. A further advantage of TT over MT is that there is no danger of instructions being delayed or lost in the post.

Using SWIFT: IMTs and EIMTs

6.17 As more and more banks become members of SWIFT, the use of mail transfer and telegraphic transfer will decline because SWIFT (introduced earlier in this section) uses its own comparable methods of payment.

(a) A 'SWIFT message' is a payment equivalent to one by **mail** transfer, where the paying bank and correspondent bank overseas are both members of SWIFT. A SWIFT message is referred to as an **International Money Transfer** (IMT).

(b) Similarly a 'priority SWIFT message' is a payment equivalent to one by telegraphic transfer. A priority SWIFT message is referred to as an Express International Money Transfer (EIMT).

The distinction between non-urgent and urgent SWIFT messages is the speed of taking action to make the settlement, not the time that it takes for the message to be transmitted.

International money orders

6.18 An **international money order** is a means of transferring comparatively small sums of money from one country to another through the agency of the Post Office or possibly an international bank (eg Barclays). Since only small amounts are involved, international money orders are best suited to small orders where the exporter asks for payment in advance since the small amount of money involved would perhaps not financially justify allowing credit to the buyer or the minimum bank charges associated with collections or letters of credit.

Question 3

Outline the main services offered by banks to the small or medium-sized business.

Answer

Bank customers can be broadly divided into **personal customers** and **business customers**. Within this broad division are several sub-groups: for example in the business sector there are small businesses and large corporates.

Business customers can operate a high interest instant access account with rates linked to money market rates and with the interest paid gross. If they have surplus funds for 3 months or more they may want certificates of deposit (CDs) which they can turn into cash if they need to at a later date.

Money transmission services. Customers want to be able to pay money in, move their money around, withdraw money and make payments.

Efficient money transmission is very important to businesses and they will make use of all the regular payment services plus one or two specific products. A firm may use the **BACS facilities** to make large payments such as wages and salaries. Firms will make more extensive use of **CHAPS** and those retail businesses accepting credit cards will need the merchant services provided by the bank to facilitate payments.

The third group of products used is **lending products**, including overdrafts, budget accounts, loans, mortgages and credit cards.

Businesses naturally need finance and this may be provided through **commercial loans, overdrafts and mortgages**. The merchant banking division would be able to offer leasing and hire purchase too.

Part D: Working capital management

Firms involved in foreign trade would be interested in foreign services. Payments can be made overseas using **SWIFT, currencies exchanged**, finance provided in **foreign currency**, and **bills of exchange discounted**, collected or negotiated.

Exam focus point

As with other aspects of working capital management, you must be prepared for **numerical questions** as well as discussions of policy issues in this area. Knowledge of **cash management models** and the **use of probabilities** in this area is needed, as is familiarity with the **impact of new technology on payment systems**.

Question 4

Which of the following services is **not** normally provided by the bank as part of a computerised corporate cash management service?

A Account reporting
B Funds transfer
C Decision support services
D Bank references

Answer

D Bank references

Chapter roundup

- Optimal **cash** holding levels can be calculated from formal models, such as the **inventory approach** and the **Miller-Orr model**.

- **Cash shortages** can be eased by postponing capital expenditure, selling assets, taking longer to pay creditors and pressing debtors for earlier payment.

- Businesses should also try to reduce **float,** the period between the time a payment is initiated and the time when funds become available.

- **Multilateral netting** can be used by groups to reduce transaction costs.

- Methods of making **international payments** include cheque, bill of exchange, banker's draft and mail and telegraphic transfers.

Quick quiz

1 Possible reasons for a lengthy float are:

   (A) .... delay

   (B) .... delay

   (C) .... delay

2 Hallas Ltd is a small manufacturing business that uses a large number of suppliers, many of which are located outside the UK. The accountant has suggested that Hallas could improve its cash position by sending payments out using surface mail rather than airmail as at present. If Hallas did this, which of the following would it be taking advantage of?

   A Lodgement delay
   B Clearance delay
   C Transmission delay
   D Collection delay

18: Cash management

3   A company wishes to make an immediate (same-day) transfer of £20,000 to a creditor in the UK. This can be achieved by CHAPS.

　　True ☐
　　False ☐

4   What is the name of: a UK system for computerised transfer of funds between banks and by companies, by which the bank customer normally supplies data on magnetic tape or disk, and which is often used for salary payments?

5   In the Miller-Orr cash management model:

　　Return point = Lower limit + ☐ × Spread

　　(Fill in the box)

6   International multilateral netting between subsidiaries of a multilateral company should:

　　(a) Reduce transaction costs - *True/False*?
　　(b) Reduce levels of transfers between different currencies - *True/False*?

7   Mrs Harris's daughter is travelling in Australia and is running out of money. Mrs Harris wishes to send her £200 within the next few days. Which of the following methods would you recommend that she uses?

　　A   Letter of credit
　　B   International money order
　　C   Banker's draft
　　D   Mail transfer

8   The formula for Baumol's model is $Q = \sqrt{\dfrac{2FS}{i}}$. What do these terms stand for?

Answers to quick quiz

1   (A) Transmission delay
　　(B) Lodgement delay
　　(C) Clearance delay

2   C   Transmission delay

3   True

4   BACS

5   One-third

6   (a) True
　　(b) True

7   B would be the quickest and cheapest method to use.

8   S = amount of cash to be used in each time period
　　F = fixed costs of obtaining new funds
　　i = Interest cost of holding cash or near cash equivalents
　　Q = total amount to be raised to provide for S

Now try the question below from the Exam Question Bank

Number	Level	Marks	Time
18	Examination	20	36 mins

Chapter 19

CREDIT CONTROL POLICIES

Topic list	Syllabus reference	Ability required
1 What is credit control?	(iv)	Evaluation
2 Total credit	(iv)	Evaluation
3 The credit cycle	(iv)	Evaluation
4 Payment terms and settlement discounts	(iv)	Evaluation
5 Methods of payment	(iv)	Evaluation

Introduction

The previous chapters have discussed some of the issues of managing cash, and you will have noted the **time lag** between the provision of goods and services and the receipt of cash for them. This time lag, as we have seen, can result in a firm making considerable demands on its bank to finance its working capital. Any increase in the time lag can make it significantly more difficult for a business to pay its own debts as they fall due.

An important decision in this area is whether to offer **settlement discounts** in return for quicker payment. Calculation of the effect of settlement discounts, and discussion of their advantages, will be tested frequently in this paper.

Learning outcomes covered in this chapter

- Identify debtor management policies and procedures for an organisation
- Evaluate debtor and creditor policies

Syllabus content covered in this chapter

- The credit cycle from receipt of customer order to cash receipt
- Payment terms
- Evaluating settlement discounts
- Methods of payment, eg cash, BACS, cheque, banker's draft, standing order, direct debit, credit card, debit card

1 WHAT IS CREDIT CONTROL?

1.1 There are two aspects to **credit** we shall consider here.

(a) **Trade credit**

This is credit issued by a business to another business. For example, many invoices state that payment is expected within thirty days of the date of the invoice. In effect this is giving the customer thirty days credit. The customer is effectively borrowing at the supplier's expense.

(b) **Consumer credit**

This is credit offered by businesses to the end-consumer.

(i) Many businesses offer **hire purchase terms**, whereby the consumer takes out a loan to repay the goods purchased. Failure to repay will result in the goods being repossessed.

(ii) In practice, much of the growth in consumer credit has been driven not so much by retailers as by banks. **Credit cards** are largely responsible for the explosive growth in consumer credit.

1.2 Credit control issues are closely bound up with a firm's management of liquidity, discussed in earlier chapters. Credit is offered to enhance turnover and profitability, but this should not be to the extent that a company becomes illiquid and insolvent.

1.3 Credit is also vital in securing orders in certain specified situations.

(a) **Economic conditions** can influence the type and amount of credit offered. In 'boom times, when customers are queuing with orders' (Bass, in *Credit Management Handbook*), new customers can be asked for security, and risk can be minimised. In other times, credit must be used to entice customers in, and so the credit manager's job is to control risk.

(b) **High-risk or marginal customers** require flexible payment arrangements. High risk customers are often profitable, but the risk has to be managed. The customer may require a credit limit of £50,000, on standard terms, but may only deserve £35,000. The supplier might choose instead to offer a £30,000 credit limit, together with a discount policy to encourage early payment.

1.4 Just as there is a relationship between offering credit and securing sales, so too there has to be a suitable working relationship between credit control personnel and sales and marketing staff. This is because, in the words of Bass, 'a sale is not complete until the money is in the bank' and the cost of chasing after slow payers and doubtful debts is considerable.

A firm's credit policy

1.5 A firm should have policies for credit and credit control.

Part D: Working capital management

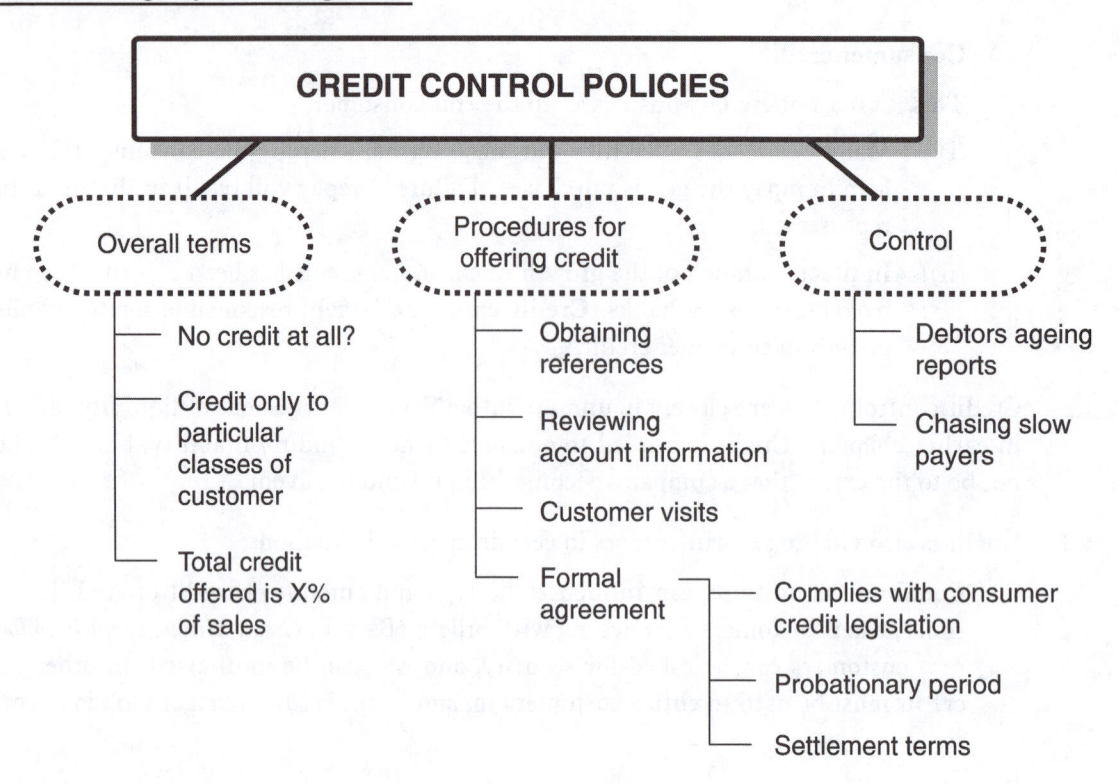

```
                        CREDIT CONTROL POLICIES
         ┌───────────────────────┼───────────────────────┐
    Overall terms          Procedures for             Control
                          offering credit
      — No credit at all?    — Obtaining              — Debtors ageing
                               references                reports
      — Credit only to       — Reviewing              — Chasing slow
        particular             account information       payers
        classes of
        customer             — Customer visits
      — Total credit         — Formal     ┬── Complies with consumer
        offered is X%          agreement  │   credit legislation
        of sales                          ├── Probationary period
                                          └── Settlement terms
```

2 TOTAL CREDIT

2.1 We saw in previous chapters that a bank's decision to lend money to a customer is determined by many factors over which the customer has little control. The bank, for example, might only wish to extend so much credit to firms in a particular industry.

2.2 Similarly, the firm itself has to maintain a 'global' approach to credit control in the light of the firm's objectives for **profit, cash flow, asset use** and **reducing interest costs**.

2.3 Finding a **total level of credit** which can be offered is a matter of finding the least costly balance between enticing customers, whose use of credit entails considerable costs, and refusing opportunities for profitable sales. Firstly it helps to see what debtors, which often account for 30% of the total assets of a business, actually represent.

Measuring total debtors

2.4 There are three methods of assessing how many days sales are represented by debtors.

(a) The **days sales in debtors ratio,** sometimes called **debtors payment period** as evidenced in analysis of financial statements. It represents the length of the credit period taken by customers.

$$\frac{\text{Total debtors} \times 365}{\text{Sales in 365 days}} = \text{Days sales}$$

For example, in 20X4 X plc made sales of £700,000 and at 31 December 20X4, debtors stood at £90,000. The comparable figures for 20X3 were £600,000 (annual sales) and £70,000 (debtors at 31.13.X3).

	20X4		20X3	
Debtors represent	$\frac{£90,000 \times 365}{£700,000}$	= 47 days	$\frac{£70,000 \times 365}{£600,000}$	= 43 days

In 20X4, the company is taking longer to collect its debts.

(b) **Count-back method**. Rather than annualising, this simply assumes that the majority of debtors are most current.

Let us take an example. Assume that at the end of March total debtors stood at £1m. Sales in March were £500,000; in February, £450,000 and in January £500,000.

	£
Total debtors at the end of March	1,000,000
Less March sales	500,000
	500,000
Less February sales	450,000
	50,000
Less January sales, unpaid portion	50,000
	–

We can calculate the days outstanding as follows.

	Days
March: entire turnover	31
February: entire turnover	28
January: $\frac{50,000}{500,000} \times 31$ days	3
	62 days

(c) The **partial month method** analyses each month's sales and the unpaid portion. These are then aggregated together. Assume that at the end of June, total debtors are £1.5m. Data related to the previous months are as follows.

	Sales (a)	Unpaid (b)	Days (c)	$\frac{b}{a} \times c$
	£	£		Days
June	500,000	500,000	30	30.00
May	450,000	400,000	31	27.50
April	500,000	300,000	30	18.00
March	600,000	150,000	31	7.75
February	400,000	50,000	28	3.50
January	500,000	100,000	31	6.20
Before January	None	None	N/A	N/A
Total	2,950,000	1,500,000	N/A	92.95
		(ie Debtors)		

2.5 (a) Financial analysts will be most interested to review the **annualised figure** for debtors calculated in Paragraph 2.4(a). However, this will be of little practical interest to credit controllers.

(b) The **count-back method** also suffers perhaps because it can lead to the assumption that most debtors are necessarily recent.

(c) The **partial month method** not only provides an overall debtors ageing figure but, as importantly, it also enables an analysis broken down by month.

Effect on profit of extending credit

2.6 The main cost of offering credit is the interest expense. How can we assess the effect on profit?

2.7 Let us assume that the Zygo Company sells widgets for £1,000, which enables it to earn a profit, after all other expenses except interest, of £100 (ie a 10% margin).

(a) Aibee buys a widget for £1,000 on 1 January 20X1, but does not pay until 31 December 20X1. Zygo relies on overdraft finance, which costs it 10% pa. The effect is:

Part D: Working capital management

	£
Net profit on sale of widget	100
Overdraft cost £1,000 × 10% pa	(100)
Actual profit after 12 months credit	Nil

In other words, the entire profit margin has been wiped out in 12 months.

(b) If Aibee had paid after six months, the effect would be:

	£
Net profit	100
Overdraft cost £1,000 × 10% pa × $^6/_{12}$ months	(50)
	50

Half the profit has been wiped out. (*Tutorial note*. The interest cost might be worked out in a more complex way to give a more accurate figure.)

(c) If the cost of borrowing had been 18%, then the profit would have been absorbed before seven months had elapsed. If the net profit were 5% and borrowing costs were 15%, the interest expense would exceed the net profit after four months.

2.8 A second general point is the relation of **total credit to bad debts**. Burt Edwards argues that there is a law of 10-to-1: 'Experience in different industries shows that the annual interest expense of borrowings to support overdue debts, ie those in excess of agreed payment terms, is at least ten times the total lost in bad debts'. This is not a 'law', but has been observed to be the case over a variety of UK businesses.

Question 1

Winterson Tools Ltd has an average level of debtors of £2m at any time representing 60 days outstanding. (Their terms are thirty days.) The firm borrows money at 10% a year. The managing director is proud of the credit control: 'I only had to write off £10,000 in bad debts last year,' she says proudly. Is she right to be proud?

Answer

At the moment, Winterson Tools Ltd is paying 10% × £1m (ie $^{30}/_{60}$ days × £2m) = £100,000 in interest caused by customers taking the extra month to pay.

2.9 The level of total credit can then have a significant effect on **profitability**. That said, if credit considerations are included in pricing calculations, it may be the case that extending credit can, in fact, increase profitability. If offering credit generates extra sales, then those extra sales will have additional repercussions on:

(a) The **amount of stock** maintained in the warehouse, to ensure that the extra demand must be satisfied

(b) The **amount of money** the company **owes** to its **creditors** (as it will be increasing its supply of raw materials)

2.10 This means an increase in **working capital**. Working capital is an **investment**, just as a fixed asset (eg new machinery) is, albeit of a different kind.

2.11 To determine whether it would be profitable to extend the level of total credit, it is necessary to assess the following.

- The additional sales volume which might result
- The profitability of the extra sales
- The extra length of the average debt collection period

19: Credit control policies

- The required rate of return on the investment in additional debtors

Question 2

A company is proposing to increase the credit period that it gives to customers from one calendar month to one and a half calendar months in order to raise turnover from the present annual figure of £24 million representing 4m units per annum. The price of the product is £6 and it costs £5.40 to make. The increase in the credit period is likely to generate an extra 150,000 unit sales. Is this enough to justify the extra costs given that the company's required rate of return is 20%? Assume no changes to stock levels, as the company is increasing its operating efficiency. Assume that existing debtors will take advantage of the new terms.

Answer

The existing value of debtors is:

$$\frac{£24m}{12 \text{ months}} = £2m$$

If sales increased by 150,000 units, the value of debtors would be:

$$1\tfrac{1}{2} \times \frac{£24m + (150,000 \times £6)}{12 \text{ months}} = £3,112,500.$$

The debtors have to be financed somehow, and the additional £1,112,500 will cost £1,112,500 × 20% = £222,500 in financing costs.

The profit on the extra sales is: 150,000 units × (£6 − £5.40) = £90,000

The new credit policy is not worthwhile, mainly because existing customers would also take advantage of it.

2.12 EXAMPLE: TOTAL INVESTMENT IN DEBTORS

Russian Beard Limited is considering a change of credit policy which will result in slowing down in the average collection period from one to two months. The relaxation in credit standards is expected to produce an increase in sales in each year amounting to 25% of the current sales volume.

Sales price per unit	£10.00
Profit per unit (before interest)	£1.50
Current sales revenue per annum	£2.4 million

The required rate of return on investment is 20%.

Assume that the 25% increase in sales would result in additional stocks of £100,000 and additional creditors of £20,000. Advise the company on whether or not it should extend the credit period offered to customers, in the following circumstances.

(a) If all customers take the longer credit of two months

(b) If existing customers do not change their payment habits, and only the new customers take a full two months' credit

2.13 SOLUTION

The change in credit policy would be justifiable, in the context of this question, if the rate of return on the additional investment in working capital exceeds 20%.

Part D: Working capital management

Extra profit
Profit margin £1.50/£10 = 15%
Increase in sales revenue £2.4m × 25% £0.6 million
Increase in profit (15% × £0.6m) £90,000

The total sales revenue is now £3m (£2.4m + £0.6m)

(a) *Extra investment, if all debtors take two months credit*

	£
Average debtors after the sales increase (2/12 × £3 million)	500,000
Current average debtors (1/12 × £2.4 million)	200,000
Increase in debtors	300,000
Increase in stocks	100,000
	400,000
Increase in creditors	(20,000)
Net increase in 'working capital'	380,000

$$\text{Return on extra investment } \frac{£90,000}{£380,000} = 23.7\%$$

(b) *Extra investment, if only the new debtors take two months credit*

	£
Increase in debtors (2/12 × £0.6 million)	100,000
Increase in stocks	100,000
	200,000
Increase in creditors	(20,000)
Net increase in working capital investment	180,000

$$\text{Return on extra investment } \frac{£90,000}{£180,000} = 50\%$$

In both case (a) and case (b) the new credit policy appears to be worthwhile.

Furthermore, the cost profile of the product can also support extra sales. If the firm has high fixed costs but low variable costs, the extra production and sales could provide a substantial contribution at little extra cost.

Debtor quality and liquidity

2.14 Another objective of any credit control system is to minimise any risks to **cash flow** arising from insolvent debtors. The **quality** of debtors has an important impact on a firm's overall liquidity. Debtor quality is determined by their **age** and **risk**.

2.15 Some **industries** have a higher level of risk than others, in other words, there is a higher probability that customers will fail to pay. Some markets are riskier than others. Selling goods to a country with possible payment difficulties is riskier than selling them in the home market.

2.16 For many customers, delaying payment is the cheapest form of finance available and there has been much publicity recently about the difficulties that delayed payments cause to small businesses. There is no easy answer to this problem.

Policing total credit

2.17 The total amount of credit offered, as well as individual accounts, should be policed to ensure that the senior management policy with regard to the total credit limits is maintained. A **credit utilisation report** can indicate the extent to which total limits are being utilised. An example is given below.

Customer	Limit	Utilisation	
	£'000	£'000	%
Alpha	100	90	90
Beta	50	35	70
Gamma	35	21	60
Delta	250	125	50
	435	271	
		62.2%	

This might also contain other information, such as days sales outstanding and so on.

2.18 Reviewed in aggregate, this can reveal the following.

- The number of customers who might want more credit
- The extent to which the company is exposed to debtors
- The 'tightness' of the policy
- Credit utilisation in relation to total sales

2.19 It is possible to design credit utilisation reports to highlight other trends.

- The degree of exposure to different countries
- The degree of exposure to different industries

Trade debtors' analysis as at 31 December

Industry	Current credit utilisation	% of total debtors	Annual sales	As a % of total sales
	£'000	%	£ million	%
Property	9,480	25.0	146.0	19.2
Construction	7,640	20.2	140.1	18.4
Engineering	4,350	11.5	112.6	14.8
Electricals	4,000	10.6	83.7	11.0
Electricity	2,170	5.7	49.2	6.5
Transport	3,230	8.5	79.9	10.5
Chemicals, plastics	1,860	4.9	43.3	5.7
Motors, aircraft trades	5,170	13.6	105.8	13.9
	37,900	100.0	760.6	100.0

Analysis

(a) An industry analysis of credit exposure shows in this case that over 45% of the company's trade debtors (about £17 million) are in the property and construction industries. Management should have a view about this exposure to industry risk.

(b) The size of the exposure to property and construction could seem excessive, in view of the cyclical nature of these industries, the current economic outlook, and the comparatively slow payment rate from these customers. (These industries account for only 37.6% of annual sales, but 45.2% of trade debtors.) Management might wish to consider whether the company should try to reduce this exposure.

(c) A decision might also be required about whether the company should be willing to accumulate trade debtors in these sectors, in order to sustain sales, or whether the credit risk would be too high.

Conclusion

2.20 The amount of **total credit** that a business offers is worthy of consideration at the highest management levels. Two issues are:

- The firm's working capital needs and the investment in debtors
- The management responsibility for carrying out the credit control policy

Question 3

Your company is concerned about the effect of inflation, which (you should suppose) currently stands at 6%, on its credit control policy. Outline the main points to consider, for discussion with your manager.

Answer

Inflation accentuates the importance of credit control, because the cost of the investment in debtors, in real terms, is higher. If a company grants credit of £100,000 for 3 months, and the rate of inflation is 6% per annum, the value in 'today's money' of the eventual receipts in 3 months' time would be about 1½% less - ie about £1,500 less. If the rate of inflation went up to, say, 12%, the value of the same receipts in 3 months' time would be about £3,000 less. In other words, the cost of granting credit increases as the rate of inflation gets higher. Also, with higher inflation, customers have an increased incentive to pay late.

3 THE CREDIT CYCLE

The credit cycle

3.1 The credit control function's jobs occupy a number of stages of the **order cycle** (from customer order to invoice despatch) and the **collection cycle** (from invoice despatch to the receipt of cash), which together make up the **credit cycle.** The job of the credit control department can comprise all those activities within the dotted line **in the diagram on the next page**.

(a) **Establish credit status for new customers or customers who request a credit extension.**

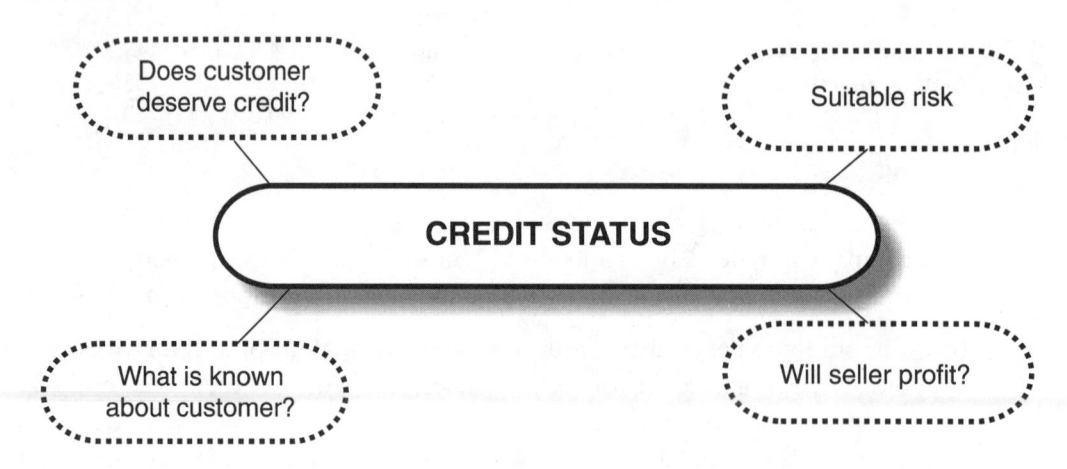

```
      Does customer              Suitable risk
      deserve credit?
                    \           /
                    CREDIT STATUS
                    /           \
      What is known              Will seller profit?
      about customer?
```

(b) **Check credit limit**

If the order is fairly routine, and there is no problem with credit status, then credit control staff examine their records or at least the sales ledger records to see if the new order will cause the customer to exceed the credit limit. There are a number of possible responses, as follows.

(i) **Authorisation**

If the credit demanded is within the credit limit, and there are no reasons to suspect any problems, then the request will be authorised.

(ii) **Referral**

It is possible that the credit demanded will exceed the limit offered in the agreement.

(1) The firm can simply **refuse the request for credit**, at the risk of damaging the business relationship. However, credit limits are there for a reason - to protect the business's profitability and liquidity.

(2) The firm can offer a **revised credit limit**. For example, the customer may be solvent and a regular payee, therefore a low risk. The company might be able to offer a higher credit limit to this customer.

Stages in the credit cycle

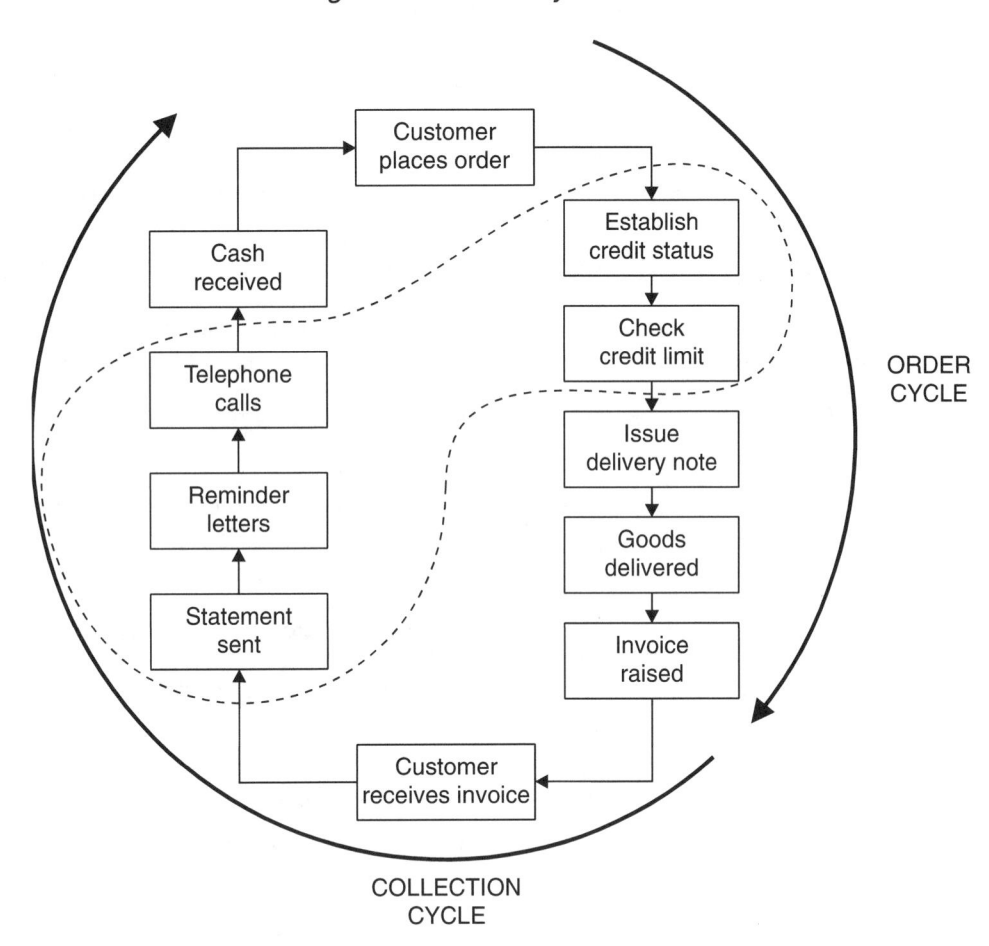

```
                    Customer
                    places order
                         |
    Cash            Establish
    received        credit status
      ^                  |
      |             Check
   Telephone        credit limit        ORDER
   calls                |               CYCLE
      ^             Issue
      |             delivery note
   Reminder             |
   letters          Goods
      ^             delivered
      |                  |
   Statement         Invoice
   sent              raised
      ^                  |
      |             Customer
      +---- receives invoice

              COLLECTION
              CYCLE
```

(3) The firm can **contact the customer**, and request that some of the outstanding debt be paid off before further credit is advanced.

(c) **Issuing documentation**

Issuing the delivery note, invoicing and so on is not the job of the credit control department, but the credit control department will need to have **access to information** such as invoice details to do its job.

(d) **Settlement**

The credit control department takes over the collection cycle, although the final payment is ultimately received by the accounts department. Collection involves reviewing overdue debts, and chasing them.

Part D: Working capital management

Question 4

See if you can explain the likely effects of a company's credit control policy on the control of working capital in general.

Answer

Working capital includes stock, debtors, creditors and cash. The effect of credit policy on working capital is that if **more credit** is granted, there will be a **slowdown** in the **inflow of cash** (unless the extension of credit also results in an increase in sales). **Discounts** for **early payment** would also affect cash flows. Similarly, **tightening up on credit** and so granting less credit will result in a **speeding up** of **cash inflows**, provided that there is no reduction in sales as a consequence of the restriction of credit.

The total amount of working capital should be kept under control because the investment in working capital must be financed, and so excessive debtors are unnecessarily costly and would reduce the organisation's return on capital employed.

Credit policy is therefore significant both from the point of view of **liquidity** (cash flow) and the **management of finance** (investment).

4 PAYMENT TERMS AND SETTLEMENT DISCOUNTS   Pilot paper, 11/01

4.1 An important aspect of the credit control policy is to devise suitable **payment terms**, covering when should payment be made and how this should be achieved.

(a) Credit terms have to take into account the **expected profit** on the sale and the seller's cash needs.

(b) Credit terms also establish when **payment is to be received,** an important matter from the seller's point of view.

> **TERMS AND CONDITIONS OF SALE**
> - **Nature of goods to be supplied**
> - **Price**
> - **Delivery**
> - **Date of payment**
> - **Frequency of payment**
> - **Discounts**

4.2 The credit terms the seller offers depend on many factors.

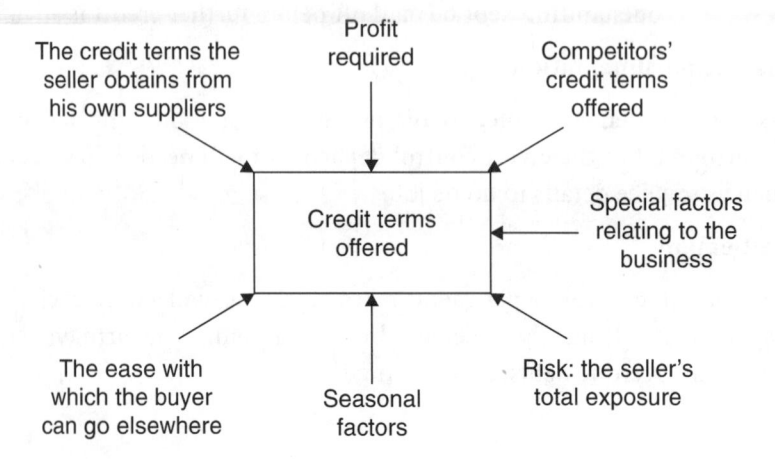

Factors influencing **Credit terms offered**:
- The credit terms the seller obtains from his own suppliers
- Profit required
- Competitors' credit terms offered
- Special factors relating to the business
- The ease with which the buyer can go elsewhere
- Seasonal factors
- Risk: the seller's total exposure

4.3 The terms must be simple to understand and easily enforceable. If the seller does not enforce his terms he is creating a precedent.

4.4 All sale agreements are **contracts**, as described earlier: credit terms are part of the contract. Although contracts do not have to be in writing, it helps if they are, and these are confirmed by the invoice.

PAYMENT TERMS	
Payment a specified number of days after delivery	Eg Net 10 (10 days)
Weekly credit	All supplies in week must be paid for by a specified date in next week
Half monthly credit	All supplies in one half of month must be paid for by specified date in next
10th and 25th	Supplies in first half of month must be paid for by 25th, supplies in second half must be paid for by 10th of next month
Monthly credit	Payment for month's supplies must be paid by specified date in next month; if date 7th might be written Net 7 prox. Some monthly credit called Number MO; 2MO means payment must be in next month but one
Delivery	Certain payment terms geared to delivery • **CWO** Cash with order • **CIA** Cash in advance • **COD** Cash on delivery • **CND** Cash on next delivery

Methods of payment

4.5 **Payment** can be accepted in a variety of forms.

- Cash
- BACS
- Cheques
- Banker's draft
- Travellers' cheques or Eurocheques
- Postal orders
- Standing order
- Direct debit
- Credit cards
- Debit card
- Bills of exchange, promissory notes

Payment times: settlement discounts

4.6 Some firms offer settlement discounts if payment is received early.

(a) If sensibly priced, they encourage customers to pay earlier, thereby avoiding some of the financing costs arising out of the granting of credit. Thus they can affect **profitability**.

(b) The seller may be suffering from cash flow problems. If settlement discounts encourage earlier payment, they thus enable a company to **maintain liquidity**. In the short term, liquidity is often more important than profitability.

(c) Settlement discounts might, conceivably, **affect the volume of demand** if, as part of the overall credit terms offered, they encourage customers to buy.

Part D: Working capital management

4.7 However discounts can have certain disadvantages.

  (a) If a discount is offered to **one customer**, the company may have to offer it to other customers.

  (b) **Discounts** may be **difficult to withdraw**.

  (c) They establish a **set settlement period**, which might otherwise be lowered in the future.

4.8 To consider whether the offer of a discount for early payment is financially worthwhile it is necessary to compare the **cost** of the discount with the **benefit** of a reduced investment in debtors.

4.9 EXAMPLE: SETTLEMENT DISCOUNTS

Wingspan Limited currently has sales of £3m, with an average collection period of two months. No discounts are given. The management of the company are undecided as to whether to allow a discount on sales of 2% to settle within one month. The company assumes that all customers would take advantage of the discount. The company can obtain a return of 30% on its investments.

Advise the management whether or not to introduce the discount.

4.10 SOLUTION

In this example the offer of a discount is not expected to increase sales demand. The advantage would be in the **reduction of the collection period**, and the resulting saving in the working capital investment required.

Our solution will value debtors at sales value.

(a) *Change in debtors*

	Debtors valued at sales price £
Current value of debtors (2/12 × £3m)	500,000
New value of debtors (1/12 × £3m)	250,000
Reduction in investment in debtors	250,000

(b) The cost of reducing debtors is the cost of the discounts, ie

2% × £3 million = £60,000

(c) The reduction in debtors of £250,000 would cost the company £60,000 per annum. If the company can earn 30% on its investments, the benefit is:

30% × £250,000 = £75,000

The discount policy would be worthwhile, since the benefit of £75,000 exceeds the cost of £60,000.

4.11 The percentage cost of an early settlement discount to the company giving it can be estimated by the formula:

FORMULA TO LEARN

$$\left(\frac{100}{100-d}\right)^{\frac{365}{t}} - 1$$

where:

d is the discount offered (5% = 5, etc)
t is the reduction in payment period in days

4.12 In the example above, the formula can be applied as follows.

$$\text{Cost of discount} = \left(\frac{100}{100-2}\right)^{\frac{365}{30}} - 1$$

$$= 27.9\%$$

Since 27.9% is less than the 30% by which the company judges investments, offering the discount is worthwhile.

Question 5

Gamma grants credit terms of 60 days net to customers, but offers an early settlement discount of 2% for payment within seven days. What is the cost of the discount to Gamma?

Answer

Gamma is offering customers the option of paying £98 after seven days per £100 invoiced, or payment in full after 60 days.

Using the formula

$$\text{Cost of discount} = \left(\frac{100}{100-d}\right)^{\frac{365}{t}} - 1$$

$$= \left(\frac{100}{100-2}\right)^{\frac{365}{53}} - 1$$

$$= 14.9\%$$

4.13 As far as an **individual debtor** is concerned, the principles are similar. For example, assume Boris Ltd has an average £10,000 outstanding, representing two months sales. You offer Boris a 1% settlement discount which would reduce the average amount outstanding to £5,000 (before discounts). You borrow money at 5%. A 1% discount on annual sales of £60,000 would cost you £600. Overdraft interest saved is £250 (£5,000 × 5%) so it is not worth offering the discount.

Late payment

4.14 It has been suggested that businesses should charge interest on overdue debts, however:

(a) **Charging for late payment** might be misconstrued (The supplier might assume that charges for late payment give the customer the authority to pay late.)

(b) Statutory **rate for interest** on overdue debts has not been established in the UK

Part D: Working capital management

(c) Charging for payments relates only to the effect of the late payment on **profitability**, not on liquidity

Question 6

Thinking back to topics covered in earlier chapters, explain how good cash management may realise each of the following benefits.

(a) Better control of financial risks
(b) Opportunity for profit
(c) Strengthened balance sheet
(d) Increased confidence with customers, suppliers, banks and shareholders

Answer

(a) **Better control of financial risk.** By determining and maintaining the proper level of cash within a company in accordance with the organisation's financial procedures and within defined authorisation limits.

(b) **Opportunity for profit.** By reducing to a minimum the opportunity cost associated with maintaining cash balances in excess of company's operating needs. Earnings (or surpluses) are improved by freeing up surplus cash for investment purposes while reducing interest charged through minimising borrowing.

(c) **Strengthened balance sheet.** By reducing or eliminating cash balances in excess of target balances and putting surplus cash to work by investing it (eg in the overnight money market); by reducing or eliminating cash borrowing and keeping interest costs as low as possible.

(d) **Increased confidence with customers, suppliers, banks and shareholders.** By having access to funds to disburse to suppliers (creditors), banks (interest, fees and principal payments) and shareholders (dividends) when due. By providing good instructions to customers (debtors) to enable the organisation to convert receipts into usable bank deposits.

Question 7

Your company has been growing rapidly over the last two years and now wishes to introduce a more formal credit control policy. You are asked to give a brief presentation on the factors involved in setting up such a policy.

Answer

The factors involved in establishing a credit control policy are as follows.

(a) **A total credit policy** must be **decided**, whereby the organisation decides how much credit it can and should allow to debtors in total. Debtors should not be excessive in relation to total sales turnover, and the cost of financing debtors should also be considered. The debtor policy that is established will include maximum periods for payment.

(b) A **credit policy** must be **set** for deciding credit terms for individual customers. This will include establishing a system of credit rating, and procedures for deciding the maximum credit limit and terms for the payment period.

(c) The **purpose of allowing credit** is to **boost sales demand**. Management must consider how 'generous' credit terms should be to encourage sales, whilst at the same time avoiding excessive increases in bad debts, and problems with chasing payment from slow payers.

(d) Granting credit will inevitably mean that **problems will arise with slow payers** and bad debts. Procedures must be established for collecting debts from slow payers and writing off bad debts.

(e) **Discounts** might be **offered** for **early payment of debts**, and a decision should be taken as to how much discount, if any, should be offered to encourage early payment, thereby reducing the volume of debtors.

5 METHODS OF PAYMENT

Cheques

5.1 Cheques are one of the most significant means by which a business's customers will pay their debts, and by which a business will pay its suppliers. Cheques may either be produced manually (with one or two signatures required, depending on value) or by computer. Counterfoils provide a **record** of payments.

> **Exam focus point**
> You may already have learned about cheques but a few reminders are in order here.

Bars to payment of cheques

5.2 (a) **Legal bars to payment** of a customer cheque include: the customer's subsequent death; the customer's bankruptcy; and court orders against the customer.

(b) A customer is entitled to **stop payment** of a cheque by giving instructions, confirmed in writing, to the bank given before the cheque is paid, **unless by using his cheque guarantee card** in issuing the cheque, the customer committed his bank to honour the cheque.

Sufficiency of funds

5.3 A bank has **no** obligation to honour a customer's cheque unless the customer has a credit balance or an agreed overdraft which suffices to provide funds for the payment of the cheque. However cheques issued under the **cheque guarantee scheme** must be honoured even if the customer has an unauthorised overdraft.

Cheque guarantee scheme

5.4 A cheque guarantee card creates a contract by which the bank, through the customer as its agent, undertakes to pay the holder of the cheque the lesser of its value or a fixed amount (£50, £100 or £250, as shown on the cheque card). A cheque guarantee card is not itself a method of payment: it is a **guarantee that a cheque will be** paid.

Debit cards

5.5 **Debit cards** are designed for customers who like paying by plastic card but do not want credit. Many customers now hold multi-function plastic cards which act as ATM, debit and cheque guarantee card in one, so that they can be used to withdraw money from a current account in three ways: cash, payment by debit card to a third party accepting such cards, or payment by cheque, supported by the guarantee card.

5.6 Debit cards are designed to be used in EFTPOS systems (**Electronic Funds Transfer at Point of Sale**) which, as the name suggests, can initiate an immediate transfer of funds from the customer's account to that of the person providing him with goods or services. In practice, in the UK, debit card transactions are not exclusively processed in EFTPOS systems. There are two main brands, Switch and Delta.

Part D: Working capital management

Credit cards

5.7 **Credit cards** provide credit to cardholders. A credit card holder uses the card to purchase goods or services **within a total credit limit**. A monthly statement will be issued to the cardholder by the card company. The cardholder must pay at least a certain minimum amount. Interest is charged on unpaid amounts. (They are not the same as **charge cards**, such as American Express, whose balance must be paid in full every month.)

5.8 Credit cards also provide a means of payment (ie money transmission). Traders who sell goods or services to customers with a bank's credit card are reimbursed by the card company, which takes a commission. It is therefore the banking organisations that give the credit, and not the traders.

5.9 The trader forwards his Visa or Mastercard sales vouchers to a **merchant acquirer** who processes the transaction in return for a **merchant service charge** from the retailer (averaging about 1.8% of the sales value). The merchant acquirer has to pay about 1% of the sales value to the credit card issuer, which bears the cost of fraud.

Banker's draft

5.10 This is a method of payment which is available on request (and on payment of a fee) to customers who need to eliminate the risk of a cheque being 'bounced'. The **banker's draft** is effectively a cheque drawn on the bank by itself, payable to a person specified by the customer.

Standing orders

> **KEY TERM**
>
> A **standing order** is an order for the supply of goods and services as need or opportunity arises, usually limited by a stated maximum. In banking: a customer's instruction to pay a stated amount to another person on specified dates. *(OT 2000)*

5.11 **Standing (or banker's) orders** are a means of making a series of payments at a **known date** to a **known recipient**. The bank asks the customer to fill in a standard form giving the recipient's bank account details (or the customer uses the recipient's pre-printed form) and the bank then automatically makes the payments as directed until the customer directs it to stop or until the final date stated on the instructions. The **customer** is in complete control of payments. When the amount payable changes, the customer has to inform the bank in writing of the new amount. Standing orders are now mainly processed via BACS (see below).

Direct debits

> **KEY TERM**
>
> A **direct debit** is a direct claim on an individual or organisation by a creditor, and paid by the individual's or organisation's bank on each occasion. Variations in period claims are admissible. *(OT 2000)*

5.12 **Direct debits** are similar to standing orders in that they allow the customer to make regular payments automatically. However, as well as authorising the bank to make the payment, the customer gives his bank details to the **creditor** (eg local authority, insurance company, hire purchase company) which then tells the bank how much to debit to the customer's account.

5.13 **Examples of payments frequently made by direct debit**

- Mortgage and other loan repayments
- Insurance and personal pension premiums
- Minimum amounts due to credit card issuers
- Subscriptions to large clubs and associations
- Utilities (gas, electricity, telephone)
- Equipment rental and maintenance

All of these payments are likely to vary (for example, because of changes in interest rates or the basic rate of tax), and so the alternative would often be to pay by cheque or cash rather than standing order. This is less convenient and more expensive for all parties.

5.14 Direct debits, like automated standing orders, are mostly processed by BACS (see below). The debit to the customer's account is made simultaneously with the credit to the originator's account (unlike cheque clearing). The refusal of a direct debit is known more quickly than the dishonouring of a cheque.

BACS

> **KEY TERM**
>
> **BACS** (Bankers Automated Clearing Services) is an electronic bulk clearing system generally used by banks and building societies for low value and/or repetitive items such as standing orders, direct debits and automated credits such as salary payments.
>
> *(OT 2000)*

5.15 As mentioned earlier, BACS is a company owned by the high street banks which operates the electronic transfer of funds between accounts within the banking system.

Clearing House Automated Payments System (CHAPS)

> **KEY TERM**
>
> **CHAPS** or Clearing House Automated Payment System, is a method for the rapid electronic transfer of funds between participating banks on behalf of large commercial customers where transfers tend to be of significant value.
>
> *(OT 2000)*

5.16 **CHAPS** is a computerised system to enable **same-day** clearing, guaranteed if instructions are received before 2pm.

Part D: Working capital management

Question 8

What do the payment terms CND stand for?

A   Campaign for nuclear disarmament
B   Cash next day
C   Cash on next delivery
D   Cash net of discount

Answer

B   Cash on next delivery

Chapter roundup

- **Credit control** deals with a firm's management of its working capital. **Trade credit** is offered to business customers. **Consumer credit** is offered to household customers.

- **Total credit** can be measured in a variety of ways. Financial analysts use days sales in debtors, but as this is an annualised figure it gives no idea as to the make-up of total debtors. Many firms need to consider the **cost of excess credit**.

- The **total investment in debtors** has to be considered in its impact on the general investment in working capital.

- The **credit control department** is responsible for those stages in the collection cycle dealing with the offer of credit, and the collection of debts.

- A firm must consider suitable **payment terms** and **payment methods**. **Settlement discounts** can be offered, if cost effective and if they improve liquidity.

- **Direct debits** are useful for companies which sell goods on credit, or they can collect amounts directly from customers' accounts.

Quick quiz

1   Goods and Chattels Ltd are considering increasing the period of credit allowed to customers from one calendar month to two months. Annual sales are currently £2.4m, and annual profits are £120,000. It is anticipated that allowing extended credit would increase sales by 20%, while margins would be unchanged. The company's required rate of return is 15%. What is the financial effect of the proposal?

    A   Reduction in profit of £102,000
    B   Reduction in profit of £42,000
    C   Increase in profit of £102,000
    D   Increase in profit of £144,000

2   The .... cycle and the .... cycle together make up the .... cycle. *Fill in the blanks*, using the following words: credit; collection; order.

3   How can we calculate the number of days sales represented by debtors?

4   What matters should the terms and conditions of sale cover?

5   What is meant by COD?

6   What is meant by EFTPOS?

7   What is the name for an arrangement similar to a standing order, but by which the creditor informs the bank how much to take from the debtor's bank account?

8   What is the following type of payment called?

    'A cheque drawn on the bank by itself, payable to a person specified by the customer.'

    A   Banker's draft
    B   Standing order
    C   Direct debit
    D   Banker's order

Answers to quick quiz

1. C

Existing debtors	£2.4m ÷ 12	£200,000
New level of debtors	£2.4m × 1.2 ÷ 6	£480,000
Increase in debtors		£280,000
Additional financing cost	£280,000 × 15%	£42,000
Additional revenue	£2.4m × 1.2 × 5%	£144,000
Net increase in profit	£144,000 – £42,000	£102,000

2. The order cycle and the collection cycle together make up the credit cycle.

3. $\dfrac{\text{Total debtors}}{\text{Annual credit sales}} \times 365 = \text{Days sales}$

4. Price, delivery, date of payment, frequency of payment (if instalments), discount

5. Cash On Delivery

6. Electronic Funds Transfer at the Point Of Sale

7. Direct debit

8. A Banker's draft

Now try the question below from the Exam Question Bank

Number	Level	Marks	Time
19	Examination	20	36 mins

Chapter 20

ASSESSING CREDITWORTHINESS

Topic list	Syllabus reference	Ability required
1 Minimising the risk of default	(iv)	Analysis
2 Externally generated information: bank and trade references, and agencies	(iv)	Analysis
3 Internally generated information: financial and accounting analysis	(iv)	Analysis
4 Internally generated information: customer visits	(iv)	Analysis
5 Using credit control information	(iv)	Analysis
6 Data protection and consumer credit legislation	(iv)	Analysis

Introduction

The previous chapter discussed the application of the firm's credit policy overall, with a review of total credit outstanding, and total credit by industry sector. In practice, a firm's credit control policy can only be implemented at the level of the individual credit customer. A **firm's decision to grant a customer credit** depends on the firm's overall policy, the status of the particular customer, and the size and type of the customer's order. The chief consideration is the evaluation of **risk** that the debt will go bad. As well as knowing about the different sources of information available, you need to consider how strong each is.

Learning outcomes covered in this chapter

- Identify debtor management policies and procedures for a customer
- Interpret the creditworthiness of a customer
- Analyse trade debtor information

Syllabus content covered in this chapter

- Assessing a customer's creditworthiness, eg sources of credit status information (eg bank references, trade references, internal credit rating information)

1 MINIMISING THE RISK OF DEFAULT

> **KEY TERM**
>
> **Credit risk** means that there is a possibility that the debt will go bad.

20: Assessing creditworthiness

1.1 (a) A debtor with a low credit risk is likely to be able to pay his or her debts when they fall due. Offering credit to a low risk debtor means that there is little chance that the creditor's profitability or liquidity will be threatened.

(b) A debtor who is a high credit risk is more likely to be unable to pay, and so there is a greater threat to the company's liquidity and profitability.

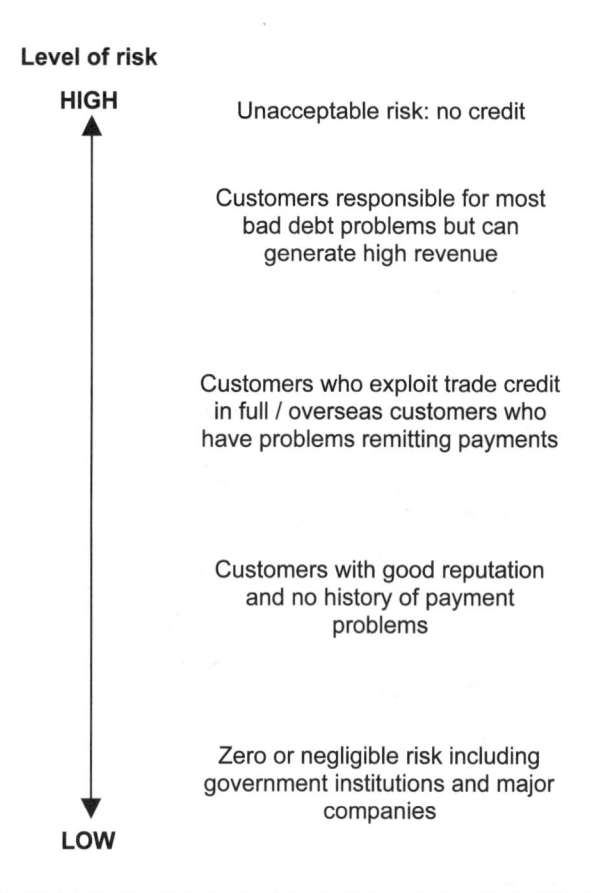

Level of risk

HIGH — Unacceptable risk: no credit

Customers responsible for most bad debt problems but can generate high revenue

Customers who exploit trade credit in full / overseas customers who have problems remitting payments

Customers with good reputation and no history of payment problems

Zero or negligible risk including government institutions and major companies

LOW

> **KEY TERM**
>
> A **credit assessment** is a judgement about the creditworthiness of a customer. A credit assessment provides a basis for a decision as to whether credit should in fact be granted.

1.2 The nature of the credit assessment a firm is able to carry out will therefore vary.

(a) Some firms will simply **write** to the **debtor's bank** asking for a **letter,** or at best write to a credit reference agency.

(b) Some firms, especially if lending to a large business, are able to spend time **examining the customer's accounts**.

1.3 Earlier in this Study Text, we looked at a bank's canons of lending, summarised as **CAMPARI**. These might be relevant to the credit controller.

2 EXTERNALLY GENERATED INFORMATION: BANK AND TRADE REFERENCES, AND AGENCIES

2.1 Standard practice in the UK is often to invite the customer who is applying for credit to provide references (eg the customers bank, and/or other suppliers). Many suppliers have a standard form which prospective customers should fill in. An example of such a form is **shown below**. The supplier will send it to the customer who will fill it in.

To: Britline Carriers PLC
Sutton Lane, Liverpool
LW6 9BC
0151 - 324 - 7345/6

Please open a credit account in the name of:
_____

Address _____

_____ Telephone _____

Below are supplied the names and addresses of referees of whom the customary trade enquiries may be made.

I / We note your credit terms as set out in your Standard Conditions of Sale *and agree to pay in accordance therewith for any goods services supplied by you. These terms are as follows.*

> All accounts are strictly net and payable at the end of the month following the month of invoicing.

Expected maximum amount of credit required	Signature
_____ In total*	_____
Weekly*	(position) _____
Monthly*	(NB: If a partnership, all partners should sign.)

* delete non-applicable

Our contact on accounts matters _____

Bankers
Name of bank _____ Full branch address
_____
_____

Trade references

(1) Name _____ Address _____
_____

(2) Name _____ Address _____
_____

Bank references

2.2 **Bank references** are useful, but banks are naturally cautious.

2.3 When writing to the bank it is necessary to be *precise* as to the credit you are offering.

Wrong

'Do you consider X Ltd to be able to pay its debts?'

Right

'Do you consider X Ltd to be good for a trade credit of £1,000 per month on terms of 30 days?'

This gives the bank manager a reasonable idea as to the amount of money required, and the terms. The manager is then more able to give an opinion.

2.4 Typical bank opinions, in declining order of favour, are as follows.

	Opinion	Notes
Best	Undoubted	No worries - the best opinion
	Considered good for your figures	Fine, but less favourable than 'undoubted'
	Respectably constituted business which should prove good for your figures	'Should' suggests that the business is fine, but resources might be strained
	Respectably constituted business whose resources would appear to be fully employed: we do not think they would undertake something they felt they could not fulfil	This is not encouraging, as the bank makes no reference to the credit asked for
Worst	Unable to speak for your figures	This implies that the bank may consider the company potentially overstretched

2.5 Other comments might qualify these statements, for example as follows.

(a) 'There are charges registered' normally implies that some of the business's assets are security for a debt (eg a bank loan).

(b) 'Considered good for your amount if taken in a series.' This implies that the customer will be able to pay off the sum in instalments. Some clarification might also be needed.

Trade references

2.6 **Trade references** are obtained from other businesses that the customer deals with. The following points should be borne in mind when following them up.

(a) Some customers may name as trade references suppliers with whom they **deliberately maintain an excellent**, and otherwise untypical, payments record, simply in order to obtain good references.

(b) The **trade referee** should offer **similar terms** to those the customer is requesting from the supplier.

(c) A **well-known company** given as a referee should always be **followed up**. An **unknown company's reference** should be treated with **more caution**, in case of collusion.

(d) The enquirier should enclose a **stamped addressed envelope**, and perhaps the enquiry should be couched as a questionnaire.

BRITLINE CARRIERS PLC
Sutton Lane
Liverpool LW6 9BC
(0151-324 7345/6)

To: Credit controller
    A Big Company plc

Dear Sir,

We have recently received a request for credit from ....Ltd ('the firm'), a customer of ours,

> who gave yourselves as a reference. I would be most grateful if you could help me by answering the following questions, and returning them in the stamped addressed envelope provided.
>
> 1   For how long has the firm been trading with you?
>   ..... Years .....Months
>
> 2   Did the firm supply you with suitable trade and other references when it opened its account with you?
>   Yes/No
>
> 3   What are your normal credit terms for the firm?
>   Amount: £.......
>   Terms: Cash, weekly, monthly, other (please detail)
>
> 4   Does the firm make payments in accordance with your terms?
>   Yes/No/Slow payer
>
> 5   Have you ever had to suspend credit facilities with the firm?
>   Yes/No
>
> If Yes, when?
>
> Please give below or overleaf any more information which you consider relevant.
>
> Yours faithfully,

Credit ratings

2.7   **Credit ratings** are formal opinions of the creditworthiness of an entity (eg a government, government agency, financial institution or large company). They are used mainly by **investors** and **banks** to assess a company's creditworthiness.

2.8   Companies or entities are given different grades according to security they offer. Some rate commercial paper (relevant to short-term investment) according to security. AAA, for example, is very secure. C might indicate default.

2.9   Credit ratings are only of limited use to trade creditors and credit controllers, but they **do** indicate certain basic facts about a company. A company with a low credit rating is having difficulty paying its banks - trade creditors are far less important.

2.10   For trade credits, however, which require to be paid back in 30 days, and which may be owed to small customers with little clout, they are not particularly helpful.

Credit reporting agencies (credit bureaux)

2.11   **Credit bureaux** provide information about businesses so that their creditworthiness can be assessed by suppliers. Credit reporting agencies in the UK include **CCN, Infolink, Equifax Europe,** and **Dun & Bradstreet.** Others specialise in a particular industrial or commercial sector.

2.12   Agency reports are useful to the credit controller to the extent that they are:

(a)   A **summary** of some, but not all, of the **information available**

(b) One of **several sources of information** which can be used to **cross-check** other information obtained, giving additional reassurance, especially where large credits are concerned

2.13 A typical agency report will contain the following details.

(a) **Legal data**

The legal status is important, if there are restrictions on operations outlined in the company's memorandum and articles.

(b) **Commercial data**

This includes details of the latest annual report.

(c) **Credit data**

(i) Bankers' opinions

(ii) Suppliers' opinions, if available

(iii) Possibly, the agency's:

(1) Own credit rating of the customer
(2) Suggested credit limit for the customer

(iv) Possibly, the agency might keep records of credit offered by its members.

(v) Dun & Bradstreet offer a **'payment' profile service**. This contains information about payments records of companies.

2.14 The **problems with agency reports** are as follows.

(a) **Up-to-date information** which would be relevant to the credit decision may **not** have **reached** its way on to the **system** (eg the collapse of a major customer).

(b) **Suppliers' references** may be **too old** to be relevant.

(c) **Newly established concerns** will **not have much** of a **track record** on which a judgement can be made.

Question 1

Clinton Ltd supplies a unique kind of herbal medicine, the Billary Pill. Each jar costs about £400 to make and is sold to chemists for £600. One day Clinton Ltd receives a request for credit from Triad Pharmaceuticals, a chain of chemist shops, comprising 20 stores in the West Midlands. They are asking for a credit limit of £6,000 on 30 days terms. They supply a bank reference, and two trade references.

(a) The bank says: 'Respectably constituted, and should prove good for your figures.'

(b) The first trade reference features a £1,000 credit limit, payable in 60 days. There have been no problems with the account.

(c) The second trade reference is not a supplier at all but one of Triad's customers. The customer's surname, Cyborg, is the same as that of the managing director of Triad Ltd.

What should Clinton Ltd do with this request?

Answer

The bank reference is hardly damning, but it is not an overwhelming endorsement either: Triad *should* prove to be a good customer. Therefore the quality of the trade reference is more important. The first reference, while indicating no problems, is of limited usefulness as the credit facility offered is much lower than that which Clinton Ltd is asked to provide. The second credit reference, from Triad's customer, who may be a relative, is worthless.

Part D: Working capital management

The request should not be dismissed out of hand, but more investigation is needed.

2.15 There are a number of other sources of data about companies which can be converted into useful credit control information.

(a) **The press**

Companies produce annual financial statements and offer a half yearly report. The basics of these results, together with informed comment, is often published in papers such as the *Financial Times*.

(b) **Historical financial data**

(i) Extel became famous for Extel cards describing the basic financial data of a company, updated for important events such as recent results or rights issues.

(ii) Some stockbrokers publish reviews for particular business sectors.

(c) **Companies Registry search**

All companies have to file certain financial information with Companies House. However, small and medium sized companies can file accounts which omit certain information, such as the profit and loss account. However, a Companies House search provides valuable evidence as to any secured lending.

(d) **County Court records**

These could be inspected to see if the company has ever defaulted on a debt.

(e) **Analysing company accounts**

A company's financial statements can generate important and useful information. For example, most companies publish a **cash flow statement** which does indicate the extent to which a company has in the past relied on borrowing, in a prescribed accounting format. Other calculations which we shall examine in the next section can also yield useful information

Question 2

Explain how a credit rating agency can help in providing a credit assessment of a customer.

Answer

Credit rating agencies, of which Dun and Bradstreet is perhaps one of the best known, can provide:

(a) A same day analysis, if required, perhaps by an on-line computer link on to a VDU in the credit controller's office

(b) Ratio analysis of the business of the customer being assessed, plus

(c) Comment on the customer's credit position

Individual customers (especially non-corporate customers) can be asked to provide the names of referees who can be approached for references. One referee will usually be the customer's **bank**. Another might be the **customer's accountant**. The initial procedure is for the referee to be asked if in his opinion the individual is reliable up to certain levels of credit. Usually, this is a low amount to start with, but as confidence develops, so the amount may well be increased.

3 INTERNALLY GENERATED INFORMATION: FINANCIAL AND ACCOUNTING ANALYSIS

Ratio analysis

3.1 The credit controller is interested in a whole variety of **accounting ratios**, to build up, where possible, a broad picture of the customer. However, the credit controller is only interested in the accounts insofar as they affect a business's ability to pay its debts on time. The credit controller has no real concern with some of the more arcane aspects of financial reporting.

3.2 A **problem with financial ratio analysis** is that historical information about profits, assets and liabilities is used for an assessment of a *future* cash flow position, when they offer only an uncertain guide.

3.3 For the credit controller, a firm's **profitability** and **return on capital employed (ROCE)** are not immediately relevant to whether a debt will be paid. However, they do indicate that, overall, the company is healthy and is able to manage its operating cycle.

Working capital

3.4 **Working capital**, as we have seen, is the difference between current assets (mainly stocks, debtors and cash) and current liabilities (such as trade creditors and a bank overdraft).

3.5 The credit analyst will be particularly interested in a number of calculations. For example, if the stock turnover period gets longer or if the debt collection period gets longer, the total amount of stocks or of debtors will increase. (Similarly, if the period of credit taken from the suppliers gets longer, the amount of creditors will become bigger. From the point of view of the credit analyst, examining the accounts as an **outsider**, both of these developments are important as they suggest **growing liquidity problems** in the potential debtor.

Question 3

Wing Ltd's liquidity has declined significantly over the last 12 months. The following financial information is provided:

	Year to 31 December	
	20X2	20X3
	£	£
Sales	573,000	643,000
Cost of goods sold	420,000	460,000
Cash/(overdraft)	5,000	(10,000)
Debtors	97,100	121,500
Creditors	23,900	32,500
Stocks	121,400	189,300

All purchases and sales were made on credit.

Required

(a) Analyse the above information, which should include calculations of the operating cycle (the time lag between making payment to suppliers and collecting cash from customers) for 20X2 and 20X3.

(b) Prepare a brief report on the implications of the changes which have occurred between 20X2 and 20X3.

Part D: Working capital management

Notes

(a) Assume a 365 day year for the purpose of your calculations and assume that all transactions take place at an even rate.

(b) All calculations are to be made to the nearest day.

Answer

(a) The information should be analysed in as many ways as possible, and you should not omit any important items. For example, the current and quick ratios are fine, when compared with the guidelines above. However, these only tell part of the story, as the dramatic change in turnover periods indicate. The relevant calculations would seem to be as follows.

(i)

	20X2 £	20X3 £
Sales	573,000	643,000
Cost of goods sold	(420,000)	(460,000)
Gross profit	153,000	183,000
Gross profit percentage	26.7%	28.5%

(ii) Size of *working capital and liquidity ratios* (in 20X3, the bank overdraft has been added to creditors):

	£	£
Cash	5,000	(10,000)
Debtors	97,100	121,500
Stocks:	121,400	189,300
	223,500	300,800
Creditors	(23,900)	(32,500)
Working capital	199,600	268,300

Current ratio: $\dfrac{£223,500}{£23,900} = 9.3:1$ $\dfrac{£310,800}{£42,500} = 7.3:1$

Quick ratio: $\dfrac{£102,100}{£23,900} = 4.2:1$ $\dfrac{£121,500}{£42,500} = 2.8:1$

(iii) Turnover periods

	20X2		20X3	
		days		days
Stock	$\dfrac{121,400}{420,000} \times 365 =$	105	$\dfrac{189,300}{460,000} \times 365 =$	150
Debtors' collection period	$\dfrac{97,100}{573,000} \times 365 =$	62	$\dfrac{121,500}{643,000} \times 365 =$	69
Creditors' payment period	$\dfrac{23,900}{420,000} \times 365 =$	(21)	$\dfrac{32,500}{460,000} \times 365 =$	(26)
Operating cycle		146		193

(b) **Sales were about 12% higher** in 20X3 than in 20X2 and the cost of sales was about 9% higher. The investments in stocks and debtors minus creditors (ie working capital ignoring cash) rose from £194,600 to £278,300, ie by £83,700 or nearly 44%. This is completely out of proportion to the volume of increase in trade, which indicates that working capital turnover periods are not being properly controlled.

The **increase in working capital** by £83,700 means that the **net cash receipts** from profits in 20X3 were £83,700 less than they would have been if there had been no increase at all in stocks and debtors (less creditors) during 20X3. The company's overdraft of £10,000 is therefore unnecessary. Furthermore, arguably the current ratio is excessive. Although the current and quick ratios appear healthy as they stand, the trend is worrying, with the quick ratio declining rapidly. This would not be necessary, if the company controlled debtors and stock better.

The causes of the increase in working capital in 20X3 are:

(i) The **increase in sales**, but mainly

20: Assessing creditworthiness

(ii) The **increased length of turnover periods**

Debtors, already allowed 62 days to pay in 20X2, were allowed 69 days in 20X3 and this would seem to be an excessive length of time. The most serious change, however, is the increase in the **finished goods stock turnover** period from 105 days to 150 days and it is difficult to see an obvious reason why this should have occurred, although there may have been a temporary build-up at the end of 20X3 in preparation for a big sales drive.

Part of the increase in stocks and debtors has been financed by an **increase in the creditors payment period**, from 21 to 26 days. This doesn't seem too bad, but in practice it might be worse. Cost of goods sold includes more than just raw materials, and if we knew the level of raw materials purchases, say, the position might appear worse. For the credit controller there are two worries:

(i) The **increase** in the **creditors' payment period**

(ii) The **overall change in working capital** out of all proportion to the growth of business activities, suggesting growing problems in liquidity, even though the current and quick ratios are healthy in themselves at the moment

Gearing

3.6 Gearing is important to the credit controller because trade debts generally take lower priority in a company's planning than interest payments on other forms of debt. If a company becomes insolvent, it is secured loans that are dealt with first.

3.7 As mentioned earlier, gearing is important also to a bank that is considering a lending decision. The bank will usually treat **overdraft finance** as part of a company's total indebtedness.

Question 4

You are given summarised information about two firms in the same line of business, A and B, as follows.

BALANCE SHEETS AT 30 JUNE

	A			B		
	£'000	£'000	£'000	£'000	£'000	£'000
Land			80			260
Buildings		120			200	
Less depreciation		40			-	
			80			200
Plant		90			150	
Less depreciation		70			40	
			20			110
			180			570
Stocks		80			100	
Debtors		100			90	
Bank		-			10	
		180			200	
Creditors	110			120		
Bank	50			-		
	160			120		
			20			80
			200			650

Part D: Working capital management

	A		B	
	£'000	£'000	£'000	£'000
Capital brought forward		100		300
Profit for year (after interest)		30		100
		130		400
Less drawings		30		40
		100		360
Land revaluation		-		160
Loan (10% pa)		100		130
		200		650
Sales		1,000		3,000
Cost of sales		400		2,000

Produce a table of six ratios calculated for both businesses.

Answer

Tutorial note. More than six ratios can be calculated from the information given; we have given all of the most obvious ratios.

			A	B
1	Gross profit margin =	$\dfrac{\text{Gross profit}}{\text{Sales}}$	$\dfrac{1{,}000 - 400}{1{,}000}$ = 60%	$\dfrac{3{,}000 - 2{,}000}{3{,}000}$ = 33%
2	Net profit margin =	$\dfrac{\text{Net profit}}{\text{Sales}}$	$\dfrac{30}{1{,}000}$ = 3%	$\dfrac{100}{3{,}000}$ = 3.3%
3	Asset turnover =	$\dfrac{\text{Sales}}{\text{Capital employed}}$	$\dfrac{1{,}000}{200}$ = 5 times	$\dfrac{3{,}000}{650}$ = 4.6 times
4	Return on capital employed (ROCE) =	$\dfrac{\text{Net profit before interest}}{\text{Total long term capital}}$	$\dfrac{30 + 10(10\% \times 100)}{200}$ = 20%	$\dfrac{100 + 13(10\% \times 130)}{650}$ = 17.3%
5	Gearing =	$\dfrac{\text{Debt}}{\text{Equity}}$	$\dfrac{100}{100}$ = 100%	$\dfrac{130}{520\,(160 + 360)}$ = 25%
	or	$\dfrac{\text{Debt}}{\text{Total capital}}$	$\dfrac{100}{200}$ = 50%	$\dfrac{130}{650}$ = 20%
6	Current ratio =	$\dfrac{\text{Current assets}}{\text{Current liabilities}}$	$\dfrac{180}{160}$ = 1.125	$\dfrac{200}{120}$ = 1.667
7	Quick ratio =	$\dfrac{\text{Current assets - stock}}{\text{Current liabilities}}$	$\dfrac{100}{160}$ = 0.625	$\dfrac{100}{120}$ = 0.833
8	Debtors' turnover period =	$\dfrac{\text{Debtors} \times 365}{\text{Sales}}$	$\dfrac{100 \times 365}{1{,}000}$ = 36½ days	$\dfrac{90 \times 365}{3{,}000}$ = 11 days
9	Stock turnover period =	$\dfrac{\text{Stock} \times 365}{\text{Cost of sales}}$	$\dfrac{80 \times 365}{400}$ = 73 days	$\dfrac{100 \times 365}{2{,}000}$ = 18 days

			A	B
10	Creditors' turnover period =	$\dfrac{\text{Creditors}}{\text{Cost of sales}}$	$\dfrac{110 \times 365}{400}$ = 100 days	$\dfrac{120 \times 365}{2{,}000}$ = 22 days

Question 5

Write the material for a report briefly outlining the strengths and weaknesses of the two businesses in the previous activity. Include comment on any major areas where the simple use of the figures could be misleading.

Answer

Although A and B have similar net profit margins, B has a **lower gross profit margin**. A must therefore have a much higher percentage of overheads than B. A's turnover is, however, much lower than B's and so its net profit is also much lower in absolute terms.

A also has a **higher ROCE**. This is because it makes more efficient use of its assets, as shown by its **high asset turnover**. However, B's asset turnover is reduced by the revaluation of its land.

A is **considerably more highly geared** than B because its long-term debt is currently as high as its proprietors' equity, whereas B's capital is nearly four times higher than its debt. Thus, A is a higher risk for a potential investor or lender.

B appears to **manage its working capital** much more efficiently than A. A turns its stock over five times a year but B is about four times as efficient. It may be as a result of this difference in working capital management that B does *not* have an overdraft while A's is quite high. B's liquidity is very much better.

However, we are not told in **which industry** A and B operate. If, for instance, they are both retailers, it may be that A is an antiques shop while B is selling food or clothes, which turn over much faster but at a lower margin. We are also ignorant of the **ownership** of each business. If the owners of one business work in it, then part of their drawings are effectively wages and so their profits should be adjusted to be comparable with the other firm.

Another proviso is that **A's bank overdraft** may effectively be part of its **long-term debt**, in which case ROCE and gearing should all be adjusted accordingly. This leads on to the problem that one balance sheet on its own is not necessarily representative. Ideally, a series should be examined, so that trends can be identified and conclusions can be considered better founded.

A further difficulty in looking at the accounts of unincorporated businesses is that they are **not required** to give a **true and fair** view and so are not governed by SSAPs. The accounting policies applied may therefore be quite different in each case.

Finally, we have no idea whether or not A's assets could also be **revalued upwards**. If so, its ROCE is almost certainly overstated, and its asset turnover deceptively high.

A tentative conclusion, in spite of the above reservations, would be that A is a more profitable but less solvent firm than B. This makes it a riskier proposition for lending or investing, especially as it has a much smaller capital base.

Cash flow and credit risk

3.8 A creditor should focus its attention on how strong the company's cash flows appear to be. We can use the classification below. Remember that, as a creditor, you might have advanced credit for an item of capital equipment.

Part D: Working capital management

Item	Comment
Net operational cash flow	Should be positive
− Priority payments	
= Cash for discretionary spending	Should normally be positive
− Investment spending	
= Cash after investment spending	If negative, the company must obtain money from non-trading sources, perhaps by borrowing

Good times and bad times

3.9 Bear in mind that many companies go through periods of growth followed by periods of decline and cut-back, within the general business cycle for their industry. In the recession of the early 1990s, many companies experienced a severe downturn in business and had to cut operational expenditures to remain cash-positive.

Question 6

What data would you look for in the financial statements of a new customer who asks for credit?

Answer

For *new customers* about whom nothing is known the credit controller can go to Companies House to obtain financial statements on a corporate customer (ie copies of past annual reports and accounts of the customer which have been filed at Companies House). These accounts can then be analysed to assess the financial position of the customer, and changes in this position over time.

Items that might be studied and ratios that might be calculated

(a) The amount of annual profit

(b) The net assets of the customer's business

(c) The return on capital employed achieved by the customer

(d) The profit/sales ratio

(e) Asset turnover ratios, in particular:

    (i) The current ratio (current assets: current liabilities)
    (ii) The acid test ratio (current assets excluding stock: current liabilities)
    (iii) Debtors' payment period
    (iv) Credit period taken from creditors (estimated as $\frac{\text{creditors}}{\text{cost of sales}} \times 365$ days)
    (v) Stock turnover period

(f) Gearing ratio (the ratio of 'prior charge capital' to equity capital)

(g) Debt ratio (the ratio of current and long term debts to total assets)

(h) The percentage increase in annual sales turnover

Weaknesses of this approach to credit risk assessment

(a) The reports and accounts filed at Companies House show an **out-of-date situation**. The customer's financial position might now be completely different

(b) Sending someone to Companies House to make the investigation **takes time**

(c) **Not all customers are corporate customers**, and so information about them will not be held at Companies House

4 INTERNALLY GENERATED INFORMATION: CUSTOMER VISITS

4.1 In addition to the accounting analysis described above, it is sometimes necessary to visit the client, so that any information gaps can be filled. Such a visit has two purposes.

(a) Any specific queries arising from the credit reference data can be discussed.
(b) The credit controller can get a feel for the business and the people running it.

4.2 The sales manager might accompany the credit manager. The credit manager should take a look around the business, and needs to speak to people at a suitable level, perhaps the financial controller.

5 USING CREDIT CONTROL INFORMATION

5.1 Having analysed the relevant accounting data, visited the client, and having received guarded assurances from a bank, we are now in a position to use this information. First of all, a new customer will be offered a set level of credit, on terms that the credit controller found appropriate.

(a) Credit might be **granted provisionally** subject to a formal review at a later date.

(b) The company may or may not wish to **grant the customer's request** in its entirety. For example, assume Joe Soap wanted a credit limit of £1,000 and 30 days. As a preliminary, the supplier might offer:

   (i) £500 repayable within 30 days
   (ii) £1,000 repayable within 15 days

Only after the customer has established a suitable payments record should this be increased. (Types of credit terms were discussed in the previous chapter.)

5.2 The **payment record** must be **monitored** continually. This depends on successful sales ledger administration.

(a) **Invoices** must be posted at the right time.

(b) **Receipts** should be posted when they arrive, and allocated specifically to the invoices to which they relate.

(c) Any **queries** (eg customers debiting their own credit balance with a debit note as 'notification' to the supplier) need to be dealt with quickly.

(d) Orders should *always* be **vetted against credit limits**: this indicates the importance of prompt updating, as above.

(e) A **customer history analysis** can be prepared: this is like a statement, but with:

   (i)   Total annual sales, on a rolling twelve month basis
   (ii) Outstanding amounts owed
   (iii) Days sales outstanding at each month end

The advantage of this is that trends in the account can be monitored, as can also the ageing of the debtor balance.

Part D: Working capital management

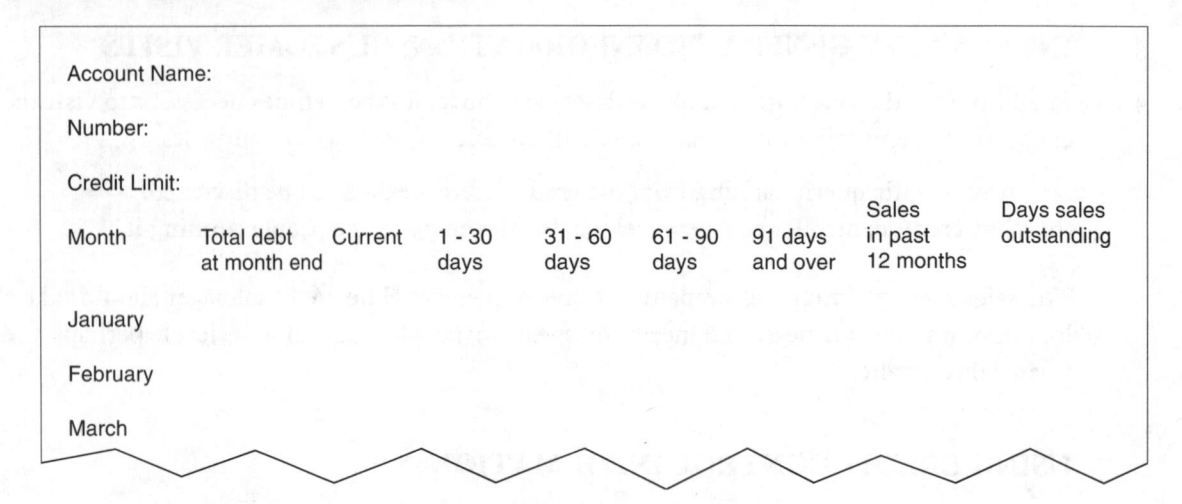

Account Name:								
Number:								
Credit Limit:								
Month	Total debt at month end	Current	1 - 30 days	31 - 60 days	61 - 90 days	91 days and over	Sales in past 12 months	Days sales outstanding
January								
February								
March								

5.3 With this information it should be possible to develop in-house credit ratings.

In-house credit ratings

5.4 Credit monitoring can be simplified by a system of **in-house credit ratings**. For example, a company could have five credit-risk categories for its customers. These credit categories or ratings could be used to decide either individual credit limits for customers within that category or the frequency of the credit review. Guidelines could be provided to help credit controllers decide into which category a customer belongs.

5.5 Over time, the payment habits of a customer can be assessed, and the customer's credit rating (and credit limits) can be set accordingly. Any deterioration in a customer's payment record could raise concerns about the customer's creditworthiness.

5.6 A **credit taken ratio** can be used to monitor the credit limits of customers. This compares the amount currently owed by a customer with the annual sales turnover in his account.

Example

5.7 A company has two debtors, Able and Baker. Each customer owes £20,000. Annual sales to Able are about £200,000, and annual sales to Baker are about £100,000.

5.8 The credit taken ratio is 10% for Able (20,000 ÷ 200,000 × 100%) and 20% for Baker. Baker could be regarded as a higher credit risk. The company might wish to keep the credit-taken ratio for customers below a certain limit. If this limit were 20%, a request from Baker for further credit would be refused until the outstanding debts are settled. The company would be willing, however, to consider a request from Able for more credit.

Credit reviews

5.9 A customer's payment record and the debtors aged analysis should be examined regularly, as a matter of course. Breaches of the credit limit, or attempted breaches of it, should be brought immediately to the attention of the credit controller.

5.10 Otherwise, the credit controller will not have the time to examine *each* customer's account thoroughly every month. The credit controller's efforts will be expended on customers thought to be higher risk. The credit situation will be reviewed more frequently, and a decision taken as to whether the credit should be extended. Illustrative internal weightings, review periods and credit offered are indicated below.

Rating	Payment record	Financial indicators	Frequency of credit reviews	Credit limit (as % of customer's annual purchases)
A Very high risk	Accounts overdue by 60 + days	Low profits Poor liquidity Highly indebted		Cash only (payment with order)
B High risk	Accounts overdue by 30 - 60 days	Deteriorating profitability, liquidity, or gearing High credit taken ratio	Monthly	Reduce to 10% of annual purchases
C Average risk	Accounts overdue up to 30 days	Stable position	Quarterly	15% of annual purchases
D Below average risk	Accounts paid on time	Stable or improving position	Six-monthly	25% of annual purchases
E Low risk	Accounts paid early Public sector customers	Strong financial position, or public sector ownership	Annually	For negotiation with the customer

Question 7

Suppose that you work for an accountancy firm, and you have been asked to advise a manufacturing company client on guidelines for a credit control system. Make brief notes for a presentation to the client on possible guidelines, covering the following points.

(a) Categorisation of debtor risk
(b) Assessment of individual customers' risk categorisation
(c) Procedures to check that the customer has received goods and an invoice

Answer

(a) A simple system for categorising debtor risk would be to establish four categories of debtor:

  (i) Strong
  (ii) Average
  (iii) Marginal
  (iv) Weak/poor

  Different credit terms might then be offered to a customer according to how that customer is categorised, with strong customers being allowed most credit and weak customers not being allowed any credit at all (ie cash sales only).

(b) Procedures should be in place for **assessing any individual customer's** risk categorisation. Since circumstances change over time, the risk category of existing customers should be reviewed from time to time. All new customers should be put into one of the credit controller's categories.

(c) Procedures should exist for checking that **goods and an invoice** have been **sent to the customer**, and when customers pay any invoice so that:

  (i) The **credit control section** is kept **up-to-date** about the current debt position for every customer

  (ii) The **debt collection staff** can be **notified** when debts become overdue

Part D: Working capital management

6 DATA PROTECTION AND CONSUMER CREDIT LEGISLATION

6.1 Credit controllers need to be aware of data protection legislation (in the UK the Data Protection Act, 1998), the limits imposed on processing data about individuals and the rights of individuals to view data about themselves.

6.2 Consumer credit legislation is also important. In the UK the Consumer Credit Act 1974 is the key legislation.

Credit reference agencies and the individual consumer

6.3 Any person running a credit reference agency needs to be **licensed under the Consumer Credit Act**. Such reference agencies were brought within the Act's scope so as to ensure that people were able to access and correct information held about them. To some extent the same ground is covered by the Data Protection Act 1984, discussed above, from which they are exempt (because they are covered by the Consumer Credit Act).

6.4 The extent of the **information held by credit reference agencies** is great and its use can have a great effect on an individual; he may find that credit is not extended to him for reasons which are stated by the agency but of which he may not be aware or which may be wrong. However, the 1974 Act gives the individual access and correction rights.

(a) Any consumer is entitled to be told by the creditor, owner or negotiator with whom he deals of the name and address of the **credit reference agency** being used. He does not have to be seeking credit at the time. If the request is made in writing, it is an offence not to comply.

(b) The consumer is then entitled to make **a written request** to the credit reference agency for a **copy of the file** relating to him. If a trader is approached for credit, the consumer has a right to be given the name and address of any agency which he intends to contact.

(c) A consumer may require the agency to **correct or remove information** held about him if he feels he is likely to be prejudiced by it not being corrected or removed. The agency should do so and report that it has done so within 28 days; alternatively the debtor may require the agency to file a correcting notice, of not more than 200 words, drawn up by the consumer, who may seek an order from the Director General of Fair Trading if the agency does not comply. Disobeying such an order is a criminal offence.

Question 8

Which of the following is the most appropriate way to word a request to a bank for a credit reference?

A   Do you consider A Ltd to be able to pay its debts?
B   Do you consider A Ltd to be good for a trade credit of £2,000 per month?
C   Do you consider A Ltd to be good for a trade credit of £2,000 per month on terms of 30 days?
D   All of the above are equally appropriate

Answer

C   The bank manager will be more able to give an opinion if he has a reasonable idea of the amount of money required and the terms.

Chapter roundup

- **Credit risk** is the possibility that a debt will go bad. High risk customers can be profitable, but need to be managed carefully.
- **Data about potential debtors** can be obtained from a number of sources.
  - Banks owe a **duty of care** to their customers and to the enquirer: their assessments of a debtor's credit status are likely to be precisely worded.
  - **Trade references** are useful, but should not be used uncritically.
  - **Credit reference agencies** supply a variety of legal and business information thereby saving time for the enquirer. An agency might give its own suggested rating.
- Some companies are able to employ **credit analysts** to examine a firm's **financial accounts**. As these are historical statements, they are no guide to a debtor's **future creditworthiness**. However, **ratio analysis** can give some idea as to trends and highlight areas for further investigation.
- **Visits to the customer's premises** can provide useful information.

Quick quiz

1 When analysing the accounts of a potential credit customer, which of the following ratios would be the **least** relevant?

   A   Gearing
   B   Interest cover
   C   Debt ratio
   D   Gross profit margin

2 Place the following bank opinions on potential customers in order, starting with the most favourable.

   A   Considered good for your figures
   B   Undoubted
   C   Unable to speak for your figures
   D   Respectably constituted business which should prove good for your figures

3 What is a 'credit rating'?

4 How is the debtors turnover period calculated?

5 Which UK Act of Parliament covers credit reference agencies?

6 Name five potential sources of credit control information other than bank, trade and credit references.

7 What types of information is a credit bureau's report likely to include?

8 What equation can be used to assess the underlying strength of a company's cash flow?

Answers to quick quiz

1   D   Gross profit margin

2   B, A, D, C.

3   An opinion of the creditworthiness of an entity, as set by a specific credit rating agency.

4   Debtors turnover period = $\dfrac{\text{Total debtors}}{\text{Annual credit sales}} \times 365 \text{ days}$

5   Consumer Credit Act 1974

Part D: Working capital management

6   (a) The press
    (b) Historical financial data
    (c) Companies registry search
    (d) County Court records
    (e) Analysis of company accounts

7   (a) Legal data
    (b) Commercial data
    (c) Credit data

8   Net operational cash flow *less*

    Priority payments *equals*

    Cash for discretionary spending *less*

    Investment spending *equals*

    Cash after investment spending

Now try the question below from the Exam Question Bank

Number	Level	Marks	Time
20	Introductory	n/a	35 mins

Chapter 21

MONITORING AND COLLECTING DEBTORS

Topic list	Syllabus reference	Ability required
1 Maintaining information on debtors	(iv)	Analysis
2 Collecting debts	(iv)	Analysis
3 Credit insurance, factoring and invoice discounting	(iv)	Analysis

Introduction

We have already seen that the credit controller should obtain information from a variety of sources in order to decide whether or not to grant credit and, if credit is granted, what that level should be. The credit controller's job does not end there, however. After all, a customer may become less (or more) creditworthy over time. One of the principal instruments a credit controller uses is the **aged debtors listing**.

The last section of the chapter deals with ways of limiting or managing the risk from bad debts. As they can have a significant financial impact, they will be examined frequently. You may be asked to calculate the consequences of factoring debts, or describe and compare different means of managing risk.

Learning outcomes covered in this chapter

- Analyse trade debtor information

Syllabus content covered in this chapter

- Present and interpret an age analysis of debtors
- The stages in debt collection, eg reminder, statement, telephone call, personal visit, legal action, debt collection agency, interest on overdue debts
- Establishing collection targets on an appropriate basis, eg motivational issues in managing credit control
- Factoring and invoice discounting

1 MAINTAINING INFORMATION ON DEBTORS

Debtors age analysis

1.1 An **aged debtors listing** will probably look very much like the schedule illustrated below. The analysis splits up the total balance on the account of each customer across different columns according to the dates of the transactions which make up the total balance. Thus, the amount of an invoice which was raised 14 days ago will form part of the figure in the column headed 'up to 30 days', while an invoice which was raised 36 days ago will form part

Part D: Working capital management

of the figure in the column headed 'up to 60 days'. (In the schedule below, 'up to 60 days' is used as shorthand for 'more than 30 days but less than 60 days'.)

HEATH LIMITED

AGE ANALYSIS OF DEBTORS AS AT 31.1.X2

Account number	Customer name	Balance	Up to 30 days	Up to 60 days	Up to 90 days	Over 90 days
B004	Brilliant Ltd	804.95	649.90	121.00	0.00	34.05
E008	Easimat Ltd	272.10	192.90	72.40	6.80	0.00
H002	Hampstead Ltd	1,818.42	0.00	0.00	724.24	1,094.18
M024	Martlesham Ltd	284.45	192.21	92.24	0.00	0.00
N030	Nyfen Ltd	1,217.54	1,008.24	124.50	0.00	84.80
T002	Todmorden College	914.50	842.00	0.00	72.50	0.00
T004	Tricorn Ltd	94.80	0.00	0.00	0.00	94.80
V010	Volux Ltd	997.06	413.66	342.15	241.25	0.00
Y020	Yardsley Smith & Co	341.77	321.17	20.60	0.00	0.00
Totals		6,745.59	3,620.08	772.89	1,044.79	1,307.83
Percentage		100%	53.6%	11.5%	15.5%	19.4%

1.2 An age analysis of debtors can be prepared manually or, more easily, by computer. In theory this should represent actual invoices outstanding, but there are problems, which we shall discuss later in this chapter, of unmatched or 'unallocated' cash and payments on account.

1.3 The age analysis of debtors may be used to help decide what action to take about older debts. Going down each column in turn starting from the column furthest to the right and working across, we can see that there are some rather old debts which ought to be investigated.

1.4 A number of **refinements** can be suggested to the aged debtors listing to make it easier to use.

(a) A report can be printed in which **overdue accounts** are seen first: this highlights attention on these items.

(b) It can help to aggregate data by **class of customer**.

(c) There is no reason why this should not apply to individual debtor accounts as below. You could also include the date of the last transaction on the account (eg last invoice, last payment).

Account number	Customer name	Balance	Up to 30 days	Up to 60 days	Up to 90 days	Over 90 days	Sales revenue in last 12 months	Days sales outstanding
B004	Brilliant Ltd	804.95	649.90	121.00	0.00	34.05	6,789.00	43

1.5 We can see from the age analysis of Heath Ltd's debtors given earlier that the relatively high proportion of debts over 90 days (19.4%) is largely due to the debts of Hampstead Ltd. Other customers with debts of this age are Brilliant Ltd, Nyfen Ltd and Tricorn Ltd.

1.6 **Additional ratios** which might be useful in debtor management, in addition to day's sales outstanding, are as follows.

(a) **Overdues as a percentage of total debt.** For example, assume that Heath Limited (Paragraph 1.2) offers credit on 30 day terms. Brilliant Ltd's debt could be analysed as:

$$\frac{£121.00 + £34.05}{£804.95} = 19.3\% \text{ overdue.}$$

(b) **If debts are disputed,** it is helpful to see what proportion these are of the total debtors and the total overdue. If, of Heath's total debtors of £6,745.59, an amount of £973.06 related to disputed items, the ratio of disputed debts to total outstanding would be:

$$\frac{£973.06}{£6,745.59} = 14.4\%$$

As a percentage of total items *over* 30 days old:

$$\frac{£973.06}{£6,745.59 - £3,620.08} = 31\%$$

An increasing disputes ratio can indicate:

(i) Invoicing problems
(ii) Operational problems

Debtors' ageing and liquidity

1.7 Also of interest to the credit controller is the *total* percentage figure calculated at the bottom of each column. In practice the credit controller will be concerned to look at this figure first of all, in order to keep the ageing figures consistent. Why might a credit controller be worried by an increase in the **ageing**? If the credit controller knows the customers are going to pay, should it matter?

1.8 Think back to your work on cash forecasting. This is based on the expectation that a company's debts will be paid within, say, 30 days after payment. In other words revenue booked in Month 1 would be followed up by cash in Month 2. The cash forecast also has an outflow side. Any reduction in the inflow caused by an overall increase in the debtors period affects the company's ability to pay its debts and increases its use of overdraft finance: unauthorised overdrafts carry a hefty fee as well as interest.

Delays in payments to specific customers

1.9 It may be the case that an increase in the overall debtors ageing is caused by the activities of one customer, and there is always the possibility that cut-off dates for producing the report can generate anomalies. (For example, a customer might pay invoices at the end of every calendar month, whereas the debtors ageing analysis might be run every 30 days.)

1.10 However, the credit controller should try and avoid situations where a customer starts to delay payment. He or she should review information from:

- Sales staff regarding how the company is doing
- The press for any stories relevant to the company
- Competitors
- The trade 'grapevine'

These can supply early warning signals.

1.11 If, however, there is a persistent problem, the credit controller might have to insist on a **refusal of credit**.

(a) This is likely to be resented by sales staff who will possibly receive less commission as a result of lower sales.

(b) However, if there is a possibility of default, the loss of a *potential* sale is surely less severe than the failure of *actual* money to arrive.

2 COLLECTING DEBTS

> **Exam focus point**
>
> A question might require you to evaluate different methods of debt collection and to recommend the most appropriate method.

2.1 Collecting debts is a two-stage process.

(a) Having agreed credit terms with a customer, a business should issue an invoice and expect to receive payment when it is due. **Issuing invoices** and **receiving payments** is the task of sales ledger staff. They should ensure that:

- The **customer is fully aware** of the terms.
- The **invoice is correctly drawn up** and issued promptly.
- They are aware of any **potential quirks** in the customer's system.
- **Queries** are **resolved quickly.**
- **Monthly statements** are **issued promptly.**

(b) If payments become overdue, they should be 'chased'. Procedures for pursuing overdue debts must be established, for example:

(i) **Instituting reminders or final demands**

These should be sent to a named individual, asking for repayment by return of post. A second or third letter may be required, followed by a final demand stating clearly the action that will be taken. The aim is to goad customers into action, perhaps by threatening not to sell any more goods on credit until the debt is cleared.

(ii) **Chasing payment by telephone**

The telephone is of greater nuisance value than a letter, and the greater immediacy can encourage a response. It can however be time-consuming, in particular because of problems in getting through to the right person.

(iii) **Making a personal approach**

Personal visits can be very time-consuming and tend only to be made to important customers who are worth the effort.

(iv) **Notifying debt collection section**

This means not giving further credit to the customer until he has paid the due amounts.

(v) **Handing over debt collection to specialist debt collection section**

Certain, generally larger, organisations may have a section to collect debts under the supervision of the credit manager.

(vi) **Instituting legal action to recover the debt**

Premature legal action may unnecessarily antagonise important customers.

21: Monitoring and collecting debtors

(vii) **Hiring external debt collection agency to recover debt**

This is covered in Chapter 22.

Customer awareness of terms

2.2 Any business can increase its chances of getting paid by ensuring, at various stages, that **the customer has no right to plead ignorance** of the due date, or that the seller attaches no importance to it.

(a) **Payment dates** and **terms** should be **discussed** during the initial negotiations.

(b) When the **order** is **confirmed in writing, payment terms should be clearly stated.**

(c) When a customer account is set up, the credit agreement should contain a clause whereby a customer **acknowledges agreement** to the supplier's terms and conditions.

(d) The **invoice** should **state boldly** the **payment terms**.

(e) **Payment terms** should also be prominently displayed on the monthly **statement**.

Proper invoicing

2.3 Slip-ups in invoicing by a supplier might create delays in payment by a customer, because the internal controls in the customer's procedures for paying the debt prevent the debt from being paid because of the discrepancies or faults.

Knowledge of customer payment systems

2.4 It helps to have some ideas as to **how customers pay**.

(a) Some customers have an **invoice run** on a **monthly basis**. There is an inevitable cut-off point after which data cannot be input to the system. Delays might be caused by a bureaucratic backlog.

(b) Other customers, regardless of their actual obligations, ration the amount paid out per month.

(c) Some customers will only pay when sent a **reminder** or when specifically asked by suppliers.

(d) Other customers will not pay until threatened with **legal action**.

Statements

2.5 Invoices are usually followed by a **monthly statement** to customers which will:

- List the new invoices during the month
- Indicate the cash received
- Indicate the outstanding balance due
- Analyse the debts by age
- Serve as a reminder to the customer about payment

Special cases

'Key account' customers

2.6 In most businesses, major **'key account' customers** will receive special treatment in the sales effort, and it is appropriate that special treatment is also given in managing the debts

Reconciliation and 'on account' payments

2.7 A problem you might encounter is a customer who pays a round sum to cover a variety of invoices. The round sum may be a **payment 'on account'**: in other words, the customer might not state which invoices the payment refers to. This might occur because the customer is having liquidity problems. Unallocated payments on account, which have not been agreed, should be investigated.

Receipts on long-term contracts

2.8 You may have read or heard about the disputes between Eurotunnel plc and TransManche Link, the consortium which carried out the construction work on the Channel Tunnel. This was an example of some of the problems that might be encountered on **long-term contracts** of any kind. Such long-term contracts generally feature **precise terms**, and a **requirement of third-party verification** (eg an architect's certification) for payments to be made.

2.9 There is always scope for argument, and the normal conditions of credit control do not necessarily apply. Simply refusing to continue to provide a service to a customer who is a slow payer may involve significant costs, especially if resources have been allocated to the project. Furthermore, the creditor firm is still concerned to maintain a healthy commercial relationship for the duration of the project.

2.10 As contracting firms devote substantial resources to certain contracts, the results of not being paid for work done can be catastrophic. The person running the cash and credit control side of the business needs to be aware of the implications in cash flow terms and perhaps needs to demand regular payments.

3 CREDIT INSURANCE, FACTORING AND INVOICE DISCOUNTING 11/01

Credit insurance

3.1 Companies might be able to obtain **credit insurance** (**default insurance**) against certain approved debts going bad through a specialist credit insurance firm.

3.2 When a company arranges credit insurance, it must submit specific proposals for credit to the insurance company, stating the name of each customer to which it wants to give credit and the amount of credit it wants to give. The insurance company will accept, amend or refuse these proposals, depending on its assessment of each of these customers.

3.3 Credit insurance is normally available for only up to about 75% of a company's potential bad debt loss. The remaining 25% of any bad debt costs are borne by the company itself. This is to ensure that the company does not become slack with its credit control.

Domestic credit insurance

3.4 **Export credit insurance** was discussed in Chapter 15. **Credit insurance** for **domestic** (ie not export) businesses is available from a number of sources.

21: Monitoring and collecting debtors

3.5 Insurance companies are prepared to assume for themselves the risk of the debt going bad, and they hope to profit from this. Furthermore, they are less vulnerable, as institutions, to the possibility that debt will ruin their business.

3.6 Most insurance companies will spend a considerable effort in examining a company's books and systems before they will accept any of the risks.

(a) The insurer will examine the entire sales ledger to look at the overall portfolio of risk, if, for example, insurance is provided against the entire sales ledger.

(b) The firm's credit control, debt collection and sales ledger administration will also be scrutinised to ensure that the firm is not lax in its credit control policy and that all efforts are taken to reduce the possibility of debts going bad.

3.7 There are several types of credit insurance on offer. These are briefly described below.

'Whole turnover' policies

3.8 **Whole turnover policies** can be used in two ways.

(a) It can **cover** the **firm's entire sales ledger**, although, normally speaking, the actual amount paid out will rarely be more than 80% of the total loss for any specific claim.

(b) Alternatively, the client **can select** a **proportion of its debtors** and insure these for their entire amount.

In other words, perhaps 80% of each debt is insured; or the entire amount of the debts incurred, say, by perhaps 80% of the customers.

3.9 Premiums on a whole turnover policy are usually **1% of the insured sales**.

Question 1

Gibbony Whey Ltd has a whole turnover policy for its debts. The policy is underwritten by Broaken Amis Assurance plc and is on a whole turnover basis, whereby 80% of the sales ledger is covered, provided that the total credit offered to customers does not exceed £1m. In the first quarter of 20X4, the company made total sales of £4m: at the end of the quarter debtors for credit sales stood at £1.4m. Gibbony Whey has traded with Sloe Pears Ltd: the underwriters approved a credit limit for Sloe Pears of £1,700. At the end of the quarter, Sloe Pears had outstanding debts of £2,100. Sloe Pears turns into a 'bad debtor' when the company's buildings are completely destroyed by a falling asteroid.

Gibbony Whey writes to Broaken Amis claiming for the bad debt. How much will Gibbony Whey be entitled to as compensation?

Answer

£1,700 × 80% = £1,360.

Gibbony Whey gave more credit than was underwritten by the insurance company.

Annual aggregate: excess of loss

3.10 Under an **annual aggregate excess of loss policy**, the insurer pays 100% of debts above an agreed limit. This is similar to motor insurers requiring that the first amount (eg £50) of a loss is borne by the insured.

Part D: Working capital management

Specific account policies

3.11 Insurance can be purchased to cover a **specific debtor account** in the event of some contingency. For example, a policy might depend on the debtor being formally declared insolvent.

Factoring   Pilot paper

> **KEY TERM**
>
> **Factoring** is an arrangement to have debts collected by a factor company, which advances a proportion of the money it is due to collect.

3.12 Some businesses might have difficulties in financing the amounts owed by customers (debtors). There are two main reasons for this.

(a) If a business's **sales** are rising **rapidly**, its **total debtors** will **rise quickly too**. Selling more on credit will put a strain on the company's cash flow. The business, although making profits, might find itself in difficulties because it has too many debtors and not enough cash.

(b) If a business grants **long credit** to its customers, it might run into **cash flow difficulties** for much the same reason. Exporting businesses must often allow long periods of credit to foreign buyers, before eventually receiving payment, and their problem of financing debtors adequately can be a critical one.

3.13 **Factors** are organisations that offer their clients a financing service to overcome these problems. They are prepared to advance cash to the client against the security of the client's debtors. The business will assign its debtors to the factor and will typically ask for an advance of funds against the debts which the factor has purchased, usually up to 80% of the value of the debts.

3.14 For example, if a business makes credit sales of £100,000 per month, the factor might be willing to advance up to 80% of the invoice value (here £80,000) in return for a commission charge, and interest will be charged on the amount of funds advanced. The balance of the money will be paid to the business when the customers have paid the factor, or after an agreed period.

3.15 This service gives the business immediate cash in place of a debt (which is a promise of cash in the future). If the business needs money to finance operations, borrowing against trade debts is therefore an alternative to asking a bank for an overdraft.

3.16 **The main aspects of factoring**

We looked at these aspects briefly in Chapter 15. They are as follows.

(a) Administration of the client's invoicing, sales accounting and debt collection service.

(b) Credit protection for the client's debts, whereby the factor takes over the risk of loss from bad debts and so 'insures' the client against such losses. This service is also referred to as '**debt underwriting**' or the '**purchase of a client's debts**'.

(c) Making payments to the client in advance of collecting the debts. This is sometimes referred to as 'factor finance' because the factor is providing cash to the client against outstanding debts.

3.17 The appeal of factor financing to **growing firms** is that factors might advance money when a bank is reluctant to consider granting a larger overdraft. Advances from a factor are therefore particularly useful for companies needing more and more cash to expand their business quickly.

The advantages of factoring

3.18 **Benefits of factoring for a business customer**

(a) The business can **pay** its **suppliers promptly**, and so be able to take advantage of any early payment discounts that are available.

(b) **Optimum stock levels** can be **maintained**, because the business will have enough cash to pay for the stocks it needs.

(c) **Growth** can be **financed** through **sales** rather than by injecting fresh external capital.

(d) The business gets **finance linked** to its **volume of sales**. In contrast, overdraft limits tend to be determined by historical balance sheets.

(e) The managers of the business do **not** have to **spend their time** on the **problems of slow paying debtors**.

(f) The business does **not incur** the **costs** of running **its own sales ledger** department.

3.19 An important **disadvantage of factoring** is that debtors will be making payments direct to the factor, which is likely to present a **negative picture of the firm**.

Invoice discounting

> **KEY TERM**
>
> **Invoice discounting** is the sale of debts to a third party at a discount, in return for prompt cash. The administration is managed in such a way that the debtor is unaware of the discounter's involvement and continues to pay the supplier. *(OT 2000)*

3.20 **Invoice discounting** is related to factoring and many factors will provide an invoice discounting service. For example, if your business had just redecorated the Town Hall it might have sent the Council an invoice for £5,000. This would be an easy invoice to sell on for cash because the Council are very likely to pay. An invoice for £5,000 sent to 'A Cowboy & Co' would not be so easy to sell for immediate cash!

3.21 The invoice discounter does **not** take over the administration of the client's sales ledger, and the arrangement is purely for the **advance of cash**. A business should only want to have some invoices discounted when it has a temporary cash shortage.

3.22 **Confidential invoice discounting** is an arrangement whereby a debt is confidentially assigned to the factor, and the client's customer will only become aware of the arrangement if he does not pay his debt to the client.

Question 2

The Managing Director, the Chief Accountant and the Chief Internal Auditor were meeting to discuss problems over debt collection recently identified in the Forward Company. One point made strongly by the Chief Internal Auditor was that his staff should be involved in much more than the routine verification tasks normally undertaken. It is, therefore, agreed that the internal audit section should look

Part D: Working capital management

at the problem and consider the possibility of using the services of a factor to take over some, or all, of the work of the debtors credit section.

Required

Outline the advantages and disadvantages of using the services of a factor.

Answer

The decision to factor the debts should only be taken once a wide ranging assessment of the costs and benefits of so doing has been carried out. This will involve the following steps.

(a) Find out **which organisations** provide debt factoring services. These may include the firm's own bankers, but there might be specialist agencies available who could also do the job.

(b) **Some assessment** of the **services provided** should also be made. Factors take on the responsibility of collecting the client firm's debts. There is a variety of factoring services.

  (i) **With recourse factoring**. This is the most basic service, whereby the bank undertakes to collect the debts and offer an advance, perhaps 80% thereon. The remainder is paid over once the cash has been received from customers. If the debt cannot be collected, the bank can claim back the advance from the client firm.

  (ii) **No recourse factoring**. The bank undertakes to pay the debts, but cannot claim the advance back from the client if the debt does not prove collectable.

  (iii) Some factors are willing to **purchase a number of invoices**, at a **substantial** discount. The factor would not be taking responsibility for the client's overall credit administration. In a way, this is like receiving an advance from a debt collector.

(c) The **costs of the factoring** service can then be assessed. The cost is often calculated as a percentage of the book value of the debts factored, so that if the factor took over £1,000,000 of debt at a factoring cost of 1.5%, then the client would pay a fee of £15,000. Moreover interest might also be charged on the advance, in some cases, before the debt was recovered.

(d) This can then be compared with the **costs of doing nothing**. If the choice is between either employing a factor or leaving things as they are, then the costs included in the decision include administration, salaries, interest costs on the overdraft, and other cash flow problems (eg delayed expenditure on purchases owing to bad debts, might mean that the company cannot take advantage of settlement discounts offered).

(e) However, before any final decision is taken, the organisation can try to ensure that factoring is still better value than other choices. These can include:

  (i) The **introduction** of **settlement discounts** as an inducement to pay early might improve the collection period, and hence reduce the outstanding debt

  (ii) The **use** of **credit insurance** in some cases

  (iii) A **stronger credit control policy**

  (iv) Perhaps **appointing more credit control staff** might in the long run be cheaper than factoring if the collection rate increases

There may well be operational or management solutions to this problem. These should be investigated first as customers might not like dealing with a third party.

Question 3

You are the Credit Controller of Andrews plc, whose normal trading terms are 30 days net. Most business is in the home market, but there are a small number of customers in Eastern Europe. Looking down the latest sales ledger report dated 30 April, you note that no payment has yet been received from a customer in Bulgaria who was invoiced in February and who has a 90 day LC. What action would you take to recover the debt?

A   Chase payment by telephone
B   Send the rep to visit
C   Refer the debt to a debt collection agency
D   Do nothing

Answer

D   Although the normal trading terms have been exceeded, this is to be expected since the debt is covered by a 90 day letter of credit. This means that payment will be received during May, and the debt can be ignored.

Exam focus point

The management of debtors and other elements of working capital gets right down to the day-to-day practicalities of running a business. In questions involving working capital management, you should always consider whether any proposed course of action really makes business sense.

Chapter roundup

- For control purposes, **debtors** are generally analysed by age of debt.

- There should be efficiently organised procedures for ensuring that **overdue debts** and **slow payers** are dealt with effectively.

- The earlier debtors pay the better. **Early payment** can be encouraged by good administration and by discount policies. The risk that some debtors will never pay can be partly guarded against by insurance.

- **Credit insurance** can be obtained against some bad debts. However, the insurers will rarely insure an entire bad debt portfolio - as they are unwilling to bear the entire risk. Also the client's credit control procedures should be of a suitable standard to avoid any unnecessary exposure.

- Some companies use **factoring** and **invoice discounting** to help short-term liquidity or to reduce administration costs

- Some customers are **reluctant** to pay. The debt collector should keep a record of every communication. A **staged process** of reminders and demands, culminating in debt collection or legal action, is necessary.

Quick quiz

1   Which of the following would be the last document issued to a customer in the order processing and debt collection cycle?

   A   Statement
   B   Reminder
   C   Advice note
   D   Invoice

2   List typical column headings that you would expect to see in an aged analysis of debtors.

3   List four types of credit insurance policy.

4   What service involves collecting debts of a business, advancing a proportion of the money it is due to collect?

5   What service involves advancing a proportion of a selection of invoices, without administration of the sales ledger of the business?

6   Which of the following is likely to be the most effective way of obtaining payment from a difficult customer?

   A   Personal visit
   B   Telephone request
   C   Sending a fax reminder
   D   Sending an e-mail reminder

Part D: Working capital management

7   In what order would a company normally undertake the following actions to collect debt?

   A   Hiring an external debt collection agency to recover the debt
   B   Notifying the debt collection service
   C   Sending a reminder
   D   Instituting legal action to recover the debt

8   The premium for whole turnover policies is usually ...% of insured sales, and whole turnover policies rarely cover more than ...% of the total loss.

Answers to quick quiz

1   B   The normal sequence is advice note, invoice, statement, reminder.

2   • Account number
    • Customer name
    • Total balance
    • Up to 30 days
    • Up to 60 days
    • Up to 90 days
    • Over 90 days

3   Whole turnover; annual aggregate; excess of loss; specific account

4   Factoring

5   Invoice discounting

6   A   This is the most expensive option, but is the most likely to obtain results. It is therefore recommended in the case of high value debtors.

7   C   Sending a reminder
    B   Notifying the debt collection service
    D   Instituting legal action to recover the debt
    A   Hiring an external debt collection agency to recover the debt

8   The premium for whole turnover policies is usually **1%** of insured sales, and whole turnover policies rarely cover more than **80%** of the total loss.

Now try the question below from the Exam Question Bank

Number	Level	Marks	Time
21	Introductory	n/a	30 mins

Chapter 22

REMEDIES FOR BAD DEBTS

Topic list	Syllabus reference	Ability required
1 Bad and doubtful debts	(iv)	Analysis
2 Third party involvement and going to Court	(iv)	Analysis
3 Bankruptcy: an outline	(iv)	Analysis
4 Insolvency: an outline	(iv)	Analysis
5 Provisions and write-offs	(iv)	Analysis

Introduction

On completion of this chapter you will be able to monitor information on the incidence of **bad and doubtful debts**. You will learn how to use **debt recovery methods** appropriate to the circumstances of individual cases and in accordance with the organisation's procedures. Recommendations to **write off bad and doubtful debts** should be based on a realistic analysis of all known factors.

In the exam you may have to recommend a course of action for dealing with specific doubtful debts.

Learning outcomes covered in this chapter

- Analyse trade debtor information
- Evaluate debtor and creditor policies

Syllabus content covered in this chapter

- Remedies for bad debts, eg credit insurance, debt collection agencies, specialist solicitors, guidance in taking legal action, negotiated settlements, an outline of the differences between bankruptcy and insolvency (no legal aspects to be examined)

1 BAD AND DOUBTFUL DEBTS

1.1 **Credit control** necessarily involves an **expense** to the business. Its costs include the salary of credit control staff, the extra time spent in administration, and the extra expense of obtaining other sources of working capital to cope with the delays in receiving payment.

1.2 All this can be justified for two reasons.

(a) It enables customers to spend.

(b) The extra administration can be compensated for by savings in time and inconvenience spent handling cash, cheques etc.

1.3 Even the best-run credit control system, however, cannot ensure that a business which is offered credit is *never* exposed to the risk of bad and doubtful debts, which increase the cost

Part D: Working capital management

to a business of offering credit. It might be helpful to distinguish between doubtful debts and bad debts: not all doubtful debts turn bad. They entail different costs for the business.

1.4 A debt is said to be **doubtful** when there is some uncertainty as to whether it will be paid: the key criterion is **uncertainty**. The debtor might still pay up but this is obviously much less certain than when the debtor was offered credit. In other words, the debt appears to be more risky than it appeared when the credit was first offered.

1.5 A **bad debt**, on the other hand, is a debt which will not be paid.

> **KEY TERMS**
>
> A **doubtful debt** is a debt for which there is some uncertainty as to whether it will be paid.
>
> A **bad debt** is a debt which is, or is considered to be, uncollectable and is therefore written off either as a charge to the profit and loss account or against an existing doubtful debts provision. *(OT 2000)*

1.6 Doubtful debts and bad debts reduce profits. (Normally, a debtor is defined as a 'current asset' which should be liquidated within 12 months.)

(a) A **provision** may have to be made **against doubtful debtors** in the accounts, either against specific debtors or as a percentage of total debtors, based on past experience.

(b) Even if the doubtful debt is eventually repaid in full, there will still be **additional expenses** relating to:

   (i) The effect on cash flow, especially if the debt is large
   (ii) The administration expenses of debt recovery procedures

(c) Bad debts, which will never be recovered, can be **written off against profits**. Bad debts relating to a specific customer are allowable for tax purposes, although general provisions are not.

1.7 It should also be noted that the expense of 'chasing' some small debtors to the extent, for example, of taking them to court may well exceed the debt itself. Although offensive to principle, it might be **expedient** just to write them off.

Warning signs

1.8 We have dealt with establishing credit risk in an earlier chapter. Circumstances change, however and, as has been suggested, the risk offered by a particular debtor may increase for any number of reasons which could not have been easily foreseen at the time. Here are some examples.

Personal customers

1.9 **Warning signs** of 'bad debts' relating to debts incurred by personal customers might include the following.

- Any sudden or unexpected change in payment patterns
- Requests for credit extension
- Notice of court action for personal bankruptcy
- Refusal to communicate or reply to correspondence and/or phone calls

Question 1

Jot down as many factors as you can think of which would increase the risk of a debt from a personal customer going 'bad'.

Answer

Here are some examples.

(a) Divorce: joint financial arrangements are unwound; both parties suffer hardship
(b) Long-term illness, resulting in a fall in the customer's income
(c) Redundancy, leading to a reliance on state benefits
(d) The income of a self-employed person might in poor economic conditions
(e) Bankruptcy
(f) Death (obviously)
(g) Redundancy of one partner can adversely affect the income of the entire family unit
(h) Fines or imprisonment imposed by the court, or substantial civil damages
(i) Other factors (eg a rise in interest rates and hence mortgage payments)

Business customers

1.10 With **business customers**, a debt can become doubtful or go 'bad' for any number of reasons. Some examples are provided below.

- The sudden loss of a major customer, hurting your customer's own cash flow
- The failure of your customer's own customers to pay on time in a timely fashion
- Disaster, such as a fire
- Industrial action, in some cases
- Sudden changes in overdraft terms, affecting the business customer's liquidity

1.11 The following tell-tale signs can indicate to the credit controller that there are problems with an account.

- Slow payment, or perhaps slower payment; some customers are always 'slow payers'
- Similar payment difficulties reported by other suppliers
- Information acquired 'on the grapevine' by the supplier's sales representatives
- A sense of impending doom, poor morale etc, at the customer's place of business
- Newspaper articles highlighting closures, reorganisation, profitability
- County court judgements
- Adverse comments from credit vetting agencies
- Cheques that 'bounce' indicate liquidity problems

Warning signs in financial statements

1.12 The credit controller, with the good fortune to have enough time, can pore over a firm's **annual financial statements** for any warning signs. A problem, though, is that when a company is having difficulties, financial statements are at their least reliable.

(a) The **accounts** might be **late**.

(b) There might be pressure on auditors to **sanction imprudent accounting policies**.

(c) Some of the **accounting ratios** calculated may be **contradictory**. For example, the company may post an increase in *sales* whereas in fact it is overtrading and running out of cash.

(d) Financial statements need only be published annually, and so might be out of date for the credit controller's purposes.

1.13 Other more sophisticated techniques can be used which take into account other aspects of the business's behaviour.

1.14 **Z-scoring**, which we discussed in a previous chapter, is one such method.

1.15 **A-scoring** is more subjective, but is based on three main pillars.

(a) **Defects**. Before they collapse, companies display a number of defects, which include the following.

- The company is dominated by a single individual.
- The posts of Chairman and Chief Executive are combined.
- Other directors do not have much of a say.
- The Board of Directors does not contain a broad spectrum of expertise.
- The Finance Director is weak.
- There are few professional managers below Board level.
- The company has poor accounting systems.
- The company is not responsive to change in certain key areas.

(b) **Mistakes**. The company perhaps:

- Borrows too much so that it is vulnerable to sudden misfortune
- Expands faster than it really can afford to (overtrading)
- Depends on the success of a big project

(c) **Symptoms**

- Financial ratios, Z-scores etc in decline
- Sudden changes of accounting policies
- Non-financial signs (eg fall in market share)

Warning signs revealed in internal review

1.16 It is likely that the first indication that a debt is going bad will come from a company's own sales ledger, through a review of the aged debtors' listing or late payments. A suggested procedure is as follows.

(a) Maintain a list of customers to which the firm is most exposed (ie important clients). **ABC analysis** is a technique of focusing on the most important customers.

(b) Any unusual or delayed transactions should be followed up more closely.

1.17 The credit controller needs to ensure that this information is conveyed to the appropriate personnel.

(a) The **finance department** should be told so that:

(i) Any necessary accounting entries can be made to provide against or write off the debt

(ii) The firm's cash flow forecast can be altered, and any new borrowing arranged

(b) If the debt is large, then the **Finance Director** might also be told if it has a material effect on profits.

(c) The **sales department** needs to know, so that no further losses arising from trading with this particular debtor are made.

Question 2

You have just been given the aged debtors listing, which no-one has looked at for ages. The account for one of your customers, who is not normally a slow payer, shows some peculiarities.

	Current	30+	Days 60+	90+	Total
Amount outstanding	1,000	-	-	400	1,400

You investigate further and find out that the customer always pays within the 30 day period and has paid all recent invoices, so the £400 outstanding seems rather odd.

What should you do?

Answer

Before contacting the customer and accusing the customer of default, it is best to eliminate other explanations for the discrepancy.

(a) Is there any **unallocated cash**? In other words, have payments been received which, for whatever reason, have not been matched with the invoice? (In some computer systems an error of 1p prevents matching.)

(b) Have invoices been **posted correctly**? In other words, does the discrepancy arise out of a clerical error? Payment might inadvertently have been posted to the wrong account.

(c) Are there **matters in dispute**? Review of the file should indicate existing correspondence on any items.

(d) Did the customer **return the goods** and send a debit note, which has not reached the system?

Once you are sure of the case, assemble all the relevant information and contact the customer: this customer is generally reliable, so it is best to act to preserve the commercial relationship.

2 THIRD PARTY INVOLVEMENT AND GOING TO COURT

2.1 There comes a point when the debtor has no alternative but to threaten **legal action** and, if this does not produce a suitable result, has to take a variety of measures to collect a debt. The firm may go to court immediately, but it is often cheaper to use a debt collection agency first of all.

Debt collection agencies

2.2 **Debt collection agencies** (alternatively called 'credit collection agencies') are the most effective way of pursuing debts. Some debt collection agencies offer a variety of credit control services, include running the credit control department in its entirety. There are over 250 such agencies in the UK. The **Credit Services Association** is a professional body for debt collectors.

2.3 Unlike other sources of third party assistance, most debt collection agencies are happy to be **paid by results**. In other words, *most* debt collectors offer a 'no collection, no fee' basis. Most receive a straight percentage. Commissions can vary between 1% and 25%, depending on the value of the debt.

2.4 Any collection agency will employ suitable techniques, depending on the client.

(a) Some collect on a letter and telephone basis. This is often the case where the client has passed on a large number of **consumer debts**.

(b) Others, especially for more difficult cases, collect 'on the doorstep'.

Part D: Working capital management

Question 3

You are considering employing the services of a debt collection agency. List the main considerations in this decision.

Answer

A debt collection agency provides a variety of services, but these have their costs.

(a) What commission is charged by the agency? Debts which are harder to collect might require a higher price.

(b) The mere involvement of a third party might encourage some debtors to pay.

(c) The cost of a solicitor should be compared with the cost of the debt collector if legal action has to be taken.

(d) The collection agency should keep the client informed about progress.

Specialist solicitors

2.5 A business might choose to use a firm of **specialist solicitors**. Debt collection agencies are considered to be normal business services, and the use of a collection agency is unlikely to result in the end of a commercial relationship. Rightly or wrongly, however, employing a solicitor is seen as being more serious.

Going to court

2.6 Before going to the expense and hassle of going to court, a firm must be sure of its case, and should therefore do the following.

(a) Be sure that the debtor is a genuine *debtor* rather than a dissatisfied customer: if the latter, the customer's complaints should be examined and dealt with if possible.

(b) Check who the debtor is (individual, firm, limited company).

(c) Ensure the name is correct. For unincorporated businesses, it is helpful to use a form of words such as 'Joe Bloggs trading as Bloggs Enterprises'.

(d) Before suing, it is advisable to check the original credit information. Is the customer likely to have sufficient assets?

2.7 The threat of a court case may encourage the other party to save themselves expense and inconvenience by sending a **negotiated settlement** (see later in this section).

Which court?

2.8 The **Small Claims Court** generally deals with amounts under £5,000. The parties can refer the case to an **arbitrator**, whose award is recorded as a county court judgement.

2.9 **County Courts** deal with all actions in contract below £25,000, and some between £25,000 and £50,000. The **High Court** deals with amounts over £50,000 and some cases where the amounts disputed lie between £25,000 and £50,000. The decision as to whether the action shall go to the High Court or the County Court depends on:

- The type of transaction
- Any public interest issues
- The legal and factual complexity of the case
- The speed at which the case can be tried

Enforcement

2.10 Whilst obtaining a county court judgement is fine in itself, we must not forget the purpose of the exercise, which is to collect money. The county court judgement must therefore be enforced, which may need to be achieved by one of the following methods.

(a) **Warrant of execution.** The court bailiff can seize the debtor's goods and sell them by public auction.

(b) **Attachment of earnings.** The court can order a specific weekly amount to be deducted from the debtor's wages.

(c) **Garnishee order.** A person owing money to the debtor is instructed to pay it instead to the creditor.

(d) **Petition for bankruptcy.** This is described in Section 3 of this Chapter.

(e) **Administrative order.** A debtor with multiple debts not exceeding £5,000, at least one of which is a judgement debt they are unable to settle immediately, discharges all obligations by making regular payments into court.

(f) **Charging order.** If the court orders a charge on the debtor's property, for example their house, this means that the property cannot be sold or transferred by the debtor: if the debt is not settled within six months, the creditor can have the property sold.

Other remedies: sale of goods

2.11 A contract for the sale of goods is covered by the Sale of Goods Acts. It does provide certain remedies, providing the contract is drawn up in the right way.

(a) **Lien.** A seller who is unpaid and who still has possession of the goods can hold on to them (eg in case of insolvency).

(b) **Retention of title.** Some contracts specify that the supplier retains title to the goods until the supplier has been paid. However, this is subject to many restrictions.

Commercial arbitration

> **KEY TERM**
>
> An **arbitration agreement** is defined in the Arbitration Act 1950 as 'a written agreement to submit present or future differences to arbitration, whether an arbitrator is named therein or not'.

2.12 **Arbitration** is an alternative to litigation in commercial disputes. As a process, it has much more in common with a business's other commercial activities than does litigation. It is often preferred by business people for that reason. A matter may be referred to arbitration in four ways:

(a) By order of the court
(b) By Act of Parliament
(c) By agreement of the parties
(d) By way of arbitration proceedings in the County Court (small claims procedure)

2.13 Some of the **advantages** of arbitration are set out below.

(a) The **proceedings** are **less formal** and **more flexible** than litigation, and are cheaper.

Part D: Working capital management

    (b) In some cases, arbitration may be **quicker** and **cheaper** than litigation.

    (c) The parties can *select* **an arbitrator** in whom they have confidence (eg an expert).

    (d) The arbitrator is likely to be **familiar** with the **commercial activities** of the parties.

    (e) The hearing is most often in **private**, so avoiding publicity.

    (f) The atmosphere of an arbitration is **more friendly** than that of a court action. This is a point of some importance if the parties are intending to continue their commercial dealings with each other.

2.14 Nevertheless, arbitration suffers from some **disadvantages** compared with litigation.

    (a) Plaintiff and defendant in an action are bound to **observe certain time limits** in preparing their cases, and so an arbitration procedure may provide more scope for deliberate time-wasting by a defendant.

    (b) A judge has power to grant interim relief (eg an injunction) to the parties or curtail proceedings by means of a summary judgement. An arbitrator's powers are **less extensive**.

    (c) Judges exercise their profession after many years of training in the process of weighing evidence and interpreting law. Arbitrators may be **unqualified** in such matters, and hence their decision may be subjective.

Negotiated settlements

2.15 Most commercial disputes do not make it to court. Apart from cases covered by arbitration procedures negotiations between the parties may be conducted at any time and settlements may result. They may even occur during trials.

3 BANKRUPTCY: AN OUTLINE

> **KEY TERM**
>
> **Bankruptcy** is the legal status of an individual against whom an adjudication order has been made by the court primarily because of inability to meet financial liabilities.
>
> *(OT 2000)*

3.1 There may come a time whereby, for whatever reason, a person or business is unable to serve the debts that have been incurred. Sometimes, the only course available to a creditor or group of creditors is to use bankruptcy and insolvency legislation to obtain payment or, perhaps at best, part-payment. This means that the assets of the person administered by someone else can be sold.

3.2 The procedures dealing with an individual's **bankruptcy** on the one hand and a limited company's insolvency on the other differ significantly. Insolvency and bankruptcy legislation in the UK is based on the Insolvency Act 1986 and subsequent amendments.

> **Exam focus point**
>
> You are only required to have an outline knowledge of these topics.

Voluntary arrangements

3.3 A **voluntary arrangement** enables an individual to make binding agreements with creditors, minimising official involvement.

3.4 A voluntary arrangement can either be an alternative to bankruptcy, before it gets started; or a way of ending a situation of bankruptcy, so that the voluntary arrangement takes over from the bankruptcy proceedings.

Bankruptcy petition

3.5 Three weeks before creditors petition a court for a bankruptcy order, they must issue a **statutory demand**. The debtor might offer a settlement. The court will refuse to declare the debtor bankrupt if the creditor 'unreasonably' refuses. Otherwise the court will issue a bankruptcy order, once the **petition** is received.

3.6 The consequences of the petition are as follows.

(a) With a few exceptions, if the debtor pays money to creditors or disposes of property, such transactions are void.

(b) Any other legal proceedings relating to the debts or the debtor's property are held in abeyance.

(c) An **interim receiver** is appointed. This may be the official receiver (a civil servant) or another qualified insolvency practitioner. The interim receiver is mainly concerned to protect the estate (eg by selling goods that will diminish in value).

The process of bankruptcy

3.7 Once the petition is granted, the consequences of a bankruptcy order are as follows.

(a) The **official receiver** takes custody and control of the bankrupt's property, until (d) below.

(b) A **statement of affairs**, detailing the bankrupt's assets and liabilities is drawn up within 21 days.

(c) Within 12 weeks of the date of the order, the official receiver summons a meeting of creditors.

(d) These **creditors** (or on occasion the court or the Secretary of State) appoint a **trustee in bankruptcy** (normally within 12 weeks of the order). The trustee has a number of powers, similar to those that the debtor had over his or her own property, before being made bankrupt.

(e) The **debtor's assets** are **realised**.

(f) A **distribution** is made to **creditors**.

The creditor's position

3.8 Creditors should submit a written claim to the trustee, detailing how the debt is made up. The creditor may also need to substantiate any claim with documentary evidence. Creditors will be sent a form on which details can be given.

3.9 Different groups of creditors have different claims and are ranked in order. Claims are paid in rank order, as follows.

Part D: Working capital management

(a) Fees paid by an apprentice or articled clerk relating to an unexpired period of training are reimbursed first.

(b) **Preferential creditors.**

- The Inland Revenue for PAYE (12 months)
- Subcontractors in the building industry
- Customs and Excise for VAT
- Car tax, and other excise duties
- National insurance contributions
- Pension scheme contributions
- Employees' wages for four months, up to £800 per employee

(c) Ordinary creditors (all others).

(d) Any remainder is allocated as follows.

- Statutory interest
- Debts incurred between spouses
- The bankrupt

Discharge

3.10 Bankruptcy as a legal state is ended by **discharge**. Normally, the bankrupt is discharged automatically three years after the order was made, unless the court determines otherwise. The bankrupt receives a **certificate of discharge**. Discharge releases the bankrupt from his bankruptcy debts.

4 INSOLVENCY: AN OUTLINE

> **KEY TERM**
>
> **Insolvency** is the inability of a debtor to pay debts when they fall due. *(OT 2000)*

4.1 The term 'unable to pay its debts' is defined in s 123 of the Insolvency Act 1986 as follows.

(a) A **creditor (owed over £750)** has served on the company, by leaving at the company's registered office, a **written demand** (in the prescribed form) requiring the company to pay the sum and the company has for three weeks failed to do so.

(b) A **court order** in favour of a creditor of the company is returned **unsatisfied** in whole or in part.

(c) It is demonstrated to the satisfaction of the court that the company is **unable to pay** its debts as they fall due.

(d) A company is also deemed unable to pay its debts if it is proved to the satisfaction of the court that the **value of the company's** assets is **less** than the **amount of its liabilities**.

4.2 Soon its creditors may want to recover their money from the company in some way. There are three main routes.

(a) **Liquidation**. This means winding the company up, in other words selling off its assets, and closing it down.

(b) **Receivership** or **administrative receivership**. Secured creditors (see Paragraph 4.3 below) call in the receiver to run the business so that they can be paid. The business is then handed back to the directors.

(c) **Administration**.

4.3 In the last section, we noted that different classes of creditors have different rights in respect of the bankrupt's assets. In a company this is also true.

(a) **Secured creditors** have a **charge** of the assets of a business. For example, a bank may lend a business money secured on its factory premises so that if the loan is not repaid, the bank has the right, subject to other legal issues, to sell the factory.

> **KEY TERMS**
>
> A **fixed charge** is a form of protection given to secured creditors relating to specific assets of a company. The charge grants the holder the right of enforcement against the identified asset (in the event of default on repayment) so that the creditor may realise the asset to meet the debt owed. Fixed charges rank first in order of priority in receivership or liquidation.
>
> A **floating charge** is a form of protection given to secured creditors which relates to the assets of the company which are changing in nature. Often current assets like stock or debtors are the subject of this type of charge. In the event of default on repayment the charge-holder may take steps to enforce the charge so that it crystallises and becomes attached to the current assets to which it relates. Floating charges rank after certain other prior claims in a liquidation. *(OT 2000)*

(b) **Unsecured creditors** have no such charge.

Compulsory liquidation

> **KEY TERM**
>
> **Liquidation** is the winding up of a company in which the assets are sold, liabilities settled as far as possible, and any remaining cash returned to members. Liquidation may be voluntary or compulsory. *(OT 2000)*

4.4 **Compulsory winding up or liquidation** is carried out by a **liquidator**, on behalf of the shareholders and/or creditors of the firm. The court decides that the company should be liquidated, usually as a result of a petition from a shareholder or creditor.

Voluntary liquidation

4.5 A **voluntary winding up** or **liquidation** occurs when shareholders and/or creditors decide to do so. Creditors have the decisive role, however, as they have prior claim over the company's assets, to the extent that their debts are paid.

The liquidation committee

4.6 A **liquidation committee** may be appointed in a compulsory liquidation and in a creditors' voluntary liquidation. The general function of the committee is to work with the liquidator, to supervise his accounts, to approve the exercise of certain of his statutory powers and to fix his remuneration.

Powers of liquidators

4.7 A liquidator *must* be appointed in a compulsory liquidation and *may* be appointed in a voluntary liquidation. The liquidator's basic function is to obtain and realise the company's assets to pay off its debts.

Order of application of assets in liquidation

4.8 The **order of application of assets in liquidation** is as follows.

(a) **Secured creditors** who have **fixed charges** are entitled to be paid out of their security so far as it suffices. If the security is insufficient in value to pay the debt in full the creditor ranks as an unsecured creditor for the balance.

(b) The **costs of winding up** are paid next - they rank before floating charges.

(c) **Preferential unsecured debts** are paid next. They rank equally. If there are insufficient funds to pay them all, they are pro-rated. They include:

 (i) PAYE and VAT owing (for the last 12 and 6 months respectively)
 (ii) Wages, up to £800 per employee or four months pay
 (iii) Excise duties etc

(d) **Debts secured by floating charges** come next in order.

(e) **Unsecured non-preferential debts** come next (eg trade).

(f) **Deferred debts** (eg unpaid dividends to shareholders) come last in order.

Alternatives to liquidation

4.9 We have seen that winding up a company is a fairly drastic step involving the cessation of trading, the disposal of assets and the final dissolution of the company. In many cases, these steps arise from the fact that the company cannot pay its debts, even though such inability to pay may be temporary or as a result of a 'one-off' disaster from which the company is basically sound enough to recover. What then are the alternatives to full-blown liquidation when a company is insolvent to some degree?

(a) **Administrative receivership**

A company's secured creditor, in preference to presenting a winding up petition, may appoint a **receiver** (under a fixed charge) or an **administrative receiver** (under a floating charge). This may well result in the secured creditor receiving payment but it can often result in a healthy company being destroyed for the sake of the secured creditors when it could have continued trading to the benefit of all concerned.

(b) **Administration**

Under this procedure a moratorium is imposed by the court on creditors' actions against the company while an insolvency practitioner attempts to secure a good resolution.

(c) **Voluntary arrangement with creditors**

By means of this the company itself, under the supervision of an insolvency practitioner, arranges with creditors for a way of sorting out the problems surrounding it.

5 PROVISIONS AND WRITE-OFFS

5.1 It is reasonable to assume that, if matters have gone as far as receivership, administration or liquidation, the company cannot pay off all its debts. In many liquidations, receiverships and administrations, the creditors are unlikely to receive in full the amount they are owed, especially if they are unsecured or non-preferential creditors.

5.2 There are two alternatives to dealing with bad and doubtful debts in the accounts and accounting records.

(a) They can be written off completely.

(b) They can be provided against. This means that the gross debtor is still maintained, in the sales ledger control account and in the sales ledger, but that a counterbalance credit is set up to provide against them.

KEY TERM

A **doubtful debts provision** is an amount charged against profit and deducted from debtors to allow for the estimated non-recovery of a proportion of the debts. *(OT 2000)*

5.3 Clearly **provisions and write offs** should only be made after consideration of all suitable factors. It is too easy to be hasty, and a slight delay in receiving payment is no excuse for writing off the debt. Factors to be considered are: the success of attempts to collect the debt; the expense of pursuing the debt (which may well be more than the debt is worth); likelihood of insolvency proceedings and communication from liquidators, receivers or administrators as to the collectibility of the debt.

5.4 The proportion of bad debts can be measured in two ways.

KEY TERM

$$\text{Bad debts ratio} = \frac{\text{Bad debts} \times 100\%}{\text{Turnover on credit}}$$

The numerator and denominator should be moving annual totals. This indicates the significance of bad debts as a proportion of credit sales.

Alternatively

$$\text{Bad debts ratio} = \frac{\text{Bad debts} \times 100\%}{\text{Total debtors at a point in time}}$$

This indicates the significance of bad debts as a proportion of debtors. *(OT 2000)*

Monitoring bad debts: bad debts/sales ratios

5.5 It is helpful for the credit controller to monitor the overall level of bad debts encountered by a firm. The following report format might be adopted.

	Jan	*Feb*	*March*	*April*
Sales	£1,000	£2,000	£1,000	£4,000
Bad debts recognised	£20	£50	-	£10
% of sales	2%	2½%	-	0.25%

Part D: Working capital management

	Jan	Feb	March	April
Bad debts originated	£50	£30	£40	?
% sales	5%	1.5%	4%	N/A

(a) **Bad debts recognised** refers to the time when the debt went bad.
(b) **Bad debts originated** refers to the date when the sale was initially made.

5.6 The purpose of such a report is to record the bad debt expense in the correct period, and to monitor the effectiveness of credit control in certain months. An increasing ratio of bad debts to sales implies a deteriorating quality of credit control, unless it results from policy to sell to higher risk customers.

Question 4

You are owed £5,000 by a customer who is refusing to pay. Which court will hear this action?

A High Court
B County Court
C Small Claims Court
D Magistrates Court

Answer

B County Courts deal with all actions in contract below £25,000. The Small Claims Courts usually deal with amounts below £3,000.

Chapter roundup

- A **debt** can go **bad** for a variety of reasons. It might have been '**high risk**' in the first place. **Unforeseen circumstances** can arise, although for both business and personal customers, it is often possible to detect warning signs of impending disaster. Existing customers might take longer to pay.

- There are some sophisticated **scoring systems** available for analysing companies, which input data from financial accounts into a model.

- **Debt collection agencies** collect debts, for a commission.

- If it comes to **court**, a county court may issue a default summons. The judgement may be enforced in a variety of ways, including bailiffs, garnishee orders, or insolvency proceedings.

- **Bankruptcy** is where an individual's property is sold for creditors' benefit. **Insolvency** is when the assets of a company are taken over by a third party appointed by creditors. The company is run until the debts are paid, or may be wound up.

Quick quiz

1 You have just obtained a county court judgement in your favour in respect of a customer who is refusing to pay his account. Which of the following would be an **inappropriate** method of enforcing the judgement?

   A Charging order
   B Warrant of execution
   C Attachment of earnings
   D Out of court settlement

2 What is a bad debt?

3   Z-scoring is primarily:

    A   A way of rating personal customers' creditworthiness
    B   A method of predicting corporate failure
    C   A method for establishing the level of provision against doubtful debts
    D   A method for establishing whether it is worthwhile to pursue bad debts

4   A court action to settle a dispute over an amount of £12,000 in the UK will be heard in:

    A   The Small Claims Court
    B   The County Court
    C   The High Court
    D   Chancery Division

5   List three methods of enforcing a County Court judgement.

6   Which of the following is **not** a route that a creditor might choose to follow as a means of recovering money from an insolvent company?

    A   Administrative receivership
    B   Liquidation
    C   Arbitration
    D   Administration

7   Bad debts ratio = $\dfrac{\ldots}{\ldots} \times 100\%$

8   Bad debts ratio can also = $\dfrac{\ldots}{\ldots} \times 100\%$

Answers to quick quiz

1   D   This is an alternative to going to court in the first place, not a method of enforcement.

2   A debt which will not be paid.

3   B   A method of predicting corporate failure

4   B   The County Court

5   Any three of:

    (a) Warrant of execution
    (b) Attachment of earnings
    (c) Garnishee order
    (d) Petition for bankruptcy
    (e) Administrative order
    (f) Charging order

6   C   Arbitration is an alternative to litigation in commercial disputes. It is not a means of debt recovery in the event of insolvency.

7   Bad debts ratio = $\dfrac{\text{Bad debts}}{\text{Turnover on credit}} \times 100\%$

8   Bad debts ratio can also = $\dfrac{\text{Bad debts}}{\text{Total debtors}} \times 100\%$

Now try the question below from the Exam Question Bank

Number	Level	Marks	Time
22	Examination	20	36 mins

Chapter 23

MANAGING CREDITORS AND STOCK

Topic list	Syllabus reference	Ability required
1 Managing creditors	(iv)	Evaluation
2 Methods of paying creditors	(iv)	Evaluation
3 Managing stocks	(iv)	Evaluation
4 Purchasing	(iv)	Evaluation

Introduction

On completion of this chapter you should be able to explain the need to monitor **creditors**, and to describe **payment methods and procedures**. As with debtors, calculations of the effect of taking discounts will be important.

You should be able to apply the **EOQ** model for stock ordering; it is likely to feature somewhere in every paper. As well as doing the calculations, you need to explain its assumptions and the components of stock costs.

We also discuss in overview the impact of **lean manufacturing** and **just-in-time** on stock control.

Learning outcomes covered in this chapter

- Evaluate creditor policies
- Evaluate appropriate methods of stock management

Syllabus content covered in this chapter

- The payment cycle from agreeing the order to making payment
- Payment terms as part of the order
- Centralised versus decentralised purchasing
- Present and interpret an age analysis of creditors
- The link between purchasing and the budget for cost centres
- The relationship between purchasing and stock control
- The Economic Order Quantity (EOQ) model (ie reorder levels, reorder quantities, safety stocks and evaluating whether bulk order discounts should be accepted)

1 MANAGING CREDITORS 5/02

Trade credit

1.1 **Trade creditors** are those creditors who are owed money for goods and services which they have supplied for the trading activities of the enterprise. For a manufacturing company, trade creditors will be raw materials suppliers.

23: Managing creditors and stock

1.2 The **management of trade creditors** involves:

- Attempting to obtain satisfactory credit from suppliers
- Attempting to extend credit during periods of cash shortage
- Maintaining good relations with regular and important suppliers

Question 1

What might your firm have to do to obtain credit from a supplier?

Answer

A firm would have to provide good references, maintain a good payment record, allow the supplier to pay a visit, and generally be *known* to be a successful business and a good credit risk.

1.3 **Taking credit** from suppliers is a normal feature of business. Nearly every company has some trade creditors waiting for payment. Trade credit is a source of short-term finance because it helps to keep working capital down. It is usually a cheap source of finance, since suppliers rarely charge interest. However, trade credit *will* have a cost, whenever a company is offered a discount for early payment, but opts instead to take longer credit.

Trade credit and the cost of lost early payment discounts

1.4 Trade credit from suppliers is particularly important to small and fast growing firms. The costs of making maximum use of trade credit include:

(a) The loss of suppliers' goodwill
(b) The loss of any available cash discounts for the early payment of debts

1.5 The cost of lost cash discounts can be estimated by the formula:

FORMULA TO LEARN

$$\left(\frac{100}{100-d}\right)^{\frac{365}{t}} - 1$$

where d is the size of the discount. For a 5% discount, d = 5.
       t is the reduction in the payment period in days which would be necessary to obtain the early payment discount

1.6 EXAMPLE: TRADE CREDIT

X Ltd has been offered credit terms from its major supplier of 2/10, net 45. That is, a cash discount of 2% will be given if payment is made within ten days of the invoice, and payments must be made within 45 days of the invoice. The company has the choice of paying 98p per £1 on day 10 (to pay before day 10 would be unnecessary), or to invest the 98p for an additional 35 days and eventually pay the supplier £1 per £1. The decision as to whether the discount should be accepted depends on the opportunity cost of investing 98p for 35 days. What should the company do?

Part D: Working capital management

1.7 SOLUTION

If the company refuses the cash discount, and pays in full after 45 days, the implied cost in interest per annum would be approximately:

$$\left(\frac{100}{100-2}\right)^{\frac{365}{35}} - 1 = 23.5\%$$

Suppose that X Ltd can invest cash to obtain an annual return of 25%, and that there is an invoice from the supplier for £1,000. The two alternatives are as follows.

	Refuse discount £	Accept discount £
Payment to supplier	1,000.0	980
Return from investing £980 between day 10 and day 45: $£980 \times \frac{35}{365} \times 25\%$	(23.5)	
Net cost	976.5	980

It is cheaper to refuse the discount because the investment rate of return on cash retained, in this example, exceeds the saving from the discount.

1.8 Although a company may delay payment beyond the final due date, thereby obtaining even longer credit from its suppliers, such a policy would be inadvisable (except where an unexpected short-term cash shortage has arisen). Unacceptable delays in payment will worsen the company's credit rating, and additional credit may become difficult to obtain.

Other creditors

1.9 There is usually less scope for flexibility with other types of short-term creditors. Things like rent and tax and dividends have to be paid out in full on certain specific dates.

Examples

(a) Rent is commonly payable on the quarter days 25 March, 24 June, 29 September and 25 December.

(b) Corporation tax normally has to be paid 9 months after the end of a company's accounting year.

(c) Employees expect to be paid regularly, usually at the end of each calendar month.

(d) Income tax collected from employees has to be paid over to the Inland Revenue by the 19th of every month.

(e) VAT collected by a business has to be paid over every 3 months.

1.10 'Management' in such cases is a matter of ensuring that what is due gets paid on time and that the finance is available when needed.

Age analysis of creditors

1.11 You will be able to appreciate what an age analysis of creditors is, having looked at the age analysis of debtors earlier in this Study Text.

1.12 EXAMPLE: AGE ANALYSIS OF CREDITORS

Here is an age analysis of creditors for Heath Limited.

			Up to 30	Up to 60	Up to 90	Over 90
\multicolumn{7}{c}{HEATH LIMITED}
\multicolumn{7}{c}{AGE ANALYSIS OF TRADE CREDITORS AS AT 31.1.X2}
Account code	Supplier name	Balance	Up to 30 days	Up to 60 days	Up to 90 days	Over 90 days
V001	Vitatechnology plc	3,284.00	2,140.00	1,144.00	-	-
P002	Prendergast Tubes plc	1,709.50	1,010.50	699.00	-	-
G072	Gerald Printers Ltd	622.64	622.64	-	-	-
P141	Plates of Derby Ltd	941.88	510.92	290.75	-	140.21
P142	Plates of Derby Ltd	604.22	514.42	-	-	89.80
G048	Greenlands Centre	34.91	-	-	-	34.91
Totals		7,197.15	4,798.48	2,138.75	-	264.92
Percentage		100%	66%	29.7%	0.0%	3.7%

1.13 Various points of analysis and interpretation could arise from an age analysis of creditors.

(a) Is the company **paying its suppliers earlier** than it needs to?

(b) Is the company taking **advantage of suppliers' discounts** where this is advantageous?

(c) Do older amounts represent **disputes**, disagreements or accounting errors that ought to be looked into?

(d) In the case of Heath Limited, is it possible that the fact that there are two accounts for Plates of Derby Ltd has led to confusion, perhaps resulting in the older unsettled items?

The purchasing cycle

The purchasing cycle proceeds as follows: Raise requisition → Purchasing department raise order → Receive goods → Carry on production → Raise goods received note → Accounts department match GRN to invoice → Record and account for invoice → Send payment → Supplier will extend credit in the future → (back to Raise requisition).

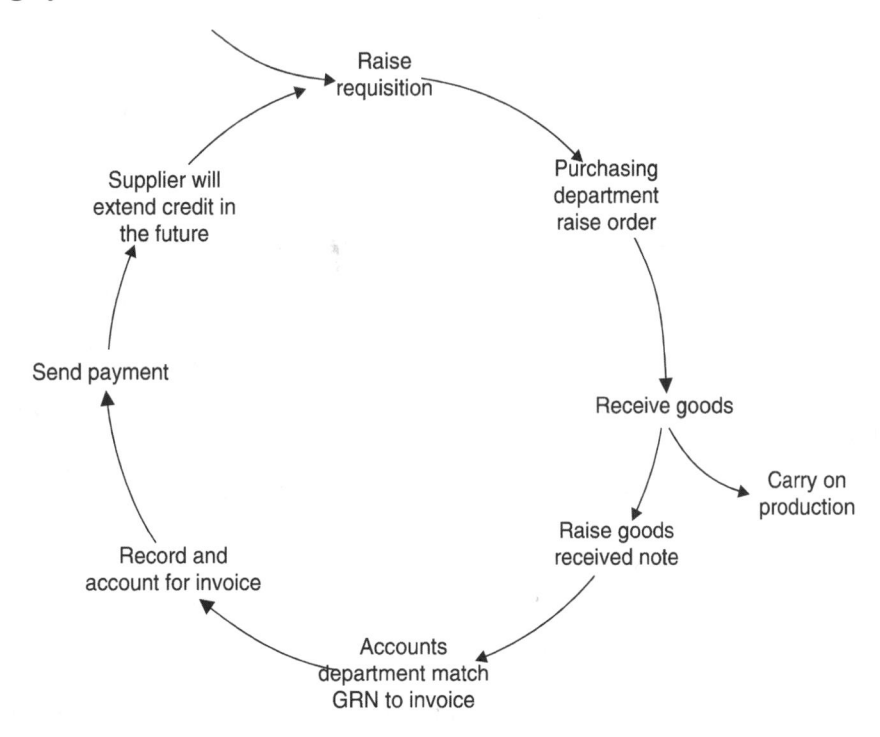

1.14 The purchasing business is now the customer, which has its credit status checked, takes delivery of goods and invoice, and pays for the goods or services.

Payment terms as part of the order

1.15 The **payment terms** offered by or agreed with the supplier form part of the contract with the supplier. Payment terms were discussed in Chapter 19 of this Study Text.

Part D: Working capital management

2 METHODS OF PAYING CREDITORS

Introduction

2.1 We should bear in mind that the methods that a business uses to **make payments** for goods and services, wages and salaries, rent and rates and so on are broadly the same as the methods of **receiving payments**. However, a business is likely to use some methods of payment much more often than others, and the most commonly used are **cheque** and **BACS** (especially for salaries and wages). **Other payment methods** are cash, banker's draft, standing order, direct debit, mail transfer and telegraphic transfer.

Payments by cash

2.2 **Cash payments** are used quite often by a business:

(a) For **small payments** out of petty cash
(b) For **wages**

2.3 Using cash to pay large amounts of money to suppliers ought to be very rare indeed.

(a) Cash needs to be kept **secure**: it is easily stolen.

(b) Cash can get **lost in the post**.

(c) It will be difficult to keep **control over cash** if it is used often for making payments.

(d) Unless a supplier issues a **receipt**, there will be no evidence that a cash payment has been made. This is bad for record keeping.

Advantages and disadvantages of paying by cheque

2.4 Cheques are widely used in business to pay for supplies and other expenses. It is worth thinking briefly about the advantages and disadvantages of using cheques as a method of payment.

Advantages of cheque payments	Disadvantages of cheque payments
Cheques are **convenient to use** for payments of any amount (provided sufficient money is in the bank, or the organisation has a large enough overdraft facility).	There are **security problems** with keeping cheques safe from theft and misuse (forged signatures), although cheques are certainly more secure than cash as a method of payment.
The cheque **counterfoil** and cheque number can be used to provide a useful method for tracing past payments whenever any queries arise.	Cheques can be a **slow method of payment**, and a supplier might insist on a different method that is more prompt and reliable, such as standing order.
They are commonly used and **widely accepted**.	

Bank giro credits

2.5 Bank giro credits (**credit transfers**) are a means by which payments might be **received** from customers. Bank giro credits can be used by businesses to **make payments**.

2.6 In practice, bank giro credits are rarely used by businesses to pay suppliers, except in cases where the supplier sends an invoice with a detachable preprinted bank giro credit transfer

23: Managing creditors and stock

paying-in slip. Suppliers who use their own preprinted bank giro credit transfer forms include the various utility companies.

2.7 Bank giro credit transfers are sometimes used by small companies to pay monthly salaries.

Payments by banker's draft

2.8 A supplier might sometimes ask a customer to pay by **banker's draft**. Banker's drafts are not used for small value items, but might be used when a large payment is involved, such as for the purchase of a company car.

Standing orders

2.9 Standing order payments might be used by a business to make regular payments of a fixed amount.

(a) **Hire purchase (HP) payments** to a hire purchase company (finance house), where an asset has been bought under an HP agreement

(b) **Rental payments** to the landlord of a building occupied by the business

(c) Paying **insurance premiums** to an insurance company

Direct debits

2.10 Direct debits, like standing orders, are used for **regular payments**. They differ from standing orders mainly for the following reasons.

(a) It is the **person who receives the payments who initiates each payment**, and informs the paying bank of the amount of each payment.

(b) Payments can be for a **variable amount** each time, and at irregular intervals, as well as for fixed amounts at regular intervals.

2.11 Payments by direct debit **might** be made by some companies for regular bills such as telephone, gas, electricity and water bills. The company being paid by direct debit will inform the payer of the amount and date of each payment in a printed statement.

Payments by Telegraphic Transfer (TT) or Mail Transfer (MT)

2.12 Occasionally, payments by a company can be arranged by means of an **electronic funds transfer** between the payer's and the payee's bank accounts. The transfer of funds is arranged between the banks concerned.

2.13 Electronic funds transfers are made quickly, and so are suitable in cases where a supplier wants **immediate payment**. They will only be used for large payments and usually at the insistence of the person being paid. Electronic funds transfers can be to a payee in a foreign country as well as within the UK.

Question 2

Libra Ltd has to make the following payments.

(a) £6.29 for office cleaning materials bought from a nearby supermarket.

Part D: Working capital management

(b) £231.40 monthly, which represents hire purchase instalments on a new van. The payments are due to Marsh Finance Ltd over a period of 36 months.

(c) £534.21 to Southern Electric plc for the most recent quarter's electricity and standing charge. A bank giro credit form/payment counterfoil is attached to the bill. There is no direct debiting mandate currently in force.

(d) £161.50 monthly for ten months, representing the business rates payable to Clapperton District Council, which operates a direct debiting system.

(e) £186.60 to Renton Hire Ltd for a week's hire of a car on company business by the Sales Director from Edinburgh Airport. The Sales Director must pay on the spot, and does not wish to use a personal cheque or cash.

(f) £23,425.00 to Selham Motors Ltd for a new car to be used by the Finance Director. Selham Motors will not accept one of the company's cheques in payment, since the Finance Director wishes to collect the vehicle immediately upon delivering the payment in person and Selham Motors is concerned that such a cheque might be dishonoured.

Recommend the method of payment which you think would be most appropriate in each case, stating your reasons.

Answer

(a) This is a small business payment which should be paid out of petty **cash** for the sake of convenience.

(b) A **standing order** is convenient for regular fixed payments. Once the standing order instruction is made, the bank will ensure that all payments are made on the due dates and will stop making payments at the date specified in the instruction. Some finance companies may insist on a standing order being set up, as it is convenient for them to receive instalments regularly without having to issue payment requests or reminders.

(c) **Pay by cheque at the bank**, accompanied by the bill and completed bank giro credit form. The bank clerk will stamp the bill as evidence that the payment was made. Paying by cheque is safer than paying by cash and is more usual for such a large payment. Handing the cheque over at the bank will be convenient and evidence of payment will be obtained. If the payment is made at a bank other than that at which Libra holds an account, the bank receiving the payment will probably make a small charge for processing it. An alternative method is to send a **crossed cheque by post**, enclosing the payment counterfoil.

(d) The **direct debit mandate** will allow the Council to debit the amounts due direct from Libra's bank account on the due dates. The mandate will be effective until it is cancelled. The Council must inform Libra in advance of the amounts it will be debiting.

(e) Payment by **credit card** or **charge card** avoids the need to pay immediately by cash or cheque. The amount paid will appear on the monthly statement for the card used. If the Sales Director's personal card is used, he will claim payment later from the company, which may pay him by cheque or with his monthly salary payment. If a company credit or charge card is used, the company will be responsible for paying the amounts shown on the monthly statement.

(f) A **banker's draft** cannot be stopped or cancelled once it is issued. Being effectively like a cheque drawn on the bank itself, it is generally accepted as being as good as cash. It is therefore most likely to be accepted by Selham Motors.

BACS

2.14 When a business uses **Bankers' Automated Clearing Services (BACS)**, it sends information (which will be input into the books of the business) to BACS for processing. Many different business use BACS; even small businesses can do so because their bank will help to organise the information for BACS. To give examples, BACS is widely used for monthly salaries by an employer into employees' bank accounts, as already mentioned, and for standing order payments, as well as for payments to suppliers.

3 MANAGING STOCKS

3.1 Almost every company carries stocks of some sort, even if they are only stocks of consumables such as stationery. For a manufacturing business, stocks (sometimes called inventories), in the form of **raw materials, work in progress** (goods or projects on which work has been carried out but which are not yet ready for sale) and **finished goods**, may amount to a substantial proportion of the total assets of the business.

3.2 Some businesses attempt to control stocks on a scientific basis by balancing the costs of stock shortages against those of stock holding. The 'scientific' control of stocks may be analysed into three parts.

(a) The **economic order quantity (EOQ) model** can be used to decide the optimum **order size** for stocks which will minimise the costs of ordering stocks plus stockholding costs.

(b) If **discounts** for **bulk purchases** are **available**, it may be cheaper to buy stocks in **large order sizes** so as to obtain the discounts.

(c) Uncertainty in the demand for stocks and/or the supply lead time may lead a company to **decide to hold buffer stocks** or **safety stocks** (thereby increasing its investment in working capital) in order to reduce or eliminate the risk of 'stock-outs' (running out of stock).

> **KEY TERM**
>
> **Safety stock** is the quantity of stocks of raw materials, work in progress and finished goods which are carried in excess of the expected usage during the lead time of an activity. The safety stock reduces the probability of operations having to be suspended due to running out of stocks. *(OT 2000)*

Stock costs

3.3 Stock costs can be conveniently classified into four groups.

(a) **Holding costs** comprise the cost of capital tied up, warehousing and handling costs, deterioration, obsolescence, insurance and pilferage.

(b) **Procuring costs** depend on how the stock is obtained but will consist of **ordering costs** for goods purchased externally, such as clerical costs, telephone charges and delivery costs.

(c) **Shortage costs** may be:

(i) The loss of a sale and the contribution which could have been earned from the sale

(ii) The extra cost of having to buy an emergency supply of stocks at a high price

(iii) The cost of lost production and sales, where the stock-out brings an entire process to a halt

(d) The **cost of the stock** itself, the supplier's price or the direct cost per unit of production, will also need to be considered when the supplier offers a discount on orders for purchases in bulk.

3.4 Businesses need to be aware of rates of **consumption/usage, and lead times**, the time between placing an order with a supplier and the stock becoming available for use.

Re-order quantities: the basic EOQ model

> **KEY TERM**
>
> **Economic order quantity (EOQ)** is the most economic stock replenishment order size, which minimises the sum of stock ordering costs and stockholding costs. EOQ is used in an 'optimising' stock control system. *(OT 2000)*

3.5 Let D = the usage in units for one year (the demand)
C_o = the cost of making one order
C_h = the holding cost per unit of stock for one year } relevant costs only
Q = the reorder quantity

Assume that:

(a) Demand is constant
(b) The lead time is constant or zero
(c) Purchase costs per unit are constant (ie no bulk discounts)

The total annual cost of having stock (T) is:

Holding costs + ordering costs

$$\frac{QC_h}{2} + \frac{C_o D}{Q}$$

3.6 The order quantity, Q, which will minimise these total costs (T) is given by the following formula. (You do not need to know how this formula is derived. Note that it is similar in form to the formula for the optimum sale quantity in Baumol's cash management model, which we looked at in Chapter 18.)

> **EXAM FORMULA**
>
> Economic Order Quantity EOQ = $\sqrt{\dfrac{2C_o D}{C_h}}$
>
> Where C_o = cost of placing an order
> C_h = cost of holding one unit in stock for one year
> D = annual demand

3.7 EXAMPLE: ECONOMIC ORDER QUANTITY

The demand for a commodity is 40,000 units a year, at a steady rate. It costs £20 to place an order, and 40p to hold a unit for a year. Find the order size to minimise stock costs, the number of orders placed each year, and the length of the stock cycle.

3.8 SOLUTION

$Q = \sqrt{\dfrac{2C_o D}{C_h}} = \sqrt{\dfrac{2 \times 20 \times 40{,}000}{0.4}} = 2{,}000$ units. This means that there will be

$\dfrac{40{,}000}{2{,}000} = 20$ orders placed each year, so that the stock cycle is once every $52 \div 20 = 2.6$

weeks. Total costs will be $(20 \times £20) + (\frac{2,000}{2} \times 40p) = £800$ a year.

Uncertainties in demand and lead times: a re-order level system

> **KEY TERM**
>
> **Re-order level** = maximum usage × maximum lead time.
>
> It is the measure of stock at which a replenishment order should be placed. Use of the above formula builds in a measure of safety stock and minimises the possibility of the organisation running out of stock, a **stock-out**.

3.9 When the volume of demand is uncertain, or the supply lead time is variable, there are problems in deciding what the re-order level should be. By holding a **safety stock**, a company can reduce the likelihood that stocks run out during the re-order period (due to high demand or a long lead time before the new supply is delivered). The **average annual** cost of such a safety stock would be:

Quantity of safety stock × Stock holding cost
(in units)   per unit per annum

3.10 The diagram below shows how the stock levels might fluctuate with this system. Points marked 'X' show the re-order level at which a new order is placed. The number of units ordered each time is the EOQ. Actual stock levels sometimes fall below the safety stock level, and sometimes the re-supply arrives before stocks have fallen to the safety level, but on average, extra stock holding amounts to the volume of safety stock. The size of the safety stock will depend on whether stock-outs (running out of stock) are allowed.

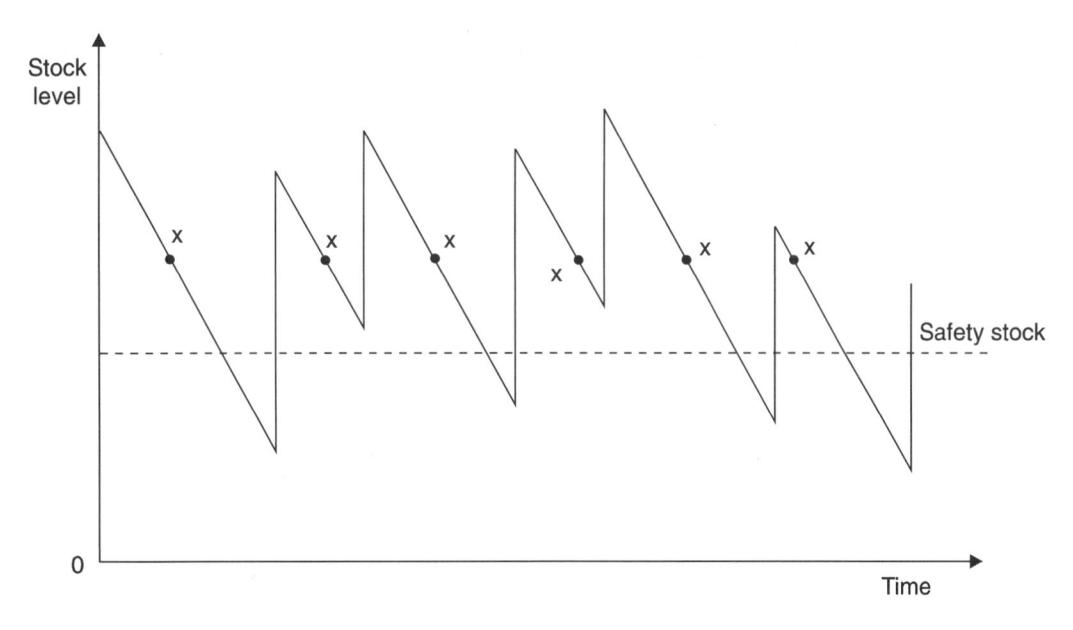

3.11 In the modern manufacturing environment stock-outs can have a disastrous effect on the production process. Nevertheless you may encounter situations where the risk of stock-outs is assumed to be worth taking. In this case the re-order level may not be calculated in the way described above.

Part D: Working capital management

Finite number of re-order levels

3.12 You may see a question where you are given a list of the re-order levels from which the business will select one. For each **possible re-order level**, and therefore each level of buffer stock, **calculate**:

- The **costs of holding buffer stock** per annum
- The **costs of stock-outs** (Cost of one stock-out × expected number of stock-outs per order × number of orders per year)

3.13 The expected number of stock-outs per order reflects the various levels by which demand during the lead time could exceed the re-order level.

3.14 EXAMPLE: POSSIBILITY OF STOCK-OUTS (1)

If re-order level is 4 units, but there was a probability of 0.2 that demand during the lead time would be 5 units, and 0.05 that demand during the lead time would be 6 units, then Expected number of stock-outs = $((5 - 4) \times 0.2) + ((6 - 4) \times 0.05) = 0.3$.

Demand normally distributed

3.15 Alternatively you may be told that demand is normally distributed. If this is the case you need to know:

- Average weekly demand
- Standard deviation of demand
- Lead time
- Acceptable risk levels

3.16 Re-order level = (Average weekly demand × lead time) + $x\sigma$

Where x = number of standard deviations that correspond to the chance business wishes to have of avoiding stock-outs

σ = standard deviation of demand

3.17 EXAMPLE: POSSIBILITY OF STOCK-OUTS (2)

Average weekly demand is 200 units, the standard deviation of demand (σ) is 40 units and demand is normally distributed. Lead time for orders is one week. What re-order levels should the business set if it wishes to have

(a) A 90% chance
(b) A 95% chance
(c) A 99% chance

of avoiding running out of stock. The relevant values from normal distribution tables are respectively:

(a) 1.28
(b) 1.65
(c) 2.33

3.18 SOLUTION

Re-order level = (Average weekly demand × lead time) + xσ

(a) Re-order level = (200 × 1) + (1.28 × 40)
= 251.2 units

(b) Re-order level = 200 + (1.65 × 40)
= 266 units

(c) Re-order level = 200 + (2.33 × 40)
= 293.2 units

Maximum and minimum stock levels

> **KEY TERM**
>
> **Maximum stock level** = re-order level + re-order quantity − (minimum usage × minimum lead time)
>
> It is the stock level set for control purposes which actual stockholding should never exceed.

3.19 The maximum level acts as a warning signal to management that stocks are reaching a potentially wasteful level.

> **KEY TERM**
>
> **Minimum stock level** or **safety stock** = re-order level − (average usage × average lead time)
>
> It is the stock level set for control purposes below which stockholding should not fall without being highlighted.

3.20 The minimum level acts as a warning to management that stocks are approaching a dangerously low level and that stockouts are possible.

> **KEY TERM**
>
> **Average stock** = Minimum level + $\dfrac{\text{re} - \text{order quantity}}{2}$

3.21 This formula assumes that stock levels fluctuate evenly between the minimum (or safety) stock level and the highest possible stock level (the amount of stock immediately after an order is received, safety stock and reorder quantity).

The effect of discounts

3.22 The solution obtained from using the simple EOQ formula may need to be modified if bulk discounts (also called quantity discounts) are available.

Part D: Working capital management

3.23 To decide mathematically whether it would be worthwhile taking a discount and ordering larger quantities, it is necessary to minimise the total of:

- Total material costs
- Ordering costs
- Stock holding costs

3.24 The total cost will be minimised:

- At the pre-discount EOQ level, so that a discount is not worthwhile, or
- At the minimum order size necessary to earn the discount

3.25 EXAMPLE: BULK DISCOUNTS

The annual demand for an item of stock is 45 units. The item costs £200 a unit to purchase, the holding cost for one unit for one year is 15% of the unit cost and ordering costs are £300 an order. The supplier offers a 3% discount for orders of 60 units or more, and a discount of 5% for orders of 90 units or more. What is the cost-minimising order size?

3.26 SOLUTION

(a) The EOQ ignoring discounts is:

$$\sqrt{\frac{2 \times 300 \times 45}{15\% \text{ of } 200}} = 30 \text{ units}$$

	£
Purchases (no discount) 45 × £200	9,000
Holding costs 15 units × £30	450
Ordering costs 1.5 orders × £300	450
Total annual costs	9,900

(b) With a discount of 3% and an order quantity of 60 units costs are as follows.

	£
Purchases £9,000 × 97%	8,730
Holding costs 30 units × 15% of 97% of £200	873
Ordering costs 0.75 orders × £300	225
Total annual costs	9,828

(c) With a discount of 5% and an order quantity of 90 units costs are as follows.

	£
Purchases £9,000 × 95%	8,550.0
Holding costs 45 units × 15% of 95% of £200	1,282.5
Ordering costs 0.5 orders × £300	150.0
Total annual costs	9,982.5

The cheapest option is to order 60 units at a time.

Note that the value of h varied according to the size of the discount, because h was a percentage of the purchase cost. This means that total holding costs are reduced because of a discount. This could easily happen if, for example, most of h was the cost of insurance, based on the cost of stock held.

Question 3

A company uses an item of stock as follows.

Purchase price:	£96 per unit
Annual demand:	4,000 units
Ordering cost:	£300

Annual holding cost: 10% of purchase price
Economic order quantity: 500 units

Should the company order 1,000 units at a time in order to secure an 8% discount?

Answer

The total annual cost at the economic order quantity of 500 units is as follows.

	£
Purchases 4,000 × £96	384,000
Ordering costs £300 × (4,000/500)	2,400
Holding costs £96 × 10% × (500/2)	2,400
	388,800

The total annual cost at an order quantity of 1,000 units would be as follows.

	£
Purchases £384,000 × 92%	353,280
Ordering costs £300 × (4,000/1,000)	1,200
Holding costs £96 × 92% × 10% × (1,000/2)	4,416
	358,896

The company should order the item 1,000 units at a time, saving £(388,800 − 358,896) = £29,904 a year.

Just-in-time (JIT) procurement   5/02

3.27 **Just-in-time procurement** means obtaining goods from suppliers at the **latest possible time** (ie when they are needed on the production line), thus **avoiding the need to carry** any materials or component stock. **Deliveries** will be **small and frequent** rather than in bulk.

3.28 **Just-in-time procurement** thus implies a mutually beneficial working relationship with suppliers. The aim is that suppliers **guarantee to deliver** raw materials components of **appropriate quality** always **on time**. In return the suppliers receive a long – term commitment to purchase their goods. **Unit purchasing prices** may need to be **higher** than in a conventional system to meet more rigorous quality and delivery requirements. However savings in production costs and reductions in working capital should offset these costs.

3.29 **Lean manufacturing** implies a smooth and predictable production flow, with setup costs and time minimised. The aim is to **match production** with ultimate **demand**, and so work is only carried out in response to customer wishes.

3.30 Production should be organised so that **transfer times** of raw materials and work-in-progress are **kept** to an **absolute minimum**. The maintenance programme should be sufficiently rigorous to stop machinery breaking down.

3.31 The **workforce** is a key element in lean manufacturing. **Flexibility** and **multi-skilling** will minimise production delay caused by shortage or absence of staff. There also needs to be an emphasis on **eliminating poor quality production**, as scrapping work in progress and producing additional units can lead to delays.

3.32 Introducing JIT/lean manufacturing might bring the following potential benefits.

- Reduction in stock holding costs
- Reduced manufacturing lead times
- Improved labour productivity
- Reduced scrap/rework/warranty costs

Part D: Working capital management

- Price reductions on purchased materials
- Reduction in the number of accounting transactions

3.33 JIT will not be appropriate in all cases. For example, a restaurant might find it preferable to use the traditional economic order quantity approach for staple non-perishable food stocks but adopt JIT for perishable and 'exotic' items. In a hospital, a stock-out could quite literally be fatal and JIT would be quite unsuitable.

4 PURCHASING

4.1 Purchases can account for a major part of a company's expenditure, but rarely get subjected to the planning and control constraints that are experienced by other business functions. This comment is not true of all branches of industry and commerce. In high street stores, 'buying' is recognised as one of the most important functions of the business.

4.2 The effectiveness of the purchasing function affects profit in three ways.

(a) Effective purchasing ensures the best **value for money** is obtained by the firm.

(b) Effective purchasing assists in **meeting quality targets**. Again this has an impact on a firm's long-term marketing strategy, if quality is an issue.

(c) An effective purchasing strategy minimises the amount of purchased **material held in stock**.

The purchasing mix

4.3 The purchasing manager has to obtain the best purchasing **quantity, quality, price,** and **delivery arrangements**. Purchasing may be **centralised** or **decentralised**. The **purchasing mix** has implications for JIT and quality management.

PURCHASING MIX	
Quantity	Size and timing of orders dictated by balance between delays in production caused by insufficient stock and costs of stock-holding
Quality	Quality of goods required for the manufacturing process, and the quality of goods acceptable to customers
Price	Short-term trends may influence, but best value over period of time is most important
Delivery	Lead time between placing and delivery of an order and reliability of suppliers' delivery arrangements

Question 4

If a company operates a JIT production system, what does this imply for purchasing?

Answer

(a) JIT systems and stockless production require the receipt of goods from suppliers at the latest possible time (ie when they are needed), to avoid the need to carry any materials or components in stock.

(b) JIT seeks to avoid defects. Supplies must be of high quality to eliminate waste, as the quality of components can affect the quality of the end product.

Thus reliability of delivery and certainty of quality are as important (if not more so) as price.

23: Managing creditors and stock

SUPPLY STRATEGY	
Sources of supply	Available sources, their location, reliability, importance of yourself to them
Spread of supply	Single source to get bulk discounts and minimise costs, or dual sourcing to avoid lost production and complacency
Cost of supplies	Speed of achievement of cost discounts through volume purchases
Make or buy decision	More efficient to make goods in-house?
Suitability of existing supplier	Producing goods to required standard, ability to improve quality
Image or reputation of supplier	Selling point to buyer's customers eg makes of car supplied by car rental firms

Building supplier relationships

4.4 Many companies are seeking to build up **long-term relationships with suppliers**, often offering them advice and help with product development, manufacturing processes and quality. This often leads to a reduction in the number of suppliers a firm deals with. This policy is a means of **ensuring consistency** of bought-in component quality, and facilitates JIT production.

(a) **Advantages** of closer relationships with suppliers include:

- Sharing of information
- Better co-ordination
- The security of the relationship enables long-term planning
- Equipment and components are consistent and compatible
- Convenience for ordering supplies
- Discounts for bulk purchases
- Preferred customer status and better service agreements
- Products, upgrades and advice tailored to specific needs

(b) **Disadvantages**

- Dependence on a supplier inhibits a firm's freedom
- It may turn out more expensive
- The balance of power might be unequal

Question 5

Walker plc is entering into a rental agreement for the use of a new building. Payments to the landlord will be made quarterly. What is the best payment method for Walker to use?

A   Cheque
B   Standing order
C   Direct debit
D   Bankers draft

Answer

B   Standing orders provide for regular payments to be made by the bank to the supplier. They are preferable to direct debits because control of the amount of the payment is retained by the person making the payment.

Part D: Working capital management

Chapter roundup

- Effective management of **trade creditors** involves seeking satisfactory credit terms from suppliers, getting credit extended during periods of cash shortage, and maintaining good relations with suppliers.

- Trade creditors are a useful and cheap **source of finance,** but a successful business needs to ensure that it is seen as a good credit risk by its suppliers. Some creditors must be paid on specific dates. This must be remembered and cash must be available.

- A business will use a variety of methods to make payments. Ignoring payroll (wages and salaries) and petty cash, the most common and convenient methods of payment are by **cheque** and by **BACS**. **Other payment methods** are often arranged at the insistence of the supplier, and this explains much of the use of banker's drafts, standing orders and telegraphic transfers. **Direct debits** are not often used for payments by businesses, but might occasionally be used for convenience.

- Some businesses have a substantial proportion of their total assets tied up in **stocks**. Financial aspects of stock management consist of keeping the costs of procuring and holding stock to a minimum. The aim of **Just-in-Time** is to hold as little stock as possible and production systems need to be very efficient to achieve this.

- Purchasing may be **centralised** or **decentralised**. The optimal mix of **quantity, quality, price** and **delivery arrangements** should be sought.

Quick quiz

1. Cost of lost cash discount = $\left(\dfrac{100}{100-d}\right)^{\frac{365}{t}} - 1$. What do d and t represent?

2. Avery Ltd has been offered a cash discount of 2% by one of its suppliers if it settles its accounts within 10 days. Avery currently takes 60 days credit from the supplier. What is the implied cost in interest per annum to the nearest whole % if Avery decides not to take the discount?

    A   2%
    B   12%
    C   16%
    D   24%

3. The basic EOQ formula for stocks indicates whether bulk discounts should be taken advantage of.

    True ☐
    False ☐

4. What do BACS and CHAPS stand for?

5. Identify the potential benefits of JIT manufacturing.

6. The Economic Order Quantity can be expressed as follows:

    $$\sqrt{\dfrac{2C_oD}{C_h}}$$

    What does C_h describe in this formula?

    A   The cost of holding one unit of stock for one year
    B   The cost of placing one order
    C   The cost of a unit of stock
    D   The customer demand for the item

7. Using the following information:

    Max lead time = 5 days
    Min lead time = 2 days
    Average lead time = 3 days
    Reorder level = 100 units

Reorder quantity = 150 units
Maximum usage = 60 units
Average usage = 30 units
Minimum usage = 20 units

Calculate the maximum level of stock.

8 Calculate the minimum level of stock.

Answers to quick quiz

1   d is the percentage discount given.
    t is the reduction in payment period to obtain this discount (in days)

2   C   In this case:

$$\left(\frac{100}{100-2}\right)^{\frac{365}{50}} - 1 = 15.9\%, \text{ say } 16\%$$

3   False. It may be necessary to modify the formula to take account of bulk discounts.

4   Bankers' Automated Clearing Services; Clearing House Automated Payment System.

5   (a) Reduction in stock holding costs
    (b) Reduced manufacturing lead times
    (c) Improved labour productivity
    (d) Reduced scrap/rework/warranty costs
    (e) Price reductions on purchased materials
    (f) Reduction in the number of accounting transactions

6   A   The cost of holding one unit of stock for one year

7   Maximum level of stock = re-order level + re-order quantity − (minimum usage × minimum lead time)
    = 100 + 150 − (20 × 2)
    = 210 units

8   Minimum level of stock = re-order level − (average usage × average lead time)
    = 100 − (30 × 3)
    = 10 units

Now try the question below from the Exam Question Bank

Number	Level	Marks	Time
23	Examination	20	36 mins

Appendix
Mathematical tables and exam formulae

PRESENT VALUE TABLE

Present value of £1 ie $(1+r)^{-n}$ where r = interest rate, n = number of periods until payment or receipt.

Periods (n)	\multicolumn{10}{c}{Interest rates (r)}									
	1%	2%	3%	4%	5%	6%	7%	8%	9%	10%
1	0.990	0.980	0.971	0.962	0.952	0.943	0.935	0.926	0.917	0.909
2	0.980	0.961	0.943	0.925	0.907	0.890	0.873	0.857	0.842	0.826
3	0.971	0.942	0.915	0.889	0.864	0.840	0.816	0.794	0.772	0.751
4	0.961	0.924	0.888	0.855	0.823	0.792	0.763	0.735	0.708	0.683
5	0.951	0.906	0.863	0.822	0.784	0.747	0.713	0.681	0.650	0.621
6	0.942	0.888	0.837	0.790	0.746	0.705	0.666	0.630	0.596	0.564
7	0.933	0.871	0.813	0.760	0.711	0.665	0.623	0.583	0.547	0.513
8	0.923	0.853	0.789	0.731	0.677	0.627	0.582	0.540	0.502	0.467
9	0.914	0.837	0.766	0.703	0.645	0.592	0.544	0.500	0.460	0.424
10	0.905	0.820	0.744	0.676	0.614	0.558	0.508	0.463	0.422	0.386
11	0.896	0.804	0.722	0.650	0.585	0.527	0.475	0.429	0.388	0.350
12	0.887	0.788	0.701	0.625	0.557	0.497	0.444	0.397	0.356	0.319
13	0.879	0.773	0.681	0.601	0.530	0.469	0.415	0.368	0.326	0.290
14	0.870	0.758	0.661	0.577	0.505	0.442	0.388	0.340	0.299	0.263
15	0.861	0.743	0.642	0.555	0.481	0.417	0.362	0.315	0.275	0.239
16	0.853	0.728	0.623	0.534	0.458	0.394	0.339	0.292	0.252	0.218
17	0.844	0.714	0.605	0.513	0.436	0.371	0.317	0.270	0.231	0.198
18	0.836	0.700	0.587	0.494	0.416	0.350	0.296	0.250	0.212	0.180
19	0.828	0.686	0.570	0.475	0.396	0.331	0.277	0.232	0.194	0.164
20	0.820	0.673	0.554	0.456	0.377	0.312	0.258	0.215	0.178	0.149

Periods (n)	Interest rates (r)									
	11%	12%	13%	14%	15%	16%	17%	18%	19%	20%
1	0.901	0.893	0.885	0.877	0.870	0.862	0.855	0.847	0.840	0.833
2	0.812	0.797	0.783	0.769	0.756	0.743	0.731	0.718	0.706	0.694
3	0.731	0.712	0.693	0.675	0.658	0.641	0.624	0.609	0.593	0.579
4	0.659	0.636	0.613	0.592	0.572	0.552	0.534	0.516	0.499	0.482
5	0.593	0.567	0.543	0.519	0.497	0.476	0.456	0.437	0.419	0.402
6	0.535	0.507	0.480	0.456	0.432	0.410	0.390	0.370	0.352	0.335
7	0.482	0.452	0.425	0.400	0.376	0.354	0.333	0.314	0.296	0.279
8	0.434	0.404	0.376	0.351	0.327	0.305	0.285	0.266	0.249	0.233
9	0.391	0.361	0.333	0.308	0.284	0.263	0.243	0.225	0.209	0.194
10	0.352	0.322	0.295	0.270	0.247	0.227	0.208	0.191	0.176	0.162
11	0.317	0.287	0.261	0.237	0.215	0.195	0.178	0.162	0.148	0.135
12	0.286	0.257	0.231	0.208	0.187	0.168	0.152	0.137	0.124	0.112
13	0.258	0.229	0.204	0.182	0.163	0.145	0.130	0.116	0.104	0.093
14	0.232	0.205	0.181	0.160	0.141	0.125	0.111	0.099	0.088	0.078
15	0.209	0.183	0.160	0.140	0.123	0.108	0.095	0.084	0.074	0.065
16	0.188	0.163	0.141	0.123	0.107	0.093	0.081	0.071	0.062	0.054
17	0.170	0.146	0.125	0.108	0.093	0.080	0.069	0.060	0.052	0.045
18	0.153	0.130	0.111	0.095	0.081	0.069	0.059	0.051	0.044	0.038
19	0.138	0.116	0.098	0.083	0.070	0.060	0.051	0.043	0.037	0.031
20	0.124	0.104	0.087	0.073	0.061	0.051	0.043	0.037	0.031	0.026

Mathematical tables

CUMULATIVE PRESENT VALUE TABLE

This table shows the present value of £1 per annum, receivable or payable at the end of each year for n years $\frac{1-(1+r)^{-n}}{r}$.

Periods (n)	\multicolumn{10}{c}{Interest rates (r)}									
	1%	2%	3%	4%	5%	6%	7%	8%	9%	10%
1	0.990	0.980	0.971	0.962	0.952	0.943	0.935	0.926	0.917	0.909
2	1.970	1.942	1.913	1.886	1.859	1.833	1.808	1.783	1.759	1.736
3	2.941	2.884	2.829	2.775	2.723	2.673	2.624	2.577	2.531	2.487
4	3.902	3.808	3.717	3.630	3.546	3.465	3.387	3.312	3.240	3.170
5	4.853	4.713	4.580	4.452	4.329	4.212	4.100	3.993	3.890	3.791
6	5.795	5.601	5.417	5.242	5.076	4.917	4.767	4.623	4.486	4.355
7	6.728	6.472	6.230	6.002	5.786	5.582	5.389	5.206	5.033	4.868
8	7.652	7.325	7.020	6.733	6.463	6.210	5.971	5.747	5.535	5.335
9	8.566	8.162	7.786	7.435	7.108	6.802	6.515	6.247	5.995	5.759
10	9.471	8.983	8.530	8.111	7.722	7.360	7.024	6.710	6.418	6.145
11	10.368	9.787	9.253	8.760	8.306	7.887	7.499	7.139	6.805	6.495
12	11.255	10.575	9.954	9.385	8.863	8.384	7.943	7.536	7.161	6.814
13	12.134	11.348	10.635	9.986	9.394	8.853	8.358	7.904	7.487	7.103
14	13.004	12.106	11.296	10.563	9.899	9.295	8.745	8.244	7.786	7.367
15	13.865	12.849	11.938	11.118	10.380	9.712	9.108	8.559	8.061	7.606
16	14.718	13.578	12.561	11.652	10.838	10.106	9.447	8.851	8.313	7.824
17	15.562	14.292	13.166	12.166	11.274	10.477	9.763	9.122	8.544	8.022
18	16.398	14.992	13.754	12.659	11.690	10.828	10.059	9.372	8.756	8.201
19	17.226	15.679	14.324	13.134	12.085	11.158	10.336	9.604	8.950	8.365
20	18.046	16.351	14.878	13.590	12.462	11.470	10.594	9.818	9.129	8.514

Periods (n)	\multicolumn{10}{c}{Interest rates (r)}									
	11%	12%	13%	14%	15%	16%	17%	18%	19%	20%
1	0.901	0.893	0.885	0.877	0.870	0.862	0.855	0.847	0.840	0.833
2	1.713	1.690	1.668	1.647	1.626	1.605	1.585	1.566	1.547	1.528
3	2.444	2.402	2.361	2.322	2.283	2.246	2.210	2.174	2.140	2.106
4	3.102	3.037	2.974	2.914	2.855	2.798	2.743	2.690	2.639	2.589
5	3.696	3.605	3.517	3.433	3.352	3.274	3.199	3.127	3.058	2.991
6	4.231	4.111	3.998	3.889	3.784	3.685	3.589	3.498	3.410	3.326
7	4.712	4.564	4.423	4.288	4.160	4.039	3.922	3.812	3.706	3.605
8	5.146	4.968	4.799	4.639	4.487	4.344	4.207	4.078	3.954	3.837
9	5.537	5.328	5.132	4.946	4.772	4.607	4.451	4.303	4.163	4.031
10	5.889	5.650	5.426	5.216	5.019	4.833	4.659	4.494	4.339	4.192
11	6.207	5.938	5.687	5.453	5.234	5.029	4.836	4.656	4.486	4.327
12	6.492	6.194	5.918	5.660	5.421	5.197	4.988	4.793	4.611	4.439
13	6.750	6.424	6.122	5.842	5.583	5.342	5.118	4.910	4.715	4.533
14	6.982	6.628	6.302	6.002	5.724	5.468	5.229	5.008	4.802	4.611
15	7.191	6.811	6.462	6.142	5.847	5.575	5.324	5.092	4.876	4.675
16	7.379	6.974	6.604	6.265	5.954	5.668	5.405	5.162	4.938	4.730
17	7.549	7.120	6.729	6.373	6.047	5.749	5.475	5.222	4.990	4.775
18	7.702	7.250	6.840	6.467	6.128	5.818	5.534	5.273	5.033	4.812
19	7.839	7.366	6.938	6.550	6.198	5.877	5.584	5.316	5.070	4.843
20	7.963	7.469	7.025	6.623	6.259	5.929	5.628	5.353	5.101	4.870

EXAM FORMULAE

Valuation models

(i) Irredeemable preference share, paying a constant annual dividend, d, in perpetuity, where P_0 is the ex-div value:

$$P_0 = \frac{d}{k_{pref}}$$

(ii) Ordinary (equity) share, paying a constant annual dividend, d, in perpetuity, where P_0 is the ex-div value:

$$P_0 = \frac{d}{k_e}$$

(iii) Ordinary (equity) share, paying an annual dividend, d, growing in perpetuity at a constant rate, g, where P_0 is the ex-div value:

$$P_0 = \frac{d_1}{k_e - g} \text{ or } P_0 = \frac{d_0[1+g]}{k_e - g}$$

(iv) Irredeemable (undated) debt, paying annual after tax interest, i(1 – t), in perpetuity, where P_0 is the ex-interest value:

$$P_0 = \frac{i[1-t]}{k_{d\,net}}$$

or, without tax:

$$P_0 = \frac{i}{k_d}$$

(v) Future value of S, of a sum X, invested for n periods, discounted at r% interest per annum:

$$S = X[1 + r]^n$$

(vi) Present value of £1 payable or receivable in n years, discounted at r% per annum:

$$PV = \frac{1}{[1+r]^n}$$

(vii) Present value of an annuity of £1 per annum, receivable or payable for n years, commencing in one year, discounted at r% per annum:

$$PV = \frac{1}{r}\left[1 - \frac{1}{[1+r]^n}\right]$$

(viii) Present value of £1 per annum, payable or receivable in perpetuity, commencing in one year, discounted at r% per annum:

$$PV = \frac{1}{r}$$

(ix) Present value of £1 per annum, receivable or payable, commencing in one year, growing in perpetuity at a constant rate of g% per annum, discounted at r% per annum:

$$PV = \frac{1}{r - g}$$

Exam formulae

Cost of capital

(i) Cost of irredeemable preference capital, paying an annual dividend d in perpetuity, and having a current ex-div price P_0:

$$k_{pref} = \frac{d}{P_0}$$

(ii) Cost of irredeemable debt capital, paying annual net interest $i(1-t)$, and having a current ex-interest price P_0:

$$k_{d\,net} = \frac{i[1-t]}{P_0}$$

(iii) Cost of ordinary (equity) share capital, paying an annual dividend d in perpetuity, and having a current ex div price P_0:

$$k_e = \frac{d}{P_0}$$

(iv) Cost of ordinary (equity) share capital, having a current ex div price, P_0, having just paid a dividend, d_0, with the dividend growing in perpetuity by a constant g% per annum:

$$k_e = \frac{d_1}{P_0} + g \quad \text{or} \quad k_e = \frac{d_0[1+g]}{P_0} + g$$

(v) Cost of ordinary (equity) share capital, using the CAPM: $k_e = R_f + [R_m - R_f]\beta$

(vi) Weighted average cost of capital, k_0: $k_0 = k_e\left[\dfrac{V_E}{V_E + V_D}\right] + k_d\left[\dfrac{V_D}{V_E + V_D}\right]$

Stock management

(i) Economic Order Quantity $EOQ = \sqrt{\dfrac{2C_oD}{C_h}}$

Where C_o = cost of placing an order $\qquad$ D = annual demand
C_h = cost of holding one unit in stock for one year

Cash management

(i) Optimal sale of securities, Baumol model:

$$\text{Optimal sale} = \sqrt{\frac{2 \times \text{Annual cash disbursements} \times \text{Cost per sale of securities}}{\text{Interest rate}}}$$

(ii) Spread between upper and lower cash balance limits, Miller-Orr model:

$$\text{Spread} = 3\left[\frac{\frac{3}{4} \times \text{transaction cost} \times \text{variance of cash flows}}{\text{Interest rate}}\right]^{\frac{1}{3}}$$

Other

Theoretical ex-rights price

$$\text{TERP} = \frac{1}{N+1}((N \times \text{cum rights price}) + \text{issue price})$$

Where n = number of shares required to buy one new share

Exam question and answer bank

Exam question bank

Examination standard questions are indicated by marks.

1 CORPORATE OBJECTIVES *20 mins*

Explain whether a quoted company's directors seek only the maximisation of the company's profit.

2 FINANCIAL INTERMEDIATION *20 mins*

Explain in detail the various functions performed by financial intermediaries in the financial markets.

3 MARKET EFFICIENCY *20 mins*

Explain the implications for market efficiency of the fact that very few financial intermediaries are able to out-perform the market on a regular basis.

4 KM PLC (Pilot paper) *36 mins*

The finance director of KM plc has recently reorganised the finance department following a number of years of growth within the business, which now includes a number of overseas operations. The company now has separate treasury and financial control departments.

Required

(a) Describe the main responsibilities of a treasury department, and comment on the advantages to KM plc of having separate treasury and financial control departments. **14 Marks**

(b) Identify the advantages and disadvantages of operating the treasury department as a profit centre rather than a cost centre. **6 Marks**

Total Marks = 20

5 PRIMULA PLC *30 mins*

Primula plc is an all equity financed, listed company which operates in the food processing industry. The Primula family owns 40% of the ordinary shares; the remainder are held by large financial institutions. There are 10 million £1 ordinary shares currently in issue.

The company has just finalised a long-term contract to supply a large chain of restaurants with a variety of food products. The contract requires investment in new machinery costing £24 million. This machinery would become operational on 1 January 20X2, and payment would be made on the same date. Sales would commence immediately thereafter.

Primula is considering a 2-for-5 rights issue to finance the new investment.

Required

(a) Calculate the issue and ex rights share prices of Primula plc assuming a 2-for-5 rights issue is used to finance the new project at 1 January 20X2. Ignore taxation.

(b) Write a report to the directors of Primula plc which:

(i) Discusses the advantages and disadvantages of using a rights issue to raise the necessary funds.

(ii) Explains and evaluates the appropriateness of the following alternative methods of issuing equity finance *in the specific circumstances* of Primula plc:

(1) A placing
(2) An offer for sale
(3) A public offer for subscription

6 KB PLC (Pilot paper) *36 mins*

(a) KB plc has a paid-up ordinary share capital of £1,500,000 represented by 6 million shares of 25p each. It has no loan capital. Earnings after tax in the most recent year were £1,200,000. The P/E ratio of the company is 12.

Exam question bank

The company is planning to make a large new investment which will cost £5,040,000, and is considering raising the necessary finance through a rights issue at 192p.

Required

(i) Calculate the current market price of KB plc's ordinary shares.

(*Note:* Market price = Price/earnings ratio × Earnings per share) **2 Marks**

(ii) Calculate the theoretical ex-rights price, and state what factors in practice might invalidate your calculation. **6 Marks**

(iii) Briefly explain what is meant by a deep-discounted rights issue, identifying the main reasons why a company might raise finance by this method. **3 Marks**

(b) As an alternative to a rights issue, KB plc might raise the £5,040,000 required by means of an issue of convertible loan stock at par, with a coupon rate of 6%. The loan stock would be redeemable in seven years' time. Prior to redemption, the loan stock may be converted at a rate of 35 ordinary shares per £100 nominal loan stock.

Required

(i) Explain the term *conversion premium* and calculate the conversion premium at the date of issue implicit in the data given. **4 Marks**

(ii) Identify the advantages to KB plc of issuing convertible loan stock instead of the rights issue to raise the necessary finance. **5 Marks**

Total Marks = 20

7 FEATURES *36 mins*

(a) Briefly explain the main features of the following.

(i) Sale and leaseback
(ii) Hire purchase
(iii) Financial leasing **6 Marks**

(b) Prime Printing plc has the opportunity to replace one of its pieces of printing equipment. The new machine, costing £120,000, is expected to lead to operating savings of £50,000 per annum and have an economic life of five years. The company's after tax cost of capital for the investment is estimated at 15% and operating cash flows are taxed at a rate of 30%, one year in arrears.

The company is trying to decide whether to fund the acquisition of the machine via a five-year bank loan, at an annual interest rate of 13%, with the principal repayable at the end of the five-year period. As an alternative, the machine could be acquired using a finance lease, at a cost of £28,000 pa for five years, payable in advance. The machine would have zero scrap value at the end of five years.

Note. Due to its current tax position, the company is unable to utilise any capital allowances on the purchase until year one.

Required

Assuming that writing-down allowances of 25% pa are available on a reducing balance basis, recommend, with reasons, whether Prime Printing should replace the machine, and if so whether it should buy or lease. **14 Marks**

Total Marks = 20

8 CRYSTAL PLC *35 mins*

The following figures have been extracted from the most recent accounts of Crystal plc.

BALANCE SHEET AS ON 30 JUNE 20X9

	£'000	£'000
Fixed assets		10,115
Investments		821
Current assets	3,658	
Less current liabilities	1,735	
		1,923
		12,859

		£'000	£'000
Ordinary share capital			
Authorised: 4,000,000 shares of £1			
Issued: 3,000,000 shares of £1			3,000
Reserves			6,542
Shareholders' funds			9,542
7% Debentures			1,300
Deferred taxation			583
Corporation tax			1,434
			12,859

Summary of profits and dividends

Year ended 30 June:	20X5	20X6	20X7	20X8	20X9
	£'000	£'000	£'000	£'000	£'000
Profit after interest and before tax	1,737	2,090	1,940	1,866	2,179
Less tax	573	690	640	616	719
Profit after interest and tax	1,164	1,400	1,300	1,250	1,460
Less dividends	620	680	740	740	810
Added to reserves	544	720	560	510	650

The current (1 July 20X9) market value of Crystal plc's ordinary shares is £3.27 per share cum div. An annual dividend of £810,000 is due for payment shortly. The debentures are redeemable at par in ten years time. Their current market value is £77.10 per cent. Annual interest has just been paid on the debentures. There have been no issues or redemptions of ordinary shares or debentures during the past five years.

The current rate of corporation tax is 30%, and the current basic rate of income tax is 25%. Assume that there have been no changes in the system or rates of taxation during the last five years.

Required

(a) Calculate the cost of capital which Crystal plc should use as a discount rate when appraising new investment opportunities.

(b) Discuss any difficulties and uncertainties in your estimates.

9 TOVELL PLC

15 mins

The selection of appropriate discount rates for capital investments has frequently been a problem for the finance director of Tovell plc. The company has adopted a strategy of diversification into many different industries, in order to reduce risk for the company's shareholders. This has resulted in frequent changes in the company's gearing level and widely fluctuating risks of individual investments.

The current project under appraisal, an investment in the fast food industry where Tovell has no other investments, is expected to generate pre-tax operating cash flows of £420,000 in the first year, rising by 5% per year for the five year expected life of the project. After five years the land and buildings are expected to have a realisable value of £1,250,000 (after any tax effects), the same as their original cost, but in order to continue operations major new investment in equipment would be required at that time. Other fixed assets would have negligible value after five years. The total initial outlay of the project (net of issue costs) is £2.3 million.

The project would be financed by a £800,000 fixed rate loan from a regional development agency at a subsidised interest rate of 3% less than Tovell could borrow at in the capital market. The remainder of the finance would be provided by an underwritten rights issue at a 10% discount on current market price, with total underwriting and issue costs of 5% of gross proceeds. The investment is believed to add £1 million to the company's debt capacity.

Current financial data for Tovell and the fast food industry includes the following.

	Tovell plc	Fast food industry (average)
P/E ratio	12	20
Dividend yield	5%	3%
Gearing (debt/equity):		
Book values	1.1 to 1	1.6 to 1
Market values	0.4 to 1	1 to 1
Share price	470 pence	n/a
Number of ordinary shares	3.5 million	n/a

Exam question bank

Required

Explain whether you would support the company's strategy of diversifying into many different industries.

10 D PLC (Pilot paper amended) *36 mins*

The summarised balance sheet of D plc at 30 June 20X9 was as follows.

	£'000	£'000
Fixed assets		15,350
Current assets	5,900	
Creditors falling due within one year	(2,600)	
Net current assets		3,300
9% debentures		(8,000)
		10,650
Ordinary share capital (25p shares)		2,000
7% preference shares (£1 shares)		1,000
Share premium account		1,100
Profit and loss account		6,550
		10,650

The current price of the ordinary shares is 135p ex dividend. The dividend of 10p is payable during the next few days. The expected rate of growth of the dividend is 9% per annum. The current price of the preference shares is 77p and the dividend has recently been paid. The debenture interest has also been paid recently and the debentures are currently trading at £80 per £100 nominal. Corporation tax is at the rate of 30%.

Required

(a) Calculate the gearing ratio for D plc using:

  (i) Book values
  (ii) Market values

  Note: Gearing = $\dfrac{\text{Prior charge capital}}{\text{Prior charge capital} + \text{Equity}}$

  Prior charge capital is preference shares and debentures.

  For the book value calculation, equity is ordinary share capital, share premium account and profit and loss account.

  For the market value calculation, equity is *just* the market value of ordinary shares (ignore share premium and profit and loss account). **4 Marks**

(b) Calculate the company's weighted average cost of capital (WACC), using the respective market values as weighting factors. **6 Marks**

Assume that D plc issued the debentures one year ago to finance a new investment.

(c) Discuss the reasons why D plc may have issued debentures rather than preference shares to raise the required finance. **4 Marks**

(d) Explain what services a merchant bank may have provided to D plc in connection with the raising of this finance. **6 Marks**

Total Marks = 20

11 YEAR-END STATISTICS *36 mins*

The directors of X plc are comparing some of the company's year-end statistics with those of Y plc, the company's main competitor. X plc has had a fairly normal year in terms of profit but Y plc's latest profits have been severely reduced by an exceptional loss arising from the closure of an unsuccessful division. Y plc has a considerably higher level of financial gearing than X plc.

The board is focusing on the figures given below.

	X plc	Y plc
Share price	450p	525p
Nominal value of shares	50p	100p
Gross earnings yield	8.89%	5.33%
Gross dividend yield	5%	4%
Price/earnings ratio	15	25
Proportion of profits earned overseas	60%	0%

In the course of the discussion a number of comments are made, including those given below.

Required

Discuss comments (a) to (e), making use of the above data where appropriate.

(a) 'There is something odd about the p/e ratios. Y plc has had a particularly bad year. Its p/e should surely be lower than ours.' **4 Marks**

(b) 'Y plc's earnings yield is lower than ours. This gives them the benefit of a lower cost of capital.' **4 Marks**

(c) 'One of the factors which may explain Y plc's high p/e is the high financial gearing.' **4 Marks**

(d) 'The comparison of our own p/e ratio, gross dividend yield and gross earnings yield with those of Y plc is not really valid. The shares of the two companies have different nominal values.' **4 Marks**

(e) 'These figures will not please our shareholders. The dividend yield is below the return an investor could currently obtain on risk-free government bonds.' **4 Marks**

Total Marks = 20

12 YIELDS *36 mins*

(a) Describe what a yield curve is. **6 Marks**

(b) Explain the extent to which the shape of the yield curve depend on expectations about the future. **14 Marks**

Total Marks = 20

13 MARKETABLE SECURITIES *35 mins*

RT plc has forecast the following cash movements for the next six months.

Cash available now	£2,000,000
Inflow in two months	£4,000,000
Outflow in four months	£2,000,000
Outflow in six months	£4,000,000

Assume that all movements of cash take place on the *last day* of each two-month period.

The structure of short-term interest rates is as follows.

Current		Expected in 2 months		Expected in 4 months	
Maturity period	Annual yield %	Maturity period	Annual yield %	Maturity period	Annual yield %
2 months	7.3	2 months	8.0	2 months	8.3
4 months	7.4	4 months	8.1	4 months	8.4
6 months	7.5	6 months	8.2	6 months	8.3

The company invests surplus cash balances in marketable securities. Company policy is to hold such securities to maturity once they are purchased. Every purchase transaction of marketable securities costs £100.

Tasks

(a) Calculate which securities should be purchased to maximise income.

(b) Discuss the criteria that would influence a company's procedure for selecting marketable securities.

Exam question bank

14 A BRICKIE (BUILDERS) LTD *30 mins*

A Brickie (Builders) Ltd is a medium-sized private company to which you have recently been appointed as the assistant financial controller. The company is currently engaged in a business expansion programme for which additional finance will be required. It is not currently feasible to raise additional equity finance, consequently debt finance is being considered. The decision has not yet been finalised whether this debt finance will be short or long term and if it is to be at fixed or variable rates. The financial controller has asked you, as part of your first assignment, to assist her in the preparation of information for a forthcoming meeting of the Board of Directors.

Required

Prepare a draft report to the Board of Directors which identifies and briefly discusses:

(a) Four main factors to be considered when deciding on the appropriate mix of long-term or short-term sources of debt finance for the company.

(b) Two main advantages of fixing interest rates on debt.

15 AARDVARK LTD *20 mins*

Aardvark Ltd has been having some difficulty with the collection of debts from export customers. At present the company makes no special arrangements for export sales.

As a result the company is considering either employing the services of a non-recourse export factoring company, or insuring its exports against non-payment through an insurer. The two alternatives also provide possible ways of financing sales.

An export factor will, if required, provide immediate finance of 80% of export credit sales at an interest rate of 2% above bank base rate (the base rate is 8%). The service fee for debt collection is 3% of credit sales. If the factor is used, administrative savings of £35,000 a year should be possible.

A comprehensive insurance policy costs 35 pence per £100 insured and covers 90% of the risk of non-payment for exports. The insurer will probably allow Aardvark Ltd to assign its rights to a bank, in return for which the bank will provide an advance of 70% of the sales value of insured debts, at a cost of 1.5% above base rate.

Aardvark's annual exports total £1,000,000. Export sales are on open account terms of 60 days credit, but on average payments have been 30 days late. Approximately 0.5%, by value, of credit sales result in bad debts which have to be written off. The company is able to borrow on overdraft from its bank, unsecured, at 2.5% above base rate. Assume a 360 day year.

Required

Recommend which combination of export administration and financing Aardvark Ltd should use.

16 WORKING CAPITAL *36 mins*

(a) Define what is meant by the term 'overtrading' and describe some of the typical symptoms.

6 Marks

(b) Gustaffson plc is a toy manufacturing company. It manufactures Polly Playtime, the latest doll craze amongst young girls. The company is now at full production of the doll. The final accounts for 20X9 have just been published and are as follows. 20X8's accounts are also shown for comparison purposes.

PROFIT AND LOSS ACCOUNT Y/E 31 DECEMBER

	20X9	20X8
	£'000	£'000
Sales	30,000	20,000
Cost of sales	20,000	11,000
Operating profit	10,000	9,000
Interest	450	400
Profit before tax	9,550	8,600
Tax	2,000	1,200
Profit after tax	7,550	7,400
Dividends	2,500	2,500
Retained profit	5,050	4,900

BALANCE SHEET AS AT 31 DECEMBER

			20X9			20X8
	£'000	£'000	£'000	£'000	£'000	£'000
Fixed assets			1,500			1,400
Current assets						
Stock	7,350			3,000		
Debtors	10,000			6,000		
Cash	2,500			4,500		
		19,850			13,500	
Current liabilities						
Overdraft	2,000			–		
Dividends owing	2,500			2,500		
Trade creditors	4,200			2,500		
		(8,700)			(5,000)	
Net current assets			11,150			8,500
8% debentures			(1,200)			(3,500)
Net assets			11,450			6,400
Ordinary shares (25p)			5,000			5,000
Profit and loss a/c			6,450			1,400
			11,450			6,400

(i) By studying the above accounts and using ratio analysis, identify the main problems facing Gustaffson. **11 Marks**

(ii) Provide possible solutions to the problems identified in (i). **3 Marks**

Total Marks = 20

17 VX COMPANY
30 mins

The VX Company has produced the following information from which a cash budget for the first six months of next year is required.

The company makes a single product which sells for £50 and the variable cost of each unit is as follows.

Material	£26
Labour (wages)	£8
Variable overhead	£2

Fixed overheads (excluding depreciation) are budgeted at £5,500 per month payable on the 23rd of each month.

Notes

(a) Sales for the last two months of this year.

November	December
1,000	1,200

(b) Budgeted sales for next year.

January	February	March	April	May	June
1,400	1,600	1,800	2,000	2,200	2,600

(c) Production quantities for the last two months of this year.

November	December
1,200	1,400

(d) Budgeted production units for next year.

January	February	March	April	May	June
1,600	2,000	2,400	2,600	2,400	2,200

(e) Wages are paid in the month when output is produced.

(f) Variable overhead is paid 50% in the month when the cost is incurred and 50% the following month.

(g) Suppliers of material are paid two months after the material is used in production.

Exam question bank

    (h) Customers are expected to pay at the end of the second month following sale.

    (i) A new machine is scheduled for January costing £34,000, this is to be paid for in February.

    (j) An old machine is to be sold for cash in January for £1,200.

    (k) The company expects to have a cash balance of £35,500 on 1 January.

Tasks

    (a) Prepare a month by month cash budget for the first six months of next year.

    (b) Discuss the actions management might take in the light of the cash budget you have prepared.

    (c) Explain how depreciation would affect the following.

        (i) A cash budget
        (ii) The calculation of profit in a business

18 MILLER-ORR MODEL *36 mins*

(a) Explain the advantages and disadvantages to a company of paying suppliers by using an electronic funds transfer system instead of cheques by post. **5 Marks**

(b) The treasurer of a local government department is reviewing her cash management procedures. She plans to introduce the use of cash management models and has asked you to investigate their applicability to the department. The following information is available.

    (i) The department has agreed with its bank that it will maintain a minimum daily cash balance of £15,000. Severe financial penalties will apply if this balance is not maintained.

    (ii) A forecast of daily cash movements for the next twelve months shows a standard deviation of daily cash flows of £3,000.

    (iii) The daily interest rate is at present 0.0236% and this is not expected to change for the foreseeable future.

    (iv) The transaction cost for each sale or purchase is £25.

Assume you are a newly recruited accountant in the department.

Required

Write a report to the treasurer which discusses:

    (i) The advantages of cash management models over more traditional methods of cash forecasting, making specific reference to their applicability to a public sector organisation such as a local authority; **6 Marks**

    (ii) How one such model, the Miller-Orr, would operate in practice, using the information given above. Your report should include calculations of the upper and lower limits for cash balances and the return point. Assume a spread of £26,820. **9 Marks**

Note. You do not need it to calculate the spread as this is given above, but you should explain the terms used in the Miller-Orr model.

Total Marks = 20

19 ABC LTD (Pilot paper) *36 mins*

ABC Ltd is a small manufacturing company which is suffering cash flow difficulties. The company already utilises its maximum overdraft facility. ABC Ltd sells an average of £400,000 of goods per month at invoice value, and customers are allowed 40 days to pay from the date of invoice. Two possible solutions to the company's cash flow problems have been suggested.

- **Option 1** The company could factor its trade debts. A factor has been found who would advance ABC Ltd 75% of the value of its invoices immediately on receipt of the invoices, at an interest rate of 10% per annum. The factor would also charge a service fee amounting to 2% of the total invoices. As a result of using the factor, ABC Ltd would save administration costs estimated at £5,000 per month.

- **Option 2** The company could offer a cash discount to customers for prompt payment. It has been suggested that customers could be offered a 2% discount for paying by cash.

Exam question bank

Required

(a) Identify the services that may be provided by factoring organisations. **4 Marks**
(b) Calculate the annual net cost (in £) of the proposed factoring agreement. **6 Marks**
(c) Calculate the annualised cost (in percentage terms) of offering a cash discount to customers. **3 Marks**
(d) Discuss the relative merits of the two proposals. **7 Marks**

Total Marks = 20

20 FLOWER POTS LTD *35 mins*

(a) (i) A customer has asked for trade credit, on a 30 day basis. You write to the bank asking for a reference. Describe the bank's likely response.

 (ii) Identify which of the following bank references would make you more happy to offer trade credit to a customer.

   (1) Considered good for your figures
   (2) Respectably constituted which should prove good for your figures

 (iii) List the type of data you might see in a report from a credit reference agency and explain the drawbacks of such a report.

(b) Flower Pots Ltd manufactures a variety of plastic goods for the domestic market - principally plant pot holders, buckets and bowls, which they sell mainly to garden centres, supermarkets and private ironmongers' shops.

The balance sheets produced for the past three years reveal the following trends.

	31 March 20X6	31 March 20X7	31 March 20X8
Net profit / Sales	2.4%	2.1%	2.0%
Credit given	28 days	30 days	60 days
Credit taken	30 days	35 days	65 days
Working capital ratio	1.24	1.20	1.16
Stock turnover	10 weeks	12 weeks	13.5 weeks
Net worth	£43,200	£43,100	£42,650

Present overdrawn bank balance = £27,294. (The authorised overdraft limit is £25,000.)

Describe the conclusions that you would draw from these figures.

21 DEBT COLLECTION TARGETS *30 mins*

(a) Using an example, describe how you would devise a system of targets for credit control staff to ensure a consistent debtors ageing ratio.

(b) Describe the features of debt factoring, and explain why small, rapidly growing firms might employ a debt factor.

22 THE LAX COMPANY *36 mins*

The Lax Company began trading in 20X7 and makes all its sales on credit. The company suffers from a high level of bad debts and a provision for doubtful debts of 3% of outstanding debtors is made at the end of each year.

Information for 20X7, 20X8 and 20X9 is as follows.

	Year to 31 December		
	20X7 £	20X8 £	20X9 £
Outstanding debtors at 31 December	44,000	55,000	47,000
Bad debts written off during year	7,000	10,000	8,000

Exam question bank

Required

(a) State the amount to be shown in the profit and loss account for bad debts and provision for doubtful debts for the years ended 31 December 20X7, 20X8 and 20X9. **4 Marks**

(b) State the value of debtors which would be shown in the balance sheet as at 31 December in each of these years. **4 Marks**

(c) Recent research has shown that a large percentage of small company failures were due to poor financial management skills and poor credit management.

Required

Explain the problems faced by small companies in respect of credit management, and discuss internal actions which they could take to minimise the effects of these problems. **12 Marks**

Total Marks = 20

23 SF LTD (Pilot paper) *36 mins*

SF Ltd is a family-owned private company with five main shareholders.

SF Ltd has just prepared its cash budget for the year ahead, details of which are shown below. The current overdraft facility is £50,000 and the bank has stated that it would not be willing to increase the facility at present, without a substantial increase in the interest rate charged, due to the lack of assets to offer as security.

The shareholders are concerned by the cash projections, and have sought advice from external consultants.

All figures, £'000

	J	F	M	A	M	J	J	A	S	O	N	D
Collections from customers	55	60	30	10	15	20	20	25	30	40	55	80
Dividend on investment						10						
Total inflows	55	60	30	10	15	30	20	25	30	40	55	80
Payments to suppliers		20		20		25		28		27		25
Wages and salaries	15	15	15	15	15	20	20	15	15	15	15	15
Payments for fixed assets			2		5	10		15				
Dividend payable			25									
Corporation tax									30			
Other operating expenses	5	5	5	5	7	7	7	7	7	7	8	8
Total outflows	20	40	22	65	27	62	27	65	52	49	23	48
Net in or (out)	35	20	8	(55)	(12)	(32)	(7)	(40)	(22)	(9)	32	32
Bank balance (overdraft)												
Opening	20	55	75	83	28	16	(16)	(23)	(63)	(85)	(94)	(62)
Closing	55	75	83	28	16	(16)	(23)	(63)	(85)	(94)	(62)	(30)

The following additional information relating to the cash budget has been provided by SF Ltd.

(i) All sales are on credit. Two months' credit on average is granted to customers.

(ii) Production is scheduled evenly throughout the year. Year-end stocks of finished goods are forecast to be £30,000 higher than at the beginning of the year.

(iii) Purchases of raw materials are made at two-monthly intervals. SF Ltd typically takes up to 90 days to pay for goods supplied. Other expenses are paid in the month in which they arise.

(iv) The capital expenditure budget comprises:

Office furniture	March	£2,000
Progress payments on building extensions	May	£5,000
Car	June	£10,000
New equipment	August	£15,000

Required

Assume you are an external consultant employed by SF Ltd. Prepare a report for the board advising on the possible actions it might take to improve its budgeted cash flow for the year, and the possible impact of these actions on the company's business. Your report should also identify possible short-term investment opportunities for the cash surpluses identified in the first part of the budget year.

20 Marks

Exam question bank

24 SWANSEA PLC   *36 mins*

Question 24 is a question with help provided covering different areas of the syllabus.

(a) Swansea plc has entered into a long-term contract under which it will be required to make a number of cash disbursements of £1 million each at a steady rate over the following twelve months. The company holds only a very small amount of cash at the present time.

Requirebnd

(i) Evaluate the following two alternative methods of providing for the payment of these amounts. (Ignore taxation and the time value of money.)

(1) *Sale of securities.* Swansea expects to make an average rate of return of 10% on its holdings of securities over the next year. A sale of securities gives rise to a cost per sale of securities of £20, and following the sale the company will earn 4.5% per annum interest on the amount deposited. The optimal amount of cash raised by a sale of securities is given by the following formula.

$$\sqrt{\frac{2 \times \text{Annual cash disbursements} \times \text{Cost per sale of securities}}{\text{Interest rate}}}$$

(2) *Loan.* It would be possible for Swansea to borrow the £1 million required for payments at an interest rate of 13% of the amount loaned per annum. The arrangement fee of £6,000 for such a loan could be paid from existing cash resources. The amount borrowed would be placed as a term deposit at an interest rate of 8%, for drawing down when needed. **9 Marks**

(ii) What are the possible limitations of the cash management model which Swansea plc is using in part (a)(i). **4 Marks**

(b) Mumbles Ltd, a subsidiary of Swansea, wishes to install computerised equipment with a four year life which would involve an outlay of £5 million (residual value: nil). The Financial Director has carried out a study which shows that the project has a positive net present value when this is calculated using the shareholders' required rate of return as a discount rate.

Mumbles has asked Castles Leasing Limited ('Castles'), a subsidiary of a major bank, for a quotation for the acquisition of the equipment on a leasing contract under which maintenance of the equipment would be provided by Castles.

Castles has quoted an annual rental of £1,800,000. The maintenance services would cost Mumbles £190,000 annually if it had to obtain them from another source.

Mumbles pays corporate tax at a rate of 33%, and the tax becomes payable 12 months after the relevant cash flow. A writing down allowance can be claimed on a 25% reducing balance basis. A pre-tax borrowing rate of 18% applies to Mumbles.

Required

(i) Disregarding the savings in maintenance costs, evaluate whether Mumbles Ltd should lease the equipment from Castles or borrow money to purchase the equipment itself. **5 Marks**

(ii) Calculate whether a different evaluation should be made if the savings in maintenance costs for Mumbles Ltd are accounted for. **2 Marks**

Total Marks = 20

Approaching the answer

You should read through the requirement before working through and annotating the question as we have done so that you are aware of what things you are looking for.

(a) Swansea plc has entered into a long-term contract under which it will be required to make a number of cash disbursements of £1 million each at a *steady rate* over the following twelve months. The company *holds only a very small amount of cash* at the present time.

- *steady rate* → This information will be significant
- *holds only a very small amount of cash* → Can't use surplus cash holdings

Exam question bank

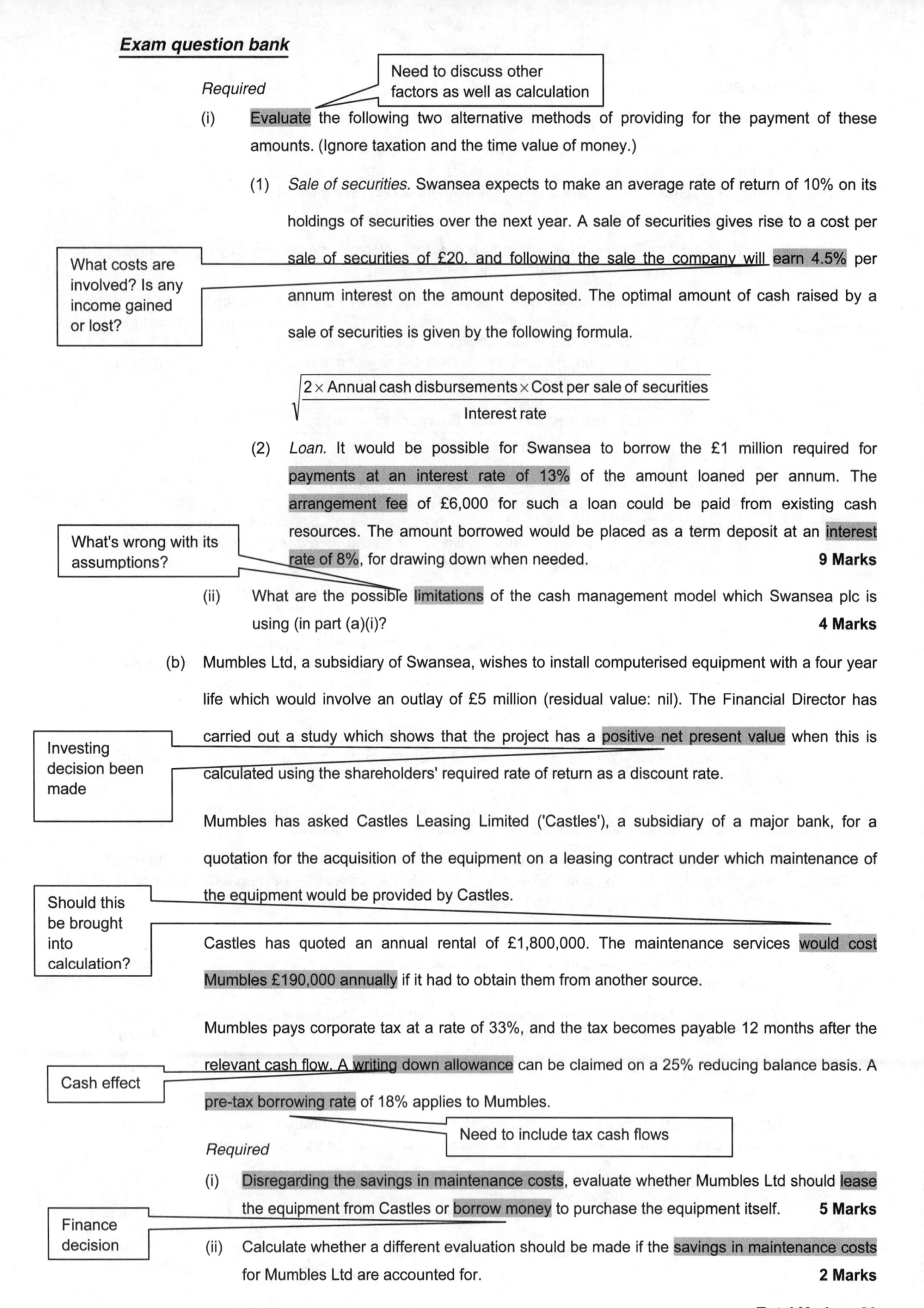

Required

(i) Evaluate [*Need to discuss other factors as well as calculation*] the following two alternative methods of providing for the payment of these amounts. (Ignore taxation and the time value of money.)

(1) *Sale of securities.* Swansea expects to make an average rate of return of 10% on its holdings of securities over the next year. A sale of securities gives rise to a cost per sale of securities of £20, and following the sale the company will earn 4.5% per annum interest on the amount deposited. The optimal amount of cash raised by a sale of securities is given by the following formula. [*What costs are involved? Is any income gained or lost?*]

$$\sqrt{\frac{2 \times \text{Annual cash disbursements} \times \text{Cost per sale of securities}}{\text{Interest rate}}}$$

(2) *Loan.* It would be possible for Swansea to borrow the £1 million required for payments at an interest rate of 13% of the amount loaned per annum. The arrangement fee of £6,000 for such a loan could be paid from existing cash resources. The amount borrowed would be placed as a term deposit at an interest rate of 8%, for drawing down when needed. [*What's wrong with its assumptions?*]

9 Marks

(ii) What are the possible limitations of the cash management model which Swansea plc is using (in part (a)(i)?

4 Marks

(b) Mumbles Ltd, a subsidiary of Swansea, wishes to install computerised equipment with a four year life which would involve an outlay of £5 million (residual value: nil). The Financial Director has carried out a study which shows that the project has a positive net present value when this is calculated using the shareholders' required rate of return as a discount rate. [*Investing decision been made*]

Mumbles has asked Castles Leasing Limited ('Castles'), a subsidiary of a major bank, for a quotation for the acquisition of the equipment on a leasing contract under which maintenance of the equipment would be provided by Castles. [*Should this be brought into calculation?*]

Castles has quoted an annual rental of £1,800,000. The maintenance services would cost Mumbles £190,000 annually if it had to obtain them from another source.

Mumbles pays corporate tax at a rate of 33%, and the tax becomes payable 12 months after the relevant cash flow. A writing down allowance can be claimed on a 25% reducing balance basis. A pre-tax borrowing rate of 18% applies to Mumbles. [*Cash effect*]

[*Need to include tax cash flows*]

Required

(i) Disregarding the savings in maintenance costs, evaluate whether Mumbles Ltd should lease the equipment from Castles or borrow money to purchase the equipment itself. [*Finance decision*]

5 Marks

(ii) Calculate whether a different evaluation should be made if the savings in maintenance costs for Mumbles Ltd are accounted for.

2 Marks

Total Marks = 20

Exam question bank

Framework for your answer

Part (a)(i)

The net costs of selling the securities are:

- Transaction costs (you need to calculate number of transactions using the formula)
- Less interest received on cash balances held (calculated on average balances)
- Plus interest foregone on securities (again calculated on average balance)

Answer also brings out problems of selling securities – the evaluation required is more than just financial calculations.

The net costs of using the loan finance are:

- Interest paid (on full loan balance)
- Less interest received on cash balance held (calculated on average balance)
- Plus arrangement fee

Again the answer mentions wider issues, in this case repayment problems.

Part (a)(ii)

The answer takes each element of the formula in turn, discusses the assumptions made and then considers whether the model misses anything out.

Part (b)(i) and (ii)

It is easier to show the payments for each year in a single column. Bringing tax in means that you have to use an after tax discount rate and consider the tax implications of all revenues and payments. Don't assume that the sole tax implication is the ability to claim capital allowances. Your answer will be incomplete if you do not calculate the total net present value **and** make appropriate comparisons.

Exam answer bank

1 CORPORATE OBJECTIVES

> **Pass marks.** You may well get a part question on objectives in your exam, and the topic may need to be brought into discussions in other areas, for example how well does an investment that you have appraised fit in with the company's objectives.
>
> The question is answered with a clear structure:
>
> (a) The **extent** to which profit maximisation is the primary corporate objective
>
> (b) The **problems** with the objective
>
> (c) Other **financial** objectives
>
> (d) Other **non-financial** objectives
>
> The question is confined to what the directors of the company should seek. In practice they may pursue other objectives that are in their own, but not necessarily the company's, best interests, for example maximisation of their own rewards. You were only allocated twenty minutes to answer the question, which is typical of the sort of timescale that you would get in the exam. The scope of the question is quite wide for the length of time available, so you must make sure your answer has sufficient breadth, and you do not spend all your time discussing profit maximisation.

As a general rule, increases in a company's profits will be in the interests of the shareholders. However, the maximisation of profits should not be the only goal, and it may be beneficial to aim for profits below the maximum possible.

The limitations of profit as a measure of performance

The profits shown in a company's accounts are **not a wholly objective measure** of the company's performance. The final figure depends on policies chosen on, for example, depreciation and the writing off of development expenditure. In the short term, profits can be increased by capitalising development expenditure, but such policies do not really increase the company's worth.

It is very hard to work out what profit could have been attained. Comparisons with an industry average may be useful, but comparisons with exceptional performers in the industry may be inappropriate. Profits need to be adjusted to reflect the resources used to earn them. A company which doubles its capital and increases its profits by 50% has probably done badly, not well.

Profits are computed annually, with half-yearly interim results. Investments which are highly profitable in the long term but are loss-makers initially could be rejected if management is concerned only with next year's profits.

Alternative financial objectives

A company must **ensure** its **financial stability** both in the short term and in the long term. Targets for the reduction of gearing or the retention of profits may therefore be appropriate. Of key importance is the **solvency** of the company. Profitable investments must be rejected if the expenditure required would leave the company unable to pay its debts.

Non-financial objectives

A company's directors may legitimately take into account a range of **non-financial objectives**, including the **welfare of employees** and **of society**, the provision of a **service to** the public and environmental goals. In some cases the pursuit of such objectives may lead to increased profits, for example when an environmentally responsible company attracts customers who share such concerns.

2 FINANCIAL INTERMEDIATION

> **Pass marks.** You may get part of a longer question on financial intermediaries as well as MCQs. Think of what they do in terms of the problems faced by a lender or borrower; matching with someone who wants to borrow or lend the right amount for the same period of time, and also minimising the risk.
>
> The instructions you are given (explain in detail), the time allowed and the number of functions you can discuss indicate that you will have to develop the points in some depth rather than provide a brief sentence on each.

The following functions are performed by financial intermediaries.

(a) **Go-between**

Firms with economically desirable projects might want funds to finance these projects, but might not know where to go to find willing lenders. Similarly, savers might have funds that they would be willing to invest for a suitable return, but might not know where to find firms which want to borrow and would offer such a return. Financial intermediaries are an obvious place to go to, when a saver has funds to save or lend, and a borrower wants to obtain more funds. They act in the role of **go-between**, and in doing so, save time, effort and transaction costs for savers and borrowers.

(b) **Maturity transformation**

Lenders tend to want to be able to realise their investment and get their money back at fairly short notice. Borrowers, on the other hand, tend to want loans for fixed terms with predictable repayment schedules. Financial intermediaries provide **maturity transformation**, because savers are able to lend their money with the option to withdraw at short notice, and yet borrowers are able to raise loans for a fixed term and with a predictable repayment schedule. Financial intermediaries such as banks and building societies are able to do this because of the volume of business they carry out.

(c) **Risk transformation**

When a lender provides funds to a borrower, he must accept a risk that the borrower will be unable to repay. Financial intermediaries provide **risk transformation**. When a saver puts money into a financial intermediary, his savings are secure provided that the intermediary is financially sound. The financial intermediary is able to bear the risks of lending because of the wide portfolio of investments it should have.

(d) **Parcelling up**

Borrowers tend to want larger loans than individual savers can provide. For example, a firm might want to borrow £10,000, but the only savers it finds might be able to lend no more than £1,000 each so that the firm would have to find ten such savers to obtain the total loan that it wants. Financial intermediaries are able to '**parcel up' small savings** into big loans, so that the discrepancy between small lenders and large borrowers is removed by the intermediary.

3 MARKET EFFICIENCY

> **Pass marks.** The efficient market hypothesis may be the subject of a part question in Paper 4. An answer focusing on a technical concept should always start with a clear definition of that concept, including as appropriate the key assumptions. Here the answer goes on to discuss the various forms of the efficient market hypothesis, concentrating on the differences between them (the amount of information available).
>
> It is also important when discussing a theory that attempts to model actual behaviour to bring in evidence of how much it applies in practice. Here there is a key distinction between the strong form and other forms.
>
> If a theory does not appear to work in practice, you need to indicate why this might be so, or at least that there is no obvious explanation why the theory does not work. Here the strong form hypothesis does not work, so you consider why when discussing the hypothesis. In addition there is the general point that some financial institutions do perform better than expected. Because this applies to all forms of the efficient market hypothesis, and because the subject is highlighted in the question, you need a separate paragraph covering why performance of financial institutions might deviate from what is anticipated. Generally written questions will benefit from a conclusion that sums up the answer and is supported by the preceding discussion.

The efficient market hypothesis contends that some capital markets (in the UK and US for instance) are 'efficient markets' in which the prices at which securities are traded **reflect** all **the relevant information** available. In other words, this information is freely available to all participants in the market and is fully reflected in share prices. Further, it is assumed that **transaction costs** are **insignificant** and do not discourage trading in shares, and that **no single individual** or group of individuals dominates the market.

The theory exists in three forms: weak form, semi-strong form and strong form.

Exam answer bank

Weak form efficiency

Weak form efficiency contends that prices only change when **new factual information** becomes **available**. Thus if a takeover bid is anticipated, the share prices of the participants will not change until the bid is actually announced. Information is in the public domain and equally available to all players in the market, and thus if this form of the hypothesis is correct, no one player should be able to outperform the market consistently. Thus the fact that financial institutions rarely outperform the market on a **regular basis lends weight** to this form of the theory.

Semi-strong form efficiency

The **semi-strong form** of the theory holds that in addition to responding to information that is publicly available, the market also reflects **all other knowledge** that **is publicly available** and relevant to the share valuation. Thus to take the example used above, the share prices of companies involved in a takeover bid will change in advance of the bid being formally announced as the market anticipates the bid. Once again, this form of the theory is based upon the assumption that all the knowledge upon which share price movements are based is in the public domain and freely available. Thus no single player or group of players should be able consistently to outperform the market. This form of the theory is supported by empirical research which suggests that share price movements do anticipate merger announcements. The fact that the neither the financial institutions nor any other group of investors regularly beat the market also supports this version of the hypothesis.

Strong form efficiency

The **strong form** of the theory holds that the market price of securities reflects **all information that is available**. This includes knowledge of past performance and anticipated events as in the semi-strong form, and also 'insider' knowledge not publicly available. This form can be tested by investigating the effect on the share price of releasing a piece of information previously confidential to the firm; if the strong form of the hypothesis is valid, then this should already be factored into the share value and a significant price movement should not result. The implication is that this sort of information is only available to specialists who are in regular contact with the company, such as investment trust managers, and that as a result they could use their privileged position to outperform other investors. Empirical work suggests that this form of the hypothesis is not valid, and this is what one would expect since insider dealing is illegal in the UK.

Conclusion

Thus the fact that the financial institutions in general do not consistently outperform the market supports both **the weak and semi-strong forms** of the efficient market hypothesis. The fact that a number of institutions do consistently perform well is probably more related to the fund managers' understanding of the structure of the industries and markets in which they invest, and their ability to hold a more widely diversified portfolio than the small investor. This means that they are in a better position to avoid the risk of large losses. The fact that they are in daily contact with the markets also means that they are in practice able to react more quickly to new information that becomes available than is the small investor.

4 KM PLC

> **Pass marks.** This question requires a factual knowledge of the role of the treasury department and the ways in which this function may be managed within the company. To answer it well, you should also take account of the specific circumstances of KM plc. When considering the role of the treasury department, think about the main financial transactions that the business undertakes. Note how many advantages of a centralised treasury department are economies of scale; advantages because of its size.
>
> The advantages of being a profit centre mostly relate to the increased financial discipline. The disadvantages mostly relate to the treasury department acting in ways that are inconsistent with the objectives of the rest of the organisation – having a different attitude to risk or over-charging for its services.

(a) **Treasurership** has been defined as 'the function concerned with the provision and use of finance. It includes provision of capital, short-term borrowing, foreign currency management, banking, collections and money market investment'.

The main responsibilities of the treasury function include:

(i) **Liquidity management**

- Working capital and money transmission management
- Banking relationships and arrangements
- Money management

This involves making sure that the organisation has the liquid funds it needs and invests any surplus funds, even for very short terms. The treasurer should maintain a good relationship with one or more banks to ensure that negotiations are as swift as possible, and that rates are reasonable.

(ii) **Funding management**

- Funding policies and procedures
- Sources of funds
- Types of funds

Funding management is concerned with all forms of borrowing, and alternative sources of funds, such as leasing and factoring.

(iii) **Currency management**

- Exposure policies and procedures
- Exchange dealing, including futures and options
- International monetary economics and exchange regulations

(iv) **Corporate finance**

- Equity capital management
- Business acquisitions and disposals
- Project finance and joint ventures

(v) **Corporate taxation**

(vi) **Risk management and insurance**

(vii) **Pension fund investment management**

The **financial control function** is concerned with determining whether the various activities of the organisation are meeting their financial objectives. This function will therefore be interested in a wide variety of **stakeholder relationships**, for example, with customers, suppliers and employees. By contrast, **the treasury function** is mainly concerned with the relationship of the company to the **providers of finance**. In a geographically dispersed company such as KM plc, it is likely that financial control functions will exist at a variety of local levels, while the treasury department will be centralised at the head office. The advantages of having a specialist treasury department include the following.

(i) **Centralised liquidity management avoids** having a **mix of cash surpluses** and **overdrafts** in different localised bank accounts, particularly in a company such as KM plc, which now includes a number of overseas operations.

(ii) **Bulk cash flows** are possible, allowing lower bank charges to be negotiated.

(iii) **Larger volumes of cash** are **available** to invest, giving better short term investment opportunities.

(iv) Any **borrowing** can be **arranged in bulk**, at lower interest rates than for smaller borrowings.

(v) **Foreign currency risk management** should be improved, with matching of cash flows in different subsidiaries being possible. This means that there should be less need to use expensive hedging instruments such as option contracts. This is particularly valuable in a company such as KM plc where there are a number of overseas operations.

(vi) A **specialist department** can **employ staff** with a greater level of expertise than would be possible in a local, more broadly based, finance department.

(vii) Centralisation will allow the company to **benefit** from the **use** of **specialised cash management software**.

(viii) Access to treasury expertise should **improve** the quality of **strategic planning** and decision making.

Exam answer bank

(b) The advantages of operating the treasury department as a **profit centre** rather than a cost centre include the following.

(i) This approach recognises the fact that some companies are able to make **significant profits** from their treasury activities. Treating the department as a profit centre may make treasury staff more motivated to achieve the best possible return for the company.

(ii) If it is treated as a profit centre, the department will have to **charge for** its services to other parts of the organisation. This may make the subsidiaries more aware of the true cost of the services they use, and encourage them to use the department more efficiently.

The main disadvantages are as follows.

(i) Treasury staff may be **tempted** to **speculate**, and to ignore the risk criteria that they should be using.

(ii) Internal charging may mean that **some subsidiaries go outside** the **organisation** for treasury services and thus reduce the overall benefit to the organisation of having a centralised treasury function.

(iii) **Performance evaluation** may be **difficult**, since the success of the function may sometimes involve the avoidance of costs rather than the maximisation of profits.

(iv) **Administrative costs** may be **increased**.

5 PRIMULA PLC

> **Pass marks.** Note the step by step approach in (a).
>
> *Step 1.* Calculate number of shares
> *Step 2.* Calculate issue price
> *Step 3.* Calculate ex-rights price
>
> In part (b) you need to do more than describe the various alternatives. You must ensure that all your discussions are related to the circumstances of Primula plc. Your answer needs to bring out the potential difficulties with whatever choice the directors make. Note how the change in financing can have quite wide implications (the impact on strategy of restrictive covenants and a change in the ownership structure). The issue of change in control is also important when we consider the alternative methods of issuing shares.
>
> The conclusion here brings out that the other methods suggested are unlikely to be used and in practice the rights issue is the most likely option.

(a) There are currently 10m shares in issue. A 2 for 5 rights issue would mean that **4m additional shares** would have to be issued (10m × 2/5).

The rights issue must raise £24m. Therefore the new shares must be issued at a price of **£6 per share** (£24m/4m).

Using the formula

$$\text{Theoretical ex rights price} = \frac{1}{N+1}((N \times \text{cum rights price}) + \text{issue price})$$

$$= \frac{1}{2.5+1}((2.5 \times 6.60) + 6.00)$$

$$= 6.43$$

(b) To: Chairman
From: Finance Director
Date: 20 November 20X1
Subject: Financing alternatives for the new investment

Introduction

The new contract is large in relation to the size of the company, and therefore the new external source of finance could have a **significant effect** on the existing **capital structure** of the business, and on its **ownership and control**. The rights issue is the main source of finance being discussed and this will be considered in more detail below. The final section of the report will consider some further methods of raising equity finance that are available to Primula plc.

Rights issue versus debenture issue

Ownership

The rights issue is large in relation to the existing equity in issue, and requires a significant additional investment on the part of the shareholders. If shareholders are likely to be unwilling or unable to exercise their rights, the company should consider underwriting the issue. The underwriters will then take up any shares that remain unsold, but this could result in a **change** in the **balance of control**.

Problems with all equity financing

The company is currently 100% equity financed, and this would continue to be the case in the event of a rights issue. This means that the **level of financial risk** faced by the shareholders is **low**. However, it also means that they cannot take advantage of the **lower cost and tax benefits** of debt finance, and that therefore the potential returns to equity are lower than they might be if some debt were to be used.

Issue costs

The calculations ignore issue costs. These may be **significant** for a **rights issue,** amounting on average to 4% of the finance raised, although this percentage rises for small issues.

Flexibility

Equity funding would not be linked to restrictive covenants limiting the company's further ability to raise finance.

(ii) **Further methods of raising equity finance**

(1) **A placing**

This is an arrangement whereby the shares are not all offered to the public, but instead, the sponsoring market maker arranges for **most of the issue** to be **bought by a small number of investors**, usually institutional investors such as pension funds and insurance companies. The **issuing costs** would be **lower** than for a **rights issue**, but the position with regard to **pre-emption rights** of the existing shareholders may have to be resolved. There could be a significant effect on the **control** of the business if the new shares are concentrated in the hands of a small number of institutional investors.

(2) **Offer for sale**

This means that Primula plc would **allot new shares** to an **issuing house**. The issuing house would then offer the **shares for sale** on the basis of a prospectus, either at a **fixed price** or by **tender**. The **issuing costs** would be significantly **higher** than for a rights issue. This is particularly true for fixed price offers where there is a higher risk that not all the shares will be subscribed. However, the **effect** on the **control of the company** is likely to be less than for a placing.

(3) **Public offer for subscription**

This is the **direct offer** of shares to the **public** by the company using a **prospectus**. **Issuing costs, underwriting** and **publicity costs** are **high**. It is only appropriate for **large issues** of shares.

Conclusion

Although alternative routes are available for raising equity, in this case the rights issue is the most likely choice.

Exam answer bank

6 KB PLC

> **Pass marks.** This question tests your knowledge of the theory surrounding rights issues and convertibles.
>
> In (a) (i) we tell you how to do the calculation because you have not encountered earnings per share and the price/earnings ratio yet. Once you have learnt about these in chapter 11, expect to be asked to calculate market price without being told the method you should use.
>
> When considering in (a)(ii) the likely price following the rights issue, you should take into account stock market factors as well as the performance of the company. Does the market view the company rationally? Is the company competing for funds?
>
> Don't forget in (a) (iii) that shares can never be issued below their nominal value; you need to mention this as it does limit the discounts on deep discounted issues.
>
> In (b) (i) you are after a figure for how much loan stock you will need to purchase a single share on conversion.
>
> (b) (ii) is a very good summary of the factors you should take into account when considering any new source of finance. One thing that will concern the business is how likely it is to obtain the funds it seeks, so don't forget to look at things from the finance provider's viewpoint.

(a) (i) The current market price can be found by multiplying the earnings per share (EPS) by the price/earnings (P/E) ratio.

EPS is £1.2m/6m = 20 pence per share

P/E ratio is 12

Market price of shares is 12 × 20p = **£2.40 per share**

(ii) In order to raise £5,040,000 at a price of 192 pence, the company will need to issue an additional 2,625,000 (£5,040,000/£1.92) shares.

Following the investment, the total number of shares in issue will be 8,625,000 (6,000,000 + 2,625,000).

At this point, the total value of the company will be:

(6m × £2.40) + £5,040,000 = £19,440,000

The theoretical ex-rights price will therefore be £19.44m/8.625m = **£2.25**.

The following factors might invalidate this in practice.

(1) The **costs of arranging the issue** have not been included in the calculations.

(2) The **market view** of the quality of the new investment will affect the actual price of the company's shares.

(3) If the issue is **not fully subscribed** and a significant number of shares remain with the underwriters, this will depress the share price.

(4) The effect of the new investment on the **risk profile** of the company and the expected future dividend stream could also cause the share price to differ from that predicted.

(5) The price of the shares depends not only on the **financial performance** of the company, but also on the **overall level of demand** in the stock market. If the market moves significantly following the announcement of the issue, this will affect the actual price at which the shares are traded.

(iii) In a **deep-discounted rights issue**, the new shares are **priced at a large discount** to the current market price of the shares. The purpose of this is to ensure that the issue is well subscribed and that shares are not left with the underwriters, and thus this form of issue pricing is attractive when the stock market is particularly volatile. However, the shares cannot be issued at a price which is **below their nominal value**.

The main drawback to this approach is that **a larger number of shares** will need to be issued in order to raise the required amount of finance, and this will lead to a larger dilution of earnings per share and dividends per share.

(b) (i) The conversion premium is the measure of the additional expense involved in buying shares via the convertible stock as compared with buying the shares on the open market immediately.

In this case, £100 loan stock can be converted into 35 ordinary shares. The effective price of these shares is therefore £2.86 (£100/35) per share.

The current market price of the shares is £2.40. The conversion premium is therefore £2.86 − £2.40 = **46 pence**. This can also be expressed in percentage terms as **19%** (0.46/2.40).

(ii) The advantages to KB plc of issuing convertible loan stock as compared with a rights issue include the following.

(1) **Convertibles** should be **cheaper** than equity because they offer greater security to the investor. This may make them particularly attractive in fast growing but high-risk companies.

(2) **Issue costs** are **lower for** loan stock than for equity.

(3) **Interest on** the **loan stock** is **tax deductible**, unlike dividends on ordinary shares.

(4) There is **no immediate change** in the existing structure of control, although this will change over time as conversion rights are exercised.

(5) There is **no immediate dilution** in earnings and dividends per share.

7 FEATURES

> **Pass marks**. Discussion about different types of leases may be part of a longer question and the knowledge is also frequently tested in MCQs. Your answer needs to bring out the financial consequences including the taxation effect and also what will happen to the borrower's balance sheet.
>
> The suggested solution to part (b) contains the full cash flows for each alternative form of finance. It would be equally correct and quicker to leave out the operating cash flows in this part of the answer, but if you choose to do this you must be careful to include the tax effects of the capital allowances. You may therefore find it safer to take the longer route.

(a) (i) **Sale and leaseback** is an arrangement which is similar to mortgaging. A business which already owns an asset, for example a building or an item of equipment, **agrees to sell** the asset to a financial institution and then immediately to **lease it back** on terms specified in the agreement. The business has the benefit of the funds from the sale while retaining use of the asset, in return for regular payments to the financial institution.

The principal benefit is that the company **gains immediate access** to liquid funds; however this is at the **expense of the ability to profit** from any capital appreciation (potentially significant in the case of property), and the capacity to borrow elsewhere may be reduced since the balance sheet value of assets will fall.

(ii) **Hire purchase (HP)** is a form of **instalment credit** whereby the business purchases goods on credit and pays for them by instalments. The periodic payments include both an **interest element** on the initial price and a **capital repayment element**. At the end of the period, **ownership** of the asset **passes to the user**, who is also able to claim capital allowances on the basic purchase cost of the asset. The mechanics of the transaction are as follows.

(1) The supplier of the asset sells it to a finance house.

(2) The supplier of the asset delivers it to the customer who will be the user and the eventual owner.

(3) The hire purchase agreement is made between the finance house and the customer.

(iii) **Finance leases** are similar to HP contracts in that the **asset is sold** not to the user but to an **intermediary** who then leases the asset to the user in return for periodic payments. However, unlike with HP, **ownership** of the asset **does not transfer** to the user at the end of the lease period, but is retained by the **purchaser**. The **purchaser** (not the user) can **claim capital allowances**, which may be passed on to the user in the form of a reduction in the periodic payments. A further difference is that although the user does not own the

Exam answer bank

asset, **entries appear** in the user's balance sheet and profit and loss account to reflect the capital element of the lease, the interest element of the payments, and the remaining lease commitment. This is to ensure that all forms of long-term debt are fully reflected in the balance sheet.

Many finance leases are structured into a 'primary period' which covers the major part of the economic life of the asset, and a 'secondary period' during which the user continues to lease the asset, but at a much lower (often only nominal) rate.

(b) This is a two stage decision. Prime Printing must first establish whether there is a business case for the acquisition of the equipment. If there is, then the second stage is to establish the most appropriate form of financing.

(i) The first step is to calculate the capital allowances.

Year	Qualifying balance £	25% allowance £	
1	120,000	30,000	
2	90,000	22,500	
3	67,500	16,875	
4	50,625	12,656	
		82,031	
5	Balancing	37,969	(120,000 – 82,031)

These can then be used to calculate the annual tax liability. This will be paid one year in arrears.

	Year 1 £	Year 2 £	Year 3 £	Year 4 £	Year 5 £
Cash savings	50,000	50,000	50,000	50,000	50,000
Capital allowance	30,000	22,500	16,875	12,656	37,969
Taxable profits	20,000	27,500	33,125	37,344	12,031
Tax at 30%	6,000	8,250	9,938	11,203	3,609

The acquisition of the machine can now be calculated by discounting the annual incremental cash flows at the after tax cost of capital (15%).

	Year 0 £	Year 1 £	Year 2 £	Year 3 £	Year 4 £	Year 5 £	Year 6 £
Capital cost	(120,000)						
Cash savings		50,000	50,000	50,000	50,000	50,000	
Tax			(6,000)	(8,250)	(9,938)	(11,203)	(3,609)
Net cash flow	(120,000)	50,000	44,000	41,750	40,062	38,797	(3,609)
15% discount factor	1.000	0.870	0.756	0.658	0.572	0.497	0.432
Present value	(120,000)	43,500	33,264	27,472	22,915	19,282	(1,559)

The total NPV of the proposal is **£24,874**.

Since the NPV is positive, the company should proceed with the acquisition.

(ii) The next stage is to evaluate the alternative methods of financing the acquisition. If the machine is purchased using the bank loan, the cash flows will be the same as those calculated above. However, the discount rate to be used must be the after-tax cost of borrowing ie 13% × (1.00 – 0.30) = 9.1%. This will be approximated to 9%.

	Year 0 £	Year 1 £	Year 2 £	Year 3 £	Year 4 £	Year 5 £	Year 6 £
Capital cost	(120,000)						
Cash savings		50,000	50,000	50,000	50,000	50,000	
Tax			(6,000)	(8,250)	(9,938)	(11,203)	(3,609)
Net cash flow	(120,000)	50,000	44,000	41,750	40,062	38,797	(3,609)
9% discount factor	1.000	0.917	0.842	0.772	0.708	0.650	0.596
Present value	(120,000)	45,850	37,048	32,231	28,364	25,218	(2,151)

The total NPV of the proposal is **£46,560**.

If the machine is acquired using a finance lease, the cash flows change since capital allowances will not be available, but the lease payments will be allowable against tax. The annual tax that will be saved is £8,400 (£28,000 × 0.30).

Exam answer bank

	Year 0 £	Year 1 £	Year 2 £	Year 3 £	Year 4 £	Year 5 £	Year 6 £
Lease payments	(28,000)	(28,000)	(28,000)	(28,000)	(28,000)		
Tax savings on lease payments		8,400	8,400	8,400	8,400	8,400	
Cash savings		50,000	50,000	50,000	50,000	50,000	
Tax on cash savings			(15,000)	(15,000)	(15,000)	(15,000)	(15,000)
Net cash flow	(28,000)	30,400	15,400	15,400	15,400	43,400	(15,000)
9% discount factor	1.000	0.917	0.842	0.772	0.708	0.650	0.596
Present value	(28,000)	27,877	12,967	11,889	10,903	28,210	(8,940)

The total NPV of the proposal is **£54,906**.

Since the NPV of the leasing arrangement is higher than that of purchase, this means that leasing is the preferred alternative.

8 CRYSTAL PLC

> **Pass marks**. (a) demonstrates the complications that may occur in weighted average cost of capital calculations. When you calculate the cost of equity, you will need to do more than just plug the figures into the formula. Don't forget to check whether shares are quoted **cum or ex div**.
>
> With debentures, the most serious mistake you can make is to treat redeemable debentures as irredeemable. Because the debentures are redeemable, you need to carry out an IRR analysis. Remember this calculation is done from the viewpoint of the investor. The investor pays the market price for the debentures at time 0, and then receives the interest and the conversion value in subsequent years. You must bring tax into your calculation, although you could have assumed that tax was paid with a one year time delay.
>
> Lastly don't forget that the weightings in the WACC calculation are based on **market values, not book values**.
>
> (b) demonstrates that the calculation of the weighted average cost of capital is not a purely mechanical process. It makes assumptions about the shareholders, the proposed investment and the company's capital structure and future dividend prospects. Given all the assumptions involved, the result of the calculations may need to be taken with a large pinch of salt!

(a) The post-tax weighted average cost of capital should first be calculated.

(i) **Ordinary shares**

	£
Market value of shares cum div.	3.27
Less dividend per share (810 ÷ 3,000)	0.27
Market value of shares ex div.	3.00

The formula for calculating the cost of equity when there is dividend growth is:

$$k_e = \frac{D_0(1 + g)}{P_0} + g$$

where k_e = cost of equity
D_0 = current dividend
g = rate of growth
P_0 = current ex div market value.

In this case we shall estimate the future rate of growth (g) from the average growth in dividends over the past four years.

$810 = 620 (1 + g)^4$

$(1 + g)^4$ = $\dfrac{810}{620}$

= 1.3065

$(1 + g)$ = 1.069

g = 0.069 = 6.9%

Exam answer bank

$$k_e = \frac{0.27 \times 1.069}{3} + 0.069 = 16.5\%$$

(ii) **7% Debentures**

In order to find the post-tax cost of the debentures, which are redeemable in ten years time, it is necessary to find the discount rate (IRR) which will give the future post-tax cash flows a present value of £77.10.

The relevant cash flows are:

(1) Annual interest payments, net of tax, which are £1,300 × 7% × 70% = £63.70 (for ten years)

(2) A capital repayment of £1,300 (in ten years time)

It is assumed that tax relief on the debenture interest arises at the same time as the interest payment. In practice the cash flow effect is unlikely to be felt for about a year, but this will have no significant effect on the calculations.

	Present value £'000
Try 8%:	
Current market value of debentures (1,300 at £77.10 per cent)	(1,002.3)
Annual interest payments net of tax £63.70 × 6.710 (8% for ten years)	427.4
Capital repayment £1,300 × 0.463 (8% in ten years time)	601.9
NPV	27.0
Try 9%:	£'000
Current market value of debentures	(1,002.3)
Annual interest payments net of tax 63.70 × 6.418	408.8
Capital repayment 1,300 × 0.422	548.6
NPV	(44.9)

$$RR = 8\% + \left[\frac{27.0}{27.0 - -44.9} \times (9 - 8)\right]\%$$

$$= 8.38\%$$

(iii) **The weighted average cost of capital**

	Market value £'000	Cost %	Product
Equity	9,000	16.50	1,485
7% Debentures	1,002	8.38	84
	10,002		1,569

$$\frac{1,569}{10,002} \times 100 = 15.7\%$$

The above calculations suggest that a discount rate in the region of 16% might be appropriate for the appraisal of new investment opportunities.

(b) Difficulties and uncertainties in the above estimates arise in a number of areas.

(i) **The cost of equity**. The above calculation assumes that all shareholders have the same marginal cost of capital and the same dividend expectations, which is unrealistic. In addition, it is assumed that dividend growth has been and will be at a constant rate of 6.9%. In fact, actual growth in the years 20X5/6 and 20X8/9 was in excess of 9%, while in the year 20X7/8 there was no dividend growth. 6.9% is merely the average rate of growth for the past four years. The rate of future growth will depend more on the return from future projects undertaken than on the past dividend record.

(ii) **The use of the weighted average cost of capital**. Use of the weighted average cost of capital as a discount rate is only justified where the company in question has achieved what it believes to be the **optimal capital structure** (the mix of debt and equity) and where it intends to maintain this structure in the long term.

(iii) **The projects themselves**. The weighted average cost of capital makes **no allowance** for the **business risk** of **individual projects**. In practice some companies, having calculated

Exam answer bank

the WACC, then add a premium for risk. In this case, for example, if one used a risk premium of 5% the final discount rate would be 21%. Ideally the risk premium should vary from project to project, since not all projects are equally risky. In general, the riskier the project the higher the discount rate which should be used.

9 TOVELL PLC

> **Pass marks**. You would not get a full question on portfolio theory and diversification in this paper; nevertheless this question does demonstrate the important points that you need to appreciate in this paper and in Paper 13. The most important point is stressed first; that investors can be a lot more flexible in their investment choices than companies. Companies may run into problems when straying from areas that they know best.
>
> Nevertheless you also need to say that diversification may help companies reduce their risks even if they are not as efficient at diversification as investors.

Diversification by investors

The stated objective that Tovell has in adopting a strategy of diversifying into many different industries is to reduce risk for the company's shareholders. However, except where restrictions apply to direct investments, investors can probably reduce investment risk more efficiently than companies, and they should already be seeking to be well-diversified in order to **minimise unsystematic risk**. The cost of diversifying is likely to be much higher for a company than for an individual investor, and therefore Tovell's diversification strategy is unlikely to contribute to the primary financial objective of maximising the wealth of the ordinary shareholders.

Other arguments against diversification

Other practical arguments against a high level of diversification by companies include the following.

(a) Managers employed by a company will normally have acquired skills and experience in one or two business sectors. If they are required to work in areas outside their direct experience their **effectiveness** is likely to be **reduced**, at least while they are going through the learning curve. Co-ordination of the different areas and effective financial control are also much harder in a fully diversified business.

(b) For the reasons outlined above, **performance** in the individual divisions of a conglomerate is **unlikely to be much above** the average for the industry. Conglomerates may therefore be vulnerable to takeover and unbundling whereby the individual businesses are sold off one by one at a profit.

Benefits of diversification

On the other hand, there may be some benefits to shareholders in diversification by Tovell.

(a) **Volatility** in the internal cash flows is **reduced**. This makes it possible to service a higher level of debt without undue risk than might otherwise be possible. As a result the overall cost of capital can be reduced, to the benefit of the ordinary shareholders.

(b) Companies may be able to **diversify** into areas which are **inaccessible** to individual investors, for example in foreign countries which have exchange controls or other barriers to direct investment.

(c) The **probability of failure is lower** in a **well-diversified company** due to the reduced overall level of risk. This may be attractive to shareholders, particularly if they are risk-averse.

Exam answer bank

10 D PLC

> **Pass marks.** (a) requires the calculation of gearing ratios and weighted average cost of capital of a company that includes both preference shares and debentures in its capital structure. You are given details in this question of how to calculate the gearing ratios, as this topic is not covered in detail until Chapter 11. Normally it would be up to you to identify the right items, and you should be careful in your treatment and explain your reasoning. You should always state the formula you are using since more than one approach is possible.
>
> Hopefully you should not have been put off in (b) by having to bring in preference shares as well. You are supplied with the weighting (market value) and the information necessary to calculate the preference shares cost of capital (% and market value). You will often be expected to use the dividend valuation model to find the cost of equity.
>
> In (c) you should consider the needs of investors as well as the position of the company, since these will be relevant in ensuring the success of the issue.
>
> In (d) note that the merchant banks provide advice on every aspect of the issue.

(a) The gearing ratio can be calculated using the following expression:

$$\text{Gearing} = \frac{\text{Prior charge capital}}{\text{Prior charge capital} + \text{equity}}$$

(i) Using book values, prior charge capital includes:

	Book value £'000
9% debentures	8,000
7% preference shares	1,000
	9,000
Equity:	
Ordinary share capital	2,000
Share premium account	1,100
Profit and loss account	6,550
	9,650

$$\text{Gearing} = \frac{9,000}{9,000 + 9,650} = 48.3\%$$

(ii) Using market values, prior charge capital includes:

	Market value £'000
9% debentures @ 80p per £1	6,400
7% preference shares @ 77p per £1	770
	7,170
Equity:	
Ordinary shares @ £1.35 per 25p nominal value	10,800

$$\text{Gearing} = \frac{7,170}{7,170 + 10,800} = 39.9\%$$

(b) The weighted average cost of capital (WACC) can be found using the following expression:

$$\text{WACC} = k_e \frac{V_E}{V_E + V_D} + k_d \frac{V_D}{V_E + V_D}$$

where:

k_e = cost of equity
k_d = cost of debt (after tax)
V_E = market value of equity in the firm
V_D = market value of debt in the firm

In this case, there are three sources of capital to be included. k_d and V_D will therefore be replaced by k_p (cost of preference shares) and P (market value of preference shares), and k_g (cost of debentures) and G (market value of debentures).

The next step is to calculate the cost of the different sources of capital in D plc:

Cost of equity (k_e)

This can be found using the dividend growth model:

$$k_e = \frac{d_0(1+g)}{P_0} + g$$

where:

d_0 = current level of dividends
g = dividend growth rate in perpetuity
P_0 = current market price of equity

$$k_e = \frac{10(1+0.09)}{135} + 0.09$$

$$k_e = 17.1\%$$

Cost of preference shares (k_p)

This can be found by dividing the preference dividend rate by the market price of the shares:

$$k_p = \frac{7}{77}$$

$$k_p = 9.1\%$$

Although preference shares are included with prior charge capital, the dividend is not allowable for tax, and therefore no adjustment needs to be made for this.

Cost of debentures (k_d)

The after tax cost of the debentures can be found using the following expression:

$$k_d = \frac{i(1-t)}{P_0}$$

where:

i = rate of debenture interest
P_0 = market price of debentures
t = rate of corporation tax

$$k_g = \frac{9(1-0.3)}{80}$$

$$k_g = 7.9\%$$

The WACC can now be calculated:

$$\text{WACC} = \frac{(17.1 \times 10{,}800)}{17{,}970} + \frac{(9.1 \times 770)}{17{,}970} + \frac{(7.9 \times 6{,}400)}{17{,}970}$$

$$\text{WACC} = 13.5\%$$

(c) Possible reasons why D plc may have chosen to raise additional finance using debentures rather than preference shares include the following.

    (i)   **Debentures** are a **cheaper form of finance** than preference shares because debenture interest is tax deductible, unlike preference dividends.

    (ii)   **Debentures** are **more attractive** to investors because they are secured against the company's assets.

    (iii)   **Debenture holders** rank before **preference shareholders** in the event of a liquidation.

    (iv)   **Issue costs** should be **lower** for **debentures** than for preference shares.

(d) Services that might have been provided by a merchant bank in this situation include the following.

    (i)   Advice on the **most appropriate form** of capital to be raised, i.e. equity or debt.

Exam answer bank

    (ii)   Advice on the **precise form** that the issue of debt should take, for instance, whether it should be secured, and if so, against which assets; whether the issue should be made more attractive to investors by the use of devices such as warrants.

    (iii)   Advice on the **price** at which the issue should be made.

    (iv)   Advice on the **coupon rate** and term of the debenture.

    (v)   Identifying **appropriate investors** and marketing the issue.

    (vi)   **Administration** of the issue, including making sure that the terms of the issue comply with statutory and regulatory requirements.

11   YEAR-END STATISTICS

> **Pass marks**. The question is asking you to refute some commonly held misconceptions about financial ratios. It is therefore helpful to state clearly the correct definitions of the ratios and terms used, and then to argue from these definitions in criticising the statements made.
>
> (a) makes what can be an important point, the price-earnings ratio does not compare like with like if future earnings are expected to be very different from what has just happened. How efficient the market is will determine how much influence future expectations have on share prices.
>
> The key point in (b) is that the cost of capital influences the share price and not the other way around.
>
> In (c) the director's misconception is explained, but even if he was correct in assuming that gearing had some influence on the share price, it is questionable how much.
>
> (d) is proved quite simply by demonstrating how the ratios are calculated; the nominal value of shares does not enter into the equation.
>
> In (e) the current market price is itself an indication of investor views, and its high level indicates that the company is viewed positively.

(a)   **P/E ratio**

The **P/E ratio** measures the **relationship** between the **market price** of a share and the **earnings per share** (on a net basis). Its calculation involves the use of the share price, which is a reflection of the market's expectations of the future earnings performance, and the historic level of earnings.

If Y plc has just suffered an abnormally bad year's profit performance which is not expected to be repeated, the market will price the share on the basis of its expected future earnings. The earnings figure used to calculate the ratio will be the historic figure which is lower than that forecast for the future, and thus the ratio will appear high.

(b)   **Earnings yield**

The **earnings yield** is effectively the inverse of the P/E ratio. As explained above, the key factors in calculating the ratio are the historic level of earnings and the current market price of the shares.

The **cost of capital** is the **opportunity cost of finance**. It is the **cost of funds** that a **company uses** and the **return** that **investors expect to receive** in return for providing funds to the company. It is thus the **minimum return** that a **company must make** on its own activities to provide sufficient cash flow to pay the investors. It can be seen therefore that the company will want the cost of capital to be as low as possible. In practice the actual cost of capital will depend on the financial structure of the company, the market rate of return and the perceived level of risk to investors inherent in the company's activities.

The actual level of the share price will therefore be a consequence of the cost of capital, and not a causative factor. Similarly, it can be seen that the earnings yield is a consequence and not a cause of Y plc's lower cost of capital.

(c)   **Financial gearing**

The **financial gearing** of the firm expresses the **relationship** between **debt** and **equity** in the capital structure. A high level of gearing means that there is a high ratio of debt to equity. This means that the company carries a high fixed interest charge, and thus the amount of earnings available to equity will be more variable from year to year than in a company with a lower gearing level. Thus the shareholders will carry a higher level of risk than in a company with lower gearing.

All other things being equal, it is therefore likely that the share price in a highly geared company will be lower than that in a low geared firm.

The P/E ratio is dependent upon the **current share price** and the **historic level of earnings**. A high P/E ratio is therefore more likely to be found in a company with low gearing than in one with high gearing. In the case of Y plc, the high P/E ratio is more probably attributable to the depressed level of earnings than to the financial structure of the company.

(d) **Comparison of ratios**

The three ratios are calculated as follows.

$$\text{P/E ratio} = \frac{\text{Market share price}}{\text{Earnings per share}}$$

$$\text{Dividend yield} = \frac{\text{Dividend per share}}{\text{Market share price}}$$

$$\text{Earnings yield} = \frac{\text{Earnings per share}}{\text{Market share price}}$$

The **nominal value** of the shares is **irrelevant** in calculating the ratios. This can be proved by calculating the effect on the ratios of a share split - the ratios will be unchanged. Thus if all other factors (such as accounting conventions used in the two firms) are equal, a direct comparison of the ratios is valid.

(e) **Comparison with risk free securities**

As outlined in (d) above, the **dividend yield** is the relationship between the **dividend per share** and the **current market price** of the share. The market price of the share reflects investor expectations about the future level of earnings and growth. If the share is trading with a low dividend yield, this means that investors have positive growth expectations after taking into account the level of risk. Although the government bonds carry no risk, it is equally likely that they have no growth potential either, and this means that the share will still be more attractive even after the low dividend yield has been taken into account.

12 YIELDS

> **Pass marks**. You would probably not get a full question on the yield curve, but both parts (a) and (b) represent the sort of part questions that might be set on this area. In (a) your explanation does need to be supplemented by a diagram, although you also need to explain about maturities.
>
> (b) firstly explains why expectations are so important (because other possible influences tend to remain constant). The answer then explains how expectations impact upon investor behaviour. Expectations of changes in inflation need to be discussed separately.

(a) A **yield curve** is a curve that can be drawn showing the relationship between the **yield on an asset** (usually long-term government stocks) and the **term to maturity** of that same asset. It shows how the rate of interest (yield) varies with different maturities. To construct a yield curve you need to gather information about the interest rates on short-term stocks, medium-term stocks and long-term stocks. These rates can then be **plotted on a diagram** against the maturity dates of those same stocks.

A normal yield curve looks like Figure 1.

Exam answer bank

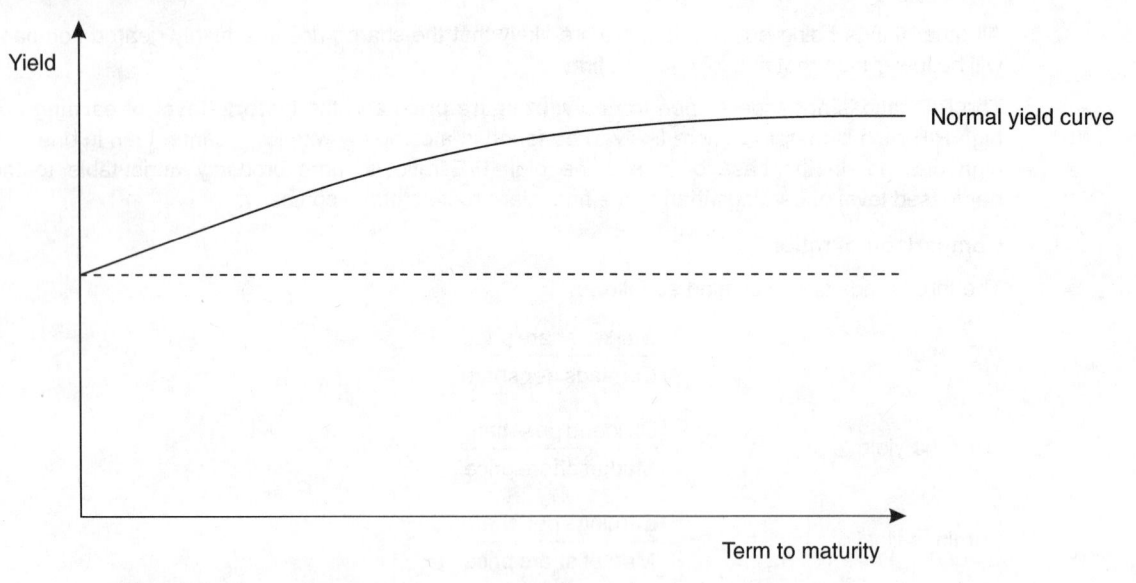

Figure 1 — Normal yield curve (Yield vs Term to maturity)

(b) **Importance of expectations**

The **shape of the yield curve** depends very much on **expectations about the future.** Reward for loss of liquidity is likely to remain fairly constant. Reward for possible default is likely to remain constant also. Reward for the risk of having to cash in before maturity and suffering a loss are also likely to stay fairly constant. The only factor which will vary widely is expectations - in particular, expectations about future short-term interest rates.

Expectations about the future level of short-term interest rates are the most important factor in determining the shape of the yield curve. Although the normal yield curve is upward sloping, with higher yields being expected for longer maturity periods, expectations of rises in future interest rates can cause the yield curve to be steeper than the normal curve. Expectations of falls in interest rates can cause the yield to flatten, or, if substantial falls are expected, to become downward-sloping (Figure 2).

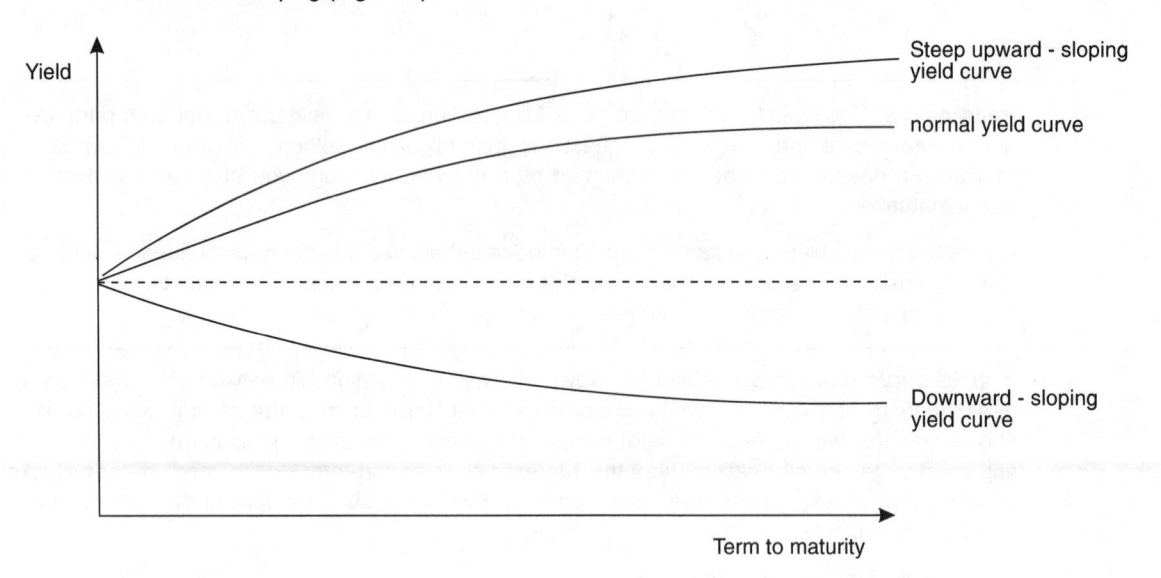

Figure 2 — Steep upward-sloping yield curve, normal yield curve, Downward-sloping yield curve (Yield vs Term to maturity)

Rising interest rates

If interest rates are now **expected to rise**, investors will not wish to lock in to lower interest rates and will therefore sell short. Borrowers will wish to borrow at lower long-term rates to avoid exposure to the higher rates expected in the future. These demand and supply factors will result in a shortage of long-term funds, which will push up long-term money market rates, and to an excess supply of short-term funds, which will lead to a reduction in short-term rates. The resulting yield curve will be more steeply upward-sloping than the normal curve.

Exam answer bank

Falling interest rates

If there are **new expectations that interest rates will fall,** investors will prefer to lock in at higher long rates, while borrowers will not wish to be committed to higher long term rates and will prefer to borrow short. There will be an excess supply of funds at long maturities and a shortage of funds at short maturities. This will tend to lower the yield curve, possibly resulting in a flat curve or even in a downward-sloping curve.

Inflation

Short-term interest rates are in turn determined partly by **expectations of inflation** rates in the near future. If high inflation is expected, investors will seek higher nominal rates of interest in order to achieve a real return. If people believe that inflation is falling, then they will not require such a high return.

13 MARKETABLE SECURITIES

> **Pass marks.** It helps to plan this answer carefully and check that you are investing exactly the amounts available for each period of two months. The plan will also show you that there are limits to the points you can make in the second half of the question so you can devote the bulk of your time to finding the best combination of investments.
>
> In (b) the focus is on selecting the appropriate (low) level of risk. As the investments are only for the short-term, the transaction costs and resources used in managing them should also be low.

(a) Since interest rates are forecast to rise, the best solution is likely to be one in which only short-term deposits are made, thus allowing advantage to be taken of the rise in rates. Options structured in this way include the following.

	Amount £'000	Month invested	Period (in months)	Rate	Value £
1	2,000	0	2	7.3%	24,333
	6,000	2	2	8.0%	80,000
	4,000	4	2	8.3%	55,333
	Transaction costs				(300)
					159,366
2	2,000	0	4	7.4%	49,333
	4,000	2	4	8.1%	108,000
	Transaction costs				(200)
					157,133
3	2,000	0	4	7.4%	49,333
	4,000	2	2	8.0%	53,333
	4,000	4	2	8.3%	55,333
	Transaction costs				(300)
					157,699
4	2,000	0	2	7.3%	24,333
	2,000	2	2	8.0%	26,667
	4,000	2	4	8.1%	108,000
	Transaction costs				(300)
					158,700
5	2,000	0	6	7.5%	75,000
	2,000	2	4	8.1%	54,000
	2,000	2	2	8.0%	26,667
	Transaction costs				(300)
					155,367

Exam answer bank

	Amount £'000	Month invested	Period (in months)	Rate	Value £
6	2,000	0	6	7.5%	75,000
	4,000	2	2	8.0%	53,333
	2,000	4	2	8.3%	27,667
	Transaction costs				(300)
					155,700

It can be seen that option 1 yields the best return.

(b) When selecting marketable securities, the company is normally doing so with the aim of maximising the return on short-term cash surpluses. With this aim in mind, the criteria are likely to include the following.

(i) The **level of risk** should be as **low as possible** since the company is not seeking a speculative gain, but to ensure that funds which are intended for specific purposes in the future do not lie idle.

(ii) The **level of return** should be as **high as possible** within the class of risk which the company is prepared to accept.

(iii) The **level of transaction costs** and the **degree of complexity** of administration should be as low as possible.

(iv) Ideally the securities will be **easily marketable** so that if the funds are required at an earlier date than anticipated this can be achieved without significant loss of revenue.

(v) The amount of funds to be invested will **influence** the types of security that will be appropriate.

14 A BRICKIE (BUILDERS) LTD

> **Pass marks.** Make sure that you match your answer to the information provided in the question. For example, we know that the company in question is a private company that requires funds for business expansion. Discussions on areas such as the effect on the share price are therefore inappropriate.

To: Board of Directors of A Brickie (Builders) Ltd
From: Assistant Financial Controller
Date: 29 January 20X1
Subject: Factors to be considered in deciding the financing mix

Introduction

The purpose of this report is to identify the main factors to be considered when deciding on the appropriate mix of long-term or short-term sources of debt finance, and to consider the advantages of fixing interest rates on debt.

Main factors to be considered

1 **The purpose of the borrowing**

The type of funds must be matched to the **purpose** for which they are required. The **business expansion programme** is likely to **require finance** both for the purchase of additional fixed assets, and for an increase in the level of working capital. In general cheaper **short-term funds** should only be used to **finance short-term requirements**, such as a larger level of fluctuations in the level of working capital. Short-term debt, usually in the form of an overdraft, is repayable on demand, and it would therefore be risky to finance long-term capital investments in this way.

2 **Flexibility**

Short-term finance is a **more flexible** source of finance; there may be penalties for repaying long-term debt early. However, we do have to be sure that further short-term debt will be available if we need to renew our facility.

3 **Our ability to borrow and repay**

We must be able to convince a lender of our ability to service the debt and to repay it at the end of the term. We must therefore put together a **business plan** for the expansion that shows how earnings from the additional sales will be sufficient to cover interest costs, and also shows how we intend to fund repayment at the end of the loan period. We must also confirm that we have the **legal capacity** to borrow in the manner required by checking the articles of association, and that we will not breach any restrictive covenants on our existing borrowings.

4 The cost of the debt and the repayment terms

The **relative costs** of the alternative sources of finance must be considered. For example, short-term debt is usually cheaper than long-term debt, but will carry a higher level of risk, as discussed above. The interest rate charged will also depend on the **perceived risk** of the investment to the lender, and this is another reason for putting together a comprehensive business plan. The **repayment terms** must also be **matched** to the pattern of cash flows coming from the new enterprise.

5 The effect on gearing

The gearing of the business is a measure of the amount of debt relative to equity. If a company is seen as being too highly geared, finance providers will judge that the **risk of default** is high, and are likely to seek higher compensation for this risk. This could take the form of a higher interest rate, restrictive covenants, or shorter repayment terms. If they perceive the risk to be high, some finance providers may be unwilling to lend at all. If gearing is likely to be a problem, we could consider acquiring some of the new assets using leases, since operating leases are not included in the company's balance sheet.

The advantages of fixing interest rates on debt

The two main advantages of fixed interest rates are as follows:

1 Cash flow planning

With a fixed rate loan, we will know exactly how much we need to pay, and when. This will make it easier to **plan** the **cash flow** and to ensure that we have **funds available** when required.

2 Cost

If we believe that interest rates are likely to rise over the period of the loan, then taking out a **fixed rate loan** will **limit our interest rate liability.**

Conclusions

The key factor in the choice of financing method is the purpose for which the funds are required. A detailed business plan for the new investment should be prepared in order to identify the most appropriate financing mix, and to support our case to potential lenders.

15 AARDVARK LTD

> **Pass marks.** This is easier than an exam question would be, but you might need to carry out some of the calculations in a larger question. Possible traps include:
>
> - Forgetting to include the saving in administrative costs or including it as part of the calculation on use of the insurer
>
> - Failing to include the bad debts saved when considering the two options involving the export factor
>
> - Incorrect treatment of the complexities involving interest; it's best to work slowly through this part of the calculation

Aardvark Ltd has the following options.

(a) It can **continue its existing policy**.

(b) It can **use the export factor**, either in combination with its existing overdraft, or using the 80% finance offered by the factor.

(c) It can **use the insurer** with the assignment of policy rights (since cheaper finance is available at no extra cost.

It is assumed that all export debts will be financed by an overdraft or by special lending arrangements.

(a) **Use of the export factor for debt collection only**

	£
Service fee (3% × £1,000,000)	(30,000)
Bad debts saved (by insurance) (0.5% × £1,000,000)	5,000
Administration costs saved	35,000
Net saving	10,000

(b) **Use of the export factor for debt collection and finance**

That there will be a saving in finance charges of 0.5% a year on 80% of the average debtors required.

	£
Service fee for debt collection	(30,000)
Interest costs saved (0.5% × 80% × £1,000,000 × 90/360)	1,000
Bad debts saved	5,000
Administrative costs saved	35,000
Net saving	11,000

(c) **Use of the insurer**

If the insurer was used, there is a saving of 1% on 70% of the finance required, since 70% of finance will be obtained at just 1.5% above base rate, instead of 2.5% above base rate.

	£
Insurance costs (0.35% × £1,000,000)	(3,500)
Savings in bank interest (1% × 70% × £1,000,000 × 90/360)	1,750
Savings in bad debts (90% × 0.5% × £1,000,000)	4,500
Net saving	2,750

Conclusion

Aardvark Ltd should use the services of the export factor, and obtain finance for 80% of export credit sales from the factor.

16 WORKING CAPITAL

> **Pass marks**. The six marks available for (a) is a lot for a definition part question so your description in (a) needs to be fairly full. Although you are directed to describe the symptoms of overtrading, you would have mentioned them even if you had not been asked.
>
> (b) should be approached by using your calculations to determine whether overtrading exists rather than just calculating random ratios. This means examining the short-term ratios in company finance, as well as sales growth, profit margins, liquidity ratios and working capital ratios. Do not be surprised however if not all the ratios show the same results; here the company is keeping up its payment schedule to creditors despite its other problems.
>
> (b) (i) concludes by highlighting the most important indicators of overtrading. It is important to do this in an answer where you have given a lot of detail, as you need to pick out where the greatest threats to the business lie. In this question the threats highlighted at the end of part (b) will be those for which remedies are identified in (b) (ii).

(a) **Overtrading**

'**Overtrading**' refers to the situation where a company is **over-reliant** on **short-term finance** to support its operations. This is risky because short-term finance may be withdrawn relatively quickly if creditors **lose confidence** in the business, or if there is a general tightening of credit in the economy, and this may result in a liquidity crisis and even bankruptcy, even though the firm is profitable. The fundamental solution to overtrading is to replace short term finance with longer term finance such as term loans or equity funds.

Problems of rapid expansion

The term overtrading is used because the condition commonly arises when a company is expanding rapidly. In this situation, because of increasing volumes, **more cash** is frequently **needed to pay input costs** such as wages or purchases than is currently being collected from debtors. The result is that the company runs up its overdraft to the limit and sometimes there is **insufficient time** to arrange an **increase in facilities** to pay other creditors on the due dates.

Exam answer bank

Lack of control

These problems are often compounded by a general lack of attention to **cost control** and **working capital management**, such as debt collection, because most management time is spent **organising selling or production**. The result is an unnecessary **drop in profit margins**.

Under-capitalisation

When the overdraft limit is reached the company frequently raises funds from other **expensive short term sources**, such as debt factoring or debtor's prompt payment discounts, and delays payment to creditors, instead of underpinning its financial position with equity funds or a longer term loan. The consequent under-capitalisation **delays investment in fixed assets and staff** and can further harm the quality of the firm's operations.

(b) (i) The company has become significantly more reliant on short term liabilities to finance its operations as shown by the following analysis:

	20X9		20X8	
	£'000		£'000	
Total assets	21,350		14,900	
Short-term liabilities	8,700	40.7%	5,000	33.6%
Long term funds (equity and debt)	12,650	59.3%	9,900	66.4%
	21,350		14,900	

Overtrading

A major reason for this is classic overtrading: sales increased by 50% in one year, but the operating profit margin fell from 9,000/20,000 = 45% in 20X8 to 10,000/30,000 = 33% in 20X9.

Refinancing

However, the effect is **compounded** by the **repayment** of £2.3 million (66%) of the 8% debentures and replacement with a £2 million bank overdraft and increased trade creditor finance. Although this may be because the interest rate on the overdraft is cheaper than on the debentures, it is generally not advisable in the context of the risk of short term debt.

However, if it is felt that the current sales volume is abnormal and that, when the Polly Playtime doll reaches the end of its product life cycle, sales will stabilise at a lower level, the use of shorter term debt is justified.

Liquidity ratios

As a result of overtrading, the company's **current ratio** has deteriorated from 13,500/5000 = 2.7 in 20X8 to 19,850/8700 = 2.28 in 20X9. The **quick assets ratio** (or 'acid test') has deteriorated from 10,500/5,000 = 2.1 to 12,500/8,700 = 1.44. However these figures are acceptable and only if they continue to deteriorate is there likely to be a liquidity problem. In the 20X9 accounts the company continues to have a healthy bank balance, although this has been achieved partly by halting dividend growth.

Investment in fixed assets

The company has **not maintained an investment in fixed assets** to match its sales growth. Sales/fixed assets has increased from 20,000/1,400 = 14.3 times to 30,000/1,500 = 20 times. This may be putting the quality of production at risk, but may be justified, however, if sales are expected to decline when the doll loses popularity.

Working capital ratios

An investigation of working capital ratios shows that:

(1) **Stock turnover** has **decreased** from 20,000/3,000 = 6.67 times to 30,000/7,350 = 4.08 times. This indicates that there has been a large investment in stock. The question of whether this is justified again depends on expected future sales, but the strategy appears to be the opposite of that adopted for fixed assets.

(2) The **average debtors payment period has increased** from 6,000/20,000 × 365 = 110 days to 10,000/30,000 × 365 = 122 days, indicating a lack of credit control. This has contributed to a weakening of the cash position. There appears to be no evidence of prompt payment discounts to debtors.

Exam answer bank

(3) The **payment period to creditors** (roughly estimated) has **decreased** from 2,500/11,000 × 365 = 83 days to 4,200/20,000 × 365 = 77 days. This result is unexpected, indicating that there has been no increase in delaying payment to creditors over the year. Creditors are being paid in a significantly shorter period than the period of credit taken by customers.

Conclusion

In summary, the main problem facing Gustaffson is its increasing overdependence on short term finance, caused in the main by:

(1) A major investment in stock to satisfy a rapid increase in sales volumes
(2) Deteriorating profit margins
(3) Poor credit control of debtors
(4) Repayment of debenture capital

(ii) **Future sales**

Possible solutions to the above problems depend on **future sales** and **product projections**. If the rapid increase in sales has been a one-product phenomenon, there is little point in over-capitalising by borrowing long term and investing in a major expansion of fixed assets. If, however, sales of this and future products are expected to continue increasing, and further investment is needed, the company's growth should be underpinned by an injection of equity capital and an issue of longer term debt.

Better working capital management

Regardless of the above, various working capital strategies could be improved. **Debtors** should be encouraged to **pay more promptly**. This is best done by instituting **proper credit control procedures**. **Longer credit periods** could probably be negotiated with creditors and quantity discounts should be investigated.

17 VX COMPANY

> **Pass marks**. It is important to adopt a systematic approach to this question. Start by heading up a sheet for workings and then work carefully through the information given, calculating each cost and revenue and determining and noting when the cash flow will occur.
>
> Make sure that you produce a clearly labelled cash budget. Do not expect the examiner to search among your workings for the final answer. You must show the opening and closing balances for each month at the bottom of each column.
>
> Often the cash budgets you produce for questions will show a shortage of cash. A discussion part asking you for remedies for that shortage will be common. You should be thinking primarily of shorter-term measures, particularly better management of working capital.

(a) *Initial workings*

(i) *Sales value*

	Nov	Dec	Jan	Feb	Mar	Apr
Sales units	1,000	1,200	1,400	1,600	1,800	2,000
Sales value at £50 (£)	50,000	60,000	70,000	80,000	90,000	100,000

Sales revenue will be received two months after the sale is made.

(ii) Production costs

	Nov	Dec	Jan	Feb	Mar	Apr	May	June
Production units	1,200	1,400	1,600	2,000	2,400	2,600	2,400	2,200
	£'000	£'000	£'000	£'000	£'000	£'000	£'000	£'000
Wages at £8			12.8	16.0	19.2	20.8	19.2	17.6
Variable o/h at £2	2.4	2.8	3.2	4.0	4.8	5.2	4.8	4.4
50% paid in month	1.2	1.4	1.6	2.0	2.4	2.6	2.4	2.2
50% in following month		1.2	1.4	1.6	2.0	2.4	2.6	2.4
Total payment			3.0	3.6	4.4	5.0	5.0	4.6
Material at £26	31.2	36.4	41.6	52.0	62.4	67.6	62.4	57.2
Payment after two months			31.2	36.4	41.6	52.0	62.4	67.6

CASH BUDGET FOR FIRST SIX MONTHS OF NEXT YEAR

	Jan	Feb	Mar	Apr	May	June
	£'000	£'000	£'000	£'000	£'000	£'000
Receipts						
Sales revenue	50.0	60.0	70.0	80.0	90.0	100.0
Sale of old machine	1.2	-	-	-	-	-
	51.2	60.0	70.0	80.0	90.0	100.0
Payments						
Wages	12.8	16.0	19.2	20.8	19.2	17.6
Variable overhead	3.0	3.6	4.4	5.0	5.0	4.6
Material	31.2	36.4	41.6	52.0	62.4	67.6
Fixed overhead	5.5	5.5	5.5	5.5	5.5	5.5
New machine		34.0				
	52.5	95.5	70.7	83.3	92.1	95.3
Net cash flow	(1.3)	(35.5)	(0.7)	(3.3)	(2.1)	4.7
Opening cash balance	35.5	34.2	(1.3)	(2.0)	(5.3)	(7.4)
Closing cash balance	34.2	(1.3)	(2.0)	(5.3)	(7.4)	(2.7)

(b) The cash budget shows that the company will require more cash than is available from February onwards. Management might decide to arrange an overdraft to cover the deficit. Alternatively they could reduce or avoid the deficit by taking actions such as the following.

   (i) **Negotiate credit facilities** or stage payments for the purchase of the machine.

   (ii) **Defer** the **purchase** of the **machine** or lease it instead of buying.

   (iii) **Defer payments** to **material suppliers**, although the company already takes two months credit for these purchases.

   (iv) **Attempt to collect payments** from debtors more quickly.

(c) (i) **Depreciation** is not a cash flow and so would have no effect on a cash budget.

   (ii) **Depreciation is charged** in the **profit and loss account** for the year and therefore reduces the profit of a business.

Exam answer bank

18 MILLER-ORR MODEL

> **Pass marks.** Your answer to (a) can usefully start with a definition of EFTS, although this shouldn't be too long; you need to leave yourself time to discuss the advantages and disadvantages.
>
> In (b) (i) you must refer to the situation described in the question; failing to mention the local authority would mean you would gain little or no credit for this part of the question. You need to bring out how the concept of balancing liquidity is brought into cash management models.
>
> (b) (ii) is unusual in that questions on the Miller-Orr model are most likely to require you to use the formula. The answer starts by explaining what the model is doing, differentiating it from the cash management models. It then goes on to describe the upper and lower limits; however to demonstrate how the model works in practice, you would have to show how transfers work when the upper and lower limits are reached. The marking would be weighted towards the last part of the answer.

(a) **EFTS**

Electronic funds transfer systems (EFTS) enable funds to be transferred between bank accounts on the same day. Examples in the UK include BACS (Bankers Automated Clearing System) and CHAPS (Clearing House Automated Payment System). International transfers can be made via SWIFT (Society for Worldwide Interbank Financial Telecommunications).

The usual alternative is payment by cheque or bankers draft, which results in delays as the documentation passes through the postal, banking and clearing systems.

Advantages of EFTS

From the payer's point of view, the advantages of EFTS are **savings** in **processing time** and paperwork and **hence** in **administration** costs.

Disadvantages of EFTS

The disadvantages to payers are as follows.

(i) The prompt processing means here is **no excuse** for **delayed payment** (eg the postal system cannot be blamed) and hence there will possibly be an effective reduction in the free credit period and an increase in interest costs.

(ii) If processing is carried out in batches, an urgent request for payment by one customer may cause a whole batch of payments to be made early, again resulting in an increased interest cost.

(b) To: The Treasurer
From: A N Recruit, Accounts   Date: 15 May 20X2
Subject: Cash management models

(i) **Liquidity and return**

Cash management models take into account the trade-off between **the rate of return** which can be earned on surplus funds and the **need to maintain liquidity**. For example, a company will need to keep a certain amount of cash in a non-interest or low-interest current account in order to meet known and expected liabilities. If, however, the balance in this account becomes unnecessarily high, the company is losing the interest which could be earned by transferring the funds to a higher interest deposit account or other form of investment.

Cash management in the public sector

For our department, this is particularly important as the more we can earn in additional interest the more we have to spend on the local community. Local authorities are increasingly being asked to demonstrate **efficiency and effective** use of resources and one of our largest resources is cash.

Similarity to stock models

Cash management models effectively regard **surplus cash** as a form of stock. Stock management models attempt to minimise the sum of stock-holding costs, stock ordering costs and stock-out costs. Equivalent costs can be identified for cash balances. The cash model which is closest to the 'Economic Order Quantity' stock model is the **Baumol model**, but this is unrealistic in that it assumes that cash is used up at an even rate.

(ii) **Miller-Orr model**

The **Miller-Orr model**, illustrated below, is more useful because it deals with receipts and payments of cash and provides trigger points for transferring cash to and from investment accounts when the current account balance becomes too high or low respectively. It does, however, make an unrealistic assumption that **cash flows** are entirely **unpredictable**.

Lower and upper limits

We have already agreed with our bank that the minimum balance on our current account will be £15,000. This is referred to as the 'lower limit'. Thus when the balance falls to that level we will need to transfer money out of the investment account into the current account. To compute the 'upper limit' the Miller-Orr model uses three data items:

- The transaction cost for each cash transfer in or out of the account: £25
- The variance of daily cash flows: $(£3,000)^2 = £9,000,000$
- The daily interest rate on invested cash: 0.0236%

Using these items of data it can be shown that the 'spread' between the upper and lower limits is £26,820. This means that the upper limit is £15,000 + £26,820 = £41,820. When the current account reaches this high level, money will be transferred out into the investment account.

Transfers

The final question is how much needs to be transferred in and out when the lower and upper limits are reached. The Miller-Orr model sets the 'return point' at a figure one third of the way between the upper and lower limits.

The return point is £15,000 + ⅓ × £26,820 = £15,000 + £8,940 = £23,940.

In summary, then, when the balance falls to £15,000, £8,940 is transferred into the account to bring it up to £23,940. When the balance rises to £41,820, £17,880 is transferred out of the account to return the balance to £23,940.

Signed: AN Recruit

Pass marks. You do not need to compute the spread in this question because it is given to you. Using the formula for the Miller-Orr model, the spread is

$$3 \left[\frac{3}{4} \times \frac{\text{transaction cost} \times \text{variance of cash flows}}{\text{interest rate}} \right]^{1/3}$$

Hence the spread is $3 \left(\frac{3/4 \times 25 \times 9,000,000}{0.0236\%} \right)^{1/3} = £26,827$

---

19 ABC LTD

Pass marks. (a) represents basic knowledge that should provide very easy marks. (b) and (c) require you to calculate the cost of the two proposals in different ways, one being an actual annual cost and the other an annualised percentage. This means that you cannot make a comparison of the two in cost terms on the basis of these calculations. However, remarks can still be made about costs (20% is evidently a lot). However you also need to bring out in (d) the uncertainties involved, principally how customers will react, and the constraints imposed by the need to remain competitive.

(a) A factor normally **manages the debts** owed to a client on the client's behalf. The main services provided by factoring organisations are as follows.

(i) **Administration** of the **client's invoicing, sales accounting and debt collection service**.

(ii) **Credit protection** for the client's debts, whereby the factor takes over the risk of loss from bad debts and so 'insures' the client against such losses. The factor usually purchases

Exam answer bank

these debts 'without recourse' to the client, which means that if the client's debtors do not pay what they owe, the factor will not ask for the money back from the client.

(iii) **'Factor finance'** may be provided, the factor advancing cash to the client against outstanding debts. The factor may advance up to 85% of approved debts from the date of invoice.

A **confidentiality agreement** may be offered to conceal the existence of the arrangement from customers.

(b) It will be assumed that the factor finance will not be replacing any existing credit lines, and therefore the full interest cost of the agreement will be relevant when determining the cost of factoring.

Annual sales are £400,000 × 12 = £4.8m

Daily sales are £4.8m/365 = £13,151

The annual cost of factoring can now be found:

	£
Interest (£13,151 × 40days × 75% × 10%)	39,453
Service fee (£4.8m × 2%)	96,000
Total annual charge	135,453
Less internal cost savings (£5,000 × 12)	60,000
Net annual cost	75,453

(c) Cost of offering discount $= \left(\dfrac{100}{(100-d)}\right)^{\frac{365}{t}} - 1$

$= \left(\dfrac{100}{(100-2)}\right)^{\frac{365}{40}} - 1$

$= 20.2\%$

(d) **Key issues in the discounting option**

- The **proposal is expensive**. The company should be able to get cheaper overdraft finance than this, and longer-term debt should cost even less.

- The company may need to **offer a discount** in order to make its terms competitive with other firms in the industry.

- The **level of take-up** among customers is **uncertain**, and will affect the cash flow position.

- Problems may arise when customers take both the **discount** and the **full forty day credit period**. This will increase **administrative costs** in seeking repayment.

Key issues in the factoring option

- The **factor** may be able to exercise **better credit control** than is possible in a small company.

- The **amount of finance** that will be received is **much more certain** than for the discounting option as 75% of the value of the invoices will be provided immediately.

- The **relationship** with the **customers may deteriorate** due partly to the reduction in the level of contact with the company, and partly to the historical view of the factor as the lender of last resort.

The final decision must take into account all the above issues. However, the most important points to consider are the ability of each proposal to meet the financing requirements, and the relative costs of the different sources of finance.

20 FLOWER POTS LTD

> **Pass marks**. Questions (a) (i) and (ii) could have been reworked as plausible MCQs and you should note the points that they make. List questions such as (a) (iii) are generally about getting as many points down as quickly as possible, so do a brief plan to collect your thoughts and then get writing.
>
> In (b) because information has been given to you selectively, you should be looking to comment on all of it. More challenging questions might give you a full profit and loss account and balance sheet and ask you to select the relevant details. Note how the answer brings out the links between the different figures (extension of credit given period appears to have led to an increased overdraft) and suggests various explanations for the change in figures, commenting on their implications. A conclusion, highlighting what is likely to happen in the near future, is helpful here.

(a) (i) As you have not quoted the **amount** of the credit, the bank is in no position to offer any opinion at all, favourable or otherwise.

(ii) Of the two options, (1) is the better reference. This is because (2) contains an element of doubt ('*should* prove').

(iii) **Credit reference agency** reports are useful to the credit controller.

(1) They summarise some (but not all) of the information available.

(2) They can be used to *cross-check* other information obtained, giving additional reassurance especially where large credits are concerned.

A typical agency report will contain the following details.

(1) **Legal data**

- Full name and registered address of the business
- Names of directors, partners, proprietors
- Authorised and issued share capital
- Parent company, if part of a group
- Secured charges
- County court judgements recorded

(2) **Commercial data**

- Types of business
- Location of offices, factories, branches etc
- Main features of latest annual report
- Details of latest annual report
- Annual turnover
- Balance sheet abstracts

(3) **Credit data**

- Bankers' opinions
- Suppliers' opinions, if available
- Possibly, the agency's:
  - Own credit rating of the customer
  - Suggested credit limit for the customer
- Possibly, the agency might keep records of credit offered by its members.

(4) Dun & Bradstreet offer a 'payment' profile service. This contains information about payment records of companies. This information is obtained from clients and fed into Dun & Bradstreet's computer database at regular intervals.

A **payment score report** can be obtained from this data. This is a numerical score that rates a company's performance in paying its bills.

The problems with agency reports are as follows.

(1) **Up-to-date information** which would be **relevant** to the credit decision may **not** have reached the system (eg the collapse of a major customer).

Exam answer bank

      (2) **Suppliers' references** may be **too old** to be relevant.

      (3) **Newly established concerns** will **not have much of a track record** on which a judgement can be made.

(b) **Profitability and net worth**

The company's profitability seems to be declining as its net profit margin has fallen by 20% over two years. This may be because sales are worsening and overheads are fixed or it may indicate poor control of overheads. Possibly gross **profit margins** have been **cut** by increased competition or slacker consumer demand.

Credit given

There seems to have been a **change in credit terms** with the result that customers now take on average two months to pay instead of one. This may have been necessary to attract a large order from a retail chain. (If so, there may be over-reliance on this customer.) However, **cash flow** must have been **badly affected** and there is a possibility of **increased bad debts**. Possibly credit control has been given less priority.

Credit taken

This has also **doubled**, presumably as a result of the increase in the debt collection period. If negotiated, this may not be a problem, but if unagreed with suppliers, **bad will** may have arisen. If the extra credit has been granted as an incentive to place large orders with one supplier, then there may be **over-reliance** on this one supplier, which is risky. If credit control has slipped, then it seems likely that extra credit has been taken to mitigate the effect on cash flow. The company could have liquidity problems.

Working capital ratio

Liquidity is falling, although not yet markedly. Current assets are falling to the level of current liabilities.

Stock turnover

This is decreasing, indicating **poor working capital management** and/or **obsolescence problems** and/or **falling sales**. Stockholding is expensive. However, the business is probably seasonal and stocks will then have to be built up for the summer months. Possibly, therefore, the March year end falls at a time of unusually high stocks, thus distorting the figures.

Bank balance

The **overdraft limit** has been **exceeded**. It would seem that the business is being financed by the bank overdraft and trade credit. How are capital items financed? What is the gearing ratio? This would have to be established.

Conclusion

If the overdraft increases, **interest** and **bank charges** will reduce profit margins even further. It seems likely that the company would benefit from medium or long-term finance. However, to make this worthwhile, management would have to tighten financial controls, especially in respect of trade debtors and stock levels. This may be difficult to achieve.

21 DEBT COLLECTION TARGETS

> **Pass marks**. (a) requires some imagination; you have to think how the target might be set and how it could be achieved. Note our example is more complicated than merely collecting the previous month's debts, and does emphasise the importance of collecting the oldest debts first.
>
> (b) gives you further practice in discussing factoring. The time available gives you the chance to discuss credit protection in some debt. However most time is spent on factor finance since this is the most important service for small, rapidly growing, firms. The answer carefully explains why it is useful.
>
> Your answer to (c) needs to bring out the lack of financial clout small companies have which means they often lack formal control systems or employees looking after credit control full time. Nevertheless there are plenty of steps that can be taken including trying to get more benefits from relationships with customers.

(a) Debtors are assets which it is hoped can be converted into cash, and many companies promote the use of **cash targets** as aids to motivate credit controllers. A cash target is the amount that should be collected in order to arrive at an 'ideal' figure for debtors' ageing. For example, assume at the end of November that debtors outstanding of £2m amount to approximately 61 days. This figure is made up as follows.

		£
November	30 days	900,000
October	31 days	1,100,000
		2,000,000

There are no debts older than this.

Sales in December are £700,000, and the target debtors' ageing at the end of December is 55 days. The December sales add £700,000 which would mean that if no money were collected total debtors at the end of December would be £2,700,000 or 92 days. Therefore, to reach a target of 55 days debtors outstanding requires that the oldest 37 days debtors (92 - 55) should be collected. These are:

		£
October	31 days	1,100,000
November	6 days $^6/_{30}$ × £900,000	180,000
Cash to be collected		1,280,000

The firm should thus aim to collect £1,280,000. Note the emphasis on collecting the oldest debts. If we simply aggregated the figures for December we would have a target debtors of 55/92 × £2,700,000 = £1,614,130 suggesting a cash recovery of only £1,085,870.

The advantages of highlighting efforts on the oldest debts are that:

(i) Older debts imply that customers are taking more credit.

(ii) Staff are not encouraged to ask for *early* payment as a special favour from recent customers.

(iii) Effort is expended on debts which are proving hard to collect anyway.

(b) **Factoring** is a service that does not have a concise definition. A factor is defined as 'a doer or transactor of business for another', but a factoring organisation specialises in trade debts, and so manages the debtors of a client (business customer) on the client's behalf. There are the following aspects of factoring.

(i) **Administration** of the **client's invoicing, sales accounting and debt collection service**.

(ii) **Credit protection** for the **client's debts**, whereby the factor takes over the risk of loss from bad debts and so 'insures' the client against such losses. This service is also referred to as 'debt underwriting' or the 'purchase of a client's debts'.

(1) The **factor might purchase** these **debts 'without recourse'** to the client, which means that, in the event that the client's customers are unable to pay what they owe, the factor will not ask for his money back from the client.

(2) Not every factoring organisation will purchase approved debts without recourse and **'with recourse' factoring might be provided**, especially in cases where the size of the debt is particularly high, or the factor would not approve the debts for a 'without recourse' agreement.

(3) **Credit protection is credit insurance** and so the factoring organisation will want to give its approval to a credit sale before it goes ahead; in other words, the factoring organisation will want to act as a credit controller.

(iii) **Making payment** to the **client** in advance of collecting the debts. This might be referred to as 'factor finance' because the factor is providing cash to the client as a prepayment of outstanding debts.

A factoring organisation might be asked by a client to **advance funds** to the client against the **debts** which the factor has purchased, up to 80% of the value of the debts. This service gives the client **immediate cash** in place of a debt (which is a promise of cash in the future). The remainder, less the fees, is received later. If the client needs money to finance operations, borrowing against trade debts is therefore an alternative to asking a bank for an overdraft, although the factor will probably charge higher interest. Whereas a bank overdraft would have shown in the client's balance sheet as a current liability, factor financing does **not show up** in the client's balance sheet at all.

Exam answer bank

In the client's balance sheet, the amount of **debtors** would be **reduced** and **cash** would initially **increase** by the same amount (although the cash would be used immediately by the client to buy more stocks, make more sales, and create even more debtors - ie the cash advance from the factor would be to put to operational use). For this reason, advances from a factor are particularly useful for **rapidly-growing companies**, that need more and more cash to expand their business quickly, by purchasing more stocks and allowing more credit sales than they would otherwise be able to do. The appeal of factor financing to growing firms is that factors might advance money when a bank is reluctant to consider granting a larger overdraft.

22 THE LAX COMPANY

> **Pass marks**. (a) and (b) give you some practice in accounting for bad debts. This is one area in which your bookkeeping skills may be tested in this paper. You should keep separate in your workings the provisions for bad debts, and the provisions for doubtful debts.

(a) *Initial working: provision for doubtful debts*

		£	£
31 December			
20X7 Provision required	= £44,000 × 3%	1,320	
20X8 Provision required	= £55,000 × 3%	1,650	
Increase in provision - charge to P & L			330
20X9 Provision required	= £47,000 × 3%	1,410	
Decrease in provision - credit to P & L			(240)

Profit and loss account charge
Year ended 31 December

	20X7 £	20X8 £	20X9 £
Bad debts	7,000	10,000	8,000
Provision for doubtful debts	1,320	330	(240) credit

(b)

Balance sheet extracts as at 31 December

	20X7 £	20X8 £	20X9 £
Debtors	44,000	55,000	47,000
Less provision for doubtful debts	1,320	1,650	1,410
Balance sheet value	42,680	53,350	45,590

(c) Small companies face a number of **problems in respect of credit management**, as follows.

  (i) Small companies are often **under pressure** from **large customers** to give over-generous credit facilities. Sometimes these customers negotiate long payment periods and sometimes they just take them. The average small company has little bargaining power to resist such pressures.

  (ii) The business is **too small** to **justify the appointment** of a **skilled credit controller**. If the job is only part of someone's overall responsibilities, it may be shelved behind other more pressing tasks. It is not always obvious to employees that prompt collection of cash has an impact on profitability and the situation may be allowed to drift until the company reaches its overdraft limit.

  (iii) Small companies do **not usually have documented systems** on their credit control policies. Neither do they invest much in training their staff in financial skills and awareness of credit problems. This may result in the granting of credit to high-risk customers.

  (iv) Many small companies are **undercapitalised** and operate with a bank overdraft as the main source of external finance. Consequently poor cash collection will quickly result in the overdraft limit being reached and recurrent problems with the bank.

The following actions could be taken to minimise the effects of these problems.

  (i) Ensure that all **top management** are **adequately trained** in the importance of cash and credit management to the profitability, liquidity and survival of the company.

(ii) Obtain **benchmark figures** for payment periods and bad debts to determine how efficient the company is compared with others in the same industry.

(iii) Analyse the company's strengths and weaknesses to see whether it is able to exercise **more bargaining power** with large customers. A company with above-average products and services will be able to operate a stricter credit control policy than one which is only average.

(iv) Decide whether **credit control** should be **managed in-house** or whether it should be passed to an external expert, such as a factoring company or even a freelance credit consultant.

(v) If credit is to be managed internally, invest in designing and documenting a **proper system**, assigning clear responsibilities and training the appropriate staff. Ensure that customers are informed of the new rules.

(vi) Consider **discount schemes** for prompt payment.

(vii) Consider a **strategic alliance** with a larger company in order to gain more bargaining power with large customers.

23 SF LTD

> **Pass marks**. The first thing to pick up when you read part (a) of this question is that the company is a **small family owned private** company and not a large plc listed on the Stock Exchange. Your suggestions should reflect this and be ones that such a company might reasonably be expected to adopt.
>
> You need to approach this question by making an assessment of the underlying profitability of the business, and trying to understand the key reasons for the cash flow problems before proposing possible solutions.
>
> The solution works down the balance sheet suggesting possible ways of improving each element of working capital and obtaining further finance. The suggestions you put forward should make as much use as possible of the data given in the question, for example highlighting the implications of the seasonal nature of sales. At the same time there are also other general suggestions that can be made; a company in financial difficulties can almost always think about tightening its credit control procedures for example. Note that the answer includes assessment of how effective the various ways of improving the situation could be.
>
> The conclusion highlights the most urgent action required as well as commenting on the company's overall state of health.

To: Board of directors, SF Ltd
From: External consultant
Date: 12 November 20X1
Subject: Cash flow budget

Introduction

The budget shows that the company will experience a **positive cash position** for the first quarter of the year, there being a net inflow of cash during this time as well as no use of the overdraft facility. However, thereafter the position deteriorates, with the company being forecast to exceed its overdraft limit from August to November. By the end of the year, the company's cash reserves will be £50,000 lower than at the start of the period.

Possible remedial actions

1 **Production scheduling**: Sales show a **cyclical movement**, with receipts from customers being highest during the winter months. However, production is scheduled evenly throughout the year. If production could be scheduled to match the pattern of demand, the cash balance would remain more even throughout the year. Any resulting increase in the overall level of production costs could be quantified and compared with the savings in interest costs to assess the viability of such a proposal.

2 **Reducing the debt collection period**: SF Ltd currently allows its customers two months' credit. It is not known how this compares with the industry norms, but it is unlikely to be excessive.

However, there may be some scope for reducing the credit period for at least some of the customers, and thereby reducing the average for the business as a whole.

3   **Tightening the credit control procedures**: It is not known what **level of bad debts** is incurred by SF Ltd, but even if it is low, tightening up the credit control and debt collection procedures could improve the speed with which money is collected.

4   **Factoring the sales ledger**: The use of a factor to administer the sales ledger might **reduce** the **collection period** and **save administration costs**. An evaluation of the relevant costs and benefits could be undertaken to see whether it is worth pursuing this option.

5   **Reduce the stockholding period**: At present it is forecast that stocks will be £30,000 higher by the end of the year. This represents three months' worth of purchases from suppliers. It is not clear to what extent this increase is predicated upon **increasing sales**, although since the building is being extended it is assumed that there will be some increase in the level of production and sales in the near future. However, the size of the increase seems excessive.

6   **Increase the credit period taken**: Since SF Ltd already takes 90 days credit, it is unlikely that it will be able to increase this further without **jeopardising the relationship** with its suppliers.

7   **Defer payment for fixed assets**:

- Presumably the **purchase** of the office furniture could be **deferred**, although the sums involved are relatively insignificant.

- The **progress payment** on the building extension is likely to be a **contractual commitment** that cannot be deferred.

- The **purchase of the car could** reasonably be deferred until the cash position improves. If it is essential to the needs of the business, the company could consider spreading the cost through some form of leasing or hire purchase agreement.

- It is not clear why the new equipment is being purchased. Presumably some form of investment appraisal has been undertaken to establish the financial benefits of the acquisition. However, if it is being purchased in **advance** of an **increase in production** then it may be possible to defer it slightly. The company could also look at alternative methods of financing it, as have been suggested in the case of the car.

8   **Dividend**: SF Ltd is a private company, and therefore the shareholders could agree to forego or defer the dividend. The practicality of this will depend on the **personal situation** of the five shareholders.

9   **Defer the corporation tax payment**: This might be possible by **agreement** with the **Inland Revenue**. The company should consider the relative costs of the interest that would be charged if this were done, and the cost of financing the payment through some form of debt.

10   **Realise the investment**: The dividend from this is £10,000, and therefore assuming an interest rate of, say, 5%, it could be worth in the region of £200,000. It is not clear what form this takes or for what purpose it is being held, but it may be possible to **dispose** of a part of it without **jeopardising** the long term **strategic future** of the business.

11   **Inject additional long term capital**: The budget assumes that both fixed and working capital will increase by £30,000 during the year, and the directors should therefore consider seeking additional long term capital to finance at least the fixed asset acquisitions. Possible sources of capital include:

- Injection of funds from the existing shareholders
- The use of venture capital
- Long term bank loan, debenture or mortgage

Conclusions

It can be seen that there are a number of avenues that SF could explore. It appears that the company is fundamentally profitable, given the size of the corporation tax bill, and the fact that were it not for the fixed asset additions and the investment in stock the cash balance would increase by £10,000 during the year. However, the liquidity issues must be addressed now to avoid exceeding the overdraft limit.

The company should also consider investing its cash surpluses during the first quarter of the year to earn at least some interest, although this will be restricted by the short periods for which funds are likely to be available. Possible investments include:

- Bank deposits

- Short term gilts
- Bills of exchange

24 SWANSEA PLC

(a) (i) The two alternative policies will be evaluated separately to determine the most beneficial choice in financial terms.

> Work out best cash management policy

(1) Selling securities

The first step is to determine the optimal amount of cash that will be raised in each transaction, and hence the number of transactions and the level of transaction costs.

$$\text{Optimal sale} = \sqrt{\frac{2 \times \text{Annual cash disbursements} \times \text{Cost per sale of securities}}{\text{Interest rate}}}$$

where: Interest rate   10%
        Cash disbursements   £1m
        Cost per sale   £20

$$\text{Optimal sale} = \sqrt{\frac{2 \times £20 \times £1m}{10\%}}$$

$$= £20,000$$

Sales made = $\frac{£1 \text{ million}}{20,000}$ = 50

Transaction costs = 50 × £20 = £1,000

Average level of cash balances = $\frac{£20,000}{2}$ = £10,000

Interest on cash balances = £10,000 × 4.5% = £450

Average portfolio balances = $\frac{£1,000,000}{2}$ = £500,000

Income lost on portfolio securities = 10% × £500,000 = £50,000

Total costs

	£
Transaction costs	1,000
Interest received on cash balances	(450)
Income lost on portfolio securities	50,000
	50,550

(2) Secured loan

Average value of remaining cash = $\frac{£1,000,000}{2}$ = £500,000

Interest received = £500,000 × 8% = £40,000

Exam answer bank

Total costs

	£
Interest paid (£1 million × 13%)	130,000
Interest received	(40,000)
Arrangement fee	6,000
	96,000

The figures suggest that the policy of **selling securities** is to be preferred since this has a net cost of £50,550, which is £45,450 less than the cost of taking out a secured loan for the period.

The company should also take into account the following other factors associated with the policies.

(1) The **value of the short-term securities** is likely to **fluctuate** and Swansea must consider the possibility that the **value** could **fall** to below that required to meet the cash payments.

(2) **Use of the securities** will **eliminate them** as a future source of finance.

(3) If Swansea takes out the loan it must have **funds available** with which to repay it at the end of the period.

[Key point for loan finance]

(ii) **Limitations** of the model include the following.

(1) It assumes that the **level of transaction costs** is **independent** of the size of the transaction. Again this is unlikely to be true in practice.

(2) In reality, **payments** will **not be made continuously** but at regular intervals. The effect of this 'stepped' effect on the operation of the model should be considered.

(3) It **assumes a steady rate of return** from the securities although this may be very uncertain. Swansea should consider the effect of fluctuations in this rate on the model.

(4) It **does not allow** for a **buffer stock of cash** but assumes that further securities will only be sold when the cash balance reduces to zero. This is unlikely to be realistic in practice.

(b) (i) The approach is to calculate the net of tax present value of the two options available to Mumbles. The discount rate to be used will be the cost of borrowing net of tax. 18% × (1 – 0.33) = 12%.

Purchasing outright

[Easier to show each year's payments in single column]

Year	0	1	2	3	4	5
	£'000	£'000	£'000	£'000	£'000	£'000
Initial outlay	5,000					
Tax savings on capital allowances (W)		413	310	232	174	522
Net cash flow	(5,000)	413	310	232	174	522
Discount factor at 12%	1.000	0.893	0.797	0.712	0.636	0.567
PV of cash flow	(5,000)	369	247	165	111	296

Exam answer bank

Working

Year of claim	Allowance	Tax saved	Year of tax payment
0	5,000 (1,250) ――― 3,750	413	1
1	(938) ――― 2,812	309	2
2	(703) ――― 2,109	232	3
3	(527) ――― 1,582	174	4
4	(1,582) ――― -	522	5

Thus the **NPV cost of purchasing** outright is £3,812,000.

Leasing

Year	0	1	2	3	4
	£'000	£'000	£'000	£'000	£'000
Annual rental	(1,800)	(1,800)	(1,800)	(1,800)	-
Tax savings (rental × 33%)	-	594	594	594	594
Net cash flow	(1,800)	(1,206)	(1,206)	(1,206)	594
Discount factor at 12%	1.000	0.893	0.797	0.712	0.636
PV of cash flow	(1,800)	(1,077)	(961)	(859)	378

Tax implications of rental

Thus the **NPV cost of leasing** is **£4,319,000**. This is £506,000 more than the NPV cost of direct purchase over the life of the equipment, and direct purchase therefore appears more attractive on financial grounds.

Comparison and conclusion

(ii) The cost of purchase can be re-evaluated to take into account the **additional maintenance costs** of £190,000 per year. These costs are assumed to start in year 1, with the associated tax saving coming through in the subsequent year.

State assumption

Year	0	1	2	3	4	5
	£'000	£'000	£'000	£'000	£'000	£'000
Initial outlay	(5,000)					
Tax savings on capital allowances (above)		413	310	232	174	522
Maintenance costs		(190)	(190)	(190)	(190)	
Tax saving			63	63	63	63
Net cash flow	(5,000)	223	183	105	47	585
Discount factor at 12%	1.000	0.893	0.797	0.712	0.636	0.567
PV of cash flow	(5,000)	199	146	75	30	332

Tax implications of maintenance

If the maintenance costs are taken into account, the NPV cost of purchase rises to £4,218,000, which is slightly less (by £100,000) than the cost of leasing. Although the decision is not reversed, the **relative costs** are **marginal**, and other factors should also be considered, for instance the **reliability** and **availability** of the **different maintenance options**.

Comparison and conclusion

Multiple choice question and answer bank

Multiple choice questions

1. You are part of a team that is measuring the economy, efficiency and effectiveness of a primary school. As a part of your study, you are analysing class sizes. Which of the following categories does this fall into?

    A   Inputs
    B   Outputs
    C   Impacts
    D   Implications

2. Ms Douglas has inherited £5,000 which she wishes to invest in equities prior to using it as a deposit on a house in a few years' time. Which of the following would you recommend?

    A   She uses the money to buy as many shares as she can afford in her favourite 'blue chip' company.

    B   She takes a £5,000 stake in an internet business being set up by her best friend.

    C   She puts the money a building society account.

    D   She invests in a unit trust.

3. The dividend growth model can be expressed as:

    $$P_0 = \frac{d_0(1+g)}{k_e - g}$$

    What is 'd_0' in this formula?

    A   This year's dividend
    B   Next year's expected dividend
    C   Last year's dividend
    D   Cost of equity

4. Ultra plc can earn a profit after tax of 15% on the capital employed, and the shares are trading at £1.50. The capital structure is as follows:

	£
400,000 ordinary shares of £1 each	400,000
Retained earnings	600,000

    What is the present earnings per share?

    A   3.9 pence
    B   4.5 pence
    C   30 pence
    D   37.5 pence

5. Mr Franco holds some warrants that can be used to subscribe for ordinary shares on a one for one basis at an exercise price of £3.25 during a specified future period. The current share price is £3.00 and the warrants are quoted at 75 pence. What is the warrant conversion premium?

    A   £0.25
    B   £0.50
    C   £1.00
    D   £2.50

6. Omega Plastics plc has issued 100,000 units of convertible debentures, each with a nominal value of £100 and a coupon rate of interest of 8% paid annually. Each £100 of convertible debentures may be converted into 50 ordinary shares of Omega Plastics plc in three years time. Any stock not converted will be redeemed at 108.

    What is the likely current market price for £100 of the debentures, if investors require a pre-tax return of 7%, and the expected value of ordinary shares in Omega Plastics plc on the conversion date is £2.50 per share?

    A   £108
    B   £123
    C   £125

Multiple choice questions

D £133

7 Mr Singh has just paid £2,600 (excluding commissions) for some 9% debentures in Scandia plc. The debentures are currently quoted at £130 per £100 nominal value. How much interest can Mr Singh expect to receive each year?

A £304
B £234
C £180
D £90

8 Which of the following is a disadvantage of acquiring capital equipment using a finance lease?

A The lease will be included in the lessee's balance sheet.
B The cost of the asset is spread over its useful life.
C The lessee can claim capital allowances on the equipment.
D The interest charges are included in the pre-tax profit.

9 The Starlodge Hotel has decided to purchase a new computerised reservation system at a cost of £10,000. The system has an estimated operational life of three years, with a scrap value of zero. The hotel has been offered a three year leasing agreement with annual payments of £4,000. Tax is payable at 30% on operating cash flows one year in arrears, and the hotel's after tax cost of capital is 10%. What is the net cost to the company of entering into the agreement?

A £12,000
B £10,000
C £9,948
D £7,235

10 Ratchet plc has just made its annual payment of debenture interest which amounted to £80,000 in total. The debentures have a nominal value of £1m, and are currently trading at £105 per £100. The rate of corporation tax is 30%, and the rate of income tax is 20%. What is the annual cost of the debentures in percentage terms?

A 5.3%
B 6.1%
C 7.6%
D 8.0%

11 Triangle plc has the following capital structure:

	£
Ordinary shares (nominal value £1)	2,000,000
Reserves	5,000,000
10% irredeemable debentures	1,000,000

The shares are currently trading at £2.00, and the debentures are trading at par. The cost of equity capital for the company is 15%, and the rate of corporation tax is 30%. What is the weighted average cost of capital for Triangle plc?

A 14.4%
B 14.2%
C 14.0%
D 13.4%

12 In portfolio theory, what is the curved line in the graph below known as?

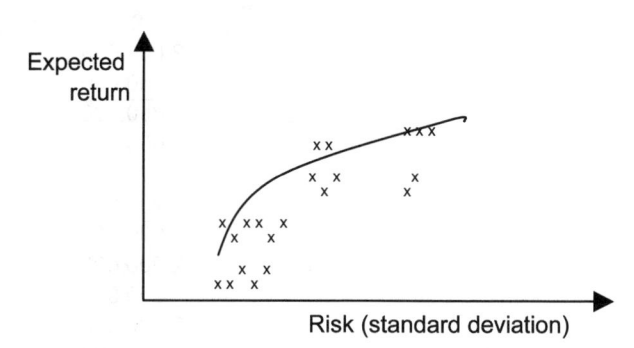

Expected return ↑ (curve above scatter of x points) → Risk (standard deviation)

- A Efficient frontier
- B Indifference curve
- C Capital market line
- D Market portfolio

13 Mrs Cox has just invested £1,000 in security A and £3,000 in security B. The securities have the following expected returns:

Probability	Security A Return	Security B Return
0.1	10%	20%
0.8	25%	25%
0.1	60%	30%

What is the rate of return that she can expect from her portfolio?

- A 20.00%
- B 21.25%
- C 25.00%
- D 25.50%

14 If the price of a share rises at twice the market rate, what would be the beta factor of that share?

- A 0.0
- B 0.5
- C 1.0
- D 2.0

15 Miss Drake is planning to construct a portfolio of shares in a bear market. Friends and colleagues have given her a number of helpful suggestions. Which of them would you advise her to follow?

- A Invest in shares with high beta factors
- B Invest in shares with average beta factors
- C Invest in shares with low beta factors
- D Invest in a small number of high technology stocks

Multiple choice questions

The following figures have been extracted from the accounts of Frobisher plc and apply to questions 16 and 17.

	£
Profit on ordinary activities	2,000,000
Interest	150,000
	1,850,000
Taxation	650,000
	1,200,000
Dividend	200,000
Retained profit	1,000,000
Ordinary shares (£1 nominal)	2,000,000
Share premium account	250,000
Profit and loss account	2,500,000
8% debentures	500,000
Mortgage on property	200,000
Current market price of ordinary shares	£6.00

16 What is the P/E ratio?

- A 12
- B 10
- C 6.5
- D 6

17 What is the gearing ratio based on book values (using total capital as the denominator)?

- A 9.5%
- B 12.8%
- C 14.5%
- D 20%

18 Mr Brown has invested £5,000 at 5% compound interest per annum. What will his investment be worth at the end of three years?

- A £5,250
- B £5,750
- C £5,788
- D £6,077

19 What type of term structure of interest rates does the curve in the graph below describe?

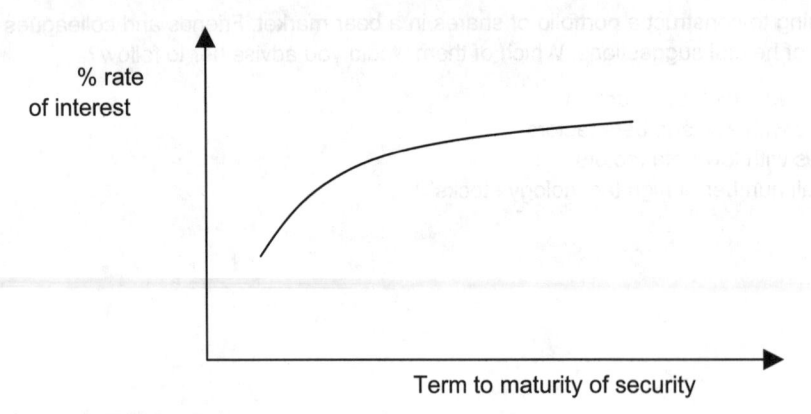

% rate of interest

Term to maturity of security

- A Normal yield curve
- B Reverse yield curve
- C Downward sloping yield curve
- D Reverse yield gap

20 The following securities are currently trading as follows:

8% Treasury Stock 2013   £135.2246
8% Exchequer Stock 2003   £109.5398

To what principle can the difference in the market prices be attributed?

- A They are different types of stock
- B The efficient markets hypothesis
- C The reverse yield gap
- D The pull to maturity

21 Which of the following statements provides the best definition of the term 'interest yield'?

- A The amount of interest paid on £100 of stock in one year
- B The quoted percentage rate of interest on a stock
- C The interest rate on a stock quoted as a percentage of the market price
- D The coupon rate

22 In the following graph, what does the point 'a' represent?

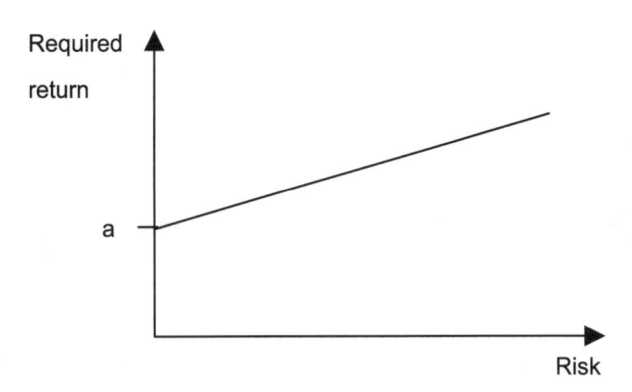

- A Market rate of return
- B Capital market line
- C Average rate of return
- D Risk free rate of return

23 A bank's decision as to whether or not to lend will be based on a number of factors. What is the mnemonic commonly used to remember these factors?

- A DUBONNET
- B CAMPARI
- C VODKA
- D SHERRY

24 Which of the following is a **disadvantage** of using a medium-term loan instead of an overdraft?

- A There is a regular repayment schedule
- B The term of the loan is fixed
- C The loan is included when calculating the capital gearing
- D There is normally a facility letter that sets out the precise terms of the agreement

25 Which of the following could normally be covered under a company's export credit insurance policy?

- A All its export business on a regular basis
- B Selected parts of its export business
- C Occasional, high value export sales
- D All of the above

Multiple choice questions

The figures below have been extracted from the accounts of Premier Ltd and apply to questions 26 to 29.

	£
Turnover	750,000
Cost of sales	500,000
Gross profit	250,000
Current assets	
Stocks	75,000
Trade debtors	100,000
Other debtors	10,000
Cash at bank and in hand	5,000
	190,000
Current liabilities	
Overdraft	30,000
Dividend	40,000
Trade creditors	80,000
Other creditors	10,000
	160,000
Net current assets	30,000

26 What is the current ratio?

  A   0.72
  B   0.82
  C   1.19
  D   1.58

27 What is the debtors' payment period?

  A   48.67 days
  B   53.53 days
  C   73.00 days
  D   80.30 days

28 What is the creditors' payment period?

  A   38.9 days
  B   43.8 days
  C   58.4 days
  D   65.7 days

29 What is the stock turnover period?

  A   36.50 days
  B   54.75 days
  C   109.50 days
  D   171.09 days

30 Frosty Ice Cream Ltd had sales in the last year of £150,000, and purchases of £115,000. At the start of the year stocks were £15,000, debtors were £5,000 and creditors were £10,000. At the end of the year stocks were £10,000, debtors were £8,000 and creditors were £12,000.

What was the operating profit for the period?

  A   £30,000
  B   £32,000
  C   £34,000
  D   £40,000

31 Speciality Chemicals plc produces quarterly cash forecasts. It uses 1,500 units of Chemical A per quarter, for which it currently pays £20 per unit. The price of Chemical A is expected to rise by 3% per quarter for the foreseeable future, and Speciality Chemicals plans to increase production by 2% per quarter for the next year.

It is now nearing the end of quarter 1. What figure for Chemical A should be included in the cash flow forecast for Quarter 3 (to the nearest £)?

A £34,792
B £33,116
C £32,467
D £31,518

32 Delights Ltd is a specialist delicatessen chain with average daily takings of £10,000. The shops are open for six days each week and takings are banked every other day. The overdraft rate is 10% simple interest. What is the annual cost to Delights Ltd of not banking daily?

(You can assume that the shops are open for six days a week throughout the year, and that the banks are open every day that the shops are open. Work to the nearest £.)

A £156
B £427
C £855
D £1,560

33 The percentage cost of an early settlement discount to the company giving it can be estimated by the formula:

$$\left(\frac{100}{100-d}\right)^{\frac{365}{t}} - 1$$

What does 'd' represent in this formula?

A The number of days credit allowed with the discount
B The number of days credit allowed without the discount
C The reduction in days credit allowed with the discount
D The discount offered

34 Centra plc is offering customers the option of paying £98.50 after seven days per £100 invoiced, or payment in full after 45 days. What is the cost of this policy in percentage terms?

A 1.5%
B 12.4%
C 14.4%
D 15.6%

35 You are the Credit Controller of WTP Ltd. The Sales Manager has asked you to open accounts for four new customers (A,B, C and D), and he is suggesting payment terms of 30 days with a credit limit of £10,000 for each customer. You have extracted the following information from their accounts. Which of the customers would you feel the most confident in supplying as requested?

	Cost of goods sold	Trade creditors
A	£1,800,000	£450,000
B	£180,000	£45,000
C	£120,000	£10,000
D	£1,200,000	£100,000

36 What is the maximum percentage of bad debt loss that will normally be covered by a credit insurance policy?

A 65%
B 75%
C 85%
D 95%

37 Which of the following would **not** be a preferential creditor in the event of a bankruptcy?

A Subcontractors in the building industry
B Pension scheme contributions
C Preference shareholders
D Customs and Excise for VAT

Multiple choice questions

38 The annual demand for an item of stock is 90 units. The item costs £225 a unit to purchase, the holding cost for one unit for one year is 10% of the unit cost, and ordering costs are £200 per order. What is the economic order quantity?

- A 20 units
- B 30 units
- C 40 units
- D 50 units

39 The annual demand for an item of stock is 90 units. The item costs £225 a unit to purchase, the holding cost for one unit for one year is 10% of the unit cost, and ordering costs are £200 per order. The economic order quantity is 40 units, but the company has decided to accept the offer of a 2% discount for orders over 45 units. What will be the total annual purchasing costs?

- A £21,257
- B £21,156
- C £21,150
- D £20,751

40 Which of the following effects is the **least likely** to be associated with the introduction of a just-in-time procurement system?

- A Improved labour productivity
- B Reduction in the number of goods inwards transactions
- C Reduction in stock holding costs
- D Reduced manufacturing lead times

Answers to multiple choice questions

1 B An output is the result of an activity, measurable as the service actually produced.

2 D Unit trusts cater for small investors who wish to spread their investment risk over a wide range of securities, but have insufficient funds to create such a portfolio by themselves. This will be less risky than investing in a single business. A building society account would be the least risky alternative, but this is not an equity investment.

3 A This year's dividend

4 D The earnings at present are 15% of £1m = £150,000. This gives earnings per share of 37.5 pence (£150,000 ÷ 400,000).

5 C

	£
Cost of warrant	0.75
Exercise price	3.25
	4.00
Current share price	3.00
Premium	1.00

6 B If the shares are expected to be worth £2.50 each on conversion day, the value of 50 shares will be £125. This is more than would be received if the stock was redeemed, and therefore it can be assumed that the debentures will be converted into shares. The expected market value can be found as follows:

Year		Cash flow	Discount factor	Present value
1	Interest	8	0.935	7.48
2	Interest	8	0.873	6.98
3	Interest	8	0.816	6.53
3	Value of 50 shares	125	0.816	102.00
				122.99

7 C £2,600 × 100/130 × 9% = £180

8 A The capital value of the asset, and the liability to the lessor must both be included in the lessee's balance sheet. This may reduce the ability of the lessee to obtain credit from other sources.

9 D It is assumed that the lease payments are tax-allowable in full.

Year		Cash flow	Discount factor	Present value
1-3	Lease costs	(4,000)	2.487	(9,948)
2-4	Tax savings (× 30%)	1,200	2.261	2,713
				(7,235)

10 A The cost can be found using the expression:

$$k_d = \frac{i(1-t)}{P_0}$$

where k_d = cost of debt (net of tax)

i = annual interest payment

P_0 = current market price of debt capital ex interest

t = rate of corporation tax

In this case:

k_d = 80,000(1 − 0.3)/1,050,000

k_d = 5.3%

Answers to multiple choice questions

11 D The following formula can be used:

$$WACC = k_e \left[\frac{V_E}{V_E + V_D}\right] + k_d \left[\frac{V_D}{V_E + V_D}\right]$$

where:

k_e = cost of equity
k_d = cost of debt
V_E = market value of equity
V_D = market value of debt

In this case:

k_e = 15%
k_d = 10% (since the debentures are trading at par)
V_E = £4m
V_D = £1m

$$WACC = \frac{(15\% \times 4m)}{5m} + \frac{(10\% \times 0.7 \times 1m)}{5m}$$

$$WACC = 13.4\%$$

12 A Efficient frontier

13 D The first step is to calculate the expected return from each security:

		Security A		Security B	
Probability		% return	EV %	% return	EV%
0.1		10	1.0	20	2.0
0.8		25	20.0	25	20.0
0.1		60	6.0	30	3.0
			27.0		25.0

The expected return from the portfolio can be calculated by weighting the returns by the value of the investment:

Return = (27% × ¼) + (25% × ¾) = 25.50%

14 D 2.0

15 C A bear market means that average market returns are falling. It is therefore advisable to invest in shares with low beta factors since prices of these shares should fall at a slower rate than will the market as a whole.

16 B The price earnings ratio is the market price of the share in pence divided by the earnings per share in pence. This is the same as the total market value of the equity divided by the total earnings.

In this case:

Total market value of equity = 2m × £6 = £12m

Total earnings after interest and tax = £1.2m

P/E ratio = £12m/£1.2m = 10

Answers to multiple choice questions

17 B The gearing ratio can be calculated as the ratio of prior charge capital to total capital employed.

In this case:

Prior charge capital	=	debentures + mortgage = £700,000
Total capital employed	=	ordinary shares + share premium account + profit and loss account + prior charge capital
	=	£2m + £0.25m + £2.5m + £0.5m + £0.2m
	=	£5.45m
Gearing	=	£0.7m/£5.45m = 12.8%

18 C Using the formula $S = X(1 + r)^n$

where:

- S = the sum invested after 'n' periods
- X = original sum invested
- n = number of periods
- r = interest rate

In this case:

$S = £5,000(1 + 0.05)^3$

$S = £5,000 \times 1.1576 = £5,788$

19 A This is a normal yield curve because the longer the term of an asset to maturity, the higher the rate of interest paid on the asset.

20 D Both securities are similar in that they are British Government stocks.

These stocks are always redeemed at their nominal value of £100, and therefore the closer the date gets to the redemption date, the closer the price of the stock will approach £100.

21 C The interest rate on a stock quoted as a percentage of the market price.

22 D Risk free rate of return.

23 B **C**haracter of the customer

Ability to borrow and repay

Margin of profit

Purpose of the borrowing

Amount of the borrowing

Repayment terms

Insurance against the possibility of non-payment

24 C A medium-term loan will increase the company's gearing and can therefore reduce its ability to raise further debt finance. Overdrafts are not normally included in the calculation since they are a form of short-term debt.

25 D All of the above.

26 C The current ratio is the ratio of current assets to current liabilities.

In this case: £190,000 ÷ £160,000 = 1.19

27 A The debtors' payment period is calculated as:

$$\frac{\text{Trade debtors}}{\text{Credit sales turnover}} \times 365$$

Answers to multiple choice questions

In this case it is assumed that there are no cash sales:

$$\frac{100{,}000}{750{,}000} \times 365 = 48.67 \text{ days}$$

28 C The creditors' payment period is calculated as:

$$\frac{\text{Trade creditors}}{\text{Purchases}} \times 365$$

In this case the purchases figure is not known, and therefore the cost of sales will be used as an approximation:

$$\frac{80{,}000}{500{,}000} \times 365 = 58.4 \text{ days}$$

29 B The stock turnover period is calculated as:

$$\frac{\text{Average stock}}{\text{Cost of sales}} \times 365$$

In this case it is assumed that the closing stock approximates to the average stock figure:

$$\frac{75{,}000}{500{,}000} \times 365 = 54.75 \text{ days}$$

30 A

	£	£
Sales		150,000
Less cost of sales		
Purchases	115,000	
Add opening stock	15,000	
Less closing stock	(10,000)	
		(120,000)
Operating profit		30,000

31 B Usage of Chemical A:

Current   1,500.0 units
Quarter 2   1,530.0 units
Quarter 3   1,560.6 units

Price of Chemical A per unit:

Current   £20.00
Quarter 2   £20.60
Quarter 3   £21.22

Cost of Chemical A for Quarter 3:   1560.6 units × £21.22 = £33,116

32 B There are three days each week when there is £10,000 unbanked, ie 156 days per year.

The daily rate of overdraft interest is 10%/365 = 0.0274%

The annual cost is therefore £10,000 × 156 × 0.0274% = £427.44

33 C The reduction in days credit allowed with the discount.

34 D The following formula can be used:

$$r = \left(\frac{100}{100 - d}\right)^{\frac{365}{t}} - 1$$

where: r = percentage cost of policy
         d = discount offered
         t = reduction in payment period in days

Answers to multiple choice questions

In this case:

$$r = \left(\frac{100}{98.5}\right)^{\frac{365}{38}} - 1$$

$$= 15.6\%$$

35 D Companies A and B both have creditor payment periods of three months (£45,000 × 12/£180,000), which is well in excess of the terms that would be offered, and suggests that there may be problems with collection.

Companies C and D both pay their suppliers within one month (£10,000 × 12/£120,000) and would therefore cause less concern over collection. However, Company C only purchases £120,000 in total, and therefore a monthly credit limit of £10,000 is too high. Company D will therefore give the least cause for concern.

36 B 75%

37 C Preference shareholders

38 C Use the EOQ model:

$$EOQ = \sqrt{\frac{2C_0 D}{C_h}}$$

Where:

C_0 = cost of placing an order
D = annual demand
C_h = cost of holding one unit of stock for one year

In this case:

$$EOQ = \sqrt{\frac{2 \times 200 \times 90}{22.50}}$$

$$EOQ = \sqrt{1,600}$$

$$EOQ = 40 \text{ units}$$

39 D It is assumed that the company will order 45 units at a time.

		£
Purchases	90 × £225 × 98%	19,845
Holding costs	45 × 0.5 × £22.50	506
Ordering costs	2 × £200	400
		20,751

40 B There are likely to be more deliveries by suppliers since goods are only obtained just before they are needed, and stock levels are reduced.

Index

Index

Note: **Key Terms** and their references are given in **bold**.

ABC analysis, 354
Account reporting, 285
Acid test ratio, 242
Administration, 362
Administrative order, 357
Administrative receiver, 362
Advance fee fraud, 56
Agency relationship, 11
Agency theory, 11
Alternative Investment Market (AIM), 21
Altman, 250
Amount of the loan, 213
Annual percentage rate (APR), 176
Arbitration agreement, 357
Arbitration, 357
A-scoring, 354
Asset cover, 168
Asset value per share, 168
Association of Corporate Treasurers, 49
Attachment of earnings, 357
Average stock, 377

BACS, **317**, 370, 372
Bad debt, 304, 352
Bad debts ratio, 363
Balance sheet, 271
Balanced portfolio, 146
Bank giro credits, 370
Bank references, 322
Banker's acceptance facilities, 211
Banker's draft, 296, 316, 370, 371
Banking Act 1987, 195
Bankruptcy, 358
Banks, 257
Basic earnings per share, 158
Baumol's model, 287
Beta factor, 140, **146**, 150, 151
Bill of exchange, 202, 224, 295
Bond, 204
Bonus issue, 76
Borrowing, 257
Bought deal, 70
Budget period, 258
Buffer, 190
Building Societies Act 1986, 195
Building societies deposits, 195
Bulk discounts, 377
Business angel financing, 27
Business customers, 353
Business failure, 250
Business risk, 126, 141

Buying, 380
   by banker's draft, 371
   by cash, 370

CAMPARI, 211
Capital asset pricing model, 140, 144, **149**
Capital funding planning, 4
Capital gain, 34
Capital market line, 139
Capital markets, 20, 63
Capital resource planning, 4
Capital structure, 75, **95**, 162, 166, 220
Cash, 255, 370
Cash budget, 258
Cash cycle, 240
Cash flow forecasts, 241
Cash flow problems, 283
Cash flow, 240
Cash forecasting, 257
Cash management models, 191, 283
Cash management policy, 190
Cash management, 51
Centralised cash management, 51
Certificate of deposit, 201
CHAPS, 317
Character of the borrower, 212
Charging order, 357
Chartists, 38
Cheque guarantee cards, 315
Cheque guarantee scheme, 315
Cheques, 315
Cleared funds cash forecast, 269
Clearing banks, 19
Clearing House Automated Payments System (CHAPS), 317
Collecting debts, 342
Collection cycle, 308
Commercial paper, 205, 324
Committed facility, 211
Compound annual rate (CAR), 176
Compulsory winding up, 361
Conglomerate, 140
Consensus theory, 7
Constituents of the firm, 11
Consumer Credit Act, 336
Consumer credit, 301
Contingency funding, 258
Conversion premium, 91
Conversion value, 91
Convertible debentures, 92

Convertible loan stock, 90
Correlation between investments, 133
Cost centre, 54
Cost of capital, 113, 123
Cost of debt capital, 118
Cost of equity, 115
Cost of floating rate debt, 122
Cost of preference shares, 118
Countertrade, 230
County Court, 326, 356
Coupon, 85, 157, 204
Credit assessment, 321
Credit cards, 316
Credit control, 301
Credit creation, 18, 19
Credit cycle, 308
Credit insurance, 344
Credit notes, 223
Credit policy, 301
Credit ratings, 205, 334
Credit reference agency, 324
Credit risk, 223, 320, 352
Credit transfers, 370
Credit utilisation report, 306
Creditors' days ratio, 243
Creditors' payment period, 243
Creditors' turnover period, 243
Creditors, 367
Cumulative preference shares, 78
Currency of invoice, 233
Current assets, 244
Current ratio, 242
Customer payment systems, 343

Day-of-the-week effects, 43, 152 262
Debenture, 86
Debit cards, 315
Debt collection agencies, 355
Debt ratio, 163, 167
Debt with warrants, 94
Debtors age analysis, 339
Debtors ageing, 341
Debtors' days ratio, 242
Debtors' payment period, 242, 243
Debtors' turnover period, 243
Decision support services, 285
Deep discount bond, 87
Default insurance, 344
Deferred ordinary shares, 64
Devaluation, 55
Dilution, 70
Direct debit, 316, 370, 371
Discount rate, 123

Discounting bills, 203
Discounts, 377
Diversification, 133
Dividend cover, 161
Dividend growth model, 35, 115
Dividend payout ratio, 161, 162
Dividend per share, 157
Dividend valuation model, 114
Dividend yield, 157
Dividend, 8
Documentary credits, 226
Domestic credit insurance, 344
Doubtful debt, 352
Doubtful debts provision, 363

Earnings per share, 158
Earnings yield, 158
Economic order quantity (EOQ), 374
Economic policy, 12
Economy, 14
Effectiveness, 14
Efficiency, 14
Efficient market hypothesis, 39
Efficient portfolios, 135
Electronic Data Interchange, 294
Electronic funds transfer (EFT), 294, 371
Enhanced, 76
Equity instrument, 64
Equity share capital, 64
Equity shares, 64
Equity, 64
Eurobond, 29
Eurocurrency markets, 28
Eurocurrency, 28
Eurodollars, 28
Euro-equity, 29
Exceptional items, 255
Excess of loss, 345
Exchange rate risk, 233
Ex-dividend, 200
Exercise price, 80
Expectations, 185
Expected return of a porfolio, 132
Export Credit Guarantee Department, 227
Export credit insurance, 227

Factoring, 224, 346
Finance company deposits, 195
Finance lease, 100
Financial control, 3, 4
Financial gearing, 163
Financial intermediary, 17
Financial leverage/gearing, 164

Financial management, 3
Financial modelling package, 275
Financial planning, 4
Financial risk, 95, 126, 163
Financial targets, 9
Finished goods, 373
Fixed charge, 88, 361
Fixed interest securities, 34
Flat yield, 197
Float, 269
Floating charge, 88, 361
Floating rate debentures, 87, 126
Foreign exchange risk, 232
Foreign trade, 223
Forfaiting, 225
Fraud, 55
Fundamental analysis, 35
Fundamental theory of share values, 34, 38, 115
Funds transfer, 285

Garnishee order, 357
Gearing ratios, 163
Gilts, 198
Government organisations, 123
Government securities, 198
Government, 12
Guarantees, 214

Hedging, 232
High Court, 356
High interest cheque accounts, 194
High interest deposit accounts, 194
High street bank deposits, 194
Hire purchase contract, 102
Hour-of-the-day effects, 43

Index numbers, 273
Index, 273
Index-linked gilts, 198, 199, 200
Indifference curve (investor's), 134
Inflation, 273
In-house credit ratings, 334
Insolvency, 360
Institutional investors, 23
Insurance against the possibility of non-payment, 213
Insurance companies, 24
Interest cover, 167
Interest rates, 183
Interest yield, 157, 197
Interest, 173

International capital markets, 28
International money markets, 28
International money order, 297
International Money Transfer, 297
Inventories, 373
Investment decisions, 5
Investment trusts, 24
Invoice discounting, 347
Irregular items, 255
Issuing houses, 66

Just in Time, 380

Key account customers, 343
Keynes, 190

Lagged payments, 233
Lead payments, 233
Leasing, 99
Legislation, 12
Lien, 357
Liquidation, 361
Liquidator, 361
Liquidity preference, 184
Liquidity ratios, 245, 250
Liquidity, 202
Loan capital, 85
Loan stock, 85
Local authority stocks, 201
London Business School, 151
Long-term contracts, 344
Loss of credit, 226

Machine replacement, 141
Mail transfer and telegraphic transfer, 370
Mail transfer, 296, 371
Management fraud, 56
Managerial model, 7
Marginal cost of capital, 127
Market portfolio, 137
Market risk premium, 148
Market risk, 145
Market segmentation theory of interest rates, 185
Market segmentation theory, 185
Markowitz, 131
Matching receipts and payments, 232
Maximum level, 377
Mean-variance inefficiency, 134
Merchant banking, 19
Methods of payment, 311

Miller-Orr model, 289
Minimum level, 377
Modern portfolio theory, 131
Money market hedges, 233
Money market, 20, 21, 204
Month-of-the-year effects, 43
Mortgages, 90
Multilateral netting, 293

Nationalised industries, 12
Negotiated settlement, 356, 358
Nominal, 176
Nominated Adviser, 23
Non-financial objectives, 9
Non-systematic risk, 145
Not-for-profit organisations, 13

Offer for sale, 66
Offers for sale by tender, 67
On account payments, 344
Open offer, 75
Operating cycle, 215, 240
Operating gearing or leverage, 167
Operating lease, 100
Operational cash flow, 255
Optimal cash balance, 191
Option deposits, 195
Ordinary shares, 64
Over-capitalisation, 245
Overdraft facility for day to day trading, 217
Overdraft facility, 190, 211
Overdraft, 211, 215
Over-the-counter (OTC) market, 23
Overtrading, 218, 246

P/E ratios, 140
Participating preference shares, 78
Pension funds, 24
Permanent interest bearing shares (PIBS), 205
Personal customers, 352
Personal guarantee, 214
Petition for bankruptcy, 357
Placing, 4, 66, 69
Portfolio management, 150
Portfolio theory, 131
Portfolio, 207
Precautionary motive, 190
Pre-emption rights, 70
Preference shares, 77
Preferred ordinary shares, 64
Price earnings (P/E) ratio, 159

Prior charge capital, 77, 164
Private companies, 122
Profit centre approach, 54
Profit centre, 54
Profit maximisation, 6
Profitability, 9
Profits and cash flows, 255
Prospectus issue, 69
Public sector, 194
Pull to maturity, 196
Purchases, 380
Purchasing mix, 380
Pyramid scheme frauds, 57

Quantity discounts, 377
Quick ratio, 242

Random walk theory, 38
Ratio analysis, 212, 327
Raw materials, 373
Receiver, 362
Redemption yield, 197, 198
Redemption, 89
References, 322
Regular items, 255
Re-order level, 375
Repayment terms, 213
Retention of title, 357
Return on capital employed (ROCE), 9
Revenue items, 255
Reverse yield gap, 186
Revolving facility, 211
Rights issue, 70
Risk of a portfolio, 132
Risk premium, 149
Risk, 320
Risk-free investments, 136
Risk-free rate of return, 113
Risk-free securities, 146
Risk-return trade-off, 186
Running Yield, 197

Safety stock, 373
Sale and leaseback, 101
Sale of Goods Acts, 357
Scrip dividend, 76
Scrip issue, 76
Security, 205, 213
Semi-strong form efficiency, 40
Sensitivity analysis, 274, 275
Share ownership, 12
Share price behaviour, 34

Index

Share price crash, 43
Share, 33
Shareholders and management, 11
Shareholders' preferences between risk and return, 141
Short-term finance, 219
Short-termism, 248
Simple, 173
Slow payers, 353
Small Claims Court, 356
Smaller companies, 25
Solicitors, 356
Specific account policies, 346
Speculation, 54
Speculative motive, 190
Spreadsheet model, 275
Stakeholders, 10
Standing order, 316, 370, 371
Statement, 343
Stock Exchange introduction, 69
Stock exchange, 21
Stock market ratios, 156
Stock splits, 76
Stock turnover period, 244
Stock turnover, 244
Stock, 86, 373
Stockholding period days, 243
Strategic financial management, 5
Strategic plan, 5
Strong form efficiency, 40
SWIFT, 294
Swinging account, 215
Systematic risk, 144, 145

Taxation, 120
Technical analysis, 38
Teeming and lading, 56
Telegraphic Transfer (TT), 296, 371
Term loan, 211
Term structure of interest rates, 184
Theoretical ex-rights price, 72
Trade credit, 300, 367
Trade creditors, 219
Trade references, 323
Trading cycle, 240
Treasury bill, 199
Treasury departments, 48
Treasury management, 48
Turnover periods, 245

Uncommitted facility, 211
Underwriters, 69
Unexceptional items, 255
Unit trusts, 24
Unsystematic risk, 144, 145

Valuation, 8
Value for money (VFM), 14
Value of rights, 73
Vendor consideration issue, 75
Vendor placing, 75
Venture capital, 26
Venture capital funds, 26
Venture capital trusts, 27
Voluntary arrangements, 359, 362

Warrant conversion premium, 81
Warrant of execution, 357
Warrant, 80
Weighted average cost of capital (WACC), 123, 124
Whole turnover policies, 345
Work in progress, 373
Working capital, 211, 239, 327
Working capital cycle, 240
Working capital requirement, 249

Yield curve, 184

Z scores, 250
Zero coupon bond, 88

CIMA – Intermediate Paper 4: Finance (7/02)

REVIEW FORM & FREE PRIZE DRAW

All original review forms from the entire BPP range, completed with genuine comments, will be entered into one of two draws on 31 January 2003 and 31 July 2003. The names on the first four forms picked out on each occasion will be sent a cheque for £50.

Name: _____   Address: _____

How have you used this Text?
(Tick one box only)
- [ ] Self study (book only)
- [ ] On a course: college (please state) _____
- [ ] With 'correspondence' package
- [ ] Other _____

Why did you decide to purchase this Text?
(Tick one box only)
- [ ] Have used BPP Texts in the past
- [ ] Recommendation by friend/colleague
- [ ] Recommendation by a lecturer at college
- [ ] Saw advertising
- [ ] Other _____

During the past six months do you recall seeing/receiving any of the following?
(Tick as many boxes as are relevant)
- [ ] Our advertisement in CIMA *Insider*
- [ ] Our advertisement in *Financial Management*
- [ ] Our advertisement in *Pass*
- [ ] Our brochure with a letter through the post
- [ ] Our website www.bpp.com

Which (if any) aspects of our advertising do you find useful?
(Tick as many boxes as are relevant)
- [ ] Prices and publication dates of new editions
- [ ] Information on product content
- [ ] Facility to order books off-the-page
- [ ] None of the above

Which BPP products have you used?

Text	[ ]	MCQ cards	[ ]	i-Learn	[ ]
Kit	[ ]	Tape	[ ]	i-Pass	[ ]
Passcard	[ ]	Video	[ ]	Virtual Campus	[ ]

Your ratings, comments and suggestions would be appreciated on the following areas.

	Very useful	Useful	Not useful
Introductory section (Key study steps, personal study)	[ ]	[ ]	[ ]
Chapter introductions	[ ]	[ ]	[ ]
Key terms	[ ]	[ ]	[ ]
Quality of explanations	[ ]	[ ]	[ ]
Case examples and other examples	[ ]	[ ]	[ ]
Questions and answers in each chapter	[ ]	[ ]	[ ]
Chapter roundups	[ ]	[ ]	[ ]
Quick quizzes	[ ]	[ ]	[ ]
Exam focus points	[ ]	[ ]	[ ]
Question bank	[ ]	[ ]	[ ]
MCQ bank	[ ]	[ ]	[ ]
Answer bank	[ ]	[ ]	[ ]
Index	[ ]	[ ]	[ ]
Icons	[ ]	[ ]	[ ]
Mind maps	[ ]	[ ]	[ ]

Overall opinion of this Study Text	Excellent	[ ]	Good	[ ]	Adequate	[ ]	Poor	[ ]

Do you intend to continue using BPP products?   Yes [ ]   No [ ]

On the reverse of this page are noted particular areas of the text about which we would welcome your feedback.

Please note any further comments and suggestions/errors on the reverse of this page. The BPP author of this edition can be e-mailed at: nickweller@bpp.com

Please return this form to: Nick Weller, CIMA Range Manager, BPP Publishing Ltd, FREEPOST, London, W12 8BR

CIMA – Intermediate Paper 4: Finance (7/02)

Please note any further comments and suggestions/errors below.

FREE PRIZE DRAW RULES

1. Closing date for 31 January 2003 draw is 31 December 2002. Closing date for 31 July 2003 draw is 30 June 2003.

2. Restricted to entries with UK and Eire addresses only. BPP employees, their families and business associates are excluded.

3. No purchase necessary. Entry forms are available upon request from BPP Publishing. No more than one entry per title, per person. Draw restricted to persons aged 16 and over.

4. Winners will be notified by post and receive their cheques not later than 6 weeks after the relevant draw date.

5. The decision of the promoter in all matters is final and binding. No correspondence will be entered into.

See overleaf for information on other
BPP products and how to order

CIMA Order

To BPP Publishing Ltd, Aldine Place, London W12 8AW
Tel: 020 8740 2211. Fax: 020 8740 1184
www.bpp.com   Email publishing@bpp.com
Order online www.bpp.com

Mr/Mrs/Ms (Full name) _____
Daytime delivery address _____
Postcode _____
Daytime Tel _____   Email _____   Date of exam (month/year) _____

		7/02 Texts	1/02 Kits	1/02 Passcards	9/00 Tapes	7/00 Videos	Virtual Campus	7/02 i-Pass	7/02 i-Learn	MCQ cards
FOUNDATION										
1	Financial Accounting Fundamentals	£20.95 ☐	£10.95 ☐	£6.95 ☐	£12.95 ☐	£25.95 ☐	£50 ☐	£24.95 ☐		£5.95 ☐
2	Management Accounting Fundamentals	£20.95 ☐	£10.95 ☐	£6.95 ☐	£12.95 ☐	£25.95 ☐	£50 ☐	£24.95 ☐		£5.95 ☐
3A	Economics for Business	£20.95 ☐	£10.95 ☐	£6.95 ☐	£12.95 ☐	£25.95 ☐	£50 ☐	£24.95 ☐		£5.95 ☐
3B	Business Law	£20.95 ☐	£10.95 ☐	£6.95 ☐	£12.95 ☐	£25.95 ☐	£50 ☐	£24.95 ☐		£5.95 ☐
3C	Business Mathematics	£20.95 ☐	£10.95 ☐	£6.95 ☐	£12.95 ☐	£25.95 ☐	£50 ☐	£24.95 ☐		£5.95 ☐
INTERMEDIATE										
4	Finance	£20.95 ☐	£10.95 ☐	£6.95 ☐	£12.95 ☐	£25.95 ☐	£80 ☐	£24.95 ☐	£34.95 ☐	£5.95 ☐
5	Business Tax (FA 2002)	£20.95 ☐ (10/02)	£10.95 ☐	£6.95 ☐	£12.95 ☐	£25.95 ☐	£80 ☐	£24.95 ☐	£34.95 ☐	£5.95 ☐
6	Financial Accounting	£20.95 ☐	£10.95 ☐	£6.95 ☐	£12.95 ☐	£25.95 ☐	£80 ☐	£24.95 ☐	£34.95 ☐	£5.95 ☐
6i	Financial Accounting International	£20.95 ☐	£10.95 ☐	£6.95 ☐		£25.95 ☐				£5.95 ☐
7	Financial Reporting	£20.95 ☐	£10.95 ☐	£6.95 ☐	£12.95 ☐	£25.95 ☐	£80 ☐	£24.95 ☐	£34.95 ☐	£5.95 ☐
7i	Financial Reporting International	£20.95 ☐	£10.95 ☐	£6.95 ☐		£25.95 ☐				£5.95 ☐
8	Management Accounting – Performance Management	£20.95 ☐ *	£10.95 ☐	£6.95 ☐	£12.95 ☐	£25.95 ☐	£80 ☐	£24.95 ☐	£34.95 ☐	£5.95 ☐ *
9	Management Accounting – Decision Making	£20.95 ☐ *	£10.95 ☐	£6.95 ☐	£12.95 ☐	£25.95 ☐	£80 ☐	£24.95 ☐	£34.95 ☐	£5.95 ☐ *
10	Systems and Project Management	£20.95 ☐	£10.95 ☐	£6.95 ☐	£12.95 ☐	£25.95 ☐	£80 ☐	£24.95 ☐	£34.95 ☐	£5.95 ☐
11	Organisational Management	£20.95 ☐	£10.95 ☐	£6.95 ☐	£12.95 ☐	£25.95 ☐	£80 ☐	£24.95 ☐	£34.95 ☐	£5.95 ☐
FINAL										
12	Management Accounting – Business Strategy	£20.95 ☐	£10.95 ☐	£6.95 ☐	£12.95 ☐	£25.95 ☐				
13	Management Accounting – Financial Strategy	£20.95 ☐	£10.95 ☐	£6.95 ☐	£12.95 ☐	£25.95 ☐				
14	Management Accounting – Information Strategy	£20.95 ☐	£10.95 ☐	£6.95 ☐	£12.95 ☐	£25.95 ☐				
15	Case Study									
	(1) Workbook	£20.95 ☐			£12.95 ☐	£25.95 ☐		11/02 ☐ 5/03 ☐		
	(2) Toolkit		£19.95 ☐ (For 11/02: available 9/02. For 5/03: available 3/03)					11/02 ☐ 5/03 ☐		
	Learning to Learn (7/02)	£9.95 ☐								

Total _____

* For paper 8 and 9, separate editions are available for the November 2002 and May 2003 exams. Please tick the exam you will be sitting.

POSTAGE & PACKING

Study Texts	First	Each extra
UK	£3.00	£2.00 £ ___
Europe***	£5.00	£4.00 £ ___
Rest of world	£20.00	£10.00 £ ___

Kits/Passcards/Success Tapes	First	Each extra
UK	£2.00	£1.00 £ ___
Europe*	£2.50	£1.00 £ ___
Rest of world	£15.00	£8.00 £ ___

MCQ cards	£1.00	£1.00 £ ___

CDs each		
UK	£2.00	
Europe*	£2.00	
Rest of world	£10.00	

Breakthrough Videos	First	Each extra
UK	£2.00	£2.00 £ ___
Europe*	£2.00	£2.00 £ ___
Rest of world	£20.00	£10.00 £ ___

Grand Total (Cheques to *BPP Publishing*) I enclose a cheque for (incl. Postage)   £ _____

Or charge to Access/Visa/Switch

Card Number ☐☐☐☐ ☐☐☐☐ ☐☐☐☐ ☐☐☐☐

Expiry date ☐☐☐☐   Start Date ☐☐☐☐

Issue Number (Switch Only) ☐☐

Signature _____

We aim to deliver to all UK addresses inside 5 working days. A signature will be required. Orders to all EU addresses should be delivered within 6 working days. All other orders to overseas addresses should be delivered within 8 working days. *Europe includes the Republic of Ireland and the Channel Islands.